SCOTS LAW FOR JOURNALISTS

EIGHTH EDITION

SCOTS LAW FOR JOURNALISTS

EIGHTH EDITION

by

Rosalind McInnes
Principal Solicitor, BBC Scotland

Previous Edition by

Alistair J. Bonnington

Rosalind McInnes

Bruce McKain

W. GREEN  **THOMSON REUTERS**

Seventh edition © A. Bonnington R. McInnes & B. McKain 2000
Reprinted 2005, 2007

Published in 2010 by
Thomson Reuters (Legal) Limited
(Registered in England and Wales,
Company No 1679046
Registered office and address for service
100 Avenue Road, Swiss Cottage,
London, NW3 3PF) trading as W. Green

Typeset by Keith Thaxton at W. Green, Edinburgh
Printed and bound in the UK by CPI William Clowes, Beccles

No natural forests were destroyed to make this product;
only farmed timber was used and re-planted

A catalogue record for this title is available from the British Library

ISBN 978-0-414-01621-7

Thomson Reuters and the Thomson Reuters logo are
trademarks of Thomson Reuters

© 2010 Thomson Reuters (Legal) Limited

Crown copyright material is reproduced with the permission of the Controller of HMSO
and the Queen's Printer for Scotland

In loving memory of John McInnes,
September 7, 1939 to October 24, 2001

PREFACE

In the 10 years since the last edition of *Scots Law for Journalists* there has, inevitably, been dramatic change. The freedom of information legislation has come into force. Contempt of court poses less of a risk to the Scottish media than it has ever done. New defamation defences are available—if not yet reliable. On the other hand, the rise in privacy-based actions against the media, and the uncertain development of the law in this area, creates a new threat, as does the legislative response to terrorism.

Some significant changes have been made to this book itself. Originally written by, as well as for, journalists, it is increasingly used by solicitors and even judges in our small jurisdiction. For this reason, and because nowadays so much more legal material is available online for journalists and lawyers alike, more case citations and references to legislation have been included. As well, because some of the most important media law developments, especially in the fields of privacy and the Albert Reynolds defence in defamation, have yet to be the subject of much home-grown litigation, there is more English case law than before. It is hoped that neither the lawyers nor the southerners have taken over, as this book is intended, first and foremost, for Scottish journalists.

The most regretted change in this edition is the loss of Bruce McKain, co-author of the past four editions, to the Faculty of Advocates, and of Alistair Bonnington, co-author of the 6th and 7th editions, to golf and travel. Their surviving contribution to the book is major.

In their place stand five new contributors. Chapters 1, 2 and 3, with a helicopter view of the Scottish legal system, were produced by Douglas Mill, Director of Professional Legal Practice, School of Law, University of Glasgow and principal, Douglas Mill Consulting. David McKie of Levy & McRae wrote Chapter 4 on the country's criminal courts, as well as Chapters 35 and 42 on advertising and race relations. Duncan Hamilton, Advocate, contributed Chapters 5 and 6, concerning the civil courts and tribunals of Scotland. Colin Miller of Biggart Baillie provided Chapters 32 and 42, dealing with intellectual property in the conventional media and the virtual world. Laura CR MacPhee of Lady Margaret Hall, Oxford, wrote Chapter 38 on official secrets.

Additional thanks are due to Michael Anderson, Legal Secretary to the Lord President; Craig Mavor, Kirsteen MacDonald and Philip Rodney of Burness; Lynne Phillips; Douglas Milne and Fiona Sasan of Morton Fraser; Grazia Robertson of Liam Robertson & Co; and Lesley Thomson, Area Procurator-Fiscal, Glasgow for answering questions in their areas. Elizabeth Cutting, Public Information Officer to the Scottish Judiciary, has provided deeply appreciated assistance in the way of access and information. Jill Hyslop and Kirsty Price of W Green Ltd have been very patient and supportive editors. Thanks to Campbell Deane of Bannatyne Kirkwood France and to Kenneth Lang of Mellicks.

Special thanks are due to Elaine EM Robertson BA MSSP of the BBC Scotland Legal Department for her work in the preparation of this manuscript, its structuring and research tasks.

An incalculable debt is owed to very many fellow workers in the journalistic and legal fields, for tip-offs about obscure cases, copies of pleadings and collegiate war stories. The lawyers know who they are and the journalists know who everyone is.

Rosalind McInnes
October 2010

CONTENTS

PART 5: Photography and Audio-taping

PART 6: Matrimonial Proceedings and Children

PART 7: Defamation

PART 8: Intellectual Property

PART 9: The Print Media and the Broadcasters

PART 10: The Human Rights Act 1998,
Privacy and Breach of Confidence

PART 11: The Journalist and the State:
Politics, Terrorism and Official Secrets

PART 12: The Internet

TABLE OF CASES

TABLE OF UK STATUTES

xxix

TABLE OF ACTS OF THE SCOTTISH PARLIAMENT

TABLE OF UK STATUTORY INSTRUMENTS

TABLE OF SCOTTISH STATUTORY INSTRUMENTS

PART 1: SCOTS LAW AND THE COURTS SYSTEM

CHAPTER 1

INTRODUCTION TO THE SCOTTISH LEGAL SYSTEM

BY DOUGLAS MILL

SCOTS LAW

HISTORY

Scotland has a well regarded, interesting and unique system of law. 01.01
Despite sharing a common legislature with its southern neighbour for
over 300 years, its sources, history and the reintroduction of its own
Parliament have meant that Scots law has managed to maintain its
characteristics.

Ironically whilst the Romans managed to conquer England their 01.02
legal system made little impact.

The English system—known throughout the World as the 01.03
"Common Law system"—is one of the main lasting impacts of the
period of British Empire. It has influenced legal systems in the United
States, Australia, Canada, and New Zealand and can be said to be the
primary international mercantile system of law. In largely
unconquered Scotland we enjoy a system rooted philosophically in
Roman law, but which has developed and is now fairly described as a
mixed system of law.

"Civil" can be a difficult term in the law. Whilst used to distinguish 01.04
European systems from their Common Law counterparts, it is also
used to describe that area of the law and legal system which is not
criminal. In other words, it is concerned with matters of contract,
status, personal relationships and damages. It is to an extent "private
law", in other words determining rights and duties between legal

1

entities—as opposed to "public law", which relates to the relationship between the State and the citizen.

01.05   Prior to the establishment of law schools in Scottish universities, Scots wishing to study law generally went to the Continent and in particular the Low Countries. Not surprisingly the impact of, for instance, Dutch law in the development of Scots law is not insignificant.

SOURCES

01.06   After the Union of the Parliaments in 1707 it was established that three main areas would continue to define distinctive Scottish heritage, namely the church, education and the law. Scotland's law and court system maintained their integrity. Scots law was open to European influences and the work of a number of leading academic authors known as Institutional Writers. However, particularly in the 19th and 20th centuries, Westminster was the source of primary legislation and in many areas of the law there has been an assimilation of the two systems. Indeed very broadly there are areas such as company law and tax law which may be called "UK" law whilst Scots law is preserved in areas such as conveyancing, criminal law and family law.

01.07   Whilst many people think of Acts of Parliament as being the main source of law there are many other forms such as case law, institutional writings and secondary legislation, local authority byelaws and other regulations. Courts generally play a useful function in "fleshing out" the law by interpreting statutes and trying to deduce the intention of Parliament where Acts remain debatable or silent.

01.08   The hierarchical court system in Scotland involves case precedent, i.e. decisions made in higher courts are generally "binding" on lower courts. Decisions at a similar level may be described as "persuasive".

01.09   The law is therefore massively complex and it would be quite simply impossible for any one individual to develop a comprehensive knowledge of all the areas of the law. Indeed this is now recognised in the law schools in Scotland where the pace of change—particularly in the volume of primary legislation—has meant a concentration on how to source, understand and interpret the law rather than a slavish recitation of its terms at any one time.

Present day legislation

International law

01.10   The United Kingdom is a signatory to a large number of international treaties. However the general position is that these international treaties do not become part of UK law until such time as legislation has been enacted to give effect to them.

Europe

Scotland is one of the very few jurisdictions whose law is being 01.11 developed by a Scottish Parliament at Holyrood, the UK Parliament at Westminster and institutions of the European Union. There are in fact "two legal Europes". First there is the Council of Europe which is the sponsor organisation for the European Convention on Human Rights and secondly there is the European Union which is concerned largely with social, economic and political issues and which has a smaller membership but much broader competence.

The Human Rights Act 1998 and the Scotland Act 1998 have both 01.12 given effect in Scots domestic law to the rights contained in the European Convention.

The vehicle for giving effect to European Union Law is the 01.13 European Communities Act 1972.

In terms of the European Communities Act 1972, EU law is 01.14 gradually replacing Parliament as the supreme source of law in the United Kingdom. The influence of the European Parliament, the Council of Europe and the European Court of Human Rights in Strasbourg has profoundly impacted on law in the United Kingdom and Scotland.

The European scene is complex as there are a number of institutions 01.15 such as the Council of Europe, the Council of the European Union, the European Union, the European Court of Justice, the European Parliament and the European Commission which has a useful website available by way of a link from the Law Society of Scotland's website *http://www.lawscot.org.uk* [Accessed September 13, 2010].

The European Parliament comprises 736 members of the European 01.16 Parliament (MEPs). The Parliament and Council form the highest legislative body within the European Union. It meets both in Strasbourg, France and in Brussels, Belgium with the Commission Secretariat being based in both Luxembourg and Brussels.

One of the principal areas of impact has been in the field of human 01.17 rights. The Convention for the Protection of Human Rights and Fundamental Freedoms (ECHR) was adopted under the auspices of the Council of Europe in Rome in 1950. This was a seminal development in the protection of the citizens of Europe following upon the Second World War.

All Member States are expected to ratify the Convention at the 01.18 earliest opportunity and indeed the UK Parliament introduced the Human Rights Act 1998 providing that it would be unlawful for public authorities to act in any way which was incompatible with the Convention rights.

01.19   The establishment of a court against violation of human rights is an important and innovative development. The European Court of Human Rights is situated in Strasbourg and is composed presently of 40 judges elected by the Parliamentary Assembly of the Council of Europe for a period of six years. There is no restriction on the number of judges from each country as they sit on an individual basis. Their restrictions are that no judge can sit beyond the age of 70 years of age and they must not engage in any activity which is incompatible with their independence or impartiality.

01.20   There are a number of Convention articles such as art.5 (the right to liberty and security), art.6 (the right to a fair trial) and art.8 (privacy) which are often the subject of court and press scrutiny. In addition to these there are Convention Protocols dealing with issues such as education, free movement and the abolition of the death penalty which impact on domestic legal systems.

01.21   The United Kingdom has been a regular litigant in Strasbourg. For example, freedom of expression issues dealt with in art.10 were examined in the case of *The Observer and The Guardian v United Kingdom* (1991) ("the *Spycatcher* case") and *Appleby v United Kingdom* (2003) [see **Chapter 36**].

United Kingdom

01.22   Ever since the Scotland Act 1998, the UK Parliament remains a fundamental source of legislation for Scotland. The UK Parliament is a bi-cameral (two chamber) system with the House of Commons acting as the lower chamber and the House of Lords as the upper chamber. Whether deriving from government policy, Private Members' Bills or otherwise, new legislation meanders through a complex system of consultation, committee work and readings in each House of Parliament. Eventually a Bill which meets all approval will receive the Royal Assent at which time it becomes an Act. Historically the House of Lords had the ability to reject proposed legislation from the Commons but this power is now merely a power to delay legislation. Proceedings in the UK Parliament are generally protected from the law of defamation and contempt of court.

Scotland

01.23   There prevailed a feeling for a long time that the UK Parliament seldom had sufficient legislative time to acknowledge the separate nature of Scots law and Scottish issues were often "tacked on" at the end of English Acts. The reinstatement of a national legislative chamber was therefore an opportunity for Scots law to refresh and update itself.

01.24   The Scottish Parliament is different in its nature being a uni-cameral system—in other words it has simply one chamber. Scottish legislation in areas which are not reserved to the UK Parliament has a different parliamentary process with much of the work being done, at least in theory, at an early stage in committee.

The work done by the Scottish Law Commission in proposing 01.25 reform is essential to the future development of Scots law.

The Scotland Act 1998 (c.46) received the Royal Assent on 01.26 November 19, 1998. It sets out the legislative competence of the Scottish Parliament which is restricted in several ways.

First, certain matters are reserved to Westminster. Within these 01.27 areas it is not competent for the Scottish Parliament to legislate. There are general reservations under Sch.5 of the Act namely:

- the Constitution and political parties;
- foreign affairs and European Union;
- public service;
- defence;
- treason.

In addition to this under Pt 2 of Sch.5 there are specific reservations 01.28 many of them quite detailed under the general headings of:

- financial and economic matters;
- home affairs;
- trade and industry;
- energy;
- transport;
- social security;
- regulation of professions;
- employment;
- health and medicine;
- media and culture;
- miscellaneous.

It should be noted that the regulation of the legal profession in 01.29 Scotland is not one of the reserved areas.

Secondly there are other general reservations, and most importantly 01.30 it links back to s.29 of the Act and confirms that any provision of the Scottish Parliament would be incompetent if it was incompatible with any provisions of the European Convention on Human Rights or with EU law.

A number of human rights issues have been tested in the Scottish 01.31 courts including the question of the independence of part-time sheriffs (in the case of *Starrs v Ruxton* **(2000)**) and the prison slopping out cases. It is fair to say that tabloid newspapers have branded the European Convention "a Nutters' Charter" and a number of issues involving ECHR compliance remain sensitive.

Generally speaking proceedings in the Scottish Parliament are 01.32 protected from the law of defamation and contempt of court. The

Cabinet Minister responsible for legal affairs is the Minister of Justice. Justice issues coming before the Scottish Parliament are dealt with initially by the Justice Committee, the work of which is broad ranging and at the time of going to press is dealing with licensing, criminal justice, sexual offences and a review of civil justice.

ASSIMILATION AND GLOBALISATION OF LAW

01.33   No legal system stands as an island. Scots law whilst retaining its essential identity in areas such as property, divorce and crime, like any other system within the United Kingdom, the European Union and an increasingly globalised commercial world, requires to be open to change. In the last generation the amount of personal foreign travel, immigration and emigration and global trade has meant that many of Scotland's leading legal firms require to be expert also in English and other foreign laws. This has accelerated the need for specialisation within legal firms.

COMPLEXITY AND SPECIALISATION

01.34   Whole areas of legal specialisation have grown in the last 20 or 30 years which did not formerly exist, such as intellectual property, sports law and media law. The volume of law produced by three legislative bodies along with subordinate legislation and a regular flow of case law means that no individual solicitor can realistically expect in this day and age to be a general practitioner of the law. It has therefore become profoundly difficult to maintain the type of general local legal practice which has traditionally been offered to the citizens of Scotland.

FINDING THE LAW

01.35   This is difficult enough for qualified lawyers and for journalists a near impossibility. A basic awareness however of some of the publications, websites and other sources is essential. One of the best starting points is the Law Society of Scotland's website—*http:// www.lawscot.org.uk* [Accessed September 13, 2010]. The Law Society is the primary regulatory body for Scotland's 10,000 solicitors and will provide a useful port of call for any initial enquiry from a journalist. It is also an excellent portal as it provides links for approximately 30 useful websites such as *http:// www.scotcourts.gov.uk* [Accessed September 13, 2010], the Scottish Court Service website, *http://www.opsi.gov.uk* [Accessed September

13, 2010], the Office of Public Sector Information and *http://
www.bailii.org* [Accessed September 13, 2010], the British and Irish
Legal Information Institute. For issues in the profession and
challenging comment *http://www.firmmagazine.com* [Accessed
September 13, 2010], is useful.

The Law Society of Scotland publishes both in paper and online   01.36
format a monthly journal which will give journalists an indication of
ongoing issues in the profession. It provides a very useful public
information section with general advice on using a solicitor, buying
or selling a house and making a will. The website is, too, the first port
of call for any queries in relation to the disciplinary system for
solicitors and any prosecutions before the independent Scottish
Solicitors' Discipline Tribunal.

The Society has a number of departments such as Education and   01.37
Training, Professional Practice and Law Reform which are geared to
assist, not just the profession but the public and their Corporate
Communications Department will act as a willing source of direction
where journalists are seeking information or experts to comment on
developments or cases.

It will also be a useful starting point for any research required into   01.38
individual cases. Scotland enjoys a number of excellent regular
publications such as the *Scots Law Times* and the *Scottish Civil* and
Scottish Criminal Case Reports which can be of great assistance to
journalists dealing with matters in court.

Scottish legal libraries have evolved over the last decade or so away   01.39
from paper and towards CD and online availability. The
sophistication of search engines and the significant upgrading of
websites over the last decade has meant that basic information in
relation to, for instance, the three Parliaments serving the people of
Scotland is readily available and updated. *Hansard* remains the
definitive source of Westminster information and the Scottish
Parliament website is easily navigated and detailed in its reports on
committees, Bills and official reports.

CHAPTER 2

THE LEGAL PROFESSION

BY DOUGLAS MILL

INTRODUCTION

02.01 For a profession with such a conservative image and thought to be resistant to change, the legal profession has seen a number of fundamental alterations to its constitution over the last 20 years or so. The broad division into solicitors and advocates remains, but now with a great degree of blurring.

SOLICITORS

02.02 Solicitors in Scotland were traditionally "men of business" and dealt broadly with all client affairs. Indeed the word "solicitor" in Scotland is a relatively recent English importation as historically people carrying out this work were known as "writers" or "procurators". There are currently in Scotland approximately 10,000 practising solicitors, almost a third of whom operate in an employed capacity as in-house lawyers working for the Crown Office and Procurator Fiscal Service, the Government Legal Service, local authorities and in financial services and industry.

02.03 The majority of solicitors operate in private practice—in approximately 1,300 practice units ranging from sole practitioners (of which there are almost 550) to large firms based in Glasgow and Edinburgh with 200–400 lawyers. There is an increasing division between the size and nature of legal work being carried out by "high street" lawyers and "big firm" lawyers, though all branches of the solicitor profession share a common training and common regulation, principally by the Law Society of Scotland. At the moment only solicitors are entitled to be partners in (proprietors of) legal firms though there is a move towards what is known as alternative business structures (ABS)—in other words what is seen as a "liberalisation" of ownership which will allow anyone to own a firm of solicitors. This is a profound step and goes well beyond the debate of the last 10 years on multi-disciplinary proprietorship (MDPs) which proposed association between solicitors and accountants and other professions. The introduction of ABS could potentially end the collegiate nature of the solicitor branch of the legal profession in Scotland and the collective guarantees which it provides to the public.

All firms of solicitors require compulsory professional indemnity insurance. The Law Society of Scotland appoint brokers who arrange the policy on an annual basis and this gives the public the assurance that any solicitor with whom they contract is insured for acts of negligence. 02.04

A second major regulatory "pillar" is the Law Society of Scotland's guarantee fund. This is subscribed to by the approximately 5,500 partners in private practice and guarantees the public against acts of fraud by solicitors which are not otherwise covered. These are important public protections and give the people of Scotland security. Solicitors are bound by a range of statutory provisions, codes and ethics and central to these are the core values of independence, acting in the best interests of the client and the avoidance of conflicts. Despite public perception there are only three areas of work wholly reserved to solicitors, namely, applications for confirmation (estate work), registration of deeds (aspects of conveyancing) and appearance work in court. These issues are under regular review. 02.05

Solicitors act as a first port of call for the client, covering a broad range of legal work largely within their own practice but where appropriate take advice from or refer to accredited specialists, solicitor advocates and members of the Faculty of Advocates. 02.06

Solicitors, who broadly share a common training with advocates, will largely have gained an LLB degree from one of the 10 providing universities namely Glasgow, Strathclyde, Glasgow Caledonian, Stirling, Edinburgh, Napier, Dundee, Abertay, Robert Gordon and Aberdeen. On graduation they require to spend a further year gaining a diploma in professional legal practice which is now available from the Universities of Aberdeen, Robert Gordon, Stirling, Dundee, Edinburgh, Glasgow and Strathclyde. Full qualification is gained after a further two year period of in-office training. The route to qualification is currently under review by the Law Society of Scotland. 02.07

For some time now the majority of entrants into the legal profession have been female and the continuation of this trend should see women in the majority in the solicitor branch of the profession within a period of 5–10 years. 02.08

Solicitors are tightly regulated principally by the Law Society of Scotland, which can act as prosecutor before the independent Scottish Solicitors' Discipline Tribunal. The Scottish Legal Complaints Commission deals with issues of poor service by solicitors and advocates which were formerly dealt with by the two respective professional bodies and the Scottish Solicitors' Discipline Tribunal. Further detail is given in **para.06.63**. 02.09

02.10   Whilst regulated nationally, solicitors are free to join a number of local bar associations or faculties. There are approximately 45 of these in Scotland generally organised on sheriff court jurisdictional lines and ranging from small rural associations to large historical groupings, such as the Royal Faculty of Procurators in Glasgow, the Society of Advocates in Aberdeen and in Edinburgh the Writers to the Signet and the Society of Solicitors in the Supreme Courts.

02.11   Many solicitors go through a relatively automatic process of qualification as a notary public. This is an important office which allows for the proper execution of formal documents and administering of oaths.

ADVOCATES

02.12   Referred to as "Counsel" the majority of advocates these days are already qualified as solicitors in Scotland and thereafter undertake additional examinations and training including a period known as "devilling". When admitted they become members of the Faculty of Advocates in Scotland of whom there are approximately 450 in practice. Regulation is principally by the Faculty of Advocates and the recently introduced Scottish Legal Complaints Commission.

02.13   The equivalent English expression is "Barrister" and whilst the English profession is chambers-based, the Scottish faculty is what is known as a "Library-based" grouping which is historically centred in Parliament House in Edinburgh.

02.14   Advocates for practical purposes tend to join "stables"—groupings which facilitate instructions and feeing, and in recent years there has been an increase in the number of stables and indeed their profiles.

02.15   Advocates have traditionally carried out referral and opinion work for the solicitor branch of the profession and also until fairly recently enjoyed exclusive rights of audience in the highest courts. The increasing complexity of the law over the last 20 or 30 years has seen a tendency towards specialisation at the Bar and indeed a growing need for the solicitor branch of the profession to be able to access independent experts. Further, the increasing globalisation of the law and the porous nature of the border between Scotland and England has seen a growing number of advocates qualified dually as English barristers. Whilst there has been a recent move towards the direct instruction of advocates by non-solicitors in some cases, the majority of instruction continues to be by firms of solicitors who are seeking to assist their clients by adding independence and expertise where necessary.

SOLICITOR-ADVOCATES

The blurring between the two main branches of the profession started 02.16
with the Law Reform (Miscellaneous Provisions) (Scotland) Act 1990
which granted solicitors, suitably qualified and experienced, rights of
audience in the higher courts. They operate under rules drawn up by
the Law Society of Scotland and approved by the Lord President and
separate systems exist for the criminal and civil courts.

There has been a very significant uptake by the solicitor branch of 02.17
the profession of these extended rights—particularly in the area of
criminal law where approximately 130 solicitor-advocates have been
granted rights to appear in the High Court. Rights to appear in the
Court of Session and House of Lords have been granted to
approximately 140 with only a few being dually qualified.

Solicitor-advocates are to be found both in-house—for example in 02.18
the Crown Office and Procurator Fiscal Service—and in private
practice.

QUEEN'S COUNSEL

Historically the preserve of members of the Faculty of Advocates, 02.19
solicitor-advocates are now entitled to apply to "take Silk" and
become Queen's Counsel. This is not a separate division of the
profession but to an extent a quality mark and QCs are generally
involved in more complex and high profile work. In cases of
significance representation is often by both senior and junior counsel.

PARALEGALS

An increasing amount of legal work within firms of solicitors and in- 02.20
house is carried out by paralegals. As a jurisdiction, Scotland has been
slower than England (where they are referred to as legal executives) in
the development of paralegals though moves are currently afoot to
examine the possibility of rationalising training and qualification and
regulation.

TRANSFERS WITHIN THE PROFESSION

Whilst historically the majority of advocates are pre-qualified as 02.21
solicitors and it remains impossible to hold the status of solicitor and
advocate jointly, there has over the last few years been considerable
blurring round the edges of status. At the moment in fact the Lord
Advocate, Elish Angiolini, is somewhat refreshingly neither a Lord

nor by training, an advocate. Indeed her predecessor Colin Boyd QC on demitting office restored his name to the Roll of Solicitors in Scotland and became a consultant in one of Scotland's big firms. At least one high profile QC has transferred back to the solicitor branch of the profession again joining a larger firm. The Faculty of Advocates has also admitted as members the current Solicitor General, Frank Mulholland, and some time after she took up office, Elish Angiolini, the Lord Advocate.

CHAPTER 3

THE JUDICIARY, PROSECUTION AND GOVERNMENT LEGAL SERVICES—AN OVERVIEW

BY DOUGLAS MILL

Scotland has a unique system of law reflected in its court system, the 03.01
prosecution of crime and the composition and nature of its Judiciary.
The court system for both criminal and civil matters is hierarchical
with, broadly, the most basic criminal matters being dealt with in
justice of the peace courts. These are lay courts where a justice of the
peace (JP), who is not legally qualified and sits with a legally qualified
clerk, gives advice on matters of law and procedure. In Glasgow, some
courts are presided over by a legally qualified stipendiary magistrate
who has higher sentencing powers. These courts were created by the
Criminal Proceedings etc. (Reform) (Scotland) Act 2007 and
replaced the former district courts which were operated by local
authorities. These courts operate much the same way as before and
are often, though erroneously, still referred to as district courts. The
majority of criminal and civil work is handled again locally in sheriff
courts with more serious criminal issues being dealt with by the High
Court of Justiciary. In criminal matters there is no further appeal.

In civil issues the majority of work is initiated in the sheriff court 03.02
with appeals to a sheriff principal and thereafter to the Court of
Session in Edinburgh. The Court of Session itself is both a court of
first instance for matters of higher value and legal complexity, and
the Court of Appeal. Appeals lie thereafter to the newly established
Supreme Court (see below). This body was established in October
2009 replacing the Appellate Committee of the House of Lords as the
highest court in the United Kingdom. The Supreme Court has 12
justices who sit in the former Middlesex Guildhall on the western side
of Parliament Square. The Supreme Court is the highest civil court for
all of the United Kingdom in civil cases and for England, Wales and
Northern Ireland in criminal cases. It also has jurisdiction over
devolution issues for Scotland, Wales and Northern Ireland. Of the
12 justices two are Scots, namely, Lord Hope of Craighead appointed
in 1996 and Lord Rodger of Earlsferry appointed in 2001.

JUDGES

The Court of Session is the highest civil tribunal in Scotland. There are 03.03
approximately 30 Senators of the College of Justice in Scotland. They

can sit either in civil matters in the Court of Session or in criminal matters in the High Court of Justiciary. The principal judge in Scotland is Lord Hamilton who in civil matters is known as the Lord President, and when sitting in the High Court is known as the Lord Justice General. The second senior judge is the Lord Justice-Clerk, Lord Gill. Within the Court of Session a hierarchical system operates with a distinction being made between Inner House judges and Outer House judges. The Inner House can sit as a First Division comprising the Lord President and four other judges and the Second Division comprising the Lord Justice-Clerk and a similar number. The majority of other judges sit in the Outer House as Lords Ordinary.

03.04   The Court of Session is situated in the High Street in Edinburgh in the building known as Parliament House. With the return of the Scottish Parliament, which is situated at Holyrood approximately half a mile away, this can cause some geographical and terminological confusion.

03.05   The same judges also sit in criminal matters at the High Court of Justiciary. This sits as a court of first instance principally in Edinburgh, Glasgow and Aberdeen and also goes "on circuit" throughout Scotland as may be required to deal with significant matters such as murders. It also acts as an Appellate Court disposing of appeals against both conviction and sentence.

03.06   Formerly appointed by the Lord Advocate, judges are now appointed by the Queen on the advice of the First Minister whose recommendations are in turn based on the recommendations of the Judicial Appointments Board for Scotland. This body has recently been placed on a statutory footing.

SHERIFFS

03.07   There are approximately 50 sheriff courts in Scotland divided into six sheriffdoms, namely Glasgow and Strathkelvin, Grampian, Highlands and Islands, Lothian and Borders, North Strathclyde, South Strathclyde, Dumfries and Galloway and Tayside, Central and Fife. Each sheriff court area has a sheriff principal who is assisted by an appropriate number of sheriffs. The sheriff principal deals with appeals and some cases at first instance. These sheriffdoms vary greatly in geographical extent, population and the number of courts within their area. They range for example from Glasgow Sheriff Court (one of the busiest courts in Europe) with approximately 25 full-time sheriffs sitting essentially five days a week to some of the more outlying courts such as Kirkwall, Lerwick, Lochmaddy and Portree which tend to conduct business either one day per week or even as and when required. These courts are likely to share sheriffs and fiscals.

In volume terms, the bulk of Scotland's civil and criminal court work is carried out in the sheriff courts. Whilst in some larger sheriff courts a degree of specialisation is developing, broadly sheriffs are qualified to hear both civil and criminal business. Sheriffs are now appointed by the Queen on the advice of the First Minister whose recommendations are in turn based on the recommendations of the Judicial Appointments Board for Scotland and there are approximately 142 full-time sheriffs. This number is supplemented by 80 part-time appointments. These solicitors or advocates will assist the Scottish Courts Service by sitting where there is need occasioned by holidays, illness or volume of business.   03.08

SUPREME COURT

The House of Lords judicial functions have now been transferred to a newly established Supreme Court. There are approximately 12 Lords of Appeal in Ordinary two of whom are Scots, Lord Hope of Craighead and Lord Rodger of Earlsferry. In addition, a number of retired Lords of Appeal in Ordinary are still eligible to hear appeals. From a Scottish perspective they deal with purely civil business. The Supreme Court has an extremely useful website—*http://www.supremecourt.gov.uk* [Accessed September 13, 2010]   03.09

OTHER COURTS AND TRIBUNALS

These are dealt with in detail in **Chapter 6**.   03.10

In addition to the main courts, Scotland has a number of specialist courts, for example, the Restrictive Practices Court, the Registration Appeal Court and the Court of the Lord Lyon.   03.11

Over the years much civil work has been transferred to tribunals. The work of many formerly separate tribunals is now being done by a First-tier Tribunal from which there is a right of appeal on a point of law to the Upper Tribunal. In addition there are a number of separate subject-specific tribunals such as the employment tribunals, and the children's hearing system. Additionally the Scottish Criminal Cases Review Commission was established on April 1, 1999. It is an independent executive non-departmental public body with the responsibility for reviewing and investigating alleged miscarriages of justice, referring appropriate cases to the High Court for determination.   03.12

CROWN OFFICE AND PROCURATOR FISCAL SERVICE

03.13   The prosecution of crime in Scotland is headed by the Lord Advocate presently the Rt. Hon. Elish Angiolini QC. The second in command is known as the Solicitor General for Scotland, presently Francis Mulholland QC. Since devolution the political aspects of these posts have changed though the day-to-day responsibilities in relation to criminal law remain. Before the Scotland Act 1998, the government in power at Westminster would appoint Scottish Law Officers sympathetic to their political views. This appeared to continue initially after devolution but there are signs that political affiliation may no longer be important. Refreshingly the Scottish National Party, when it succeeded Labour as the controlling administration in Holyrood, continued the appointment of Elish Angiolini as Lord Advocate. The interface between the political and legal responsibilities of the Lord Advocate is likely to be a continuing area of tension.

03.14   The Crown Office is based in Chambers Street in Edinburgh and controls a regionalised Procurator Fiscal Service. There are approximately 600 procurators fiscal situated throughout the country, constituting the largest single grouping of lawyers in Scotland. Procurators fiscal operate principally in the sheriff courts in the prosecution of crime and in liaison with the police authorities. Private prosecution in Scotland is an extremely rare event and legally very complex. The last private prosecution in Scotland occurred almost 30 years ago.

LAW OFFICERS

03.15   In addition to the Lord Advocate whose duties extend beyond prosecution of crime to giving general legal advice to Scottish Ministers and the Solicitor General, there is also the post of Advocate General (currently Lord Wallace of Tankerness). This person acts as principal legal adviser to the United Kingdom Government on matters of Scots law. He currently sits in Dover House in London and the office arose as part of the devolutionary process which resulted in the Scotland Act 1998.

GOVERNMENT LEGAL SERVICES

03.16   Since devolution there has been a great increase in the number of lawyers engaged in the service of the State. There are now six constituent offices of the Government Legal Service for Scotland

(GLSS), namely, the Scottish Government Legal Directorate, the Office of the Solicitor to the Advocate General for Scotland, the Legal Secretariat to the Lord Advocate, the Legal Secretariat to the Advocate General, the Scottish Parliament Legal Services and the Scottish Law Commission.

Excluding procurators fiscal, there are approximately 100 lawyers 03.17 currently in the employment of GLSS. To put that number in context, were GLSS a private legal firm it would be the sixth biggest in Scotland. The workload demands on these lawyers is extensive with an average of 15 Acts of the Scottish Parliament and 600 statutory instruments requiring scrutiny each year.

CHAPTER 4

CRIMINAL COURTS AND PROCEDURE

BY DAVID McKIE

JURISDICTION

04.01   In dealing with courts the word "jurisdiction" constantly occurs. Its basic meaning is simply a power to hear and decide. Territorial jurisdiction describes the area of Scotland over which a particular court has jurisdiction. A court has original jurisdiction if it has power to hear and decide cases coming before it directly, at first instance and appellate jurisdiction if it has power to hear and decide appeals. Justice of the peace ("JP") courts (formerly district courts) and sheriff courts have restricted jurisdiction over an area defined by statute. The High Court, however, has jurisdiction over the whole of Scotland.

SUMMARY AND SOLEMN JURISDICTION

04.02   Courts of summary jurisdiction deal with the less serious crimes. Proceedings begin with a complaint (sometimes called a summons) and there is no jury. The punishment which can be imposed is limited. The courts of summary jurisdiction in Scotland are the sheriff courts and JP courts, although the sheriff court can also deal with solemn (jury) cases.

04.03   Courts of solemn jurisdiction deal with the more serious crimes. Proceedings take place on an indictment, which starts with a private hearing on petition, and there is always a jury of 15 (the one exception to this is the Lockerbie prosecution, which proceeded in the special circumstances of an Order in Council allowing this case to be heard in Holland before a panel of three Scottish judges sitting without a jury). The sheriff courts and the High Court of Justiciary are the only courts of solemn jurisdiction in Scotland. The sheriff court has both summary and solemn jurisdiction, the sheriff sitting alone in summary cases and with a jury in solemn cases.

JUSTICE OF THE PEACE COURTS

04.04   A JP court is a lay court in which an unqualified magistrate sits with a legally qualified clerk. The clerk advises the justice on legal and procedural issues. The maximum sentence which a JP can impose is: 60 days' imprisonment or a fine not exceeding £2,500; and in Glasgow only, some courts are presided over by a legally qualified stipendiary magistrate, who can impose 12 months' imprisonment or a fine not exceeding £10,000. These courts were created by the Criminal Proceedings etc. (Reform) (Scotland) Act 2007 and replace district courts, which were run by councils. The purpose of the change was to unify the organisation of sheriff and district courts. The changes were introduced on a sheriffdom-by-sheriffdom basis from 2008–2010.

Justice of the peace courts have jurisdiction over a wide range of minor offences, such as breach of the peace and many offences under local authority byelaws. 04.05

Prosecutions are conducted by the procurator fiscal who must comply with directions given by the Lord Advocate regarding prosecutions in the JP court and must report to the Lord Advocate, if called upon to do so, on matters concerning the discharge of his functions. The clerical work of the court is the responsibility of the clerk of the court, who may be full time or part time, and must be an advocate or a solicitor. The clerk also acts as legal assessor in the court, advising the justices about the law and procedure. In busy courts such as Glasgow, the clerk carries out this function through part-time depute assessors. 04.06

The procedure and rights of appeal in JP courts are similar to those in summary procedure in the sheriff courts and will be considered later. 04.07

Children's hearings are not really courts at all, although they do in fact deal with most offences committed by children [see **Chapter 6**]. "Children" for this purpose means anyone under the age of 18. The policy behind the Social Work (Scotland) Act 1968, which introduced children's hearings, is based on therapy rather than punishment. The law on children's hearings is now to be found in the Children (Scotland) Act 1995. 04.08

In certain circumstances children may be "in need of compulsory measures of care". These circumstances include cases where the child is beyond the control of his or her parent; where through lack of parental care he or she is falling into bad associations or is exposed to moral danger; where he or she has been the victim of certain offences (such as cruelty); or where he or she has failed to attend school regularly without reasonable excuse. 04.09

The circumstances also include the commission of an offence, and in fact a large proportion of the cases brought before children's hearings are brought on the offence ground. The hearing does not, however, conduct trials. If the grounds of referral are accepted by the child and his or her parent the hearing proceeds to decide what course would be in the best interests of the child; it may, for example, decide to place him or her under the supervision of a local authority social work 04.10

department, or it may decide to send him or her to a residential establishment. But if the grounds are not accepted—as would be the case if the referral was based on the belief that the child had committed an offence but the child denied committing the offence— the children's hearing does not proceed. Instead it must either discharge the referral or have the case referred to the sheriff for a finding as to whether the grounds are established.

04.11   A referral hearing before a sheriff takes the form of a proof as in a civil court. Witnesses are put on oath and their evidence is subject to cross-examination. The standard of proof which the sheriff applies is the same as in civil courts on a balance of probabilities. It is important to note that the sheriff does not dispose of the case himself even if he is hearing a referral. If he finds the facts established he simply remits the case back to the children's hearing for disposal. To use a criminal analogy (although it is not entirely appropriate), the sheriff decides on conviction, but not sentence.

04.12   The same result follows if the hearing considers that the grounds have not been understood by the child. This can be a case where the child is too young to understand. In some cases new-born babies have been taken into care if the social work authorities believe the parents are not capable of taking care of the child or if the child is in some form of danger. For example, an elder brother or sister may have been assaulted or abused in the past. If the sheriff finds the ground established the case goes back to a children's hearing for the appropriate measures to be taken. Hearings also have power to deal with cases referred under the Solvent Abuse (Scotland) Act 1983.

04.13   The Antisocial Behaviour etc. (Scotland) Act 2004 also gave hearings the power to restrict a child or young person's movement. This involves intensive support and monitoring services (monitoring is facilitated by an electronic "tag") where the young person is restricted to, or away from, a particular place. The electronic tag must be supported by a full package of intensive measures to help the young person change their behaviour.

04.14   The people who sit on children's hearings are lay volunteers drawn from carefully selected children's panels. The organisation of hearings and the referral of cases to them are the responsibility of an officer called (rather confusingly) "the reporter", who is appointed and paid by the local authority. Procedure at the hearings is quite informal. The public is not admitted, but bona fide press representatives may attend. There is a strict ban on identifying any child in any way concerned in a hearing [see **Chapter 25**].

04.15   It is increasingly common for the children involved in hearings or court proceedings to be separately represented from their parents. One method of achieving this end is to appoint a "safeguarder" to the child, who will usually be a solicitor or someone with a social work background. It is necessary for a sheriff or a children's panel hearing a case involving a child to consider the necessity of appointing a safeguarder. The safeguarder must represent the child's interests in the proceedings. But a safeguarder is not a legal role. It is the safeguarder's task to ascertain the whole family circumstances of the child. The safeguarder must represent the child's interests as opposed to that of the parents or other family members, although on many occasions these interests may coincide. By using safeguarders, the Scottish system hopes to live up to the United Nations Convention on the Rights of the Child 1989 which requires domestic courts to afford a child involved in proceedings the right to have his or her views taken into account. In most cases, the safeguarder's task is completed by summarising the views and interests of the child in question and reporting these to the court or hearing. Safeguarders do not require to attend the hearing itself, although in practice many do so.

Another method of having a child's interests protected is for the hearing or the sheriff to appoint a curator ad litem to the child. Again the aim is to make sure that the views of the child are placed before the hearing or the court. The appointment of a curator ad litem is a more formal step than the appointment of a safeguarder. A curator ad litem will almost invariably be a legally qualified person, who will appear at the hearing or court and assist the court in coming to a decision. It should be noted that the curator ad litem, which is a much more well-established concept than that of safeguarder, has the task of representing the child's interests rather than the child's views. 04.16

Appeal from any decision of the children's hearing lies to the sheriff. Appeal from any decision of the sheriff in relation to the children's hearing lies to the Court of Session by way of stated case (explained later) on a point of law or in respect of any irregularity in the conduct of the case. 04.17

The role of the media in covering children's hearings was a central issue in the long-running inquiry, beginning in August 1991, into allegations of child sex abuse on Orkney. Some sections of the media were severely criticised for "taking the side" of parents whose children were said to have been abused. The conduct of the media was given as one of the reasons why place of safety orders could not continue in force and children had to be returned home. The case illustrated the extreme difficulties of producing balanced reports in this type of case where one side feels unable to comment because of confidentiality. Because of what happened in the Orkney case, submissions were made to Lord Clyde, the judge in charge of the inquiry, that the media should no longer be allowed to attend children's hearings. Lord Clyde did not accept these submissions and the media continue 04.18

to be allowed to attend children's hearings under the provisions of the Children (Scotland) Act 1995.

SHERIFF COURTS

04.19 The sheriff courts deal with most criminal cases in Scotland. The judge is either the sheriff or the sheriff principal. Both are appointed by the Judicial Appointments Board, which was set up in 2002, replacing the previous system whereby the Lord Advocate was directly involved in the decision making process. Both must be advocates or solicitors of at least 10 years' standing. There are six sheriffdoms in Scotland: Grampian, Highland and Islands; Tayside, Central and Fife; Lothian and Borders; Glasgow and Strathkelvin, North Strathclyde; and South Strathclyde, Dumfries and Galloway. Each is headed by a sheriff principal who, in addition to his judicial functions, has a general duty to secure the speedy and efficient disposal of business in the sheriff courts of his sheriffdom and who has correspondingly wide administrative functions. During the 1980s and 1990s the increased use of temporary sheriffs meant that it was highly likely that an accused person would be tried by a temporary sheriff rather than by a full-time sheriff. Temporary sheriffs were solicitors and advocates to similar standing of full-time sheriffs. However, they held a commission to act as temporary sheriffs on a year-to-year basis. They could sit on any court in Scotland. They were paid a daily fee for their work. They were not prevented from appearing for accused persons or as prosecutors on the days when they were not sitting as temporary sheriffs. Temporary sheriffs could hold their commission for a period of 12 months only. There was concern that this form of tenure may not accord with the requirements of art.6 of the European Convention on human rights which requires judges to be "independent". In the case of *Starrs* **(1999)** the High Court ruled that temporary sheriffs did not comply with the requirements of the Convention (art.6) as their continued tenure was within the gift of the Lord Advocate who was also prosecutor in the case. This breached the "fair and impartial tribunal" part of art.6. It is important to note that the High Court proceeded on the basis of perception of justice being done rather than the standards of justice achieved in courts where "temps" were sitting. It was announced following the *Starrs* decision that part-time sheriffs would be appointed to replace temporary sheriffs. The part-time sheriff would enjoy secure tenure, avoiding the kind of objection taken in the *Starrs* case to the "temps". Most part-time sheriffs continue their role as solicitors or advocates and "float", i.e. travel to different jurisdictions from where they normally practise. They are paid on a daily basis.

The sheriff courts have a very wide criminal jurisdiction, both   04.20
solemn and summary. There are three limitations. First, the
jurisdiction is limited geographically. As a general rule a sheriff can
deal only with crimes committed within his sheriffdom. Secondly, the
jurisdiction does not extend to certain crimes, of which the most
important are treason, murder and rape. Thirdly, the sheriff's powers
of punishment are limited in most summary cases. From December
10, 2007, with the introduction of the Criminal Proceedings etc.
(Reform) (Scotland) Act 2007, the maximum penalty that may be
imposed in summary cases is 12 months' imprisonment or a £10,000
fine, in solemn cases five years' imprisonment or an unlimited fine. A
higher sentence in solemn cases may be imposed by referring the
matter to the High Court of Justiciary.

The prosecutor in the sheriff court is almost invariably the   04.21
procurator fiscal or his depute. In cases of considerable seriousness,
an advocate depute, the Solicitor General, or even the Lord
Advocate, might appear. The administrative work is done by the
sheriff clerk and his deputes.

Sheriff court: summary and solemn procedure
There are two forms of procedure followed in the sheriff court when   04.22
dealing with criminal cases. In summary cases the sheriff sits alone
without a jury. This procedure is used for the vast majority of
criminal prosecutions. There is no need for advance notification of
the witnesses who will be called, no need for shorthand notes or any
formal record and no need to lodge productions prior to the trial diet.
The only record kept of the proceedings are the sheriff's notes and any
minutes the clerk of court may be instructed to make by the sheriff.

Appeals from a summary case are normally taken by way of stated   04.23
case to the High Court. These can be against conviction, or sentence,
or both. This involves the accused person asking the sheriff to state in
writing the reasons for the conviction or the sentence imposed. As with
solemn cases leave to appeal to the High Court is required from a
single "sifting" High Court judge.

In solemn procedure the sheriff sits with a jury of 15. In this case   04.24
proceedings are formally recorded by tape recorder or a shorthand
writer. The procedure followed is basically the same as that to be
found in the High Court when sitting as a trial court.

Although there are no opening speeches in Scottish cases many   04.25
sheriffs think it useful to give an explanatory introductory address to
the jury regarding their function in the case. There are closing speeches
from the Crown and then the defence. In solemn procedure unlike
summary procedure if there is a conviction it is necessary for the
Crown to move for sentence before sentence will be pronounced.
Sentencing is automatic in summary cases. It is a very rare event in

solemn procedure for the Crown not to move for sentence, but it does occasionally happen, for example if the accused has spent time in custody awaiting trial but is only found guilty of a very minor part of the indictment.

No case to answer submission

04.26   In both solemn and summary procedure it is possible for the defence to make a motion at the end of the Crown case that there is no case to answer. This submission concerns the quantity of evidence which has been led. Quality is not an issue at this point. It should be noted that a no case to answer submission will only be successful if the evidence led by the Crown does not justify conviction on the charge/charges or any other competent charge/charges. Accordingly a no case to answer submission would fail in a housebreaking case if the Crown had brought forward enough evidence to justify a conviction on a charge of reset. It would be perfectly possible for the defence to make a submission to the effect that a conviction of reset only would be competent. But that would be a different form of submission. A no case to answer submission is restricted to the circumstances where conviction on any competent charge cannot follow on from the evidence which the Crown has led in the case.

Trial within a trial

04.27   The trial within a trial procedure had fallen into disuse until the landmark decision in the case of *Thomson v Crowe* **(1999)**. That five judge decision made it clear that a trial within a trial is competent, and indeed necessary, in certain circumstances in both solemn and summary procedure. A trial within a trial is necessary when one party questions the admissibility of evidence which the other proposes to adduce before the court. In almost all cases it will be the defence who are claiming that evidence is inadmissible, e.g. because the police forced a confession out of the accused person by means of threats or inducements. In these circumstances the sheriff will hear the evidence from the witnesses and hear submissions at the end of this section of the evidence on the admissibility of that evidence. In the case of a jury trial the sheriff will hear the evidence outwith the presence of the jury. If the sheriff decides that evidence is admissible it would be necessary to bring the jury back into court and then recall all the relevant witnesses and have them go through their evidence once more because the jury did not hear the evidence on the first occasion. Reporting evidence led during the trial within a trial procedure may be a contempt risk, even if the judge/sheriff forgets to put the requisite reporting restriction in place [see **Chapter 15**]. If the evidence is inadmissible, the jury should be unaware of it.

HIGH COURT OF JUSTICIARY

The judges of the High Court of Justiciary are the Lord Justice   04.28
General (who is the same person as the Lord President of the Court
of Session), the Lord Justice-Clerk and Lords Commissioners of
Justiciary. All are also judges of the Court of Session and Senators of
the College of Justice, which means they cover both criminal and civil
business. The 1990 Law Reform Act also made provision for
"temporary" High Court judges, leading to the appointment of two
leading QCs and two sheriffs. The number of temporary judges soon
increased to eight. These temporary Court of Session and High Court
judges were not used following the **Starrs (1999)** decision [see
para.04.19]. But the challenge to temporary judges failed.
Temporary judges hold their commission for three years rather than
the temporary sheriffs' one year. Also they are appointed by the Lord
Justice General rather than the Lord Advocate. **Kearney v HM
Advocate (2006)** was a significant case for temporary judges. The
appellant argued that he had been denied a fair trial as it had taken
place before a judge who was not independent considering his
appointment and period of tenure. It was further argued that the
Lord Advocate, under s.57(2) of the Scotland Act 1998, had no
power to conduct a prosecution before a tribunal lacking
independence and impartiality. The temporary judge, an advocate,
was appointed for three years by the Scottish Ministers after
consultation with the Lord Justice General. The appeal was
dismissed on the basis that a reasonable observer would not consider
the judge to be biased. The fact that it was the Lord Justice General,
and not the Lord Advocate, who determined the workload of judges,
together with his security of tenure during the period of his
appointment, was enough to satisfy the requirements of
independence and impartiality.

The seat of the High Court is at Parliament House in Edinburgh, but   04.29
it also goes on circuit to other parts of Scotland. All of the judges do
not, of course, sit in each case. Normally there is only one but difficult
cases can be heard by two or more. In 1999 the unusual precedent for a
Scottish court sitting outside the United Kingdom was seen in the
Lockerbie case. However, strictly speaking, either Camp Zeist or
Kamp van Zeist in Holland was legally designated to be part of
Scotland.

The High Court deals with the most serious crimes and is the only   04.30
court which can try treason, murder or rape. Prosecutions are
conducted by the Lord Advocate, the Solicitor General, or, more
usually, an advocate depute.

04.31 The High Court also has jurisdiction to hear appeals from and review the decisions of cases heard on summary procedure. When sitting for this purpose it consists of at least two judges and is commonly referred to as the Justiciary Appeal Court. It has the important duty of reviewing proceedings in all inferior criminal courts with a view to seeing that justice is done.

Rape cases

04.32 Judges of the High Court of Justiciary normally "close the doors" while the evidence of an alleged victim of rape or attempted rape is being heard, the object being to protect the witness from anything which might inhibit her in giving evidence. It has also become the practice of the judges to allow reporters covering the proceedings to remain in court provided they do not identify the witness in their reports.

04.33 This practice was judicially recognised in a case in 1983 in which Lord Avonside said:

> "In our courts a victim alleged to have been raped almost invariably gives evidence behind closed doors. In such a situation the public is not permitted to hear her evidence. It has been the practice, particularly in Glasgow, to allow the Press reporters to remain. They are asked to exercise a wise discretion, and, in my experience, this they do admirably. The trial judge could, of course, if he thought it desirable, exclude the Press and clear the court completely".

04.34 Besides the powers the judges have under statutes of the Scottish Parliament under the Criminal Procedure (Scotland) Act 1975 they may, from the opening of the evidence in a rape trial "or the like", clear the court of all persons except those actually involved in the proceedings. Judges can now also give directions to prohibit publication of "a name or other matter" where they were already able merely to prohibit disclosure of it in open court.

04.35 The law in England on rape reporting has a much more chequered history, perhaps illustrating the wisdom of a voluntary code.

04.36 In England identification in court reports of the alleged victim of rape or attempted rape was banned and it became an offence to identify the accused in such cases unless and until he was convicted. The absurd consequences emerged in a number of cases, in particular in a case in 1986 when a man charged and named by the police in connection with a series of murders became anonymous when he was charged also with rape. Apart from the difficulties this created for the media, the police were hampered in circulating details of the man wanted for the crimes. It became clear also that a man acquitted of rape and convicted of murdering his victim could be jailed for life but not identified by the media, which, however, would be free in law to name the victim.

Following the Ealing Vicarage rape case in London in which the victim was identified in a number of reports, major changes were made in England under the Criminal Justice Act 1988. The Act did away with the anonymity of rape accused and increased restrictions on identifying the victim. The law is now contained in the Sexual Offences (Amendment) Act 1992, which protects the victims of other sexual attacks. 04.37

The position in England now is that after an allegation of a rape offence, the name, address, or picture of the woman cannot be published in her lifetime if this is likely to lead to her being identified by members of the public as an alleged victim. Also, after a person is accused of rape, or information is laid before a magistrate accusing him of rape, nothing may be published in the woman's lifetime to identify her as an alleged victim. 04.38

The restrictions apply in cases of rape, attempted rape, aiding, abetting, counselling or procuring rape or attempted rape, incitement to rape, conspiracy to rape and burglary with intent to rape. They also apply in civil cases, for example if the woman claims damages for rape. 04.39

The restrictions may be lifted in certain circumstances, for example if the woman was charged with a criminal offence arising from the rape allegation, such as wasting police time because of a false allegation. 04.40

The woman may also be named if, before trial, the accused satisfies a Crown Court judge that this is necessary to bring witnesses forward and the defence will be prejudiced if the restriction is not lifted; the court is satisfied that anonymity places an unreasonable restriction on reporting the trial; or the alleged victim gives her written consent. 04.41

COURT OF CRIMINAL APPEAL

Strictly speaking, there is no such court in Scotland. However, the "Scottish Court of Criminal Appeal" is a convenient term frequently used instead of the more correct but cumbersome "High Court of Justiciary sitting as a Court of Criminal Appeal". The court hears appeals against conviction or sentence in trials heard on solemn procedure. Traditionally, it is the highest Scottish criminal court. There is no appeal to what was traditionally known as the House of Lords but is now under the umbrella of the Supreme Court. But under the Scotland Act 1998 a "devolution issue" can now be taken to the Supreme Court, which was formerly the Judicial Committee of the House of Lords and comprises the country's 12 most senior justices. There is now a "sift" procedure whereby it is necessary for an appellant to obtain leave to appeal before proceeding to the full 04.42

hearing. The sift takes place on the basis of the documents lodged by the appellant's solicitors. If the single "sifting" judge rejects the appeal, the appellant can apply to a quorum of the High Court for a review of the single judge's decision. Experience has shown that few appellants take this course of action. Current information suggests that about three-quarters of all appeals are dismissed by the sifting judge.

04.43   In addition to appeals at the instance of the accused person, cases may be referred to the High Court by the Scottish Criminal Cases Review Commission. Such cases are treated by the court in the same way as a normal appeal. The Scottish Criminal Cases Review Commission will normally only consider a case once a first appeal has been taken and rejected by the High Court.

04.44   Although not strictly appeal, another form of procedure occasionally found is a reference by the Lord Advocate to the High Court on a point of law. The High Court's decision in this case does not overturn a decision of a lower court. However, it may give guidance as to the conduct of future cases. Some significant matters have been considered by the High Court in this way. In 1992 the High Court decided that crime carried out as a joke still attracted criminal penalties. In 1995 the court decided that the supply of a controlled drug to someone who dies as a result of taking that drug was a good legal basis for a charge of culpable homicide.

04.45   Of those appeals which proceed to the full court hearing, sentencing appeals are disposed of by a bench of two judges and appeals involving conviction by three judges. Occasionally in a case of importance a larger bench of five or more judges will be convened.

SCOTTISH CRIMINAL PROCEDURE

04.46   Although the details of criminal procedure can be left to the lawyer, the journalist should know the steps in outline so that he can tell what is happening and what is about to happen. In this field the laws of Scotland and England are very different. To take only one example, private prosecutions are common in England but very rare in Scotland. An outstanding case occurred in 1982 when, after the Crown had decided not to prosecute three youths following a particularly vicious attack upon a woman in Glasgow, the High Court granted her authority to bring a private prosecution (by the old process of issuing a bill for criminal letters). The case went to trial and resulted in convictions for rape against one youth and for indecent assault against two others. It was the first private prosecution to have been allowed under this procedure in Scotland since 1909. The three judges who authorised the private prosecution described the case as strange and unique, the Crown having earlier dropped proceedings against the youths following a psychiatric report that the risk of damage to the victim's health if she appeared in court made it inadvisable that she be called as a witness. The court's decision to allow her to proceed was reached after the judges were satisfied that she would after all be able to appear and give evidence, without which it was originally thought a prosecution could not succeed. The court ruled that there was no doubt the woman had the necessary title and interest to prosecute privately, and this course was not opposed by the Lord Advocate. This so-called Glasgow rape case has not been followed by other private prosecutions. In 1992 a woman who claimed she had been raped in her own home by three men applied to the court for authority to take private proceedings against them. However, her application for a bill of criminal letters to prosecute the three men privately was refused by the High Court.

The Lord Advocate, assisted by the Solicitor General for Scotland, is responsible for the investigation and prosecution of crime in Scotland. Both are appointed by the Crown. In terms of the Scotland Act 1998, both the Lord Advocate and the Solicitor General for Scotland are members of the Scottish Parliament ex officio. The Lord Advocate and the Solicitor General have the function of supplying legal advice to the Scottish Government, i.e. the Scottish Ministers. In practice the Lord Advocate delegates most of his responsibility in criminal matters to advocates depute who work, along with a staff of officials, at the Crown Office in Edinburgh. The procurators fiscal investigate crime at the local level under the general supervision of the Crown Office. In the case of minor offences the procurator fiscal has a discretion whether or not to prosecute, or to issue a formal written warning, with the implied sanction of a prosecution if the warning is not heeded. He can also impose a fixed penalty for minor offences, similar to road traffic law, which avoids the time and expense of a criminal trial. He reports more serious crimes to the Crown Office which decides whether to prosecute and, if so, in which court. 04.47

Two general principles should be noted at this stage. The first is that everyone is innocent until he is proved guilty beyond reasonable doubt (and in Scotland the proof must normally be by the evidence from two independent sources—known as corroboration). The second is a principle of great importance to journalists which will be dealt with in more detail later. It is that there must be no publicity which may seriously prejudice a person's trial (which can constitute either the case not proceeding and/or the publisher being found guilty of a contempt of court) [see **Chapter 15**]. 04.48

As already noted there are two types of criminal procedure— summary and solemn. Different rules apply but the preliminary steps 04.49

are the same. The first stage is generally the police investigation under the authority of the procurator fiscal. Newspapers have sometimes played an active part in the exposure of crime but there is a grave risk of contempt of court if anything is published after arrest has been made or a warrant granted for arrest which creates a substantial risk of seriously prejudicing or impeding the course of justice. Journalists should understand that it is the creation of the risk of prejudice which constitutes contempt of court. It is not necessary that a journalist has created actual prejudice.

04.50   The police often enlist the help of the media in their inquiries and there is probably no danger in assisting as requested. In certain cases, however, it may be wise to check that the request has been cleared by the procurator fiscal. This would be advisable, for example, if the request is to publish a photograph of a wanted man in a case where the question of identification could arise at a later stage. Even if the Crown approves the release of a photograph, or an identikit likeness, it should be remembered that the defence can independently raise the issue of contempt. However, a finding of contempt would be extremely unlikely in these circumstances.

04.51   The investigations may result in an arrest. Normally a warrant is required but some statutes allow arrest without warrant. A policeman can arrest without warrant when he finds a person committing or attempting to commit a serious crime or when he is told by the victim or a credible eyewitness that this has just occurred. He can also arrest without warrant in cases of breach of the peace or threatened violence or in certain circumstances when he finds a person in possession of stolen goods and unable to give a satisfactory explanation.

SUMMARY PROCEDURE

04.52   Where the accused has not been arrested, but has simply been cited to appear, he may plead in person, through a solicitor or by letter. If he pleads guilty in his absence, he may, subject to certain safeguards, be sentenced there and then. If he pleads not guilty a date will be fixed for a trial. If the accused is refused bail, the trial must commence within 40 days of his first appearance in court [see **para.04.59**].

04.53   If an accused person has pled "not guilty", the court will hold an intermediate diet three weeks prior to the trial diet. The purpose of the intermediate diet is to ascertain the state of preparation of the parties. The sheriff will wish to ascertain if there are areas of the evidence which can be agreed so that certain witnesses need not be called to give evidence at the trial proper. It is perfectly possible for an accused person to choose to plead "guilty" at the intermediate diet. There is no evidence led at the intermediate diet. An early plea of guilty entitles the accused to a discount in sentence.

The procedure at the trial is straightforward. The prosecutor calls   04.54
his first witness and examines him. The defence can cross-examine (leading questions, which are questions with a "yes" or "no" answer, are allowed at this stage), after which the prosecution has a limited right to re-examine. After all the evidence for the prosecution has been led, the defence may advance a "no case to answer submission" which argues that there is insufficient evidence to convict the accused of the crime charged or any competent alternative [see **para.04.26**]. If there is no such submission, or if it is unsuccessful, then the evidence for the defence is led. The defence is not compelled to lead evidence. Even if they do so, the accused need not go into the witness box. After the hearing of all evidence the prosecutor addresses the court, followed by the accused or his agent and the judge pronounces his finding. This may be either guilty, not guilty or not proven. A finding of not proven has the same effect as a finding of not guilty. It is used where the court is not satisfied that the man is innocent but the prosecution has failed to prove that he is guilty. (Note that the correct terminology is "the charge was found not proven". It is not "the accused was found not proven".) If the accused is found guilty he is allowed to address the court before sentence is pronounced. Normally this is done by his solicitor, who tenders a "plea in mitigation" to the court.

CRIMINAL PROCEDURE (SCOTLAND) ACT 1995

Criminal procedure in Scotland is consolidated in the Criminal   04.55
Procedure (Scotland) Act 1995, as amended by the Crime and Punishment (Scotland) Act 1997 the Bail, Judicial Appointments etc. (Scotland) Act 2000 and the Criminal Proceedings etc. (Reform) (Scotland) Act 2007. In the legislation, there is to be found provision on anonymity of children involved in criminal cases as accused or victims [see **Chapter 6**].

The 1995 Act gives police powers to detain a suspect for up to six   04.56
hours while they make investigations to enable them to decide whether there is sufficient evidence to arrest him. The strict liability rule under the contempt of court law does not come into operation until the arrest stage is reached or a warrant is granted or an indictment/complaint served, but the journalist must still exercise great caution about what he reports at the detention stage. Publication of information which creates a serious risk of prejudice to any future trial before an arrest is made or a warrant issued may be regarded as contempt at common law [see **Chapter 15**].

04.57   There are safeguards for the detainee: he is not obliged to answer any questions other than those intended to find out his name and address; he has to be told the nature of the suspected offence; he is entitled to have his detention intimated to a solicitor and one other person of his choice; and if not arrested at the end of six hours' detention he must be released and cannot again be detained on the same grounds. If he is arrested he is entitled to have this fact intimated to a person named by him without unnecessary delay. There are special safeguards for children. At the time of publication, it is anticipated that his rights will be extended to include the right to have access to legal advice before any interview takes place under caution.

04.58   The Act gives an accused the right to petition the sheriff to have an identification parade held where the prosecutor has not already made arrangements for one and the sheriff considers it reasonable.

04.59   In summary cases an accused who is refused bail by the court and is kept in custody must not be detained for more than 40 days after his initial court appearance. The court, however, has power to grant an extension for reasons similar to those provided under solemn procedure (referred to below), and subject to a right of appeal by either side.

SOLEMN PROCEDURE

04.60   In solemn procedure the accused's first appearance in court is on petition in chambers before a sheriff, and all that can be published about the proceedings at this stage, besides the identity of the accused (unless he is a child) is a general indication of the nature of the charges, supplied usually by the procurator fiscal. It is important to remember that the fiscal may later proceed on an amended charge, or charges, or even drop proceedings altogether, although this is unusual. The accused may apply for bail at this hearing. If bail is refused the accused will be detained "for further inquiries" for a period of up to eight days. When brought back to a second private hearing in the sheriff's chambers (called the full committal diet) he may apply for bail again. If bail is refused the accused is detained "until liberated in due course of law".

04.61   There is legal presumption in favour of bail being granted. But a bad record of previous convictions or reasonable belief that the accused might abscond or interfere with evidence or witnesses would point towards bail being refused.

04.62   Journalists must note that the reasons for a refusal of bail cannot normally be revealed until the trial is completed, although the bare decision of a grant or a refusal of bail is normally reportable. The

United Kingdom Government conceded in the European Court of Human Rights in Strasbourg in February 2000 that the provisions in United Kingdom domestic law preventing someone from applying for bail if appearing in court on a second charge having already been convicted on a previous occasion were in breach of the Convention. In practice it is unlikely that persons accused of such serious offences (culpable homicide, attempted murder, rape, attempted rape) would be granted bail if already convicted of one of these crimes. However, from February 2000 they were allowed to make the application. The position was regularised in terms of statute in the Bail, Judicial Appointments etc. (Scotland) Act 2000.

Pleading diets occur automatically in sheriff and jury cases. In the other form of solemn procedure, namely that before the High Court and a jury, there will only be a preliminary diet if one of the parties asks for this. Usually, a preliminary diet is requested where there is a preliminary legal matter which the defence wish to argue. For example, they may claim that the terms of the indictment lack specification, i.e. there is insufficient detail. They might also argue that the indictment does not disclose a crime known to the law of Scotland. However, a preliminary or pleading diet can explore any legal matter if the court is willing to listen. 04.63

It is also open for there to be a judicial examination as a method of discovering, at a hearing in private before a sheriff, what explanation or comment the suspect may have on any incriminating statement he is alleged to have made. He can be questioned by the fiscal under the control of the sheriff who must ensure questioning is fair. The accused has a right to be represented by a solicitor and to consult him before answering any question, and the solicitor may ask him questions to clear up any ambiguity. A shorthand record is kept of the examination and a copy of the transcript must be made available to the accused. As an additional safeguard, a tape recording of the proceedings is kept. The record, or any part of it, may be used in evidence. The journalist is not allowed into these proceedings and will have to rely on the procurator fiscal or the defence agent for information as to what took place. In that situation, particular care must be taken with any report. 04.64

In Scotland, if someone is accused of a crime under solemn procedure, very strict legal time limits apply. The indictment, which details the charges which the accused will face, must be served on him within 80 days of the accused being fully committed in custody. Where the case is to proceed before a sheriff and jury, the trial must start within 110 days of full committal. A first diet must take place not less than 10 days before the trial. That calling of the case allows the court the opportunity to establish the state of preparation of both Crown and defence. The procedure and time limits are different in High 04.65

Court cases. There, the next step after full committal is the preliminary hearing which must occur within 110 days from the point of full committal. This hearing gives the judge an opportunity to assess the extent of preparation of both sides, and he will only allow the case to go ahead to trial if both sides are ready. The trial in custody cases must begin within 140 days.

04.66   The Act requires that a trial under solemn procedure must start within 12 months of the accused's first appearance on petition; otherwise he must be discharged and cannot be charged again with the same offence unless delay has been caused by his failure to appear or an extension has been granted by the court.

04.67   If during the trial the court decides that, because of the accused's misconduct, a proper hearing cannot take place unless he is removed, it may order that the trial proceed in his absence, although he must be legally represented.

04.68   In court the accused is sometimes called "the panel". The trial takes place before a judge and a jury of 15. Neither Crown nor defence now have any challenges to the jurors called unless on cause shown. Once the jury is empanelled, the trial will begin. The clerk reads out the indictment to the jurors and puts them on oath to "well and truly try the accused according to the evidence". A juror may wish to affirm rather than take the oath. Normally, jurors are given copies of the indictment and copies of any special defence (alibi, incrimination, insanity and self-defence) lodged. There are no opening speeches in Scottish criminal procedure. The Crown calls its witnesses and the defence are entitled to cross-examine. The prosecutor may re-examine. The judge may ask questions to clarify points of confusion. After the Crown case is complete, if the defence pleads that insufficient evidence has been led to convict the accused, they can advance a submission of "no case to answer". It is important, as noted above, for journalists to understand that this submission is based purely on the question as to whether or not in law a sufficient quantity of evidence has been led to go to the jury. It does not deal with the question of the quality of the evidence.

04.69   The prosecution and the defence address the jury in turn and the judge charges the jury. The general principle is that the jury are masters of the facts and the judge master of the law. His main duty in charging the jury is to set out the law applicable to the case but he may also make fair and impartial comments on the evidence. After the charge the jury retire to consider their verdict. The verdict need not be unanimous, it may be by a majority, even eight to seven. The verdicts available to the jury are "guilty", "not guilty" or "not proven". In the rare case where the accused is found to have been insane at the time of the alleged crime, he will be found not guilty on the ground of insanity. An accused person found not guilty on the ground of insanity can still be made subject to a hospital order by the court. Such a hospital order may require its subject to be detained in the state hospital at Carstairs. An individual subject to a hospital order has the right to appeal on an annual basis to the sheriff of the area in which he is detained for review of his detention. The terms of the mental health legislation required that the person detained had to be receiving some form of medical treatment to justify continued detention. This famously caused controversy with the release of Noel Ruddle in July 1999 when the weight of psychiatric evidence brought before Sheriff Douglas Allan at Lanark Sheriff Court was to the effect that Mr Ruddle was not being treated within Carstairs. The Scottish Parliament rushed through amending legislation aimed at ensuring that in future sheriffs could refuse to release such persons if it was felt their release would cause a danger to the safety of the public. This legislation has survived a challenge to its competency based on the European Convention on Human Rights.

SENTENCING

If the verdict is "guilty" then, after the prosecutor has moved for 04.70 sentence and any previous convictions have been admitted or proved, the accused or his counsel or solicitor may make a plea in mitigation of sentence. The judge will then pronounce sentence, but if the trial has been in the sheriff court and the sheriff thinks the offence merits a heavier sentence than he can impose, he can remit to the High Court for sentence.

After the initial petition procedure but before service of the 04.71 indictment the accused may inform the Crown that he wants to plead guilty and have his case be disposed of as quickly as possible. He gets a shortened form of indictment and appears for sentence on what is known as a s.76 hearing.

The only sentence for murder is life imprisonment except where the 04.72 person convicted is under 18, in which case the sentence is detention without limit of time in a place and under conditions to be directed by the First Minister. If he is over 18 but under 21, the sentence is detention for life at first in a young offenders' institution and then in prison. Where the sentence passed is for life the judge may recommend the minimum term to be served and must give his reasons if he does so; a recommendation is appealable as part of the sentence. The Crime and Punishment (Scotland) Act 1997 makes provision for the imposition of life imprisonment for certain offenders—namely those who have been convicted of a "qualifying offence" committed after "the relevant date". "The relevant date" is the date on which s.1 of the 1997 Act is brought into force. At the time of writing, this section has not been brought into force. Qualifying offences are such things as culpable homicide; attempted murder; incitement to commit murder or conspiracy to commit murder; rape or attempted rape; sodomy or attempted sodomy; assault to severe injury of the danger of life; robbery with a weapon; various firearms offences; lewd, indecent or libidinous practices; unlawful intercourse with a girl under the age of 13 years. In light of the incorporation of the European Convention into the domestic Scots law it seems increasingly unlikely that this provision will ever be activated. The actual length of the sentence will be decided by the court and will generally be determined by a period depending on the nature of the crime, the impact on the victim, personal circumstances of the offender and the timing of the plea. Unlike in England for those over 21, there is no unlimited period for a life term. The maximum period is 30 years and the minimum period 12 years.

04.73   No prison sentence may be imposed on a person over 21 who has not previously been so sentenced to detention, unless the court thinks no other course is appropriate. No-one under 21 may be sent to prison, and borstal training was replaced by detention in a young offenders' institution.

04.74   As already noted at the close of the prosecution evidence in either solemn or summary procedure the accused is entitled (in solemn procedure in the absence of the jury) to submit a plea that there is no case to answer. If the plea is sustained the accused is acquitted, if refused the trial proceeds to defence evidence. Any report of submissions made on such a plea in a solemn case can be safely published only after the proceedings have ceased to be "active" [see **Chapter 15**].

COMPENSATION

04.75   Offenders can be ordered to pay compensation to their victims, either instead of or in addition to any other method the court may select for dealing with them, for personal injury, loss or damage caused by their offences. The provisions do not apply to loss resulting from death or from a road accident unless caused by the convicted person. There is no limit to compensation under solemn procedure, but in summary cases the limits are set by statute. Where the convicted person's means are insufficient to meet a fine besides compensation, priority is given to compensation. A compensation order is treated as a sentence for appeal purposes.

DIFFERENCES BETWEEN SOLEMN
AND SUMMARY PROCEDURE

The main differences between summary and solemn procedure can be   04.76
summed up as follows. In summary procedure there is no jury and also
no petition for committal. Proceedings begin with the complaint. In
solemn procedure there is usually a petition for committal and
proceedings are on indictment. Cases under summary procedure are
heard in the sheriff courts or JP courts. There is no jury. Cases on
solemn procedure are heard in the sheriff or High Court and there is a
jury. Appeal in summary procedure is by stated case or bill of
suspension to three judges sitting as the Justiciary Appeal Court.
Appeal in solemn procedure is to at least three judges of the High
Court sitting as a Court of Criminal Appeal.

Summary appeals
Summary appeals against conviction normally proceed by a method   04.77
called "a stated case". Occasionally where the appeal is based on the
argument that the court has done something which is incompetent, the
method will be bill of suspension. The initial step is an application for a
stated case, note of appeal (against sentence only) or bill of suspension,
which must take place within one week of the decision under appeal
(the stage at which the proceedings again become active under the
Contempt of Court Act 1981).

The draft stated case prepared by the sheriff or justice is subject to   04.78
adjustments proposed by either side if they are agreed at a hearing
arranged for this purpose. The judge stating a case for appeal must
give his reasons if he refuses any adjustments, and these may be taken
into account by the appeal court, which also has power to hear
additional evidence or order that this be heard by a person it appoints
for the purpose. The appeal court may also appoint an assessor with
expert knowledge to assist in deciding an appeal.

There is also a right of appeal against conviction by way of bill of   04.79
suspension where the stated case procedure would not be appropriate
or competent. The prosecutor may appeal against acquittal or
sentence on grounds, in either case, of alleged miscarriage of justice.
The court may remit a case back with directions to affirm the verdict,
quash the verdict and authorise a new prosecution (to be begun within
two months) on the same or similar charges as before. Where an
appeal against acquittal is sustained the court may convict and
sentence the respondent, remit the case back to the court below with
instructions to do so, or remit back to the lower court with the appeal
court's opinion and direction.

04.80   As stated above, all criminal appeals by the accused now require leave of a single "sifting" judge of the High Court before they can proceed to a full appeal hearing. Summary appeals have a particularly high rejection rate at the "sift" stage.

Solemn appeals

04.81   Where the appeal court in solemn procedure has allowed an appeal against conviction on the ground that there has been a miscarriage of justice, a new prosecution may be brought within two months charging the accused with the same or any similar offence arising out of the same facts. However, no sentence may be passed which could not have been passed in the original proceedings.

04.82   In the first case to be brought under this provision, a man who had been charged in 1982 with the murder of his wife's lover was convicted of culpable homicide in the High Court at Inverness. He appealed successfully, on the ground that a misdirection by the trial judge had led to a miscarriage of justice. Under the old law he would have been freed, but under the provisions introduced by the Criminal Justice (Scotland) Act 1980 the Lord Advocate was granted authority by the appeal court to bring a fresh prosecution, commonly referred to as a "retrial". This time, the man was charged with culpable homicide and the second trial took place at Edinburgh to avoid the risk of prejudice from local knowledge, in Inverness, of the original hearing and conviction. The charge was found not proven and the accused was released. Evidence at the two trials was for the most part identical. A somewhat surprising use of this power came in the case of *Alexander Hall*. An ex-police officer, Mr Hall had served 12 years' imprisonment for the crime of murder when his second appeal, heard in 1998, was successful. The Crown asked for and were granted authority to bring a fresh prosecution, which they did in May 1999. The fresh prosecution was unsuccessful.

04.83   While in theory there is no limit to the number of retrials in any case, in practice more than one is unlikely. The High Court will take various factors into account in deciding whether or not to grant authority to bring a fresh prosecution. Experience has shown that it is the exception rather than the rule for the High Court to allow a second prosecution. Even in cases where the error in the lower court has not been the Crown's but that of the judge (in misdirecting the jury), the court will not necessarily grant authority.

04.84   The procedure is exceptional, compared to practice in England where retrials are relatively common, but the 1980 Act brought to an end the fundamental rule in Scotland that an accused could not be tried more than once on the same charge. In such a case the proceedings remain active under the Contempt of Court Act 1981 from the time authority for a new prosecution is granted by the court, until a new trial is concluded or a decision is taken to drop further proceedings. There are however a few instances of retrials in Scottish procedure.

These present particular difficulties for the journalist in making sure   04.85 that nothing printed or broadcast prejudices the forthcoming retrial proceedings. A great deal of the information is already in the public domain. However, journalists would do well to remember that courts accept the point that the public mind is "notoriously short". Journalists cannot proceed on the basis that, because something has already been printed in a newspaper, it can be reprinted prior to the second trial. Journalists must exercise considerable discretion in dealing with these difficult situations. It must be remembered that contempt of court can be committed by raising a risk that the evidence of witnesses will be affected by what is read in newspapers, heard on radio or seen on TV. Contempt is not restricted to prejudicing the minds of jurors. No doubt this was the main reason why, in 1999, journalists were extremely careful not to re-visit the facts which came out at the original trial in 1985 of former policeman Alexander Hall, when the High Court overturned his conviction but allowed the Crown authority to bring a fresh prosecution [see **Chapter 15**].

An accused may appeal against conviction, sentence, or both, on   04.86 grounds of alleged miscarriage of justice, and formal notice has to be lodged at the Justiciary Office in Edinburgh within two weeks. This has special significance when the question of publicity arises after the end of a trial. The appeal court may uphold the verdict, quash the conviction, substitute an amended verdict of guilty (and pass a different sentence from that already passed), or, as we have seen, set aside the verdict and grant authority for a new prosecution. Where the appeal is against sentence the court has power not only to reduce but also to increase the original sentence.

Since October 1993 the Crown has had a right of appeal against   04.87 (what it feels) are unduly lenient sentences in solemn cases. An appeal can be taken by the Crown against a sentence imposed by either a sheriff or a High Court judge. The appeal court has made it clear that it will only increase a sentence if, "the sentence must be seen to be unduly lenient. That means that it must fall outside the range of sentences which the Judge at first instance, applying his mind to all the relevant factors, could reasonably have considered appropriate". Sentencing appeals are now heard by two judges.

Where an accused is found not guilty, that is (currently) the end of   04.88 the matter, although at the time of publication, a Scottish Law Commission report looks to have persuaded the Scottish Government to legislate to allow those acquitted of serious offences to be re-tried.

04.89   In both solemn and summary appeals there is provision for the hearing of additional evidence not available at the trial, and in either situation the Crown may appeal by bill of advocation. The High Court also has power under ss.106 (solemn cases) and 175 (summary cases) of the Criminal Procedure (Scotland) Act 1995 to allow the hearing of new evidence of any witnesses whether or not they were called at the trial. The applicant must provide an explanation as to why this evidence was not brought to the attention of the trial court. However, the legal test for admitting fresh evidence was lowered in 1997 and it already appears that the Appeal Court is willing to look at new evidence more readily than under the old legislation. The 1997 legislation followed a somewhat embarrassing public disagreement between the then Lord Justice General, Lord Hope, and the then Lord Justice-Clerk, Lord Ross, over the interpretation of the old test for admitting fresh evidence. In *HM Advocate v Church* **(1995)** Lord Hope put a very liberal interpretation on the old legislation, while Lord Justice-Clerk Ross, presiding over a court of five judges a few weeks later in *HM Advocate v Elliot* **(1995)** followed the traditional, more strict approach. That controversy has, however, been superseded by the new test, which came into force in 1997. The law is now found in s.106 (solemn) and s.175 (summary) of the Criminal Procedure (Scotland) Act 1995.

04.90   The High Court considered the new legislation in the high-profile case of *Campbell and Steele v HM Advocate* **(1998)**, the so-called ice-cream wars case. In that case the appeal was based in part on the change of evidence of a material witness. The majority of the judges took the view that, under the new legislation, the applicant was still required to provide a reasonable explanation to the court as to why the fresh evidence was not heard at the trial. The Lord Justice-Clerk and Lord Sutherland went on to say that only if they were satisfied by the applicant's reasonable explanation on that point would they go on to consider a second explanation from the witness as to why the fresh evidence now being proffered to the court had not been given at the original trial. That explanation, like the first, would have to be "reasonable". The third judge, Lord McCluskey, did not feel that this two-stage approach was necessary. However, in a subsequent appeal, when fresh expert witness evidence was produced, both Campbell and Steele's verdicts were overturned on the basis of a misdirection of the original trial judge.

SCOTTISH CRIMINAL CASES REVIEW COMMISSION

04.91   Since April 1, 1999 an accused person who has exhausted all rights of appeal may apply to the Scottish Criminal Cases Review Commission.

The purpose of applying is to request the Commission to refer the case back to the High Court sitting as the Court of Appeal. The Commission itself has no powers to overturn a conviction.

BAIL

An accused person is presumed innocent until proved guilty and should not, without good reason, be deprived of his or her liberty before conviction. It is reasonable, however, that if he goes free he should be required to give some security that he will appear at later stages in the proceedings. Bail is a means to this end.   04.92

Until the passing of the Bail etc. (Scotland) Act 1980, the normal security took the form of a payment of money under a bail bond, but the Act effectively abolished money bail except in special circumstances. Bail is now granted subject to conditions, laid down by the court or the Lord Advocate, to which the bail applicant must subscribe.   04.93

These will, for example, be that he will appear at a court diet when required, does not commit an offence while on bail or interfere with witnesses or obstruct the course of justice in any other way. He may also be required to make himself available to enable inquiries to be made or a report prepared to assist the court, or be required to report regularly at a police station, or stay away from his wife or family or other person(s) specified in the conditions attached to his bail. In special circumstances either the accused or someone on his behalf may be required to lodge money in court to ensure his attendance at a future hearing. The money may be forfeited if he fails to attend.   04.94

Liberation on bail may also be granted by the police after arrest on a summary charge, (often done where minor offences or more detailed technical ones are involved, where further investigation is necessary) and if the accused is refused bail at this stage he may apply to the court for bail. Because the conditions of bail are contained in a document, a copy of which the accused must receive, and which must show also his normal place of residence, access to the addresses of accused persons is more readily available to the media under the terms of the Bail Act than before it, when the accused was frequently cited at the sheriff clerk's office.   04.95

In deciding whether or not to grant bail the court may take into account the type of crime charged whether, for example, it involves alleged interference with witnesses or whether the applicant has a criminal record, and if so what bearing that may have upon the possibility of his being in breach of conditions attached to bail. In each case the court has to balance the right of the untried person to   04.96

the presumption of innocence against the risk of justice being frustrated by his failure to keep his part of the bargain.

04.97   For breach of his undertaking, the person granted bail may be fined and jailed for a maximum of three months in a summary case in the sheriff court, or a similar sum and 60 days in the JP court. If he is charged on indictment, he is liable to a fine (with no maximum laid down) and imprisonment up to two years. Any penalty imposed may be in addition to the sentence passed by the court in respect of the original offence.

04.98   Traditionally in Scots law, murder and treason were not bailable crimes. Exceptionally, a person accused of one of these crimes could be released by authority of the Lord Advocate or the High Court. However, the list of non-bailable crimes was considerably extended by the Criminal Procedure (Scotland) Act 1995 (s.26). In terms of that statute, a person accused for a second time of the following charges was to be automatically refused bail: attempted murder; culpable homicide; rape; attempted rape. But these rules of Scots law breached the rights of accused persons under the European Convention on Human Rights. The Scottish Parliament dealt with the matter in the Bail, Judicial Appointments etc. (Scotland) Act 2000. Now all accused persons have the right to apply for bail even if they are accused of the most serious crimes such as murder, rape and treason. Previous convictions of serious crimes are no longer an automatic bar to bail being granted. However, the seriousness of the charge and the existence of previous convictions make a grant of bail much less likely.

04.99   In addition to the provisions for pre-trial bail, anyone convicted and sentenced to jail or detention may be granted bail pending disposal of an appeal. However, it should be noted that a convicted person who lodges an appeal does not automatically return themselves to the position of a person accused of a crime at the outset of proceedings. Once a person has been convicted and sentenced to imprisonment, they have a difficult task in persuading the court that they should be released pending the appeal hearing.

04.100   There is a right of appeal against refusal or against the conditions attached to the granting of bail. The Crown may appeal against the granting of bail. In either case the appeal is normally heard by a High Court judge in chambers. The proceedings are kept private to protect the accused from possible prejudice arising from publicity given to statements made as a necessary part of information required by the judge. These may relate to the accused's record or other matters likely to influence the minds of potential jurors or witnesses at a subsequent trial. This kind of information must not appear in any report at this stage. Reporters, however, have a right of access to the decision, and this information is usually supplied by the Justiciary Office.

KEY POINTS

1. There are three criminal courts: High Court, sheriff JP   04.101
   (formerly district). The Lord Advocate is responsible for the
   investigation and prosecution of crime. Private prosecutions
   are extremely rare.
2. Solemn procedure (dealing with the most serious cases) begins
   by way of a petition and cases are heard by a judge or sheriff
   and a jury of 15. The maximum sheriff court sentence is three
   years. Certain cases such as murder and rape must be taken in
   the High Court. There is no opening speech and the verdict
   can be by a simple majority.
3. Summary cases start with a complaint and are heard by justice
   or sheriff sitting alone. Appeal against conviction involves
   initially a "sifting" single judge and then if leave is granted to
   three High Court judges or two judges in sentence only
   appeals. In certain cases the Appeal Court can grant
   authority for a retrial.

CHAPTER 5

CIVIL COURTS AND PROCEDURE

BY DUNCAN HAMILTON

THE GILL REVIEW

05.01 In February 2007, the then Minister for Justice announced that the Lord Justice-Clerk, Lord Gill, was to head a review of the civil courts. That review was published on September 30, 2009. It made many wide reaching recommendations which were anticipated to radically alter the administration of civil justice in Scotland. The proposals were broadly welcomed by the Scottish Government and by all parties in the Scottish Parliament. Nevertheless, financial constraints due to the reduction in the Scottish Government budget meant that some of the more substantial proposals will either not be adopted or their implementation will be significantly delayed.

THE PROPOSALS

05.02 The proposals are extensive in scope. Broadly, they cover changes to the civil court system, the introduction of case management, the increased use of information technology, the increased role of mediation as an alternative to formal court proceedings, pre-action protocols to avoid cases going to court at all and new mechanisms for ensuring that when cases do go to court, they settle very quickly. There is also a proposal for a Civil Justice Council for Scotland to draft and review rules of court and keep under review all the various changes being proposed. Finally, there are proposals for a new approach to judicial review.

05.03 The most relevant changes in the context of the journalist attempting to understand the proposals for new procedure are probably contained in Chapters 4 and 5 of the *Report of the Scottish Civil Courts Review* (The Stationery Office, 2009), Vol.1. They include:

- The designation of sheriffs as specialists in particular areas of practice, including solemn crime, general civil, personal injury, family and commercial (see paras 64, 66).

- The creation of a national Sheriff Appeal Court to hear summary criminal appeals and civil appeals from district judges and sheriffs (see para.79).
- The increase in the privative (i.e. exclusive) jurisdiction of the sheriff court from its current level of £5,000 to £150,000 (see para.123).
- The creation of a specialist personal injury court, based at Edinburgh Sheriff Court but with jurisdiction throughout Scotland. Pursuers will thus have the choice between local access to justice or the advantages of a sheriff court with an all-Scotland jurisdiction (see para.154).
- The creation of district judges who would sit in the sheriff court and hear summary criminal business and civil claims of modest value (see para.176).
- The introduction of a docket system in the Court of Session and sheriff court. A case would be allocated to a particular judge or sheriff, who would deal with all hearings in that case (see paras Ch.4, 44, 45, 62, 72, 73).
- With certain exceptions, that all actions should be subject to judicial case management. A case management hearing should be fixed shortly after defences are lodged. It would normally take place by means of a telephone conference call (see paras Ch.5, 48, 74, 77–81).
- In the sheriff court actions will be transferred to a court in which a sheriff with the relevant specialism is resident. Procedural business will be conducted by email, telephone, video conferencing or in writing (see Ch.5, para.76).
- District judges will have jurisdiction to hear housing actions, actions for payment of £5,000 or less, and referrals and appeals from children's hearings, and concurrent jurisdiction with sheriffs in family actions (see Ch.5, para.71).
- There should be a single new set of rules for cases for £5,000 or less (called "the simplified procedure"). The new rules should be based on a problem solving or interventionist approach in which the court should identify the issues and specify what it wishes to see or hear by way of evidence or argument. The rules should be written in plain English and drafted for party litigants rather than legal practitioners (see Ch.5, paras 125–127, 131).
- There should be a special procedure for dealing with multiple claims which give rise to common or similar issues of fact or law, for example, litigation arising out of a mass disaster or liability for defective products. Detailed recommendations are made regarding the features that such a procedure would

have, including special funding arrangements for multi-party actions to be administered by the Scottish Legal Aid Board (see Ch.13, paras 64–119).

05.04　These proposals will not necessarily all be introduced, or if they are it is likely that they will be further modified. For example, the raising of the privative jurisdiction of the sheriff court to £150,000 has already provoked controversy. Nevertheless, if and when funding allows and after the Scottish Parliament has fully considered the matter, significant and radical change can still be expected. The Scottish Governement published its response to the Review on November 11, 2010, accepting the principles and most of the detailed recommendations made. It did, however, suggest that some of the substantial changes would require to be made over a prolonged period of years.

05.05　In the meantime, however, the existing system and procedures will be maintained and it is accordingly vital that the journalist be aware of the status quo.

SHERIFF COURT

05.06　Scotland is divided into six regional sheriffdoms containing a total of 49 sheriff courts. Each sheriffdom has a sheriff principal who, as well as hearing appeals in civil cases, is responsible for the way business is conducted in the courts.

05.07　The sheriff court has a very wide civil jurisdiction extending to almost all types of action—such as divorce, adoption of children, liquidation of companies, club and gaming licence applications, bankruptcies and fatal accident inquiries. Exceptions such as actions of reduction of deeds require to be raised in the Court of Session. Actions involving amounts under £5,000 must be brought in the sheriff court. They cannot be heard by the Court of Session. This is what is known as the privative jurisdiction of the sheriff court. There is no upper limit to the value of cases which can be dealt with in the sheriff court. Civil jury trial in the sheriff court was abolished in 1980.

05.08　An important part of the sheriff court's work is its commissary jurisdiction involving the appointment and confirmation of executors to administer the estates of people who have died. Only when he has obtained confirmation is an executor entitled to ingather and administer the estate.

05.09　Procedure in civil cases in the sheriff court was modified by the introduction of the summary cause in 1971 and again by the introduction of the small claims procedure in 1988. Certain cases including all actions for payment of sums of money between £3,000 and £5,000 (excluding interest and expenses) are known as summary causes. They are begun by filling in a printed form of summons. All such forms are available from the court or on the Scottish Courts website. Evidence in these summary cause cases is not recorded. If a party loses and wishes to appeal, they can do so from a judgment of the sheriff to the sheriff principal on any point of law, and then from the sheriff principal to the Inner House of the Court of Session if the sheriff principal certifies the case as suitable for such an appeal.

The small claims procedure applies to actions where the money   05.10
value does not exceed £3,000. It was introduced after criticism of court procedures by the consumer lobby, which claimed that even the summary cause procedure was too difficult for lay people to understand. In small claims cases both pursuers and defenders are encouraged to "do it yourself". There is a preliminary hearing at which the sheriff tries to determine the issue between the parties. This takes the form of an informal discussion involving the sheriff, pursuer and defender or their representatives. If matters cannot be resolved at this stage the case is adjourned for a proof hearing at which, again, the emphasis is on informality. There is a right of appeal on a point of law to the sheriff principal, although appeals in small claims cases are extremely rare. The recent raising of the small claims limit from £750 to £3,000 was a response to the criticism that the original limits had been rendered too low as a consequence of not having been increased since 1988.

The procedure in ordinary causes, including actions for amounts   05.11
over £5,000, is more formal and follows the lines of Court of Session procedure, with some modifications which are noted later. Appeal is either to the sheriff principal and from there to the Inner House of the Court of Session, or else direct to the Inner House of the Court of Session.

COURT OF SESSION

The Court of Session sits in Edinburgh and consists of the Lord   05.12
President, Lord Justice-Clerk and 32 other judges. The total number of judges was increased to 34 in 2004. The personnel are the same as that of the High Court of Justiciary. Judges in the Court of Session are known also as "Senators of the College of Justice" or "Lords of Council and Session". Each judge takes the courtesy title of "Lord" or "Lady" followed by their surname or a territorial title. Because of pressure of business, the 1990 Law Reform Act provided for temporary judges to sit in the High Court and Court of Session. They sit on the Bench dressed as QCs—Queen's Counsel (i.e. senior advocates)—and do not wear the traditional judges' robes. Judges are now appointed after recommendation by the Judicial

Appointments Board. The criteria against which candidates are assessed and the statutory role of the Board are set out in the Judiciary and Courts (Scotland) Act 2008.

05.13 The court is divided into an Inner House which is largely an appeal court, and an Outer House which deals with cases at first instance. The Court of Session remains one court, however. The division between Inner and Outer House is not a strict one. Judges from the Inner House may sit as single judges in the Outer House to help with pressure of work, and judges from the Outer House may be brought in to make up an additional appellate bench, known as the Extra Division. In theory, the court could still sit as a whole court to hear cases of particular difficulty but the raising of the number of judges and limitations of space have made this impracticable.

05.14 The Inner House is in turn divided into two divisions of equal status, the First Division and the Second Division. The First Division consists of the Lord President and three judges. The Second Division consists of the Lord Justice-Clerk and three judges. The Outer House consists of judges who sit singly and are known as Lords Ordinary. The reason for this peculiar name is that at one time there were two types of judges in the Court of Session, Ordinary Lords and Extraordinary Lords, the latter being nominees of the King and needing no legal qualifications. The power of appointing Extraordinary Lords was lost in 1723. The Outer House is where most cases are heard at first instance across the entire spectrum of civil work. There are designated judges to deal with intellectual property disputes and commercial actions. The further development of specialist courts also forms part of the recommendations of the Gill Review.

05.15 The Inner House is mainly an appeal court, hearing appeals from the sheriff courts and from the Outer House as well as from various other special courts and tribunals. It also has an original jurisdiction in certain types of petition including many petitions to the *nobile officium*—the inherent power of the court to grant a remedy where none is otherwise available.

05.16 The Court of Session has a general power to review the judgments of inferior courts and tribunals on the ground that they have exceeded their jurisdiction or have failed to observe fundamental rules of justice, such as the rule that both parties must be heard before a decision is given.

05.17 The Judiciary and Courts (Scotland) Act 2008 has made significant changes in a number of key areas. First, the Act provides a statutory guarantee of the continued independence of the judiciary in Scotland. Every person responsible for the administration of justice in Scotland—including the First Minister, his Cabinet, Members of the Scottish Parliament and the Lord Advocate—is now statutorily bound to uphold the independence of the judiciary. Secondly, the Act unifies the judiciary under the leadership of the Lord President and gives specific powers and responsibilities to the holder of that office ranging from the efficient disposal of business in the Scottish courts to the welfare, training and guidance of judges. Thirdly, the Judicial Appointments Board for Scotland is established in statute and the factors influencing appointment as a judge are laid out in the Act. That is a deliberate attempt to provide transparency in the process which the Scottish Parliament believes to be important for public confidence. Fourthly, and often as important from a public perspective, the Act deals with complaints about the judiciary and matters such as conduct, suspension and removal from post. The procedures around complaints about the judiciary are perhaps of potential journalistic importance given the frequency of, and coverage given to, disaffected litigants or interested parties in both the civil and criminal courts. Fifthly, a range of important structural questions are addressed in the Act—setting out the new procedure for aspects such as altering the boundaries of sheriffdoms—areas where the Lord President's consent to change is now required. In short, whilst some of the changes are simply putting in statute what was already in place, other aspects of this Act are of significance in terms of transparency and accountability—two aspects of immediate interest to the journalist. Other new powers such as those to revise the structure and governance of the courts may yield significant change in the years to come.

SUPREME COURT

In civil cases, unlike criminal, there has long existed an appeal from the 05.18 Court of Session to the House of Lords. That appeal is now to the new Supreme Court, established in October 2009 under the Constitutional Reform Act 2005.

An appeal must be lodged within three months of the judgment 05.19 appealed from. The Scottish Government has previously expressed a view that it might consider introducing measures to remove the right of appeal to the Supreme Court and thus establish the Inner House of the Court of Session as the final court of civil appeal in Scotland. In December 2008, a review was announced by the Scottish Government into that potential reform under the chairmanship of Professor Neil Walker of the University of Edinburgh. The Walker Report (*Final Appellate Jurisdiction in the Scottish Legal System* (The Stationery Office, 2010)) was published in January 2010 and whilst accepting the desirability of a new, self-standing Scottish Supreme Court in the event of Scotland becoming independent, concluded that under the current constitutional set up, the most attractive option is a quasi-federal Supreme Court. Under that option, those Scottish cases, both civil and criminal, that raise common UK issues would be heard by the quasi-federal Supreme Court at a Scottish location, while those Scottish cases, again both civil and criminal, which address distinct questions of Scots law can be dealt with solely and conclusively by the indigenous Scottish courts. The Scottish Government will now consider what proposals, if any, to bring forward.

PROCEDURE IN CIVIL CASES IN SCOTLAND

05.20 What follows is merely an outline designed to give a general picture of the steps involved in getting a case into court. The person who brings an ordinary civil action is called the pursuer, the person against whom it is brought, the defender.

05.21 In the case of ordinary actions in the Court of Session, the first step is for the pursuer's solicitor or counsel to prepare a summons. This is, in essence, a document summoning the defender to appear at court, setting out the pursuer's claim and asking the court to give judgment in his favour. A copy of the summons is served on the defender, usually by recorded delivery or registered post. There is then a period of grace, known as the *induciae*, to give the defender time to take legal advice and decide on his course of action.

05.22 When this period expires, the pursuer's solicitor lodges in the court offices what is known as "the process", which consists of the summons and various other documents which will be needed later in the proceedings.

05.23 The next stage is that the case appears in the calling list of the Court of Session. This is the first public announcement of the action. The only details given are the names and addresses of the parties and the names of the pursuer's solicitors. The calling list is available online at the Scottish Courts website and is physically attached to the walls of the Court of Session for all to examine.

05.24 If the defender does not defend, the court will normally give judgment for the pursuer—a decree in absence. Exceptions to that rule include actions affecting status, such as an action for divorce or declarator of death where decree will not be given until the grounds of action have been proved by sufficient evidence. If the defender does wish to defend, he must enter appearance and lodge defences containing his answers to the pursuer's allegations.

05.25 Those written claims and defences are contained in a single document known as the record (pronounced as in "to record"). The record contains numbered paragraphs setting out each aspect of the case. The defender answers each numbered paragraph with one of his own. A period of time is then allowed for the written pleadings which set out the respective cases of the parties to be altered by them in light of ongoing investigations, and in response to the case the other side is putting forward. During this period the record is open for adjustment and is accordingly known as the "open record".

After the parties have completed their adjustments, the court makes 05.26 an order closing the record. A "closed record" is then printed and added to the process.

The next steps in the procedure vary. There may be a preliminary 05.27 dispute about further procedure and this may have to be decided by a judge. In the normal course of events, the case will eventually be heard by a judge alone or, more rarely, by a judge and jury. There are certain types of cases—including personal injuries and actions for libel or defamation—which must be sent to jury trial unless the parties otherwise agree or one party (usually the defender) convinces the court that the case is especially complex and difficult. In civil cases, the jury numbers 12 and may return a majority verdict [see **para.05.58**]. The Scottish Government recently concluded a consultation on criminal jury numbers and announced that it was unpersuaded by the argument to alter the requirement of 15 people for a criminal jury. Regardless, the civil jury numbers will remain unaffected—partly, it is assumed, because there are so few civil trials.

To sum up, the procedure in an ordinary civil action in the Court of 05.28 Session is, in rough outline: summons; lodging of process; case in calling list; appearance; defences; open record; closed record; proof or jury trial.

At a proof there are no opening speeches. The case commences with 05.29 the calling of the first witness. Counsel make submissions at the end of the evidence. The judge may give an immediate decision, or, more likely, take time to consider the case in general and produce a decision in writing at a later date. That is what is known as the judge taking the case to *avizandum.*

There is an important distinction between cases which are dismissed 05.30 and those in which decree of *absolvitor* are granted. If the defender wins a decree of *absolvitor* that is a higher degree of success than dismissal since it prevents the pursuer from suing the same defender again over the same case. In the case of dismissal it is possible for the pursuer to find another remedy against the same defender.

Apart from damages for financial loss or loss of property 05.31 (commonly referred to as patrimonial loss) a court may make an award for the pain and suffering (*solatium*) endured by an injured pursuer, and a loss of society award to compensate a bereaved relative for the death of someone who has died because of the defender's negligence. A loss of society award is intended to compensate for the loss of companionship and guidance. The court can also make an award for aspects such as future care costs of an injured person or to reflect services which they now require to have fulfilled by family members.

05.32   The procedure in an ordinary civil action in the sheriff court is broadly similar. The pursuer's solicitor draws up an initial writ instead of a summons and a copy is served on the defender. There is no calling list as such and the defender must, if he wishes to defend, enter appearance within the *induciae*. Thereafter he must lodge defences. Adjustments are now exchanged between parties only. They are not lodged in court. When adjustments are complete the sheriff closes the record and the case will proceed to debate or proof.

05.33   As with the Court of Session, anxiety about the length of time being taken for ordinary actions to reach their conclusion in the sheriff court has resulted in the use of "options hearings" to allow the court to set future procedure and focus the issues between the parties. The theme of judicial management and greater efficiency has, of course, underpinned many of the recommendations of the Gill Review.

PERSONAL INJURY CASES

05.34   Given that about two-thirds of all summons in the Court of Session relate to personal injury actions, it is understandable that much attention has been focused on the efficient disposal of these cases in order to free court time for other matters. Chapter 43 of the Rules of the Court of Session sets out the reforms originally promoted by a working party on Court of Session procedure under Lord Coulsfield in 2000. The rules finally came into full effect in 2003. The effect has been to encourage limited factual pleading, to ensure early disclosure of documents, to require adherence to a strict court timetable and to facilitate early resolution of cases through the use of negotiated pre-trial meetings. The procedure in relation to personal injury cases is now held up by many as an example of efficiency and early resolution.

COMMERCIAL COURT

05.35   In response to the needs of the business community, the Commercial Court seeks to provide access to specialist judges to handle commercial cases quickly and flexibly. That can involve any transaction or dispute of a business or commercial nature. There are currently four designated commercial judges led by Lord Glennie. The procedures for the Commercial Court are set out in Ch.47 of the Rules of the Court of Session.

PETITIONS

There are, of course, special procedures in special types of case. The 05.36
procedure for cases brought by petition differs from that outlined
above. The person presenting the petition is called the petitioner and
the person opposing it is known as the respondent. Often, the merit of
a petition can be decided by a judge at the first hearing. The reason for
that is that the factual context may not be in dispute between parties—
and accordingly no evidence needs to be disputed in court. A petition
may therefore be whether in an agreed set of facts, one party was
entitled to act as they have, as a matter of law. Should there be a
factual dispute between the parties, a hearing on the disputed
evidence can be arranged.

STANDARD OF PROOF

There is an important distinction between the standards of proof 05.37
demanded by the law in criminal and in civil cases. In criminal
proceedings generally proof must be "beyond reasonable doubt". In
civil cases the court has to be satisfied merely on a "balance of
probabilities"—in other words, the judge or jury has to decide which
of two conflicting stories is more probable.

JUDICIAL REVIEW

A simplified procedure for dealing with petitions for judicial review of 05.38
administrative decisions came into operation in the Court of Session in
1985. Since then, a great many cases have been heard under the new
procedure and many of them have been of important news value,
involving as it often does a decision of the government or another
public body. Recent examples include a petition on behalf of the
victims of Hepatitis C seeking to force a public inquiry and petitions
on behalf of prisoners seeking to end practices such as "slopping out"
for those on remand. Judicial review is the exercise by the Court of
Session of its inherent supervisory jurisdiction. In other words, the
Court of Session retains the authority to review decisions made.

In these cases it can be disputed that a body has acted "ultra vires" 05.39
(beyond its powers) or alternatively where it is not disputed that the
body making the decision had the power to do so, it is argued that the
decision reached was unreasonable—although that test (known as
Wednesbury unreasonableness) is a high one. In terms of that abuse
of discretion, there are a host of factors which might be relevant—

including the decision maker acting in bad faith, with dishonesty, taking account of irrelevant material or ignoring relevant material.

05.40   Other common grounds for judicial review include:

- breach of legitimate expectations;
- fettering of discretion;
- being contrary to natural justice.

05.41   The case of **West v Secretary of State for Scotland (1992)** remains the most fundamental statement of the position in Scotland as a decision of the Inner House of the Court of Session. It continues to be applied in the most recent case law.

05.42   There it was said:

- that the Court of Session had power, in the exercise of its supervisory jurisdiction, to regulate the process by which decisions were taken by any person or body to whom a jurisdiction, power or authority had been delegated or entrusted by statute, agreement or other instrument;
- that the sole purpose for which the supervisory jurisdiction might be exercised was to ensure that the person or body did not exceed or abuse its jurisdiction, power or authority or fail to do what that required;
- that judicial review was available, not to review the merits of a decision, nor for the court to substitute its own opinion, but to ensure that a decision maker did not exceed or abuse his powers or fail to perform his duty.

05.43   It is important to note that legal aid remains available for judicial review and indeed the awarding of legal aid in some cases has in itself proved to be controversial and worthy of coverage—such as in the case of three convicted rapists (the so-called Fernieside Three) who sought, and were granted, legal aid to judicially review the refusal of the Scottish Criminal Cases Review Commission to consider referring their cases back to the High Court (**M, Petitioner (2006)**)

05.44   The remedies open to the court in judicial review are wide ranging but rarely include the award of damages. They can include interim orders such as interim liberation and interim interdict.

05.45   The media itself can become involved in judicial review—for example the BBC initially succeeded in reviewing a decision of the Broadcasting Standards Commission when that body held that Dixons, the electrical retailer, had a right to privacy in relation to undercover journalism (**R v Broadcasting Standards Comission (2001)**). The BBC lost that case in the Court of Appeal, as did the news presenter Anna Ford in her attempt to review a decision of the Press Complaints Commission in 2001 (**R (on the application of Ford (2001)**). Both bodies were in principle capable of being reviewed, albeit that neither case resulted in success for those seeking to challenge the respective decisions. The fact that there have been few recent challenges perhaps suggests that the bar is accepted as being high.

As noted above, there is the real prospect of further change to the 05.46 procedures surrounding judicial review as a consequence of the Civil Justice Review chaired by Lord Gill.

Of particular note is the attempt to change the categories of 05.47 potential litigants. The Civil Justice Review specifically notes that the current law is overly restrictive and should be replaced by a single test, namely, whether the petitioner has demonstrated a sufficient interest in the subject matter of the proceedings (see Ch.2, para.25).

More restrictively, it is also proposed that petitions for judicial 05.48 review should be brought within a period of three months (see paras 38, 39) and that a requirement to obtain leave to proceed with an application for judicial review should be introduced. The test should be whether the petition has a real prospect of success (see Ch.2, paras 51, 52).

From a journalistic point of view, one further change which may 05.49 make for more cases of public interest coming to court is the recommendation that the court should have power to make special orders in relation to expenses in cases raising significant issues of public interest (see Ch.2, para.73).

POLITICAL COVERAGE

Broadcasters are often reviewed in the course of political campaigns— 05.50 notable attempts include the Scottish National Party (now forming the Scottish Government) seeking to interdict a party leaders debate on Scottish Television and Grampian Television from going ahead without the inclusion of Alex Salmond MP, now First Minister of Scotland. Whilst failing on the merits, that decision is interesting also because the petition was said to be incompetent seeking, as it did, interim interdict against the broadcasting of the programme. Given that the television companies had obligations under the Broadcasting Act 1990, the correct procedure according to the court, would have been to seek judicial review of the exercise of their powers and discretion under the Act (*Scottish National Party v Scottish Television Plc* **(1998)**). This issue was once again raised in the context of the first televised Prime Ministerial debates in the 2010 UK general election. The SNP were not invited to participate in those debates prompting fresh legal action. The petition this time sought interim interdict against the debates on the basis of the BBC being in breach of its obligations of impartiality under its founding Royal Charter and in terms of its own election guidance. The petition failed, Lady Smith finding that the BBC had offered planned coverage for the SNP throughout the campaign which satisfied the requirement of impartiality and that moreover the attempt at securing interim interdict in the third of three UK leaders debates was too late. The SNP, she found, should have acted sooner, and at the outset of the three debates rather than focusing solely on the third debate broadcast by the BBC. The SNP maintained that their appeal to the BBC Trust had only recently been dismissed and that to have brought the action earlier would have been premature. The court disagreed (*Petition of SNP* (2010)). The arguments will continue, not least with the prospect of Westminster and Holyrood elections planned for the same day in 2015. This area will therefore generate considerable media focus for the foreseeable future.

SCOTLAND ACT 1998

05.51 Unlike Westminster, the Scottish Parliament at Holyrood has its powers defined by statute. It is a devolved Parliament with a specified set of powers. If the Scottish Parliament acts beyond those powers— for example to legislate in an area where power is reserved to Westminster such as defence, pensions, foreign affairs, the constitution of the United Kingdom—the Scottish courts are entitled to strike down the legislation. This is also true in relation to legislation which is not compatible with aspects of European law such as human rights, which is discussed below.

05.52 The first significant challenge was in the case of *Adams v Scottish Ministers* (2004), which related to the highly controversial ban on hunting with dogs in Scotland.

05.53 The recent, and ongoing, challenge to the Damages (Asbestos-related Conditions) (Scotland) Act 2009 (*Axa General Insurance Ltd* (2010)) provides a more comprehensive review of the law in this area. In short, the case is authority for resisting the argument that legislation passed by the Scottish Parliament can be challenged at common law on the grounds of irrationality except in the most extreme of circumstances. The petitioners additionally failed to convince the court that the legislation was a breach of either art.6 of the European Convention on Human Rights (regarding state interference and the right to a fair trial) or art.1 to the First Protocol to the Convention (which enshrines the right to peaceful enjoyment of property). At the time of writing, that decision is under appeal to the Inner House. It will probably be further appealed to the new Supreme Court. A second important recent challenge has been launched by tobacco companies seeking to challenge the Tobacco and Primary

Medical Services (Scotland) Act 2010 which seeks to ban the use of cigarette vending machines and the display of cigarettes and cigars in shops. The result of that judicial review, proceeding on the basis that the Scottish Parliament acted beyond its powers, will also probably lead to appeal to the Inner House and thereafter to the Supreme Court. Although technical, these are matters of real public and constitutional significance and will attract media coverage in the coming years. To date, however, we can say that success in a judicial review of Scottish Parliamentary legislation has been an elusive prize.

CIVIL JURIES

In Scotland, in certain circumstances, there remains the statutory right 05.54 to a civil jury trial.

The right to jury trial in Scotland in both criminal and civil cases 05.55 appears to date from the 14th century, but fell into disuse in civil cases during the 17th century and was not revived until the passing of the Jury Trials (Scotland) Act 1815. It was already in operation in England and was brought to Scotland experimentally and, at first, for a limited period only. The Scottish civil jury in modern times is based on the English model, which explains why there are 12 jurors and not the traditional Scottish figure of 15. The Law Reform (Miscellaneous Provisions) (Scotland) Act 1980 abolished civil jury trial in the sheriff court.

In England, it was eventually decided by the courts themselves that 05.56 jury trial in civil cases would not in future be permitted except by specific authority of the court. In Scotland, on the other hand, the position remains that, if a party with a statutory right to jury trial insists on this form of procedure, unless there is some "special cause" why it should not be allowed, there must be a jury trial.

"Special cause" usually consists of difficult questions of law or 05.57 mixed fact and law which would be difficult for a jury to deal with, or undue delay in raising the action, resulting in special problems in assessing the reliability of evidence given by witnesses whose recollection is dimmed by the passage of time. For example, in the case of *Shanks v BBC* **(1993)**, a defamation action arising out of a TV programme, the BBC successfully asked the Court of Session to have the case conducted before a judge sitting alone without a jury. The case involved allegations about share dealings, which, the court felt, a jury would have difficulty in understanding.

A virtue of the old Scottish jury was that it had 15 members, making 05.58 it possible to achieve a majority verdict. A recent review launched by the Scottish Government confirmed that Scotland will remain unique in the world as having 15 member juries in criminal cases. In civil cases with a jury of 12 derived from England there is always the risk of a "hung" jury with the vote equally divided. This happened in one case in the Court of Session in 1973 when a jury was discharged after failing to reach a verdict after three hours.

05.59 In practice civil juries are most often used to decide claims for damages for injuries caused by accidents of various kinds—for example at work or on the roads. Recent cases have shown, however, that juries are becoming equally popular for dealing with defamation cases. Since the Interest on Damages Act 1971 the verdicts of juries in civil cases are easier to understand than they used to be. Juries now have to return a verdict, if they make an award of damages, divided into separate sums for each element of damages—for example past and future loss of earnings and pain and suffering.

05.60 Perhaps reflecting its English ancestry, the procedure in a civil trial is different in several important respects from cases dealt with by a judge sitting alone. The hearing is opened by an address to the jury by junior counsel for the pursuer who outlines the circumstances of the case and explains the basis of his client's claim. The jury then hears the evidence for the pursuer before being addressed by junior counsel for the defender, who, in turn, introduces the evidence for his client. At the end of the evidence senior counsel for each side sums up the case for the jury and the judge completes the hearing by directing the jury on questions of law. As in a criminal case the judge makes it clear that the jury are sole judges of the facts.

05.61 Sometimes during a trial the jury are taken from the courtroom while counsel make submissions to the judge on a question of law. If the case is not ultimately withdrawn from the jury, care must be taken not to publish reports of statements made by counsel which could be read by jurors before the case is finished. It could be argued that such a report amounted to an interference with the course of justice or that it is a contempt of court because it prejudiced the case of one side or the other. Ordinarily, in those circumstances the judge should make an order in relation to postponement on reporting under s.4(2) of the Contempt of Court Act 1981. The leading case in this field remains that of *R. v Horsham Justices Ex p. Farquharson* **(1982)**, in which Lord Denning firmly established the purpose of the provision was to provide the media with certainty. He put it thus:

> "Section 4 (2) retains the common law about the occasions when a report (otherwise fair and accurate) may be a contempt of court—but with this improvement: Nothing is to be left to implication. It is for the court to make an order telling the newspapers what things they are not to publish."

He continued: 05.62

> "Unless the court makes such an order then the newspaper is
> given complete protection by section 4 (2) from being subjected
> to proceedings for contempt of court."

That approach was approved more recently by the Court of Appeal in 05.63
R. v Times Newspapers Ltd **(2008)**. Even in the absence of a specific
s.4(2) order, however, it is advisable to exercise journalistic
responsibility.

The starting point for a journalist looking at the law is s.2(2) of the 05.64
Contempt of Court Act 1981. That means that, "publication which
creates a substantial risk that the course of justice in the proceedings
in question will be seriously impeded or prejudiced" may be a
contempt, regardless of whether a s.4(2) order is in place or not.

But Parliament created an exception for contemporary reports of 05.65
proceedings in s.4(1). It did so explicitly in the public interest and
accordingly journalists who make a, "fair and accurate report of
legal proceedings held in public, published contemporaneously and in
good faith" will be protected. If the court believes that even despite
such fair and accurate reporting, "it appears to be necessary for
avoiding a substantial risk of prejudice to the administration of
justice" it can order that the proceedings be postponed for a specified
period.

The journalistic rule of thumb should be to adopt the principle that 05.66
any publication meeting the high test in s.2(2) is always potentially a
contempt. Nevertheless, in the absence of a s.4(2) order, the statutory
right to give a fair and accurate report of legal proceedings maintains.
Parliament granted that right in the public interest and with a view to
ensuring public justice.

Appeal against the verdict of a civil jury is taken by way of a motion 05.67
for a new trial. This is heard in the Inner House and may be on a
variety of grounds such as misdirection by the trial judge,
insufficiency of evidence or because of a perverse verdict by the jury.
The appeal may be against the amount of damages awarded either as
too high or too low. The appeal judges may order a new trial before a
fresh jury or, if they agree unanimously that the jury is not entitled to
find in favour of the pursuer and that there is no fresh evidence to put
before a jury, find in favour of the defender. As this book goes to print,
the recent defamation jury trial in the case of **Sheridan v News
International** **(2006)** is a recent and high profile example of a civil
jury awarding the pursuer, a Scottish politician, £200,000 in respect
of allegations made by the *News of the World* newspaper about his
sexual conduct. The appeal remains sisted (essentially procedurally
frozen) pending the result of a criminal trial in which Mr Sheridan
and his wife are charged with various crimes including attempting to

pervert the course of justice in relation to the evidence they gave at the original defamation trial [see **Chapter 26**].

05.68   The issue of the role of civil juries and the level of awards was discussed and clarified by the House of Lords in the case of *Girvan v Inverness Farmers Dairy* **(1997)**. A jury at the Court of Session awarded Mr Girvan, a sheep farmer and former champion clay pigeon shooter, damages of £193,080 after he suffered a disabling elbow injury in a road accident. Of that total, the jury awarded £120,000 for pain and suffering which was successfully challenged as excessive. A second jury awarded £165,530 pounds, including £95,000 for pain and suffering. That £95,000 award was again challenged as too high and the case went to the House of Lords. The House of Lords judges decided that the proper approach was still the same as adopted by the Court of Session in the case of *Landell v Landell* **(1841)**—the award of damages must be so excessive that the court could say the jury had committed a gross injustice or reached a palpably wrong result. That remains the position.

JUDICIAL COMMITTEE OF THE PRIVY COUNCIL

05.69   The Judicial Committee of the Privy Council is a body of distinguished lawyers, including senior judges and former judges, acting as a court of appeal from the supreme courts of Commonwealth countries. It was formerly the final court of appeal in the British Empire, and still decides appeals from New Zealand, Singapore, the Channel Islands and most of the Caribbean countries. In 2006, for example, the Privy Council struck down the mandatory death sentence imposed on those convicted of murder in the Bahamas, as being in breach of the constitution (*Bowe & Davis v The Queen (The Bahamas)* **(2006)**)

05.70   Within the United Kingdom, the Judicial Committee hears appeals from the decisions of English ecclesiastical courts and various professional disciplinary bodies such as the Disciplinary Committee of the General Medical Council.

05.71   The Judicial Committee also has hitherto had jurisdiction to hear and determine "devolution issues" or in other words issues relating to the power and functions of the Scottish Parliament. Whilst that can relate to questions of legislation and whether a particular Bill is within the competence of a devolved Parliament in Edinburgh, it also provides a mechanism for review of a range of criminal appeals with wide ranging ramifications. For example, in one recent case from 2008 before the Judicial Committee, the question of disclosure of evidence by the Crown was challenged on the basis that the failure of the Lord Advocate in Scotland to disclose evidence ahead of trial breached the accused's human rights under the ECHR—something the devolved

administration, including the Law Officers, are not allowed to do
(*MacDonald v HM Advocate* (2008)).

As a consequence of the provisions of the Constitutional Reform 05.72
Act 2005, from October 2009 the jurisdiction of the Judicial
Committee of the Privy Council in respect of devolution issues under
the Scotland Act 1998 was exercised by the new Supreme Court.

EUROPEAN COURT OF JUSTICE

The court's powers are laid down in the European Economic 05.73
Community Treaty, and one of the consequences of the United
Kingdom joining the Community in 1972 was that the court assumed
jurisdiction to give preliminary rulings on any question raised before a
Scottish or English court, criminal or civil. A domestic court may in
certain circumstances request the European Court to give a
preliminary ruling. The national court must be satisfied that a
decision by the European Court is necessary to enable it to give a
judgment in the case before it.

The national court or tribunal may take this course either at the 05.74
instance of any party in the case or on its own initiative. Once the
ruling has been given the case returns to the court or tribunal where it
began. The procedure is likely to be adopted in situations where the
national law appears to be incompatible with Community law. The
proceedings before the originating court are halted meantime.

Figures from the ECJ up to the end of 2007 show that there is little 05.75
more than a trickle of these cases from Scotland. In fact, since 1972,
there have been only seven. The UK as a whole has made 434
references. To put that in context, Denmark, a country of similar size
to Scotland, had made 116 referrals and Germany 1,601 (Anna Poole,
"ECJ in the Fast Lane" (2008) 53(12) JLSS 58). The courts are
however relaxing that stance somewhat from the initial test of
"necessity" to refer to a more open test of "complete confidence"—in
other words asking whether the court has complete confidence not to
refer. This area of referral may therefore yet develop. Recent examples
include questions of the right to compensation in relation to the
destruction of diseased fish stocks and the proportionality of
regulations in relation to beef production.

HUMAN RIGHTS

Not to be confused with the European Court of Justice, which 05.76
deliberates in Luxembourg and is part of the apparatus of the
European Union, is the European Court of Human Rights which sits
in Strasbourg. Whereas the Court of Justice is concerned with the

interpretation of European Community rules, often of a highly technical nature, the Court of Human Rights handles a broad range of cases frequently of great significance for the life and liberty of individual citizens. A list of some of the cases involving the United Kingdom confirms this. The court has been asked to rule on issues such as the lack of an effective investigation into shootings in Northern Ireland, the failure of social services to remove children from neglectful parents, the requirement of a father's consent for the continued storage and implantation of fertilised eggs, corporal punishment in schools, the closed shop, pensioners' rights, contempt of court, the use of "plastic bullets" and telephone tapping.

05.77   For journalists *Lingens v Austria* **(1986)** remains fundamental in so far as it recognised that public figures (such as politicians) must expect and accept vigorous criticisms. That case has been confirmed on numerous occasions and the case of *Lombardo v Malta* **(2009)** provides a useful restatement of the position. In that case the question was criticism by a local paper from three councillors in relation to the activities of the council. Not only was *Lingens* upheld, but reference was also made to *De Haes v Belgium* **(1998)** in which the editor and journalist of a weekly magazine which criticised three judges of the Antwerp Court of Appeal for awarding custody of children to a Belgian notary accused by his wife of incest and child abuse, succeeded in persuading the court that their criticism was severe but proportionate [see **Chapter 36**].

05.78   The court is part of the machinery set up under the European Convention on Human Rights. The court itself has existed since 1959. Since 1998 it has operated on a full-time basis with 47 judges, one for every state party to the Convention. The judges are elected for six-year terms by the Parliamentary Assembly of the Council of Europe. The process was dramatically altered by the adoption of changes in 2004 to speed up the process—a recognition of the need to deal with the ever greater number of cases being taken to Strasbourg by citizens.

05.79   It is of course important to recognise that the impact of the Convention is not just in cases taken to Strasbourg. The Human Rights Act 1998 incorporated the Convention into our domestic law. The human rights legislation provides that all courts and tribunals must interpret legislation passed in the United Kingdom in a way which is compatible with Convention rights. It also makes it unlawful for government or public authorities—whether the Scottish Parliament or the Metropolitan Police—to act in a way which is incompatible with Convention rights.

05.80   Precisely those arguments have been addressed in the two recent cases of judicial review (in relation to the Damages (Asbestos-related Conditions) (Scotland) Act 2009 and the Tobacco and Primary

Medical Services (Scotland) Act 2010) arising from Scottish Parliamentary legislation noted earlier in the chapter.

If the Court of Session or the High Court in Scotland decides   05.81
something in a Westminster Act is not compatible with a Convention right they will be able to make a declaration to that effect. Since the doctrine of Westminster sovereignty remains, the courts will not be able to strike out incompatible parts of Westminster legislation as they can do with an Act of the Scottish Parliament if it is ruled to be beyond the powers of the legislature and therefore of no effect.

The right to apply to the Strasbourg Court is still available, even   05.82
after the introduction of the Human Rights Act 1998 into Scots law. But most of the academic evidence to date has concluded that generally the Scottish courts are applying the law consistent with the Convention rights and it may be that as such, the success of that incorporation will see a reduced flow of cases. Of those cases which have relied on the Convention, there appear to be clusters of decisions in relation to immigration control, prison conditions and children.

In a journalistic context, it is particularly important to note   05.83
provisions such as s.12 of the Human Rights Act 1998 which relates to the freedom of expression. That section provides protection from court remedies being granted which restrict freedom of expression in the absence of the defender or respondent. Moreover, it sets out in s.12(3) additional and specific protection for the Convention right to freedom of expression where the proceedings related to material which is "journalistic, literary or artistic". This aspect and the developing case law is discussed more fully at **Chapter 28**.

CHAPTER 6

MISCELLANEOUS SPECIAL COURTS AND TRIBUNALS

By Duncan Hamilton

06.01 According to the Contempt of Court Act 1981, contempt can apply to "any tribunal exercising the judicial power of the state". That phrase carries a deliberate vagueness which should cause the journalist to pause and consider whether the coverage of any inferior court or tribunal comes within that definition.

06.02 The leading case remains that of *Att Gen v BBC* **(1981)** when the essentially administrative (as opposed to judicial) function of the Lands Valuation Court, allowed the House of Lords to find that it was not a tribunal within the 1981 Act. Lord Denning in that case explored the aspects which might determine whether a body was covered by the definition—a planning enquiry and commercial arbitration being examples of the kinds of things which would not be covered but anything done with the authority of Parliament or the Crown might be. The involvement of a judicial, legal element is important but not determinative as was seen in a later case *General Medical Council v BBC* **(1998)** in which the General Medical Council was held not to be such a forum because it did not "exercise the judicial power of the state". If in doubt, the wise path is to take legal advice. It really never is too early to consult a solicitor!

06.03 Even if a court or tribunal does not itself have the power to punish for contempt, a report by a journalist of such a court or tribunal may still be open to a finding of contempt in the High Court or Court of Session, under exercise of the supervisory jurisdiction.

06.04 Turning to consider a few specific special courts:

LANDS VALUATION APPEAL COURT

06.05 The Lands Valuation Appeal court is the court of appeal against the decisions of the local valuation appeal committee (where appeals against the valuation made by the local assessor are considered) in relation to the assessed valuation of property for rating purposes. The Lands Valuation Appeal Court consists of three nominated judges of the Court of Session, whose decision is final.

COMPETITION APPEAL TRIBUNAL

The Competition Appeal Tribunal (CAT) was created under the Enterprise Act 2002 which came into force on April 1, 2003. Its function is to deal with a number of different types of case, including to hear appeals on the merits in respect of decisions made by the Office of Fair Trading (OFT) and the regulators in the telecommunications, electricity, gas, water, railways and air traffic services sectors. The CAT also hears actions for damages and for money under the Competition Act 1988, and reviews decisions made by the Secretary of State, OFT and the Competition Commission in respect of merger and market references or possible references under the Enterprise Act 2002. A high profile recent example is the appeal by a group of investors in Halifax Bank of Scotland (HBOS) against the decision to allow a merger with Lloyds TSB Plc (*Merger Action Group v Secretary of State for Business, Enterprise and Regulatory Reform* (2008)). The tribunal consists of three members—one who is a senior lawyer (often a judge of the Chancery Division of the High Court in England) and the other two as ordinary members who have expertise in law, business, accountancy, economics or some other related field.

06.06

THE UPPER TRIBUNAL

The Upper Tribunal is a newly created court of record with jurisdiction throughout the United Kingdom. A court of record simply means that its decision is a binding decision on the tribunals and public authorities below. It has been established by the Westminster Parliament under the Tribunals, Courts and Enforcement Act 2007. It now hears many appeals to the courts, the Social Security and Child Support Commissioners and other similar bodies, made against the decisions of local tribunals. It also has assumed some of the supervisory powers of the courts to deal with appeals against the actions of tribunals and of government departments and other public authorities which otherwise previously would have been heard, in a Scottish context, in the Court of Session. The tribunal judiciary are all judges and include one from Scotland. The Upper Chamber is created as part of the redrawing of the tribunal system throughout the UK. All tribunals covered by it will eventually have "first tier" tribunals with appeals being to the various chambers of the Upper Tribunal. Those are being gradually introduced on the basis of subject areas. The Administrative Appeals Chamber, for example, started work on November 3, 2008 and the Finance and Tax Chamber on April 1, 2009.

06.07

06.08   In a Scottish context, it is important to note that this has necessitated changes to the Court of Session and its supervisory role. Specifically, in the context of judicial review, many of the decisions made in the Court of Session will now be passed to the Upper Chamber. Rule 58.7A of the Rules of the Court of Session deals with where there is, as from November 3, 2008, mandatory transfer from the Court of Session. It is there made clear that where several conditions set out under s.20 of the Tribunals, Courts and Enforcement Act 2007 are satisfied, the application for judicial review will be transferred. Importantly, however, r.41.59 of the Rules of the Court of Session also still allows an appeal in the Court of Session against a decision of the Upper Tribunal, albeit only in very limited circumstances which amount largely to whether or not there is a compelling reason or point of principle. It may be expected that there will rarely be so.

ELECTION COURTS

06.09   The function of these courts is to hear petitions complaining against irregularities in the conduct of elections. In Scotland, the election court in relation to a parliamentary election consists of two judges of the Court of Session, nominated by the Lord President. In a local government election, the judge will be the sheriff principal of the relevant sheriffdom. The courts can try prosecutions for corrupt (e.g. bribery, threats of force) and illegal (e.g. paying money to transport electors to the poll, voting when disqualified) practices. Chapter 69 of the Rules of the Court of Session sets out the appropriate procedure.

REGISTRATION APPEAL COURT

06.10   This court relates to disputes over the registration of voters. The type of case with which it deals can perhaps best be illustrated through the example in 2007 of a convicted prisoner appealing to the court against a decision to exclude him from the register of voters for the Scottish Parliamentary elections (*Smith v Scott* (2007)). In that case, the court found that refusal was incompatible with the human rights of the convicted prisoner and accordingly issued a declaration of incompatibility in relation to the 2007 elections. The elections proceeded and were not in the event successfully challenged in relation to their legality but the example remains a strong one of some of the lesser known courts generating stories of real journalistic and public interest.

SCOTTISH LAND COURT

This court deals with disputes over agricultural holdings and as a   06.11
consequence of the Agricultural Holdings (Scotland) Act 2003, the
court can now determine the existence, termination and disputes in
relation to such holdings. It can therefore grant decree of interdict or
removal. It also has the leading role to play in relation to crofting
disputes—whether on boundaries, rent or access. The chairman has
the same rank and tenure as a Court of Session judge. There is an
appeal on a point of law to the Court of Session.

LYON COURT

The Court of the Lord Lyon has jurisdiction over all heraldic business   06.12
and the right to bear arms in Scotland. An Act of the Scottish
Parliament of 1592 gave the Lord Lyon responsibility for prosecuting
as a criminal offence anyone who uses unauthorised arms. The court
has its own procurator fiscal, an independent official prosecutor. In
1672 a further Act of the Scottish Parliament authorised the creation
of the Public Register of All Arms and Bearings in Scotland. No
armorial bearings may be used in Scotland unless on the Register.
Occasionally business in the court can be both contentious and
newsworthy, such as the dispute between two cousins in 1996 over the
title "11th Earl of Selkirk" and the reported £500,000 worth of family
heirlooms that go with the title (see *Hamilton, Petitioner* **(1996)**). An
appeal from a decision of the Lyon Court is to the Inner House of the
Court of Session and thereafter to the House of Lords.

LICENSING BOARDS

The Licensing (Scotland) Act 2005 represented the greatest shake up   06.13
in licensing laws for 30 years but essentially continues to rely on the
judgment of licensing boards comprising members of the relevant
local councils to decide on all aspects of the granting, revoking,
extensions and variations of licences for the retail sale of alcohol and
supply of alcohol in members clubs. Appeal from a decision of a
licensing board continues to be to the sheriff court and then to the
Court of Session.

CHURCH COURTS

In Scotland, it is necessary to distinguish between the courts of the   06.14
Church of Scotland and the courts of every other church.

06.15   That is because unlike any other church, the Church of Scotland has statutory jurisdiction set out in the Church of Scotland Act 1921 over a wide spectrum of church affairs including discipline and "matters spiritual". In those matters, the civil courts cannot interfere. The extent, and limitations, of that exclusive jurisdiction has been tested in a number of cases in both the Court of Session (*Logan v Presbytery of Dumbarton* (**1995**)) and the House of Lords (*Percy v Church of Scotland Board of National Mission* (**2006**)). The internal courts of the Church of Scotland are the Kirk Session of a particular church, the Presbytery (consisting of the Ministers and Elders within a particular geographical area), the Synod consisting of the members of several Presbyteries and finally the General Assembly with representatives from the whole church.

06.16   The other churches, having no statutory protection, are open to the full range of civil remedies in the Scottish courts—whether on matters of contractual, property or employment law—as would be available against any other club or society. The courts will not, however, enter into the vexed world of doctrinal disputes. The courts' jurisdiction is in matters of law.

06.17   One recent case illustrating the courts intervening in a property dispute involved a dispute within the Free Church leading to the creation of a separate entity known as the Free Church (Continuing) which claimed that the original church had breached its own constitution and accordingly was no longer entitled to the property and assets of the Church. A long and bitter public dispute was finally resolved when the action was dismissed (*Free Church of Scotland (Continuing) v General Assembly of the Free Church of Scotland* (**2005**)).

COURTS MARTIAL

06.18   The Armed Forces Act 2006 brought together what had previously been three separate statutory frameworks of discipline relating to the Royal Navy, the Army and the Royal Air Force. Those have now been combined into one framework covering criminal conduct and disciplinary matters. Traditionally, commanding officers (CO) have played a central role in discipline and their jurisdiction in less serious offences remains under the new statute. They now have the power to impose a sanction up to 90 days' detention.

06.19   More serious offences require to be tried by court martial.

06.20   In brief, the Act creates offences and provides for the investigation of alleged offences, the arrest, holding in custody and charging of individuals accused of committing an offence, and for them to be dealt with summarily by their CO or tried by court martial. Instead of (as previously) courts martial being set up to deal with particular cases, the Act provides for a standing court martial, called the Court Martial. Rather like the High Court in Scotland, the court may sit in more than one place at the same time, and different judge advocates and service personnel will make up the court for different trials.

More serious cases must be notified to the service police and passed direct to the independent Director of Service Prosecutions (DSP) for a decision on whether to prosecute. In other cases the CO will consider whether to deal with the matter summarily (if it is within his jurisdiction) or to refer the case to the DSP with a view to proceeding to a trial by the Court Martial. In all cases which it is intended should be tried by the Court Martial, it will be the DSP who takes the decision to prosecute and determines the charge or charges. Those facing charges with which the CO intends to deal summarily have a right to elect trial by the Court Martial, or, if they agree to be dealt with summarily and the charge is found proved, to appeal to the Summary Appeal Court. A person convicted by the Court Martial will be able to appeal to the Court Martial Appeal Court.   06.21

The Court Martial deals with both offences against the civilian criminal law and specifically military offences. In all cases, a judge advocate conducts the trial which is broadly similar to the English civilian Crown Court trial, even when dealing with a minor disciplinary or criminal offence. The jury, known as the board, comprises three, five or more commissioned officers or warrant officers. Having listened to the judge advocate's directions on the law and summary of the evidence, they are responsible for finding those accused guilty or not guilty. Following a finding or plea of guilty, the board joins the judge advocate to decide on sentence. A court martial has the same sentencing powers in relation to imprisonment as a Crown Court, including life imprisonment.   06.22

The avenue of appeal for someone convicted, subject to obtaining permission to appeal, is to the Court Martial Appeal Court and ultimately to the House of Lords.   06.23

A Service Civilian Court (SCC) has also been established to deal with officials attached to the services overseas or dependants of service personnel resident overseas.   06.24

The interface between these procedures and art.6 of the European Convention on Human Rights (the right to a fair trial) continues to present both considerable legal difficulty and, consequently, good copy for the journalist. Recent examples include ***Bell v United Kingdom* (2007)** (in which the summary procedure under a commanding officer breached the ECHR) and ***Thompson v United Kingdom* (2005)** (where the commanding officer was held not to be an independent figure and so the procedure in breach of arts 5 and 6).   06.25

TRIBUNALS

06.26 Increasing emphasis is placed on the role and importance of tribunals as an alternative to the more traditional court setting. In general, they are deemed to be quicker, cheaper and more informal than courts, although often no less important.

06.27 The Administrative Justice and Tribunals Council was created by the Tribunals, Courts and Enforcement Act 2007 and replaces the Council on Tribunals. The Scottish Committee of that body has a particular interest in administrative justice and tribunals in Scotland, including those UK-wide tribunals which sit in Scotland, and some 20 tribunals which are constituted under separate Scottish legislation. These cover a wide range of subjects including education appeal committees, mental health tribunals for Scotland, additional support needs tribunals for Scotland and National Health Service discipline committees in Scotland as well as those tribunals which exist only in Scotland such as children's hearings. An annual report to the Scottish Ministers is laid before the Scottish Parliament.

06.28 Since most tribunals are set up under the authority of Parliament, a fair and accurate report of tribunal proceedings will normally be protected by qualified privilege. However, many tribunals are designed to be informal and one consequence is that witnesses or parties can often make allegations which would not be allowed in a court of law. One obvious example is that many tribunal hearings do not require those involved to be placed under oath. It is therefore even more important that the journalist exercise care and good judgment as to whether some of the more extreme allegations made in a tribunal setting form part of a fair and accurate report. The defence of privilege does not protect material which is not of public concern and the publication of which is not for the public benefit.

06.29 Can a journalist be held in contempt of a tribunal? Yes—but crucially, as we have seen, it depends on whether that tribunal or body is exercising the power of the State.

06.30 On this, see also **Chapter 15**.

EMPLOYMENT TRIBUNALS

06.31 Employment tribunals (previously known as industrial tribunals) deal with a range of issues of interest to the journalist—including redundancy, equal pay, sexual and racial discrimination at work and health and safety. They deal also with questions of unfair dismissal and can order the reinstatement of an employee or an award of compensation. The tribunal sits in public but in exceptional circumstances (national security, breach of confidence or to prevent information being made public which would damage an employer) can take evidence in private.

The tribunal consists of a legally qualified chairman and two   06.32
members selected from a panel with specialist knowledge or experience. The Employment Appeal Tribunal hears appeals on questions of law from employment tribunals and under the Employment Protection Act 1975, consists of judges (including at least one from the Court of Session) and members having special knowledge or experience of industrial relations. The current Scottish judge is Lady Smith. The rules are currently set out in the Employment Tribunals (Constitution and Rules of Procedure) Regulations 2004 (SI 2004/1861).

The Employment Tribunals Act 1996 attempts to deal with the   06.33
coverage of allegations of sexual misconduct and should be fully read before the journalist attempts to cover such a hearing. Section 11 makes provision for a restrictive reporting order banning the identification of specified individuals. Journalists should note both the breadth of that potential identification (including as it does "any matter likely to lead members of the public to identify him as a person affected by, or as the person making, the allegation") and also the financial sanction which may be taken for breach. Those sanctions will be against the proprietor, editor and publisher of a newspaper, or the body corporate and editor of a broadcasting programme. Avoiding exposing senior management to the wrath of the tribunal is highly recommended.

The definition of "sexual misconduct" includes sexual offences,   06.34
sexual harassment and "other adverse conduct of whatever nature relating to sex". It also includes behaviour based on the sex of the person against whom the behaviour is directed or the sexual orientation of that person. A case involving the Metropolitan Police in 2003 (*X v Commissioner of Police of Metropolis* **(2003)**) took that further by holding that, "the case simply had to appear to involve allegations of the commission of a sexual offence". The order can be made at any time before the tribunal decision is promulgated—the date on which the notice announcing the tribunal's decision is sent to the parties. The order stays in force until promulgation of the decision, unless the tribunal has revoked it earlier. An application to lift the restriction in circumstances where settlement has been reached outwith the tribunal can be made—as indeed successfully happened in 2006 in relation to the actor Kevin Costner. Mr Costner allegedly exposed himself to a spa worker who was subsequently dismissed. She took her case to tribunal but settled before the hearing. The press successfully applied for a lifting of the reporting restriction.

The practical application of these provisions has been laid out in *R.*   06.35
v London (North) Industrial Tribunal Ex p. Associated Newspapers

***Ltd* (1998)**. In the present context it is important to note what is said there in attempting to balance the power to grant the order against the background of the general notions of freedom of expression granted to the press.

06.36   Mr Justice Keene put it thus at [1998] ICR 1212 at 1223:

> "In arriving at a conclusion as to what that purpose was, both sides agree that in this case it is proper to have regard to the ministerial statements as reported in *Hansard*. Those statements, referred to earlier, show that the purpose of these provisions was to enable complaints of sexual harassment at work to be brought and witnesses to give evidence about incidents of sexual harassment without being deterred by fear of intimate sexual details about them being publicised. I am not sure that it is possible to define persons 'affected by' such allegations simply in terms of categories, such as alleged victim, alleged perpetrator and witness of the incident, although it seems that these were the persons whom Parliament principally had in mind. The right approach is to deal with the individual case and to ask whether a particular person is 'affected by' the allegation, given the purpose of the legislation. It would not be right for this court to seek to substitute some definition of its own for the words Parliament has chosen to use."

06.37   His Lordship goes on to suggest that any restriction on the general freedom of the press should be very narrowly construed.

> "Applying this approach to the interpretation of section 11, one can see that the power to make a restricted reporting order will normally exist so as to prevent anything likely to lead to the identification by members of the public of the victim of the alleged sexual misconduct and the alleged perpetrator. (I stress in passing that at this stage I am dealing simply with the legal power to make an order and not with the exercise of that discretionary power.) The power may exist in an appropriate case so as to protect the identity of a witness of a sexual incident, where the disclosure of the identity of that witness would be capable of preventing the proper conduct of the tribunal hearing. It may be that other witnesses are also capable, in appropriate cases, of coming within the meaning of those words 'a person affected by' the allegation. But in all cases the approach should be to see whether the individual is clearly such a person, given the purpose of section 11 and the need to respect the importance of the freedom of the press."

06.38   That approach was approved and adopted in the Scottish case of ***Scottish Daily Record & Sunday Mail Ltd v M* (2001)**. Importantly, that case also establishes that it will be a relevant factor to rejecting the imposition of an order if both parties have already put the matter in the public domain. In that case both a former topless model and her employer had previously co-operated willingly with the publication of previous articles. The restricted reporting order was refused despite both now wishing it granted in her case of sexual harassment. It will always, however, depend on the particular facts and circumstances.

One added complication has been identified recently in *A v B*   06.39
(2010). That case related to dismissal after allegations of an employee having sex with children in Cambodia. It threw up what the Employment Appeal Tribunal in England referred to as the "remarkable anomaly" of the legislative provisions which seem to suggest that whilst s.11 can be used in relation to the original tribunal, authority does not exist in the related legislation for a permanent anonymity order to be made in relation to the appeal proceedings. There, and in other cases, reliance has instead been placed on the Convention rights of the individual. From a media perspective there is plainly interest in such cases but caution must be exercised precisely because as *A v B* illustrates, the courts are often ready to show flexibility and creativity to defend the anonymity of individuals in certain circumstances.

Broadly similar orders can be made under s.12 in relation to   06.40
disability—a term defined in the Disability Discrimination Act 1995. Disability is defined as physical or mental impairment which has a substantial and long-term effect. A tribunal can make an order where it is likely to hear, "any evidence of a medical, or other intimate, nature which might reasonably be assumed to be likely to cause significant embarrassment to the complainant if reported".

NHS TRIBUNALS

In Scotland, under the Smoking, Health and Social Care (Scotland)   06.41
Act 2005 (and also new regulations passed by the Scottish Parliament in 2004 and 2006), the powers and procedures for an NHS Tribunal to investigate cases where it is claimed that a doctor, dentist, pharmacist or optician should be removed from the NHS list have been significantly altered. The general power of these tribunals derives from the National Health Service (Scotland) Act 1978. In practical terms, the chairman must be an advocate or solicitor of at least 10 years standing. There are two other members. If the tribunal decides to refuse to hold an inquiry or decides that the practitioner should remain on the list, the matter is at an end. If it supports removal, the

practitioner can appeal to the Court of Session under s.11 of the Tribunals and Inquiries Act 1992.

TRANSPORT

06.42　The Traffic Commissioner for Scotland is appointed by the Secretary of State for Transport. Decisions of the Traffic Commissioner on issues such as HGV operator licences go to the Transport Tribunal. That tribunal is currently in the process of being moved to the new Upper Tribunal. (On the Upper Tribunal see **para.06.07**.)

LANDS TRIBUNAL

06.43　The Lands Tribunal deals with issues such as the discharge or variation of title conditions, tenants' rights to purchase their public sector houses, disputed compensation for compulsory purchase of land or loss in value of land caused by public works, valuations for rating on non-domestic premises and appeals against the Keeper of the Registers of Scotland. Parties may additionally refer a range of related matters to the tribunal to act as arbiter. The president is Lord McGhie and there are three other members. Appeal on a point of law lies to the Court of Session.

INQUIRIES

06.44　Inquiries into matters of national importance can take three forms—a tribunal of inquiry, a committee of inquiry or a royal commission.

TRIBUNALS OF INQUIRY

06.45　These are appointed by Parliament to inquire into matters of urgent public importance. Ordinarily they sit in public. They have the power to order witnesses to attend and to give evidence. There is also the power to refer cases of contempt of the tribunal to the Court of Session for consideration and punishment.

06.46　　One recent example which explains the legal framework and purpose is the decision of the Scottish Government in March 2008 to set up "the Fingerprint Inquiry" which arose as a consequence of the case of Shirley McKie and which is looking at the potential shortcomings of how fingerprint evidence is collected and used in criminal trials. Given the impact on a number of existing convictions in other cases and the need for public confidence in the prosecution of crime, the public importance was clear. This is a public judicial inquiry set up by Scottish Ministers under the Inquiries Act 2005. The Act sets out how an inquiry is established, and various matters to do with its proceedings, such as evidence and procedure. Under the same Act, Scottish Ministers have created the Inquiries (Scotland) Rules 2007 (SSI 2007/560) which govern all aspects of the proceedings. At the time of writing, a final report has still to be produced.

ROYAL COMMISSIONS

Royal Commissions are often set up where the object is to set the scene 06.47 for future policy reform. For example, there have been royal commissions on such things as the press, capital punishment, the constitution and divorce. These commissions in practice usually sit in public but they are not compelled to publish all evidence they receive.

LOCAL INQUIRIES

Planning inquiries are amongst the most common type of these local 06.48 inquiries—dealing with vexed questions of where to site a local supermarket or where best to build a motorway. These are held by reporters who then makes findings and recommendations to the Scottish Ministers. One controversial recent example is the Beauly–Denny public inquiry into the erection of new electricity transmission line running down the spine of Scotland. That controversial and long-running series of hearings was announced in August 2006 and only recently reported. On January 6, 2010, Scottish Ministers finally gave approval for the power line to be built.

FATAL ACCIDENT INQUIRIES

The Fatal Accidents and Sudden Deaths Inquiry (Scotland) Act 1976 06.49 sets out the law on fatal accident inquiries in Scotland. Around 14,000 deaths are reported every year. About half of them are investigated by the procurator fiscal as part of the work of the Crown Office and Procurator Fiscal Service. Public inquiries are held where there has been a fatal accident at work, a death in legal custody or where the Lord Advocate considers that it is in the public interest on the ground that the death was sudden, suspicious or unexplained, or occurred in circumstances such as to give rise to serious public concern. Since devolution between 35 and 80 fatal accident inquiries are held each year. Therefore, in practice the need for a fatal accident inquiry (FAI) arises only in a very small fraction of these cases.

06.50   The purpose of an FAI is to establish the time, place and cause of a death. Such inquiries do not attribute blame or guilt in either the civil or criminal sense. The procurator fiscal leads evidence at the inquiry, which is held in the sheriff court. At the conclusion of the inquiry, the sheriff will issue a determination which will contain findings about the circumstances of the death. The sheriff may also make recommendations as to how such deaths may be avoided in future. These recommendations are not legally binding. Sheriffs make such recommendations in around a third of all FAIs.

06.51   It is, however, important to note that a major review of the current system was carried out under Lord Cullen of Whitekirk. The *Review of Fatal Accident Inquiry Legislation* (Scottish Government, 2009) was published in November 2009. Lord Cullen described the recommendations as "fine tuning" but they do make some significant changes, not least the holding of such inquiries outwith court buildings, the changes designed to improve the transparency for families of the deceased and the expansion of the categories of people for whom such inquiries are appropriate. The Scottish Parliament is currently considering the changes.

LOCAL AND PARLIAMENTARY OMBUDSMAN

06.52   In a UK context, complaints about the service provided by a UK Government department, agency or other organisation acting on their behalf can be addressed by the UK Parliamentary Ombudsman. In a Scottish context, complaints about councils, the National Health Service, housing associations, the Scottish Government and its agencies and departments, colleges and universities and most Scottish public bodies **are dealt with by the Scottish Public Services Ombudsman.** That office was set up in 2002 as a "one-stop-shop". It replaced three previous offices—the Scottish Parliamentary and Health Service Ombudsman, the Local Government Ombudsman for Scotland and the Housing Association Ombudsman for Scotland.

PROFESSIONAL DISCIPLINARY BODIES

06.53   There are a range of professional bodies which supervise discipline within their own professions. The purpose of these groups is to ensure that only those fit to be a member of a particular profession are allowed to be registered as being so.

06.54   Decisions to strike off a professional are open to appeal but the professions can be subdivided into two groups—those with an appeal to the Privy Council and those with an appeal to the Court of Session. Reports should always state that the name of the professional will be removed "failing the entry of an appeal to the Privy Council within 28 days" or to the Court of Session as the case may be.

In the legal world, the position of solicitors and advocates in Scotland has undergone radical change. The office of the **Scottish Legal Services Ombudsman** was abolished in September 2008 and replaced by the **Scottish Legal Complaints Commission** (SLCC) which opened on October 1, 2008. The SLCC was set up under the Legal Profession and Legal Aid (Scotland) Act 2007 to investigate complaints made by members of the public about services provided by legal practitioners in Scotland. It operates wholly independently of the legal profession, provides a single gateway for taking a complaint forward and offers the services of trained mediators to aid resolution. Previously, legal complaints not resolved by the appropriate professional body could be taken to the Scottish Legal Services Ombudsman (SLSO). The Ombudsman was able to investigate how the complaint was handled, but not the actual complaint. 06.55

Simply put, the job of the SLCC is to receive complaints about the *service* received from a legal practitioner, and decide whether to investigate those complaints. Whilst the Law Society of Scotland (in the case of solicitors or solicitor advocates) or the Faculty of Advocates (for advocates) will still deal with matters of professional misconduct or unsatisfactory conduct, the SLCC will oversee how such conduct complaints are investigated and prosecuted. Therefore, the SLCC has an important role to play in influencing the conduct processes, including the powers to audit and recommend changes. Nevertheless, the primary source of discipline in relation to conduct remains the relevant professional body. 06.56

In investigating a service complaint, the SLCC can listen to both the person making the complaint and the legal practitioner, examine certain documents or demand explanations in connection with the complaint, and reach an outcome it considers fair and reasonable. This means it must take account of the relevant law (including levels of damages awarded by courts in similar circumstances) and relevant codes of practice, professional rules, standards and guidance. 06.57

Where a complaint is either upheld or not upheld, the SLCC must notify the person making the complaint, and any practitioner or practice involved in the complaint, in writing of its decision. It can also publish a report of the investigation. 06.58

The SLCC has the power to answer the service complaint by awarding the complainer up to a set limit of £20,000 for any loss, inconvenience or distress resulting from the inadequate professional service. It can also require the relevant legal practices and practitioners to reduce fees, re-do work and rectify any mistakes, at their own expense. If the SLCC feels that the practitioner shows a 06.59

lack of competence relating to any area of the law or legal practice, it can report the matter to the relevant professional body.

06.60   Appeal against a decision of the SLCC is to the Court of Session within 28 days.

06.61   The 2007 Act also specifies that an appeal can be made to court against any decision of the SLCC, and sets out various conditions for such an appeal, including that it must be made within 28 days of the SLCC's decision.

06.62   Questions of a solicitor's conduct are still dealt with by the Law Society of Scotland.

06.63   Complaints against solicitors in Scotland are channelled first through the Scottish Legal Services Complaints Commission who will refer conduct matters to the Law Society of Scotland, which carries out an initial investigation and can decide to prosecute more serious cases before the Scottish Solicitors' Discipline Tribunal (SSDT). The SSDT is an independent body which mainly deals with serious disciplinary issues. The most severe sanction available to the Tribunal is to strike an individual off the Roll of Solicitors, which effectively removes the individual's right to practise as a solicitor in Scotland. The tribunal normally sits with two solicitor members and two lay members: solicitor members cannot also be members of the Council of the Law Society. All members are appointed by the Lord President of the Court of Session—Scotland's most senior judge. The tribunal is governed by a new set of rules known as the Scottish Solicitors Discipline Tribunal Procedure Rules 2008.

06.64   Conduct issues amongst members of the Scottish Bar will continue to be referred to the Dean of Faculty. In recent years, efforts have been made to make those hearings more open—for example in 2007 when Donald Findlay QC was cleared of professional misconduct over allegations of insensitive jokes about the Pope. That hearing is believed to have been one of the first to have been heard in public—an implicit recognition by the Faculty that greater transparency in these matters is essential for confidence in the system of discipline it enforces.

06.65   The appointment and removal of judges is now governed by the Judiciary and Courts (Scotland) Act 2008.

PART 2: THE COURT REPORTER

CHAPTER 7

THE COURT REPORTER

BY ROSALIND MCINNES

RIGHTS AND RESPONSIBILITIES

The aim here is to present a guide, for quick reference, to cover the 07.01
situations most likely to cause difficulty or raise doubts for journalists
reporting the courts in Scotland. Over the years, there have been
statements by judges on many important aspects of the court
reporter's work, but these are only pieces in the jigsaw. Decisions of
the courts and Acts of Parliament leave unanswered vast areas of
difficult and dangerous territory. Common sense is as important as a
detailed knowledge of the law.

Few members of the public have the time to attend and see for 07.02
themselves that justice is being done. In the civil courts in
particular—including the Court of Session, the supreme civil court in
Scotland—the public are often entirely absent. The desire to ensure
that justice is not only done, but seen to be done, can hardly be
achieved if the only people allowed to be present in court are counsel
and solicitors and the judges themselves.

As Lord Macfadyen said, when the Inner House refused the 07.03
application of murderer William Beggs (***Beggs v Scottish Ministers***
(2006)) that his reclaiming motion (appeal) in a civil case he brought
over his transfer to Peterhead Prison be heard in private with the press
excluded:

> "The relevant general principle is that court proceedings should
> be held in public ... In circumstances in which it is thought
> proper to exclude the public, it is normal to allow representatives
> of the press to be present to preserve the pubic nature of the
> proceedings. It would be an extreme step indeed for us to
> exclude the press."

07.04 The importance of the right to report is not restricted to the trial, but extends to earlier proceedings, according to the English decision in *Re T* **(2009)**. Arbitrations are in an entirely different position, with extensive witness anonymity afforded by s.15 of the Arbitration (Scotland) Act 2010, and, for privacy reasons, are popular in certain business disputes.

07.05 Where so much is at stake—not only the reputations of people named in the journalist's reports but possibly also the journalist's own career and liberty—the court reporter must have a sound grasp of what information can be safely used.

FAIRNESS AND ACCURACY

07.06 The essential ingredient of a court report is that it is fair and accurate. This is important not just from the point of view of fair play to everyone involved in the case—parties, witnesses, counsel and the judge. A fair and accurate contemporaneous report of proceedings held in open court is protected from a defamation action even though it contains defamatory information. It is also protected against contempt of court [see **Chapter 15**].

07.07 The reporter must not fall into the trap of believing that as long as a report is accurate it is safe—that is, protected by privilege. It must also be fair. Fairness implies not only that there should be a proper balance between the claims of both sides, but also to third parties who are not present or represented in court and therefore have no opportunity to reply.

PLEAS IN MITIGATION

07.08 The classic example is the plea in mitigation made by counsel on behalf of an accused person, based on information from the accused. Counsel has no opportunity to check the truth of these statements. One example is what has become known as the Portsmouth defence, where the accused alleges that the victim of an assault made a homosexual advance. If there is a guilty plea, the victim may not be in court and may find out about the allegation for the first time when he sees his name in the paper. Where statements of this kind form an essential part of the story and must be published, it should be made clear in any report that they are allegations and not necessarily statements of fact.

07.09 Denials made out of court by someone offended by the plea, or demands for a right to reply, would not be protected by privilege. They may be protected by other defences in defamation, such as reply to attack [see **paras 26.79, 27.45, 29.03** and *Carroll v BBC*; *Curran v Sunday Mail*].

Although Scotland has so far been spared legislation on the subject, 07.10
the Criminal Procedure and Investigations Act 1996 (s.58) was
introduced in England in an effort to postpone for a year the
reporting of derogatory claims made in pleas in mitigation. The Act
applies to Scottish newspapers and broadcasters when they are
reporting English proceedings. Section 58(4) states that a postponing
order may be imposed:

> "Where there are substantial grounds for believing: (1) that an
> assertion forming part of the speech or submission is derogatory
> to a person's character (for instance because it suggests that his
> conduct is or has been criminal, immoral or improper) and
> (2) that the assertion is false or that the facts asserted are
> irrelevant to the sentence."

This does not cover derogatory statements made in the prosecutor's 7.11
statement and an order cannot be made if the claim made during
mitigation was previously made at the trial at which the accused was
convicted, or during any other proceedings relating to the offence.

The power seems to be rarely used. An order was refused by Judge 07.12
John Machin at Lincoln Crown Court in 2007 in relation to a woman
who had admitted offences but claimed that she was a victim of
domestic violence, the judge saying: "There has to come a time when
the press is able to make a balanced report."

CIVIL CASES AND REPLY

The great majority of civil cases are argued in the presence of both 07.13
parties and their lawyers. Normally, claims made by one side against
the other will be answered, and the reporter has the opportunity
(which it will be unwise to pass up) of including the reply where one is
given. But if one side makes an allegation in the presence of the other,
and there is no reply, the newspaper is as free to publish the allegation
as if a reply had been made. The point is that there was an opportunity
to reply which was not taken. In that situation, justice would be on the
side of the journalist, provided, of course, that the report was fair and
accurate. It would probably be appropriate to indicate in the report
that no reply was made.

BALANCE

A court report should leave out nothing which is essential for a 07.14
balanced report, viewed from the position of both sides in the case.

To achieve this balance, the court reporter may have to include dull or uninteresting information. For example, it may be important to say in an interim interdict hearing that one side was not represented in court, otherwise it may look as if that side has no defence to put forward.

07.15   The reporter should always remember, however, the important distinction between details which could lead to a court action and information which merely causes annoyance or irritation. Many complaints about press reports have no merit, and the journalist has to be ready for, and to recognise, the groundless protest when it arises. The journalist should also remain detached; the trap of feeling sympathy for one side is that you may be in danger of causing prejudice to the other.

07.16   Depending on the kind of organisation the reporter works for, it may not always be necessary to report every piece of information the law allows. As a matter of taste rather than law it might, for example, be preferable in certain circumstances not to identify someone who was clearly psychologically disturbed. When the reporter does decide to omit from a report information which would normally be regarded as newsworthy, whether the name of a party or an allegation, that decision should be capable of justification.

07.17   If a reporter is approached by someone involved in a court case with the suggestion that details of the case should not be published, the reporter should inform the news editor. In the meantime the report should be written up as if no approach had been made. The duty to write the story is the reporter's, that of deciding whether to publish it is the editor's. Requests by interested parties to publish an explanation or correction in a case before the court should be treated with great caution. This might suit the interests of one side but interfere with those of the other. It would also not be privileged if it was not part of the court proceedings.

CLOSED DOORS

07.18   While proceedings are sometimes held behind closed doors in special circumstances, it is one of the fundamental principles of the Scottish system that the judicial process is public. It is only in this way that justice may not only be done but may be seen to be done. Two Acts of the original Scottish Parliament—the Evidence Act 1686 and the Court of Session Act 1693—are still in operation. The first of these lays down that there shall be "publication of the testimonies of witnesses". The second provides that:

> "[I]n all tyme comeing all bills, reports, debates, probations, and others relating to processes shall be considered, reasoned, advised, and voted by the Lords of Session with open doors ...

but with this restriction, that in some speciall cases the said Lords shall be allowed to cause remove all persons except the parties and their procurators".

The types of "special cases" that are in practice taken in private are 07.19 few. In criminal law, for example, bail appeals, although they may be heard in court, are usually heard in chambers because the judge deciding whether to grant bail may be given information such as details of previous convictions. Appearances by an accused on petition in solemn criminal cases, both first appearance and the subsequent full committal diet, are held in private.

Cases involving the adoption of children are, with rare exceptions, 07.20 heard in private—s.109 of the Adoption and Children (Scotland) Act 2007. Referral hearings before a sheriff are held in the sheriff's chambers. According to *Sloan v B* **(1991)**, which dealt with the Orkney "ritual abuse" investigations, under an older version of the children's hearing rules, the press can attend, but the sheriff has a discretion to refuse to admit the media if s/he thinks it proper.

Actions of declarator of nullity of marriage sometimes involve 07.21 evidence thought to be better given in private.

The doors may be closed in any case on the order of the judge for 07.22 part of the hearing where it appears necessary for the doing of justice, but it should not be a decision which is often reached. A judge may decide on this for reasons other than the particular character of the evidence, for example, where there is reason to anticipate a demonstration in the courtroom which might disrupt the proceedings, or any conduct among members of the public which would distract the attention of the court, counsel or witnesses. It is not usual for the media to be excluded in cases of this kind.

A very high importance has been given to open justice, even in the 07.23 post-Human Rights Act 1998 world of privacy, and the exercise of such a discretion against the media is likely to be challenged. On June 17, 2008, BBC Scotland successfully challenged an order purporting to exclude journalists from a sheriff court while the complainer, a 14-year-old boy, gave evidence in *PF v Richard Taylor* **(2008)**. On July 28, 2009, the BBC, STV, the *Herald*, the *Daily Record* and the *Evening Times* challenged an order purporting to close a criminal trial to "all persons other than those essential to the case"—*PF v Harkness* **(2009)**. The order was amended to make it clear that accredited media representatives would be welcome in court. The sheriff may have taken the view originally that the media counted as, "persons ... essential to the case".

Section 93 of the Police, Public Order and Criminal Justice 07.24 (Scotland) Act 2006 is startling. It purports to give the court power to exclude any person other than a judge, party, court officer or involved lawyer, or, "any person ... who does not, in the opinion of the court, have a sufficiently direct interest in the proceedings to justify that person's presence", and "to prohibit the publication of any matter relating to the proceedings (including the fact that the referral has been made)."

07.25   The court can only make such an order if it thinks that it is necessary to protect the safety of any person and in the interests of justice. Section 93 is designed to cover cases where a person has pled guilty and had the case referred back to the court for reconsideration of the sentence, upwards or downwards, because s/he has, or has not, co-operated with the police.

07.26   It is not difficult to imagine a case in which some details, e.g. the current address, of a criminal who has co-operated with police would be concealed to protect the criminal or informant's safety, but very hard indeed to see that it could be appropriate, in the interests of justice, to exclude an accredited media representative from criminal proceedings of, potentially, particularly strong public interest. Still less to order the media to conceal that the criminal court proceedings have taken place at all. There has been one attempt to exclude the media under these provisions, in September 2008 at Kilmarnock Sheriff Court. The BBC challenged it and the Crown took steps which meant that the order fell. It is likely that a provision of this sort could per se be challenged on human rights grounds by judicial review, given its breadth and potential impact on open justice in criminal proceedings.

07.27   The media are admitted to sittings of the Court of Session when it sits during court holidays. The judge and counsel do not normally wear wig and gown, and the court deals with urgent business.

SUMMARY TRIAL PROCEDURE

07.28   There is a kind of short-cut procedure in the Court of Session known as summary trial provided for by s.26 of the Court of Session Act 1988, by which parties, by agreement, may bring their dispute before a Court of Session judge of their choice for a speedy decision, and without right of appeal. In the great majority of such cases the procedure, so far as reporters are concerned, does not differ significantly from that of a proof under the ordinary procedure—evidence and counsel's speeches are heard, and the judge delivers a judgment (which, however, is final).

07.29   In 1967, under the "old" summary trial rules (s.10 of the Administration of Justice (Scotland) Act 1933), a petition was brought before the court to determine who was the heir male of the late Lord Sempill, and the procedure appears to have been unique in that it took place entirely in secret. The decision of the case depended on the sex of Ewan Forbes-Sempill, who was registered in infancy as female but underwent a change of sex as an adult. The petition, which was brought under the s.10 procedure, was heard by Lord Hunter in a solicitor's office, no decision or judgment was ever issued, and no press report of the case was therefore possible.

Following press reaction to this unusual method of avoiding publicity, the Lord Advocate said that under s.10(3) of the 1933 Act, the course taken by the court was justified in view of the "purely private" nature of the matter. It seemed to him that somewhat similar considerations to those operating in nullity cases justified the secret hearing. The view of Lord Kilbrandon, then Chairman of the Scottish Law Commission, was that s.10 was intended to provide a kind of judicial arbitration, whereby people could take their private disputes before the judge they had selected and get a final decision. The judge's opinion need not be published, any more than the deliverance of an arbiter. The Commission, he said, saw no reason to amend s.10. 07.30

Subsection (3) of s.10 provided that the judge might, on cause shown, hear and determine in chambers any dispute or question submitted for his decision under the section. Subsection (8) laid down, however, that the section shall apply to any dispute or question "not affecting the status of any person". In other words, actions of divorce or nullity of marriage could not, and cannot, be dealt with by summary trial procedure. Perhaps the most remarkable aspect of the procedure, as applied to the *Forbes-Sempill* case, is that the choice (with the judge's consent) lies with the parties themselves. The analogy with arbitration is questionable; the parties pay an arbiter often for reasons of privacy (usually commercial), whereas judges and courts are funded by the public. Issues of personal privacy may be protected in other ways, e.g. under the Judicial Proceedings (Regulation of Reports) Act 1926 [see **Chapter 24**], and it is not difficult to envisage an abuse of summary trial, e.g. where the issue was maladministration of a public works contract. It is a device for maintaining secrecy in judicial proceedings which one would like to believe would be rarely if ever invoked since it is so directly in conflict with the principle that justice should be seen to be done. 07.31

Section 10 was repealed and re-enacted in s.26 of the Court of Session Act 1988. It does not mention a chambers hearing, but the rules of court for summary trial allow the judge to hear the case "in court or in chambers". 07.32

RAPE AND OTHER SEX CASES

07.33   The Scottish media have never disclosed the identity of an alleged victim of a sexual offence unless the latter has consented. (It is recommended that such consent should be given explicitly, either on tape or in writing.) In any case, they are now obliged to anonymise under the Sexual Offences (Amendment) Act 1992 [see **para.20.38**].

07.34   The public are normally excluded from court when the alleged victim gives her evidence in a rape trial. Reporters are allowed to stay. Section 92(3) of the Criminal Procedure (Scotland) Act 1995 states:

> "From the commencement of the leading of evidence in a trial for rape or the like the judge may, if he thinks fit, cause all persons other than the accused and counsel and solicitors to be removed from the courtroom".

07.35   In *X v Sweeney* (1982), in a judgment concerning the Glasgow rape case [see **para.04.46**], Lord Avonside said:

> "In our courts a victim alleged to have been raped almost invariably gives evidence behind closed doors. In such a situation the public is not permitted to hear her evidence. It has been the practice, particularly in Glasgow, to allow press reporters to remain. They are asked to exercise a wise discretion, and in my experience, this they do admirably. The trial judge could, of course, if he thought it desirable, exclude the press and clear the court completely."

07.36   In *HM Advocate v Mola* (2007), which concerned the trial of a man accused of knowingly infecting his partner with the HIV virus, Lord Rodger, without having heard argument on the matter, observed:

> "The practice so described is, in my experience, the norm in the High Court wherever it is sitting. It is clear from that passage that his Lordship is describing a practice which is within the power of the court to allow the press to remain, but again, as Lord Avonside states, the practice does not limit the power of the court to order complete closure under Section 92(3)".

07.37   Both *Sweeney* and s.92(3) pre-date the passing of the Human Rights Act 1998, which "brings home" the art.6 right in the European Convention on Human Rights. Article 6 guarantees a "public hearing" of criminal charges and the art.10 right to receive and impart information. However, it also brings here the art.8 right to privacy and the protection of alleged victims of sexual assault raises privacy considerations of a high order. How these would play out if a court wished to hear a rape trial in secret (contrary to Scottish practice) remains to be seen.

The Contempt of Court Act 1981 gives the courts power to 07.38
postpone parts of a court report, in the case of s.4, and, in the case of s.11, to direct non-publication of a name "or other matter" which it was already able to allow to be withheld from the public during the hearing of a case. This is more fully dealt with in **Chapter 15**.

EMPLOYMENT APPEAL TRIBUNALS

In *Dallas McMillan v A & B* **(2008)**, the Employment Appeal Tribunal 07.39
in Scotland held that a journalist had no right to seek recall of a restricted reporting order in a sexual harassment tribunal once the tribunal had settled. It was suggested that, if there was a journalistic interest in such a tribunal, the journalist could be sisted as a party to the action, i.e. could "join in" the tribunal. Otherwise, once the tribunal has settled, the journalist has no way in to lift the order—the proceedings do not exist any more. That said, being "sisted as a party" would be an elaborate step for a court reporter to take. The decision is, from the media's point of view, unsatisfactory, given that it is the media who are (and will remain) bound by such an order [see **paras 06.31 to 06.40**].

THE REPORTER'S PRIVILEGE

The right to report judicial proceedings in Scotland originated in the 07.40
common law. Lord President Inglis put it this way in the case of *Richardson v Wilson* **(1879)**:

> "The publication by a newspaper of what takes place in court at the hearing of any case is undoubtedly lawful; and if it be reported in a fair and faithful manner the publisher is not responsible though the report contains statements or details of evidence affecting the character of either of the parties or of other persons; and what takes place in open court falls under the same rule, though it may be either before or after the proper hearing of the cause. The principle on which this rule is founded seems to be that as courts of justice are open to the public, anything that takes place before a judge or judges is thereby necessarily and legitimately made public, and being once made legitimately public property may be re-published without inferring any responsibility."

In *Richardson* the action had appeared on the calling list. There had 07.41
been no hearing of any kind in court. But, as was pointed out in the

case of *Macleod v Lewis Justices* **(1892)**, it is what takes place in open court which may safely be published. Examples will be given later of situations in which it is not always entirely safe even to publish everything that passes in open court.

07.42   Following the case of *Cunningham* **(1986)**, reporters may be able to claim qualified privilege to publish passages from a summons referred to in open court although these have not actually been read out in court.

07.43   Lord Clyde held in *Cunningham* that a summons founded on in this way is made public—a ruling of importance to court reporters as it may be applied also to documents other than the summons, although not necessarily, as the judge observed, to court productions.

07.44   In *Barclay v Morris* **(1997)**, Lord Osborne held that showing him a medical report and a cost of care report so that he could establish the dates and that the injured pursuer would be in hospital for life, did not mean that the defender had waived confidentiality in the report. He said:

> "I respectfully agree with what Lord Clyde has said … However … a spectator of the proceedings … would have had no difficulty in understanding what was taking place. In relation to the reports concerned, reference was made to their dates and to the fact that the premise upon which they were written was that the incapax would never leave hospital. There was no question of the contents of these documents being incorporated into what counsel had said … I should point out that here I am dealing with a motion in relation to documents which are not even productions."

07.45   The importance of reporters keeping their notebooks for a reasonable period is of particular significance in court cases. What is a reasonable period will vary with the circumstances, but experience suggests that one year would not be excessive. Generally, with the rise of internet-based actions, the period of time after which a story may come back to haunt a journalist is lengthening, rather than shortening.

07.46   In one Court of Session case, a newspaper report quoted counsel as stating in court that a director of a company had been trying to sell the company's assets. Eleven months after the item appeared, a director of the company, although he was not named in the report, apparently recognised himself as the person referred to in it. He wrote to the editor of the paper, alleging he had been defamed and threatening to sue the paper for damages. Fortunately the reporter was able to find his notes, which showed that the statement complained of was indeed made by counsel in court and was accurately reported. Nothing more was heard of the matter.

A report based upon a statement made in court which is privileged 07.47
may lose that protection if it is not clearly attributed to the speaker. If
a statement from court proceedings is quoted in a press report without
attribution, the newspaper itself will bear responsibility for the
statement, and if it should prove to be actionable, the defence of
privilege will not be open to the paper.

The *Daily Record* reported a bigamy case in Edinburgh Sheriff 07.48
Court in 1971 under the headline, "Unlucky bigamist gets nine
months". The report opened with the bare statement: "Robert Hogg
was unlucky in his two attempts at a happy marriage. His first wife ran
off with another man—and his second had a child to another man".
The statement that Mr Hogg's second wife had had a child to another
man was based on a submission made in court by Mr Hogg's solicitor,
but it was denied by the woman in question, who sued the *Daily
Record* for £2,000, alleging she had been defamed.

Her complaint was that the passage in the report stood by itself as a 07.49
statement of fact by the paper and was not attributed to anyone taking
part in the sheriff court proceedings.

At a legal debate in the Court of Session, Lord Brand rejected an 07.50
argument by counsel for the paper that the passage, if read by itself,
did not identify the woman. Sending the case for trial by jury, the
judge said it was one thing for a solicitor to say in court on his client's
instructions that the woman had had an illegitimate child, but it was
quite another matter for a newspaper to make such a claim on its own
authority. In his view, the bald statement that the pursuer had a child
to another man was, on the face of it, defamatory.

He accepted that the remainder of the paper's report, duly 07.51
attributing to Mr Hogg's solicitor in court the statement that the
pursuer had had an illegitimate child, was privileged, but said it
would be for the jury to decide whether the opening passage was a
fair and accurate summary of the fuller, privileged passage which
followed.

The case in fact never went to trial, but Lord Brand's judgment 07.52
provides a useful warning on the care to be taken in publishing
possibly defamatory statements without attributing them. The
"repetition rule" in defamation means that it is not normally a
defence for a newspaper to say that it was only repeating a
defamatory statement made by someone else. Conversely, though, to
adopt an otherwise privileged defamatory statement as the
newspaper's own *will* tend to make the newspaper responsible for it.

GOOD NOTE-TAKING

07.53   Excellent note-taking is a necessity to accomplish accurate work in the courtroom (tape recorders are specifically prohibited under the Contempt of Court Act 1981). If the report is not both fair and accurate, the journalist loses the protection of absolute privilege against defamation proceedings. He or she may also suffer the danger of being held to be in contempt of court if the inaccuracy is sufficiently serious to prejudice the proceedings before the court [see **paras 07.06, 07.07 and 15.60**].

PRIVILEGED MATERIAL AND COMMENT SHOULD BE KEPT SEPARATE

07.54   If the media wish to comment upon a case as well as to report what happens during the proceedings—and, of course, especially at the end of the trial, the media will often wish to comment—the comment should be recognisably distinct. This is a good rule when reporting on any privileged material. The Court of Appeal English case of *Curistan* **(2008)** involved a mixture by the *Sunday Times* of a report of what had been said in Parliament and additional material about Peter Curistan. Adding comment does not mean that the material stops being privileged, but can affect meaning.

IMPARTIALITY AND BALANCE

07.55   The report itself should be impartial, in the sense that it should be a straightforward and balanced account of what happened in court. It should not distort either by inaccuracy or by omission. The privilege is for reporting what happens in court, not adopting all the evidence given as true, though of course once someone is convicted, he may be safely described as "a murderer" or whatever charge has been proved. The report need not be verbatim or even long. Where a newspaper merely purports to report the result of a case and does so accurately it cannot be liable in damages because it fails to narrate the steps leading up to judgment. "There is no duty on a reporter in a report of a law suit to make his report exhaustive. It is ... sufficient if the reporter gives the result of the litigation truly and correctly" (per Lord Anderson in *Duncan v Associated Newspapers* **(1929)**). When proceedings before the result are being reported, however, care must be taken to see that the report is not one-sided. A significant omission can imperil the privilege (*Wright and Greig v Outram* **(1890)**). If one party's allegations are mentioned, the other party's replies should be given equal prominence so far as possible.

In a criminal case, very often the accused will not give evidence and 07.56 there may be few defence witnesses. Practically speaking, the main opportunity for balancing there is by reporting the cross-examination of Crown witnesses, as well, obviously, as making it clear that the accused is pleading not guilty. If reported allegations are found unproved, this must always be clearly stated. Allegations and refutations available on the same day should be published together. The burden of proving that a report is fair and accurate lies on the media (*Pope v Outram* **(1909)**).

The need to preserve a fair balance between prosecution and defence 07.57 in criminal cases and between the opposing sides in a civil action is especially important for evening papers. Where the report is incomplete in one edition and presents an unbalanced picture of the case, particular care should be taken to ensure that the balance is restored in later editions or in the issues of the following day. Statements rebutting earlier assertions by the other side must be reported.

A proper balance between opposing sides does not necessarily 07.58 require the publication of equal space to each. A lengthy argument advanced by one party may be completely demolished in a single sentence. It is rare for the defence case in a criminal trial to take as long as the Crown's. The reporter, who is to put the reader, viewer or listener in a similar position to that of a person attending court proceedings, is entitled to reflect that in the allocation of space to each side, so long as the report remains fair and accurate.

HEADLINES

Care should be taken with headlines in reports of judicial proceedings. 07.59 If these take the form of comment on the case, they cannot be regarded as part of the report and will not be privileged. They should therefore always be justified by the facts reported so as to be protected by the defence of fair comment. Sub-editors should be mindful of this.

REFERENCE TO DOCUMENTS

It is often impossible to understand a case completely without 07.60 reference to the various documents connected with it. How far are statements derived from this source protected? The answer varies with the circumstances. In civil cases a report of statements made in an open record [see **Chapter 9**] is completely unprivileged and the same would seem to apply to reports derived from a closed record which has not yet been referred to in open court. In practice, of course, there are many circumstances where it may be judged safe to publish information from a closed record at this stage but the law seems clear. A litigant who sends pleadings (whether the record is closed or not) to a newspaper for publication is not privileged in doing so. "If the pleadings so published are slanderous, then the paper publishing them, and the person sending them for publication, are liable in damages for slander" (per Lord Young in *Macleod v JPs of Lewis* **(1892)**). The same principles would apply to the indictment or complaint in criminal cases. Once the case comes up in open court, the position is different. Publication of a document actually read out in open court is, of course, privileged and privilege should also protect statements derived from documents which are merely referred to expressly or impliedly in open court. The test here would seem to be whether the information in the documents is an essential part of the case and is merely referred to for the sake of convenience.

07.61   The point arose in *Harper v Provincial Newspapers* **(1937)**. A man called James Harper appeared in the Edinburgh Burgh Court. The clerk of court read out his name, but not his address. He was found guilty of a fairly minor offence. A reporter verified the name and took down the address from the complaint, which was shown to him for that purpose by the clerk of court. In fact the address given in the complaint was not that of the accused, but that of his father who was also called James Harper. When the report appeared, the father sued the newspaper and the question then arose whether the statement derived from the complaint was privileged. It was held that it was. The address was an essential part of the case which was omitted from the proceedings in open court simply for reasons of speed and convenience. But it was observed that different considerations might apply to information taken from documents which were merely productions in a case.

07.62   In the case of *Cunningham v Scotsman Publications Ltd* **(1986)**, Lord Clyde held that privilege applies to a document which, "is referred to and founded upon before the court with a view to advancing a submission which is being made", even if not read out in open court.

07.63   In *Nicol* **(2002)**, Lady Paton held that the breach of the Judicial Proceedings (Regulation of Reports) Act 1926 [see **Chapter 24**] did not remove the privilege for fair and accurate court reporting in a defamation action against Caledonian Newspapers.

NO PRIVILEGE FOR HEARINGS IN PRIVATE

No privilege attaches to reports of proceedings held in private. It is a   07.64
question of circumstances in each case whether proceedings are in
private or in public. In *Thomson v Munro and Jamieson* **(1900)**, it
was held that when a statutory examination of a bankrupt took place
in public in the sheriff clerk's room, this "was for the occasion a public
court".

An interesting question arises regarding children's hearings. They   07.65
are not open to the public, but bona fide journalists are admitted. It
can hardly be doubted that fair and accurate reports would enjoy
privilege. The journalists are there to represent the public. A
children's hearing is a court for contempt purposes. There would
seem to be the strongest reasons for according privilege to the only
source of information on the proceedings available to the public.

INTERRUPTIONS IN COURT

Situations may arise where there is doubt whether remarks form part   07.66
of the proceedings. Thus in one English case (*Hope v Leng Ltd* **(1907)**)
a witness shouted from the well of the court that the plaintiff's evidence
was "a pack of lies". It was held in this case that a report containing
this statement was nonetheless privileged. It is clear, on the other
hand, that a report of a conversation between two spectators at the
back of the court would not be privileged. The journalist must
exercise discretion in deciding whether or not the interruptions can
properly be regarded as part of the proceedings [see **para.22.17**].

It is not unusual, in the real life drama of a courtroom, for an   07.67
interjection of this sort to happen—a protestation of innocence by
the relatives of someone who has been convicted; insults or worse
between the relatives of victims and the convicted person (in either
direction); occasionally a physical collapse, due to health problems or
stress, by an accused person or witness, or even, as in the case of
Michael Ross **(2008)**, when convicted of the murder of an Orcadian
waiter, an attempted escape from court. Most such incidents occur
after the verdict and/or are seen by the jury as they happen. There is
rarely much factual dispute as to what happened and, typically,
limited reputation to damage. A report of them might, conceivably,
influence a juror or witness in unusual circumstances.

Given that the journalist in court is encouraged to put the public in   07.68
the same position as they would be if they were physically present,
though, there is an additional and strong argument that this sort of
behaviour does form part of an absolutely privileged court report,
even though it is not an intended part of proceedings. It would always

be open to the court to order a postponement of the reporting of such events under s.4(2) if a contempt risk arose.

PARTY LITIGANTS

07.69   Special care has to be taken in reporting statements made by people conducting their own case, either because they do not wish or cannot afford to be represented by counsel. The judges invariably are less strict in enforcing rules of procedure than they would be with a lawyer.

07.70   The difficulty is that party litigants tend to bring in irrelevant statements and sweeping allegations which have no direct bearing on the questions before the court. The reporter may have to exclude these from a report. Where these statements or allegations implicate third parties who have not the opportunity to reply and are patently irrelevant to the issue under consideration, they may not form part of a fair and balanced report of the proceedings.

07.71   The reporter who has some background knowledge of a case from an outside source should remember that if that information is included in the report, it will not be protected by privilege.

INTERPRETATION

07.72   The court reporter has to be especially careful in interpreting, condensing, or translating into lay language passages from legal proceedings. It may be relatively simple to copy accurately and reproduce what a speaker says, but the exact reproduction of language used in court would rarely be acceptable, particularly for the tabloid press or for radio and television reports.

07.73   In "translating" legalese into lay terms the reporter must understand the meaning of the information and use precisely the words which will convey the idea intended by the speaker. For example, a trust disposition and settlement can simply be called a will, and someone who alienates heritable subjects can normally be said to be selling a house. The most common terms are included in the glossary at the end of this book.

07.74   Apart from offering a kind of translation of legal jargon, the reporter will often find it necessary to condense the normal verbosity of legal terminology, especially when a report is based upon written pleadings in a civil action. Written judgments of the court may have to be distilled from 100 or more pages to a few hundred words before they appear in print or on a news bulletin. Again, the reporter must understand what the judge's decision means and the reasoning by which the decision was reached.

Where the judge has had to wrestle with difficult legal questions, 07.75
perhaps involving lengthy citation of cases, the reporter's job will
vary according to the kind of organisation for which s/he works. In
many cases the paper will be satisfied with the bare result, but other
newspapers will wish to give their readers some sort of explanation of
the reasoning which lies behind a decision. For the bald decision in a
case may sometimes seem, on the face of it, unjust or unfair. A report
of the reasoning which led to the decision may explain the apparent
anomaly.

KEY POINTS

1. It is a fundamental principle of Scots law that unless there are 07.76
   exceptional circumstances the courts sit in public.
2. A fair and accurate report of legal proceedings held in public is
   generally protected against defamation or contempt of court
   actions. This privilege may be lost if a statement that would be
   defamatory outside the courtroom is not clearly attributed to
   the person who makes it.
3. Reports based on information from a calling list, summons or
   open record are not privileged and could lead to a defamation
   action. There will, however, be instances where a case can be
   safely reported in some detail at the calling list, summons or
   open record stage. The closed record, though not legally
   privileged in itself, can be used as the basis for a fair, accurate
   and balanced report once a case has come into open court. The
   record is not normally read out and it is important to check
   that it is up to date.
4. Special types of cases, such as adoption hearings, are
   conducted behind closed doors.
5. Alleged victims in sex cases should not be named without their
   consent.
6. Special care is needed in reporting statements of people
   conducting their own cases. It can also be highly dangerous
   to mix up background knowledge with what is said in court.

CHAPTER 8

REPORTS OF ENGLISH COMMITTAL
AND PRE-TRIAL HEARINGS

By ROSALIND McINNES

08.01   England has its own legal system with its own range of specific reporting restrictions designed to protect children, alleged victims of sexual offences, vulnerable witnesses, and so on. In some cases, there could be prosecutions in Scotland if the Scottish media were to breach such an order in reporting English proceedings. In proceedings arising out of the *Stephen Lawrence* case (*R v D* (2010)), for instance, an order was granted on September 7, 2010 in the English Court of Appeal under s.82 of the Criminal Justice Act 2003 which was binding throughout the UK. An attempt to lift it was unsuccessful on October 5, 2010.

08.02   No attempt is made to cover all such reporting restrictions here. Instead, this chapter is designed to assist Scottish journalists sent to cover the opening stages of English criminal cases with a Scottish "hook". At the time of writing, the trials of Peter Tobin, Scottish serial killer, north and south of the border, are very much in mind. This chapter points out some of the major traps to avoid in such cases.

08.03   At its most basic, in either jurisdiction: if the case could end up before a jury, and the jury is not there, and what is being said in court could make the accused look bad, do not publish before taking advice from a local lawyer.

COMMITTAL HEARINGS

08.04   Under the Scottish criminal procedure, early preliminary proceedings are held in private. In England, by contrast, the magistrates' courts hold preliminary hearings to decide the future procedure in more serious cases, which could end up in the Crown Court, for a jury trial. These preliminary hearings deal with bail and preparation for trial. In "either-way cases" (charges could be tried by a magistrates' court or by a Crown Court), the magistrates' court also has to decide whether the case needs to be tried in a Crown Court and to ask the defendant how s/he intends to plead to the "either-way" charge. If jury trial is chosen—the defendant can insist on trial by jury—the case is adjourned for a committal hearing. Indictable offences, such as murder, rape and robbery are triable only at the Crown Court.

96

In a committal hearing, the magistrates examine the evidence to see   08.05
if there is enough for the defendant to be "committed for trial" to the
Crown Court. Some of the evidence presented to the magistrates may
not feature in the trial. It may be ruled inadmissible. Such material
might be prejudicial, e.g. a confession which the defence successfully
argue was improperly obtained. The magistrates may also be told
about previous convictions or suspicions that the defendant may
have committed other unsolved crimes, when they are deciding on
bail. Witnesses used to give evidence at committal hearings, but now
there are only written witness statements.

Reporting restrictions in s.8 of the Magistrates' Courts Act 1980   08.06
aim to ensure that potential jurors at a future Crown Court trial are
not swayed by what they see or hear in media reports. The reporting
restrictions apply to both "either-way" offences and indictable
offences.

WHAT CAN BE REPORTED FROM A COMMITTAL HEARING?

The details which may be included in a report, even though it is   08.07
published before the trial, are restricted to the following points:

(1) the identity of the court and the names of the examining
    justices;
(2) the names, addresses and occupations of the parties and
    witnesses and the ages of the accused and witnesses;
(3) the offence or offences, or a summary of them, with which the
    accused is or are charged;
(4) the names of the legal representatives involved in the
    proceedings;
(5) any decision of the court to commit the accused or any of the
    accused for trial, and any decision of the court on the disposal
    of the case of any of the accused not committed;
(6) where the court commits the accused for trial, the charge or
    charges, or a summary of them, on which he is committed
    and the court to which he is committed;
(7) where the committal proceedings are adjourned, the date and
    place to which they are adjourned;
(8) any arrangements as to bail on committal or adjournment,
    and this includes any bail conditions. If bail is refused,
    though, the media should not report why it was refused;
(9) whether a right to representation funded by the Legal Services
    Commission as part of the Criminal Defence Service was
    granted to any of the accused, i.e. whether the accused got
    legal aid.

08.08 The media will also usually publish a straight denial of guilt or the accused's choosing trial by jury. A certain amount of bland scene setting may be indulged in with impunity, e.g. that the accused wore a white skirt or that the hearing lasted 20 minutes.

08.09 In 1996 the former editor and the owners of the *Citizen* newspaper in Gloucester were each fined £4,500 over a story of the first appearance before magistrates of the mass murderer Fred West. Although the report was accurate it included a statement that West had admitted killing his daughter. In 2008, the publisher of the *Jewish Chronicle* was fined £1,000.

WHEN COMMITTAL HEARING REPORTING RESTRICTIONS ARE LIFTED

08.10 The restrictions no longer apply if the magistrates decide not to commit any of the accused for trial; the court decides to try the accused summarily (as regards that accused only); when they have all finally been tried at Crown Court or one of the accused asks for restrictions to be lifted. If there is more than one accused, all are allowed to make submissions before a decision is taken on whether restrictions should be lifted. If one accused objects, reporting restrictions will be lifted only if it is decided to be in the interests of justice to do so. The kind of consideration the court might have to have in mind in deciding whether to lift restrictions is whether one accused wants publicity in the hope of encouraging an important defence witness to come forward.

PRE-TRIAL HEARINGS IN SUMMARY PROCEEDINGS

08.11 When a charge is going to be tried by magistrates, and the plea is not guilty, the magistrates may hold a pre-trial hearing to rule on points of law, the admissibility of evidence, procedural or bail issues. These pre-trial hearings are subject to extensive, automatic reporting restrictions under s.8C of the Magistrates' Courts Act 1980. This is on the off-chance that the case in fact ends up before a jury, e.g. because the magistrates discover that the alleged crime is worse than it first seemed, or that it is closely linked to another case which is going to trial at the Crown Court already.

08.12 As with committal or other preliminary hearings, pre-trial hearings of this sort could touch upon previous convictions or inadmissible evidence. Thus, during the relevant period, the media can only report the name of the court, the magistrates' names, the names, ages, home addresses and occupations of the accused and witnesses, the offences charged, the names of counsel and solicitors, bail arrangements, whether legal aid was granted and, if the proceedings are adjourned, to when and where they are adjourned.

These reporting restrictions can be lifted at the magistrates'   08.13
discretion, as they were in the MPs' expenses case (for background,
see *R. v Chaytor, Morley, Devine and Hanningfield* (2010)).
Otherwise, they come off automatically when the case is disposed of
by acquittal, conviction, dismissal or the prosecutorial decision not to
proceed.

CROWN COURT HEARINGS

When a case is definitely in the Crown Court, and there is a not guilty   08.14
plea, there are hearings before the jury becomes involved. These
include applications for a case to be dismissed for insufficient
evidence, and "preparatory hearings" in complicated cases. There are
automatic reporting restrictions covering such hearings which limit
reporting to the name of the Crown Court and the judge; the names,
ages, home addresses and occupations of the accused and witnesses;
the offences charged; the names of counsel and solicitors; bail
arrangements; whether legal aid has been granted; and, where the
proceeding are adjourned, to when and where they have been
adjourned.

In some fraud cases, "relevant business information" of a fairly   08.15
anodyne kind, e.g. registered office of a company, can also be
reported. There are other "pre-trial hearings" to which automatic
reporting restrictions apply. These stop the media reporting rulings
on admissibility of evidence or any other question of law. The judge
has discretion to remove the reporting restrictions. Otherwise, they
lapse at the end of the trial.

Those accused of a crime in the Crown Court can be "arraigned",   08.16
i.e. asked how they are pleading, in a pre-trial hearing or a preparatory
hearing. If there are several accused of several charges, and all plead
guilty, the pleas can be reported, as there will be no trial. If they all
plead not guilty, that, too, can be safely reported.

SECTION 4(2) ORDERS

A mixture of guilty and not guilty pleas can be reported unless the   08.17
judge makes a s.4(2) order under the Contempt of Court Act 1981
[see **Chapter 20**] to postpone reporting of any guilty pleas about
which a jury should not know, e.g. in a related trial.

The coverage of committal proceedings can also be affected by   08.18
s.4(2), which gives courts power to postpone publication of reports of
proceedings to avoid prejudicing other proceedings which are pending

or imminent. In an appeal against an order made by Horsham Justices under the section in 1981, the English High Court ruled that magistrates must not make an order that is wider than necessary to prevent prejudice to the administration of justice [see **Chapter 20**]. In deciding that the magistrates' order was too wide, the court said it should have been limited to sensitive matters disclosed during the committal hearing.

THIRD PARTY COSTS ORDERS

08.19   Since the Courts Act 2003, publishers in England and Wales may also face a "third party costs order" where "serious misconduct" affects a case—such as a publication which results in the abandonment of a trial midway. This could run into millions, and might apply even where the statutory test for publication contempt is not met [see **Chapter 16**]. Thus far, this has not been a major problem for the media.

KEY POINTS

08.20   1. Under s.8 of the Magistrates' Courts Act 1980, there are stringent restrictions on what can be reported at English preliminary hearings.

PART 3: INFORMATION AND ACCESS

Chapter 9

ACCESS TO INFORMATION

By Rosalind McInnes

COURT DOCUMENTS

In reporting the civil courts one of the most common problems for the journalist is gaining access to documents. 09.01

Court records are the subject of an absolute exemption under the Freedom of Information (Scotland) Act 2002. 09.02

The Rules of the Court of Session, however, state "a writ ... may be inspected by any person having an interest" (r.4.11). There are some types of application where the Rules of Court expressly provide that the documents in the case are to be confidential, e.g. r.67.3, which deals with adoption. By implication, therefore, most court writs are not confidential. This does not mean, however, that the journalist has an automatic right to be given a copy—still less that it is safe to quote from such a document. 09.03

Arguably, a journalist who needs a document in order properly to report on or to understand a case taking place in open court is entitled to it as an implicit aspect of the media's role of "watchdog" [see **para.27.85**] under the art.10 right to freedom of expression. Until recently, the European Court of Human Rights has been slow to interpret the art.10 right to receive information as creating a free-standing right to access documents, but times are fast changing in this respect. The UK Government made a "friendly settlement" with Harriet Harman (then a solicitor with the National Council for Civil Liberties) in the mid-1980s after she was held to be in contempt of court for passing on documents received during litigation to a journalist, notwithstanding that the documents had been read out in open court. Lord Roskill said in that case in the House of Lords: 09.04

101

> "The only exception [to the rule that a solicitor who received documents as part of the "discovery" process in litigation, by which enforced access to some of the other side's documentation is given, is subject to an implied obligation only to use that documentation for the purposes of the litigation] would be in favour of those who engage in day-by-day reporting, whether for press agencies, as representatives of the media, or as law reporters. It is well known ... that Counsel and solicitors have always, and as I think rightly, been ready to help reporters of all kinds who desire to ensure that their day-by-day reports should be fair and accurate by showing them particular documents ... I would prefer to regard [this] assistance ... in the interests of fair and accurate reporting, as being for the immediate purpose of the litigation in question ..." (*Home Office v Harman* (1981)).

09.05   Lord Clyde said in the Scottish defamation case of *Cunningham v Scotsman Publications* (1986), about whether a newspaper report which included allegations in a summons which had been the basis of an interim interdict application, but had never been read out in open court, was entitled to privilege:

> "The pursuer's counsel argued that on the defenders' approach the reader of the reporter's account ... would have an advantage over the person listening in court who would only have had a reference to the document ... But it may be that in this matter the newspaper reporter has a responsible role to play in enabling both those within and those without the walls of the court to be equally well informed of what has taken place."

09.06   His Lordship evaded the question of just who was a "party interested" and thus entitled to inspect a process under the then Rules of Court, but stated, "My attention was not drawn to any provision which prohibits the inspection of a document which has been founded upon in open court" (*Cunningham v Scotsman Publications* (1986)).

09.07   In *Chan U Seek v Alvis Vehicles* (2005) in England, the *Guardian* applied for copies of documents from the court file. The parties had agreed confidential terms of settlement. The *Guardian* reporter wanted to see the witness statements. Mr Justice Park said that there was a strong presumption that there should be as few impediments as possible to the reporting of cases:

> "[N]ot just by specialist law reporters but also by the national and local press ... it is through the press identifying the newsworthy cases, keeping itself well-informed about them and distilling them into stories or articles in the newspapers that the generality of the public secure the effects and, I trust, the benefits of open justice."

He pointed out that, increasingly, the courts were using written 09.08
materials, rather than having oral hearings. That being so, the
Guardian had an entirely legitimate interest in the pleadings and
witness statements, given that its core business was as a newspaper.
He also pointed out, shrewdly, that open justice was often the last
thing which the parties want:

> "I am sure that Alvis, which certainly did not want to be sued by
> Mr Chan and which has now settled the case, would much prefer
> it if The Guardian was not taking the interest which it is ...
> However, the proceedings ... were not a private arbitration.
> They were proceedings in open court, and unwelcome publicity
> ... is not uncommonly a consequence" (*Chan U Seek v Alvis
> Vehicles Ltd* (2005)).

Very similar points were made in the English family court case of *Re* 09.09
Brandon Webster (2006), where Munby J. said:

> "If the media are to be permitted to attend a hearing ... then the
> very same public interest requires, in my judgement, that the
> media should be allowed to see documents such as [Norfolk
> County Council's solicitor's] position statement. For if the
> media ... are not permitted to see [this] the ability of the media
> ... to understand what took place during the hearing would be
> severely compromised ...".

The *Guardian* is, at the time of writing, appealing in England the 09.10
refusal in April 2010 of its request for access to documents about the
extradition of Jeffrey Tesler, an English solicitor, to the United States.

Thus, giving journalists access to the documents referred to in a 09.11
court case to facilitate fair and accurate reporting is, as a general rule,
not only legitimate, but judicially desirable. None of this, though, adds
up to a straightforward right of access in practice, and some of the time
journalists will be reduced to begging or borrowing—stealing is not
recommended—documents vital to a proper understanding of a court
case.

In principle, the practice in the sheriff courts should be the same as in 09.12
the Court of Session; although relatively few civil cases appear to be
reported from the sheriff courts, which is unfortunate since this may
be a rich source of (local, in particular) news.

The most important documents which a reporter may have to refer 09.13
to before it is possible to write a fair, accurate and balanced report of a
case at its various stages are the calling list, court rolls, petitions,
records and judgments. A wide variety of other documents may
come, with the assistance of lawyers or court authorities, into the
hands of reporters. These include copies of wills, contracts, letters
and minutes. In general, these may be safely quoted only where their

contents have been referred to and seen by the judge in open court, and the reporter wants to see them to check the accuracy of notes.

THE ROLLS OF COURT

09.14   The Rolls of Court show the allocation of civil and criminal cases in the Court of Session and High Court of Justiciary in Edinburgh. There is (1) a "long" roll published at the beginning of each session (usually in September, January, and April) showing in advance the dates for hearings on the evidence such as proofs and jury trials, and procedure rolls (legal debates); (2) a weekly roll, showing next week's business; and (3) a daily roll, showing tomorrow's business.

CALLING LIST

09.15   One section of the Rolls of Court is the calling list. The calling list is usually the first public notice of a court action being raised, and a copy is displayed on the wall in Parliament House. It is now available, along with the rest of the Rolls of Court, on the Scottish Courts website (*http://www.scotcourts.gov.uk* [Accessed September 14, 2010]). Each entry contains only the names and addresses of the parties to the action, and the names of the solicitors acting for the pursuer.

09.16   Under the Contempt of Court Act 1981, civil cases only become active from the time when arrangements for a hearing are made, or when a hearing starts [see **para.16.17**]. This makes it possible to prepare a report based on information in the calling list without falling foul of the contempt law, even in the sort of civil action which can go to a jury, as *Tommy Sheridan*'s **(2006)** defamation case did.

09.17   However, there is still the risk of defamation. Unlike coverage of a case being heard in open court, a report based on inquiries at the calling list stage will not have the protection of privilege. And, since any report at this early stage may involve access to particulars contained in the summons, special care is needed to avoid publishing defamatory allegations from that source.

09.18   The reporter in the Court of Session can use the calling list as a guide to the cases likely to be available for reporting in the future. It is important to keep track of the major news stories of the day because many of them end up in the Court of Session and the first sign may be in the calling list.

SUMMONS

The appearance of a case on the calling list is the public signal that the 09.19
pursuer in the action has served a summons on the defender. The
journalist must treat a summons with great caution, particularly
before a hearing of any kind has taken place in court.

In the case of *Richardson v Wilson* **(1879)**, the Court of Session 09.20
rejected the argument that once an action appeared on the calling list
the contents of the summons could be made public. The court said that
would not be a report of judicial proceedings, but of the contents of a
writ which were at the time unknown even to the court.

The *Edinburgh Evening News* published a passage from a summons 09.21
which had appeared on the calling list. No further step in procedure
had taken place and a party mentioned in the report sued the paper.
The newspaper argued, unsuccessfully, that the paragraph which was
published was a bona fide and correct report of the claims in an action
called and pending in the Court of Session and they were entitled to
publish it (*Richardson v Wilson* **(1879)**). The pursuer maintained that
statements contained in the report (reproduced from the summons)
were untrue and defamatory. The report was not said to be in any
way unfair as a representation of the statements in the summons.

Lord Craighill said the principle was that what might be seen and 09.22
heard in court could be published. The courts were open and
accessible to all. It did not follow, however, that every step of process
in a cause from the calling to the final judgment was an occasion on
which everything which could be discovered from an examination of
the process might be published to the world. Were this so, the world
would get to know the contents of writs and productions before the
court.

The public, he said, had no right and no interest to know more than 09.23
could be learned by attendance in court. The right and the interest of
the public were concerned not with the statements which one party in a
cause might make against the other, but with the proceedings in open
court, by which justice was to be administered.

The *Edinburgh Evening News* appealed unsuccessfully to the First 09.24
Division. Lord President Inglis said the duty of the clerk in charge of
the process was at that stage plainly not to part with the summons or
give access to it, except to the parties to the case or their agents. That
was the rule in the contemporary Act of Sederunt. The present day
RCS r.4.11(1) says that: "A writ shall remain in the Office of Court
and shall not be borrowed from process, but may be inspected by any
person having an interest".

In *Cunningham v Scotsman Publications* **(1986)**, where there had 09.25
been a hearing in open court and the contents of the summons were

known to the judge, Lord Clyde decided that reporters might be able to claim the protection of qualified privilege in quoting from the summons although the summons had not been read out and only one side had been present in court.

09.26   David Cunningham, a former advocate, sued the *Scotsman*, *Dundee Courier & Advertiser* and the *Herald* for £600,000 damages, alleging they had defamed him in reporting a hearing in the Court of Session in 1984, when interim interdict was granted in his absence to ban him from dealing in certain shares. (That action was later abandoned.)

09.27   Mr Cunningham complained that the reports contained passages from the summons which had not been read out in court and were thus not covered by privilege. He argued that privilege protected only reports of the factual details of what went on in court—the identity of the parties and the judge, the nature of the proceedings, what was said by counsel and the judge and what the court actually did. Putting a document before a judge did not amount to publishing it in open court.

09.28   The newspapers argued that the summons was before the court, it was referred to by counsel, the allegations in it were founded on by counsel and the court granted an interdict in terms of one of the conclusions in the summons.

09.29   Lord Clyde, upholding the newspapers' plea that their reports could be protected by qualified privilege, said that previous Scottish cases (including *Richardson*) did not support the argument that a report must always be limited to what was said and read aloud in open court. Courts sat to hear cases and give judgment "with open doors", and it was evident that, for public confidence in the administration of justice to be maintained, the public must be able to see and hear proceedings for themselves.

09.30   The proceedings must also be intelligible. Lord Clyde added:

> "The public must have at least the opportunity of understanding what is going on and if they do not have the opportunity I do not consider that the hearing is a public one. If the hearing is a public hearing then it does not seem to me that that characteristic is destroyed simply because for perfectly proper reasons of convenience a document is referred to and not read out in full. Where a document has been incorporated into what counsel has said, the proceedings cannot be said to be open to the public unless the terms of the document can be seen by the public."

09.31   There was also a clear advantage in enabling the public to know with certainty and accuracy what had passed in court, rather than leaving them to rely on rumour or speculation, and the reporting of proceedings might be found to be unfair or misleading if access to the pleadings which had been founded upon in open court was not allowed. To make a realistic application of the principle to the circumstances of the *Cunningham* case, Lord Clyde said he could not restrict the availability of privilege to a report of what was actually read out in court. Lord Clyde continued:

> "The test is not what is actually read out—although all that is read out is published—but what is in the presentation of the case intended to be published and so put in the same position as if it had been read out. If it is referred to and founded upon before the court with a view to advancing the submission which is being made, it is to be taken as published."

To decide the scope of privileged reporting by reference to the method   09.32
of communication between counsel and judge seemed to Lord Clyde to involve adopting a standard which could be fixed by "chance, caprice or idiosyncrasy". One advocate might prefer to read passages of pleadings while another would summarise or merely make reference to them. Making publication depend on whether or not a document founded on in open court was or was not read out by counsel or judge might more easily invite suspicion of secrecy.

   Lord Clyde's judgment was obviously a significant one for the   09.33
media, but its limits should be carefully noted. The decision was not appealed and the case never went to proof. This meant that the question of whether the allegations published in the newspapers were in fact privileged in this case was never decided. All that was decided was that they might be. Lord Clyde also pointed out that it might well be that documents other than pleadings, such as productions, were in a different position. The newspapers defending Mr Cunningham's action agreed that productions could not be published unless they were led in evidence.

   Lord Clyde also made it clear that not all parts of a document would   09.34
necessarily be safely used in a court report:

> "I should not wish to exclude the possibility that cases could arise where a document contained matter which was quite distinct and separable from the point in issue before the court and neither relevant to it nor necessary for its determination and where such matter might not necessarily be published where other parts were founded upon."

ADJUSTMENT ROLL

After the summons has been served and defences lodged—none of   09.35
which takes place in open court—an action appears on what is known as the "adjustment roll". The allegations that each party

intends to prove will be spliced into an "open record" (pronounced "reCORD", accent on the second syllable). At intervals fixed by the court, the action appears on the case list of a judge who has to decide whether a continuation should be allowed for one side to answer claims put by the other. At some stage, the judge will decide that no further adjustment of the pleadings is to be allowed and order that the record be closed.

09.36   The distinction between an open record and a closed record is important for the safe reporting of civil actions. The record (containing the parties' written pleadings) remains open so long as the case is on the adjustment roll. The court reporter must check from the front cover that it is in fact a closed record before using extracts from it. In the sheriff court the cover of the record may not indicate whether it is open or closed and a check must be made with court officials or lawyers as to whether it has in fact been closed.

09.37   The closing of the record means that the pleadings of the parties to the action are in their final form, subject to anything that might be added by a minute of amendment. The reporter should be mindful of the fact that even when the record is closed and both parties have therefore stated their case fully, one cannot necessarily quote from the record with impunity. The safest view is to regard statements contained in a record as covered by privilege only if they are read out in open court. It should also be remembered that the closing of a record has the effect of making civil proceedings active in terms of the Contempt of Court Act 1981.

OPEN RECORD AND CONTEMPT OF COURT

09.38   It was decided in the case of *Young v Armour* **(1921)**, that publication of the contents of an open record in that case was an interference with the administration of justice. The action was one for damages for breach of promise of marriage. Extracts from the record were published in certain English newspapers and by one Scottish paper, the *Weekly Record*, before it had been closed. Under the heading "Love on the Golf Links", the report gave a detailed account of the facts stated in the open record. Both sides agreed there had been an interference with the due course of justice, because the case might have been settled without any of the facts having been made public.

09.39   Lord Blackburn said that the appearance of the article amounted to contempt of court since the record, while still open, was not public property. The editor of the Scottish newspaper was ordered to appear in court personally to give an explanation.

09.40   He apologised and explained that, although he knew that the contents of an open record should not be published, he had seen the article in certain English papers and had assumed, wrongly but quite honestly, that the case had been heard in court. The apology was accepted, but the judge said that if the explanation had not been satisfactory, the fine inflicted would have been severe. The court considered that, "the contempt which resulted from publication of this sort was a serious offence and one which should be met with a severe penalty".

While that case sounded a warning about the dangers of publishing 09.41 details from an open record, the reporter should not take fright at the very mention of the words open record. The Contempt of Court Act 1981 has relaxed the *Young v Armour* rule. Contempt considerations in publishing from an open record only now arise when proceedings are active under the Act, for example at a preliminary hearing [see **paras 16.17 to 16.18**], although publication from the open record could still be contempt at common law if intended to prejudice the administration of justice.

Important points of law are often debated before the closing of the 09.42 record, and if a full scale hearing takes place in open court, a report of the proceedings can be published. On the basis of the *Cunningham* decision, information from the open record could be used if it is referred to in court and the court is being asked to make a decision on it. A report based on information in the record which had nothing to do with the particular hearing would probably not be privileged.

CLOSED RECORD

A closed record is sometimes referred to as a public document, but this 09.43 does not mean that its contents can be freely published at any stage in the proceedings. It was made abundantly clear in a decision in 1892 (*Macleod v Lewis Justices* (1892)) that, until a case has come into open court, excerpts from even a closed record should not be published. Great care must be taken over information from a closed record which might be actionable.

The privilege protecting a newspaper from a defamation action over 09.44 what it publishes from a closed record operates only from the time the action has come into open court.

In the case of *Macleod v Lewis Justices* (1892), the closed record 09.45 contained defamatory statements about two justices of the peace. The justices, who were the defenders in the case, answered the statements with a general denial.

Immediately after the record was closed, an agent for the pursuer 09.46 handed to a reporter for the *North British Daily Mail* a record containing the pursuer's contentions but not the defenders' general denial. A summary of the record was published in the paper and also in the *Scottish Highlander*. The papers later published a letter from the justices stating the allegations about them in the record were "a tissue of libellous falsehoods". The pursuer complained to the Court of Session that the publication of these letters was contempt of court. The court ruled that there was no contempt, but made some observations which provide useful guidance on this aspect of court reporting.

09.47   Lord Justice-Clerk MacDonald said it might be a practice to hand complete records to the newspapers, but it was not one to be looked on with favour, and certainly to hand an incomplete record to anyone for the purpose of publication was a very gross irregularity. That was quite different from the publication by newspapers of what took place in a case when it was in open court.

09.48   Lord Young, agreeing, said it was clear that statements made in pleadings, i.e. in court, were privileged, however libellous they might appear, but there was no privilege whatever in the publication of pleadings. Reporting of proceedings was simply an enlargement of the audience which heard them in court, but which was limited by the size of the courtroom. It was therefore quite right to report, for example, a debate on the relevancy of a case, and the report would be privileged if it was fair. While a litigant was privileged in the statements made on record, he was not privileged if he sent his pleadings (whether the record was closed or not) to a newspaper for publication. If the pleadings published were defamatory, the paper publishing them, and the person sending them for publication, were liable in damages.

09.49   It is not surprising, therefore, that reporters sometimes find solicitors reluctant to hand over to them closed records in cases which have not reached the stage of a hearing in open court. Yet, where a closed record is made available, and contains nothing which could reasonably be regarded as risky to publish, or the reporter is careful not to reproduce any risky elements, there is still scope for the safe reporting of cases from this source.

09.50   The effect of the ruling in the case of **Macleod** seems to have been modified by practice in the intervening years. For example, when an action of damages opens before a judge or jury in the Court of Session it is usual for solicitors willingly to let the press have a copy of the closed record without any reservations as to which passages may be published. They do so although at a proof or jury trial, the closed record may never be read out in open court. A literal reading of **Macleod** in such cases would make adequate reporting impossible.

09.51   Since the closed record is the only reliable and practicable means of preparing a complete, fair and balanced report, it is not surprising that solicitors engaged normally hand over a copy to the press at the opening of the evidence and often at a preliminary legal debate.

Indeed, it would surprise many of them to learn that by so doing they were providing the media with something they had no legal right to publish.

The case of **Macleod** seems to assume that the closed record will 09.52 sooner or later be read out in open court. In fact, this rarely happens, since the judge has a copy, as do counsel and instructing solicitors. There may be no need for counsel to read it out, except to draw attention sometimes to a particular passage. A reporter who had to depend solely upon such desultory readings, often out of context, from one side of a case, would have great difficulty in ever achieving any semblance of fair or balanced reporting.

In short, there is a risk in publishing the contents of a closed record if 09.53 the case has not yet come into open court. From the moment a hearing has begun (whether a legal debate, proof or jury trial) the journalist can safely use the record so far as necessary for accurate reporting of the proof hearing, even if the contents of the record itself are not read out in open court. This must apply particularly when the judge, who may already have read the closed record in preparation for the hearing, tells counsel expressly that there is no need to read it out in court. In that situation the record may properly be "taken as read".

The journalist should always check, however, that the record is up- 09.54 to-date. It is important to ensure that the amount sued for has not changed and that there has been no major change in the allegations and defences put forward by the parties to the action. For example, are the parties to the action still the same and is there still a plea of contributory negligence?

COMMON SENSE

As in so many other aspects of court reporting, the journalist needs to 09.55 exercise care and common sense in deciding which passages it is safe to reproduce from the record before the case is heard in open court. Where the pleadings are read out by counsel during the proceedings, these passages, when published fairly and accurately, are privileged, but quotes from the record are not.

It is generally safe to assume that a lawyer who hands over a closed 09.56 record to a reporter without reservation is tacitly conceding that the statements, so far as the lawyer's own client is concerned, may be published without fear of reprisals. But the reporter has to keep in mind the interests of other parties to the case. Also, parties can change their lawyers, and indeed their minds.

OPEN COURT

09.57 Once the case is in open court, the reporter can normally expect to obtain a closed record from the solicitor for one party or the other. If not, the next step will be to approach the clerk of court. If the clerk is unable or unwilling to provide a copy, the reporter's next line of approach is to the Principal Clerk of Session. In the unlikely event of the Principal Clerk's refusal to help, the reporter will have to ask to see the Lord President.

09.58 This situation did occur in a case where, not only did both parties to a large property dispute refuse to hand over a record, and the clerk feel unwilling to supply one to the press, but one of the parties offered a journalist a sum of money for not publishing anything about the case. As it was impossible to report the case without access to the pleadings, Lord President Cooper was approached and instructed the Principal Clerk that the court staff should provide the press with a closed record. Otherwise, he said, the parties would be enforcing a closed doors hearing at their own hand.

09.59 Journalists should also be aware that in cases where the media have asked for eminent counsel's opinion on this issue, the view has been expressed that the provision of a closed record to reporters by the court or solicitors does not mean that every allegation in the record is covered by privilege.

09.60 The transcript of evidence taken on commission (where a witness is unable to attend court) is in a similar position to the closed record when evidence is being heard. Although the evidence may not be read out because the judge will have the actual transcript, it should, for press purposes, be taken as read, and treated as being covered by the same kind of privilege as spoken evidence. The reporter should be given access to a copy of the transcript, unless it contains the type of evidence which the court would ordinarily hear behind closed doors.

PETITIONS

09.61 A wide variety of cases are started by a petition rather than a summons. The procedure is different, and there is a separate petition department in the Court of Session. There are also certain changes of wording. With a summons the parties are pursuer and defender. With a petition, the parties are petitioner and respondent. Petitions are met with "anwers", rather than "defences". In cases where the court makes an ex parte order (i.e. in the absence of the person against whom the order is sought) a report should indicate, in the interests of fairness, that the other party was not present or represented in court and was allowed time to answer.

An ordinary action is begun by the pursuer serving a summons on 09.62
the defender, who in turn replies (if contesting the case). By contrast, a
petition is addressed to the court which orders notification to other
parties having a potential interest to lodge answers to the petition.
Petitions often relate to the winding up of companies, variation of
trusts, judicial review and child abduction.

When (and if) answers are lodged to a petition, these go through the 09.63
kind of adjustment which occurs in an ordinary action, and eventually
a document equivalent to a closed record (usually entitled "petition
and answers") is drawn up. The journalist can normally treat this in
the same way as a closed record.

INTERIM INTERDICTS

An interim interdict may be granted on the basis of a summons or a 09.64
petition.

The use of the expression "temporary order" or "temporary ban" is 09.65
not always a satisfactory way of referring to an interim interdict.
"Interim" does not necessarily mean "temporary". An interim order
is made to restrain someone from doing something until some further
development in the case. That may not take place for weeks or for
months or may never happen at all. The interim interdict could
continue in operation indefinitely and could not properly be called
temporary. It is also attributing to a court more power than it has to
say in a report of interdict proceedings that it has issued an order to
prevent some specific act. An interdict can only prohibit it.

Because interim interdicts come to court as a matter of urgency, the 09.66
summons or petition is frequently in a fairly basic state. There is also
often no opportunity for the alleged wrongdoer to be represented at
the application for an interim order. The court's decision has to be
reached upon an ex parte statement which, for the reporter, requires
special care. Only as much of such a statement as is necessary to
explain the basis of the court's decision—or as much as has been
stated in open court—may be safely published.

A person who has reason to think an interim interdict will be taken 09.67
out against him or her can, in Scotland, lodge in court what is known
as a caveat. A caveat obliges the clerk of court to contact the person
against whom an interdict is sought and ask whether the latter wishes
to appear and make submissions before the judge decides whether the
interdict should be granted.

Most newspaper and broadcasting organisations in Scotland lodge 09.68
caveats which last for a year, then are renewed. Separately, there is
now a general obligation under s.12(2) of the Human Rights Act
1998 to notify the other side where possible [see **paras 36.28**

onwards] if the party is applying for any order which might affect the exercise of freedom of expression.

09.69   If the court refuses to grant an application for interim interdict, the case for publishing no more than necessary is even stronger. Unless there is some compelling reason why the result should be reported—for example where the case has been reported at an earlier stage and there is an obligation to publish the result—petitions for interim interdict which fail on an ex parte application should only be reported with extreme care. It is possible that in refusing the application for interim interdict the judge has taken the view that the allegations contained in the writ lodged by the pursuer are unfounded, but there are a number of reasons why the court might refuse interdict at this stage. For example, the judge might feel there is a lack of specification in the pleadings or that the test of "balance of convenience" has not been satisfied.

09.70   If there is a compelling reason why the decision refusing an interim order should be published, the decision alone should be given, and it would generally be unwise to go into the detail of the allegations made by counsel in seeking the order—unless these have been stated in open court. On the other hand, where, in refusing to grant an interim interdict, the court reaches a decision which is in itself important, the reporter is justified in asking court staff for enough information about the case, including names and addresses of parties, to prepare a report.

COURT ROLLS

09.71   Cases which have come to court by way of a petition are usually indicated by "Pet" before the name of the petitioner. The name of the party who is suing comes first. Parties' names are usually followed by the names of solicitors for the parties represented in the case. An appeal from a single Court of Session judge is known as a "reclaiming motion".

09.72   A "motion" is when the court is asked to do something. Some are hotly contested, e.g. motions for discharge of a proof (the big hearing, with witnesses' evidence, in a civil case) because one side is not ready, or motions for an additional fee by the winning side. Others are largely a formality, further simplified since April 2010 in ordinary actions and personal injury actions. The rolls refer to "starred" and "unstarred motions". This is a reference to the practice of marking some court business with an asterisk. In a "starred motion", counsel are due to appear to make submissions in open court. Unstarred motions go through on the nod and there is no public appearance, and the entry in the roll indicates a formal step in procedure which is not usually reportable at all. In the Inner House, motions are called "single bills" and are marked with an asterisk where appearance is required. Although the Divisions of the Inner House are concerned largely with appeals from the Outer House and from the sheriff courts, they also deal with a wide variety of petitions.

At appeal, the court will have before it not only the closed record, or   09.73
petition and answers, but also usually an appendix containing a transcript of the evidence from the court below and a copy of the judgment delivered by the judge or sheriff, which is under appeal.

If the evidence has been given in open court, it may be useful to refer   09.74
to this and the judgment being appealed against where necessary to report the appeal.

AVIZANDUM

After the hearing of evidence or legal debate the court may give an   09.75
immediate decision or may "make avizandum", which means that it will take time to consider the case before issuing a written judgment. Occasionally the court will give its decision and produce reasons in writing later.

Strictly speaking, the judgment of the court comprises two   09.76
documents—the interlocutor and the opinion of the judge(s). In practice, the opinion is the source of news. The interlocutor is a minute kept by the clerk of court recording in formal style the precise terms of the decision. This is normally no use for publication and the reporter should refer to it only as a guide to the true effect of a decision if this is not clear from a reading of the judgment.

Decisions do not come into force until the interlocutor is signed by   09.77
the judge. In certain circumstances a judge will grant a decree, but for specific reasons will agree to delay operation of the decision for a stated period. He or she does this by "superseding extract" of the decree, in other words, delaying the process by which the successful party can obtain the extract copy of the decree which will enable it to be enforced. In these circumstances, reports of the case should make it clear that the decision does not immediately become effective.

CRIMINAL CASES

In criminal proceedings the document with which the reporter is   09.78
mainly concerned is, in cases dealt with in solemn procedure, the indictment, and in summary cases, the complaint or charge sheet. In the justice of the peace court, the complaint contains the name and address of the accused person as well as the charge against him. In the High Court where bail has been allowed the address of the accused is

normally on the indictment, and where he is in custody his address, if known, can usually be obtained from court officials.

09.79   In the case of indictments, the first point at which the media are protected against a defamation action by the statutory privilege for court reporting if they publish the whole contents of the document is when it is read out to the jury at the opening of the trial, or when the accused pleads guilty to the charge(s) contained in it.

09.80   Where charges are dropped against an accused person without trial, papers which published the charge at an earlier stage, for example when the accused appeared on petition, should publish the dropping of the charges.

09.81   When someone appears on petition, the procurator fiscal will normally inform the media of the name of the accused and provide brief details of the charge for publication. Where no plea is taken from the accused and the case is continued, these facts should be included in any report. On the question of bail, the journalist may come to have details of the submissions made to the court, e.g. the procurator fiscal opposing bail on the grounds of previous convictions. Such details should not appear in a report. All that can be said is that bail was granted or refused.

09.82   To name an accused person before he appears on petition is a defamation risk. The charge may be dropped. He may not appear in court at all and, if he does, it may be on a different charge from that originally preferred by the police—if indeed there has been a charge at all. In the ***McAvennie*** case, a newspaper reported that former footballer Frank McAvennie had been charged with assaulting his ex-wife. The newspaper accepted that there had been no charge, but offered to prove that there had been a draft charge. Mr McAvennie argued that the article meant that he had in fact committed the assault. He lost on that part, unsuccessfully appealed (***McAvennie v Scottish Daily Record and Sunday Mail Ltd* (2003)**) and the action later settled.

09.83   On one occasion, when the media were refused access to a complaint at the old Burgh Court in Edinburgh, once the case was in court for trial, the Lord Advocate of the day, John Wheatley QC, was approached. His opinion was that, although reporters had no statutory right of access to complaints, it was a matter of public policy that they should have this facility in the interests of accurate reporting of cases.

KEY POINTS

1. While a journalist has no greater right than any member of the public to attend legal proceedings, it is recognised that the reporter requires access to certain court documents at the appropriate stage in proceedings to carry out the job properly. As a matter of public policy the media are allowed access to certain papers, both in criminal and civil cases, or at least to some of the information contained in them. Where access to documents necessary for the fair and accurate reporting of a case heard in open court is refused, the reporter should raise the matter with the appropriate court authority. 09.84

2. To avoid being sued for defamation, a journalist should quote from documents which have been read out or had their quoted contents referred to in open court. A summons is not "privileged" for quoting just because it has been lodged with the court and served on the defender to the action.

3. To name an accused person before he appears in a criminal court is also a defamation risk.

CHAPTER 10

DATA PROTECTION

By ROSALIND MCINNES

10.01   The Data Protection Act 1998 aims to regulate the processing (including collecting) of personal information, set preconditions for data to be processed, and to increase the individual's right to control how information about him or her is used.

10.02   Its predecessor, the Data Protection Act 1984, required data users to register with the Data Protection Registrar, to handle data in accordance with certain principles (to do with keeping the data safe, accurate and using it for defined purposes only) and to give individuals access to information about them. The 1998 Act is similar, but wider and far more obscure.

10.03   Some lawyers thought that this Act was the end of the self regulation of the press. Publications, true or not, routinely have to be justified by a reasonable belief that publication is in the public interest. Yet compelling public interest justifications tend to emerge after investigation, not in advance of it. As with the privacy element of the Human Rights Act 1998, a major concern was the scope for interference in investigative journalism at the investigation stage, not through publication bans. The existing, nominally voluntary, codes have been given some legal force by the back door.

10.04   In practice, since the last edition of this book, the Data Protection Act 1998 has added little to the journalistic hurdles imposed by the rapid development of the law of breach of confidence [see **Chapter 37**]. Section 13 of the Act entitles an individual to compensation. Bolt-on claims for Data Protection Act breaches were made in the cases involving Catherine Zeta-Jones and Michael Douglas's wedding photographs, the article and pictures about Naomi Campbell's drug abuse and Narcotics Anonymous therapy, Danielle Lloyd's claim against Carphone Warehouse over mobile phone photographs (***Lloyd v Jagpal* (2009)**)), and J.K. Rowling's young son, but where those cases went up the English appellate ladder, the amount of court time devoted to the data protection angle noticeably decreased. Such awards as have been made for the data protection element in media cases have been modest in the extreme. Catherine Zeta-Jones and Michael Douglas, for instance, got £50 each for their Data Protection Act claims.

10.05   The Data Protection Act claim as an independent cause of action against the media has not made much of a stir mainly because it has been subsumed into the breach of confidence arguments about the respective values of privacy and freedom of expression, what constitutes the public interest and so on. For one thing, all data processing under the Act has to comply with the data protection principles [see **para.10.21**], the first of which states that personal data shall be processed "fairly and lawfully"; where a journalist, newspaper or broadcaster is found to be in breach of confidence, they are most unlikely to be able to establish that they were nonetheless "lawfully" processing the data. For another, in a case which is ultimately about personal privacy, the same damage will have been sustained by the successful claimant or pursuer, and the courts will not allow them to be compensated twice for the same consequences of the same intrusion.

Beyond that, there is a palpable reluctance on the part of the courts, and in many cases the litigants, to try to make sense of the Data Protection Act 1998. European Directives are expressed at quite a general level and require to be translated for a number of different European languages and legal systems. This does not make for clear or elegant prose and the 1998 Act is mostly a cut and paste from such a Directive. 10.06

Journalists should not, however, relax prematurely about the Data Protection Act 1998. The looseness of its drafting leads to the making of novel arguments which seek to impinge upon freedom of expression. In *Quinton v Peirce* **(2009)**, for instance, the failed Conservative candidate argued that the successful Liberal Democrat candidate was obliged, under the Data Protection Act principles of fairness and accuracy, to "rectify" the contents of an election leaflet. He failed, the English judge holding that the leaflet was not substantially inaccurate or unfair. More generally, however, he said of the Act: 10.07

"I am by no means persuaded that it is necessary or proportionate to interpret the scope of this statute so as to afford a set of parallel remedies when damaging information had been published about someone, but which is neither defamatory nor malicious."

He specifically rejected the idea that the Data Protection Act could be used to force someone to publish a correction or apology or to notify the opposition of what was in the leaflet: 10.08

"I decline ... to interpret the statute in a way which results in absurdity. Plainly, it cannot have been the intention of the legislature to require electoral candidates to give their opponents advance warning each time reference is to be made to them in a document that happens to be computer generated."

10.09   This case was not argued to be journalistic expression, so the question of the "journalistic exemption" [see **para.10.33**] did not arise, and the judge was clearly impatient with what he saw as a devious attempt to use the Act in a manner for which it was not designed. But it does show some of its potential pitfalls for free expression. In *Clift v Slough BC* **(2009)**, an English judge warned that the Data Protection Act 1998, coupled with the Human Rights Act 1998, would fundamentally alter assumptions about whether and when, for example, employment references may contain freely expressed criticism [see **para.30.01**].

10.10   The most pressing difficulty so far for journalists is that the Act may be used as a reason on the part of the police and local authorities to withhold information from the media. There is considerable leeway for the police to disclose even sensitive information, in terms of the exemptions contained in the Act, including a "Crime and Taxation" exemption; however, compelling such disclosure will be far from simple.

REFUSAL OF ACCESS ON DATA PROTECTION GROUNDS

10.11   Journalists looking for various types of information may encounter not just resistance couched in terms of the Data Protection Act, but genuine confusion on the part of the holders of that information as to whether they can hand it over, given that the Act creates a criminal offence of unlawfully obtaining or disclosing personal data, "knowingly or recklessly", without consent. There is a public interest defence. Conversely, it is not unknown for the police, while looking for information *from* journalists, to say that they are serving "a Data Protection Act notice". The journalist should be on guard against such a notice, however official looking. The Data Protection Act does give the police force special powers to process information, but not to require it from the press.

10.12   As well as the police, journalists sometimes struggle to get access to, e.g. a class photograph or CCTV of drunken misbehaviour in hospitals' accident and emergency departments. When faced with this sort of difficulty, it is worth looking closely at Schs 2 and 3 of the Act which set out the possible grounds for processing. Even with medical information, which is "sensitive personal data" [see **Appendix 5**], very often a health professional or authority will be entitled to give the material to the media.

10.13   An interesting case in point is *Michael Stone v South East Coast Strategic Health Authority* **(2006)**, where the convicted killer of Lin and Megan Russell objected to the publication of an enquiry report commissioned under the National Health Service Act 1977 on the basis that it contained details of his medical, psychiatric and social history. The judge, Davis J., took the view that the health authority, county council and probation board involved had the power to commission this enquiry and promulgate its report under the 1977 Act, so processing was justified under para.7 of Sch.3: "The processing is necessary for the exercise of any functions conferred on any person by or under an enactment." Further, it could be processed under para.8 of Sch3:

(1) The processing is necessary for medical purposes and is undertaken by—
  (a) a health professional, or
  (b) a person who in the circumstances owes a duty of confidentiality which is equivalent to that which would arise if that person were a health professional.
(2) In this paragraph "medical purposes" includes the purposes of preventative medicine, medical diagnosis, medical research, the provision of care and treatment and the management of health care services.

The judge pointed out that, "paragraph 8 focuses on the processing and the person undertaking the processing: it does not focus on the recipient of the information".   10.14

SCHOOLS

In December 2005, the Information Commissioner's Office issued a "Data Protection Good Practice Note" on taking photographs in schools. It gave as an example of media use which would not breach the Act, a photograph taken by a local newspaper of a school award ceremony with the school's agreement and the parents' awareness.   10.15

DATA PROTECTION (PROCESSING OF SENSITIVE PERSONAL DATA) ORDER 2000

Finally, the journalist looking for information held by somebody else, or looking to justify the processing of sensitive personal data, should take a look at the Data Protection (Processing of Sensitive Personal Data) Order 2000 (SI 2000/417) [see **Appendix 6**]. Para.3 covers disclosures for journalistic, artistic or literary purposes ("the special purposes") where the disclosure is "in the substantial public interest" and in connection with alleged criminality, dishonesty, malpractice, impropriety or mismanagement.   10.16

PERSONAL DATA

10.17   "Personal data", under s.1(1) of the Act, covers only information about living, identifiable individuals. The statutory definition is:

> "personal data" means data which relate to a living individual who can be identified—
> (a) from those data, or
> (b) from those data and other information which is in the possession of, or is likely to come in to the possession of, the data controller,
> and includes any expression of opinion about the individual and any indication of the intentions of the data controller or any other person in respect of the individual.

10.18   The data controller is the person or company who decides how the information is going to be used or otherwise processed.

10.19   There is a turf war of sorts over what "personal data" means. The Court of Appeal in the English case of *Durant v FSA* (2003) said that, simply because someone's name was in a document, that did not amount to "personal data". It depended on whether the information in question affected that person's privacy, was significantly biographical or focused on the person.

10.20   However, this interpretation has been criticised as being incompatible with the European Directive. So a thick haze of doubt hangs over *Durant*. The Information Commissioner issued guidance after it, which the Information Tribunal has suggested was inconsistent with the Court of Appeal approach (see *Harcup v Information Commissioner* (2007)) and the Grand Chamber of the European Court of Justice took a broad definition of "personal data" in the *Bavarian Lager* case (2010). This is a big unanswered question, untouched by the decision of the House of Lords in *CSA v Scottish Information Commissioner* (2008) [see **para.11.16**].

THE DATA PROTECTION PRINCIPLES

10.21   The Act sets out in Sch.1 the eight data protection principles. The first is the most important:

> Personal data shall be processed fairly and lawfully and, in particular, shall not be processed unless—
> (a) at least one of the conditions in Schedule 2 is met, and
> (b) in the case of sensitive personal data, at least one of the conditions in Schedule 3 is also met.

The others are concerned with the adequacy, accuracy, relevancy,   10.22
extent, use and safekeeping of personal data [see **Appendix 5**].

SENSITIVE DATA

There are special categories of "sensitive" personal data. These   10.23
include information about a person's ethnic origin, politics, trade
union affiliations, criminal record, including allegations of
criminality whether proved or not, religious "or other beliefs of a
similar nature", sexual life and physical/mental health.

Normally, in order to process sensitive personal data, it is necessary   10.24
to fit into one of the grounds set out in Sch.2 of the Act *and* one of the
grounds set out in Sch.3 of the Act [see **Appendix 5**]. These Schedules
give special grounds for special cases, such as processing for medical
purposes, for the administration of justice, for parliamentary
functions, for legal proceedings, for ethnic monitoring, "to protect
the vital interests of the data subject" (i.e. the person to whom the
information relates) and the like. The ordinary mortal, however, will
normally need "explicit consent" in order to process sensitive personal
data.

Data may include sound or image data, e.g. digital programming.   10.25
"Processing" is widely defined. It covers organising, holding,
adapting, altering, retrieving, using, disclosing, blocking, erasing and
destroying information! Although the Act was originally mainly
aimed at automated processing of information, the final hard copy
book or newspaper is part of "processing" too, according to the
Court of Appeal in *Naomi Campbell v Mirror Group Newspapers Ltd*
(2002).

The scope of "sensitive personal data" may be broader than meets   10.26
the eye. In the case where unwelcome photographs were taken of
author J.K. Rowling's toddler in an Edinburgh street *Murray v*
Express Newspapers Plc *(2008)*, it was argued that, because the
photograph showed him to be "a white Caucasian male child with no
obvious physical infirmities or defects", this was sensitive personal
data about his race and health. Mr Justice Patten said (in a decision
later overruled by the Court of Appeal, but not on this point) that if
the photograph constituted personal data, "then it is hard to escape
from the conclusion that insofar as it indicates the racial or ethnic
origin of the data subject it also consists of sensitive personal data".
(He did not agree that it was health data: "A photograph of an
apparently healthy individual in fact tells one nothing about his
actual state of health.") He suggested, however, that condition 5 of
Sch.3 would suffice here, which allows the processing of sensitive
personal data where, "the information contained in the personal data

has been made public as a result of steps deliberately taken by the data subject."

10.27　A similar argument was made, and similarly countered, in **Quinton (2009)** where it was suggested that even a colour photograph on a website of an unsuccessful Conservative candidate at a public meeting, wearing a blue rosette, would constitute "sensitive personal data" because it showed his political opinions. Both of these cases ultimately turned on different legal points, but they do hint at the width and complexity of "sensitive personal data".

PROCESSING OF NON-SENSITIVE DATA WITHOUT CONSENT

10.28　Even in relation to information which is not "sensitive", the processing needs to be done fairly and lawfully: it must meet a condition in Sch.2 of the Act, and must comply with the other data protection principles, unless a special exemption of one kind or another applies.

DATA SUBJECTS' RIGHTS UNDER THE ACT

10.29　As well, the 1998 Act gives people increased rights to be informed about information held on them. Under the 1998 Act, individuals can act directly to enforce those rights and they can also seek compensation for breach. This includes compensation where an individual has suffered distress as a result of processing for journalistic purposes.

10.30　They have a right to prevent certain types of damaging, distressing or annoying processing and to amend or to erase inaccurate information.

CRIMINAL OFFENCES

10.31　Tougher sanctions are possible for serious breaches, under the Criminal Justice and Immigration Act 2008. Section 78 provides a defence for journalistic, literary or artistic purposes, where a person can show s/he acted with a view to publication and "in the reasonable belief that in the particular circumstances then obtaining, disclosing or procuring was justified as being in the public interest". Under the original s.55, there was already a public interest defence, but the new defence requires only "reasonable belief". However, s.78 is not yet in force as at November 2010.

INFORMATION COMMISSIONER

The Information Commissioner polices data protection issues. In 10.32
England, Wales and Northern Ireland, this Commissioner also deals
with freedom of information. The Information Commissioner's
decisions are subject to review by the Information Tribunal and the
courts.

JOURNALISTIC ACTIVITY

There are a number of exemptions to the requirement to comply with 10.33
the data protection principles. The most important for the journalist is
the s.32 exemption for processing for journalistic, artistic and/or
literary purposes. This exemption only applies if the processing is
solely for these "special purposes" and (1) the information is
processed with a view to publication; (2) the newspaper, etc. ("data
controller") has a reasonable belief that, "having regard ... to the
special importance of the public interest in freedom of expression",
publication of the information is in the public interest; and (3) there is
a reasonable belief that compliance with data protection would be
incompatible with journalistic, artistic and/or literary purposes. The
journalist still requires to keep the data secure.

It is important for the journalist to show compliance with any 10.34
relevant designated code of practice. The Press Complaints
Commission (PCC) Code has been designated. So, for instance, a
journalist doing a story involving hospitals may need to take great
notice of cl.8 of the code. To some extent, the Data Protection Act
makes nominally self-regulatory codes into quasi-legal obligations.

KEY POINTS

1. The Data Protection Act 1998 aims at ensuring the accuracy, 10.35
   safety and controlled use of information about living
   identifiable individuals.
2. There is considerable dispute about what is covered by
   "personal data".
3. Thus far, for the media, data protection claims have not
   resulted in large, discrete awards, but the Act is complex and
   its use and interpretation unpredictable.
4. When journalists are refused access to information on the
   grounds of data protection objections, they should see if they
   can advance persuasive arguments using the grounds set out
   in Schs 2 and 3 of the Act and the Data Protection

(Processing of Sensitive Data) Order 2000 (SI 2000/417), but they will not be able to compel the provision of information under the Act unless it is information about the journalist as an individual. Nor can the police compel the media to provide information under the Act.

5. Special protection is given to "sensitive personal data". This category covers ethnicity, politics, trade union affiliations, criminal convictions or allegations of criminality, religious beliefs, sexual life and physical or mental health.

6. The Act creates both criminal offences and a right to compensation.

7. There is a "journalistic exemption", but its scope is restricted. It applies only to the processing of information for journalistic, artistic and/or literary purposes with a view to publication, where the journalist, etc. has a reasonable belief that publication of the information is in the public interest and compliance with the Act would be incompatible with journalism. It will be very difficult for a journalist to claim this exemption where there has been a breach of the PCC or equivalent code.

CHAPTER 11

FREEDOM OF INFORMATION

By Rosalind McInnes

The Freedom of Information Act 2000 covers UK public authorities 11.01
listed in that Act. The Freedom of Information (Scotland) Act 2002
covers Scottish public authorities listed in it [see **Appendix 7**].

The Acts have a similar structure, but there are significant 11.02
differences between them, with the Scottish Act generally considered
to be somewhat better for the information seeker. The Freedom of
Information (Scotland) Act 2002 has, on the face of it, fewer
exemptions to the right to information and those exemptions tend to
be based on claims of likely "substantial prejudice" to some interest,
as opposed to merely "prejudice" in the UK Act. This can be
overplayed. "Substantial" in the contempt of court context has, after
all, been interpreted as meaning "greater than minimal"—not much.
Applicants under the Freedom of Information (Scotland) Act 2002
have no right of appeal to the Information Tribunal, but they can
appeal to the court.

COMMISSIONERS

Importantly, there is a separate, Scottish Information Commissioner 11.03
to police the 2002 Act. The UK Information Commissioner has to
combine a data protection function—ensuring the privacy and
safekeeping of personal data—with a freedom of information
function—making public information widely available where
appropriate. There is no inherent contradiction between these roles,
but, given that both Acts contain wide-ranging and complex
exemptions to the right of public access where personal information
is concerned, there is a tightrope to walk.

EXEMPTIONS

The principle of openness in both Acts, in relation to information held 11.04
by those named public bodies, is subject to a large number of
exemptions. Some of these are absolute. Others are qualified
exemptions, i.e. the information must still be disclosed where the
public interest in disclosing the information is not outweighed by that

in maintaining the exemption. Under the Scottish legislation, there are five absolute exemptions:

(1) Information which is already accessible (even if for a fee).
(2) Information the disclosure of which is already legally prohibited.
(3) Information the disclosure of which would be in breach of confidence.
(4) Court records, including an inquiry (except a fatal accident inquiry).
(5) (a) Personal data about the requester, personal census information or a dead person's health record; and (b) about a third party, where its disclosure would breach any of the data protection principles or be likely to cause unwarranted damage or distress.

11.05 Qualified exemptions under the Scottish legislation include information held for the purposes of criminal investigations, civil proceedings and inquiries into deaths; disclosure of information likely to prejudice substantially international relations; commercial interests; law enforcement (widely defined, to include tax, charity regulations, health and safety, etc.) and national security. Section 29 protects information about the formulation of government policy, including legal advice about it.

TIMESCALES AND MONEY LIMITS

11.06 Generally, the public authorities have to provide the information within 20 working days. Under the fees regulations made in 2004 (SI 2004/467), a public authority can refuse a request on the basis that costs would be excessive. At the moment, anything above £600 counts as excessive, not counting any time spent in finding out whether the public authority has the information or considering whether it is exempt.

MINISTERIAL VETO

11.07 Both Acts provide for a ministerial veto, i.e. the government can override an entitlement to information. The ministerial veto has already been used twice, in February 2009 over Iraq War Cabinet minutes and, in December 2009, over minutes of the Cabinet Committee on Devolution from 1997. In Scotland, this veto can only be deployed by the First Minister, who has to certify that the information concerned "is of exceptional sensitivity".

WHAT MUST THE AUTHORITY DO?

According to the Inner House of the Court of Session in *Glasgow City* 11.08
Council v Scottish Information Commissioner **(2010)**, information is
what the Act offers, not the records themselves. The applicant has to
give his or her true name. Requests have to be specific, but the public
authority, under its duty to advise and assist, ought to clarify
ambiguous requests. There is a duty on the part of the public
authorities to provide advice and assistance to requesters. This has
proved unexpectedly important, with authorities being expected
actively to strive to provide something useful, even if some of what
they hold is exempt or too expensive to provide.

APPEALS

The UK Act allows a dissatisfied requester of information to appeal to 11.09
the Information Commissioner once any internal review process has
been exhausted, then to the Information Tribunal, then to the courts
on a point of law. The Freedom of Information (Scotland) Act 2002
provides for an internal review of the decision by the public
authority, then allows an appeal to the Scottish Information
Commissioner, and thence to the Court of Session on a point of law.

JOURNALISM, ART OR LITERATURE DEROGATION

The BBC and Channel 4 are public authorities, but only "in respect of 11.10
information held for purposes other than those of journalism, art or
literature". This has already embroiled the BBC in extensive
litigation over whether the Balen Report on its Middle Eastern
coverage was held for journalistic purposes. The Court of Appeal in
June 2010 held that it was, even though it was also held for other
purposes.

PUBLICATION SCHEMES

Public authorities all have to produce a "publication scheme" 11.11
committing them to publishing, regularly and without request,
certain types of information. If the information is available—even for
money and even in a form that may make it difficult for the seeker to
isolate or gather the information—a request will be met with the
exemption that the information is otherwise available.

NEWS

11.12 The Acts, together, despite their (from a journalist's perspective) leisurely timescales, and numerous exemptions, have given birth to a large number of headlines, both trivial and serious. In particular, they have brought information about politicians' financial claims on the state to the public eye. There has been a reluctance to allow the personal data exemption to shield, e.g. expenditure of public money by public servants in the course of their work. For example, the High Court in England rejected the argument that information about MPs' second homes funded under the additional costs allowance should be exempt as "personal data" (*Corporate Officer of the House of Commons v The Information Commissioner* (2008)).

11.13 In Scotland, orders to release information about why certain provisions from a 1990 Act had not yet been brought into force, and about planning consent applications, have been upheld by the court (*Scottish Ministers v Scottish Information Commissioner, Alexander, Elstone and Williams* (2007)). The legislation is particularly useful to journalists, such as special correspondents, who are able to follow a story or an area of interest over a longer investigative period.

11.14 Fiscals are covered by the Freedom of Information (Scotland) Act 2002, as is the Lord Advocate (being one of the Scottish Ministers), but the qualified exemption protecting investigations and the absolute exemption covering court records limit the journalistic usefulness of this.

TIPS FOR MAKING A REQUEST

11.15 Experience suggests that journalists should hone their requests as narrowly as possible and head off objections at the pass. A request for, "the minutes of the meeting of March 15 of the sports committee, redacting (i.e. deleting) the names of all non-councillors and any legal advice given", is more likely to get a swift and satisfactory response than, say, a request for, "all information concerning the council's decision to limit the opening hours of public gyms". Sometimes, of course, names and other potentially exempt information will be the nub of what the journalist wants, but requests should, so far as possible, be pared down and specific.

11.16 Even quite radical modes of assistance can legitimately be expected of a public authority. In *CSA* (2008), where the requester was refused information about childhood leukaemia statistics in Scottish postcodes on the basis that this might identify individual patients, the Scottish Information Commissioner contemplated the possibility that the public authority could have treated the statistics by random modification ("Barnardisation") in order to prevent such identification. Following an appeal to the House of Lords, the *CSA* case is under reconsideration by the Scottish Information Commissioner.

WHOLLY-OWNED COMPANIES

A company which is wholly owned by a Scottish public authority is 11.17 automatically caught by the Freedom of Information (Scotland) Act 2002. There is provision in the Act for the public authorities listed to be updated—new ones added and others removed—by order of the Scottish Ministers. In 2008, 11 new bodies were added, including the Commissioner for Children and Young People in Scotland, and 10 existing ones were removed, including Scottish Homes and social inclusion partnerships.

ENVIRONMENTAL INFORMATION REGULATIONS 2004

The Environmental Information Regulations 2004 (SI 2004/3391) 11.18 provide access to environmental information—very widely defined to include matters such as noise, contamination of the food chain and cultural sites, as well as obvious elements such as biodiversity and radioactive waste. In some respects, these regulations are better for information-seekers than the freedom of information legislation—for instance, there is a broader definition of "public authority". The European Court of Human Rights has also been strongly in favour of access to environmental information—*Guerra v Italy* **(1998)**.

KEY POINTS

1. There are two pieces of freedom of information legislation in 11.19 the UK. The Freedom of Information Act 2000 covers specifically listed UK public authorities. The Freedom of Information (Scotland) Act 2002 covers specifically listed Scottish public authorities. The UK Information Commissioner deals with data protection issues for the whole UK and freedom of information issues under the UK Act. The Scottish Information Commissioner deals solely with Scottish freedom of information issues under the 2002 Act.

2. The Acts include a large number of exemptions to the obligation to hand over information. The Scottish Act contains absolute exemptions for information the disclosure of which would be in breach of confidence; court records; and many kinds of personal data.
3. The Government can override a legal decision that a requester has an entitlement to information. The UK Government has already done so twice.
4. Authorities can refuse to release information on the grounds of expense, but they have in all cases a duty to provide advice and assistance to those looking for information.
5. In addition, there is a wide-ranging right to environmental information under the Environmental Information Regulations 2004 (SI 2004/3391).

CHAPTER 12

REGULATION OF INVESTIGATORY POWERS

BY ROSALIND MCINNES

REGULATION OF INVESTIGATORY POWERS ACT 2000

This Act (known as RIPA) deals with the interception of 12.01
telecommunications, surveillance use of covert human intelligence
sources and encryption. It repeals the Interception of
Communications Act 1985 and creates a new statutory framework
for telephone and email monitoring and interception, with a view to
making the latter comply with the Human Rights Act 1998. The
maximum sentence for illegal hacking into mobiles is two years in
prison and/or a fine. The *News of the World's* Clive Goodman was
jailed for four months, and his co-conspirator Glenn Mulcaine for six
months in 2007, for conspiring to intercept royal voicemails. Some of
the charges were under RIPA [see **Chapter 41**].

As well as making unauthorised interception of 12.02
telecommunications a criminal offence, RIPA allows people to sue
for interception over a private system. Emails, voicemails, pagers and
mobile phones are all covered. Where information has been encrypted,
one may be asked to disclose it in intelligible form.

Interception of communications is lawful if a warrant has been 12.03
issued. Such warrants or notices must also be justified in terms of the
Human Rights Act 1998, i.e. they must be necessary and
proportionate, not used merely for convenience where alternative
means of achieving the same end would be available.

The main concern for the media arising from RIPA is that it allows 12.04
for the interception, surveillance and disclosure of journalistic sources
without prior judicial authorisation, and, indeed, without the
journalist even knowing that the interception has taken place. The
Regulation of Investigatory Powers Act 2000 does not make it illegal
for a journalist to record a telephone call, even without the other
party's awareness. (The Press Complaints Commission (PCC) has
taken the view that such a recording does not constitute using a
"clandestine listening device" in terms of the PCC Code.)

REGULATION OF INVESTIGATORY POWERS
(SCOTLAND) ACT 2000

12.05   The Regulation of Investigatory Powers Act 2000 applies in Scotland. However, this Act of the Scottish Parliament deals with similar issues in relation to devolved matters, typically to do with crime and public health. This Act, RIPA, the Human Rights Act 1998 and the Police Act 1997 are all intended to work together to regulate the use of investigatory powers across the UK so as not to infringe privacy rights. The Regulation of Investigatory Powers (Scotland) Act 2000 seeks to impose controls on, in particular, the police's use of intensive surveillance in people's living accommodation and private vehicles. Only the chief constable can authorise this, and the authorisation must be approved by a surveillance commissioner.

12.06   The Act also seeks to create greater protection for "covert human intelligence sources", i.e. undercover agents and the like. In order to be authorised under the Act, any surveillance has to be necessary for particular purposes and proportionate to the ends to be achieved by it. The Chief Surveillance Commissioner has to make an annual report to be laid before the Scottish Parliament, but the Scottish Ministers can censor any part of it which appears to them that it would be contrary to the public interest to publish. The Act specifically states that nothing in it makes it illegal to obtain information in any way otherwise lawful.

KEY POINTS

12.07   1. The Regulation of Investigatory Powers Act 2000 and the Regulation of Investigatory Powers (Scotland) Act 2000 are intended to regulate the use of surveillance, with a view to protecting privacy.

2. Unauthorised interception of telecommunications is a crime, but it is not illegal to record a telephone call without the other person's consent.

CHAPTER 13

THE REHABILITATION OF OFFENDERS ACT 1974 AND CRIMINAL MEMOIRS

By ROSALIND MCINNES

PURPOSE OF THE REHABILITATION OF OFFENDERS ACT 1974

The purpose of this Act is to enable people with criminal convictions to 13.01
wipe certain old offences off their records and continue their lives
largely free from the constant threat of disclosure. The Act achieves
its purpose by prohibiting the telling of the truth and legalising lying.
It uses two key concepts, the "rehabilitated person" and the "spent"
conviction.

RESTRICTION OF INFORMATION ABOUT SPENT CONVICTIONS

From the journalist's point of view, one of the main effects of the Act is 13.02
that it restricts the availability of information about the spent
convictions of a rehabilitated person. A rehabilitated person is, in
general, to be treated for all purposes in law as if he had not
committed the offence in question or been charged, prosecuted,
convicted or sentenced as a result. Evidence of spent convictions is
not normally admissible in any judicial proceedings in Great Britain
and a person is not, in such proceedings, liable to be asked or bound
to answer any question relating to his past which cannot be answered
without acknowledging or referring to a spent conviction.

However, there are important exceptions to these rules. The Act 13.03
does not affect the admission of evidence as to a person's previous
convictions in any criminal proceedings before a court in Great
Britain, certain proceedings under the Sexual Offences Act 2003, in
service disciplinary proceedings, in most proceedings (such as
children's hearings, adoption, guardianship, or proceedings relating
to parental responsibilities or rights) involving children under 18,
nor, in England and Wales, proceedings concerning youth
rehabilitation orders. A party or witness in any proceedings can also
waive the protection of the Act and consent to the admission of
evidence about his spent convictions or the determination of an issue

involving such evidence. Also, where a judicial authority is satisfied that justice cannot be done in the case except by admitting or requiring evidence about a person's spent convictions, that authority can, in effect, override the Act, so as to demand that evidence be heard. Lord Drummond Young said in *Scottish Ministers v Doig* (2007) that: "I can see no reason for giving this provision a restrictive interpretation."

13.04   In most non-judicial contexts, such as applying for a job or filling in a proposal form for an insurance policy, a person is not bound to disclose spent convictions in answer to any question about the past and is not to be subjected to any legal liability or prejudice for non-disclosure. In Scotland, the Scottish Ministers have power to make orders excluding or modifying the application of these provisions in particular circumstances. There are specific exemptions from the Act, allowing certain questions to be asked to assess people's suitability for particular jobs and activities, e.g. working with children or vulnerable adults, or holding firearms. In relation to certain types of posts—a broad group, including judges, vets and traffic wardens—failure to disclose a spent conviction may still be grounds for dismissal. A similar exemption exists for "any action taken for the purpose of safeguarding national security".

13.05   It is an offence for a person, such as a court official, police officer or civil servant, who in the course of duty has access to official records, to disclose, "otherwise than in the course of those duties", information about spent convictions. There is a defence which covers disclosure to, or at the express request of, the rehabilitated person.

13.06   The phrase "otherwise than in the course of those duties" probably relates to disclosure by one official to another, and is unlikely to cover, for example, disclosure by a press officer to the press. If such disclosure to the press were regarded as covered by the phrase, the further question would arise whether the journalist receiving the information was a "person who, in the course of his official duties ... had custody of or access to any official record of the information contained there". It would be difficult to argue that he was. He would receive the information in the course of his job, but would not have custody of or access to it in the course of his official duties.

13.07   On a proper reading of the Act the obligation would seem to be on court officials, police officers and other public officials to hold back the relevant information and not on the press. This view is supported by s.9(4), which makes it an offence to obtain information about spent convictions from any official record by means of any fraud, dishonesty or bribe. The purpose of s.9 of the Act, in short, is to keep information on spent convictions within the confines of official records, and the effect of ss.4 and 9 is to restrict the information available to the press and public.

EFFECTS ON LAW OF DEFAMATION

The other main effect of the Act from the point of view of the media is   13.08
that it limits the availability of certain defences to an action of
defamation. First, a defender in such an action cannot rely on the
defence of *veritas* in relation to a spent conviction if the publication is
proved to have been made with malice.

It is not clear exactly what is meant by "malice" in this context. It   13.09
cannot include, as it does in some other areas, the lack of any honest
belief in the truth of the statement made. If, however, the dominant
motive was improper—spite being the obvious example—that would
probably amount to "malice" in law, for these purposes. Even if there
is a history of ill feeling, that would not automatically make such a
publication malicious. The publisher might genuinely believe that an
old enemy was, e.g. unfit for some job as a result of a previous
conviction. On the other hand it probably includes an intention to
injure wholly or mainly for the gratification of personal spite or ill
will. A newspaper which published details of a rehabilitated person's
spent convictions because it was annoyed by the person's unco-
operative attitude over some other matter would, if its malice could
be proved, be unable to rely on the defence of *veritas*.

Secondly, a defender in an action for defamation cannot rely on the   13.10
privilege attaching to a fair and accurate report of judicial proceedings
if it is proved that the report contained a reference to evidence which
was ruled to be inadmissible in the proceedings because it related to a
spent conviction. This provision does not apply to bona fide law
reports and reports or accounts of judicial proceedings, "published
for bona fide educational, scientific or professional purposes, or given
in the course of any lecture, class or discussion given or held for any of
these purposes".

These are the only two areas in which the law of defamation is   13.11
altered by the Act, which expressly provides that spent convictions
can be referred to in other respects to enable a defender to rely on any
defence of *veritas* or fair comment or of absolute or qualified privilege
available. Moreover, the law of defamation is not in any way altered
by the Act if the publication complained of took place before the
conviction was spent. For most purposes in the UK, an online
publication is treated as "published" every time it is downloaded
afresh [see **para.43.25**].

SENTENCES SUBJECT TO REHABILITATION

Some sentences are excluded from rehabilitation under the Act. The   13.12
convictions to which these sentences relate accordingly never become

spent convictions and the person on whom they are imposed never becomes a rehabilitated person in relation to them. Generally, these are sentences of imprisonment or detention—including youth custody or corrective training—which are for life, are indefinite in duration, e.g. for public protection, or are for more than 30 months. This includes Scottish children convicted on indictment and sentenced to more than 30 months' detention.

EFFECT OF SUBSEQUENT CONVICTION

13.13 A subsequent conviction after the rehabilitation period does not revive the earlier conviction: it remains spent.

13.14 The effect of a subsequent conviction during the rehabilitation period depends on its nature. If it is a conviction for a minor offence (in Scotland, an offence within the jurisdiction of the justice of the peace courts—the successors to the district courts), it has no effect on rehabilitation. If it is a more serious offence but does not involve a sentence excluded from rehabilitation (i.e. heavier than 30 months' imprisonment or detention), it delays the expiry of the rehabilitated period until the end of the rehabilitation period applicable to the new offence if that ends later. If the subsequent conviction involves a sentence excluded from rehabilitation then it precludes rehabilitation altogether and the old offence never becomes spent.

REHABILITATION PERIODS

13.15 The Act provides for different rehabilitation periods depending on the gravity of the sentence and the age of the offender. In the case of adult offenders the scale is set at Table A of the 1974 Act. So, for instance, a prison sentence for a term of more than six months, but less than 30 months, will normally have a rehabilitation period of 10 years.

13.16 In the case of persons under 18 these months are reduced by half. There is a special scale for certain sentences confined to young offenders (Table B).

13.17 The rehabilitation period applicable to an order discharging a person absolutely for an offence is six months from the date of the conviction and the same period applies to a discharge by a children's hearing.

13.18 If a person is conditionally discharged, bound over to keep the peace or be of good behaviour, the rehabilitation period ends one year after the date of the conviction or when the relevant period to keep the peace, etc. ends, whichever is the later.

13.19 Where a probation order is made in relation to someone over 18, the rehabilitation period is five years from the date of conviction. In the case of someone under 18, the period is either two and a half years from conviction or until the probation order ends, whichever is the longer.

A similar rule—one year or the duration of a period of care, 13.20 residential training or supervision, whichever is the longer—applies in relation to various orders dealing with children and young persons, including a supervision requirement. If a convicted person is made the subject of a hospital order under the Mental Health Act 1983 or the Criminal Procedure (Scotland) Act 1995, the rehabilitation period ends five years after the date of the conviction or two years after the hospital order ceases to have effect, whichever is later.

Finally, if a convicted person has any disqualification imposed on 13.21 him or her (such as a disqualification from driving), the rehabilitation period ends when the disqualification ceases to have effect. The same rule applies to a "disability, prohibition or other penalty".

These are the main rules on rehabilitation periods, but the Act 13.22 contains other provisions and also empowers the Scottish Ministers to make orders varying the periods. The result is a complex piece of legislation. It will often be difficult to know whether a conviction is spent.

Fortunately, from the journalist's perspective, so long as there is no 13.23 malice, and no reference in a report of judicial proceedings to evidence actually ruled to be inadmissible under the Act, the journalist has the protection in defamation of the usual defences and privileges.

"REHABILITATED PERSON" AND "SPENT CONVICTION"

On the expiry of the relevant length of time, the person concerned 13.24 becomes a rehabilitated person and the conviction becomes a spent conviction. This is subject to the rules on subsequent conviction considered above; rehabilitation under the Act is designed for those who do not commit other serious offences during the rehabilitation period. It is also subject to the sentence being served, at least in the case of imprisonment and other custodial sentences. Non-payment of a fine does not prevent rehabilitation; nor does failure to comply with any requirement of a suspended sentence, supervision order or the like. The escaped convict does not become a rehabilitated person.

APPLICATION TO SERVICE DISCIPLINARY PROCEEDINGS

Findings of guilt in service disciplinary proceedings are treated as 13.25 convictions for purposes of the Act. The rehabilitation period for cashiering, discharge with ignominy or dismissal with disgrace from Her Majesty's service is 10 years; for dismissal from Her Majesty's service, seven years; and for a sentence of service detention within the meaning of the Armed Forces Act 2006, five years. These periods are halved if the person sentenced was under 18 years of age when found guilty.

APPLICATION TO CHILDREN'S HEARINGS

13.26 Children's hearings do not convict or sentence the children who come before them. Their approach is intended to be therapeutic rather than punitive. Nevertheless, it was thought desirable that people brought before them on an offence ground should have the chance of becoming rehabilitated persons under the Act.

13.27 Accordingly, the Act provides that if a child is referred to a children's hearing on an offence ground and that ground is accepted by the child (and, where necessary, parent), or deemed established to the satisfaction of the sheriff, then the acceptance, establishment or deemed establishment of the ground shall be treated for the purposes of the Act as a conviction and any disposal of the case by a children's hearing as a sentence.

APPLICATION TO FOREIGN COURTS

13.28 The Act applies to convictions by or before courts outside Great Britain. In calculating rehabilitation periods in relation to such convictions a sentence is treated as if it were the nearest British equivalent. But a conviction by a court outside Great Britain does not delay or preclude rehabilitation in relation to a previous conviction if it was for conduct which would not constitute an offence under the law in force in the relevant part of Great Britain.

EFFECTS ON CONFIDENTIALITY AND PRIVACY

13.29 Since the Human Rights Act 1998 in particular, a number of unsuccessful attempts have been made in England to argue that, e.g. the continued endorsement of driving licences beyond the period after which convictions were spent, *R. v DVLA Ex p. Pearson* (2003), or the having regard by a council to spent convictions when deciding whether to hire as a subcontracted schools driver a woman who had offended, seriously, over 30 years ago, unjustifiably violated the art.8 rights to private life of those involved, *R. (on the application of A) v B Council* (2007).

13.30 In *Silkman v Heard* (2001) in England, Eady J. was sceptical of the argument that privacy considerations ought to obtain:

"For one thing, criminal convictions are in the public domain at least until such time as they become spent. For another, the very fact that the Rehabilitation of Offenders Act has been relied upon so rarely in libel actions has at least raised doubts as to whether the concomitant restrictions on freedom of expression can be described as 'necessary in a democratic society' …".

In an English case—*L v Law Society* (2008)—a law student argued, 13.31 again without success, that an appeal against the Law Society's decision to cancel his enrolment which would involve consideration of the student's spent convictions ought to be held in private. The Master of the Rolls said:

"The contention that the 1974 Act renders spent convictions confidential misunderstands the Act's intention and its ambit … Notwithstanding the obvious practical difficulty of rendering secret a public judgment which had been freely and properly reported in the press, the Act does not purport to have that effect … While the 1974 Act in some respects may place an individual with spent convictions in the same position as someone with no convictions, it does not do so by rendering the convictions confidential; it does so simply by putting in place a regime which protects an individual from being prejudiced by the existence of such convictions."

The Rehabilitation of Offenders Act 1974 is not the only Act in force. 13.32 The Data Protection Act 1998 treats convictions as sensitive personal data [see **Chapter 10**]. In *Chief Constable of Humberside v Information Commissioner* (2010), the Court of Appeal held that chief constables did not have to delete certain old and relatively minor convictions from the police national computer.

CRIMINAL MEMOIRS

The Coroners and Justice Act 2009 allows a Court of Session judge to 13.33 make an "exploitation proceeds order" where a criminal sells his or her story. The Act does not stop publication of memoirs or the like, but it enables the profits to be clawed back by Scottish Ministers. In deciding whether to make such an order, the court has to consider the seriousness of the offence, whether publication will cause further offence, especially to the victim or surviving family, the social, cultural or educational value of the publication and the public interest in general. The material potentially covered here would, in theory, embrace everything from a gangster's tabloid interview to thoughtful and scholarly books of the Gitta Sereny type. The court is empowered to differentiate between them.

KEY POINTS

13.34   1. The aim of the Rehabilitation of Offenders Act 1974 is to allow people with convictions to live down their past where appropriate. The rehabilitated person is generally to be treated as if he had never committed the offence. After a certain period of time, the conviction is regarded as "spent". Where a person has been sentenced to prison or detention for more than 30 months, those convictions can never be "spent".

2. Evidence of previous convictions is, however, admitted in criminal proceedings.

3. In a defamation action involving a spent conviction a journalist cannot rely on a defence of *veritas* if the publication is proved to have been made with malice. Sentences of imprisonment or detention of more than 30 months are not subject to rehabilitation.

4. Spent convictions do not become confidential information.

5. The Court of Session can make an "exploitation proceeds order" to confiscate profits made on criminals' memoirs.

CHAPTER 14

RIGHTS OF ACCESS

By Rosalind McInnes

With one or two exceptions, such as the right of admission to   14.01
children's hearings, the journalist is in exactly the same legal position
as any other member of the public. S/he can go to public places and
public meetings. In many cases, of course, reporters are given special
privileges such as reserved seats and free admission.

Certain meetings must be held in public; certain places, such as   14.02
streets and various open spaces in towns, are publicly accessible
places; certain places are private places to which the public are
invited and most places are private places to which the public are not
invited.

Notwithstanding this general principle, the Human Rights Act   14.03
1998, with its protection of art.10 freedom of expression, has a
bearing on these issues. In *R. v Secretary of State for Home
Department Ex p. Simms and O'Brien* (1999), the House of Lords
overturned the prison service's refusal to allow journalists to visit and
interview prisoners in order to investigate alleged miscarriages of
justice.

Meetings and proceedings which must normally be held in public   14.04
include court proceedings and certain local government meetings.
Under s.95 of the Representation of the People Act 1983, candidates
can use schools and meeting rooms for public meetings—so journalists
cannot be excluded from election meetings of this sort. Paragraph 15.1
of the Standing Orders of the Scottish Parliament (as required in the
Scotland Act 1998) states that meetings of the Parliament shall be
held in public. It also provides for meetings of the committees or
subcommittees to be held in public—unless "the committee decides
otherwise" (para.2.3.5). Most legislative committee business must be
in public, though such a committee meeting can be held in private for
the purpose of taking evidence.

COURT PROCEEDINGS

The general rule is that proceedings in a court of law must be in public,   14.05
unless justice demands otherwise. The Human Rights Act 1998
reinforces this approach. The principal applications of and
exceptions to this rule have been considered elsewhere in this book.
This is one context where journalists are very often allowed to

remain, even where the public at large are excluded [see **Chapter 7**]. In *R. v Wakefield* **(1975)**, where the judge had cleared the court whilst the jury viewed allegedly obscene films, the Court of Appeal in England held that the press should have been allowed to stay.

QUASI-JUDICIAL PROCEEDINGS

14.06 Most inquiries, tribunals and other quasi-judicial bodies must, as a general rule, meet in public, but there are numerous exceptions, for example under s.19 of the Inquiries Act 2005 [see **para.6.46**].

PARLIAMENT

14.07 Both Houses of Parliament normally admit public and press to their meetings, but this is merely practice and there is no legal right of admission. Both Lords and Commons have full power to regulate their own procedure and can hold secret sessions when they think it necessary. For example, many such sessions were held during the Second World War. It is a breach of parliamentary privilege to publish any report of, or to purport to describe the proceedings at, a secret session.

14.08 Each House has power to punish for breaches of privilege as a contempt of Parliament. Contempt of Parliament includes any act or omission which, directly or indirectly, includes either House of Parliament or any member or officer of such a House in performing parliamentary functions or duties. This includes, according to *Erskine May's Parliamentary Practice*, 23rd edn, edited by William McKay et al. (London: LexisNexis UK, 2004), publications which "bring the House into odium, contempt or ridicule or lowers its authority".

14.09 To publish information derived from the reports of select committees before they have been laid before the House is a breach of privilege. The committee is reporting to the House in the first place and only indirectly to the public. To reveal the contents of a report before Members of Parliament have had a chance of reading it is a breach of privilege. The same does not apply to Green and White Papers. They are addressed to the public in the first instance and, while the government in practice communicates important matters to Parliament before publication, this is a matter of courtesy alone. Although publication of witnesses' submissions should be authorised by the committee according to House of Commons Standing Orders, there is no breach of privilege involved in publishing evidence given in public.

Complaints of breach of privilege are raised in the House by a   14.10
member and are then usually referred to the Committee of Privileges
for a report. The Commons can imprison an offender, although this
has not been done since 1880. In the Withers breach [see below], the
Clerk of the House observed, "The House of Commons has not
imposed a fine since 1666. The lapse of time does not mean the power
has evaporated." (The House of Lords considered doing so in 1975
over The *Economist's* leak of a wealth tax report, though none was
levied.) Offenders can be "brought to the Bar of the House by the
Serjeant at Arms and there reprimanded by the speaker in the name
and by authority of the House"—according to the clerk, the last time
this happened to a non-member, it was the journalist John Junor, who
was rebuked for remarks in the *Sunday Express* about MPs' special
petrol allowances during the Suez crisis. Normally an offender is
merely admonished or reprimanded. Proceedings were commenced in
October 1994 against the *Guardian* editor Peter Preston over his
sending of a fax which bore the House of Commons logo, for which
he was reprimanded.

The most recent controversies over contempt of Parliament have   14.11
involved the English law firms acting for defamation claimants.
Carter Ruck in October 2009 unsuccessfully tried to stop the
Guardian from reporting a parliamentary question tabled by an MP
referring to the oil firm Transfigura's alleged dumping of toxic waste,
claiming that reporting the question would breach an injunction. In
February 2010, law firm Withers was found in contempt of
Parliament for trying to restrict what a Liberal Democrat MP, John
Henning, said in the House of Commons. An apology was held to
suffice by the Standards and Privileges Committee, which observed,
"It has long been accepted that the House should assert its privileges
sparingly". Given the human rights to liberty, fair trial and freedom of
expression embodied in the Human Rights Act 1998, this would
clearly be wise. The attempt, by MPs charged with offences relating
to their expenses claims, to argue that they could not be tried in the
criminal courts because of parliamentary privilege failed in
November 2010 in the Supreme Court—as did their earlier attempt
to have reporting restrictions put in place in relation to this plea (*R.
v Chaytor, Morley, Devine and Hanningfield* (2010)).

LOCAL AUTHORITIES

The Local Government (Access to Information) Act 1985 (s.2) gives   14.12
the public and duly accredited reporters of newspapers (which
include any organisation "systematically engaged in collecting news
for radio or television or for cable programme service") rights to

attend meetings of local authorities and their committees and subcommittees, with certain prescribed exceptions. Joint committees of two or more local authorities, and any subcommittees, are covered too. These rights do not, however, extend to the taking of photographs at meetings or the recording of proceedings for later communication to anyone not attending, "or the making of any oral report on any proceedings as they take place". The meeting has a discretion to decide whether to permit taping or photography.

14.13   Press and public may be excluded for either of two reasons. First, that it is likely confidential information will be disclosed at the meeting or secondly that the subject matter of discussion is exempt from public access.

14.14   Confidential information is defined as information which has been furnished by a government department on terms forbidding its disclosure or which is prohibited from being disclosed by any enactment or court order.

14.15   Exempt information is defined under a list of specific subjects, including such matters as adoption or fostering of particular children, financial affairs of named individuals, commercially prejudicial details of council contracts for acquisition or supply of goods or services, details of tenders for contracts, information about counsel's advice and "any action taken or to be taken in connection with the prevention, investigation or detection of crime". The list also includes "any protected informant", which means any person giving the local authority information about a crime or offence.

14.16   Exclusion of press and public on the ground of exemption can take place only where a resolution to that effect has been passed identifying the particular subject on the list. The Scottish Ministers have power to extend or curtail the exemption list.

14.17   A meeting also has power to exclude anyone to suppress disorder or other misbehaviour.

14.18   Press and public have a right to see copies of agendas, reports and other papers relating to meetings (but not those relating to confidential or exempt items). Papers must be supplied on request to the media and made open for public inspection for three days before a meeting, or, if it has been called at short notice, from the time it is convened. The papers remain open for public inspection for six years after a meeting.

14.19   Where confidential or exempt information is concerned, an official of the local authority must provide instead a written summary indicating the nature of the matters considered in private without actually disclosing the confidential or exempt information. The authority is entitled to charge for the provision of these services and also for the supply of photocopies of extracts of documents. Unreasonable refusal to allow inspection of documents is a criminal offence.

Anything defamatory contained in any document supplied to the 14.20
media is privileged under the Act unless maliciously published.

The Act leaves intact the rights of access by the media in Scotland to 14.21
meetings authorised by any other legislation. Admission to certain
other bodies is covered by the Public Bodies (Admission to Meetings)
Act 1960, as amended by the Local Government (Scotland) Act 1973.

The bodies in the 1960 Act so far as Scotland is concerned are health 14.22
boards set up under the National Health Service (Scotland) Act 1978
(so far as their executive functions are concerned), NHS Trusts, the
Council for Healthcare Regulatory Excellence and the Office of the
Health Professions Adjudicator.

There is a right in the 1960 Act to exclude members of the public 14.23
where necessary for the orderly conduct of business, even if the
unruly members of the public appear to be making a political protest:
*R. v Brent Health Authority Ex p. Francis and Community Rights
Project* **(1985)**. In that case, though, the press had been allowed to
remain.

OTHER PUBLIC MEETINGS

In the case of meetings held in public places, the journalist has the 14.24
same right to be present as any other member of the public—a right
which may be limited by byelaws as well as by the law on such
matters as breach of the peace. S/he cannot be singled out for
exclusion by the organisers of the meeting.

In the case of meetings or other proceedings, such as most sports 14.25
meetings, to which the public are invited but which are held on
private property, the journalist's rights depend on the terms of the
invitation. The organisers of such meetings may choose to exclude
the media or impose conditions on entry, such as a ban on cameras.
The whole question is really one of contract between those granting
and those seeking admission and the terms of the contract may be
express or implied. There may, for example, be an implied term that a
person can be excluded for not behaving in a proper manner.

TRESPASS

As a general rule, no-one is entitled to enter private property without 14.26
the owner's consent, but there are exceptions. Statutes give certain
people, such as police officers with search warrants, rights of entry.
Even in the case of the police pursuing a criminal, the right of a
householder to refuse admission in the absence of a warrant is fairly
strongly protected by the Scottish court. Generally, entry is allowed if
it is necessary in the public interest—to put out a fire, for example.

These exceptions will not normally benefit the journalist, who will be infringing the owner's legal rights in entering another's property, whether it is enclosed or not, without permission.

14.27   The Criminal Justice and Public Order Act 1994 made some types of trespass criminal, for example for the purpose of holding a "rave" or setting up a "New Age" encampment. It creates a complex offence where two or more people enter and remain on land (not buildings or roads) without lawful authority or occupier's consent and with the purpose of remaining there. For the offence to be committed, though, the occupier must have taken reasonable steps to ask them to leave and have called the police. The senior police officer must then reasonably believe that the people are trespassers and have caused damage to land or property, used abusive or threatening words or brought six or more vehicles on to the land. The offence is only committed when the trespassers refuse to obey a police direction to leave. The same Act creates an offence of "aggravated trespass" on land in open air (not roads) where the trespasser's conduct will intimidate those engaged in lawful activities. This is aimed at field sport saboteurs.

14.28   The Scottish Parliament's "right to roam" legislation—the Land Reform (Scotland) Act 2003—has further complicated matters, but it remains generally the case that one cannot be prosecuted under Scots law merely for unauthorised entry on to another's land [see **Chapter 41**].

14.29   This does not mean, however, that the property owner has no remedies. S/he can order an intruder to leave. If the intrusion is likely to be repeated s/he can apply to the court for an interdict, which it is contempt of court to ignore. If the intruder has caused actual damage to the property, the owner can also sue for compensation. The privacy of the home is particularly recognised in art.8 of the European Convention on Human Rights and has already featured significantly in some of the breach of confidence case law, e.g. *McKennitt v Ash* **(2006)** [see **paras 37.51 onwards**].

KEY POINTS

14.30   1. Generally, the right of the journalist to attend meetings is the same as any other member of the public.

2. The Local Government (Access to Information) Act 1985 provides the right to attend meetings of councils and subcommittees. The media may be excluded if "exempt" information is to be discussed, but this can be done only after a resolution to that effect has been passed. Copies of agendas and reports must be made available for inspection.

3. Access to various health service meetings is provided in the Public Bodies (Admission to Meetings) Act 1960.

PART 4: CONTEMPT OF COURT

Chapter 15

CONTEMPT OF COURT: THE BASICS

By Rosalind McInnes

15.01 Contempt of court can take several forms, but for the journalist the area that causes the greatest danger is the risk of compromising an accused person's right to a fair trial by publishing prejudicial information. Contempt findings within the UK are rare, at present. Nonetheless, they still pose a threat to the media, particularly in Scotland. Moreover, they pose a personal threat of a criminal sanction against the individual journalist.

15.02 Legal systems adopt entirely different approaches to the question of balancing the often conflicting interests of freedom of speech and the right to a fair hearing. In the United States, for example, a mass of detailed information about a case is often published before and during a trial.

15.03 Historically, Scots law has adopted almost exactly the opposite approach. In the *Scottish Daily Express* and *Sun* case, *HM Advocate v News Group Newspapers* **(1989)**, the Lord Justice General (Emslie) said:

> "Our system of criminal justice in Scotland depends essentially upon the proposition that jurors called to try an accused person should arrive in the jury box without knowledge or impression of facts, or alleged facts, relating to the crime charged on the indictment."

15.04 This traditional view underwent a sea-change in *Cox and Griffiths, Petitioners* **(1999)**, a case 10 years later involving the *Daily Record*. There, the judges, led by the then Lord Justice General, Lord Rodger, were prepared to give a significantly more prominent role than Scottish courts had in the past to freedom of speech as defined in art. 10 of the European Convention on Human Rights.

COX AND GRIFFITHS, PETITIONERS

The *Daily Record* story related how a number of "high risk" prisoners   15.05
were moved from one jail to another under "a massive armed police
guard". The story quoted a police insider as saying:

> "We are taking no chances with this lot. It was an impressive sight
> and part of an intricate plan to ensure these heavy-duty guys got
> to their destination. They are facing a lot of heavy charges."

When the case called at the High Court in Edinburgh a week later   15.06
counsel for one of the accused argued that the article created a
substantial risk that the course of justice would be seriously
prejudiced. Lord Bonomy agreed and imposed £1,500 fines on Peter
Cox, the duty editor of the *Record*, and Stuart Griffiths, the reporter
who wrote the story. The judge said he was in no doubt that the terms
in which the accused were described and the description of the
arrangements made for their transfer amounted to a contempt of
court.

The journalists appealed and in his report to the appeal court Lord   15.07
Bonomy said:

> "This article would, in my opinion, cause any objective reader to
> conclude that organised criminals were being put on trial.
>
> It contained language which was designed to give the reader the
> impression that each of the accused fell into that category... .
> While references to tight security arrangements do not on their
> own justify an inference that those to whom they relate are
> criminals or of bad character, in this article these have to be read
> in the context of referring to the prisoners being transferred as
> 'this lot' and 'these heavy-duty guys.'"

EXTENT AND LOCALITY OF
CIRCULATION OF NEWSPAPER

In the appeal by the journalists, Lord Rodger said the article appeared   15.08
in a paper with a wide circulation in the Edinburgh area and he had no
hesitation in deciding that it was quite likely that some of the jurors
would have read the article. He also considered it likely that any juror
who had read the article might well have still remembered it when the
trial began and made the connection between the story and the case
which he was being asked to decide.

TABLOIDS

15.09 Lord Rodger said that, at times, counsel for the journalists had appeared to ask the court to accept that readers of tabloids did not really believe what they read in their paper and that stories were written more to entertain than inform. The judge added:

> "I reject any suggestion that, because the article appeared in a tabloid newspaper, the court should apply a different (and apparently higher) standard in judging its potential for impeding or prejudicing the course of justice."

REFERENCES TO SECURITY ARRANGEMENTS

15.10 He agreed that in themselves references to high security arrangements did not amount to contempt:

> "Juries will often see that some accused are on bail, while others are held in custody, while still others are taken to and from court under conditions of particular security. There is nothing to suggest that jurors' awareness of these particular facts affects their ability to return a proper verdict based on the evidence which they have heard in court... . There is similarly no reason to suppose that an article in a newspaper referring to security precautions will interfere with a juror's ability to judge the case properly."

IMPORTANCE OF FREEDOM OF EXPRESSION

15.11 Lord Rodger noted that the trial judge had attached importance to the references to "this lot" and "these heavy-duty guys" but, having read and re-read the article, he took the view that it did not amount to a contempt:

> "It seems to me that an attentive reader of the article would be likely to carry away an abiding impression that the prisoners concerned, as a group, were facing very serious charges and were people who, for that reason and perhaps for other reasons, the police considered had to be kept under tight security conditions in case someone engineered their escape."

15.12 A reader who had formed that impression might also wonder whether the prisoners on trial were people with underworld contacts who might try to arrange their escape:

"If a juror's speculation went that far, I consider that there would be a risk of the article causing some prejudice to the course of justice in the proceedings: from the point of view of the administration of justice it would be better if these thoughts were not stimulated in the juror's mind.

It is important, however, to recall that the due course of justice is only one of the values with which the Contempt of Court Act 1981 was concerned. The other value was freedom of expression. Parliament passed the 1981 Act in order to change the law of the United Kingdom and so to bring it into conformity with the interpretation of Article 10 of the European Convention on Human Rights ... the Act was designed to regulate the boundary which had always, of course, existed between freedom of expression and the requirements of the due course of justice. ... Parliament may have re-drawn the boundary at a point which would not have been chosen by people looking at the matter primarily from the administration of justice.... But these factors simply make it all the more important that the courts faithfully observe the boundary which Parliament has settled in order to meet the international obligations of the United Kingdom."

If anything, Lord Prosser's opinion was even more "media-friendly." 15.13
He added:

"I think it worth emphasising that quite apart from the 1981 Act and quite apart from the European Convention on Human Rights, there was in my opinion never any excuse for the courts extending the boundary, and diminishing freedom of speech, on the basis that some wider boundary is more convenient, or simpler, or provides a useful cordon sanitaire or the like .... Just as Parliament, in defining the boundary, denies freedom of speech only where necessary, so the courts, in applying the limitation on freedom of speech need have no qualms about going to the boundary.... On the outer side of the boundary, and right up to it, it seems to me that the press and public are entitled to express themselves as they wish, and I would regret it if they felt that the courts were discontented or critical, or felt entitled to tell them to keep further away."

The law was not so foolish as to assume that no juror would ever 15.14
entertain a suspicion that an accused was violent or dishonest or criminal in various ways. It was largely because the law realised that jurors might well have such suspicions that they were told to stick to the evidence they heard in court and exclude other considerations

from their minds. As far as the *Daily Record* article was concerned, Lord Prosser said:

> "Anyone reading this particular article can see an element of drama, or indeed melodrama, in the way the whole events are described. One might add that it would be extremely boring if this were not so. ... The atmosphere created, or re-created by the article seems to me to be fairly typically (and acceptably) 'tabloid'—but it is an atmosphere very familiar from television and indeed an atmosphere created in the first place (deliberately or otherwise) by the way in which 'high-risk' prisoners are normally conveyed to court by the police."

JURIES ARE "HEALTHY BODIES"

15.15 Lord Prosser concluded that he had read the article a number of times:

> "On no reading have I seen anything which I would regard as creating any risk of any prejudice, far less a substantial risk of seriously impeding or prejudicing the course of justice in the proceedings... . Juries are healthy bodies. They do not need a germ-free atmosphere. Even when articles in the press do contain germs of prejudice it will rarely be appropriate, in my opinion, to bring these to the attention of the court, far less for specific directions to have to be given, far less for the issue to be treated as even potentially one of contempt... . I do not see this article as even near to the crucial boundary. The whole matter seems to me to be a harmless piece of perfectly ordinary reporting."

Lord Coulsfield agreed that the finding of contempt should be quashed.

THE *EVENING TIMES* CASE: BIG TAM

15.16 The approach in the *Daily Record* case was followed by Lord Rodger in 1999 when he dismissed an attempt by the Lord Advocate to find the *Evening Times* (**HM Advocate v Scottish Media Newspapers Ltd (2000)**) in contempt over a story about a Scots actor.

15.17 Actor Iain McColl, then well known as "Big Tam" in a Scottish sitcom, appeared on petition at Glasgow Sheriff Court on a charge of threatening sheriff officers. On the same day the *Evening Times* published an article detailing how Mr McColl spent a night in the cells after allegedly brandishing an axe when sheriff officers arrived at his flat.

Lord Rodger pointed out that the Lord Advocate now held his   15.18
appointment on the recommendation of the First Minister under the
Scotland Act 1998. He had no power to ask the court for any remedy
which would not be compatible with the European Convention on
Human Rights. The Contempt of Court Act 1981 itself, which the
Evening Times article was alleged to contravene, had been passed by
Parliament to bring our law into line with art.10 of the Convention.

TIME GAP BETWEEN PUBLICATION AND TRIAL

Lord Rodger said the court had to assess the risk of prejudice at the   15.19
time the article was published, adding:

> "In assessing the risk we have to take account of the time which
> would elapse between publication and the likely date of the
> trial.... . Here, in a case where Mr McColl was released on bail,
> trial would be likely to take place within 12 months but,
> realistically, would not be likely to take place within the first
> three months. In fact we know that it is unlikely to take place
> until around nine months after publication."

In the court's view it was impossible to say that the article was in   15.20
contempt of court. Lord Rodger went on: "We consider it rather
unlikely indeed that anyone cited to serve as a juror would even recall
the article." The case was unusual since it involved someone who
might be known to jurors as an actor on television. Where
personalities from the world of politics, sport or entertainment were
tried by a jury, the jurors might often know more about their way of
life and the background to any charge than in the normal case. That
might lead the presiding judge "to give a more pointed direction
about the need to reach a verdict based solely on the evidence", but
would not mean that there was a risk to a fair trial.

Lord Rodger's confidence in juror robustness, and concern not to   15.21
discourage proper media coverage of court proceedings, can also be
felt in relation to the making of s.4(2) orders [see **paras 20.19
onwards**].

RISK IS DECREASING, BUT STILL PRESENT

There has been a marked drop, throughout the UK, in numbers of   15.22
contempt prosecutions. Various reasons have been suggested for
this—the Human Rights Act 1998 and its emphasis on freedom of
expression; the desire on the part of the police and prosecuting
authorities to alert the public to the reality of the terrorist threat; the
growing sense that so much information is readily retrievable from the

internet that embargoes are decreasingly practical; jury research from other jurisdictions suggesting that jurors really can prefer trial evidence to media comments.

15.23   However, it would be a dangerous mistake to assume that anything goes in the 21st century in Scotland. There were four proceedings for contempt centring around Peter Tobin, who was convicted of the murders of Angelika Kluk, Vicky Hamilton and Dinah McNicol, although all were ultimately dropped. Two of the proceedings related to magazine articles with Tobin's former wife, casting him in predictably lurid light. One related to an interview with the late Father Gerry Nugent, a witness and incriminee in the Angelika Kluk murder trial. Perhaps these proceedings were instituted to chill a media frenzy around Tobin, given the two upcoming murder trials. They hung over the newspapers and magazine in question for some time. The fourth concerned the *Digger* magazine, which was charged with contempt in November 2008, during Peter Tobin's trial for the murder of Vicky Hamilton. There, articles headlined "The Paedo Files" and referring to Tobin's previous conviction for the murder of Angelika Kluk were the subject of complaint. Again, no contempt finding was made against the *Digger*, apparently because of its small circulation in Dundee, the area of the Vicky Hamilton murder trial.

THE 1981 ACT

15.24   Contempt is now largely governed by the Contempt of Court Act 1981 [see **Appendix 1**]. According to Lord Hailsham, the Lord Chancellor at the time, the aim of the Act was to make the law clearer and more liberal. The Act was passed as a result of several UK defeats before the European Court of Human Rights.

SCOTLAND AND ENGLAND

15.25   The Act was also designed to harmonise the law north and south of the border but experience has shown a wide divergence of interpretation, even allowing for the different pre-trial procedures in Scotland and England. Several stories that would have seen a Scottish editor at least heavily fined have passed without adverse comment in England.

15.26   In *HMA v Scottish Express Newspapers Ltd* (1988), for example, where the *Daily Express* was fined £30,000 for what Lord Emslie described as a disgraceful contempt, counsel for the *Express* explained that the story had been checked in Manchester by an English barrister. Lord Emslie said:

"It is perhaps unfortunate, since our system depends so much on the absence of pre-trial publicity, that advice about publication should be given ultimately not by a Scottish lawyer but an English one."

A cynical journalist might think that, however "disgraceful" the 15.27 contempt, it was not so severe as to prevent the Lord Advocate (who brought the case against the *Express*) from later prosecuting *Sindicic* (and securing his conviction). Such a combination of outcomes is less likely today, with art.10 having a stronger hold on Scottish judicial thinking on contempt.

The publishers of the *Daily Record* and the *Sun* were each fined 15.28 £5,000 in May 1997 for stories about a man called John Cronin. The *Record's* editor and the *Sun's* Scottish editor were both fined £250. The petition for contempt was brought by the Crown in the High Court after stories were published following Cronin's appearance at Haddington Sheriff Court charged with making nuisance telephone calls to female political workers (*HMA v Daily Record* (1997)).

That day the *Record* ran a story saying that Cronin was due to 15.29 appear in court and informing readers of his background, including the fact that he had been jailed for six years for an appalling attack on a woman who became known as Judy X. Following his court appearance, the *Record* and the *Sun* both carried similar stories which again went into Cronin's previous history and referred to him as "a sex beast". At that stage he had appeared on petition which meant that he was facing a jury trial, although shortly afterwards the charge was reduced to summary level and Cronin pleaded guilty.

Roy Martin QC, counsel for the *Record*, explained that there had 15.30 been no deliberate intention to interfere with the course of justice. The newspaper had taken legal advice before publishing both stories and the advice had been that the publication would not create a substantial risk to Cronin's prospects of a fair trial. The court was told:

"The Daily Record took the view that, given the nature of Cronin's public persona, given the widespread knowledge of his identity through photographs both in newspapers and on television of his whereabouts and his previous criminal activities, any risk created by publication of an article which repeated these elements would not be sufficiently substantial to result in contempt."

Mr Martin said that this reasoning had been based on the English case 15.31 in which a court had aborted a trial involving Geoff Knights, the boyfriend of actress Gillian Taylforth, because of pre-trial publicity. The saturation coverage had made frequent references to Mr Knights' "violent past". In 1996, however, the Queen's Bench

Divisional Court refused to hold five papers in contempt over stories they carried after the arrest of Mr Knights on a charge of wounding a taxi driver. The reports quoted witnesses stating in graphic terms that Knights had committed the offence—"Knights beat me to a pulp"; "Knights went berserk with an iron bar"—and referred to his previous convictions. The court said that it was taking account of the saturation coverage given over previous years to the relationship between Miss Taylforth and Mr Knights, his previous convictions and his violent behaviour in the past (*Att Gen v MGN Ltd* (1997)).

15.32   Both Cronin and Mr Knights, it was argued, had become notorious in the public eye because of widespread media publicity. However, the *Record* had now taken further legal advice and was prepared to accept that the articles had given rise to a more than minimal risk of prejudice to a fair trial. The *Sun* also accepted that what it had published amounted to contempt. The *Sun*, too, had taken legal advice before publishing, which was to the effect that the story did not constitute contempt [see **para.17.20**].

JURY ROBUSTNESS

15.33   Again, a case like this might well not be brought in Scotland today. The Scottish courts have followed through on Lord Prosser's statement in *Cox and Griffiths, Petitioners* (1998) that: "Juries are healthy bodies. They do not need a germ-free atmosphere."

15.34   In *HMA v Fraser* (2000), Lord Osborne took the view that Nat Fraser could be tried for the assault and attempted murder of his missing wife Arlene, even though the coverage of her disappearance contained "innuendo" about Nat Fraser. The judge said that the publicity was mixed, and a juror would be most unlikely to have read it all.

15.35   In *Danskin v HM Advocate* (2001), the High Court of Justiciary sitting as an Appeal Court held that standard directions to the jury would be enough to cure any difficulty created by extensive publicity concerning the earlier extortion trial involving the solicitor accused.

15.36   In *Montgomery and Coulter v HM Advocate* (2001), the Privy Council held that a fair trial was possible in relation to the murder of Surjit Singh Chhokar, despite extensive and prolonged prejudicial publicity about the case.

15.37   In *HM Advocate v Haney* (2003), the Appeal Court again refused a plea in bar of trial in relation to Mags Haney and her relatives, although the Appeal Court did express surprise that there had been no contempt proceedings against newspapers who had published references to her criminal record, together with prejudicial photographs. The court also commented that:

"The notoriety of the Haney family predated the first of these articles by a matter of years ... The background effect of that publicity is, in our view, as strong as that of the individual reports which we have had to consider in this case."

In *Sinclair v HM Advocate* (2008), the Appeal Court held that a fair trial was still possible for Angus Sinclair, accused of the World's End murders and later acquitted on a "no case to answer" submission, despite extensive references to him on the internet suggesting he was guilty and referring to his criminal record.   15.38

Scottish courts have always been highly reluctant to abort a trial because of the accused's complaints about prejudicial pre-trial publicity. What is new is the relative slowness of all concerned to mount contempt prosecutions—sometimes despite apparent judicial hints, as in *Haney* and also in *HM Advocate v Valerie Cowan* (2007), at Paisley Sheriff Court, where Sheriff Susan Sinclair suggested that the Crown should be looking at an apparently prejudicial article.   15.39

In *HM Advocate v McGee* (2005), Lord Abernethy considered a two page spread in the *Sun* making allegations about sexual and physical abuse by the accused against his wife and daughter, and photographs of all three, so prejudicial that he granted a motion for an adjournment and moved the trial. There were, however, no contempt proceedings against the *Sun*, and no attempt to argue that there could never be a fair trial. The decision was simply to adjourn the trial to the following month and to hear it in Dundee, rather than Aberdeen. The jury acquitted McGee.   15.40

Grounds of appeal in relation to pre-trial publicity were allowed in both the William Beggs (*Beggs v HMA* (2010)) and Luke Mitchell (*Mitchell v HMA* (2008)) cases after the two men were convicted, though the original coverage had not resulted in contempt findings, but both men's appeals have failed. In March 2010, the Appeal Court of the High Court of Justiciary said that the trial judge in the *Beggs* case had taken the right approach to the publicity issues and specifically endorsed his refusal to grant a s.4(2) order and his decision "not to arraign any website authors for possible contempt". Leave to appeal to the Supreme Court was refused.   15.41

INTERDICTS AND INJUNCTIONS TO PROTECT ADMINISTRATION OF JUSTICE

In 2005, the Court of Appeal lifted an injunction restraining Channel 5 from broadcasting a programme called *Gangsters*, following the fatal shooting of one of the eponymous gangsters. The chief constable had been concerned that witnesses would be deterred from coming forward, for a variety of reasons. Lord Justice Auld, lifting the   15.42

injunction, said that before an injunction could be granted there needed to be "a high standard of persuasion that there will be substantial risk that the course of justice in the proceedings in question will be seriously impeded or prejudiced" and that this was not satisfied here. The trial was months away and the victim was already notorious in the area: *Chief Constable of Greater Manchester v Channel 5 Broadcast Ltd* **(2005)**.

15.43   It is not unknown, though, for an English court to grant an injunction banning the media from interviewing witnesses for a documentary to be transmitted after the verdict (*Ex p. HTV Cymru* **(2002)**). In *Att Gen v BBC* **(2007)**, the Court of Appeal lifted an injunction against the BBC in connection with the "cash for honours" investigation. In that case, the claimed substantial risk was to the ability of the investigating police to reveal the document in question to suspects or witnesses at the time of the police's choosing. The lifting of this injunction, however, came after a great deal had been put into the public domain already.

15.44   The Scottish courts are perhaps somewhat readier to stop publication in advance where they fear a risk to the administration of justice. In *Muir v BBC* **(1997)**, an entire documentary was prohibited until after the trial of two prison officers. Neither the prison officers nor the trial were mentioned in the programme, but it featured a prison doctor who was to be a controversial witness in the forthcoming trial. An application to the European Court of Human Rights by the BBC failed (*BBC v UK* **(1996)**).

15.45   In Scotland in 2005, Lord Bracadale—clearly uncomfortable with the extremely short timescale in which he was forced to decide— granted an interim interdict against STV. *Tonight With Trevor McDonald* had been planning to show footage of the aftermath of an alleged stabbing, for which Mr Paterson was being prosecuted, but not to identify the location as Glasgow and to pixellate the accused's face. Lord Bracadale thought that the material almost certainly constituted evidence in the case and was potentially prejudicial (*Paterson* **(2005)**).

TRIBUNALS AND OTHER BODIES

15.46   "Court", for the purposes of the 1981 Act, "includes any tribunal or body exercising the judicial power of the State." The Government of the day could not undertake to provide a list of the tribunals and other bodies which fitted the definition. If the Government with its resources found the task beyond it, it is not one this book can be confident of achieving, given the great number and variety of bodies possibly involved.

A crude practical test may be to consider how powerful the body is.   15.47
If it can deprive someone of liberty, it will almost certainly be a court
for contempt purposes.

The Court Martial Appeal Court, Restrictive Practices Court and   15.48
Employment Appeal Tribunal are expressly included in the definition
of "Scottish Proceedings".

Employment tribunals and mental health review tribunals have   15.49
both been held to fall under the definition of court. In *Ewing
v Security Service* **(2003)**, in England, the Investigatory Powers
Tribunal was held to be a court [see **para.38.10**].

The problem may be simplified to some extent by leaving out of the   15.50
definition all those tribunals set up to deal with disputes or complaints
over the conduct of members of professions, trades or specialised
bodies. In most of these cases the body in question is deciding
questions of discipline, ethics or practice within the profession or
trade in question. In *GMC v BBC* **(1998)**, the Court of Appeal in
England held that the Professional Conduct Committee of the
General Medical Council was not a court for contempt purposes, and
declined to grant an injunction against a *Panorama* dealing with
Bristol doctors and paediatric heart surgery success rates. The GMC
had feared that the programme would affect the evidence of witnesses.

In *Att Gen v BBC* **(1981)**, where the House of Lords held that a local   15.51
valuation court was not a court of law, Lord Steyn said:

> "There is today a plethora of such tribunals ... In my view, it does
> not by any means follow that the modern inferior courts need the
> umbrella of contempt of court, nor that they come under it.
> Indeed, in my opinion, public policy requires that most of the
> principles relating to contempt of court which have for ages
> necessarily applied to the long-established inferior courts ...
> shall not apply to valuation courts and the host of other modern
> tribunals ... otherwise the scope of contempt of court would be
> unnecessarily extended and accordingly freedom of speech and
> freedom of the press would be unnecessarily contracted."

Lord Scarman said in the same case: 15.52

> "If the body under review is established for a purely legislative or
> administrative purpose, it is part of the legislative or
> administrative system of the state, even though it has to perform
> duties which are judicial in character."

The definition of "court" does, however, cover an appeal to a court   15.53
from a tribunal which is not itself within the category.

PUBLIC INQUIRIES AND CONTEMPT

15.54   The inquiry by Lord Cullen, the then Lord Justice-Clerk, which
        followed the massacre of 16 children at Dunblane Primary School in
        March 1996 was constituted under the Tribunals of Inquiry
        (Evidence) Act 1921 and the publication of a number of newspaper
        articles prompted the Lord Advocate, Lord Mackay of Drumadoon,
        to warn of the dangers of contempt. The Lord Advocate issued a note
        to editors expressing his concern at the tone of articles which attacked
        the conduct of individuals, including police officers, councillors and
        local authority officials whose actings might be the subject of scrutiny
        at the inquiry and who might have to give evidence. Lord Mackay said
        that in some cases publication followed "intrusive personal
        approaches" to individuals. He raised his concerns with Lord Cullen
        who agreed that any further instances of harassment of potential
        witnesses by the media or publication of material which might
        impede the investigation or interfere with the giving of evidence
        should be referred to the Lord Justice-Clerk. This would enable Lord
        Cullen to consider certifying the conduct of those responsible with a
        view to contempt of court proceedings in the Court of Session.
15.55   The Lord Advocate said he recognised that the media wished to
        discuss issues that might form the subject of recommendations by
        Lord Cullen and emphasised that he had no wish to inhibit such
        debate unless it amounted to contempt of court. By way of guidance
        he referred to the 1969 Salmon Committee on the law of contempt as
        it affected tribunals of inquiry which recognised that the publication of
        interviews with prospective witnesses raised difficult problems of
        contamination of evidence [see **para.15.63**].
15.56   Section 20 of the 1981 Act provides that it covers any tribunal to
        which the Tribunals of Inquiry (Evidence) Act 1921 from the time of
        its appointment to when it reports to Parliament, but the 1921 Act has
        been repealed and replaced by the Inquiries Act 2005.

FATAL ACCIDENT INQUIRIES

15.57   Fatal accident inquiries have statutory power to deal with contempt.
        There have been attempts to bring contempt proceedings against the
        media over the reporting of fatal accident inquiries, although these are
        held by a sheriff sitting alone without a jury. In 1990, Sheriff Principal
        John Mowat QC ordered the editor of the *Sunday Telegraph* and the
        author of an article in the newspaper to appear before him in the
        inquiry into the Lockerbie disaster.
15.58   In an article headed "Lockerbie Whitewash Warning" the *Sunday
        Telegraph* suggested that lawyers acting for the bereaved families

were trying to avoid bringing out evidence of security flaws at Heathrow airport so as not to damage a possible future compensation claim against Pan Am. Mr Brian Gill QC (now Lord Justice-Clerk), counsel for the relatives, complained that the article could influence the way in which legal representatives carried out their duties.

The sheriff principal said, however, that he was reasonably   15.59 confident that the implication in the article that he was conducting a whitewash did not impede the course of justice. He added that Mr Gill had some grounds for suggesting that he had been defamed in the article, although that was not a matter for the court.

In 1991 there were contempt hearings at Dunoon Sheriff Court   15.60 during an inquiry into the death of a Glasgow lawyer who had lost her life while hillwalking. There was a complaint by counsel for the dead woman's family that an article in the *Evening Times* previewing the inquiry had anticipated the outcome of proceedings by pointing out that the woman was an experienced hill walker who died in fair weather conditions. There was also a complaint that the *Herald* had committed contempt because inaccurate remarks had been attributed to a witness. Although it was accepted that the sheriff was an experienced professional who could dismiss the article from his mind, it was argued that witnesses could have their evidence influenced by what they had read.

Both newspapers submitted that there was no contempt since there   15.61 was no jury to be influenced at a fatal accident inquiry. To decide that witnesses might be influenced by something they had read in a newspaper was to suggest that they were not going to fulfil their oath to tell the whole truth and that would be a dangerous extension of the law. It was also argued on behalf of the *Evening Times* that the pre-inquiry publicity might in fact have had the desirable effect of bringing witnesses forward.

While it would be going too far to say that publicity in advance of a   15.62 fatal accident inquiry could never amount to contempt of court, it is clear that fatal accident inquiries are not in the same position as criminal trials. The crucial difference is the absence of a jury, but another important factor is that no-one is on trial at a fatal accident inquiry.

The authorities might, however, take a different view if the   15.63 complaint was not merely that a witness had read something in a newspaper, but that his evidence had been influenced by his being interviewed by a journalist shortly before the inquiry or trial. There could be an argument that this had changed the evidence the witness would otherwise have given. This was certainly the line taken by the Salmon Committee and raised by the Crown before the Dunblane Inquiry.

CORONERS' INQUESTS

15.64 These are confined to England and Wales, but because the 1981 Act applies to the whole United Kingdom, it may be important for journalists and publishers in Scotland to know the position of the inquest in the context of contempt law. Inquests, unlike fatal accident inquiries, can have juries. They fall under the Contempt of Court Act 1981 from the time when the inquest opens: see *Peacock v LWT* **(1986)**, which resulted in a LWT programme not being broadcast during an adjournment of an inquest into a death in police custody.

15.65 The Coroners and Justice Act 2009 sets out many of the key features but, at the time of writing, further change is contemplated, in the controversial direction of "secret inquests" and anonymisation [see **Chapter 38**].

15.66 Coroners can grant orders postponing reporting under s.4(2) of the 1981 Act. If they do not, and no other statutory order is in place, a fair and accurate report would be protected for defamation and contempt purposes.

PENALTIES FOR CONTEMPT

15.67 Where a court imposes a prison sentence for contempt it must, under s.15 of the 1981 Act, be for a fixed term, although the court retains its power to order discharge at an earlier date. The maximum prison sentence which may be imposed by the High Court or a sheriff court in cases with a jury is two years, but a fine (without statutory limit) may be imposed as well or as an alternative. Where the contempt is dealt with by a sheriff in summary or civil proceedings other than on indictment, the maximum penalty is three months' imprisonment or a fine of £2,500, or both.

APPEALING A CONTEMPT FINDING

15.68 The case in which the *Daily Express* was fined £50,000, *Express Newspapers, Petitioners* **(1999)** [see **para.16.07**], raised the question as to whether it was competent for someone who had been found in contempt and punished by three High Court judges to appeal to a larger bench by presenting a petition to the *nobile officium*. The *Express* sought an appeal on the basis that the fine was excessive. Lord Rodger, the Lord Justice General, said that the petition for contempt brought by the Lord Advocate could have been heard by a single judge, rather than a bench of three. Since the court was being asked to entertain an appeal against a decision of three judges, the court had decided that it was appropriate for the appeal to be heard by five judges.

KEY POINTS

1. Contempt law tries to balance the often conflicting interests of freedom of speech with the right to a fair trial. The traditional approach of Scots law is that pre-trial publicity should be kept to a minimum, particularly where a jury is involved. Much greater weight has been given since 1997 to freedom of speech but there remains a potent risk of a contempt finding in Scotland.   15.69

2. The Contempt of Court Act 1981 says that anything which creates a substantial risk that the course of justice in particular legal proceedings will be seriously impeded or prejudiced is contempt, where the case is active, even although prejudice was not intended. Publication of previous convictions before a trial would be likely to amount to contempt, as would publication of the accused's picture if identification was in issue.

3. Contempt law also applies to tribunals and other bodies "exercising the judicial power of the State".

4. The courts are willing, on occasion, to stop a publication in order to protect a trial.

5. The term "court" includes any tribunal or body exercising the judicial power of the State. This includes employment tribunals, but excludes a number of other bodies, even if they call themselves "courts".

6. Contempt of court will rarely be a problem in relation to a public inquiry or to a fatal accident inquiry, since these bodies do not have juries, but questions can arise in relation to witness influence.

7. Contempt is punishable by up to two years in prison and/or an unlimited fine, in serious cases.

CHAPTER 16

THE STRICT LIABILITY RULE IN ACTIVE CASES UNDER THE CONTEMPT OF COURT ACT 1981

BY ROSALIND MCINNES

STRICT LIABILITY RULE

16.01   The 1981 Act lays down a "strict liability" rule which means that a journalist can be guilty of contempt even although he did not mean to interfere with the course of justice. The risk of committing contempt under the strict liability rule applies only to a publication which creates a substantial risk that the course of justice in the proceedings in question will be seriously impeded or prejudiced.

16.02   A publication includes any speech, writing or broadcast or other communication in whatever form addressed to the public at large or any section of the public. The phrase "communication in whatever form" would include, for example, pictures, headlines and cartoons.

ACTIVE PROCEEDINGS

16.03   The risk also arises only when proceedings are active, which in a criminal case in Scotland is from the moment of arrest without warrant; the grant of a warrant to arrest; or the service of an indictment or other document setting out charges against an accused person—whichever comes first.

DETENTION POWERS

16.04   One complication for the media is that the police have the power to detain a suspect for up to 12 or even 24 hours since *Cadder v HMA* **(2010)** was decided by the Supreme Court in London. This is not an arrest and proceedings are technically not active under the 1981 Act, but any story at the detention stage would have to be written with extreme care. By the time the newspaper was published or the item broadcast the suspect might either have been released or arrested, which could lead to problems with defamation or contempt of court. The possibility of contempt at common law would also have to be considered [see **Chapter 22**]. This covers conduct intended to prejudice the administration of justice.

WHEN CONTEMPT RISK ENDS

In criminal proceedings, the risk of contempt under the Act ends when 16.05
the accused is acquitted or sentenced or with the return of any other
verdict, finding, order or decision which puts an end to the
proceedings.

Proceedings may also cease to be active because of some other 16.06
process causing them to be discontinued or by other "operation of
law". Proceedings are discontinued when they are expressly
abandoned by the prosecutor or deserted simpliciter, i.e. absolutely
or without qualification.

As the *Scottish Daily Express* discovered to its cost in 1999 16.07
(*Express Newspapers plc, Petrs* (1999)) the risk of contempt still runs
when proceedings are deserted *pro loco et tempore* (for the time being).
In a case which also confirmed that the media can appeal against a
contempt finding by way of a petition to the *nobile officium* (which
exists to provide a remedy in extraordinary or unforeseen
circumstances) the *Express* was fined £50,000, one of the biggest
amounts in Scotland for many years.

The circumstances were that the *Express* published a front page 16.08
article about a case four days after it had been deserted temporarily
by the Crown. The article dealt with the evidence in the case. The fine
was imposed by three judges at the High Court and the *Express*
appealed to a larger court against the size of the penalty.

In a hearing before five judges at the High Court in Edinburgh, Lord 16.09
Rodger, the Lord Justice General, said the newspaper now accepted
that the case had still been active under the 1981 Act, but had
originally published on the opposite and wholly mistaken view. The
reporter involved in the case had spoken to the procurator fiscal who
advised that the Crown reserved the right to re-indict the accused. A
firm of solicitors who had advised the newspaper gave advice that the
proceedings were now at an end. Counsel for the newspaper now
accepted that the legal advice was "completely indefensible".

Lord Rodger, refusing to lower the fine, added: 16.10

> "We note that the Express gave considerable prominence to the
> article. We note also that, even though the Express took legal
> advice, it is well established that ... the duty of publishers is
> actually to avoid publishing articles which create a substantial
> risk of serious prejudice to the course of justice ...".

Ironically from the point of view of the newspaper the prosecution 16.11
eventually became time-barred after a year elapsed from the first
appearance of the accused on petition.

WHEN IS SENTENCING?

16.12 An accused is sentenced when he or she is made subject to any order or decision following on conviction or finding of guilt which disposes of the case, either absolutely or subject to future events. Where a sentence is deferred for two or three weeks to enable the court, for example, to obtain background reports on the accused, the proceedings remain active during that time.

16.13   That the case remains active does not necessarily mean that the risk of a contempt finding remains the same. The Scottish media normally run their own "backgrounders", often including details such as previous convictions and photographs of the former accused, as soon as possible after the verdict, without waiting for the sentencing.

INSANITY

16.14 Criminal proceedings are also no longer active if the accused is found to be under a disability rendering him or her unfit to be tried or to plead or is found insane in bar of trial.

TWELVE MONTHS AFTER WARRANT AND NO ARREST

16.15 Criminal proceedings are no longer active 12 months after a warrant has been issued unless the person in question has been arrested within that period. If he or she is arrested after the expiry of the 12 months, the proceedings become active again.

16.16   In the Lockerbie case the sheriff in Dumfries originally issued warrants for the arrest of two Libyans in December 1991. The strict liability rule ceased to operate in December 1992 as no arrests had been made, although the possibility of common law contempt remained. The proceedings became live again when the two Libyans surrendered themselves in April 1998 for trial in the Netherlands.

CIVIL PROCEEDINGS

16.17 The Act also applies to civil proceedings which become active either from the time arrangements for the hearing are made or from the time the hearing begins, whichever happens first. Appellate proceedings in civil cases are treated in the same way as criminal appellate proceedings.

16.18   A hearing need not necessarily be the hearing of the case on its merits or for disposal of the main point. It can be a hearing to deal with an incidental or preliminary matter, such as interim interdict, amendment of pleadings, appointment of curator, etc. A fair and accurate report of such a hearing—if held in public—would be protected under s.4 of the 1981 Act [see **para.05.65**].

The making of arrangements for a hearing is defined in the Act as 16.19 meaning, in the case of an ordinary action in the Court of Session or sheriff court, when the record (the document setting out the parties' cases) is closed; in the case of a motion or application, when it is enrolled or made; and in any other case, when the date for a hearing is fixed or a hearing is allowed. Again, it is the step which happens first that has the effect of deciding when the case becomes active.

Since some of the steps referred to—such as closing the record, 16.20 enrolment of a motion or allowance of a hearing—take place usually in the offices of the appropriate court without public intimation, the journalist will have to check with either court staff or lawyers in the case as to whether any of the stages in question has been reached.

The changes made in the Act on contempt in civil cases have an 16.21 important bearing on the summons as a possible source of information for journalists. Before the passing of the Act it was understood from the case of *Richardson v Wilson* (1879) that a summons was a private document. Publication of material from a summons in that case, which had only appeared on the calling list, led to a newspaper being sued for slander. The First Division, in upholding a complaint against the paper, also ruled that it would be contempt for a lawyer to make the contents of a summons available to the press before the case had come into open court. Publication from a summons could therefore lead to a risk of contempt as well as proceedings for defamation. The 1981 Act appears to rule out the risk of contempt by the media by the publication of information from a summons. A summons will normally be issued before a date for a hearing has been fixed or any other relevant step under the Act has caused the case to become active.

But the Act does not alter the pre-existing law that it is contempt to 16.22 publish material intended to prejudice the proceedings.

There certainly have been cases since the Act was passed where 16.23 stories have appeared in the media based almost entirely on summonses which have been handed over either by lawyers or one of the parties involved in the case. This happened, for example, in cases where prison officers have been suing over injuries received in prison riots. It has also happened in the case of haemophiliacs who have been diagnosed as suffering from the AIDS virus after receiving batches of contaminated blood. No objection was taken to these reports. Few civil cases other than libel trials end up before a jury, so any risk of prejudice would be likely to be confined to witnesses only. Journalists should always bear in mind, however, that the summons may include allegations which could lead to a defamation action if prematurely published.

16.24   Civil cases remain active until they are disposed of, discontinued or withdrawn. It is also worth noting that when an action is adjourned or interrupted so that negotiations can take place, the case remains active in terms of the Act until the proceedings are settled, disposed of or withdrawn. But s.5 of the Act is designed to ensure that this fact does not preclude comment on a case while active, provided it is published "as part of a discussion in good faith of public affairs or other matters of general public interest" and so long as "the risk of impediment or prejudice to particular legal proceedings is merely incidental to the discussion" [see **Chapter 18**].

16.25   It must be remembered that some civil cases *are* heard by juries and, even where they are not, they still typically involve lay people as witnesses. The editor and publishers of *Private Eye* were each ordered to pay £10,000 in 1990 by the Court of Appeal in England for their "serious contempt" in publishing two articles about the wife of the Yorkshire Ripper while her libel action against them was pending. The allegations that Mrs Sonia Sutcliffe had provided her husband with a false alibi and defrauded the DSS were published three months before the hearing of the libel action. The Appeal Court took the view that, apart from the possibility of influencing potential jurors by blackening Mrs Sutcliffe's character, the articles were intended to deter her by what were tantamount to threats. They posed a threat to the administration of justice and clearly created a substantial risk of serious prejudice (*Att Gen v Hislop* **(1990)**).

CONTEMPT AND APPEALS

16.26   The 1981 Act extends the contempt law to cover cases at the appeal stage.

16.27   It is worth remembering, however, that there has to be a substantial risk of serious prejudice and that senior judges, rather than a jury, will be hearing any appeal. The High Court in Scotland has stated in the case of *Aitchison v Bernardi* **(1984)** that lay magistrates, far less legally-trained sheriffs and High Court judges, should be incapable of being influenced by the media. It was also made clear in Parliament during the debate on the Contempt of Court Bill that there would normally be a "free for all period" for the media between the end of a case and an appeal being lodged.

16.28   A case does not become active for contempt purposes merely because a lawyer says at the end of a case that the client intends to appeal. There must be a definite starting process such as a notice of appeal or an application for leave to appeal. Appeal proceedings are active until disposed of, abandoned, discontinued or withdrawn. However, if the appeal court grants the Crown authority to bring a fresh prosecution, the risk of prejudicing the new proceedings begins from the end of the appeal.

The issue of contempt and appeals was discussed in the unreported case of *Forbes Cowan* **(1998)** in which BBC Scotland planned to broadcast *The Skipper's Tale*, the story of the detection and arrest of the crew of a ship which had been seized by Customs officers at Troon in Ayrshire. Four accused were convicted after trial and, after they were sentenced to a total of 32 years, lodged appeals, some against both conviction and sentence. BBC Scotland announced its intention to broadcast *The Skipper's Tale*, even although it knew that appeals were pending, and, if successful, might lead to fresh prosecutions. One of the accused, Forbes Cowan, applied to the High Court claiming that the broadcast would amount to contempt. His petition specifically addressed the possibility of the case being heard by another jury in a second trial. The High Court dismissed Mr Cowan's petition without asking the BBC to present an argument. In effect, the court was saying that he had not made out even a case worthy of consideration. Without a written judgment it is not easy to work out the reasoning behind the decision, but the court did seem to be concerned about the possibility of the media not being able to discuss a much publicised case until all appeals had been exhausted, perhaps years in the future. It can be taken from this case that the launching of an appeal is unlikely to prevent the media from discussing a case in a fair and balanced way. 16.29

The refusal of the court to grant reporting restrictions on the Kim Galbraith appeal, *Scarsbrook v HM Advocate (No.1)* **(2001)**, and in *Beggs v Scottish Ministers* **(2006)**, where it was unsuccessfully argued that publicity might influence any future retrial of convicted killers, suggest that this approach is firmly rooted in the Scottish judges' thinking. 16.30

THE LOCKERBIE CASE

In 1987, Lane L.C.J. banned the showing of a Channel 4 re-enactment of hearings in the Birmingham pub bombings appeals. The programme was based on daily transcripts of what had already been said in court, but Lord Lane decided that showing it was likely to undermine public confidence in the legal system: *Att Gen v Channel Four Television Co Ltd* **(1988)**. 16.31

This approach was rejected in Scotland in the case of two Libyan nationals accused of conspiracy to murder after Pan Am flight 103 exploded over Lockerbie, killing 270 people (*Al-Megrahi v Times* 16.32

Newspapers Ltd **(2000)**). They petitioned the High Court in July 1999 asking it to hold the *Sunday Times* in contempt. The newspaper had run a story headlined: "Official: Gadaffi's Bomb Plot". The story alleged that the Libyan leader had personally instructed the head of his External Security Organisation (ESO) to organise the Lockerbie bombing as revenge for an American air raid on Tripoli. The article detailed alleged links between the head of the ESO and one of the accused and concluded: "It would be an odd sort of justice that found his cat's paws guilty of murder and let the real villain off the hook." The accused argued that a fair and dispassionate reader of the articles would be left with the impression that their guilt could be taken for granted.

16.33   Lord Cullen, the then Lord Justice-Clerk, said he had no doubt that anyone who had been committed for trial was under the protection of the court. However, as the court had pointed out in the *Daily Record* case *Cox, Petr* **(1998)**, the Contempt of Court Act 1981 had been passed to change United Kingdom law and bring it into line with the European Convention on Human Rights. "The Act represented a distinct shift in favour of freedom of expression", Lord Cullen emphasised.

16.34   Special arrangements had been made for the men to stand trial in the Netherlands before three judges. At the date of publication it was unrealistic to consider the effect on potential jurors in Scotland.

16.35   Counsel for the two men maintained however that the *Sunday Times* had still committed a contempt. They argued that the court should take action to prevent public confidence in the course of justice from being undermined. In support of their argument they relied on *Att Gen v Channel Four Television Co Ltd* **(1988)** (see above) in which Lane L.C.J. had said that the broadcasting of a TV reconstruction of a current appeal might affect the public's view of the judgment of the court and leave the accused in doubt about the effect of outside influences.

16.36   Lord Cullen said it seemed clear that this approach was an attempt to establish a general rule in the law of contempt that it was offensive for the media to "pre-judge" issues in pending cases. The problem with that was that it could not stand alongside ss.1 and 2 of the 1981 Act in which Parliament had adopted a different test. "There is nothing in the Act which enjoins the court to apply as the test the perception of others as to whether the course of justice may be affected," Lord Cullen stressed. He went on to say:

> "The administration of justice has to be robust enough to withstand criticism and misunderstanding. ... It is one thing to say that it is good law that a party to proceedings should be able to rely on there being no usurpation by any other person of the

court to decide the case according to law. ... It is quite another thing to say that what is contempt of court should be judged by reference to the perspective of that party."

Lord Cullen added that even if it had been correct to use the test of 16.37 whether public confidence in the administration of justice had been undermined, he would have decided that the test had not been met in this case:

"In this country the public and those who are the subject of criminal proceedings enjoy the benefit of an independent judiciary, the members of which are well used to concentrating on the evidence, and only the evidence, which is put before them in the proceedings, and to arrive at decisions in an impartial manner."

He refused to go as far as to rule out absolutely the risk of a 16.38 professional judge being influenced by something he had read about a case with which he was dealing. But he quoted the words of Lord Bridge of Harwich in the *Lonrho* **(1990)** case in which the judge had said this was a "very much more remote" possibility (than in a case involving a jury).

Lord Coulsfield agreed. He said it would only be in an exceptional 16.39 case that a single publication, like the *Sunday Times* story in the present case, would be regarded as so damaging that a trial could not go ahead. He warned, however, that repeated publication either by one or several newspapers over a period of time might create an atmosphere in which it would be extremely difficult for either a judge or jury to reach a proper conclusion. "Such repeated publication might properly be described as 'trial by newspaper' and might be capable of being regarded as prejudicial to the course of justice" (*Al-Megrahi v Times Newspapers Ltd* **(2000)**).

However, not even William Beggs (*Beggs v Scottish Ministers* 16.40 **(2006)**), in his unsuccessful attempt in 2006 to obtain a s.4(2) order restricting reporting of civil proceedings in which he was appealing against the court's refusal to quash an order to transfer him from Saughton to Peterhead Prison [see **para.07.03**], suggested that there was a substantial risk that appeal judges would be prejudiced by reporting (2006).

Judges are not expected to be robots. If they themselves are the 16.41 subject of disrespectful attack in their court, for instance, they will send any resultant contempt proceedings to be decided by other judges. They are, however, expected to be able to distinguish between what a newspaper says and what is evidentially or legally significant to the case before them. In the contempt proceedings (not under the strict liability rule) unsuccessfully brought against solicitor Aamer Anwar in July 2008 (***Anwar, Respondent* (2008)**)) over comments he had made following his client's conviction under the Terrorism Act 2008, Lord Osborne stated: "Judges who administer the law must expect and accept that proceedings over which they exercise control may, from time to time, be publicly and trenchantly criticised" [see **paras 22.18 onwards**].

KEY POINTS

16.42
1. The Contempt of Court Act 1981 sets out the "strict liability rule". It states that a publication which creates a substantial risk that the course of justice in active proceedings will be seriously impeded or prejudiced is in contempt of court.
2. Criminal cases are active from arrest; the grant of a warrant to arrest; or the service of an indictment or other document setting out charges against the accused. In practice, the risk normally ends with the return of the verdict.
3. Civil proceedings become active either from the time arrangements for the hearing are made, or from the time the hearing begins. The contempt risk is usually not high in a civil case, because there are rarely juries. However, defamation cases and some other personal injury cases can go before juries. As well, there can be a contempt risk if witnesses are improperly influenced by the media.
4. There is a strong and general presumption that a judge, sheriff or even lay magistrate in Scotland will not be influenced by what the media publish about court cases.
5. Criminal proceedings are no longer active 12 months after a warrant has been issued, unless the person in question has been arrested within that period.

CHAPTER 17

WHAT IS A STATUTORY CONTEMPT?

BY ROSALIND MCINNES

"SUBSTANTIAL RISK OF SERIOUS PREJUDICE"

Under the strict liability rule, it is contempt to publish something 17.01
which creates a substantial risk that the course of justice in active
proceedings will be seriously impeded or prejudiced.

Lord Diplock has expressed the view in the House of Lords in the 17.02
case of *Att Gen v English* (**1982**) that the word "substantial" in s.2 of
the 1981 Act is to be equated with "not remote". Lord McCluskey
seemed to adopt the same approach in the trial of Paul Ferris at the
High Court in Glasgow in March 1992 when he said a substantial
risk meant a risk which was not negligible.

It is impossible to give an exact definition of what the courts will 17.03
regard as a substantial risk of serious prejudice, but obvious risks are
the revealing of previous convictions or publication of any inference
that the person charged committed the offence. For example, you
could report a bank robbery and say that "a" man had been arrested
but not "the" man. Photographs of the accused, although frequently
used in court reporting in England and Wales, will tend to pose risks in
Scotland—see the *Riordan* case, below—as may photographs of
incriminees, i.e. people named by the accused as responsible for the
crime instead of him.

The closer a publication is to the trial, and the wider its distribution 17.04
in the area from which jurors (or sometimes witnesses) are likely to
come, the greater the risk of a contempt finding.

The publishers and editors of the *Milngavie and Bearsden Herald* 17.05
were each fined £250 for contempt in 1977 over a report about two
men who appeared on petition at Dumbarton Sheriff Court on
charges of assault and robbery. The newspaper reported that the two
men, whom they identified, had both been wearing masks when they
had been caught. The Crown submitted that this was a "fair
indication of their guilt" and the court accepted that there had been
an interference with the administration of justice.

175

HM ADVOCATE v SCOTSMAN PUBLICATIONS: WITNESS INTIMIDATION AND CELEBRITY

17.06   In *HM Advocate v Scotsman Publications* **(1998)** the High Court decided that the *Scotsman* had committed contempt by stating that two witnesses in a pending election fraud trial against Glasgow Govan MP Mohammed Sarwar had asked for police protection because they feared intimidation. Lord Marnoch said he was in no doubt that that the ordinary reader would be left with the impression that two "key witnesses" had asked for protection because they feared intimidation from Mr Sarwar or his associates:

> "In my opinion, where, in the context of a criminal prosecution, particularly one involving charges of election fraud and attempting to pervert the course of justice, there is reference to feared intimidation, the ordinary reader is likely to assume that the accused is ultimately the person whose intimidation is to be feared … He, after all, is the person with the most obvious interest in the outcome of the trial … I have to say that in my opinion there could hardly be a more prejudicial suggestion in advance of a trial … The fact that an accused should stoop to intimidating witnesses is one which many readers, including the ordinary reader, would regard as almost tantamount to guilt."

17.07   Once the ordinary reader had formed that impression it was an impression that was likely to "stick", particularly when applied to someone as well known as Mr Sarwar.

17.08   Lord Rodger, the then Lord Justice General, said that looking at the date of publication, the likely date of the trial and the very small readership of the *Scotsman* in the west of Scotland, he had found it harder than Lord Marnoch to be satisfied that the risk of serious prejudice to the proceedings was other than remote. However, particularly because of the high profile of Mr Sarwar which might make the story stick in a reader's mind, he had decided that it would not be right to dissent from Lord Marnoch's view.

17.09   Lord Caplan agreed that the prominence of the accused was an important factor in deciding that the article had amounted to contempt.

> "If he had been a relatively anonymous accused then I should have found it difficult to conclude that the import of the article would have been retained in the mind of a juror participating in any trial which occurs some months hence. … However, because of the publicity which has surrounded him, an adverse impression of his character, which a reader might derive from the article,

could readily be retained in his or her mind until the trial. ... What are the odds of this happening I do not know but the risk is certainly a serious one."

Lord Rodger took a somewhat different view of the effects of the "celebrity" accused in the circumstances of the Big Tam case (*HM Advocate v Scottish Media Newspapers Ltd* (2000)) [see **paras 15.16 onwards**]. 17.10

PREVIOUS CONVICTIONS

In May 1997, the publishers of the *Daily Record* and *Sun* newspapers were each fined £5,000 and their editors £250 for referring to notorious rapist John Cronin as a "sex beast" at a time when he was facing trial for making nuisance calls. The two journalists who wrote the stories were not fined, on the basis that they had taken legal advice. Both newspapers apologised to the court and admitted contempt. In today's post-Human Rights Act 1998, internet-driven world, a finding of contempt in a similar case is perhaps unlikely, but even so, relating previous convictions is a course to be followed only in highly unusual circumstances. 17.11

MOTIVE AND TIMING

In England in 2002, the *Mirror* paid out about £130,000—a £75,000 fine and the rest in Attorney General's costs—after it published an article suggesting that an assault was racist at a time when the jurors (who had been instructed that the motive was not racist) were out considering the verdict. The trial had to be aborted, costing over £1 million: *Att Gen v MGN Ltd* (2002). 17.12

In July 2008, ITV Central Ltd were fined £25,000 and agreed to pay third party costs of a postponement to the trial (of about £37,000) for publishing a news report on the morning of the trial. The piece referred to the fact that one of the accused had been convicted of murder and was serving a term of imprisonment for it: *Att Gen v ITV Central Ltd* (2008). 17.13

It will be noted that both of these lethal publications occurred at very sensitive points during the trial. This suggests that the so-called fade factor, the assumption that people forget what they may have happened to see in a broadcast or read in a newspaper months before the trial, is of the utmost importance in incurring or avoiding liability for publication contempt. 17.14

BACKGROUND INFORMATION

17.15   **Kemp, Petitioner (1982)**, where the appeal judges made a contempt finding against the *Herald* and *Scotsman*, provided some useful guidance for the media over the publication of outside information which is not part of the evidence in court. Although references to an unmarked police car and a secret address were not based on evidence that had come out in court, Lord Emslie was satisfied that their mention was not prejudicial given that there were extraordinary security precautions obviously being taken at the relevant trial, which arose out of alleged terrorism offences. They did not impact upon the credibility of the witnesses who were being given this protection.

ADAMS, PETITIONER

17.16   One rare case in which a Scottish court has followed through a finding of contempt by aborting a trial was that of Joseph Trainer at the High Court in Paisley (*Adams, Petitioner* (1987)). Trainer was on trial for the murder of his brother-in-law; his defence being that the fatal stabbing was an accident. After closing speeches, Radio Clyde reported that he had offered to plead guilty to a reduced charge of culpable homicide. This had not been said in open court and, in any case, was not consistent with a plea of accident.

17.17   Lord Allanbridge took the exceptional step of polling the jury to see how many had heard the offending broadcast and it turned out that seven out of the 15 had. The judge fined Colin Adams, the news editor of Radio Clyde, £20,000 and Gavin Bell, the freelance who had sent out the story, £5,000. He also decided the prejudice was so great that the trial must be halted.

RESPONSIBILITY OF PUBLISHER? EDITOR? JOURNALIST?

17.18   Mr Trainer was retried at the High Court in Edinburgh and acquitted. Mr Adams appealed against his fine, which was quashed by three appeal court judges. Lord Emslie said that Mr Adams had relied on the expertise of a freelance journalist with 20 years' experience and it was difficult to attach any blame to him for what had happened.

17.19   The case is also interesting for anyone trying to answer the question of who is liable for contempt. In many cases it will be the publisher and editor, but *Adams, Petitioner* (1987) illustrates that freelance reporters and other journalists can also be found liable and fined. A freelance was found guilty of common law contempt in February 1997 after he incorrectly filed a report for the *Scottish Daily Mail* and *Daily Record* and fined £750, but this finding was quashed on appeal, as he had simply misheard evidence in a crowded courtroom (*Donald, Petitioner* (1998)) [see **para.18.03**]. A BBC journalist was fined £500 in 2001 in England for accidentally naming a witness who should have been anonymised: *Att Gen v BBC* (2001). It will depend on the particular circumstances of each case.

THE IMPORTANCE OF "LEGALLING"

As we have seen in the *John Cronin* case [see **paras 15.28 onwards**], the   17.20
court decided that since the stories in question had been submitted for legal checking, the reporters could not be held responsible for what happened after that. It is obviously good practice for a journalist to get a difficult story "legalled" if there is legal advice available. If the court then takes a different view of, say, "substantial risk", the individual journalist will almost certainly be protected unless the error is a factual one due to the journalist's own misreporting [see **para.17.25**].

EVIDENCE NOT YET HEARD

Defence lawyers still sometimes complain where a publication refers   17.21
to evidence which has not yet been led in court. Unsuccessful objection was taken on this ground to a *Scotsman* headline, "Tortured for money, murdered, chopped up and dumped in sea" in February 2009 during the trial for the murder in Arbroath of Jolanta Bledaite, a Lithuanian migrant worker.

   In law, a journalist reporting court proceedings has no obligation to   17.22
follow the choreography favoured by Crown or defence lawyers. The obligation is to avoid a substantial risk of serious prejudice. However, it would be wrong to assume that it is always safe to include information from outside the courtroom in reports of criminal cases because the protection given by s.4(1) of the 1981 Act only covers a fair and accurate contemporaneous report of court proceedings. There will usually be no substantial risk where the information consists simply of facts which are already known or about to become known to members of the jury and will not therefore influence their minds in reaching their verdict. It should always be clear that it does not form part of the proceedings as such.

   Journalists must also be wary of reporting trials at an early stage   17.23
when all that has happened is that an indictment has been read to the jury. Scottish judges tend to disapprove of phrases such as, "The court was told" or "The court heard" at this stage. They take the view that

this gives the impression that evidence has been led, when in fact, it has not.

17.24   If basing a story simply on allegations in the indictment, it is safer to use a phrase such as, "The Crown alleges" or "The indictment states". To a journalist the distinction may seem artificial and pointless, but the courts regard it as important.

17.25   It can be highly dangerous to mix together background with what is said in court. In December 1991, the BBC were fined £5,000 over a television news report on a drugs trial in Shrewsbury, a report described by Watkins L.J. in the High Court as "strewn with error" (*Att Gen v BBC* (1991)). Counsel for the BBC told the court:

> "There was a series of mistakes, in no small measure due apparently to the inability of this reporter to distinguish what he had heard and seen in court on the one hand, and what he had been told some time before in briefings by Customs and Excise."

17.26   It is also possible to commit contempt through a simple misunderstanding of criminal procedure. In 1990 the Aberdeen *Press and Journal* was found guilty of contempt over a report of a murder trial which was headed: "Husband decides on no defence in wife-murder trial". This was based on the first paragraph of the story which stated that the accused had decided not to defend the charge. In fact all that had happened was that his defence counsel had decided not to call any witnesses in support of his not guilty plea. After an unqualified apology by the editor, Lord Cameron decided that the contempt had been purged.

IMPEDIMENT

17.27   A contempt risk can arise if the publication risks *impeding* the trial, rather than actually prejudicing it. In the unusual but compelling case of *Att Gen v Random House* (2009), Tugendhat J. granted an injunction to restrain publication of a book called *The Terrorist Hunters* before the jury gave their verdicts on an airline bombing plot. The judge said that he was not sure that the trial would be prejudiced, but it might be seriously impeded by jury investigations, defence applications and resultant delay.

WITNESSES

CONTEMPT IN CIVIL AND CRIMINAL CASES

It should not be forgotten that, like jurors, witnesses—or, at least, lay 17.28
witnesses—may be regarded as vulnerable to influence, of various
kinds, from the media.

IDENTIFICATION EVIDENCE

In one of the most recent Scottish contempt findings, Sheriff Douglas 17.29
Allan, in September 2007, fined the *Sun*, the *Daily Record* and STV
£1,750 each for showing a photograph of footballer Derek Riordan
during his trial for assault. Although there was no jury, Sheriff Allan
held that this created a substantial risk of serious prejudice because the
witnesses would be asked physically to identify Derek Riordan (as is
normal in a Scottish trial). Although his was a well-known face to
those in the local area who were interested in football, these
particular witnesses did not know who he was.

The *Daily Record* unsuccessfully appealed, the Appeal Court 17.30
observing:

"… it appears to us that [the photograph's] publication created a
not insubstantial risk that the memory of the witness who had
already started giving evidence, but had not yet been cross-
examined, might be reinforced and thus make his identification
of Mr Riordan more confident: and the other witness, who had
not yet started his evidence, might be assisted in his
identification by publication of the photograph" (*Scottish Daily
Record and Sunday Mail Ltd v Thomson* (2009)).

Witness identification was the issue in *Att Gen v Express Newspapers* 17.31
(2004), where the *Daily Star* was fined £60,000 for identifying two
footballers as the subject of allegations of gang rape. Warnings had
repeatedly been issued by the Attorney General and the Metropolitan
Police that identification was an issue and requests had been made that
the suspects should not be named. The alleged victim had not been able
to identify the men and the court rejected the idea that she could have
worked it out through a process of elimination based on internet
rumour.

CRITICISING, INFLUENCING OR DETERRING WITNESSES

17.32   Again, the prosecution of the *Mail on Sunday* over the interview with a priest about his relationship with murder victim Angelika Kluk presumably arose from concern that an important witness, possibly the last person other than the murderer to see her alive, was published giving a particular version of events.

17.33   The question of whether witnesses might be influenced by something they had read was also at the centre of a case at Dumbarton Sheriff Court in November 1999 in which the publishers and acting editor of the *Daily Record* were each fined £500 for contempt. The journalist who wrote the story was also found guilty of contempt but escaped with an admonition because she had no say in how her report was presented. The young age of the witnesses involved seemed to play an important part in the sheriff's decision.

17.34   Sheriff Tom Scott was told that the newspaper had published the offending article on the eve of a children's hearing into alleged ill-treatment and assault involving an eight-year-old girl. The girl was due to give evidence, along with two other family members aged under 16.

17.35   The Reporter to the Children's Panel argued that the evidence of the young girl was likely to be tainted by publication of the newspaper article at such a critical time. The *Daily Record* submitted that it was unlikely that an eight-year-old would have read the article or, even if she had, understood it sufficiently for it to colour her evidence in court. Their counsel also pointed out that the newspaper had received clear and unequivocal legal advice that the article was safe to publish.

17.36   Sheriff Scott was satisfied that the article had created a substantial risk of prejudicing the evidence of all three children. He accepted that the hearing was concerned with events that had taken place nine months previously but added: "On the very day before three children were due to give evidence one of them was branded a liar in the newspaper and that created a risk of prejudice" [see **Chapter 25**].

17.37   In *Ex p. HTV Cymru* (2000) [see **para.15.43**], the broadcasters were planning to transmit a documentary as soon as the jury had returned a verdict. It had intended to interview at least one witness who had already given evidence on behalf of the Crown. The Crown, supported by the defendant, obtained an injunction stopping the media from contacting or interviewing any witness who had given or was likely to give evidence. The court accepted that such an approach could alter the witnesses' view of the evidence they had given, particularly since several of the witnesses were clearly vulnerable and impressionable. It was even suggested that a witness might be unwilling to give further evidence at all. There was a peculiarity in this case in that at least one prosecution witness was going to have to be recalled before the Crown closed its case. It was accepted by the court that, once the evidence had closed, any risk of this sort flew off and HTV would be able to proceed.

A similar point, about possible reluctance of a witness to return to court to complete evidence, arose in *Att Gen v BBC* **(2001)**, where the BBC and one of its journalists were found in contempt for naming a Crown witness in the third of a series of trials arising out of allegations of indecent assault in an approved school in the 1950s and 60s. The witness had said that he would be happy to give evidence on the understanding that details about him would not be publicly released. It was held that this amounted to contempt because it created a substantial risk that the witness would be unwilling to return to court, that he would not do himself justice in giving evidence, or that other witnesses would be unwilling to give evidence. The BBC was fined £25,000, plus an additional penalty of up to £25,000 in costs. 17.38

Whilst the Court of Appeal lifted the injunction restraining Channel Five in the *Gangsters* documentary case discussed above [see **para.15.42**], the perceived problem there, too, was principally the effect on witnesses. 17.39

The safest advice is that interviewing witnesses needs to be approached with care, if it is done at all. In most cases, it will not be appropriate for the media to interview a witness before s/he has given evidence, and only then if there is no likelihood of recall. 17.40

Intimidation of witnesses, by anybody, is of course contempt and press harassment might also be [see in relation to Dunblane at **para.15.54**]. The courts, however, have been slow to assume that witnesses will be influenced by more subtle press behaviour. 17.41

Sheriff William Palmer said in the Dunoon Sheriff Court fatal accident inquiry into a hillwalking accident [see **para.15.60**] that the witnesses would fulfil their oaths regardless of what they read in a newspaper, but the question of influencing witnesses remains an interesting one. 17.42

It has been decided in at least one sheriff court case (*Tudhope v Glass* **(1981)**) that witnesses would not be affected by pre-trial publicity, either by having their evidence tainted or by being discouraged from coming forward. Also, in the *Stuurman* case (*HM Advocate v Stuurman* **(1980)**) Lord Emslie said: "We are not impressed by the supposed risk that the evidence of witnesses would or might be tainted by anything they had read or heard", following the arrest of the accused. He pointed out that the basis upon which any witness's evidence or opinion was given or expressed was open to the test of cross-examination. 17.43

17.44 The Court of Appeal in **R. *v Bieber* (2006)** in England rejected the notion that a television programme screened shortly after a verdict, entitled *Real Story—Death of a Policeman* and including interviews with a number of witnesses, "might in some unspecified way have contaminated the evidence that was given at the trial. This is pure speculation."

17.45 The alleged impact on witnesses of publicity was rejected in May 2008 as a factor in Luke Mitchell's appeal against his conviction for the murder of Jodi Jones (*Mitchell v HM Advocate* **(2008)**).

ESCAPED PRISONERS

17.46 Care must be taken in publishing reports about prisoners who have escaped from prison or from custody, in case what is said will prejudice their subsequent trial or proceedings taken against them for having escaped. It is by no means unknown for someone to plead not guilty to a charge of escaping from custody. An accused charged with attempting to defeat the ends of justice by escaping has the same basic right to protection from prejudice by publicity as any other person awaiting trial, but the extent of this right may be modified where the escaped prisoner has a record of violence and may be a danger to members of the public: the media would feel entitled to publish details sufficient to warn them. In fact this is often done, with photographs, at the request of the police. Although ultimately contempt is a matter for the court, this is unlikely to result in a contempt threat. Once the prisoner has been recaptured, the media ought normally to go back to a position of caution, especially as regards publication of previous convictions or photographs.

17.47 In 1981 a man serving life for murder was allowed out of Saughton Prison to visit his family under escort, escaped and, while at large, raped a woman. At the time of his escape an official of the Scottish Prisons Department was quoted as saying he was not considered dangerous. Next day a public warning was issued through the media, along with his photograph, with the consent of the Lord Advocate. After the man was caught and sentenced for the rape, the Scottish Home and Health Department stated that in future cases of the kind their advice to the media would be that, although a person's behaviour in prison did not suggest he would be a danger to the public, his record involved violent crime.

THE INTERNET

17.48 The implications of the internet are dealt with more fully in **Chapter 43**, but it is worth noting at this juncture that perhaps the most seminal judgment in the UK so far is Lord Osborne's in *HM Advocate v Beggs (No.2)* **(2002)**. In his opinion, internet archives were, in effect, continually republished, as and when they were downloaded:

"It appears to me unrealistic to make a distinction between the moment when the material is first published on the website and the succeeding period of time when it is available for access on demand by members of the public."

However, he did not consider that archived material not accessible by 17.49 the insertion of the accused's name into a search engine gave rise to substantial risk of serious prejudice. In *HM Advocate v Bermingham* **(2002)**, where Lord Hamilton refused to make a contempt finding against various media outlets, his Lordship said that it was speculative whether a juror was computer literate, had access to an internet site and how often a juror would use a search engine which could throw up information about an accused person, but at that time, far fewer people were online.

Angus Sinclair, who was acquitted of the 1977 World's End 17.50 murders on a no case to answer basis in 2007, unsuccessfully argued that he could not get a fair trial because of prejudicial material on the internet revealing his previous convictions and asserting his guilt of the World's End murders. The Appeal Court said the jury could be told in advance to advise if they had any knowledge about the case through the internet and instructed not to search online for information about the accused: "While the possibility remains that a juror ... might disobey ... the whole jury system depends on there being trust between judge and jury ..." (*Sinclair v HMA* **(2000)**).

In *Coia v HM Advocate* **(2008)**, the court rejected a similar 17.51 argument in a fraud case where the publications complained of were online, saying:

"In our opinion, criminal trials in our jurisdiction are not and cannot be conducted in a prophylactic vacuum. They are, and must be, conducted in the real world, of which the [Financial Services Authority] ... and the internet are parts".

These decisions should be borne in mind when a media outlet is asked 17.52 to consider the extreme step of purging its archive.

MISTAKES IN COURT REPORTS

In a number of other cases, the Scottish courts have decided that the 17.53 fact that a mistake has been made in a story will not necessarily lead to a finding of contempt. This should not however, be taken as a signal to relax standards of accuracy.

17.54   In a murder trial at the High Court in Kilmarnock in 1989, a reporter's story stated that the two victims had been "felled" by single blows. A sub-editor changed the word to "killed" and also used the word "killed" in the headline. Counsel for the editor of the *Daily Record* argued that any problem created by the story could be solved by a direction by the trial judge that the jury should concentrate solely on the evidence in court. Lord Kirkwood said that in the circumstances, he was not satisfied that the *Record* story had created a substantial risk of serious prejudice.

17.55   Lord Cameron reached a similar decision in a trial at the High Court in Glasgow in which the accused was alleged to have said: "I'll get life for it." The quote appeared in the *Herald* and *Evening Times* as: "I'll get life for what I've done". The second statement amounts to a confession, while the first may not.

17.56   This approach to reporting errors was summed up by Lord Cowie in the case of Daniel Pollock at the High Court in Airdrie in 1984 where the BBC reported details of charges which were no longer on the indictment before the jury. Lord Cowie accepted the argument that the realistic view of what a juror would think if he had heard the BBC report was that the reporter had got it wrong because the story did not coincide with the indictment. Any risk of prejudice could be cured by a simple direction to the jury to ignore the BBC report and decide the case solely on the evidence. *HMA v Pollack* **(1984)** illustrates the importance of checking with the clerk of court that the indictment in the hands of the reporter is the same as the one in the hands of the jury.

17.57   In *HM Advocate v Bermingham* **(2002)**, Lord Hamilton declined to make a finding of contempt against the *Daily Record*, Radio Forth, the website *icScotland.co.uk* and BBC Reporting Scotland for reporting evidence from a complainer that she had been raped, when in fact the evidence amounted to an allegation of attempted rape. Lord Hamilton said:

> "Let us say one member of the jury read the Daily Record. The reaction might be that they have got it wrong again. You expect that kind of thing with newspapers. [The juror] sat in the court and knew exactly what the [witness] said. Where is the prejudice in that?"

17.58   In the first, aborted trial of Luke Mitchell in 2004, the journalist in a national newspaper who had misreported evidence was called before the court, but, on giving an explanation for the inaccuracy, no further action was taken.

17.59   The same point came up in *HM Advocate v Brown and Wilson* **(2009)**, where a trial had to be deserted temporarily because of inaccurate reporting, including reference to a previous charge of assault which had been taken off the indictment in which a daughter was accused of murdering her mother with her boyfriend's assistance. The trial re-started and ultimately resulted in a conviction, with no contempt proceedings against the newspaper. This may be a useful instance for a journalist to cite when looking for an up-to-date indictment from a busy court official: accuracy is in everyone's interests.

In **HM Advocate v Meiklem and McFadden (2009)**, the *Digger*, a   17.60
Glasgow-based crime reporting publication, its owner and two reporters were brought to court for contempt over alleged misreporting of the cause of death in a murder trial, vital evidence over telephone records and criticism of an expert witness. There was no finding of contempt, but the *Digger* was heavily criticised and a public warning given.

A reporter would be unwise to believe, however, that all judges will   17.61
adopt the same approach when a mistake has been made. In the case of Alistair Keating at the High Court in Edinburgh in 1987, a fireman was accused of trying to kill his wife by wiring explosives into her car. The *Sun* ran a story in the middle of the trial giving the impression, wrongly, that the accused had admitted putting the explosives in place. The publishers of the *Sun* were fined £5,000 by Lord Mayfield.

KEY POINTS

1. It is contempt of court to publish something which creates a   17.62
   substantial risk that the course of justice in active proceedings will be seriously impeded or prejudiced.
2. In Scotland, photographs of the accused pose a particular contempt risk.
3. The risk of a contempt finding increases the closer one comes to the trial, the wider the circulation of the publication in the area where the trial takes place and the memorability of the publication.
4. It is widely believed that there is a greater chance of a contempt finding against a newspaper in Scotland than in the rest of the UK.
5. It will rarely be safe to refer to the previous convictions of an accused on an active case.
6. It can be assumed that judges, sheriffs, justices of the peace and other trained lay decision makers will not be prejudiced by media publications. However, there is a risk of improperly influencing potential jurors and, sometimes, also lay witnesses.

CHAPTER 18

DEFENCES UNDER THE CONTEMPT
OF COURT ACT 1981

By ROSALIND MCINNES

18.01   Fair and accurate contemporaneous court reporting is protected under the 1981 Act [see **Chapters 7 and 15**].

INNOCENT PUBLICATION

18.02   Under s.3 of the 1981 Act, the journalist is afforded a defence of innocent publication. The Act provides that the publisher of information will not be guilty of contempt if, having taken all reasonable care, he does not know and has no reason to suspect that proceedings are active. The burden of proving this defence lies on the publisher of the information. In an English case, *R. v Duffy* **(1996)**, it was said that:

> "Section 3 expects of journalists a high standard of care before they are in a position to avail themselves of that defence ... It would be rare, indeed, for a journalist, who writes an article suggesting that an identifiable person has committed a criminal offence, to be able to avail themselves of the statutory defence without specifically asking those in a position to know if there are any active criminal proceedings."

In that case, because the journalist had been working so closely with a senior policeman on the investigation, he was held entitled to assume (wrongly) that he would hear if the proceedings became active.

18.03   Section 3 was successfully used in Scotland in 1997 by the *Scottish Daily Mail* and *Daily Record* to cover a garbled report by a freelance who had misheard evidence in a noisy, crowded courtroom. In *HM Advocate v Belmonte* **(1996)**, Lord Weir suggested that the *Dumfries and Galloway Standard* should have contacted the Crown Office before publishing an article with a picture of George Belmonte headed, "This Man Is A Paedophile" and referring to his previous convictions for sex offences. The reporter had contacted the judiciary department, which had declined to assist, and the local police, who were unaware of the charges against Belmonte. The newspaper's circulation in Glasgow, the area of the trial, was so small that no contempt finding was made, but Lord Weir said that the only sure way was to contact the Crown Office. In many cases, since arrest alone makes proceedings active for contempt purposes, the police will be the better source. It is also doubtful whether the Crown Office could assist within a news timescale in many cases. Depending on the circumstances, either or both may need to be contacted to establish a s.3 defence at a later date. Some positive steps, however, would normally be necessary.

PUBLIC INTEREST

Section 5 provides a limited public interest defence. A publication made as, or as part of, a discussion in good faith of public affairs or other matters of general public interest, is not to be treated as contempt if the risk of prejudice to legal proceedings is merely incidental to the discussion.   18.04

This has proved a useful defence on some occasions, notably for the *Daily Mail* in the case of Dr Leonard Arthur, a paediatrician charged with the attempted murder of a Down's Syndrome baby. During the trial, the *Daily Mail* published an article by Malcolm Muggeridge in support of a pro-life candidate in a forthcoming by-election. The House of Lords decided in *Att Gen v English* **(1982)** that although the article, which did not specifically mention the *Arthur* case, did create a risk of prejudice to the trial, it was a discussion of public affairs written in good faith. Any prejudice was merely incidental. To decide otherwise would have meant that all media discussion of mercy killing would have been stifled from the time Dr Arthur was charged in February 1981 until his acquittal in November. "Discussion" was given a wide definition in the Arthur case, where it was made clear that the test was not whether the publication could easily have omitted reference to the active case, but whether the risk created was, "no more than an incidental consequence of expounding [the journalist's] main theme".   18.05

In England in 1989, s.5 was successfully deployed by the BBC to ward off the injunction of a programme about the West Midland Serious Crime Squad. The *Mail on Sunday* in 1983 also successfully pleaded an s.5 defence in the case of Michael Fagan, who became notorious as the man who managed to get into the Queen's bedroom. The state of security at Buckingham Palace was said to be a matter of the gravest public concern and an excellent example of the kind of information s.5 was designed to cover (*Att Gen v Times Newspapers Ltd* **(1983)**).   18.06

Clearly, any crime or allegation of criminal activity will raise matters of legitimate public interest, but it does not follow that any discussion will be protected by s.5. The test seems to be how close a link can be established between the trial in question and the   18.07

publication. In 1989, TVS Television (*Att Gen v TVS Television Ltd* **(1989)** was fined £25,000 and the publishers of the *Reading Standard* £5,000 after Lloyd L.J. rejected the argument that they were protected by s.5. The TV station broadcast a programme about sham bed and breakfast accommodation in Reading and the newspaper ran an article about the programme. As a result, a trial in Reading had to be aborted after nearly a month at a cost of £215,000. The case involved a local landlord who was charged with defrauding the DSS over bed and breakfast accommodation, and his picture featured in the TV programme. Lord Justice Lloyd said that the common sense test was to look to see how closely the subject matter of the discussion related to the particular legal proceedings. In this case the relationship between the two was very close (1989).

18.08   Section 5 has failed in England on other occasions, because the publication was too specific to a particular case (about an alleged bid to free a sex killer from a state hospital in one case (*Att Gen v Associated Newspapers Group plc* **(1989)**), and about the trial of an artist for theft of body parts in another (*Att Gen v Guardian Newspapers Ltd* **(1999)**)), or because of absence of "good faith" (in *Private Eye's* coverage of the former wife of the Yorkshire Ripper, who was suing *Private Eye* (*Att Gen v Hislop* **(1991)**)). It also failed to ward off an injunction stopping the book *Terrorist Hunters* from being published before the end of a trial about an airline bomb plot (*Att Gen v Random House* **(2009)**) [see **para.17.27**].

18.09   In *HM Advocate v Wilson* **(2001)**, Lord Reed, when considering his refusal to grant a s.4(2) order restricting reporting, said of a *Scotsman* article to which his attention had been drawn:

> "That article was a feature article, rather than a news report, concerned with the treatment by the legal system of the victims of child sexual abuse. The article was concerned with the ways in which a focus upon the rights of accused persons ... could conflict with the interest of victims ... The article seemed to me to be legitimate reporting of a matter of public interest."

18.10   Lord Reed was not considering an article in which the case was readily identifiable (the alleged victims were not named), nor was he considering s.5, but his comments are of interest in showing the Scottish judicial attitude to public interest reporting in a features context.

REPORTS OF THE SCOTTISH PARLIAMENT

18.11   The Scotland Act 1998 provides that a fair and accurate report made in good faith in proceedings of the Parliament in relation to a Bill or subordinate legislation will not amount to contempt under the strict liability rule. This is a limited protection compared to the position on reporting Westminster. It would not apply, for example, to the reporting of prejudicial comments about an active case made during a general debate, say, on law and order.

KEY POINTS

1. There is a defence of "innocent publication" where the publisher, having taken all care, does not know and has no reason to suspect the proceedings are active. Some form of enquiry to the police or Crown Office will normally be necessary.   18.12
2. There is a narrow public interest defence, covering discussions of public affairs. Its scope is limited.
3. A fair and accurate report made in good faith in proceedings of the Scottish Parliament in relation to legislation will not amount to contempt under the strict liability rule. Much greater protection is given to Westminster reports.

CHAPTER 19

PROTECTION OF JOURNALISTS' SOURCES

BY ROSALIND MCINNES

19.01   On the face of it, s.10 of the 1981 Act protects the confidentiality of journalists' sources. It states that no court may require the disclosure, nor will a person be guilty of contempt for refusing to disclose the source of information contained in a publication, unless it is established to the satisfaction of the court that disclosure is necessary in the interests of justice, national security or for the prevention of disorder or crime. According to the English courts, a journalist may also fall under s.10 protection before publication, and a photograph counts as "information" (*X Ltd v Morgan-Grampian (Publishers) Ltd* (1990); *Handmade Films v Express Newspapers* (1986)). It applies to civil as well as criminal proceedings—indeed "the interests of justice" may not involve legal proceedings at all.

19.02   Early experience of the section suggested that the exception was wider than the rule. In a number of cases the English courts declined to interpret the phrases "national security", "the interests of justice" and "the prevention of crime" in the media's favour.

19.03   In 1983 the *Guardian* came into possession of a secret government memorandum about publicity surrounding the arrival of cruise missiles in the United Kingdom. The Government asked the courts to order the return of the memo so that they could examine markings on it to try to discover who had leaked it. The *Guardian* claimed protection under s.10, but this was rejected by the House of Lords.

19.04   The court said that although there was no threat to national security in this particular case, the leaker might strike again, this time with more serious consequences. The result was that Sarah Tisdall, a Foreign Office clerk, was identified as the informant and jailed for six months under the Official Secrets Act 1911. This could, of course, have been avoided had the newspaper destroyed the document before any order for its return was made (*Secretary of State for Defence v Guardian Newspapers Ltd* (1984)) [see **Chapter 38**].

19.05   In 1988 the *Independent* newspaper was fined £20,000 after financial journalist Mr Jeremy Warner refused to answer questions put to him by inspectors appointed under the Financial Services Act 1986 to identify the source of suspected leaks from government departments. The inspectors claimed this information was necessary for the prevention of crime and that two articles written by Mr Warner suggested he was in possession of leaked information.

Lord Griffiths said in the House of Lords that the word "necessary"   19.06
in s.10 had a meaning somewhere between "indispensable" and
"useful". The nearest paraphrase was "really needed". The court's
view was that Mr Warner's evidence was really needed by the
inspectors for the purpose of their inquiry, which was the prevention
of crime. The judges also rejected the argument that the phrase
"prevention of crime" was limited to the situation in which
identification of the journalist's source would allow steps to be taken
to stop a particular, future, identifiable crime from being committed
(*Re An Inquiry under the Company Securities (Insider Dealing) Act
1985* **(1988)**).

EUROPEAN COURT OF HUMAN RIGHTS

In 1990, William Goodwin, a young trainee reporter on the *Engineer*   19.07
magazine, was fined £5,000 after refusing to hand over the notes of a
telephone conversation with his source. After he received information
about a private company's plans for refinancing, the company went to
court to stop publication and compel disclosure of the source. Lord
Bridge said that the phrase "interests of justice" might refer to a
company's wish to discipline a disloyal employee, even though legal
proceedings might not be needed to achieve that (*X Ltd v Morgan-
Grampian (Publishers) Ltd* **(1990)** [see **para.19.01**]). However, the
European Court of Human Rights in 1996 held that Goodwin's
art.10 rights had been violated (*Goodwin v United Kingdom* **(1996)**).

The European Court has also taken a consistently strong position   19.08
on the undesirability of searching journalist's homes or offices,
finding for the journalists in *Roemen and Schmit v Luxembourg*
(2003), *Ernst v Belgium* **(2003)**, *Voskuil v Netherlands* **(2007)** and
Tillack v Belgium **(2007)**. In *Tillack*, a *Stern* journalist had had 16
cases of documents (one of which the police lost for seven months),
two computers and four mobile phones seized by the police, after he
published articles about financial irregularities in the European
Union institutions.

In *Financial Times Ltd v United Kingdom* **(2009)**, the *Financial*   19.09
Times won a major protection of sources victory in Strasbourg, over
its refusal to hand over a document which could have identified a
source in connection with a story about a Belgian brewing
company—making the UK a two-time loser in the European Court
of Human Rights over the failure to protect journalistic sources. In
September 2010, the Grand Chamber of the European Court of
Human Rights gave another decision strongly in favour of protecting
journalistic sources in *Sanoma v The Netherlands* **(2010)**.

SUCCESSFUL SOURCE AND JOURNALISTIC
MATERIAL PROTECTION CASES

19.10   In the UK, over the same period, matters generally have gone much less well for journalists seeking to protect sources and other confidential material. There have been successes. Daniella Garavelli, then chief reporter of the *Newcastle Journal*, successfully pleaded a s.10 defence in a case in 1996 over her refusal to reveal to a police disciplinary tribunal the sources of a story. Lord Justice Beldam, sitting with Smith J. in the High Court, said that Ms Garavelli had put before the public fully and fairly a question of considerable public importance and the court dismissed an application for her committal to prison for contempt. The story involved allegations that senior police officers in Northumbria might be massaging crime figures: *Chief Constable v Garavelli* **(1997)**.

19.11   In *R. v Shannon* **(2000)**, the Court of Appeal upheld *News of the World* journalist's Mazoor Mahmood's refusal to disclose the identity of an informant who had provided information about an actor's involvement in drug dealing.

19.12   The Court of Appeal in *R. v Bieber* **(2006)** [see **para.17.44**] declined to order the producers of a programme to hand over to a convicted murderer the material they had available when making a documentary about the killing and the way in which it had been put together. The court said that it was "pure speculation" that the making of the programme might have contaminated the evidence of the witnesses.

... AND FAILURES

19.13   More frequently, however, source protection arguments have failed. They did in the Court of Appeal case of *Camelot Group Plc v Centaur Communications Ltd* **(1998)**, over leaked accounts relating to the National Lottery. Section 10 also failed the website operators in *Totalise v Motley Fool* **(2003)**, who were ordered to disclose the identity of a user who had posted defamatory comments on the site.

19.14   On Halloween 2007, in *Assistant Deputy Coroner for Inner West London v Channel Four Television Corporation and the Ritz Hotel Ltd* **(2008)**, Eady J. (who for some reason put both "the public interest" and "journalistic materials" in inverted commas in his judgment) granted a coroner's witness summons against Channel Four to produce journalistic documents about the death of the Princess of Wales, despite source protection arguments. The judge did, however, order disclosure only to the coroner, in the first instance.

Equivalent arguments under the Terrorism Act 2000 failed Shiv   19.15
Malik, who was writing a book, *Leaving Al-Qaeda: Inside the Mind
of a British Jihadist* (**R. (on the application of Malik) v Manchester
Crown Court (2008)**) [see **para.40.07**]. He did, though, succeed in
limiting the amount of his material he was obliged to hand over to the
authorities.

The unfortunate Robin Ackroyd, an investigative journalist of   19.16
distinction, spent most of the early years of the millennium embroiled
in litigation over his refusal to name sources who had provided him
with Ian Brady's medical records. Ultimately, in the Court of Appeal
in 2007, the protection of his sources was permitted, on fairly narrow
grounds that a good deal of time had passed and some new evidence
had emerged (**Mersey Care NHS Trust v Ackroyd (No.2) (2007)**).
The saga of who leaked Ian Brady's medical records went to the
Court of Appeal in 2000, 2003 and 2007, and to the House of Lords
in 2002, not counting the single judge decisions.

HEALTH WARNING RE PROMISING
ANONYMITY TO A SOURCE

It will be obvious that a journalist who gives a promise of anonymity   19.17
to a source may need a strong stomach, access to a full bank account
and the willingness to apply to Strasbourg, possibly from a cell. The
qualified protection given by s.10 of the 1981 Act remains a
precarious peg for the journalist's hat.

RISK TO LIFE

The Appeal Chamber of the International Criminal Tribunal for the   19.18
former Yugoslavia in 2002 set aside a summons to the *Washington
Post* reporter, Jonathan Randal, to give evidence at the trial of a
former interviewee. The court accepted the argument that such
courts should "call journalists last", i.e. only where their evidence
was vital and could not be obtained from another route.

It has to be borne in mind that, as well as compromising the ability   19.19
to carry out the journalistic function, orders which compel journalists,
directly or indirectly, to reveal their sources, put journalists' own lives
and their families' lives at risk. In 2007, the Council of Europe issued
guidelines to Member States that, to ensure their safety, journalists
should not be required to hand over notes, photographs, video or
audio in crisis situations (Recommendation No.R/2000/7 of the
Committee of Ministers to Member States on the Right of
Journalists not to Disclose Their Sources of Information).

19.20   Northern Ireland investigative reporter Suzanne Breen was allowed in June 2009 not to reveal Real IRA source material, in response to an order sought under the Terrorism Act 2000, but there was no discussion of s.10 of the 1981 Act in that case, only of art.10 and the protection given to journalistic material within the 2000 Act itself [see **Chapter 40**]. The main consideration in the decision was the genuine and continuing risk to her, her partner's and their baby's lives had she revealed the source material (*Breen* **(2009)**).

SCOTTISH CASES ON DISCLOSURE
OF JOURNALISTIC SOURCES

19.21   There has been a scarcity of decisions by the Scottish courts on s.10. In the case of *Daily Record* journalist Gordon Airs (*HM Advocate v Airs* **(1975)**), the High Court took the view that a journalist witness who refused to answer a competent and relevant question was guilty of contempt. Lord Emslie took the view that it was hard to imagine any circumstances in which a relevant question could be judged unnecessary. *Airs* predates the 1981 Act and subsequent developments.

19.22   In *Moffat v News Group* **(1999)**, a director of STV and a journalist, who were suing over allegations that they were having an adulterous affair, sought an order requiring the newspaper to say who its witnesses were. The newspaper objected that this would involve disclosing journalistic sources. Lord Eassie refused to make the order on other grounds, but added, "[s]ince the burden of establishing veritas lies with the [newspaper] any decision on their part not to lead the evidence of the primary sources ... would be to their forensic disadvantage", and therefore some special reason would probably be necessary to obtain compulsory disclosure of journalistic sources.

JOURNALISTIC MATERIAL

19.23   There is limited cultural and legal acceptance of the importance of protecting journalistic material in Scots law. The provisions in the Police and Criminal Evidence Act 1984 (PACE), which provide special protection for journalistic material in England, have no direct equivalent in Scotland, and the protection for such material given in Sch.5 Pt 1 of the Terrorism Act 2000 does not apply in Scotland [see **Chapter 40**]. A refusal to supply untransmitted journalistic material without a court order—in accordance with the BBC Guidelines and promises to contributors—to the Fraser Inquiry into the Scottish Parliament building was attacked by the counsel to the inquiry as "arrogance" in May 2004.

NO FISHING

Anyone seeking documents, tapes, etc. under a court order has to give 19.24 reasons. There can be no "fishing" request. A "specification of documents" in a court case is sometimes sought for the recovery of journalistic material. The BBC was forced to defend itself in September 2004 in the early stages of the murder trial of Luke Mitchell, after an over-broad specification of documents was sent in a blunderbuss fashion to Scottish broadcast media, looking for everything which had been broadcast on the case. Lord Nimmo-Smith granted a very much more limited order after hearing representations from the BBC and STV.

KEY POINTS

1. Section 10 of the Contempt of Court Act 1981 states that no 19.25 court may require the disclosure of a journalistic source unless it is necessary in the interests of justice, national security or for the prevention of disorder or crime.
2. The European Court of Human Rights is strongly in favour of the protection of journalistic sources and very much against searches of journalists' homes or offices.
3. However, protection given to journalistic sources in the UK has remained inconsistent and relatively weak.
4. The Scottish courts will not grant broad orders for recovery of journalistic material, even broadcast material, without adequate reason, in principle.

CHAPTER 20

PROTECTING AND RESTRICTING
COURT REPORTING UNDER THE CONTEMPT
OF COURT ACT 1981

By Rosalind McInnes

20.01 The 1981 Act states in s.4 that a fair and accurate report of legal proceedings, held in public, published contemporaneously and in good faith, will not be contempt of court.

CONTEMPORANEOUS

20.02 The exact meaning of "contemporaneous" reporting in the contempt context is still vague. However, a defamation decision in *Arthur Bennett v Newsquest (London) Ltd* (2006), in England, suggests that a relatively generous view of contemporaneous reporting may be taken—looser, at any rate, than "as soon as possible", though, for safety's sake, that remains the gold standard.

PRELIMINARY HEARINGS

20.03 In 1986 at the High Court in Edinburgh Lord Sutherland refused to hold the *Herald* newspaper in contempt over a story about mobbing and rioting in Peterhead jail. The *Herald* carried a story of a court hearing before the trial headlined, "Killer accuses prison officers" and defence counsel objected in the strongest possible terms to jurors being told that his client was a killer. He described the report as grave contempt.

20.04 Lord Sutherland pointed out, however, that the references to the accused's murder convictions had been made in open court at the preliminary hearing and what the *Herald* had done was to report the proceedings in court. Given the terms of s.4, there was no contempt.

20.05 A blanket s.4(2) order [see **para.20.28**] preventing the reporting of any of the preliminary hearings, past or future, in the perjury case arising out of Tommy Sheridan's defamation trial was successfully challenged in July 2010.

LEGAL DEBATE IN JURY'S ABSENCE

In February 1985, McCowan J., the judge trying the case of civil 20.06
servant Mr Clive Ponting, *R. v Ponting* **(1985)**, asked the Attorney
General to consider a prosecution for contempt against the *Observer*
newspaper. During the trial of Mr Ponting, who was charged with a
breach of the Official Secrets Act 1911, the newspaper published the
contents of a legal debate outwith the presence of the jury.

The judge said he had made no order banning publication, because, 20.07
"I assumed that the greenest reporter on his first day on a provincial
newspaper with a circulation of 1,000 would know that he should not
report remarks made in the absence of the jury". However, the
Attorney General later confirmed that he would not prosecute the
newspaper.

In March 1991, the publishers of the *Evening Times* were fined 20.08
£5,000 and the editor £500 at Paisley by Sheriff James Spy. The sheriff
said the newspaper had given details "for all the world to see" of
information which had been kept from a jury. The jury in the trial
had been reduced to 14 after one of their number claimed to know
one of the accused. This had been the subject of a legal debate
outwith the presence of the jury where the accused's lawyer said his
client did not know any of the jurors, and that if one of the jurors
knew his client, it could only be "by reputation".

The *Evening Times* reported what had happened outwith the jury's 20.09
presence and the sheriff halted the trial after ruling that the report had
created a substantial risk that the two accused would not receive a fair
hearing. This was disputed by the newspaper, which also argued that
despite the absence of the jury the proceedings were in public.

On appeal, the findings of contempt and the fines were set aside after 20.10
the Crown said it did not support them. Unfortunately, since no
reasons were given for the Crown's view and no written judgment
was issued by the court, it is difficult for the journalist to obtain any
guidance from the appeal.

In principle, the view at least of the English Court of Appeal is that, 20.11
whenever the court deliberately sends out the jury to keep them in
ignorance of what is said—or indeed, when before a jury has been
empanelled there are potentially prejudicial discussions in open
court—it is for the court to make an order restricting reporting. Lord
Denning said in *R. v Horsham Justices Ex p. Farquharson* **(1982)**:

> "Section 4(2) retains the common law about the occasions when a
> report (otherwise fair and accurate) may be a contempt of
> court—but with this improvement: Nothing is left to
> implication. It is for the court to make an order telling the
> newspapers what things they are not to publish ... Thus, when

the jury is sent out, the judge should tell the newspaper reporters, 'You are not to publish anything of what takes place whilst the jury are out' …".

20.12 Traditionally, the Scottish media's practice has been to exercise care over reporting legal debate in the absence of the jury, so as not to risk prejudicing a trial. A journalist who could be shown not to have published "in good faith" would not be entitled to the protection of s.4(1), which could have some bearing here. If the jury has specifically been sent out so that the admissibility of evidence may be considered by the judge, or if a plea in bar of trial is taking place, in which the defence is discussing existing prejudicial publicity, reporting obviously damaging information might be a contempt risk even if the judge has omitted to make an order.

RESTRICTIONS ON COURT REPORTS UNDER THE CONTEMPT OF COURT ACT 1981

20.13 The Privy Council in case of ***Independent Publishing Co Ltd v Att Gen of Trinidad and Tobago* (2004)** held that there was no common law power to order the postponement of court reporting—though it could nonetheless in certain situations be a common law contempt to report. The Appeal Court of the High Court of Justiciary had already said in ***Caledonian Newspapers Ltd, Petrs* (1995)** that there was no common law power to impose restrictions sought in that case.

20.14 Under s.4(2) of the 1981 Act, a court may order that a report of proceedings, or any part of them, should be postponed for as long as the court thinks necessary to avoid a risk of prejudice to the proceedings. Section 4(2) says:

> "In any [legal proceedings held in public] the court may, where it appears to be necessary for avoiding a substantial risk of prejudice to the administration of justice in those proceedings, or in any other proceedings pending or imminent, order that the publication of any report of the proceedings, or any part of the proceedings, be postponed for such period as the court thinks necessary for that purpose."

20.15 It will be noticed that the threshold for getting a reporting restriction is only "a substantial risk of prejudice", whereas the test for contempt of court is "substantial risk of serious prejudice". However, the prejudice must be to specific, pending or imminent proceedings. A fear that not to grant the order would have a generally prejudicial effect on the administration of justice would not be sufficient.

Postponements in Scotland are sometimes ordered when one 20.16
accused pleads guilty to a charge and a co-accused is to stand trial in
the near future.

In the trial of Daanish Zahid and Zahid Mohammed in November 20.17
2004 for the murder of Pollokshields teenager Kriss Donald, Lord
Philip granted an order anonymising references in the evidence to
three other suspects who had gone to Pakistan—Imran Shahid,
Mohamed Faisal Mushtaq and Zeeshan Shahid. Later, they too were
found guilty of murder. (At the first trial, Daanish Zahid was
convicted of murder, Zahid Mohammed of racially motivated
abduction and assault.)

One of the most interesting uses of a s.4(2) order in Scotland 20.18
involved a case in which a 15-year-old girl was accused of the murder
of her 18-year-old sister. She was convicted of murder in September
1998, but the media was banned from reporting anything about the
case until the end of any trial of her 14-year-old brother, who was
also suspected of having taken part in the murder. It was not until he
was acquitted in March 1999 that details of the earlier case could be
published. By that time she was 16 and her name could be published.
Defence counsel for the 14-year-old boy also agreed that the usual
restrictions on naming him in press reports should be lifted. The
background to this case, and the media's entitlement in principle to
challenge these orders before the trial judge, is set out in *Scottish
Daily Record and Sunday Mail Ltd, Petitioners* **(1998)**.

KIM GALBRAITH PRINCIPLES

In the very important case of Kim Galbraith (*HM Advocate v* 20.19
Galbraith **(2000)**) the Lord Justice General in the Appeal Court
provided welcome guidance on s.4(2) orders. He said courts must
ensure that such orders were no wider than necessary to avoid a
substantial risk of prejudice. He stressed that they covered only the
postponement of reports of court proceedings, publication of which
were fair and accurate, but nevertheless posed a substantial risk of
prejudice to the administration of justice. An order to postpone
reports of prejudicial comment not contained in a fair and accurate
report of proceedings in open court would be an abuse of the power
contained in s.4(2).

Ms Galbraith had been convicted of murdering her husband, a 20.20
policeman, and one of her grounds of appeal was that she had not
received a fair hearing because of adverse publicity during the trial
about her counsel Donald Findlay QC. One possible outcome of the
appeal was a retrial. It was argued that there should be no reporting
of the appeal proceedings, possibly until the end of any retrial. Much

of the reporting of the original trial was said to have been hostile and it was anticipated that the appeal would be reported in much the same way if no s.4(2) order were granted. A barrage of hostile media comment would be likely to poison the minds of potential jurors at any retrial. Lord Rodger pointed out, however, that comment of that kind would not be protected as a fair and accurate report of court proceedings:

> "The court's power in section 4(2) is not intended to be used to deal with such publications but to deal, rather, with reports of its proceedings which are fair and accurate but should nonetheless be postponed. It would accordingly be an abuse of this particular power to pronounce an order … not for the purpose of warding off an anticipated consequence of the fair and accurate reporting of the appeal proceedings but for the purpose of warding off prejudicial comment which those proceedings might prompt."

20.21   As to the argument that even a fair and accurate report of the appeal proceedings would substantially prejudice the right to a fair retrial, Lord Rodger said that the order sought was in the widest terms and would exclude reporting of legal arguments that would be unlikely to have any bearing on the jury's assessment of evidence at any retrial. He added, however, that the position might be different if the appeal court were dealing with prejudicial and inadmissible material, such as previous convictions. A s.4(2) order had to be narrowly drawn. The Appeal Court here refused to grant any order:

> "Even if we examine those parts of the evidence which might relate to the evidence led at the trial we see no reason to anticipate at present that a fair and accurate report of the appeal hearing would create a substantial risk of prejudice to the fairness of any possible retrial.
>
> This court and courts in other jurisdictions have frequently had occasion to express their confidence—based on accumulated experience over many years—in the ability of jurors, when properly directed, to reach their verdict on the evidence led at the trial unaffected by any extraneous considerations … We are confident that … jurors who had read and remembered reports of the appeal proceedings would still be able to reach an impartial verdict at any retrial."

20.22   Since *Galbraith*, interested parties such as editors or media lawyers can opt in to receive notice of reporting restrictions made by the Scottish courts. Such orders take effect straightaway, but do not become final until 48 hours have elapsed. During the interim, the media may approach the court—usually via the clerk—to challenge such an order as incompetent, inappropriate, over-broad, etc.

Galbraith has been influential in curbing unnecessary or over-broad 20.23 reporting restrictions. It was quoted with approval by the English Court of Appeal in the **Barot** terrorism case (**Re B (2006)**). Although a great many such orders are still granted, the senior Scottish judiciary has increasingly turned a critical eye on them.

BASRA CASE

In **BBC, Petitioners (2001)**, a s.4(2) order had been granted by the trial 20.24 judge in relation to a case where the accused (ultimately convicted) was blaming another man, who had also, originally, been arrested for the murder of shopkeeper, Mr Basra. Both the advocate depute and defence counsel unsuccessfully argued that anonymised reporting by the BBC of an element of the trial which fell under the order was a contempt. The trial judge held that it was not. The original s.4(2) restriction was withdrawn, and a more limited one put in its place. Ultimately that order, too, was withdrawn, with the approval of the Appeal Court, which emphasised the importance of open justice to the wider public interest, not just that of the parties. Lord Rodger said:

> "Of course, a court which is called upon to make an order under Section 4(2) must bear in mind that restrictions on the publication of the proceedings in our courts are exceptions to the general rule in favour of publication ... A court must be careful to bear that wider public interest in mind, especially in those cases where— for whatever reasons—the parties themselves would wish the court to make an order ... Even in those situations, the court must consider not only whether such an order is 'necessary' but also what the appropriate scope of any order might be."

In **HM Advocate v Wilson (2001)**, Lord Reed refused to make a 20.25 s.4(2) order in a complex trial involving multiple child sex abuse allegations, in the wake of a feature article in the *Scotsman* concerned with the legal system's treatment of victims of child abuse:

> "The article seemed to me to be legitimate reporting of a matter of public interest. It did not contain any details which would enable jurors readily to identify the present case as being one of those discussed ... Even if there were such a risk, it seemed to me that it would be possible to eliminate the risk by the usual directions to a jury, and if necessary ... special directions ...".

20.26   In *HM Advocate v Beggs (No.1)* (2001), Lord Osborne, following the Appeal Court in *Galbraith*, refused to grant a s.4(2) order which would have the effect of postponing the reporting of the entire trial of William Beggs, who was ultimately convicted of the murder of Barry Wallace. Senior counsel's acceptance that he would have "no problem" with fair and accurate reporting was "clearly fatal" to the motion for a s.4(2) order. The Appeal Court of the High Court of Justiciary endorsed this approach in March 2010, rejecting Beggs's ground of appeal based on prejudicial publicity.

20.27   An order was lifted by Lord Hardie at Glasgow in similar circumstances in *HM Advocate v Gavin Brown* **(2006)**. Juror robustness had to be assumed, the court re-emphasised.

20.28   In the early stages of the Tommy Sheridan libel trial, in May 2006, Lady Smith refused to grant a s.4(2) order sought for Mr Sheridan over a contempt hearing about the refusal of Alan McCombes, co-founder of the Scottish Socialist Party (SSP), to hand over the minutes of an SSP meeting, even though the libel trial itself was to be heard by a jury. A similar approach was taken by Tugendhat J. in England, refusing an order over an early hearing in a defamation case brought by Michael Jackson's bodyguard, Michael Fiddes, against Channel 4, in 2010. Also in 2010, BBC Scotland and the *Guardian* successfully sought the lifting of a s.4(2) order preventing reporting of all the preliminary hearings in the perjury case against Tommy and Gail Sheridan arising out of the libel trial. A narrower order was put in its place.

20.29   This caution in imposing and drafting reporting restrictions was echoed south of the border in October 2006 in the powerful decision by the Court of Appeal (*Re B* **(2006)** [see **para.20.23**]), to allow contemporaneous reporting of the sentencing of Barot, who had pled guilty to conspiracy to commit mass murder, despite the existence of a pending trial against his original co-defendants, at which Barot's conviction would be admissible as evidence. The Court of Appeal said:

> "In our view ... editors should be trusted to fulfil their responsibilities accurately to inform the public of court proceedings ... The risk of being in contempt of court ... is an important safeguard, and it should not be overlooked simply because there are occasions when there is widespread and ill-judged publicity in some parts of the media."

20.30   In 2009, the media resisted an attempt in England to obtain a s.4(2) order which would have prevented the reporting of the trial of Peter Tobin for the murder of Dinah McNicol, on the argument that Tobin was appealing his conviction against the murder of Scottish schoolgirl Vicky Hamilton. The McNicol trial was fully reported.

20.31   This does not mean that a s.4(2) order will never be appropriate.

In **R. v Sherwood Ex p. Telegraph Group (2001)**, the Court of   20.32
Appeal regretfully upheld a s.4(2) order covering the whole of a trial
against an individual police officer who had fatally shot an unarmed
man in his own home. This was because the policeman's senior
officers were to be tried about three months later on charges of
misfeasance in public office. The two trials had deliberately been
severed, to avoid prejudice. The Court of Appeal considered the
passage of time, a possible change of venue, the robustness of jurors,
limitations on the reporting restriction, and so on, but took the view
that it would be worse to create distorted contemporaneous reporting
through a more limited reporting restriction than simply to have a
three-month blackout. They set out a three stage test for the granting
of s.4(2) orders: (1) whether reporting would give rise to a "not
insubstantial" risk of prejudice; (2) whether a s.4(2) order would
eliminate that risk; and (3) whether, even if the answers to (1) and
(2) were both "yes", an order should be made at all. The
circumstances in *Sherwood* were admittedly unusual.

POSTPONEMENT ONLY

Section 4(2) can only be used to postpone reporting, not to prevent it   20.33
forever. In *Times Newspapers v R* **(2008)**, the Court of Appeal said:

> "Section 4(2) is designed to enable the court to prevent the
> publication of the report of proceedings where the publication
> will prejudice the conduct of those proceedings, or specific
> pending proceedings ... The section permits postponement and
> the need for postponement cannot subsist beyond the end of the
> proceedings in question."

Section 4(2) orders should not be indefinite. It will often not be   20.34
possible for the court to attach a particular calendar date at which the
order will end, but it should be able to stipulate the stage at which the
postponement ends. If it is not, it is unlikely to be a proper case for the
use of s.4(2), which is not designed to protect either privacy or the
administration of justice in the abstract. It is there to postpone
reports in order to protect specific proceedings.

SECTION 11

Section 4(2) orders are not, however, the only reporting restriction   20.35
available under the 1981 Act. There is also s.11, which reads:

> In any case where a court (having power to do so) allows a name or other matter to be withheld from the public in proceedings before the court, the court may give such directions prohibiting the publication of that name or matter in connection with the proceedings as appear to the court to be necessary for the purpose for which it was so withheld.

20.36 Section 4(2) orders can be used to postpone reporting only; s.11 orders operate as a permanent censorship of the information unless lifted. Since the s.11 order is confined to a court "having power to do so", the particular court seeking to use it should normally be able to establish such a power exists [see **para.20.13**].

20.37 Section 11 orders have been made in England and Wales since 1981 with reasonable regularity, but were not part of the Scottish landscape until 2007. Indeed, as recently as *X v BBC* **(2005)**, Lord Carloway declined at an earlier hearing to grant either a s.4(2) order or a s.11 order anonymising the pursuer. The pursuer in that case, who was attempting to prevent the transmission of a documentary about the sheriff court featuring her story, was unable to cite any case where the court in Scotland had exercised such a power in such a case, so Lord Carloway considered that he had no power to grant a s.11 order. However, in the case of *HM Advocate v Mola* **(2007)**, without having heard argument, Lord Hodge issued a judgment stating that s.11 could be used in Scotland to anonymise a complainer whose partner had knowingly infected her with HIV. Wholly predictably, other s.11 orders have followed.

20.38 This may be of limited future significance, simply because the Scottish courts thus far have tended to use them to protect complainers in sexual offences cases, who would never have been named either as an example of Scottish journalists' ethics, or, now, under the Sexual Offences (Amendment) Act 1992, an Act of England and Wales which has been extended to Scotland since the seventh edition of this book. Moreover, the Criminal Justice and Licensing (Scotland) Act 2010 gives the court a broadly based discretion to make witness anonymity orders. This will afford a third legislative route to stop the Scottish media doing what they have never done as regards naming alleged victims of sexual offences, but it goes well beyond that in its scope.

20.39 However, since s.11 is worryingly amorphous and under-analysed, some of the English case law on s.11 should perhaps be mentioned. The Court of Appeal stated in *R. v Barry George* **(2002)** that a s.11 order should only remain in force for the time necessary to fulfil its purpose. In that case (the first Jill Dando murder trial), a s.11 order prohibiting publication of photographs of the appellant's face pending identification parades had been lifted—rightly, in the view of the

Court of Appeal—once the identification parades had finished. In *R. v Times Newspapers* **(2007)**, a question had been accidentally put and answered in the public part of a trial which should have formed part of evidence heard in private. Section 4(2) can only be used to postpone reporting, not to ban it altogether. Thus a s.4(2) order was inappropriate. However, the Court of Appeal said a s.11 order could have been made instead.

In *R. (on the application of Trinity Mirror Plc) v Croydon Court* **(2008)**, the Court of Appeal refused to allow s.11 (or s.4(2)) to be used to anonymise a sex offender in order to protect his two primary school age daughters. The Court of Appeal held that s.11 was not available as the man had already been named in court and emphasised the importance of open, non-anonymised reporting of criminal trials.   **20.40**

The English courts have resisted such orders where they have been sought to spare embarrassment or commercial disadvantage. Where the information has already been revealed in open court, s.11 is not competent. In *HM Advocate v Johnson* **(2008)**, BBC Scotland successfully challenged a reporting restriction on this basis.   **20.41**

PERILS OF ANONYMISATION

Lord Steyn made it clear in the House of Lords decision in *Re S* **(2004)** [see **Chapter 25**] that: **20.42**

> "There are numerous automatic reporting restrictions ... There are also numerous statutory provisions, which provide for discretionary reporting restrictions ... Given the number of statutory exceptions, it needs to be said clearly and unambiguously that the court has no power to create by a process of analogy, except in the most compelling circumstances, further exceptions to the general principle of open justice."

The new Supreme Court has taken a critical view of what Lord Rodger called the, "deeply ingrained ... habit of anonymisation" in *HM Treasury v Ahmed* **(2010)**. Lord Rodger, delivering the unanimous judgment of the court, said: **20.43**

> "What's in a name? 'A lot', the press would answer. This is because stories about particular individuals are simply much more attractive to readers than stories about unidentified people. It is just human nature. And this is why, of course, even when reporting major disasters, journalists usually look for a story about how particular individuals are affected. Writing stories which capture the attention of readers is a matter of

reporting technique, and the European Court holds that article 10 protects not only the substance of ideas and information but also the form in which they are conveyed ... The judges are recognising that editors know best how to present material in a way that will interest the readers of their particular publication and so help them to absorb the information. A requirement to report it in some austere, abstract form, devoid of much of its human interest, could well mean that the report would not be read and the information would not be passed on."

KEY POINTS

20.44   1. Under s.4 of the Contempt of Court Act 1981, a fair and accurate report of legal proceedings, held in public, published contemporaneously and in good faith, will not be contempt of court.
           2. It is possible for the court to make an order under s.4(2) of the 1981 Act to postpone reporting of proceedings to avoid a substantial risk of prejudice to the administration of justice in those proceedings, or other pending or imminent proceedings.
           3. Section 4(2) orders cannot be used to ward against hostile reporting. They should not be granted at all unless they are necessary. Even if they are necessary, their scope should be as narrow as possible. Juries must be assumed to be robust and to take on board judicial instructions.
           4. Section 4(2) gives a power to postpone only, not permanently to censor any element of a court report.
           5. Other reporting restrictions are available to the court. The Sexual Offences (Amendment) Act 1992, which anonymises victims of certain sexual offences, now applies in Scotland. The Criminal Justice and Licensing (Scotland) Act 2010 contains provisions for witness anonymity orders.

CHAPTER 21

INTERVIEWING JURORS AND USING TAPE RECORDERS: OFFENCES

BY ROSALIND MCINNES

JURIES

Section 8 of the Contempt of Court Act 1981 protects the 21.01
confidentiality of the jury room. It is a contempt to obtain, disclose or
solicit any particulars of statements made, opinions expressed,
arguments advanced or votes cast by members of a jury in the course
of their deliberations in any legal proceedings. A journalist who
interviewed a juror about these things in a particular case would be
guilty of contempt even although nothing was ever published.

In 1994, the House of Lords decided that the prohibition applied not 21.02
just to jurors, but to anyone who published information they revealed.
They dismissed an appeal by the *Mail on Sunday* (*Att Gen v Associated
Newspapers Ltd* (1994)) against a finding of contempt after it
published interviews with jurors revealing details of jury room
discussions. The paper, editor and a journalist were fined a total of
£60,000. The European Court of Human Rights declined to criticise
this.

In *HM Advocate v Seckerson and Times Newspapers* (2009), the 21.03
newspaper and the foreman of a jury were found in contempt for
revealing that the immediate consensus of the jury was 10–2 and that
they reached their decision by "commonsense".

WHAT *CAN* BE DISCUSSED BETWEEN JURORS AND JOURNALISTS

However, a general discussion about the merits or otherwise of the 21.04
jury system would not be contempt. Nor would a discussion about
the jury in a particular case which did not depend upon asking about
or revealing particulars of their deliberations. One could ask jurors
what they thought of the judge's conduct of the case, or the sentence,
or the appropriateness of trying a child in an adult court, for example,
but one cannot stray into the territory of how such considerations
affected the jury's decision making. Great care is therefore necessary.

JOURNALISTS AS JURORS

21.05   In the *R v C* (2009) case in the Court of Appeal, the court dismissed an argument that the fact that the foreman of the jury was a *Sun* columnist meant Cornwall had not had a fair trial. Lord Justice Leveson, however, recommended that a journalist "called to serve on a jury which will have to examine issues upon which he or she has expressed strong opinions about the state of the law (rather than detection, sentence or the system generally)" should alert the judge to this.

21.06   Section 8 has not made it any easier to carry out genuine research into how juries approach their job. This is regrettable in an area like contempt where the whole approach of the courts hinges on how jurors are thought to be affected by publicity. Such research as exists from other common law jurisdictions tends to support the view that jurors are robustly un-influenced by media coverage.

TAPE RECORDERS

21.07   Section 9 makes it contempt to use a tape recorder in court, or bring one into court for use, without the court's permission. It would also be contempt to publish a recording of legal proceedings by playing it in public or to dispose of a recording with a view to publication. The section gives courts a discretion to allow tape recording under such conditions as they think fit. The courts also have power to order forfeiture of a tape recorder and any recording.

21.08   In *R. v Cullinane* (2007) in the English Court of Appeal, two men were arrested for contempt of court, one for having on his mobile phone some photographs of officers in the concourse area of the court [see **Chapter 23**] and the applicant for having a tape recorder on him on which he had recorded the bail application in a case with which he was helping. He was sentenced to four months' imprisonment for breach of s.9. The Court of Appeal plainly found this heavy handed and he was immediately released, but they did feel that some sanction was appropriate, and added that any publication of the recordings on a website would be a further contempt.

21.09   Section 9 does not apply to inquiries under the Inquiries Act 2005.

KEY POINTS

1. Section 8 of the Contempt of Court Act 1981 makes it   21.10
   contempt to obtain, disclose or solicit particulars of
   statements made, opinions expressed, arguments advanced
   or votes cast in jury deliberations. There still remains scope
   for journalists to explore jurors' experiences outwith these
   areas.
2. It may be appropriate for journalists who have adopted public
   positions on criminal justice matters to alert the court to this,
   if they are called as jurors, preferably by letting the clerk of
   court know.
3. It is contempt to use an unauthorised tape recorder in court.

CHAPTER 22

COMMON LAW CONTEMPT

By ROSALIND MCINNES

22.01   It is still possible to commit contempt of court at common law, outside the provisions of the Contempt of Court Act 1981, if the court decides that the conduct involved was intended to impede or to prejudice the administration of justice. Section 6 of the 1981 Act specifically leaves that possibility open. The kind of behaviour that the courts might regard as serious enough to amount to deliberate contempt can be seen in a case in 1988 in which the publishers of the *Sun* newspaper were fined £75,000 in England.

22.02   The authorities had decided there was not enough evidence to prosecute a doctor accused of raping an eight-year-old girl. The *Sun* financed a private prosecution and published a number of articles describing the doctor as a "beast" and a "swine". They also published his name and his picture on the front page. The doctor went to trial at Chelmsford Crown Court and was acquitted.

22.03   Lord Justice Watkins agreed with the Attorney General that the *Sun* had been guilty of contempt, even though the case was not active for the purposes of the strict liability rule. The court said that where a newspaper gave practical help to stage a private prosecution, then published a series of articles intended to prejudice a fair trial, it was guilty of contempt at common law (***Att Gen v News Group Newspapers* (1988)**).

22.04   In May 1991, the editor of the *Sport* newspaper was cleared of contempt after the Attorney General brought proceedings against him at common law (***Att Gen v Sport Newspapers Ltd* (1991)**). North Wales Police had issued a picture of David Evans, a man they wished to interview in connection with the disappearance of a schoolgirl. They asked that his previous convictions for rape and a history of sex attacks should not be published. Two days before a warrant was issued for Evans' arrest (which meant the case was not active under the 1981 Act) the *Sport* published a story headlined, "Evans was given ten years for rape".

22.05   Evans was later jailed for life for the girl's murder, and in subsequent proceedings, the High Court decided that the Attorney General had failed to show that the editor of the *Sport* had intended to prejudice a fair trial. In court, the editor defended the decision to publish Evans's record on the basis that, "he was on the run and a danger to other women".

In the course of his decision, Hodgson J. was strongly critical of the 22.06
decision in the *Sun* case. He said the decision was wrong and were it
necessary to do so, he would refuse to follow it. He warned that to
find a newspaper guilty of contempt in these circumstances could
impede investigative journalism. He added:

> "Many of the targets of investigative journalism are rich and
> powerful and who is to say that they, when attacked, will not
> respond by seeking leave to move for contempt?"

SPYCATCHER CONTEMPT

In a decision with wide-ranging implications for the media, the House 22.07
of Lords decided in April 1991 (*Att Gen v Times Newspapers* **(1991)**)
that the *Sunday Times* had been guilty of contempt at common law by
publishing extracts from the book *Spycatcher* while an injunction was
in force banning publication by a number of other newspapers. There
was no injunction restraining publication by the *Sunday Times* and the
newspaper argued that it would be an unwarranted extension of the
law to find it guilty of contempt. The newspaper maintained that
although it knew of the existence of the orders against other papers it
was not bound by them nor was it assisting a breach of the injunction
by those newspapers which were caught by the injunction. The *Sunday
Times* had received legal advice that to publish in these circumstances
would not amount to contempt.

The Attorney General, who brought proceedings against the 22.08
Sunday Times, accepted that the newspaper could not be bound by a
court order to which it was not a party. His argument, which the court
accepted, was that by publishing *Spycatcher* extracts the paper had
knowingly destroyed the whole point of the injunctions, and that was
a deliberate interference with the course of justice. Lord Ackner
pointed out that *Sunday Times* editor, Andrew Neil, knew of existing
injunctions against the *Observer* and *Guardian* and regarded
Spycatcher as "banned in Britain". To avoid the risk of an injunction
against his own paper, Mr Neil kept the *Spycatcher* extracts out of the
first edition.

Lord Ackner said that since the whole point of contempt was to 22.09
prevent interference with the course of justice, it would leave a
remarkable gap in the law if it could not deal with a situation of this
kind.

"Whatever would be the point of a court making an order designed to preserve the confidentiality of material, the subject matter of a dispute between A and B, pending the trial of the action, if, at the whim of C, the protection afforded by the court by its order could be totally dissipated?"

22.10   Lord Jauncey, one of the Scottish judges in the appeal, said he was quite satisfied that a person who knowingly acted to frustrate the operation of a court order could be guilty of contempt even though he was neither named in the order nor assisted anyone who was named to breach it. He did not accept that this necessarily converted every injunction from an order against a named person to one against the world. It was only in a limited type of case that independent action by a third party would interfere with a court order in which he was not named. (In an early decision in the *Cavendish* case (*Lord Advocate v Scotsman Publications Ltd* (1989) [see **paras 37.61 onwards**] Lord Coulsfield also suggested that this sort of publication could be contempt of court.)

22.11   However, Lord Oliver recognised the wide-ranging implications of the decision and the potential for gagging the media for a lengthy period. He stressed the importance of the courts keeping a vigilant eye on the possibility of the law of contempt being invoked in support of claims which were, in truth, insupportable. At the time, an injunction could be granted on fairly weak grounds, which would have the effect of strangling publication until the end of a trial which could be years away.

22.12   The European Court of Human Rights considered the use of injunctions in the *Spycatcher* cases. It decided that although the Human Rights Convention did not ban the use of prior restraints on publication, the dangers involved called for the most careful consideration by the court, particularly in cases where the media was involved. Nowadays, s.12 of the Human Rights Act 1998 makes it harder to get an injunction or, in Scotland, an interim interdict in such circumstances, but it is still possible [see **paras 36.28 onwards**, and see also **Chapter 38**].

22.13   Thus, even if what a journalist publishes does not fall foul of the strict liability rule, it might still interfere with the administration of justice in a *Spycatcher*-type case. In *Att Gen v Punch and James Steen* **(2003)**, the House of Lords found the *Punch* editor in contempt for publishing an article by ex-Security Services officer David Shayler in breach of an order against Shayler, rather than *Punch*. It was held that even though Steen had no intention to damage national security as such, he must be taken to have known he was undermining the court's order and pre-empting the decision it was to make on the confidentiality David Shayler owed his former employers. That was the subject of a separate litigation in relation to which the order against Shayler himself had been granted.

Similarly, in *Independent Publishing Co Ltd v Att Gen of Trinidad* 22.14 *and Tobago* **(2004)**, the Privy Council held that even though the judge in Trinidad and Tobago had no common law powers to restrict prejudicial reporting by order, a newspaper could still be in contempt if it prejudiced the administration of justice.

The Court of Appeal in *Times Newspapers Ltd v R* **(2007)**, held that 22.15 a s.11 order could cover a question and answer which had "slipped out" in public, but added that, since the effect of publishing the question and answer would be to frustrate the court's purpose in keeping that part of the evidence secret, "we consider it likely that any such [publication] would, itself, constitute a contempt of court at common law."

WILFUL BREACH OF A COURT ORDER

Deliberate breach of an injunction or interdict is itself contempt of 22.16 court, being direct disobedience of a court order. Greater Manchester Newspapers Ltd were found in contempt in 2001 (*Venables v News Group International* **(2001)**) for having breached the injunction granted, on the basis of breach of confidence, to protect the new identities of the young killers of James Bulger. Rather than giving the new identities or whereabouts of Robert Thompson and Jon Venables, they instead gave information about the respective distances of the places where they had been detained. Even though it was only partially accurate, cumulatively the information was held to be sufficient to breach the order.

CONTEMPT IN COURT

If a party to a legal action or a witness or member of the public 22.17 commits contempt by behaviour in court or makes offensive remarks or signals amounting to contempt, it will not normally be contempt for a report of the incident to be published, including quotations of what was said by the offender, provided the behaviour can be treated as relevant to the proceedings before the court. It may be a matter of degree to decide when remarks not relevant to the case are safe to publish, but proceedings for contempt are unlikely where the report is accurate. In the Moira Jones murder trial, in March 2009, the accused's manipulation of the headphones through which he was receiving simultaneous translation of the evidence—sometimes refusing to put them on—was reported. Obviously, as when an accused makes a threat to a witness in court, the jury was in a very good position to observe the behaviour, and it formed a proper part of the court report *(HMA v Harcur* (2009)). If, however, the accused throws a punch at a journalist on his way out of a Reliance van, this episode should be saved for the backgrounder.

DIGNITY OF THE COURT/"MURMURING" JUDGES

22.18   There is an old form of contempt called "murmuring judges", meaning defaming or threatening judges in relation to their professional conduct. The media would, however, be failing to meet their responsibilities if they did not criticise the judiciary and court decisions where criticism is deserved. A court would be extremely reluctant, unless in the most exceptional circumstances, to treat this as contempt of court. The Appeal Court of the High Court of Justiciary expressed themselves strongly in *HM Advocate v JT* (2005), after a storm of critical media comment about a sentence on a case reported as a "baby rape":

> "The denigration of a judge betrays gross indifference to the critical importance in a democratic society of the independence of the judiciary, and tends to harm the administration of justice ... The position is compounded when the reporting of the circumstances is inaccurate or misleading. The media have responsibilities as well as powers and duties."

22.19   There were some unusual features of that case, including harassment of the sentencing judge's family, however, and there was no attempt to bring the editors to court.

22.20   In their judgment in the Aamer Anwar case (*Anwar, Respondent* (2008)), where a solicitor had made, on his client's behalf, criticisms of a Terrorism Act 2000 conviction, the court quoted with approval what Lord President Normand had said in the earlier case of *Milburn* (1946):

> "The greatest restraint and discretion should be used by the court in dealing with contempt of court, lest a process, the purpose of which is to prevent interference with the administration of justice, should degenerate into an oppressive or vindictive abuse of the court's powers ... The court should never forget that disaffected litigants sometimes feel aggrieved and that some of them are ill-tempered, and that they may say or write things which are foolish and reprehensible. The court should be on its guard against putting an overstrained construction upon such utterances ...".

Although they said Mr Anwar's statements were misleading and 22.21
petulant, they did not find him in contempt.

Robust criticism of the efficiency of the system or the wisdom of 22.22
individuals may be acceptable, but it would be highly dangerous to
state or imply, for example, that a judge or sheriff had been guilty of
dishonest or criminal behaviour. The most likely result would be an
action for defamation.

KEY POINTS

1. Even if a publication does not fall foul of the "strict liability 22.23
   rule"—i.e. if it does not give rise to substantial risk of serious
   prejudice in relation to an active case—it could still be
   common law contempt.
2. Common law contempt covers conduct intended to impede or
   to prejudice the administration of justice.
3. Proceedings against the media for common law contempt of
   this sort have been rare, but the *Sun* was found guilty of it in
   1989 when it published prejudicial articles about a man the
   private prosecution of whom the newspaper was financially
   supporting.
4. Publication which would undermine a court order can also be
   common law contempt. In 2003, the House of Lords held the
   editor of *Punch* in contempt for publishing an article by ex-
   Security Services officer David Shayler in breach of an order
   against Mr Shayler, even though there was no order against
   Punch.
5. There is a relatively archaic form of contempt called
   "murmuring judges", but the media are entitled to criticise
   the judiciary.

PART 5: PHOTOGRAPHY AND AUDIO-TAPING

Chapter 23

PHOTOGRAPHY AND AUDIO-TAPING

By Rosalind McInnes

CONTEMPT

23.01 The publication of a photograph is just as capable as a story or a headline of creating a substantial risk of serious prejudice in terms of the Contempt of Court Act 1981. The 1981 Act makes no specific mention of pictures, but lays down rules which apply to "publications" and goes on to explain that this includes, "any speech, writing, broadcast or other communication in whatever form, which is addressed to the public at large or any section of the public". "Other communication in whatever form" will include photographs, as well as television pictures, videos, sketches, drawings or cartoons.

23.02 The 1981 Act does not, however, deal with the whole law of contempt as it affects photography, and it is still necessary to go back to the old common law for guidance, particularly over the restriction on taking or making pictures within court precincts.

23.03 It should certainly not be assumed that, although the 1981 Act is a United Kingdom statute, the Scottish courts will apply the same standards as the English in interpreting it. For example, English newspapers have always exercised much greater freedom than those in Scotland in publishing pictures of criminal suspects. Even since the passing of the 1981 Act they have continued publishing this kind of picture to an extent that would be inviting contempt proceedings in a Scottish case.

23.04 Lord McCluskey found the BBC guilty of contempt in March 1992 for broadcasting footage of Paul Ferris, a murder accused on trial at the High Court in Glasgow, being led from a police van to the court.

23.05 There might be circumstances where the risk was small, for example if the accused was well known to the public as a sports or showbusiness personality, but such cases would be uncommon. The judge added, however:

"There is only one safe route for the media to follow and it is this—do not publish any picture of an accused person in Scotland until a trial is finished or the charge has been dropped by the Lord Advocate."

The BBC submitted that viewers saw only a fleeting glimpse of Ferris   23.06
for two or three seconds and not at a peak viewing time, but Lord McCluskey said the accused had been clearly identified and there was a substantial risk that the course of justice might be seriously prejudiced.

A similar approach was taken by the Scottish Appeal Court in *HM*   23.07
Advocate v Caledonian Newspapers **(1995)**, reinforced most recently in March 2009 where the Daily Record, STV and the *Scottish Sun* had each been fined £1,750 for contempt of court after showing a photograph of footballer Derek Riordan during his summary trial. He was acquitted of assault, but the contempt findings were upheld on appeal, despite the argument that Riordan was so well known that publishing his photograph did not create a substantial risk of serious prejudice. The court said:

"Fame, celebrity—its often tawdry modern counterpart—and notoriety all carry with them the possibility of recognition by members of the public. It may be that a person will be so well known that mere mention of his or her name may be expected to bring an image to the minds of the vast majority of members of the public. But such cases will be rare ... Recognition of a person is a notoriously subtle process, one which is best described by psychologists; but our own experience in the criminal courts justifies this description. It is common experience that one may fail to recognise a person, familiar in a particular context, when seen out of context. The only safe course, where identification is an issue, is not to publish any photograph or similar image ... at least until ... there is no question of further identification evidence being given." (*Scottish Daily Record and Sunday Mail Ltd v Thomson* **(2009)**) [see **para.17.29**]

It would be wrong to treat it as a total certainty in every case that the   23.08
publication of a picture would bring contempt proceedings. There might be a degree of fame or notoriety (although clearly the Appeal Court did not think Derek Riordan had achieved it) at which the accused's face would be so recognisable to all, for all purposes, as not to give rise to a substantial risk of serious prejudice to the proceedings. There must be some cases where, from the nature of the facts, e.g. a domestic murder in domestic premises, or from the nature of the

charges, e.g. carousel fraud, identification is most unlikely to be an issue. Journalists may also ask, or be told by, the defence that identification is not in issue.

23.09   In *all* cases where the photograph of an accused is to be used, however, the journalist will be prudent to take legal advice before publishing.

SHOWING PHOTOGRAPHS AFTER THE
EVIDENCE HAS BEEN HEARD

23.10   Once all the evidence has been heard, there is no obvious reason why a photograph of the accused should not be shown, unless it is prejudicial in its content or presentation.

INCRIMINEES

23.11   Pictures of witnesses who have completed their evidence are normally permissible, but not always. In a case where there is a defence of incrimination (where the accused blames someone else for the crime), if the person being incriminated gives evidence, his or her picture should normally not be used until the evidence is complete.

CARE WITH CAPTIONS

23.12   Even if a picture is regarded as safe, care has to be taken to avoid a substantial risk of serious prejudice in writing the caption. At the risk of stating the obvious, there must be a check that the caption matches the picture. The caption itself can be prejudicial. In *HM Advocate v Haney* (2003), the showing of a photograph of the accused, Mrs Haney, captioned "Mags' Drug Throne", led the Appeal Court to express surprise that the Lord Advocate had not taken contempt proceedings, saying "the publication of photograph[s] of her clearly constituted contempt."

INSIDE THE COURT

23.13   There is no Scottish statute specifically dealing with the taking of photographs, or having a camera in court. The Criminal Justice Act 1925, which bans the taking of photographs and the publication of photographs taken in court, applies only to England and Wales. The 1925 Act provides that no-one shall take or attempt to take in any English court—apart from the Supreme Court, which replaces the House of Lords and the Judicial Committee of the Privy Council—

any photograph or, with a view to publication, make or attempt to make in any court any portrait or sketch of any person, judge, juror, witness or party to any proceedings, civil or criminal. However, the attitude towards photography in and around the courts in Scotland was, until 1992, similar to the English one. Sound recording without the court's permission was, and is, prohibited by s.9 of the Contempt of Court Act 1981 [see **para.21.07**]. Wilful disobedience of a court order or deliberate disruption of court proceedings is clearly common law contempt. Depending on the circumstances, to take a photograph in a Scottish court could fall into this category. Beyond disruption or disobedience, court photography may have objectionable consequences.

In Glasgow Sheriff Court in 1975, Peter Sweeney admitted being in 23.14 contempt of court in that, during the proceedings in a criminal case in the court, he was in possession of a camera and took photographs in the court. His solicitor said Mr Sweeney had wanted a souvenir of his first visit to a courtroom, but, after being told by an attendant to leave, which he did, he had been pursued by a detective, apprehended and detained in custody overnight. The following day the photographs he took were produced in court and Sheriff Archibald Bell QC admonished Mr Sweeney for contempt of court and confiscated the camera. He stated: "Proceedings in court cannot and should not be subject to any interruption", although Mr Sweeney's solicitor had said what his client had done was so quiet and unobtrusive that even the sheriff was "unaware and not troubled by the matter".

The advent of mobile phones with in-built cameras has brought this 23.15 issue to the fore. In November 2007, a man was arrested in connection with mobile phone footage which apparently showed the interior of the High Court in Glasgow during a murder trial. The footage had been posted on *YouTube*. In England, where the law is clearer, some stiff sentences have been handed out for taking photographs with a mobile in court—a year in prison in *R. v D* **(2004)**, where the English Court of Appeal observed that illegal photography had the potential to prejudice the administration of criminal justice because it could be used to intimidate witnesses, jurors and dock officers. A six-month jail sentence for contempt of court was given to Shaun Nash, a Bristol teenager who took video footage of a robbery trial, leading to its being aborted, in November 2004. In May 2009, comedian Jimmy Carr was investigated, although not ultimately prosecuted, for allegedly using his mobile phone to take a picture of a sign saying photographs should not be taken inside the magistrates court in Sudbury, Suffolk.

PRECINCTS OF THE COURT

23.16 In a case in which official guidance was sought in 1964, the then Lord President issued a ruling which stated: "No photographing is permitted within the precincts of the Law Courts. The precincts of the Law Courts are defined as the areas occupied by the car park and the piazza." The reference was to the portion of Parliament Square, Edinburgh, lying between St Giles Cathedral and Parliament House, and offered no guidance as to the precincts of any other law court in Scotland.

23.17 It was probably the first formal attempt to define the precincts of any Scottish court over restrictions on photography. When invited to supply a definition of precincts of the court in an earlier case, the Lord Advocate of the day, Lord Wheatley, stated that a definition was not possible because the extent of the precincts must vary with the circumstances and requirements of each case.

23.18 The police cells were held to be part of the precincts of the court in *Garrett v HM Advocate* (1993). In the *Aamer Anwar* case—where a solicitor who criticised a criminal verdict was not found to have been in contempt of court—no distinction was drawn by the court between his statement on the steps of the court and his subsequent press release and *Newsnight Scotland* interview (*Anwar, Respondent* (2008)).

TELEVISING COURT PROCEEDINGS

23.19 Justice Albie Sachs observed in *South Africa Broadcasting Corp Ltd v National Director of Public Prosecution* (2007) that broadcasting of court proceedings "should not be looked upon as an inconvenient intrusion by the public, or as a favour to be granted or withheld from the broadcasters. It involves fulfilment of an obligation …".

23.20 In 1992, the then Lord President, Lord Hope, a quiet iconoclast who now sits in the Supreme Court of the UK, revisited the matter of television in court. He said:

> "The rule hitherto has been that television cameras are not allowed within the precincts of the court. While the absolute nature of the rule makes it easy to apply it is an impediment to the making of programmes of an educational or documentary nature and to the use of television in other cases where there would be no risk to the administration of justice. In future the criterion will be whether the presence of television cameras in the court would be without risk to the administration of justice."

23.21 Lord Hope felt that technology had now reached such an advanced stage that certain court cases could probably be televised without undue interference with the proceedings, much as had happened in Parliament.

He added: 23.22

> "It is also in the public interest that people in Scotland should become more aware of the way in which justice is being administered in their own courts. There is a risk that the showing on television of proceedings in the courts of other countries will lead to misunderstandings about the way in which court proceedings are conducted in our own country."

The Lord President issued a series of guidelines under which requests   23.23
by broadcasting organisations to televise proceedings in the Court of Session and High Court would be dealt. The criterion was to be "whether the presence of television cameras in the courts would be without risk to the administration of justice." Televising trials or civil proofs while the case was ongoing was still banned, but such hearings could be filmed for broadcast at a later date "for the purpose of showing educational or documentary programmes" if all the parties involved consented and the presiding judge approved.

However, cameras were to be allowed into the courtroom to televise   23.24
appeal cases, both civil and criminal, subject to satisfactory arrangements being made about the placing of cameras and provided there was no additional lighting which would make courtroom conditions intolerable. The cameras were to be allowed in subject to the approval of the presiding judge and under his/her conditions. Ceremonial occasions might be televised in the courtroom for use in a news bulletin. The taking of television pictures (without sound) of judges on the Bench, as a replacement for still pictures, will be allowed with the permission of the judge concerned. Requests by television companies to film proceedings, including proceedings at first instance, for later showing in educational or documentary programmes, were to be given favourable consideration. However, the consent of all parties involved in the proceedings are needed, as is the approval of the presiding judge. Similar guidelines were introduced by the sheriffs principal for sheriff courts.

From a broadcaster's perspective, thus far, however, the guidelines   23.25
in Scotland have been something of a damp squib.

The first ever broadcast of a Scottish criminal trial was seen in April   23.26
1994 when BBC Scotland screened *Focal Point—The Trial*, a case in Glasgow before Sheriff Brian Lockhart and a jury. In November 1994 BBC 2 began showing a six-part series filmed in the Scottish courts. The first programme featured a murder trial. The programme was broadcast only after the accused's trial and appeal had been completed and there was no risk of prejudice to the proceedings.

23.27   In 2006, BBC Scotland screened a documentary called, *Sheriff Court*, featuring proceedings, including trial proceedings, in Glasgow Sheriff Court, which were filmed in 2003. The time gap there—although the main factor behind it was the purported withdrawal of consent by one of the featured accused (*X v BBC* (2005))—eloquently suggests the amount of time and effort, and consequently expense, involved in doing this kind of documentary.

23.28   Indeed, the present requirements for the consent of all concerned, the enormous administrative burden of projects like *Sheriff Court,* and the threat to broadcasters' editorial independence, make them highly unlikely to happen often in future. Absent radical reform, to provide public access of this sort will tend to be a thankless and unappetising activity for broadcasters. Limited filming in the drugs court and domestic violence court in Glasgow Sheriff Court has been done for BBC Scotland documentaries in 2010.

FILMING APPELLATE PROCEEDINGS

23.29   There has been more impact on appeal proceedings. Cameras were allowed into the Court of Criminal Appeal to film the judges issuing their opinions in the case of *Campbell and Joseph Steele* (1998) who alleged that their murder convictions were a miscarriage of justice. Cameras were allowed in court for the *Nat Fraser* (2008) appeal. The broadcasting of the reasoned appeal judgments in the highly controversial *Nat Fraser* murder conviction, where there were claims about concealment of evidence, did make a significant contribution to public access to that case. The dropping of the second appeal by Megrahi against his conviction for the Lockerbie bombing was televised too. Such pieces enable the public to see what is being done in the name of public justice and their continued availability online also allows the thoughtful viewer to reflect on the process and arguments.

ATTEMPTS TO BROADCAST LOCKERBIE TRIAL

23.30   The BBC went to court twice in 2000 (*BBC, Petitioners (No.1)* (2000); *BBC, Petitioners (No.2)* (2000)) to seek public access to the televising of the Lockerbie trial itself, which was refused twice. The Lockerbie trial was so unusual—no jury, taking place in the Netherlands before three Scottish judges as a result of an international agreement, and being selectively televised live to victims' relatives in Dumfries, London, New York and Washington D.C.—that to have broadcast would not have set any precedent in terms of broader televising of the courts. In the light of the ongoing controversy surrounding the trial, however, this failure on the courts' part to pick up the opportunity of a free, publicly-available, permanent full record of the trial seems especially regrettable.

TELEVISING INQUIRIES

Inquiries under the Inquiries Act 2005 may be televised at the 23.31 discretion of the inquiry chairman. Before that, in the Hutton Inquiry in 2003, Lord Hutton was televised giving his verdict, but the evidence was not filmed. Televising of opening and closing statements, in part, was allowed in Lord Cullen's inquiry into the Ladbroke Grove crash and Lord Saville's inquiry into Bloody Sunday. Lord Phillips allowed radio broadcasting of final statements in the BSE Inquiry. Permission to broadcast was refused in the Shipman Inquiry, the Arms to Iraq Inquiry and the Bristol Inquiry.

IN THE OPEN

When the judge, jury, clerk and counsel leave the courtroom, for 23.32 example to go outside to inspect a piece of evidence such as a car, the place where the inspection takes place may become, for the time being, the equivalent of the courtroom. In the Lockerbie trial, Kamp van Zeist became, for legal purposes, the equivalent of a Scottish courtroom.

Parties or witnesses or counsel walking along the street, either going 23.33 to or leaving the court buildings, are in a different position and there is no danger in taking pictures provided nothing is done that would amount to obstructing or molesting them. Any conduct by photographers which prevented a witness from coming to court to give evidence might be regarded as an interference with the course of justice and punishable as common law contempt [see **Chapter 22**].

ASSAULT, FRAUD, BREACH OF THE PEACE AND PHOTOGRAPHS

Unlawful interference with the person is assault. This may result in a 23.34 criminal prosecution or a civil action for damages. The law on assault should not be of concern to the journalist, but there have been instances of mobbing and manhandling by reporters on the trail of a story. To photograph a person is not by itself assault, even without consent, but to force someone to submit to being photographed in a certain place or in a certain pose probably would be assault. Journalists should also be aware of a case in 1989 in which a newspaper reporter in Scotland admitted a charge of fraud. She had gained access to a hospital patient by pretending to be his niece. The causing of distress to the patient would not be necessary to constitute the offence, but could be regarded as an aggravating factor by the court (see also **Chapter 41**].

23.35   In 1975 proceedings were begun, but later abandoned, against two press photographers who took pictures of a solicitor in the street outside the sheriff court at Dunfermline. The solicitor was appearing on behalf of a client at an inquiry into a suspicious death and the picture was taken during an adjournment. The solicitor complained to the procurator fiscal, on whose authority the photographers were later charged with assault and had their films confiscated.

23.36   Researches could produce only a civil case (*Adamson v Martin* **(1916)**), in which a boy aged 17, charged with a minor offence, had his fingerprints and photograph taken by the police without his parents' consent. He brought proceedings against the chief constable for defamation, claiming that his reputation had been damaged by having his fingerprints and photograph filed by the police along with those of notorious criminals.

23.37   In the Dunfermline case, the Crown Office intervened and instructed the procurator fiscal not to proceed with the case against the photographers, whose films were returned to them. The case establishes only that there has been no instance in Scotland of a successful prosecution for assault by photography. One should not ignore the very expansive common law crime of breach of the peace.

23.38   In March 1992 at Kilmarnock Sheriff Court a photographer was warned by police that if he tried to take a picture of a witness at a fatal accident inquiry he could be charged with breach of the peace. The case concerned the death of the witness's five children in a house fire, and he had made it clear to police that he did not wish to be photographed. In 1998, a *Daily Record* photographer was acquitted on a not proven verdict on a breach of the peace charge [see **paras 41.02 onwards**]. A postman was fined for breach of the peace in October 2008 after he took a photograph on his mobile phone of an Edinburgh woman vomiting in the street [see **para.41.05**]. Since the advent of the Human Rights Act 1998, any such charge could be subject both to arguments about the art.10 freedom of expression rights of the media and the audience, if taking a photograph of an unwilling subject for journalistic reasons were to be criminalised.

23.39   In England, in January 2010, a journalist—photographer Andrew Handley—who was arrested, handcuffed and detained for eight hours when he tried to take photos of a road accident, received £5,000 and an apology from Thames Valley Police when they settled his action for unlawful imprisonment and assault. In the same month, the European Court of Human Rights decided that the stop and search of freelance photojournalist Pennie Quinton under ss.44 and 45 of the Terrorism Act 2000 was a breach of her art.8 rights on the unusual grounds that stop and search powers were not adequately prescribed by law—*Gillan and Quinton v United Kingdom* (2010).

BREACH OF CONFIDENCE

Traditionally, in the UK, it has not been unlawful to photograph a 23.40 person or to publish the result (although the courts' distaste for certain types of invasive behaviour has, it is felt, influenced the awards of damages made where an actionable wrong has existed, e.g. defamation, infringement of copyright or breach of confidence). Times are radically changing here. Some of the most significant privacy cases have arisen from photography.

Campbell v MGN (2004), where the House of Lords split three 23.41 judges to two over the *Mirror* story about Naomi Campbell's drug addiction and attendance at Narcotics Anonymous, was decided mostly on the photography, even though all the photograph actually showed was Naomi Campbell in a public street. Lord Hope, the same judge who, when Lord Justice General in Scotland, brought in the filming code guidelines, said:

"Had it not been for the publication of the photographs ... I would have been inclined to regard the balance between [the privacy right of Naomi Campbell and the freedom of expression right of the newspaper and its readership] as about even ... But the text cannot be separated from the photographs."

Baroness Hale, who agreed with him, said: 23.42

"We have not so far held that the mere fact of covert photography is sufficient to make the information contained in the photograph confidential. The activity photographed must be private. If this had been, and had been presented as, a picture of Naomi Campbell going about her business in a public street, there could have been no complaint. She makes a substantial part of her living out of being photographed looking stunning in designer clothing. Readers will obviously be interested to see how she looks if and when she pops out to the shops for a bottle of milk. There is nothing essentially private about that information nor can it be expected to damage her private life. It may not be a high order of freedom of speech but there is nothing to justify interfering with it."

These photographs, however: 23.43

"[W]ere different. They showed her coming either to or from the [Narcotics Anonymous] meeting ... A picture is 'worth a thousand words' because it adds to the impact of what the words convey; but it also adds to the information given in those words. If nothing else, it tells the reader what everyone looked like; in this case it also told the reader what the place looked like."

23.44   The saga of Catherine Zeta-Jones and Michael Douglas's wedding photographs also went to the House of Lords once and to the Court of Appeal four times: privacy litigation is not for the faint hearted or poorly funded. And again, there was a three to two split among the Lords (*OBG v Allan* (2007)). The majority held that *OK!* magazine, which had paid for an exclusive, could sue *Hello!* magazine for breach of confidence when they ran a "spoiler" using photos taken by a freelance who had "infiltrated" the wedding. It was also held by the Court of Appeal that, even though Catherine Zeta-Jones and Michael Douglas had in fact sold the rights to their wedding photographs, they retained a residual right of privacy which allowed them to make a claim against *Hello!* magazine when it published covertly-obtained photographs of their wedding, the couple having granted an exclusive to *OK!* magazine.

23.45   The awards to the happy couple were modest. Bride and groom got £14,600, being £3,750 each for the distress caused by publication of unauthorised photographs, £7,000 to them both for the cost and inconvenience of having to deal hurriedly with the selection of the authorised photographs when the *OK!* publication was brought forward so *Hello!* wouldn't scoop them, and £50 damages each for breach of the Data Protection Act 1998. Madonna, who did not sell or publish her wedding photographs at the time, received a payout (October 2009) from the *Mail on Sunday* who published them shortly after her divorce from Guy Ritchie.

WHY ARE PHOTOGRAPHS TREATED DIFFERENTLY IN BREACH OF CONFIDENCE?

(I) THEY HAVE MORE IMPACT

23.46   This sense of the distinctive freight of the visual image is widely shared among the judiciary. Lord Nicholls said in the *Hello!* case:

"Photographs are much the best way of conveying an impression ... Photographs make one a spectator at the wedding. Information communicated in other ways, in sketches or descriptive writing or by word of mouth, cannot be so complete or accurate."

Only photographic information was claimed to be confidential in the   23.47
Douglas case—nothing else about the wedding was said to be secret.
Scots law from a pre-Human Rights Act 1998 timeframe, also gave
photographs some significance. In *McCosh v Crow* **(1903)**, it was
held that a photographer who had taken a photograph for a customer
was not entitled without consent to sell or to exhibit copies of it.

The Strasbourg case of *Von Hannover v Germany* **(2005)**, where the   23.48
European Court of Human Rights found for Princess Caroline of
Monaco over a series of superficially harmless photographs of her
walking, shopping, horse riding, and so on, is difficult to reconcile
with the insistence of UK courts, so far, that an individual does not
have an image right, i.e. a right to control the use of their own
picture. Even public photography of public figures could, on a strict
reading of the *Von Hannover* case, violate a person's human rights,
despite containing nothing obviously embarrassing or distressing.

In *D v L* **(2003)**, Waller L.J. also thought that a sound recording   23.49
raised similar issues:

> "Just as a photograph can make a greater impact than an account
> of the matter depicted by that photograph, so the recorded details
> of the very words of a private conversation can make more
> impact, and cause greater embarrassment and distress, than a
> mere account of the conversation in question."

The *News of the World* settled a privacy action brought by Max   23.50
Clifford over telephone tapping allegations in March 2010.

(II) THEY HAVE MORE EVIDENTIAL VALUE

As well as being more impactful, photographs are thought to carry   23.51
more credibility. Lord Hoffmann, in his dissent in the *Naomi
Campbell* case, observed that: "The picture carried a message, more
strongly than anything in the text alone, that the Mirror story was
true." Photographs are treated differently, too, in that however
widely the basic information they contain has been published, re-
publication may still be prevented on privacy grounds. Knowing and
showing are two different things.

(III) THEY MAY BE DISTINCTIVELY INTRUSIVE, EVEN ON RE-PUBLICATION

In *D v L* **(2003)** [above], an English Court of Appeal case, where an   23.52
injunction was refused where it was sought to prevent publication of
surreptitiously recorded tapes revealing the sexual proclivities of one
party to a broken marriage, taped by the other, Waller L.J. said:

"A photograph is more than the information you get from it. A court may restrain the publication of an improperly obtained photograph even if the taker is free to describe the information which the photo provides or even if the information revealed by the photograph is in the public domain ...";

which is exactly what happened in the *Theakston* (2002) case. There the newspaper was allowed to publish that the children's presenter Jamie Theakston had visited a brothel, but was not allowed to show photographs of him in the brothel.

23.53   The Court of Appeal said in *Douglas v Hello!* (2005):

"Once intimate personal information about a celebrity's private life has been widely published it may serve no useful purpose to prohibit further publication. The same will not necessarily be true of photographs. Insofar as a photograph does more than convey information and intrudes on privacy by enabling the viewer to focus on intimate personal detail, there will be a fresh intrusion of privacy when each additional viewer sees the photograph and even when one who has seen a previous publication of the photograph, is confronted by a fresh publication of it. To take an example, if a film star were photographed, with the aid of a telephoto lens, lying naked by her private swimming pool, we question whether widespread publication of the photograph by a popular newspaper would provide a defence to a legal challenge to repeated publication on the ground that the information was in the public domain."

23.54   A photograph of a dead baby which his siblings were likely to find particularly disturbing was injuncted in *Re T* (2009), an English family court decision arising out of the tragic death of Mason Tipper.

(IV) ... UP TO A POINT

23.55   Insofar as anything may be said to be a bright-line rule in privacy law, it is suggested that photographs of identifiable individuals taken without their knowledge or consent and featuring nudity, sexual activity or delicate medical treatment are out in future unless a cogent public interest exists. However, actually suppressing re-publication may be practically difficult in the internet age, even if conceptually acceptable, and judges are no keener on looking foolish in public than other famous names.

23.56   It seems quite clear from Eady J.'s comments in the *Max Mosley* case (*Mosley v News Group Newspapers* (2008)) that he would have felt justified to ban such a story in its entirety, words and pictures, on the basis of his view that sexual morality amongst consenting adults, paying or non-paying, is an extremely private matter in which there will rarely be a legitimate public interest. Nonetheless, this judge declined to grant such an injunction on the basis that hundreds of thousands of people had already seen the *News of the World's* video of Mosley and the prostitutes in the sado-masochistic "dungeon". The images would be retrievable on the internet even if they were ordered to be taken off the *News of the World* website: "The court should guard against slipping into playing the role of King Canute ... The dam has effectively burst." Beyond the mixed watery metaphors is the reality of an almost uncontrollable international medium specialising in the likes of *YouTube*. But then, Mosley was president of the *Federation Internacionale de l'Automobile* and the son of internationally notorious parents. A Scottish soap actor, comedian or politician may be able substantially to vindicate his or her privacy rights by a much more focused attack on an individual Scottish newspaper.

Of course, the last person in a position to deny that visual image 23.57 matters is a television broadcaster or photo-journalist, paparazzos, or indeed any newspaper writer or online blogger who wishes to use any kind of illustration.

Occasionally, too, the journalist can find himself the snapped, 23.58 rather than the snapper. Mazur Mahmood, the *News of the World* "fake sheikh", unsuccessfully sought an injunction against George Galloway and Ron Mackay in 2006 to ban his photographs from being kept on Galloway's Respect website. His argument that this would compromise his undercover work and endanger his life fell on deaf ears. Mr Justice Mitting said:

"If taken by the target [of the investigation] ... then it was taken in circumstances which give Mr Mahmood no right to claim privacy ... Or even if the photograph was merely taken quite innocently as part of a social occasion, it is in no sense an invasion of Mr Mahmood's right to privacy ..." (*Mahmood v Galloway* (2006)).

In June of the same year, Elton John unsuccessfully attempted to stop 23.59 publication of a photograph of him outside his house, on the street, showing his baldness.

DAMAGES

Photographs may accompany investigative journalism, as in the 23.60 *Campbell* case, or they may themselves be fought over as part of the celebrity culture, as with the Douglas wedding photographs. They may also, however, be intrusive in a more obvious sense. Sara Cox, for instance, got £50,000 plus a 40 per cent success fee (total costs of about £200,000) against MGN, Jason Fraser and Fraser-Woodward Ltd in 2006 for nude photographs of her on her honeymoon in a secluded resort (*Cox v MGN Ltd* (2006)). The PCC Code explicitly forbids intrusion with telephoto lenses and on people's holidays.

23.61   Given the status that s.12 of the Human Rights Act 1998, and s.32 of the Data Protection Act 1998, give to journalistic codes like the PCC, a newspaper which behaves in this way has little prospect of avoiding a payout in the post-Human Rights Act world of privacy. Damages, originally modest, are creeping upwards. Hugh Grant, Liz Hurley and her husband accepted damages in May 2008 of £58,000 for covert photographs of them on holiday together. Sienna Miller settled for £35,000 in 2008 for a photograph of her topless on a yacht, plus other publications about her romantic life. Kate Middleton, then Prince William's girlfriend, is estimated to have received £10,000, plus legal costs, for photographs taken of her during her Christmas 2009 holiday.

CHILDREN

23.62   Perhaps the most important "photograph" case so far in the UK came out of Edinburgh. J.K. Rowling, the author of the *Harry Potter* novels, brought a breach of confidence action on behalf of her son, David. A photograph had been taken of him in his pushchair on Princes Street, on a walk with his parents. (The PCC had previously upheld J.K. Rowling's complaint on behalf of her elder daughter, over a photograph on holiday on a beach.) The first instance judge struck out the claim. The Court of Appeal disagreed, holding that it was arguable that the toddler did have a right to protect his privacy in such a situation:

> "It may well be that the mere taking of a photograph of a child in a public place when out with his or her parents, whether they are famous or not, would not engage Article 8 of the Convention. However ... it all depends upon the circumstances ... This was not the taking of a single photograph of David in the street ... It was the clandestine taking and subsequent publication of the photograph in the context of a series of photographs which were taken for the purpose of their sale for publication, in circumstances in which [Big Pictures (UK) Ltd] did not ask David's parents for their consent ... This was at least arguably a very different case from ... [Naomi] Campbell being photographed while popping out to buy the milk."

23.63   Significant factors discussed in the case include the special protection to be accorded children, the failure to pixilate David's features, the fact that J.K. Rowling had sought to shelter her children from publicity and the regularity with which photographers stood outside the family home.

> "Thus, for example, if the parents of a child courted publicity by procuring the publication of photographs of the child in order to promote their own interests, the position would or might be quite different from a case like this, where the parents have taken care to keep their children out of the public gaze" (*Murray v Big Pictures (UK) Ltd* (2008)).

This case has now settled, so we cannot say which side would have won 23.64 at trial, but it is a potent indicator that even innocuous (so far as content goes) photographs in public can create difficulty.

Hello! paid Jude Law £9,500 plus legal costs in 2010 for 23.65 photographs of him and his children on holiday on a beach—a clear PCC Code breach.

Scottish actor Ewan McGregor got a settlement from various 23.66 newspapers, including the *Daily Record* in 2004, for photographs of him on holiday with his children.

As with the *Mosley* case, though, the point comes where the 23.67 publication is so pervasive as to make a court ban transparently futile. The English judge in the 2009 Alfie Patten case, where a 12-year-old boy was announced to have fathered a child who subsequently turned out not to have been his daughter, declined to grant an injunction to ban re-publication of photographs of the children involved there (*Re Stedman* (2009)).

There are special provisions in Scotland which may be used to stop 23.68 publication of pictures of children under 16, and sometimes older, involved in court proceedings, children's hearings and fatal accident inquiries. This is an area of particular importance to photographers and anyone involved in television journalism. A full account of the section is contained in **Chapter 25**. An Appeal Court decision in 1993 (*McArdle v Orr* (1993)) seemed to suggest that, where the legislation specifically prohibits inclusion of a picture, all pictures of children are banned even though the picture is taken from behind or the child's face is blanked out and he or she cannot be identified by most people. That may now be open to argument, either in terms of the exact wording of the relevant piece of legislation or as a matter of human rights law.

An important point to remember is that the ban on identifying— 23.69 including, specifically, any photograph of—a child will also mean that the picture of an adult involved in the case cannot be used if this would lead to the identification of the child. The ban could also extend to pictures of a school or any other area that could lead to the child's identification. In one case a 12-year-old boy appeared at the High Court in Edinburgh and admitted firearms offences. He had arrived at school one morning armed with a shotgun. Reporting restrictions were not lifted and neither the boy nor his school could be named. Reports referred only to the general area of Scotland in which the incident took place. After the case was dealt with, a photographer took pictures as the boy was driven away from court to a secure school. The boy himself could not be seen in the pictures and at least one newspaper published the picture on the understanding that the adult who was visible in the car was a social worker accompanying the boy to court. In fact it was one of the boy's parents and the newspaper had committed an offence by unwittingly identifying the child by publishing a picture of his parent.

OFFICIAL SECRETS

23.70   There is a voluntary system administered by a joint committee representing the media and civil service to restrict publication of sensitive material. Matters which are subject to restriction are listed under a series of "DA-Notices". These are dealt with in more detail in **Chapter 38**; the aspect most likely to concern photographers covers pictures of defence establishments, installations, dockyards and factories.

TERRORISM

23.71   In July 2009, the Metropolitan Police dropped the claim, made in its guidelines, that under the Terrorism Act 2000, the police had the right to inspect all images taken in public. They maintain a right to view images taken by those they reasonably suspect to be terrorists [see **para.40.07**]. In June 2010, the Met paid damages of £3,500 each to two photojournalists, Marc Vallée and Jason Parkinson, who were prevented from covering a protest outside the Greek Embassy. The police said that the service "apologised and accepted liability for a breach of freedom of expression ...".

KEY POINTS

23.72   1. Using a photograph of an accused person will normally pose a contempt risk.
2. Photography or televising of proceedings in a Scottish court is not illegal, but in practice the restrictions on doing so are onerous and deterrent, especially at trial stage. There has been more broadcasting of criminal appeals and inquiries.
3. Taking a photograph can amount to breach of the peace.

4. A number of major privacy and breach of confidence cases have arisen out of photography: the pictures of Naomi Campbell outside Narcotics Anonymous, the publication of unauthorised photographs from Catherine Zeta-Jones's and Michael Douglas's wedding and the decision by the European Court of Human Rights that photographs of Princess Caroline of Monaco in a range of trivial pursuits breached her art.8 rights to private life.
5. Photographs are often treated differently by the courts than written or spoken descriptions. Sometimes, audio-tapes are also treated in this manner. Re-publication of an available photograph may be regarded as breaching the subject's privacy.
6. Paparazzi photographs have resulted in a number of payouts to celebrities. If photographs are taken in breach of the PCC Code, there will be real legal difficulty in resisting a claim of this sort.
7. One of the most significant privacy cases involved a photograph in Princes Street, Edinburgh of J.K. Rowling's son in his pushchair. The Court of Appeal held that it was at least arguable that the toddler did have a right to protect his privacy in such a situation.
8. Photographs of children accused of or said to be the victims of crime in criminal trials, or children involved in the children's hearing system and, in some cases, child witnesses in civil and criminal cases and fatal accident inquiries, may be banned.

PART 6: MATRIMONIAL PROCEEDINGS AND CHILDREN

CHAPTER 24

MATRIMONIAL PROCEEDINGS

By Rosalind McInnes

24.01 Media reports of divorce cases in Scotland are rare for several reasons. First, the Judicial Proceedings (Regulation of Reports) Act 1926, imposes strict limits on what the media can publish about divorce, nullity and separation actions. Secondly, the overwhelming majority of divorces in Scotland are undefended and since 1978 are not normally heard in open court at all. Thirdly, breakdown of marriage is now so commonplace in Scotland that the average case is not newsworthy.

24.02 Clearly, however—as the English divorce of Paul McCartney and Heather Mills in 2008 made plain—divorce proceedings can still make headlines. It is important, therefore, that journalists should be familiar with the terms of the 1926 Act.

24.03 The 1926 Act is unusual because, rather than banning the publication of specific details of matrimonial cases, it says that reports are prohibited altogether except for four limited categories of information. Section 1(1)(a) is not restricted to divorce cases and applies to judicial proceedings of any kind. It bans the publication of any indecent material or any indecent medical, surgical or physiological details, publication of which would be calculated to injure public morals. The terms of the 1926 embargo are mandatory and probably over-broad, given that the Human Rights Act 1998 is concerned with freedom of expression as well as privacy, but the journalist may not wish to pioneer such a challenge.

24.04 The Civil Partnership Act 2004 extended its provisions to the dissolution of civil partnerships, some of which have already proved newsworthy. Matt Lucas of the *Little Britain* comedy series obtained in May 2010 an apology and damages from Express Newspapers over its coverage of his former civil partner's suicide.

TERMS OF THE ACT

The part of the 1926 Act which has most relevance to the working 24.05
journalist is s.1(1)(b) which affects reports of any judicial proceedings
for dissolution of marriage, nullity of marriage or judicial separation.
Nothing may be published about these types of case except:

- the names, addresses and occupations of the parties to the
  action and of witnesses;
- a concise statement of the charges, defences and counter-
  charges in support of which evidence has been given;
- submissions on any point of law arising during the
  proceedings, including the court's decision on the legal point;
- the judgment of the court and any observations made by the
  judge in giving judgment.

The maximum penalty for each contravention of the 1926 Act is four 24.06
months' imprisonment or a £5,000 fine or both, liability lying with the
proprietor, editor, and printer or publisher. The 1926 Act applies to
both defended and undefended divorces and undefended cases are by
far the more frequent.

PROCEDURE IN DIVORCE CASES

In undefended cases the court will accept affidavits (sworn statements) 24.07
as evidence. For instance, if both parties agree a divorce but are in
dispute over money, affidavits can be presented to the court, instead
of the spouses coming to give evidence. Such cases are often dealt
with in chambers, rather than open court.

A list of the divorces granted in undefended cases in the Court of 24.08
Session is published in the court rolls once a week. A similar list is
published in at least some sheriff courts. These lists do not contain
enough information in themselves to provide the reporter with a story.

To comply with the terms of the 1926 Act only the brief details 24.09
permitted by the Act should be used from the court documents. The
few reports published in newspapers of affidavit divorces have run to
only a few paragraphs setting out who has been divorced, on what
ground and which judge granted decree. To use further details from
the court documents would run the risk of breaching the 1926 Act.

As far as defended cases are concerned the normal practice in the 24.10
Court of Session has been to wait until the judge issues the decision in
a case before carrying a report. This is likely to be several weeks after
the hearing of evidence. The decision is normally given in writing and a
copy is made available to journalists. Divorce judgments are normally

in very full terms and provide the journalist with more than enough information to present a complete picture of a case.

24.11 There may of course be defended cases which are seen as so interesting and important that a decision is made to report them before the judgment stage. Again, this can be done only within the terms of the 1926 Act. The basic point to remember is that, unlike most other cases, a detailed account of the evidence as it unfolds cannot be given in a divorce, nullity or separation action. The 1926 Act talks about a "concise" report of claims on both sides "in support of which evidence has been given." In other words, the journalist must wait until enough has been heard of the evidence to produce a "concise" summary of the case.

24.12 The word "concise" could present some difficulty, since its exact interpretation will vary with the circumstances of each individual case. A recital of alleged incidents or allegations based on the evidence given in court would not come within the definition of "concise". Where there is doubt, or the case is complicated, the safest course is to err on the side of brevity and keep the summary to a single sentence for the charges and another for replies and counter-charges.

24.13 The restrictions in the 1926 Act apply to reports "in relation to court proceedings". In any follow-up story, such as an interview with one of the parties outside the court, it would be sensible to avoid a mere rehashing of any evidence given in court, as this could arguably be caught by the terms of the Act. The dangers of defamation should also be kept in mind since a report based on information given outside the court would not be protected by privilege.

POINTS OF LAW

24.14 Submissions on a point of law which crop up during the proceedings can provide a good source of copy. There have been several outstanding instances, for example the question of whether artificial insemination by a donor (AID) was a good defence to an action of divorce for adultery (*MacLennon v McLennon* (1958)). In the notorious Argyll divorce case, the issue arose as to whether a wife could be compelled to surrender as evidence passages in her diary containing references to her alleged association with men other than her husband (*Argyll v Argyll* (1962)).

24.15 In reporting this kind of submission the reporter must be careful that what is published is not in essence an argument on the facts but truly deals with a question of law. A legal argument must of course be based on a certain minimum amount of fact, but any report, to come within the Act, should contain no more factual information than necessary for a proper report of the legal submissions.

The next permissible category is "decision of the court" on the 24.16
submissions on any point of law. This covers judgments given by the
court at certain preliminary stages over legal issues, where the judge is
not necessarily being asked to give a final decision on the case. In the
AID case referred to above, Lord Wheatley heard preliminary debate
on issues of great legal interest and public importance. The arguments
contained a great deal of reportable and permissible material and the
judgment could be published.

In another case, a wife made a preliminary application to the court 24.17
for an advance of a very large sum of interim expenses to enable her to
bring witnesses from various countries to Scotland to help her defend a
divorce action. The judge, Lord Guthrie, said that under the 1926 Act
his judgment on the point could be legally reported provided that the
only other information published was the parties' names and
addresses as they appeared on the calling list.

In reporting such preliminary matters, as well as the judgment, 24.18
however, bear in mind that the 1926 Act prohibits the publication of
any material calculated to injure public morals, whether or not it falls
within the ambit of a concise statement, submission on law, etc.

The 1926 Act does not say that the media are allowed to publish in 24.19
matrimonial cases the name of the judge or the court in which the case
is heard or description of the parties or witnesses. But it seems a matter
of common sense that the Act cannot have been intended to ban the
publication of details of this kind, provided any descriptive material
does not amount to evidence.

Decree in Scotland becomes absolute when it is granted, subject to a 24.20
14-day period to allow for any appeal to be lodged. The term "decree
nisi" is not used in Scots law.

Divorce should not be granted until the court is satisfied that the 24.21
welfare of any children of the marriage has been addressed. The
granting of a decree can be delayed in certain cases where the court
has to look into the circumstances in which the children of the
marriage are being cared for before issuing decree.

The restrictions imposed by the 1926 Act upon the reporting of 24.22
matrimonial cases apply to the appeal stages as well as in the court
which first hears the case.

Section 14 of the Presumption of Death (Scotland) Act 1977 states 24.23
that s.1(1)(b) of the 1926 Act does not apply to an action of declarator
of death under the 1977 Act. This followed a technical breach by a
newspaper in 1956, where there was a petition for dissolution of
marriage on the ground of presumed death.

CASES UNDER THE 1926 ACT

24.24   Any doubts over the continuing validity of the 1926 legislation were removed by a case in 1996 in which the procurator fiscal in Glasgow investigated claims that the *Evening Times* and the Scottish edition of the *Daily Mail* had breached the Act over reports of a divorce action at Glasgow Sheriff Court involving a member of the Scottish bar. The reports recounted in detail what the *Daily Mail* described as "the drama of [a] bitter divorce action".

24.25   The deputy Crown Agent wrote to the director of the Scottish Daily Newspaper Society confirming that, following a complaint by the advocate involved, Strathclyde Police had been instructed by the fiscal to look into alleged contraventions of s.1 of the 1926 Act. The letter stated that Crown counsel had considered the reports by police and the fiscal and concluded that there should be no criminal proceedings. No reason was given for the decision not to prosecute. The letter continued:

> "Crown counsel are concerned that there may be some apprehension as to the continued applicability of the 1926 Act. I have therefore been asked to write to you and the editors of the two newspapers pointing out that the 1926 Act remains in force."

24.26   In *Re Moynihan* **(1997)**, the President of the Family Division, Sir Stephen Brown, of the High Court in England and Wales ruled in terms that the 1926 Act applied to proceedings in that case, which was concerned with nullity of a decree of divorce.

> "As long as the provisions of the 1926 Act remain in force it will be necessary for the prosecution authorities to consider the question of prosecution in any case which may be referred to them on a case by case basis."

24.27   Sir Stephen adopted what appeared to be an extremely liberal interpretation of how the media should approach the Act, but also pointed out that *Moynihan* was a very exceptional case. After the death of Lord Moynihan, his fourth wife Editha raised a court action to have their divorce declared null and void. On the first day of the case the media attended en masse and Sir Stephen read out the relevant parts of the 1926 Act, pointing out that in defended divorce cases the evidence could not be reported, even although it was given in open court. The statement of the charges, defences and counter-charges in support of which the evidence was given could be published, but not the details of the evidence. That meant that the nature of the charges could be published, as could the final judgment of the court in full, "without editing in any sense so that the full matter might be revealed in the course of the judgment."

Up to that point the judge's understanding of the law appears to 24.28 coincide with the views expressed so far in this chapter. However, Sir Stephen went on to say that nobody in court (including the Attorney General) had raised any substantial objections as to why details should not be made public as and when they arose. The judge said he had a great deal of sympathy with reporters but pointed out that the terms of the 1926 Act were mandatory and did not allow the court any discretion to lift reporting restrictions. He added: "The Attorney General has ... indicated that he would not be very anxious to institute criminal proceedings if by some oversight there was a breach of the strict letter of the law." He warned, however, that until Parliament intervened the Act did apply.

> "Having said that, it is quite plain that there would appear to be ample scope ... for clear and full details of the proceedings to be given, though not necessarily a line by line account of what a particular witness says at any particular time."

If the judge meant that the general gist of a witness's evidence can be 24.29 reported, even though not a line by line account, that provides greater scope for reporting divorce actions than had previously been understood. The judge also made it clear that he saw no objection to the reporting of closing submissions and the *Daily Telegraph* duly ran a report under the headline: "Wives fight for the Moynihan millions." The *Telegraph* report went into details of the evidence as rehearsed by counsel.

That was, of course, an English decision, and it remains to be seen 24.30 whether a Scottish court would take a similarly relaxed view. The first prosecution of any kind in the United Kingdom at Paisley Sheriff Court in *Friel v Scott* **(2000)** [below] suggests not.

FIRST PROSECUTION

Proceedings for a breach of the 1926 Act were taken in *Friel v Scott* 24.31 **(2000)** against the *Glasgow Evening Times*, the *Scottish Daily Mail*, the *Scottish Daily Express*, the *Paisley Daily Express* and the *Scotsman*. The charge stated that the newspapers had published reports of judicial proceedings of an action of divorce at Paisley Sheriff Court. The charge said that material had been published which was not a concise statement of the charges, defences and counterclaims in support of which evidence had been given. The action had been settled without evidence being heard, but newspapers published allegations of homosexual encounters, violence and theft from documents lodged in court.

24.32 The sheriff dismissed the complaints on the argument that Paisley Sheriff Court had no jurisdiction to try the case. He said there was no dispute that the newspapers were circulating in the Paisley area, but in his view each was printed outwith the jurisdiction.

24.33 The submission for the newspapers was that publishing occurred at the place of printing. At that point the newspaper was sold to wholesalers for onward sale. Any offence was completed when printing was completed and anything done after that to bring the newspaper into the hands of the public was not part of publication. The Crown argued that it was wrong to say that publication stopped at the door of the printing press. There was a whole chain of events up to sale and they were all part of the process of publication.

24.34 The sheriff said, however:

> "It seems to me that in the context of this criminal statute ... 'publish' occurs at one point in time and place... . It seems wrong that although the accused does nothing more once the paper is handed over that nonetheless he is to be held to be criminally responsible for matters thereafter that are beyond his control... . It is my view that publication for the purposes of the statute takes place once and that is when the paper is handed over to the wholesaler at point of printing."

24.35 The sheriff said the fact that the *Paisley Daily Express* coincidentally sold the paper directly in the sheriffdom was irrelevant if the publishing was complete at an earlier point.

24.36 The Crown appeal against the decision was rejected by three judges at the High Court in Edinburgh headed by Lord Rodger, then Lord Justice General.

24.37 In the appeal, the Crown argued that the sheriff had been wrong to rule that publication for the purposes of the 1926 Act took place once—when the paper was handed over to the wholesaler at the point of printing. According to the Crown the offence of publication involved the circulation for sale of a newspaper within the jurisdiction of the court. The argument was that publication should be regarded as a continuing offence, beginning at the printing works when the publisher handed the newspaper over for distribution to retailers and persisting when the public bought their newspapers from the retailer. A newspaper was published whenever and wherever it was offered to the public by the proprietor, the Crown maintained. In this case the publishers had offered the newspapers for sale in Paisley.

24.38 Lord Rodger said he was satisfied that the Crown approach must be rejected. In the context of the 1926 Act it appeared to him that an

editor or publisher published a newspaper at the point where it had
been printed and was offered for sale or distribution.

He said: "The origin of the Act in a desire to prevent a salacious   24.39
public being regaled with accounts of unsavoury details from judicial
proceedings is of some importance for present purposes." The Act had
been introduced not to protect the privacy of those involved in the
proceedings but to prevent injury to the morals of those who might
read the reports in the newspapers. Thus:

> "The aim of the Act is ... to prevent injury to public morals
> throughout Great Britain by the publication of unsavoury
> matters and details from judicial proceedings, wherever they
> may be held... . Nor is this surprising: in 1963, for instance,
> newspaper reports of Lord Wheatley's opinion in the Argyll
> divorce case were devoured just as eagerly in London as in
> Edinburgh where the action was heard."

Similarly, although the present divorce case was in Paisley, Parliament   24.40
must have been just as concerned to prevent injury to the morals of
readers in Edinburgh. He pointed out that by a "nice irony" the baby
whose birth gave rise to the 1926 Act—Geoffrey Russell, the
improbable result of a *mariage gris* between Lord Ampthill and
Christabel Russell—later became deputy chairman of Express
Newspapers.

Lord Rodger said that interpretation of the 1926 Act was consistent   24.41
with the statutory aim of preventing publication of reports calculated
to injure public morals. The court therefore held:

> "If any offences were committed they were committed when the
> papers were offered for sale or distribution at the publishers'
> works or offices ... They were not committed at the stage when
> the papers were circulating in Paisley; there is accordingly no
> basis for the Sheriff Court at Paisley having jurisdiction to try
> the alleged offences."

This approach, i.e. that the 1926 Act is about public decency, not   24.42
individual privacy, was endorsed by the Supreme Court in *Re
Guardian News and Media Ltd* **(2010)**, a case concerned with
suspected terrorists rather than divorces.

BREACH OF THE 1926 ACT AND DEFAMATION

In a 2002 defamation case, also involving a divorce concerning a   24.43
member of the Scottish bar—one which featured allegations of
assault, irresponsibility towards children of the marriage and lying—
Lady Paton was asked to decide how a claimed breach of the 1926 Act

would affect a newspaper's right to defend itself on the basis that the article complained of was a privileged court report. Lady Paton said that a journalist was not responsible under the 1926 Act, on the basis that he did not "print or publish" or "cause or procure" the article's printing. She also took the view that the 1926 Act did not give a divorce litigant any civil law right to recover damages from a newspaper (taking a different view from that of the English judge in the *Argyll* case, who had thought the 1926 Act a suitable basis for granting an individual like the Duchess an injunction). The Act provided only criminal sanctions. It was for the benefit of the public, not the parties. She left open the question of whether a litigant could seek an interdict against a breach of the Act. Finally, she held that a breach of the 1926 Act would not mean that a fair and accurate court report ceased to be privileged for defamation purposes (*Nicol v Caledonian Newspapers* (2002)).

RECENT ENGLISH CASE LAW ON THE 1926 ACT

24.44   In June 2009, refusing to exclude the media from a hearing about financial arrangements concerning the divorce of Earl Spencer, brother of the Princess of Wales, and his second wife, the English judge Munby J. declined to give guidance as to whether the 1926 Act applied, pointing out that this would be advisory, not judicial (*Spencer v Spencer* (2009)) [see **para.25.82**]. Five months later, McFarlane J. decided that the divorce case between Denis Morley and Alzbeta Holmokova, featuring claims that a banker had offered £500,000 to "lure" the wife away, was to be held in public. Ms Holmokova had said that she would drop the petition rather than have the case heard in public. The judge said that the restrictions in the Judicial Proceedings (Regulation of Reports) Act 1926 would be backed up where necessary by further restrictions on what was reportable.

DECLARATION OF FREEDOM AND PUTTING TO SILENCE

24.45   The old Scottish action for declarator of freedom and putting to silence—used to stop people claiming to be married to someone, a relic from the days in which irregular marriage was common in Scotland—was abolished by the Family Law (Scotland) Act 2006, although apparently the courts could still grant an interdict to the same effect.

KEY POINTS

1. The Judicial Proceedings (Regulation of Reports) Act 1926 24.46
   places strict limits on what can be reported in divorce and
   related cases. Detailed reporting of evidence is not allowed.
   Legal argument can be reported. The safest way to report
   defended divorces is to wait for a written judgment.

2. There was no prosecution under the 1926 Act in the United
   Kingdom until 1999 when the Crown took proceedings
   against five newspapers over reports of a divorce case at
   Paisley Sheriff Court. The sheriff decided that he had no
   jurisdiction to hear the case because the papers had not been
   published within the sheriffdom and his decision was upheld
   on appeal. The decision means that, for the purposes of the
   1926 Act, publication takes place once—when a newspaper is
   handed over to the wholesaler at the point of printing.

3. The 1926 Act also bans in any judicial proceedings the
   publication of indecent material the publication of which is
   calculated to injure public morals.

4. The Act is designed to protect public morals, not to allow
   individuals to sue for breaches.

CHAPTER 25

CHILDREN

By Rosalind McInnes

25.01   The law allows for the protection of anonymity for most children involved in legal proceedings on the assumption that they may be harmed by publicity. The protection is provided in various ways in criminal and civil cases, children's hearings and fatal accident inquiries.

IDENTIFYING CHILDREN IN CRIMINAL CASES

25.02   The law on identifying children in criminal cases is contained in s.47 of the Criminal Procedure (Scotland) Act 1995. When s.552 of the Criminal Justice and Licensing (Scotland) Act 2010 comes into force, no child under 12 at the time of the offence will be prosecuted for it, but many children are involved in criminal cases in one capacity or another.

25.03   Section 47 applies to any criminal court in Scotland and forbids revealing in court reports a name, address or school, or including any information calculated to lead to the identification of "any person under 16 years concerned in the proceedings" either as accused or a person "in respect of whom the proceedings are taken", i.e. an alleged victim. A court may at any stage of the proceedings dispense with the ban on identification if satisfied that this is in the public interest. The Scottish Ministers also have power, after a case has been dealt with, to make an order lifting the prohibition or to overrule an order made by the court. The ban on identification applies to pictures as well as to newspaper, radio and television reports of cases.

25.04   Prohibition on use of a picture is absolute in terms. It would include, for example, a pixilated photograph of a child, a dorsal view shot, an interview in silhouette or the like. In practice, photographs of this type are sometimes used, however.

25.05   In *McArdle v Orr* **(1994)**, the Appeal Court of the High Court of Justiciary upheld the conviction of a *Highland News* editor who had used a photograph of a child sexual abuse victim and her mother with "blacked out" faces. The prosecution was not under s.47, but under the children's hearing legislation (the predecessor to what is now s.44 of the Children (Scotland) Act 1995, below). The child's aunt—whose son was found guilty of assaulting the child—said that she recognised the girl and her mother, as did the depute reporter to the children's panel and an assistant reporter. The Lord Justice-Clerk, Lord Ross, said:

"The newspaper in question did publish a photograph as being or including a picture of this child ... It follows that the action of the appellant as editor in publishing that picture was a plain contravention of the provisions of Section 58(1) of the Act of 1968."

The present s.44 of the Children (Scotland) Act 1995 is somewhat differently worded, containing no express reference to pictures, but the court in *McArdle v Orr* (1994) observed: 25.06

"There are also findings to the effect that the Depute Reporter to the Children's Panel, an Assistant Reporter to the Children's Panel, and the aunt of the child ... recognised her from the picture in the newspaper."

CHILD WITNESSES WHO ARE NEITHER THE ACCUSED NOR THE ALLEGED VICTIMS

Where the person under 16 is involved in a criminal case as a witness only *and no-one against whom the proceedings are taken is under 16*, there is no bar on identification unless the court specifically orders one.   25.07

CHILDREN WHO FEATURE IN THE EVIDENCE BUT ARE NOT ACCUSED, ALLEGED VICTIMS OR WITNESSES

If a child is mentioned in the proceedings, but is not the accused, the victim or a witness, then s/he is not covered by s.47. In *HM Advocate v Brown and Wilson* (2009), the Crown Office withdrew a claim that the two-year-old son of one of the accused, and grandson of the victim, could not legally be named under s.47. If a child features significantly in the evidence, without being covered by a statutory reporting restriction, as did this two-year-old grandson of the victim in the "body in the burn" murder trial, a fair and accurate court report may entail identification. For example, in the March 2009 trial of his mother and her partner at Glasgow High Court in connection with the death of toddler Brandon Muir, evidence as to the hospital visits of Brandon's sister was relevant to the question of which adult was said to be responsible. (His mother was acquitted and her partner convicted of culpable homicide.) This small girl was neither an alleged victim nor a witness, so she would not fall within the usual statutory anonymity provisions. Some media outlets chose not to use her name,   25.08

though her mother, after her acquittal, named the child in a tabloid interview.

DEAD CHILDREN

25.09   In a case before the High Court in Edinburgh in (*HM Advocate v George Aitken* (1983)), in which the Crown asked for a ruling on the then current equivalent of s.47, Lord Brand held the section does not apply to dead children. He ruled that a "person" within the meaning of the section was a live person and someone who was dead could not be "concerned" in the proceedings. The judge added that, if he had decided the section did apply, he would have allowed identification in the particular case in the public interest.

REQUESTS TO LIFT STATUTORY ANONYMITY

25.10   In deciding whether or not to allow identification, the court must bear in mind the public interest. The decision will depend very much on the facts of the case and view of the individual judge. In a case in 1991 at the High Court in Edinburgh, Lord Sutherland decided that it would not be in the public interest to lift reporting restrictions in the case of a boy who had been convicted of culpable homicide the previous year, when aged 11, of a three-year-old boy. He was named by the media on his release in 1999 as Richard Keith.

25.11   In *HM Advocate v Bonini* (2005), a toddler had been tragically killed by an air gun whilst in the arms of his elder brother who, because he had been shot at, although not wounded, was also a victim in terms of the charge against Bonini. The BBC, with the consent of the older brother and his family, successfully sought to lift the normal reporting restriction covering the teenager. Naming the older boy enabled the BBC to avoid the clumsy, and sometimes misleading, formula "a boy who cannot be named for legal reasons". Naming a child perpetrator without consent obviously raises different issues from this case.

25.12   Lord Malcolm, in November 2009, refused newspapers' applications to lift the statutory anonymity of two 14-year-old girls and a 13-year-old boy convicted of torturing another young teenager at the Omni Centre in Edinburgh. The English court, in January 2010, similarly refused to remove the anonymity of the Edlington 11-year-olds convicted of torture. Given the continuing publicity surrounding Mary Bell and the Bulger killers, such reluctance is likely to persist in future in relation to children convicted of serious crimes.

25.13   The maximum penalty for contravening the section is a fine of £2,500.

RELEVANT AGE IS CHILD'S AGE AT DATE
OF COURT HEARING

The journalist must look at the child's age when the case is in court. If 25.14
the child becomes 16 on the day the case is before the court, the
automatic ban on identification no longer applies. It is now the
practice of the Crown Office in framing indictments to include the age
of the accused and victims under 16.

STATUTORY ANONYMITY PROVISIONS
TO BE TIGHTLY CONSTRUED

The section has to be read subject to its opening words: "No 25.15
newspaper report of any proceedings in a court shall reveal ...". In
Frame v Aberdeen Journals Ltd (2005), the Appeal Court of the High
Court of Justiciary held that the Aberdeen *Press & Journal* had not
broken the law by naming Luke Mitchell, teenage murderer of Jodi
Jones, when he was arrested. The newspaper was reporting his arrest;
they were not reporting court proceedings. The Appeal Court said
that, whatever the policy arguments for protecting children under 16
who were arrested and charged by the police, the terms of the statute
were clear and had to be strictly applied.

Statutory provisions—which could, after all, result in criminal 25.16
convictions—have been given a stringent and literal interpretation
both in the Luke Mitchell case and in *Clayton v Clayton* (2007).
There, the English Court of Appeal, to everyone's surprise, held that
an abducting father could identify his child as having previously been
involved in family court proceedings. The phrase "identify ... any
child as being involved" had to be construed strictly, so as to include
ongoing proceedings only. However, the court granted an injunction
banning the father from involving the child in a film he wanted to make
about the abduction and his arrest. There still could be no reference to
what had been said behind closed doors in the family proceedings.

Not only must the restrictions be construed narrowly, the orders 25.17
themselves must be specific. In the English case of *Briffet & Bradshaw
v DPP* (2002), an order which simply said "that under Section 39 of
the Children and Young Persons Act 1933 reporting restrictions
apply in respect of the Applicant herein and that this matter be listed
as ex parte 'K'" was regarded as quite inadequate. The boy in that case
had been excluded from school following an alleged sexual assault on
another child; the order had been granted in relation to judicial review
proceedings taken by his mother against his expulsion. In principle,
however, a s.39 order would have been competent in English civil
proceedings, and the case is a reminder that even children who may

have committed serious offences can expect a degree of additional protection from the law in the UK.

APPEALS

25.18   The Act makes no express provision for appeal against a court's direction either allowing or banning publication in terms of s.47, but the Scottish court is willing to hear the media, to judge from *HM Advocate v Slonaker* **(2005)** [see **para.25.42**].

CHILD RELATIVES OF ACCUSED OR CONVICTED PERSONS

25.19   A case at the High Court in Edinburgh in 1990 illustrated the unexpected problems the section can cause. A man was charged with murdering his wife, and the only person under 16 involved in the case was the wife's son by a previous marriage, who was an eyewitness to the fatal attack. The Crown asked for an order to prohibit the child's identification in media reports on the basis that he was now living with relatives at a new address and attending a new school where no-one knew of his tragic background.

25.20   Lord Milligan acknowledged the wide public interest in the free reporting of our criminal courts, but decided that in this case the boy's identity should be protected by banning publication of his name, address, or school. Reporters present in court pointed out, through the clerk, that it would be difficult, if not impossible to report the names of the accused and the victim of the alleged murder without revealing the boy's identity. They argued that it was highly undesirable to report a murder trial anonymously.

25.21   Lord Milligan stressed that his intention was that there should be no publicity only as to the fact that the boy had given evidence, the content of the evidence or that he was present when the alleged murder took place. The compromise was reached that the trial was reported with the names of the accused and the deceased but no mention whatsoever was made of the boy or his evidence.

25.22   It is unlikely that such an approach would be adopted nowadays. Lord Philip was unhappy with the Crown's suggestion during the first trial for the murder of Pollokshields teenager Kriss Donald that the media should be ordered not to report the alleged involvement of other men, who had fled to Pakistan at the time of the first trial, in the fatal attack. His Lordship (who presciently predicted that, despite the extant publicity about the missing co-accused, they would still be tried if they came back to Scotland) said: "But that's the whole nature of the crime" (2004). It is also perhaps unlikely that a report which so distorted the evidence would qualify for any protection as being "fair and accurate".

The most acute clashes between the privacy rights of children and 25.23 the right to receive and impart information have come in the context of criminal trials following domestic tragedies. There have been no Scottish cases in this vein yet, but the English courts have been extremely reluctant to anonymise a criminal defendant, regardless of the claimed consequences for his or her child. The leading case is *Re S* **(2004)**, where a mother stood accused of poisoning her small son with salt. Attempts to anonymise her, with her consent, in order to protect the privacy and to facilitate the upbringing of her surviving child, were rejected by the House of Lords.

Lord Steyn, in a ringing endorsement of open justice, said: 25.24

> "There are numerous automatic statutory reporting restrictions … There are also numerous statutory provisions, which provide for discretionary reporting restrictions: see, for example, Section 8(4) of the Official Secrets Act 1920. Given the number of statutory exceptions, it needs to be said clearly and unambiguously that the court has no power to create by a process of analogy, except in the most compelling circumstances, further exceptions to the general principle of open justice."

He said: 25.25

> "From a newspaper's point of view, a report of a sensational trial without revealing the identity of the defendant would be a very much disembodied trial … They are less likely to give prominence to reports of [such a] trial. Certainly, readers will be less interested and editors will act accordingly. Informed debate about criminal justice will suffer."

Following that, in *A Local Authority v PD and GD* **(2005)**, the 25.26 President of the English Family Division refused to anonymise a man accused of killing his wife, despite claims that his anonymity was necessary in order to protect their six-year-old daughter. In *Re LM* **(2007)**, the President of the Family Division again refused to anonymise the parents of a child—who was being put forward for adoption—in an inquest where the mother was likely to have been found to have killed the child's sister. The family had a distinctive surname and it was anticipated that it would be difficult to find adoptive parents even without the problems of publicity.

In *R. (on the application of Trinity Mirror) v Croydon Court* 25.27 **(2008)**, the Court of Appeal overturned a Crown Court injunction, which would have anonymised a sex offender to protect his two daughters (not his victims). Just a week later, the Divisional Court in

England lifted reporting restrictions anonymising Lincoln Crawford, a high-profile barrister who had been convicted of harassing his ex-wife, again granted in order to protect his own children (***Crawford v CPS* (2008)**).

25.28 In a number of these cases the facts were very distressing, and the children clearly deserving of particular care, but the courts have firmly held the line on not anonymising people alleged to have committed serious criminal offences in order to avoid what Lord Steyn said in *Re S* was an "essentially indirect" impact upon the alleged offender's own child.

25.29 This does not mean that an anonymised criminal trial can never be contemplated since the Human Rights Act 1998. Sometimes the nature of the offence—for instance, a "home alone" case—or, less often, the defence—for instance, reasonable chastisement in a trial for physical assault of a child—will point so obviously to the relationship between accused and alleged victim, that the accused ought to be anonymised. However, anonymisation of an accused in a serious criminal trial is rarely and reluctantly done. The requirements of open justice will usually triumph, unless Parliament has already passed a statutory exception.

25.30 One notable case is ***Re W* (2005)**, where the President of the Family Division granted an injunction anonymising a convicted woman and the partner she had knowingly infected with AIDS, in order to protect her two small children, who needed urgently to be found a home, against the effects and stigma of publicity. Perhaps the distinguishing factor here is that it was feared that the children themselves (certainly inaccurately in one case and probably inaccurately in the other—the baby was too young to be tested) would be stigmatised as suffering from the disease.

25.31 In ***Re X and Y (Children)* (2004)**, Munby J. granted an injunction to stop the media mentioning the handicapped and motherless twins of the criminal defendant's identical twin brother, who was being tried for sexual offences against other children, where the children's father was himself a convicted paedophile. However, photographs of both men were allowed and the trial, including the father's evidence, could otherwise be fully reported. This case was obviously very unusual on its facts and the impact upon open justice was minimal. The children were not a significant part of the trial and the main point was to stop the re-publication of previous favourable human interest stories about them and linking these to their uncle's trial.

25.32 It is not uncommon to have orders granted which purport to prevent the mention of the existence of children whose parents are involved in criminal proceedings—for instance, such an order covers one notorious child murderer's own two young daughters. The media have never sought to challenge these, it would appear, and in terms of their own codes it would rarely be self-consistent to do so.

MEANING OF "CALCULATED"

When Parliament bans publication of information "calculated" to lead to identification, that does not mean that the journalist will be excused if s/he did not actually "calculate" that identification would take place as a result of what s/he had written. The journalist must decide whether identification of the child would follow as a natural and likely result of publication. In 1982 the *Lothian Courier*, Bathgate, was fined £75 at Linlithgow Sheriff Court for naming a man in a report it carried of his conviction for assault on his 18-month-old daughter. The newspaper admitted a charge under s.47, that publication of the man's name was "calculated" to lead to the identification of the child, although that was not the paper's intention.

25.33

CHILD VICTIMS, INCEST AND JIGSAW IDENTIFICATION

Child victims are entitled to anonymity. In non-incest cases involving abuse or neglect of children, the practice in Scotland whenever possible is to name the adult accused and not to specify his/her relationship to a living child victim. Special risks arise where the nature of the case implies the victim's relationship to the offender. In reporting cases of incest or other sexual offences, the media in Scotland have followed the practice of not identifying alleged victims. This is now also covered by the Sexual Offences (Amendment) Act 1992, which has been extended to Scotland since the last edition of this book. Where the person in question is under 16 it is an offence in any case to publish his or her identity under s.47. Incest cases often come to light after many years, when the victim has grown up, and, because of the inevitable family link, protection of the complainer's identity requires particular care. If the incest is felt to be journalistically central—for example, in cases where a man has impregnated his own children during extended abuse—it will normally be necessary to anonymise the convicted person, unless the victim, once adult, waives her anonymity.

25.34

The media must take care to avoid "jigsaw identification" where two or more reports, each protecting the anonymity of a child, may disclose her identity when read together. This could happen where one report names the accused but does not disclose his relationship to the victim, while another publishes an anonymous report indicating the accused's relationship to the victim.

25.35

25.36   The Press Complaints Commission Code states that, in cases including children under 16 who are alleged victims *or* witnesses in sexual offences cases, the word "incest" must not be used where a child victim might be identified. The adult may be identified, but: "Care must be taken that nothing in the report implies the relationship between the accused and the child".

25.37   The Ofcom code says:

> "Where statutory or other legal restrictions apply preventing personal identification, broadcasters should ... be particularly careful not to provide clues which may lead to the identification of those who are not yet adult ... and who are, or might be, included as a victim, witness, defendant or other perpetrator in the case of sexual offences featured in criminal, civil or family court proceedings:
>
> by reporting limited information which may be pieced together with other information available elsewhere, for example in newspaper reports (the 'jigsaw effect');
>
> inadvertently, for example by describing an offence as 'incest'; or
>
> in any other indirect way."

25.38   Where a case of incest is reported, the practice of Scottish newspaper editors has been that the adult is identified but the word "incest" is not used, the offence being described as "a serious offence against a young child" or the like. The child is not identified and the report excludes anything implying the relationship between the accused and the child.

25.39   Similar concerns may arise with adult incest survivors. Increasingly, some child abuse survivors choose to be identified and/or to write about their experiences. Written or taped consent from the victim is advisable for the media if they wish to carry such stories.

SIBLINGS IN ABUSE CASES

25.40   In the case of sexual crime, it should also be remembered that, while an adult survivor can identify him or herself, no-one is entitled to "out" a sibling as a fellow victim of rape, etc. Pragmatically, too, there may be defamation risks in such histories, where family members often take different views of long distant events of which there is typically scant documentation. At least two "misery memoirs" have resulted in defamation actions, over Constance Bristowe's *Ugly* and Gayle Sanders's *Mummy's Witness*.

NO POWER UNDER STATUTORY PROVISIONS PROTECTING CHILDREN TO ANONYMISE AN ADULT

In *R. v Teesside Crown Court Ex p. Gazette Media Company* (2005), 25.41
the English Court of Appeal held that the child victim anonymity
legislation could not be used to prohibit, in terms, naming the
defendant, but:

> "[I]f the offender is named and the victim is described as 'an 11-
> year-old schoolgirl', in circumstances in which the offender has an
> 11-year-old daughter, it is at least arguable that the composite
> picture presented embraces 'particulars calculated to lead to the
> identification' of the victim."

The same approach has been taken to the Scottish legislation. In *HM* 25.42
Advocate v Slonaker (2005), Lady Paton refused to make a
s.4(2) order to postpone reporting until all witnesses under the age of
16 had given their evidence (for fear of possible influencing of the
young witnesses by media reports). She also refused to grant any
order specifically anonymising one of the accused, who was over 16,
despite claims that to name him would be to identify his co-accused,
who were still children. But, again, as with the *Teesside Crown Court*
case, that does not mean a newspaper is necessarily safe to name. Her
Ladyship said:

> "In relation to Section 47, a decision will have to be made by the
> media as to whether or not publication of the first accused's name
> in press reports of the trial would, or would not, be calculated to
> lead to the identification of the second and third accused."

INHERENTLY IDENTIFICATORY DETAILS

On rare occasions, the simple facts of the case may pose a risk of 25.43
identification. In May 2009, West Lothian Council sought an
interdict against various papers who had, with the mother's and
grandmother's encouragement, run stories about a girl who gave
birth at a very early age. Later, the baby's father was prosecuted for
her rape. Lord Malcolm declined to grant the interdict, but opined
that to give the girl's age at the time of the baby's birth could identify
her and thus breach s.47 (*West Lothian Council v News Group
Newspapers Ltd* (2009)).

ASBOS AND PARENTING ORDERS

Under the Anti-Social Behaviour etc. (Scotland) Act 2004, it is an 25.44
offence to publish "anywhere in the world" anything which would
identify those involved in proceedings relating to parenting orders—

specifically, the parent, the child, a sibling or any other child who is a member of the same household, the address of the parent, the address or the school of the child. The court may, in the interests of justice, relax these restrictions.

25.45   There is a defence if the person publishing did not know and had no reason to suspect that the published matter was intended, or was likely, to identify the person concerned, child, address or school. This, of course, is restricted to publishing matter about the parenting order proceedings which would identify these people. If, e.g. the parent is convicted of murder, or the child wins a swimming competition, there is nothing to stop the family's being identified, so long as the parenting proceedings are not involved. Section 111 provides, too, that a child in whose interests a parenting order has been made is also covered under s.47 of the Criminal Procedure (Scotland) Act 1995 [see **para.25.03**].

25.46   Section 138 of the same Act provides that court proceedings concerning child ASBOs or parenting orders are to be heard in private and "no person other than a person whose presence is necessary for the proper consideration shall be present", although the court can direct that the proceedings take place in public or in the presence of additional persons allowed by the court.

25.47   Given that accredited media representatives have long been permitted to attend both children's hearings and criminal cases involving children, this is one more case where the Scottish Parliament has retrenched drastically on open justice in a way which may not be Convention-compliant [see **para.36.06**].

FATAL ACCIDENT INQUIRIES

25.48   The Fatal Accidents and Sudden Deaths Inquiry (Scotland) Act 1976 states that inquiries under its terms should be held in public but where "a person under the age of 17 is in any way involved" (a provision open to wide interpretation), the sheriff may order that the child's name, address or school, or any particulars calculated to lead to the identification of the child, should not be revealed, or any picture relating to the inquiry which includes a picture of the child published or broadcast.

25.49   The wide scope of the Act can be seen from a fatal accident inquiry at Dumbarton Sheriff Court in 1984 into the death of a six-week old baby boy. The late Lord Caplan, then sheriff principal, agreed to a motion by counsel for the boy's parents that there should be reporting restrictions in the case. The result was that no-one was named in reports of the inquiry, although the names had already been published in a statutory advertisement published in the *Herald*. The reason given in court for applying reporting restrictions was to protect the three-year-old sister of the dead infant. She was said to be involved in the case because of the father's evidence that he had dropped his baby son after the little girl pulled his arm.

At Forfar Sheriff Court in 1992, during a fatal accident inquiry into 25.50 the death of a 14-year-old girl from inhaling solvent, Sheriff Kermack made an order purporting to ban the media from naming everyone involved in the inquiry under the age of 17, including the dead girl. It is difficult to see how this order could properly be made insofar as it related to the dead girl. On the analogy of Lord Brand's decision in the *Aitken* case [see **para.25.09**], the dead girl was not legally a person covered by the provision. It does not appear to have been followed in more recent cases, such as the fatal accident inquiries into the deaths of 14-year-old cadet Kaylee McIntosh and two-year-old Muireann McLaughlin in May 2009. The case law so far militates against anonymisation of adults in such circumstances with a view to protecting children. The *Re LM* (2007) decision [see **para.25.26**], which concerned an inquest, the English equivalent of a fatal accident inquiry, is likely to be persuasive in a Scottish fatal accident inquiry. There, the President of the Family Division refused to anonymise the parents of a "disturbed" child, with a distinctive surname, for whom adoption was being sought, in an inquest where the mother was likely to be found to have killed the child's sister.

CHILDREN'S HEARINGS

The Social Work (Scotland) Act 1968 abolished juvenile courts and 25.51 brought about important changes in the methods of dealing with children. It laid down that a child could be prosecuted for an offence only on the instructions of the Lord Advocate, and that no court, other than the High Court of Justiciary and the sheriff court, had jurisdiction over a child for an offence.

It requires every local authority to set up a children's panel—a pool 25.52 of suitably qualified citizens to hear cases involving children who may need compulsory measures of supervision, including children who have committed offences. The majority of cases in recent years, however, are on care and welfare grounds—children as victims, rather than offenders.

Residential establishments provide education and care for children 25.53 referred to them by children's hearings or sheriff courts. A child who poses a serious risk to him or herself, or to other people, can be placed in secure accommodation, the case to be reviewed every three months.

25.54   The Scottish Children Reporter's Administration, a non-departmental government body funded directly by the Scottish Government, employs officers known as reporters.

25.55   The 1968 Act also requires each local authority to appoint an officer to arrange children's hearings. Reporters do not have to be legally qualified. Most are from a legal or social work background. Where the reporter considers that a child may be in need of compulsory measures of supervision, it is his or her duty to arrange a children's hearing.

25.56   Cases of this kind are heard by three members of the appropriate panel. This tribunal, consisting of a chairman and two other members, must include at least one woman. It is properly termed a children's hearing and not a children's panel, which, as already explained, refers to the complete list of people from whom the members of any particular children's hearing are selected. A child can be referred to a children's hearing by anyone, but the great majority of referrals come from the police. There are various grounds of referral: that the child is beyond the control of any relevant person (typically a parent); falling into bad association or exposed to moral danger; suffering from lack of parental care; the victim of an offence or the member of the same household as the perpetrator of an offence against a child or the victim of an offender; failing to attend school regularly, without reasonable cause; has committed an offence; or is misusing drugs, alcohol or solvents. The standard of proof is the civil standard, i.e. on the balance of probabilities, except where a child is being charged with any offence, in which case proof has to be beyond reasonable doubt. Children's hearings cannot appoint curators ad litem, who can only be appointed by the courts, but can appoint a legal representative. This may be done in complex cases or where the child's liberty is at stake.

25.57   There is a right of appeal by a child or parent, or both, to the sheriff against a decision of a children's hearing, and the appeal is heard in chambers. It was decided in 1991, in a case (*Sloan v B* (**1991**)) in which it was alleged that nine children in Orkney had been ritually abused, that when a case is referred from a children's hearing to a sheriff to determine whether the grounds of referral are established, a sheriff has the discretion to allow the press into chambers to report the proceedings. Reports must not contain any information which would identify any child involved. A sheriff who is not satisfied that the decision was justified can impose another decision, but more usually the case may be sent back to the children's hearing for reconsideration, and the normal rules then apply to reports of the proceedings. Appeals from the sheriff can be made to the Court of Session or to the sheriff principal.

The present law is to be found in the Children (Scotland) Act 1995.   25.58
Although children's hearings are conducted in private, bona fide
representatives of a newspaper or news agency are entitled to attend.
The press can be excluded if it is necessary to do so, in the interests of
the child, to obtain the child's view in relation to the case, or if their
presence is likely to cause "significant distress to the child". Section
44 of the Act was extensively amended by Criminal Justice (Scotland)
Act 2003. Section 44(1) now reads:

> "No person shall publish any matter in respect of a case about
> which the Principal Reporter has from any source received
> information or any matter in respect of proceedings at a
> Children's Hearing, or before a Sheriff on an application
> [relating to child protection orders; referral to a Children's
> Hearing; exclusion orders from the child's family home for the
> child's protection; or review of establishment of grounds of
> referral] which is intended to, or is likely to, identify—
> (a) the child concerned in, or any other child connected (in any
>   way) with, the case, proceedings or appeal; or
> (b) an address or school as being that of any such child."

For these purposes, a child is anyone under *18*.   25.59
   "To publish" includes "to cause matter to be published".   25.60
   This considerably broadens the previous restrictions on reporting.   25.61
"[A]ny other child connected (in any way)" is obviously a wide
definition. There is a similar provision in the fatal accident inquiry
legislation, but there the sheriff would have to grant the order and
thus to specify the child to be protected. In many cases, the journalist
will not be in a position to know, realistically, what information the
Principal Reporter has, or which children may be indirectly involved
in a case.
   The term "case" is not defined. Clearly, though, it must be taken to   25.62
refer to a case within the children's hearing system. Children are very
often referred to the children's hearing system because of offences
committed by adults. The amendment can hardly be intended to
prevent the publication of evidence or to anonymise the accused, by
the back door, in those trials. What it does cover, however, is by no
means certain; and since the journalist is unlikely to have any idea as
to the Principal Reporter's state of knowledge, practically impossible
to comply with, regardless of how it is interpreted. This provision may
not, for that reason, survive a human rights challenge.
   Section 44(3) provides a general defence for someone accused under   25.63
s.44 who can, "prove that he did not know, and had no reason to
suspect, that the published matter was intended, or was likely, to
identify the child or ... the address or school".

25.64   Section 44 may be dispensed with by the sheriff, judge or Scottish Ministers "in the interests of justice". Breach is punishable by a maximum fine of £2,500.

WHAT CONSTITUTES IDENTIFICATION?

25.65   Disclosure of the sex and age of a child in a named village or small community or, for example, that he is the son of a policeman or teacher, could well lead to his identity being disclosed. In cases of that kind it may be necessary to leave out a local name and give instead only the name of the county or region so that the child's identity is protected. The issue inevitably arises: identifiable to whom?

25.66   English judges appear to have taken the view that it is identification to those who do not already know the story. In *Medway Council v G* **(2008)**, Sir Mark Potter, President of the Family Division, said, in deciding to name Medway Council, that all the locals would know the story: "The court must concentrate on the position of those who do not already know who the child is."

25.67   In *Re B (A Child: Disclosure)* **(2004)**, Munby J. allowed Kent County Council to be named, observing:

> "There is of course the risk that identification of a local authority will make it easier for those already in the know, or for those who are part of B's close family, domestic or social circle, to realise that something being published is in fact about her, rather than about some other child. But that is not of itself ... a sufficient reason to keep the identity of the local authority secret."

25.68   As far back as 1990, Dame Elizabeth Butler-Sloss had said in *Re M and N (Minors)* **(1990)**: "Unless there is a total ban ... someone somewhere may put the story to the person."

25.69   On the other hand, in the *Teesside Crown Court* **(2005)** case [see **para.25.41**] the "composite picture" entailed a knowledge of the detailed family circumstances of the offender. Certainly, in *McArdle v Orr* **(1994)** [see **para.25.05**], evidence as to identification was led from the child's aunt (herself the mother of the child's attacker), and two officials who had attended at the children's hearing itself. It seems likely, though, that the Appeal Court in that case regarded the inclusion of any picture, identificatory or not, as a breach of the terms of the particular legislation.

25.70   This is a difficult area of the law, because the reality is that most children have a fairly small social circle from which, sadly, their attackers (or, much less frequently, their victims) are likely to come. In other words, the reporting of the essential facts of a case involving a child, particularly where prolonged abuse or neglect is alleged, will tend to identify a small circle of possible victims, once the convicted person has been named. The most practical advice for Scottish journalists is to follow, wherever possible, the conventions in place to avoid jigsaw identification, and, specifically, to avoid any unnecessary detail which would increase the likelihood of a child victim or accused being identified to anyone who does not already "know the story".

CIVIL CASES INVOLVING CHILDREN, INCLUDING RESIDENCE AND CONTACT DISPUTES

Where a dispute over who "gets" the children is part of divorce 25.71 proceedings, reporting will be restricted under the Judicial Proceedings (Regulation of Reports) Act 1926 [see **Chapter 24**]. However, the media may be banned from identifying children in a civil hearing, even although it is not part of a divorce action.

Section 46 of the Children and Young Persons (Scotland) Act 1937 25.72 states that in relation to any proceedings in any court, the court may direct that no media report shall reveal the name, address or school, or include any particulars calculated to lead to the identification of a person under the age of 17 concerned in the proceedings. It applies to a person by or against or in respect of whom the proceedings are taken, or who is a witness. The prohibition applies to pictures of such a person in relation to the proceedings. Breach is punishable by a fine of up to £2,500. It can be used to cover a child witness in parenting order proceedings [see **paras 25.44 onwards**].

The long standing doubt over whether s.46 applied to civil cases 25.73 came about because it was originally included in a section of the 1937 Act which referred expressly to criminal proceedings. However, in the *C v S* **(1989)** case, the Inner House of the Court of Session, where divorced parents living in different countries were arguing over the care of their son, but agreed that publicity over the case would distress him, accepted that it had a wider scope. Since *C v S*, judges and sheriffs have made orders banning the identification of children on a number of occasions under s.46: see the court announcements section on the Scottish Courts website (*http:// www.scotcourts.gov.uk* [Accessed September 17, 2010]). Often they relate to orders under the Child Abduction and Custody Act 1985 involving, e.g. allegations of child abuse (*PQ, Petitioner* **(2000)**), but one has been granted in a sheriff court action for recovery of possession of a rented property (*City of Edinburgh Council v HT* **(2003)**).

In principle, civil cases involving children can be reported in an 25.74 identifiable manner. It is for the court to make an order under s.46 to say if they are not (*DM* **(2000)**)—unless of course, they are caught by other anonymising legislation. The effect of such an order is that, if the case is reported at all, it has to be in an anonymised form. Note, however, that it is only where the judge makes an order in a civil case that the media are prevented from identifying the child involved. In criminal cases, identification of a child accused of, or alleged to be the victim of, crime is banned unless the judge makes a specific order to the contrary.

25.75   Now that judgments of the Court of Session, High Court of Justiciary and often sheriff courts are regularly put on to the Scottish courts website, the High Court of Justiciary has issued a practice note (No.1 of 2007), saying when they need to be anonymised.

ADOPTION PROCEDURE

25.76   Section 109 of the Adoption and Children (Scotland) Act 2007 provides that a wide range of proceedings under the Act are heard and determined in private, unless the court directs otherwise. This includes hearings for the return of a child unlawfully removed, for the making of adoption orders, for the making, variation or revocation of permanence orders, or for orders granting authority for a child to be adopted. Likewise, all documents lodged in court in adoption proceedings are treated as confidential under the Rules of Court. The reporting of adoption proceedings is therefore extremely difficult, if not impossible, except where the court permits the hearing to take place in public. This rarely happens in practice, but occasionally, adoption proceedings have been reported on an anonymised basis.

25.77   An example of this was a case in 1973 where an important point affecting procedure to be followed in adoption cases in general was debated in the First Division. The proceedings were of sufficient importance to be reported in some newspapers, without names and addresses.

ENGLISH FAMILY PROCEEDINGS
INVOLVING CHILDREN

25.78   In the past, wardship jurisdiction exercised by the English courts over children who had been made wards of court was presumed—wrongly—to give children anonymity or other protection from the media's attention. In 1984, Balcombe J. ruled that the English High Court had power to make an anonymity order "against the world at large", i.e. the entire media (including, in effect, those Scottish media outlets with assets and circulation in England). Mary Bell had been convicted of the manslaughter with diminished responsibility of two boys, aged four and three, when she was 11 years old and living in

Newcastle. She was released on licence in 1980, made a new life for herself under a different name, and had a baby daughter who had been made a ward of court. The judge issued an injunction to stop the *News of the World* revealing the woman's identity, that of her child or of the child's father, and extended his order to apply to all the media in the interests of the ward—*Re X (A Minor) (Wardship: Injunction)* **(1985)**. When her daughter came of age, the law of breach of confidence had developed so exponentially since the advent of the Human Rights Act 1998 [see **Chapter 36**] that a further "contra mundum" injunction was granted to protect the identities of Mary Bell and her daughter—*X (formerly known as Mary Bell)* **(2003)**. In 2009, Mary Bell became a grandmother, and yet another injunction—again, based on breach of confidence—was granted to protect the anonymity of the baby and, hence, the baby's mother and grandmother. (Mary Bell would have been protected under the English law anonymising children accused of crime in 1968, when she was tried, but the judge lifted the restriction.)

Very crudely, the position in English law with family proceedings is 25.79 that there are two main provisions. Section 97(2) of the Children Act 1989 prevents identification of a child as being involved with certain proceedings. Section 12 of the Administration of Justice Act 1960 prevents publication of information relating to proceedings of a court sitting in private where the proceedings are brought under the Children Act 1989, relate to the exercise of the inherent jurisdiction of the High Court in respect of minors, or otherwise relate wholly or mainly to the upbringing of a minor.

Section 97(2) only applies while the Children Act 1989 proceedings 25.80 are ongoing, so children can be identified afterwards as having been involved in such proceedings, but the prohibition under the 1960 Act still stops publication of what happened in the court sitting in private and what it decided, unless there is permission to publish. So if details of the proceedings are to be published at all after they are over, the court has to give permission for that (because s.12 of the 1960 Act still applies), and if there is a need to anonymise anyone involved, the court has to prohibit that identification (because s.97(2) no longer applies)—see, e.g. *William Ward* **(2007)**.

OPENING UP OF THE ENGLISH FAMILY COURTS

The secrecy surrounding family proceedings in England and Wales has 25.81 created so much suspicion and confusion that a strange coalition of journalists, fathers aggrieved at not getting access to their children, parents claiming miscarriages of justice re allegations of abuse and general disquiet over the hegemony of expert diagnoses like

Munchausen's Syndrome by Proxy, has forced a radical change in the court rules, allowing the media a presumptive right to attend. The Scottish courts have routinely allowed the media access to children's hearings and family actions.

25.82   This development is in its own infancy at the time of writing, and subject to attempts to close access down again. Thus far, a bid by Earl Spencer and his latest ex-wife to exclude the media from ancillary relief proceedings in their divorce failed (*Spencer v Spencer* (**2009**)). However, another bid to exclude the media in July 2009 (*Re X* (**2009**)) from a hearing in residence and contact in relation to the daughter of a well-known couple succeeded. There, the issues to be explored were "intimate, emotional and sensitive", the child herself was said to be distressed by having read earlier reports about herself in the newspapers and the likelihood was that she would suspect one or other of her parents of having leaked the information.

BREACH OF CONFIDENCE AND CHILDREN

25.83   Even outside court proceedings, the developing law of privacy has been used to attempt to protect troubled and troublesome children. In *Green Corns v Claverley* (**2005**), another English case, Tugendhat J. granted an injunction against the publication of addresses of children's homes for vulnerable children, including some who were themselves sex offenders. The judge laid emphasis on the clauses of the PCC Code protecting children.

25.84   In *Leeds City Council v Channel Four* (**2005**), Munby J. refused an injunction against a documentary showing covertly-shot footage of unruly schoolchildren. The children were pixilated (face, hair and neck) but it was accepted that they would be identifiable to those in their immediate locality. The teacher was suspended in March 2009 by the General Teaching Council for her actions in covertly filming the children.

CHILDREN OF CELEBRITIES

25.85   The children of parents who are in the public eye for more positive reasons may also be felt to require some protection against the lens. A number of celebrities have complained to the PCC on behalf of their children over the years, but, with the advent of the Human Rights Act 1998, they may increasingly take their complaints to court. In November 2003, Ewan McGregor won an injunction in the High Court in London over photographs covertly taken of his children when the family were on holiday and published in the *Daily Record*. Damages were also to be assessed for breach of confidence and under the Data Protection Act 1998. J.K. Rowling persuaded the Court of Appeal that a photograph of her son being wheeled by her in his pushchair along Princes Street might be actionable (*Murray v Big Pictures (UK) Ltd* (2008)) [see **paras 23.62 onwards**]. Sir Anthony Clarke MR said of the photograph:

> "This was at least arguably a very different case from that to which Baroness Hale referred in her now well known example ... of [Naomi] Campbell being photographed while popping out to buy the milk".

Instead: 25.86
"[A] news agency, a freelance photographer and two newspapers had photographers outside the Murrays' house in the period before publication of the photograph and ... this was not an isolated event ... The photograph could, after all, have been published with David's features pixilated out if [Big Pictures (UK) Ltd] had wished."

He added: "The fact that he is a child is in our view of greater 25.87 significance than the judge thought", and referred to the PCC Code. He concluded:

> "It seems to us that ... the law should indeed protect children from intrusive media attention, at any rate to the extent of holding that a child had a reasonable expectation that he or she will not be targeted in order to obtain photographs in a public place for publication which the person who took or procured the taking of the photograph knew would be objected to on behalf of the child."

A reasonable expectation of privacy might, of course, be outweighed 25.88 by freedom of expression, in a particular case. J.K. Rowling has been consistently zealous in not using her children for publicity purposes. Celebrity parents who seek to control, rather than to avoid, publicity involving their children would be less likely to succeed, as the law presently stands.

Indeed, this applies not only to celebrity parents, but to any parents 25.89 trying to control publicity relating to their children for collateral purposes. In the unusual case of *Paul Dacre & Associated Newspapers v City of Westminster Magistrates Court* (2009), the English Divisional Court stayed, i.e. stopped, a private prosecution mounted by a mother who had, after being embroiled in a bitter custody dispute with her husband, formed a romantic liaison with the head of Fathers 4 Justice and participated in both a high-profile National Lottery protest stunt and an interview explaining herself. She attempted privately to prosecute the *Daily Mail* for publishing information compromising her child's right to anonymity. The court held that the mother could not take her case forward, because she had encouraged publicity which had the very same effect.

25.90   Judges in more orthodox types of family proceeding have also warned parents that they cannot, as it were, run with the hare and hunt with the hounds. Mr Justice Munby in the **Brandon Webster (2006)** case, where a child had been taken into care on wrong suspicions that his parents had injured him, made the point that parents have to accept negative publicity as well as positive. And in **Re B (2004)** [see **para.25.67**], the same judge said:

> "The mother is not necessarily entitled to set the media agenda. If she wants to put some parts of the case into the public domain, then she may have to accept that other less appealing parts of the case are also put into the public domain."

25.91   Given that the child's interests are distinct from those of the parents, there ought, logically, to be limits to the significance attached to the publicity-courting of the parents, but it remains to be seen how any such limit would be set.

CHILDREN'S RIGHTS TO FREEDOM OF EXPRESSION AND FREEDOM OF INFORMATION

25.92   The courts do not simply accord paternalistic protection to children, but, these days, take account of their positive rights, including their own right to freedom of expression. English cases where children have been heard as well as seen include **Angela Roddy (2003)**, which involved an interview with a teenage girl whose baby had been adopted against her wishes; **Kelly v BBC (2001)**, where the BBC was allowed to broadcast an interview with a 16-year-old boy who had been made a ward of court after leaving home to join a fringe religious group; and **X Council v B (2008)**, allowing a 15-year-old and a 10-year-old (with parental consent, in the case of the latter) to identify themselves as the subject of what they saw as wrongful care proceedings. Section 69 of the Freedom of Information (Scotland) Act 2002 allows children to make freedom of information requests.

CHILDREN UNDER 14 NOT ALLOWED IN PUBLIC GALLERY DURING CRIMINAL TRIALS

25.93   The Criminal Procedure (Scotland) Act 1995 s.50, states that no child under 14, except a baby, can be in court during criminal proceedings, except when required as a witness or otherwise for the purposes of justice, or when the court consents. In any proceedings involving an offence against or conduct contrary to decency or morality, where a child is called as a witness, the court can be cleared. Bona fide reporters will be allowed to remain "for the purpose of the preparation of contemporaneous reports of the proceedings."

CHILDREN'S COMMISSIONER REPORTS AND ANONYMITY

As of 2003, Scotland has a Commissioner for Children and Young   25.94
People. Under s.13 of the Act creating the post, the Commissioner has to ensure "so far as reasonable and practicable having regard to the subject matter" a report under the Act does not name or identify a child referred to in it, but this obligation is not placed on the media.

KEY POINTS

1. Section 47 of the Criminal Procedure (Scotland) Act 1995   25.95
    bans the identification of an accused or victim aged under 16
    in criminal cases. The ban can be lifted by the court and does
    not apply where the child victim is dead. Identification is
    allowed where the child is a witness only, unless (a) the judge
    orders otherwise, or (b) one of the accused is under 16.
2. The ban relates to court proceedings and does not come into
    effect at an earlier stage. In rare cases, it may sometimes result
    in a guilty adult being anonymised.
3. To protect children in incest cases, the general practice is to
    say that a named accused has been guilty of a serious sexual
    offence. The term incest is not used.
4. Children's hearings are in private but the media can attend.
    There are extensive prohibitions on identifying children
    involved in any way with cases in the children's hearing
    system (Children (Scotland) Act 1995 s.44).
5. In residence and contact cases, or other civil proceedings, the
    court can make an order banning the identification of a child
    under the age of 17 involved in the proceedings (Children and
    Young Persons (Scotland) Act 1937 s.46).
6. In fatal accident inquiries a sheriff can ban the identification of
    a child under the age of 17 in any way involved in the
    proceedings (Fatal Accidents and Sudden Deaths Inquiry
    (Scotland) Act 1976).
7. Children have their own rights to freedom of expression and
    to receive information.
8. Celebrities whose children are targeted by paparazzi have had
    some success in legal action.

PART 7: DEFAMATION

CHAPTER 26

ESSENTIALS OF DEFAMATION

By Rosalind McInnes

THE REPETITION RULE

26.01 There is no general privilege of journalism:

> "It would be a total mistake to suppose that the editor of a newspaper, who sits behind a curtain like another veiled prophet, is entitled to vote himself public accuser, to the effect of calling every member of society to account for his misdeeds and to confer upon every anonymous contributor whom he admits into his columns, the same privilege" (Lord Deas in *Drew v Mackenzie* (1862)).

26.02 A journalist cannot usually defend a publication on the basis that an article accurately reports the fact that someone else has made a defamatory allegation. This is called the repetition rule. It is not enough to prove that it is true that X said Y was a drug dealer. The journalist has to prove, typically, that Y *is* a drug dealer.

26.03 For many years, a journalist has had a privilege for reporting certain words of others, e.g. in Parliament or in court. Otherwise, broadly, journalists had no more right to spread defamatory allegations than any other citizen. (Though, of course, citizen journalism is itself on the rise, with blogging and user-generated content an increasing feature of the media landscape.)

A NEW DAWN?

26.04 Since the millennium, there has been some significant progress. In the first place, the decision of the House of Lords in the case of *Albert Reynolds v Times Newspapers* (1999) [see **paras 27.88 onwards**], recognised that a communication to the public at large might—in limited circumstances—attract the protection of qualified privilege at common law. A related defence of "neutral reportage" is beginning to assume significance. Furthermore, the European Convention on Human Rights has been "brought home" to Scots law by the Human Rights Act 1998.

The *Reynolds* case suggests that journalists will sometimes be 26.05 protected if they are responsibly reporting significant matters of public interest. Although the concept of the public figure defence has not been imported from America, it does appear that journalists are more likely to be able to plead the *Reynolds*-style defence when producing copy on individuals such as politicians and civil servants in relation to such of their activities as legitimately interest the public. The *Reynolds* approach follows the high value placed on freedom of speech by art.10 of the European Convention on Human Rights. Convention jurisprudence recognises the public figure concept in such cases as *Lingens v Austria* (1986). So both the development of common law privilege and the importation of the European Convention point towards a more sympathetic approach to the publication of critical material of public interest by newspapers and broadcasters about public figures.

In practice, though, most recent Scottish defamation cases turn on 26.06 two things: what the publication is held to mean, and whether that meaning is probably true.

WHO CAN BE SUED?

Lord Kyllachy's remark in *Wright v Greig* (1890) is still generally true 26.07 today: "A person circulating a slander is answerable equally with the author of the slander." This means that the author, editor and publisher can all be sued for the one publication. It means that both the writer of a defamatory article, report or letter and the proprietor of the newspaper in which it is published may be liable for damages and it means that the newspaper which merely repeats a defamatory statement already published in the columns of another is as liable to be sued as if it originated the allegation. By the Defamation Act 1952 s.12, however, a newspaper owner can prove in mitigation of damages that other publishers have already paid out for similar slurs.

INNOCENT DISSEMINATION

For many years the courts have recognised the need to protect 26.08 innocent disseminators of defamatory material, such as librarians and newsagents. Nowadays, s.1 of the Defamation Act 1996 provides that a person will not be legally responsible as "author", "editor" or "publisher" for the dissemination of defamatory material if only involved in printing, producing, distributing or selling printed material; processing, copying, distributing, exhibiting or selling films or sound recordings; similar activities or operations with other electronic media; broadcasting a live radio or television programme "in circumstances in which he has no effective control over the maker of the statement"; or providing access to a communications system by means of which the statement is transmitted by a person over whom he has no effective control. This would certainly cover, e.g. a telephone company. In some circumstances at least, it will cover internet service providers. However, to use this section to escape liability, the person must also demonstrate the following: (1) he or she took reasonable care in relation to publication; and (2) did not know and had no reason to believe that what he or she did caused or contributed to the publication of a defamatory statement.

26.09   On the question of "taking reasonable care", there may well be arguments as to situations where a publication or an individual is well known for making defamatory allegations. In such situations, the "innocent dissemination" defence may be more difficult to run.

26.10   In *Market & Research International Ltd v BBC* (1999) before Gray J. in the Queen's Bench Division, Gray J. instructed the jury in a case which settled dramatically after the jury had retired to consider its verdict.

26.11   The BBC's sole defence was s.1 in relation to defamatory comments about the polling organisation MORI made by the late Sir James Goldsmith during a live broadcast of *The World This Weekend*. Mr Justice Gray said that effective control meant a "real" ability to direct or determine what the speaker said: "Effective control would, you may think, certainly exist if the interviewee was also an employee of the broadcasting organisation." He also said that the jury could take into account the previous conduct and character of Sir James Goldsmith and the BBC's obligation to provide impartial political coverage. He reminded the jury not to base their views on whether the interviewer should have intervened on hindsight. He did, however, say that the jury could consider the fact that the BBC did not operate any time delay mechanism or device. In response to the BBC's argument that this would have meant that the broadcast was no longer live, and in any case a time delay of this order would only be of use to prevent, e.g. swearing, not to pick up a defamatory comment, the judge said:

> "I do not accept that a broadcast ceases to be live within the meaning of the Act merely because there was a delay of a few seconds ... Nor can I accept that the person operating such a device would be exercising 'an editorial or equivalent function'. I

consider that the function of an editor is to adapt, fashion and organise information so as to enable it to be communicated to the public in a journalistically acceptable or desirable fashion ... The person who presses the button of the delay mechanism in order to cut out the profanity or libel is not, in my judgment, exercising an editorial function in the sense I have described."

There are so few cases on s.1 that it is difficult to give guidance. It 26.12 would be odd if the consequences of a provision which was supposed to broaden freedom of expression were to discourage appropriately provocative interviewing, to censor political speech in advance or to limit online debates about matters of public controversy. It is nonetheless prudent, where possible, to pre-record interviews with "wildcards"; where not possible, to attempt to set some ground rules and "off limits" areas in advance; and to be ready to intervene promptly and unobtrusively if an apparently defamatory remark is made: "We can't go into that now"; "X isn't here to defend himself"; or the equivalent.

The position re online debates on newspaper websites is probably 26.13 simpler, in that if the website host warns in advance that defamatory content should not be published and will be removed if it is, then acts promptly on any complaint about defamatory content, the newspaper is likely to be protected, to judge from the *Godfrey v Demon Internet* **(1999)** case [see **Chapter 43**]. The *Sunday Herald* initially mounted a defence on the basis of s.1 in relation to a notice posted on its website in 2003 defaming George Robertson, the former MP and Secretary General of NATO, in relation to the Dunblane massacre, but as Lord Robertson settled out of court for £25,000 plus expenses, its applicability was never tested.

It is sometimes thought that it is safe to publish a statement if it is 26.14 stated clearly that it is merely being repeated for what it is worth. This is not so, unless a privilege exists of the "fair and accurate court report" type, or, less likely, the *Albert Reynolds* or reportage kind. Otherwise, a newspaper is as legally responsible in these circumstances as when a statement is printed and endorsed by the newspaper itself [see **para.26.02**]. It is important to note that if the opportunity to comment is given but not taken, this is no defence in itself to an action of defamation, though failure to offer a right of reply will be highly damaging to an *Albert Reynolds* defence.

CRIMINAL ASPECTS?

In Scotland, defamation is a civil wrong giving rise to an action for 26.15 damages and not a criminal prosecution. However, the Representation of the People Act 1983 makes it a criminal offence for any person before or during an election, including a European Parliamentary election, to make or publish for the purpose of affecting the return of any candidate any false statement of fact in relation to the personal character or conduct of such candidate unless the maker/publisher reasonably believed the statement to be true [see **Chapter 39**]. In theory, too, a publication tending to cause a breach of the peace might render the publisher liable to prosecution for this common law offence—although such a prosecution can almost be discounted due to the importation of the European Convention into United Kingdom law.

PUBLICATION

26.16   You can shout a slander to the waves and write reams of libellous invective—if nobody hears or reads there will be no defamation. Publication of some sort is essential. Scots law allows an action for injury to the feelings caused by an insulting and defamatory statement even if it is not made known to any third party [see **para.31.02**]. From the journalist's point of view the difference is not important. There is no technical distinction in Scots law between words published in writing and words spoken. The terms "libel" and "slander" are often interchangeably used in the older Scots case law.

DEFAMATORY

26.17   There is no clear rule on what is and what is not defamatory. Generally speaking, however, a defamatory statement involves some imputation against character or reputation, including business or financial reputation. The test most commonly quoted in Scottish cases today comes from the English House of Lords decision in *Sim v Stretch* **(1936)**: "Would the words tend to lower the plaintiff in the estimation of right-thinking members of society generally?"

26.18   There is some old case law suggesting that it is actionable to say falsely that someone is insane (*Mackintosh v Weir* **(1875)**), impotent (*Cunningham v Phillips* **(1868)**; *Friend v Skelton* **(1855)**) or a rape victim (*Youssoupoff* **(1934)**)) on the basis that the social consequence would be shunning of the pursuer, even if the response ought to be sympathetic. It is unlikely that such decisions would be reached now, but claims for so-called "false privacy" have been made in the English courts, and suggestions of physical incapacity, illness or sexual victimhood would score as highly private matters.

26.19   The fact that a statement has been regarded as defamatory in the past does not necessarily mean that it will be regarded as defamatory now [see e.g. **para.26.59**]. It is not enough that the subjects of an article have a personal objection to the behaviour attributed to them. It has to offend against mores, not just individual morals: "It is nothing to the point ... to aver that an allegation is disparaging in the section of society to which [the pursuer] belongs if it is not also disparaging in the view of society as a whole." (*Bell v Jackson* (2001)) This is true not only of fringe beliefs, but of differing practices in journalism (*Dr Sarah Thornton v Telegraph* (2010)).

CRIME

To call someone a thief or accuse him or her of some other serious crime will generally be defamatory. It would not normally be actionable to say that a man had exceeded the speed limit, but to say this of someone who makes their living from careful driving might give rise to an action.   26.20

An unusual set of circumstances led to the case of *Leon v Edinburgh Evening News* (1909). The *Evening News* reported a police court case under the headline "The Edinburgh Licensing Prosecution: Prisoners Acquitted". One of the accused referred to, who had never been in custody but had simply appeared in court in answer to a citation, sued for defamation, pointing out, quite correctly, that he had never been a prisoner. It was held that in the circumstances of the case the statement was not defamatory.   26.21

Lord Kinnear observed that: 26.22

> "The description was not technically exact. But a paragraph in a newspaper of this kind does not necessarily use technical language: and in ordinary language an accused person at the Bar of a court may not improperly be described as a prisoner. To an ordinary reader, the paragraph with its heading, would not in my opinion convey any more injurious meaning than that the pursuer had been accused and had been acquitted."

This case was successfully cited by the *Sunday Mail* when it was sued by former footballer Frank McAvennie over an allegation that he had been charged with assaulting his estranged wife. In fact, the newspaper accepted that he had not been charged. Instead, they said, a report had been sent to the procurator fiscal, containing a draft charge. The sheriff principal confirmed that it was not possible to read the article as meaning Frank McAvennie had actually assaulted his wife (*McAvennie v Scottish Daily Record and Sunday Mail Ltd* (2003)).   26.23

But whilst words like "prisoner" have been found not to be defamatory in some contexts, they may well be in others. As with   26.24

much in defamation law, it is a question of the meaning which would be taken from the words.

VIOLENCE

26.25   Allegations of violence are highly likely to be actionable. Three Scottish cases since the millennium relate to allegations of wife-beating (*Wray v Associated Newspapers Ltd* (2000) [see **para.26.78**], *McAvennie* 2003 [see **para.09.82**], *Nicol* (2002) [see **para.07.63**]); one to an allegation that a teacher had hit a pupil (*Mackellar* (2004)); one to being associated with violent organisations (*Haikney* (2006) [see **para.26.41**]) or being responsible for the Dunblane massacre (*Robertson* (2002) [see **paras 26.28, 26.47**]). In the *Woodland Trust* case, the allegations centred around claims that the Woodland Trust "massacred" or "slaughtered" deer or other wildlife (*Woodland Trust v McMillan* (2002)).

DISHONESTY

26.26   Actions have often been based on imputations of drunkenness or dishonesty—the latter covering anything from appropriating public funds to evading payment of rent. The 21st century Scottish cases of *Thomson* (2000); *Paton* (2000); *Nicol* (2002); *Woodland Trust* (2002); *Harwood, Petitioner* (2003); *Kennedy* (2005); *McCormick v Scottish Daily Record and Sunday Mail* (2006); and *Macleod* (2007) would all fall into this category. A serious attack on integrity requires serious evidence, if a defence of *veritas* is to succeed. If a man has been called a thief it is no defence to prove that long ago, as a boy, he had two convictions for petty theft (*Fletcher v Wilson* (1885)). If a man has been called a liar, it is not enough to prove that he lied on one occasion (*Milne v Walker* (1893)). It has been said not to be defamatory to call someone a "liar" or "a stranger to the truth" at all (*Carroll v BBC* (1997) [see **para.26.56**]), but, again, context is all.

HYPOCRISY

26.27   Where the behaviour alleged is neither criminal nor immoral by conventional standards, but nonetheless felt to be damaging and untrue, the allegation is often pled as being an innuendo of hypocrisy.

26.28   In the *Sheridan* (2006) case, for instance, it was suggested that saying Tommy Sheridan drank champagne, when he was known to be teetotal, amounted to an allegation of hypocrisy. In the *Robertson* (2006) case, it was argued, without success, that depicting an amicable discussion between the pursuer and the newspaper's editor, after the newspaper's editor had apologised for an anonymous posting falsely accusing him of responsibility for the Dunblane massacre, closely followed by the raising of defamation proceedings, could amount to an innuendo of hypocrisy.

SEXUAL BEHAVIOUR

Prophit v BBC (1997) featured allegations of lesbianism and fraud, 26.29 but the pursuer there was a nun; no point as to whether an allegation of homosexuality was per se defamatory was taken.

In *Quilty v Windsor* (1999), it was held that it was not. However, an 26.30 action on the basis of hypocrisy would presumably be competent if the pursuer was, e.g. married or a vocal opponent of homosexuality.

Imputations of adultery or promiscuity have traditionally been 26.31 found to be actionable. Despite recent privacy cases like *CC v AB* (2006) and *Mosley* (2008), it is not likely that the law of defamation will relax in this regard. In other words, a journalist who is sued for breach of confidence and told that it is no business of his to expose an adulterous football manager can still confidently expect to be sued for defamation if the football manager denies the adultery.

Some of the highest Scottish defamation awards have arisen as a 26.32 result of sexual allegations. When the *Sun* newspaper alleged an employee at Glenochil Prison had had an affair with a prisoner while on duty, she was awarded £50,000 (*Winter v News Scotland* (1991)). An appeal by the defenders on the amount of damages awarded was unsuccessful.

In 1999, Father Noel Barry and Annie Kerr Clinton sued the *Sun* 26.33 newspaper, again over allegations of sexual impropriety. Despite the *Sun* newspaper's proving that Father Barry had had a romantic relationship with a former nun, the jury found in his favour. They awarded Father Barry damages of £45,000. In Mrs Clinton's case they were even more sympathetic, awarding her £125,000 (*Clinton v News Group Newspapers Ltd* (1999).

In 2006, former MSP Tommy Sheridan was awarded £200,000 by a 26.34 jury over allegations that he had visited a "swingers' club" and committed adultery. This remained unpaid pending a perjury trial ongoing at the time of writing and a civil appeal by the *News of the World*.

It is noteworthy that *Winter*, *Barry/Clinton* and *Sheridan* were all 26.35 jury awards and all involved direct allegations. Judges have been known to stop a more questionable innuendo-based case from going to the jury. Lord Marnoch did this in *Hannah v Scottish Daily Record* (2000):

"While the pursuer had spent time in what is described as a 'nightclub brothel', there was no allegation that he actually succumbed to the sexual temptations on offer. Instead, all the emphasis, in my view, is on drink, drunkenness and, eventually, on the police having to be summoned. I accordingly refuse to remit to probation that particular averment" [see **para.26.28**].

IMPECUNIOSITY

26.36 This edition is being written, to borrow the financial journalist's euphemism, in troubled times. Journalists would do well to remember that imputations on solvency are often actionable, so long as the pursuer is in a position to prove damage to credit-worthiness (**Bell v Jackson (2001)** [see **para.26.19**]). They need not go as far as to allege bankruptcy. It is enough if they imply financial embarrassment. If the pursuer can demonstrate that losses occurred as a direct result of these allegations, e.g. cancellation of contracts by customers, then such losses would be recoverable.

26.37 Further, it is vital to remember that where companies are quoted on the public Stock Exchange, the value of their shares is dependent on the confidence in which they are held in the financial community. If a company could prove that its share value had plummeted as a result of an erroneous story in a newspaper it might well be able to recover substantial damages from the newspaper.

PROFESSIONAL SKILLS AND BEHAVIOUR

26.38 Numerous defamation cases have been concerned with imputations on an individual's fitness for his or her occupation or profession. To give only a few examples, it is dangerous to accuse a minister of brawling with his parishioners (**Mackellar v Duke of Sutherland (1859)**), a teacher of ignorance of his subject (**McKerchar v Cameron (1892)**), a medical practitioner of cruelty to a patient (**Bruce v Ross & Co (1901)**), and an accountant of being unfit to be a trustee in bankruptcy (**Oliver v Barnet (1895)**).

26.39 Recent cases have been brought by solicitors over allegations that they permitted fraudulent claims to be made to the Scottish Legal Aid Board (**Thomson v Ross (2001)**), and a feared allegation that one of their partners would be said to be acting in a conflict of interest (**Dickson Minto v Bonnier Media (2002)**). One Glasgow solicitor (**McCormick (2006)** [see **para.27.41**]) recovered £45,000 damages for allegations that, amongst other things, he was implicated in a cover-up of child abuse and smeared witnesses. Journalist Angus Macleod unsuccessfully sued over an allegation that he was "justly renowned for his powers of invention" [see **para.26.26**]. An action was also brought over alleged communication of defamatory statements to the Chartered Institute of Management Accountants and to the Institute of Chartered Accountants of Scotland (*Cairns v Downie* (2005)). Breach of trust and disregard for professional integrity was part of the controversy in *Hay v ICAS* (2003).

OTHER RECENT SCOTTISH CASES

More heterogeneous recent Scottish defamation cases arose out of 26.40 councillors said to have been accused of entering into a "secret" agreement committing the council, and malicious use of public money (*Brooks v Lind* (2000)), an MP accused of leaking a confidential suicide note (*Adams v Guardian Newspapers Ltd* (2003)), mis-selling techniques in relation to therapeutic beds (*Hutchinson and App A UK Ltd v Scottish Daily Record and Sunday Mail Ltd* (2008)), and racial abuse (*Moore v Scottish Daily Record and Sunday Mail Ltd* (2009)). Being the "spiteful source of disharmony" within a golf club was argued to be a defamatory matter in *Crockett v Tantallon Golf Club* (2005). In an interesting sidelight on the changing expectations of fathers, two men sued over allegations that they had evaded responsibility to their children (*Nicol* (2002) [see **para.24.43**]) and that aspersions had been cast on their paternal attitudes and abilities (*Fitchie v Worsnop* (2004)).

MEANING

In many if not most defamation cases, the parties are at odds over the 26.41 meaning of the publication, as well as its truth. Many 21st century Scottish cases have involved skirmishes over meaning (*Haikney v Newsquest* (2006); *Macleod v Newsquest* (2007); *McCue v Scottish Daily Record and Sunday Mail* (2000); *Paton v Sarwar* (2000); *Thomson v Ross* (2001); *Kennedy v Aldington* (2005); *McCann v Scottish Media Newspapers* (2000); *Robertson v Newsquest* (2006)). The pursuer must state clearly the meaning for which he or she contends before any evidence can be led; the court must be satisfied that the words complained of are capable of bearing that defamatory meaning. This is a matter of law. The test is whether the meaning is a reasonable, natural or necessary interpretation of what has been published.

The court should give the words the natural and ordinary meaning 26.42 which they would have conveyed to the ordinary reasonable reader who is neither naïve nor unduly suspicious. The court should not be too literal, nor over-analytical, nor should it accept "strained and sinister" interpretations. The publication has to be read as a whole. In the case brought by *McCann v Scottish Media Newspapers* (1999) [see also **para.26.74**], then chairman of Celtic, against the *Herald*, the late Lord Macfadyen held that the three *Herald* articles published on February 10, 1998 had to be read and made sense of all together, when "the articles were limited by references leading the reader forward from the first to the second, and from the second to the third". The English judge Sharp J. agreed with *McCann* in *Dee v Telegraph Media Group Ltd* (2010).

26.43   Even with all these uncontroversial tests applied, the parties are often in dispute about meaning. As Tom Stoppard has written, language is a finite instrument crudely applied to an infinity of ideas. The effect of emphasis, headlines, lexical choice, illustrative cartoons and significant omissions may all have their effect on the meanings selected by the court. Whether particular words (or pictures, or gestures, etc.) are capable of bearing a defamatory meaning is a matter of law for the court. Which meaning they are ultimately held to bear in a particular case is a matter of fact for the jury if there is one, or for the judge if there is not. Journalists need no reminder that language is subtle, many layered and mutable over time and context. The ultimate meaning to be attached to a journalist's words in a defamation action will typically be out of the journalist's hands once the words are out of his mouth.

26.44   Given the inherent ambiguity of language, there are often several valid contenders for the meaning of a particular phrase, and a degree of artificiality in ultimately selecting one of them, but that is how defamation law operates. For this reason, the meaning of a particular word may be defamatory in one case and not defamatory in another. In the *Woodland Trust* (2002) case, for example [see **para.26.25**], Lord Eassie said:

> "I am in no doubt that in judging whether a statement may have a defamatory meaning and whether that defamatory meaning should be attributed to it, it is necessary to bear in mind the potential meanings ascribable to the words employed and have regard to the context and tone of the statement in which they are used in order to decide the meaning which the reader should attach to the words ... To describe a man whose trade is that of selling meat as a 'butcher' is utterly different from describing the Duke of Cumberland, in the days and years after Culloden, as 'Butcher Cumberland'."

26.45   In *Moffat v West Highland Publishing Ltd* (2000), the then main board director of SMG sued over an adverse review of the STV Gaelic soap opera *Machair* which referred to him as "The Laird of

Coocadden's In-house Bully". Lord Cameron of Lochbroom, who dismissed the action, said:

> "To term a man a bully does not mean that he has been given to bullying, just as to call a man a fraud does not mean that he has committed a fraud ...".

Although humour is not a defence (*Prophit* (1997) [see **para.26.29**]), a 26.46 satirical or whimsical tone or context can radically affect how a judge or jury interprets a publication (*Moffat*; *Macleod* (2007) [see **para.26.52**]).

Crucially, the meaning of a publication depends upon its totality. 26.47 This can work against the media, as when an unintentionally juxtaposed picture creates a defamatory innuendo. It can also work for the media, as when part of a publication contains a defamatory allegation which the rest of the publication undercuts. This has been referred to as the "bane and antidote" principle. For example, in the *George Robertson* case [see **para.26.28**], the former NATO chief sued over an anonymous blog on the *Sunday Herald* online forum, suggesting that he bore responsibility for the Dunblane killings. The *Sunday Herald* settled the case. Following "gleeful reports" from other newspapers, it ran an article explaining why. Their article included a small reproduction of a *Scottish Daily Mail* article alluding to the "claims he was responsible for the Dunblane massacre". The judge rejected Lord Robertson's second defamation action, saying: "The whole tenor of the article is that the allegation ... is untrue".

INNUENDO

Journalists must be aware of the legal concept of a defamatory 26.48 innuendo. This arises in two situations. First, it can arise where words are innocent on their face but, in reality, carry a defamatory meaning. It is a question of fact in each case as to what meaning a reasonable, right-thinking person would take from the article or broadcast.

The most extreme example of this is where the words are conveyed 26.49 in such a way as to mean precisely the opposite of their ordinary meaning. The double positive "Aye, right" is famously, in the west of Scotland, a sarcastic negative.

It will be seen then that the concept of innuendo can be very 26.50 problematical for journalists, particularly those working in television and radio. An innuendo can arise from a wink, a nudge, a facial expression or intonation of voice—although, oddly, the temporary judge refused to listen to a tape-recording of the radio programme complained of in **Prophit** [above]. It is, of course, necessary for the pursuer to plead very precisely what innuendo s/he is setting out to prove. The defender has to be given proper notice of the charge of innuendo.

26.51 Secondly, a defamatory innuendo can be pled by the pursuer if the words have a special (derogatory) meaning for certain people. For example, to say that a Scottish solicitor paid promptly for office furniture by a cheque from a client's account might seem unremarkable to the general public. To other solicitors, however, it would mean that, at best, he was guilty of professional misconduct and, at worst, was a thief.

26.52 In 2007, the journalist Angus Macleod sued the *Sunday Herald* over a jocular piece in "Alan Taylor's Diary", saying, "Angus Macleod ... who, like Alexander Graham Bell, is justly renowned for his powers of invention, came close [to winning a mythical 'Tartan Bollocks Award'] with his confident prediction that Jim Wallace would still be leading the LibDems in 2007." He argued that, as a reputable journalist, he was not supposed to invent stories, rather than to investigate them. Lord Macphail dismissed the defamation claim on the basis that the reader would not have taken the piece as a serious allegation, but observed:

> "It may well be that in other circumstances, to say of a journalist that he was justly renowned for his powers of invention would lead such a reader to regard the words as a grave accusation ...".

26.53 In **McCue v Scottish Daily Record and Sunday Mail Ltd (2000)**, a *Sunday Mail* article described McCue as having "strong connections with reformed killer Jimmy Boyle" and a raid on premises linked to Mr McCue was reported. The judge, however, rejected any innuendo of involvement in criminal activity:

> "In my opinion, the article would not be read ... as implicating Mr McCue as the licence holder and tenant in dealings with counterfeit currency or with drugs ... In two different places it is said that four men and a woman were detained by the police ... There is no doubt that the word 'stash' implies secrecy ... but without any indication of where the notes were found it would not in my opinion be reasonable to infer from that statement read in the context of the whole article a link between the counterfeit money and the tenant and licensee of the premises ...".

26.54 But a few journalistic or editorial changes could have seen matters end differently:

"A reference to Mr McCue as one of those detained by the police when read in the context of other statements in the article, might well change the meaning of the article to bear the innuendo that he was in fact involved in some way with the currency. In this article as it stands there is no basis for making that link";

so the action was dismissed.

Similarly, in *Paton v Sarwar* (2001), the Inner House of the Court of 26.55 Session upheld the dismissal of an action where Peter Paton claimed it had been alleged that he was guilty of electoral fraud. The court said:

"The affidavit does not anywhere state, or, in our view, imply that the pursuer was involved in making unlawful late registration of voters or, indeed, in electoral fraud or an illegality of any kind. What it says is that the pursuer tried to persuade Badar Islam to draw attention to the alleged illegality of the irregularities committed by the defender. There is, on any fair reading of the affidavit, therefore, no basis for the innuendo ...".

Sometimes over-elaborate innuendos are pointlessly pled. In *Carroll* 26.56 (1997), the sheriff principal said:

"In an action of this kind a pursuer is required to spell out a defamatory innuendo only if the defamatory character of the statement complained of is not obvious ... The phrase 'a stranger to the truth' is a phrase in everyday use ... It *means* that the person it is applied to is a liar. It does not merely *imply* that" (italics in the original).

In *Harwood* (2003) [see **para.26.26**], Gordon Reid QC said, "An 26.57 allegation of misappropriation of company funds is an unambiguous assertion of dishonesty", and although the petitioner had said that it was defamatory, "directly and by innuendo", the judge said that any innuendo averred would not be required.

A defamatory innuendo, like defamation itself, can arise 26.58 unintentionally, but that is no defence. If the court is satisfied that an ordinary right-thinking person would draw a defamatory meaning from the words (and possibly pictures) used, then the test for defamation is satisfied. Generally, in defamation cases, a newspaper may end up trying to prove what it is deemed to have said, which is not necessarily what it meant to say.

As with all questions of meaning in a defamation case, though, it is 26.59 not enough that the words could bear the meaning alleged. The innuendo must represent what is a reasonable, natural or necessary inference from the words used, regard being had to the occasion and the circumstances of their publication (*Russell v Stubbs* (1913)). This, however, is subject to the qualification that the reader may have knowledge of special facts making an apparently innocent statement defamatory. It seems harmless to say that Mrs M gave birth to twins on a certain date but this became defamatory, to Edwardian eyes at least, when read by those knowing that she had been married for only a month (*Morrison v Ritchie* (1902); and see below).

STATEMENT

26.60   There must be a statement. It need not, however, be in words. It may be inferred from acts, as where a waxwork effigy of the pursuer was placed in a waxworks among the effigies of notorious criminals (*Monson v Tussauds* (1894)), or where a boy's photograph was placed by the police in their "rogues' gallery" (*Adamson v Martin* (1916) [see **para.26.36**]). Two Scottish cases since the millennium feature cartoons: of a Cossack kicking out his boot (*Barratt International* (2003)), and of a dismantled vintage car in the snow (*Kennedy* (2005)). The temporary judge in *Kennedy* said:

> "The cartoon, albeit not a drawing of the pursuer's vehicle, has been employed in such a way as to set the tone of the article. No doubt it is correct that the cartoon of itself is not a defamation since it is plain that the cartoon vehicle is not the same as the pursuer's. Had that cartoon been standing alone, there would have been no cause for complaint, but when it is allied to the content of the letter, it adds the colour for which the second defenders as publishers must be responsible."

26.61   Of more importance for the journalist is the possibility of inferring a defamatory statement from drawings and photographs. This clearly gives rise to a duty by the sub-editor to take care when laying out the pages. It is wise for the sub-editor to look over the whole page to see if any defamatory innuendo might arise from the juxtaposition of photographs and stories.

ABOUT A PERSON

26.62   The statement must be of and concerning the pursuer, who must show that reasonable persons would take the words to refer to him/her but need not prove that they were intended to do so (see below). Identification to a small specialised group was held sufficient in *Kennedy*, but the Inner House observed in *Brooks* (2000) [see **para.26.40**] that:

"Our view is that this article cannot be read as having a meaning such as might be apparent to those having detailed knowledge and experience of the mysteries surrounding the recent history of Monklands District Council."

INDIVIDUALS CAN BE DEFAMED WITHOUT BEING NAMED

Difficulties arise where a class of persons is defamed. The general rule 26.63
is that members of the class can sue if and only if the class is sufficiently well defined for the defamation to be applicable to the pursuer as an individual. Thus, a statement about "all prisoners" would not be actionable by someone who was a prisoner at the time (*Quilty* **1999**) [see **para.26.30**]). Even where an individual is clearly identifiable from a publication which attacks the class to which s/he belongs, that will not convert the publication to a defamatory attack on the individual.

In *Wardlaw* **(1898)**, a temperance campaigner wrote a letter to the 26.64
Dunfermline Journal complaining about publicans being elected as magistrate and as Dean of Guild:

"Publicans, as the manufacturers of criminals, are not wanted ... It is both disgraceful and deplorable that licensed poisoners ... could be allowed to compose what may practically be said to be a 'publican officialism' in our Town Council ...".

In one sense, the latter obviously did refer to the pursuers, as they were 26.65
the only Dunfermline publicans to hold those offices, but the Inner House dismissed the action on appeal on the basis that it did not defame individuals, just alluded to them as a member of a class (the newspaper itself was not sued). The judges were unanimous and robust, the word "silly" being used of all parties. As Lord Trayner summed up: "I think that the defender was foolish to write such a letter, and that the pursuers are foolish to take any notice of it."

Journalists should take particular care when dealing with a small 26.66
group of people. All members of the group may be able to sue for damages, even if none of them is named. In *Baigent v BBC* **(2001)**, three adults who were not mentioned in the programme, but who were family members involved in running the care home featured in the documentary sued on, were awarded a total of £60,000. It would be perfectly possible for a journalist to write that "all Scottish customs officers are dishonest". Such a large group would be unlikely to be allowed to sue by the courts. However, if the journalist restricted this statement to customs officers based at a particular locality in Scotland, it might transpire that there were only two or three officers serving there. These customs officers would have a claim in

defamation against the journalists which could only be defended if the journalist could prove that the statement was true.

26.67 There is no magic number, below which the defamation risk stops. It has been said in England that, in principle, the question is one of whether the person suing is recognisably and individually the person impugned, rather than the size of the group as such (*Aiken v Police Review Publishing Ltd* (1995)) but, in practice, size matters, if only for risk assessment.

26.68 In the many sparsely populated areas of Scotland, especial care will be necessary, as with any case where identification of an individual is legally problematic for reasons of contempt, privacy or statutory anonymity.

DEFAMATION AFTER DEATH

26.69 If a defamation action is raised and the pursuer dies when the case is in court, trustees can carry on the proceedings—s.3 of the Damages (Scotland) Act 1993. In this respect defamation and verbal injury actions are distinct from other damages actions for personal injury. In all other cases (except where the pursuer has been killed outright as the result of the wrongful action, e.g. careless driving), it has been possible since the Damages (Scotland) Act 1993 for trustees/executors to raise proceedings for both *solatium* (compensation for certain types of non-financial suffering) and patrimonial, i.e. financial, loss even if the deceased had not raised the action while alive. In defamation, verbal injury "or other injury to reputation" actions, the executor can only start an action to claim damages for patrimonial loss.

CORPORATE PURSUERS

26.70 A company can sue for defamation relating to its business interests but cannot, of course, recover damages for injury to feelings. As previously indicated above, the damages recoverable by a company could be substantial if it can prove loss of revenue caused by the defamatory statement. In the *Capital Life v Sunday Mail* (1978) case, the damages awarded by a Scottish court were a then record £327,000 (excluding interest and expenses) where the newspaper had unjustly accused an insurance company of unlawful business practices. The main element in the award of damages in the *Capital Life* case was the substantial loss of business the pursuers could prove to have resulted from the articles. A general award to a company for damage to its reputation is possible (*Waverley Housing Management Ltd v BBC* (1993)). In *Woodlands Trust* (2002) [see **para.26.25**], the court observed:

"While, as a limited company, the pursuers cannot have feelings ... it is in my view clear that the reputation of a body such as the pursuers is important to their ability to continue to secure financial support from the public ...".

Firms, as well as companies, can sue for business loss. In the *Baigent* 26.71 case [above], there was also a claim by the partnership which ran the nursing home for its business loss, even though the family which ran the home had raised another action for the damage to them as individuals. The losses are different, in law.

In the McLibel case, *Steel and Morris v United Kingdom* (2005), 26.72 where pamphleteers had found themselves sued for defamation by McDonald's, the European Court of Human Rights said that, like public figures, big companies had to accept more robust criticism than did private individuals.

GOVERNMENT

A local authority cannot sue, following a decision by the House of 26.73 Lords in *Derbyshire County Council v Times Newspapers Ltd* (1993). Note, though, that an individual closely associated with a local authority could sue if a publication directly reflected on his or her own reputation. To say that Glasgow City Council is corrupt would not be actionable. To say that a particular small department accepted bribes might be actionable at the hands of the individuals who worked there, if there was only a handful of them. Also, of course, certain acts of a public body will be carried out by identifiable individuals.

Even in non-political cases, the court will allow for a degree of 26.74 connection between conduct attributed to a corporate body and to an individual with a senior or representative function in the body. In *McCann v Scottish Media Newspapers* (1999) [see **para.26.42**], the judge said that the phrase "misleading behaviour" was applied directly to the actings of Celtic Plc, not to its then chairman, but Mr McCann was offering to prove that the articles in question focused on his personal involvement and that there was a strong association in the public mind between him and the activities of the company such that a reasonable reader might understand the reference to "misleading behaviour" as applying to himself.

In *Brooks* (2000) [see **para.26.40**], the leader of the Labour Party 26.75 Group of councillors in Monklands District Council sued the *Airdrie & Coatbridge Advertiser* and one of its journalists. The newspaper had quoted a letter from the leader of the Monklands Tories to the council's controller of audit, accusing Mr Brooks of "malicious misuse of public money" in an earlier defamation action brought in his name. It transpired that that defamation action, legal expenses of which had been paid for by the council prior to the early dropping of the case, had only been brought because the council wanted to close down these attacks, but was advised that it could not sue in its own name. The newspaper accepted that this contained an innuendo that the money had been used for Mr Brooks's private benefit and that this was untrue, but successfully argued that, on the face of it, the litigations were for the private benefit of those in whose names they were raised, and it was fair comment on a matter of public interest for the Tory leader to call this a malicious misuse of public money. Mr Brooks, however, won damages in relation to the unfounded suggestion that he had entered into a secret agreement committing the council to expenditure.

DERBYSHIRE COUNTY COUNCIL PRINCIPLE EXTENDED

26.76   The ***Derbyshire County Council*** principle covers central government. In ***British Coal Corporation v NUM* (1996)**, French J. in England held that British Coal was also a governmental body falling under the ***Derbyshire*** rule and so not permitted to sue for defamation. It has been extended to cover political parties: ***Goldsmith v Bhoyrul* (1998)**. It may be possible for local authorities, etc. to fund defamation actions by individual employees over allegations against them connected with their duties, but not as a back door attempt to protect the public body's own reputation. (***Comninos v Bedford BC* (2003)**).

PUBLIC FIGURES

26.77   However, under the present law, public figures can continue to pursue actions for defamation. They are expected to be robust about public criticisms of their public acts, but not their private characters.

26.78   An example of an attack on private character was the action brought by Jimmy Wray, the Labour MP, against the *Mail on Sunday* newspaper over their allegations that Mr Wray had been violent towards his former wife. Lord Johnston, in his judgment of March 2000, made it clear that although Mr Wray was a public figure he was still entitled to a remedy from the court where defamatory allegations had been made about his private life. Mr Wray was awarded damages of £60,000. Similarly, in the ***Brooks v Lind* (2000)** case, the court said:

"We do not see that reference to having entered into a secret agreement as falling within the broad tolerance which the authorities show was allowed to political exchanges. Nor do we agree that the reference does not reflect adversely on the pursuer's private character."

Contrast the *Frances Curran v Scottish Daily Record and Sunday Mail* 26.79
Ltd **(2010)** case, where calling a Scottish Socialist Party MSP a "political scab" was held not to be defamatory at all, since public figures had to accept robust criticism of their public statements. For further discussion of the public figure, see below at **para.27.46**.

TIME LIMITS FOR DEFAMATION ACTIONS

Defamation proceedings in Scotland must be raised within three years 26.80
of the defamatory statement being made. The Scots time limit is much more generous to pursuers than that afforded to claimants throughout the rest of the United Kingdom where, in terms of the Defamation Act 1996, proceedings must be raised within one year. One case has already ended up in Scotland as a result, despite the pursuer's tenuous connections with the jurisdiction (*Kennedy* **(2005)** [see **para.26.26**]).

This is likely to recur, with the exponential growth in internet 26.81
publication [see **Chapter 43**]. Journalists should remember that repetition of the publication is a fresh publication and starts the three-year period (triennium) running again. So, for example, if a broadcaster repeated a television programme after a lapse of two years, the potential pursuer could sue up to five years after the original broadcast. If each downloading is regarded as a fresh publication—which is the current position, and, again, Strasbourg has refused to reject this approach (*Times Newspapers v United Kingdom* **(2009)**)—then internet publishers are facing ongoing liability in respect of their archives, albeit that this may be tempered by carrying appropriate "notices" that the article is the subject of legal challenge [see **para.27.83**].

LEGAL AID

Since the last edition of *Scots Law for Journalists*, legal aid for 26.82
defamation has been introduced in Scotland—by the Civil Legal Aid for Defamation or Verbal Injury Proceedings (Scotland) Direction 2008—but only in limited circumstances. The would-be pursuer must establish that there is a significant wider public interest in the resolution of the case and funded representation would contribute to

it, or the case is of overwhelming importance to the person *and* that there is something exceptional about the person or the case such that without funding for public representation it would be practically impossible for the person to bring or defend the proceedings and the lack of public funding would lead to obvious unfairness in the proceedings. The index for "exceptionality" is the *Steel and Morris v United Kingdom* **(2005)** case [see **para.26.72**], where Strasbourg found in favour of two pamphleteers who had taken on the McDonald Corp and lost.

26.83   Lord Wheatley in *DW, Petitioner* **(2010)**, which related to a false allegation of murder, held that the Scottish Legal Aid Board had been fully justified in refusing legal aid, saying: "[t]he standard that has to be reached ... if legal aid is to be granted ... may be almost insurmountable", but that it was clear that this was what the legislature intended. Probably a more significant element in probable growth of defamation actions in Scotland is the willingness by some lawyers to take cases on a speculative basis.

KEY POINTS

26.84   1. A statement about a living individual which lowers his or her reputation in the eyes of the general public is defamatory. A statement can be plainly defamatory on its face or defamatory only by reason of the innuendo which it carries. A statement which is defamatory is usually presumed in law to be untrue and the burden of proving the defence of truth (*veritas*) placed on the defender.

2. A corporate body such as a firm or a company can sue for defamation. If they can prove that they have lost business as a result of the defamatory statement such a corporate pursuer could be entitled to very substantial damages. A local authority and similar public body cannot sue.

3. It is no defence to a defamation action that the journalist is merely repeating accurately what someone else has said. This is called "the repetition rule". There are some exceptions, notably for fair and accurate court reporting and parliamentary coverage.

4. Section 1 of the Defamation Act 1996 gives a defence for innocent dissemination of defamatory material. It may be of some use to live broadcasters or newspapers with online contributions from readers. To benefit from this defence, journalists have to be alert to defamation issues and react quickly to complaints.

5. The *Albert Reynolds* defence for responsible journalism also provides some potential cover for the conscientious journalist, especially in relation to stories involving political or other public figures of legitimate public interest.

6. A statement will be defamatory if it tends to lower someone in the estimation of right-thinking members of society. Allegations of violence, dishonesty, hypocrisy, sexual immorality, solvency and professional impropriety are particularly apt to result in defamation actions.

7. Many defamation actions turn over pieces, the meaning of which is disputed. What an article or programme means is what a reasonable viewer, reader or listener thinks it means—not necessarily what the journalist intended it to mean. The words are to be given their natural and ordinary meaning. The meaning depends on publication as a whole. The pursuer cannot cherry pick paragraphs which, read alone, would be defamatory. Equally, though, the journalist cannot prove that a piece as a whole is true simply because elements of it are.

8. Words which are innocent on their face may nonetheless contain a defamatory innuendo.

9. Individuals can be defamed even without being named.

CHAPTER 27

DEFENCES AND PRIVILEGE

BY ROSALIND MCINNES

ONUS OF PROOF

27.01 Scots law, like English law, proceeds on the basis that the onus of proof in a defamation action lies on the defender. Strasbourg has consistently declined so far to hold that this infringes a journalist's right to freedom of expression: *McVicar v United Kingdom* **(2002)**, ***Steel and Morris v United Kingdom* (2005)** [see **para.26.72**] (in, respectively, the *Linford Christie* and *McDonald's* cases) and most recently in *Europapress Holding Doo v Croatia* **(2010)**.

STANDARD OF PROOF

27.02 Proof is on the balance of probabilities, lower than the criminal standard of "beyond reasonable doubt". But what amounts to proof on the balance of probabilities can be quite high. In *Wray* [see **para.26.78**], the judge made it clear that in defamation cases where the "sting" of the allegations amounted to an accusation of criminal conduct (as they did here because in effect Mr Wray was being accused of the crime of assault) although the standard of proof remained "the balance of probabilities", the court would require very strong evidence before being satisfied that the newspaper had proved it was telling the truth.

VERITAS

27.03 *Veritas*, or truth, is probably the single most important defence for the journalist.

27.04   First, with a very limited exception under the Rehabilitation of Offenders Act 1974, it is a complete defence, even if the journalist is publishing a highly defamatory statement out of sheer malice.

27.05   Secondly, many defamation cases do boil down to clashing versions of events: did the pursuer take the bribe, throw the punch, have the affair?

Thirdly, in matters of investigative journalism at least, it may well 27.06
be professionally important to the journalist to prove that his or her
story is true, as opposed to merely legal.

Fourthly, accuracy as to supporting facts, or at any rate depth of 27.07
research, can be critically important to the success of other defences
to defamation actions—in particular, to fair comment and to
Reynolds privilege [see **paras 27.85 onwards**]. In other words, a
journalist may not, at the end of the day, have quite enough to
succeed in proving the truth of the publication but, in aiming high, be
able to get over the hurdles of other defences.

Defamatory statements are presumed to be false and the defender 27.08
who relies on *veritas* has, as already noted, the burden of proving
their truth.

If the pursuer founds upon two separate allegations, the defender 27.09
can prove the truth of one of them, whether or not it is possible to
prove the truth of the other (*O'Callaghan v Thomson & Co* (**1928**)).

Under s.5 of the Defamation Act 1952, a *veritas* defence in a 27.10
defamation action where the pursuer is complaining of more than
one distinct charge shall not fail "by reason only that the truth of
every charge is not proved if the words not proved to be true do not
materially injure the pursuer's reputation having regard to the truth
of the remaining charges." Under the present law, a pursuer can pick
and choose only one allegation out of several. In that case, the
journalist has no opportunity to prove the truth of the remaining
allegations so as to take advantage of s.5.

Under s.12 of the Defamation Act 1996, evidence of a conviction of 27.11
an offence by a UK court or court martial is now conclusive evidence
that the convicted person committed the offence only where the
convicted person is the pursuer/claimant and only so far as relevant
to any issue arising in relation to his or her defamation action. Proof
of the conviction of any other person is still admissible, but will no
longer be conclusive. It appears that Parliament wanted to cover such
cases as those in which investigative journalists who have criticised the
conduct of police officers are then sued for defamation by these
officers. Often such cases relate to the arrest of accused persons. If
these accused persons have been convicted, the law as it stood prior
to 1996 precluded the defence from giving evidence to the effect that
the accused persons were innocent—because the police officers had
fabricated the evidence against them. The 1996 legislation allows the
defence to challenge the correctness of the conviction of a third party,
i.e. a person who is not the pursuer in the defamation case before the
court.

The Rehabilitation of Offenders Act 1974 adds a slight 27.12
complication to *veritas* in relation to criminal offences. If the offence
in question is the subject of a "spent conviction" the defender in an

action of defamation by the rehabilitated person cannot rely on *veritas* if the publication is proved to have been made with malice—though malice is quite a hurdle for the pursuer [see **paras 27.48 onwards**].

27.13   The defence of *veritas* can be a very difficult one. Even where charges seem justified, they may not be easy to prove. It can also be an unwise defence if there is serious risk of failure as it means that the defamation is persisted in and this is a factor which can aggravate damages. Scots law does not recognise the concept of exemplary or punitive damages, but it does recognise the concept of aggravated damages. Although in **Sarwar v News Group Newspapers Ltd (1999)** the temporary judge, Gordon Coutts, said "[i]t is going too far to state that by merely pleading veritas damages are aggravated", he awarded aggravated damages in **Baigent v BBC (2001)** [see **para.26.66**] when the defender persisted in the defamation right up to the end of the court proceedings.

RIXA AND VULGAR ABUSE

27.14   Words spoken in *rixa* are words uttered in the heat of a quarrel. Even if apparently defamatory they will not be actionable, unless it would appear to third parties that a specific charge was being seriously made. It is rare, but not unknown, for this to be pled with regard to written words (**Lovi v Wood (1802)**) or broadcast statements (**Carroll v BBC (1997)** [see **para.26.56**]).

27.15   The defence of vulgar abuse is a different aspect of the same principle. If the words used are clearly a crude and unthinking gross insult, the reasoning is that they will not be taken seriously by third parties. Therefore, they will not damage the pursuer's reputation. The odd result of this is that extreme language may not give a good basis for a defamation action.

27.16   It is possible that these defences may prove useful in uninhibited online debates. The English judge, Eady J. said in **Smith v ADVFN (2008)** of bulletin board postings:

> "From the context of casual conversations, one can often tell that a remark is not to be taken literally or seriously and is rather to be construed merely as abuse. That is less common in the case of more permanent written communication, although it is by no means unknown. But in the case of a bulletin board thread it is often obvious to casual observers that people are just saying the first thing that comes into their heads and reacting in the heat of the moment. The remarks are often not intended, or to be taken, as serious" [see **paras 27.27 and 43.31**].

This reflects the general importance in defamation of the meaning 27.17
which will be taken by the listener, viewer or reader.

FAIR COMMENT

The defence of fair comment is of great importance to newspapers and 27.18
broadcasters but its limitations should be understood by journalists.
The phrase "fair comment" is both misleading and, often, misused.
Indeed, following the Court of Appeal's observations in the *Dr
Simon Singh* **(2010)** case, it may be on the brink of re-christening as
"honest opinion". The media are perfectly entitled to comment on
matters of public interest, but if purporting to be based on fact, the
"facts" alluded to must be accurate. The defence is more likely to
succeed in features work or reviews than in news stories.

PUBLIC FIGURES AND FAIR COMMENT

Fair comment is a particularly relevant defence when dealing with 27.19
stories on public figures. There is a belief amongst many journalists
that people in public life must accept that they will be criticised in the
media. The Scottish courts have already accepted that journalists have
a degree of latitude when commenting on the public actions of those
who perform a public role or occupy an official position in society,
e.g. a politician. In *Mutch v Robertson* **(1981)**, Lord Stott said:

> "The appellant has chosen to be in the public limelight and having
> aspired to the position of chairman of a regional council cannot
> ... assume that chairmanship will be immune from criticism."

This thinking was a major element in the court's dismissal of Frances 27.20
Curran's case [see **para.26.79**] against the *Sunday Mail* for publishing
Tommy Sheridan's calling her a "scab". The temporary judge said
that this was no more than a robust criticism of political disloyalty,
not a personal attack on her.

It is not just political roles which fall under this heading. It also 27.21
covered Alistair Moffat, then main board director of the Scottish
Media Group, of whom Lord Cameron of Lochbroom said in a 1999
defamation action:

> "The pursuer is a man who holds a position which on behalf of
> those who employ him, has brought him into the public notice in
> a way akin to those who take part in public business. Indeed he is
> described ... as occupying a position of professional
> responsibility in the media world. In that respect he may require
> to suffer that which might be described as rough language or

unmannerly jests so long as such statements do not attack his private character ... or indeed disparage his business reputation" [see **para.27.23**].

27.22 Personal attacks beyond vulgar abuse, however, stand on a different footing. Lord McLaren said in *McLaughlan v Orr, Pollock & Co* **(1894)** that:

> "It is hardly necessary to point out that the constitution of this country tolerates the utmost freedom in the discussion of the conduct and motives of those who take part in its public affairs, whether in the higher plane of statesmanship or in the conduct of local affairs. ... It is only when private character is attacked, or when the criticism of public conduct is combined with the suggestion of base or indirect motives that redress can be claimed on the ground of injury to reputation."

27.23 Alistair Moffat also sued another newspaper in 1999 for suggesting that he was having an adulterous affair (*Moffat v News Group Newspapers Ltd* **(1999)**). No-one appears to have argued that, in his position, he had to tolerate that sort of false imputation.

27.24 The decision in *Reynolds v Times Newspapers* from the House of Lords [see **paras 27.85 onwards**] makes it clear that defamation law in the United Kingdom has not as yet recognised a public figure defence per se. Though Scots law has long recognised that a public figure or public official can be attacked as regards the performance of their role to a degree that would be unacceptable against a private citizen (*Langlands* **(1916)**; *Waddell* **(1973)**), politicians can and do sue in defamation in Scotland, as the cases brought by Irene McAdam, Jimmy Wray, Councillor Brooks, George Robertson, Tommy Sheridan and Frances Curran show [see **paras 27.37, 26.78, 26.75, 43.24, 05.67 and 26.79**]. In *Brooks* [see **para.26.40**], the Inner House of the Court of Session said:

> "'Secret agreement' ... in our view implies that there was an agreement which the pursuer deliberately kept from the knowledge of other councillors. We do not see that reference to having entered into a secret agreement as falling within the broad tolerance which the authorities show is allowed to political exchanges. Nor do we agree that the reference does not reflect adversely on the pursuer's private character ... Nor are we dealing with a deception, such as a lie, which might have arisen in the heat of political debate. The conduct attributed to the pursuer could only have been deliberative conduct and protracted over a period of time."

In awarding Jimmy Wray £60,000 damages for allegations that he 27.25 beat his wife, Lord Johnston said:

> "The pursuer has a high profile ... a long and dedicated career in the public sector ... In this day and age when not every member of the Westminster Parliament has been shown to have clean hands with regard to public life and his private life, the type of allegation in this article must reflect very seriously on the political position of an MP ... That, however, in the case of persons in public life, has to be compensated by the fact that they require to have thick skins, although not necessarily in relation to untruthful allegations about their domestic life";

which suggests that the target's status as a public figure can be a double-edged sword and is certainly not an all-purpose shield.

FAIR COMMENT AND PUBLIC DEBATE

The nature of a public figure's duties may have a bearing upon what 27.26 can be said about his private life (see, e.g. *Nicol* **(2002)** [see **para.07.63**], where the defenders argued that, since the pursuer himself was a former procurator fiscal, allegations of a criminal nature against him were legitimately newsworthy). But the position is not straightforward. In the context of the fair comment defence, a factor is not so much whether the target of the comment is a public figure, but rather whether they have opened themselves up to public debate. When Sara Keays, former mistress of Lord Cecil Parkinson, sued the *Guardian* over a comment piece implying that she was publicising her illegitimate daughter's health problems as a vindictive reminder of Lord Parkinson's abandonment of mother and child, the English judge, Eady J., found it relevant that she had publicised extensively the matter of her former lover's behaviour (*Keays v Guardian Newspapers Ltd* **(2003)**).

Where a person or business offers something for review—a play, a 27.27 book, a restaurant—a great licence has always been extended to criticism of it. Lord Nicholls said in the Privy Council case of *Tse Wai Chun Paul* **(2001)** that "a critic need not be mealy-mouthed ... He is entitled to dip his pen in gall for the purposes of legitimate criticism". In *Associated Newspapers v Burstein* **(2007)**, the English Court of Appeal unanimously held that a review in the *Evening Standard* of an opera which the composer claimed meant he was a terrorist sympathiser, must be fair comment. In the English case of *Smith v ADVFN* **(2008)** [see **paras 27.16 and 43.31**], Eady J. said:

> "Opinions may be expressed and exaggerated in strident terms; the only requirement is that they be honestly held. It is fanciful to suppose that any of these people did not believe what they were saying. Even if they reached their conclusions in haste, or on incomplete information, or irrationally, the defence would still avail them."

27.28 In 2010, that court again dismissed the action brought by the British Chiropractic Association against science writer **Dr Simon Singh (2010)**. Dr Singh had written, "it happily promotes bogus treatments" and made claims for treatments "even though there is not a jot of evidence". The Court of Appeal denounced the association's action as apparently an endeavour to silence its critics in an area of legitimate controversy.

LIMITS TO THE FAIR COMMENT DEFENCE

27.29 First, the matter complained of must be comment—the defence does not protect defamatory statements of fact (cf. **Waddell v BBC (1973)**).

27.30 Secondly, the comment must be such as an honest person could have made. Comment, however, does not cease to be fair merely because it represents a stupid, partisan or eccentric point of view. Cranks can have their say. Nor does comment become actionable merely because it is couched in strong or vituperative language (**Archer v Ritchie & Co (1891)**).

27.31 Thirdly, the comment must be based on facts and, if these are stated, they must be accurately stated. Thus, even a review has to be accurate. A restaurant critic can call a meal over-priced, old-fashioned and tasteless, but a claim of food poisoning would need to be proved. Under the Defamation Act 1952 s.6, however, a defence of fair comment will not fail only because the truth of every allegation of fact is not proved, if the expression is fair comment in view of such facts as are proved.

27.32 Fourthly, the comment must be on a matter of public interest. This has a wide scope. It clearly covers comment on affairs of central and local government, the administration of justice and the conduct of those holding or seeking public office. It also covers comment on sport and criticism of books, and of films, plays and other public entertainments. It does not, however, necessarily cover observations on matters such as the private lives of private citizens:

> "[While] it is in the public interest that the Press should exercise freely its right of criticism in regard to public affairs, it is equally important that the right of a private individual to have his character respected should be maintained, and that people

should not as private persons be exposed to unjustifiable and arbitrary comment" (according to Viscount Haldane in *Langlands v Leng* (1916)).

In that case, the House of Lords unanimously dismissed an action 27.33 brought by an architect in private practice who acted for a school board under a system whereby he automatically got alteration work, but new building went out to tender. The *Dundee Advertiser* criticised this system. The architect sued, saying that the article meant he was giving advice favouring alterations corruptly for his personal benefit. The court held that this was fair comment on the system, not an attack on the integrity of the architect.

PERILS OF THE FAIR COMMENT DEFENCE

Like the *Reynolds* privilege [see **paras 27.88 onwards**], "fair 27.34 comment" sounds more permissive than it has proved to be in practice. The distinction between fact and comment is neither clear nor watertight. It is relatively easy, by way of innuendo or otherwise, for a pursuer to argue that what a journalist believes to be comment bears a defamatory factual meaning. There is also a perception among media lawyers—again, difficult to test, given s.8 of the Contempt of Court Act 1981 [see **Chapter 21**]—that juries do not accept fair comment defences unless they happen to agree with the comment.

A "comment" is not exactly to be equated with an opinion (though 27.35 even the Defamation Act 1952 uses the word "opinion" in this context). It has been said to be "a deduction, inference, conclusion, criticism, remark, observation, etc." It can include a statement about someone's supposed motive. It was also warned in an English case, *Lowe v Associated Newspapers* (2006), that:

"[A] bald comment, made in circumstances where it is not possible to understand it as an inference, is likely to be treated as an assertion of fact which will only be susceptible to a defence of justification or privilege."

A journalist cannot comment on the hypothesis that the factual 27.36 statements of others are true: *Galloway v Telegraph* (2006).

TIPS FOR USING THE FAIR COMMENT DEFENCE

27.37   It helps if a journalist can do the following:

- choose a context labelling that something is intended to be comment rather than fact, e.g. by placing it in an editorial, leader, or indeed review section;
- spell out (accurate) facts on which the comment is based, e.g. "having voted against the Bill, he is guilty of the deaths of the innocent" is easier to defend than, "he is guilty of the deaths of the innocent". It was never necessary in Scotland to set out all the facts on which the comment is based (*Wheatley* (1927), per Lord Anderson), a line which the English courts finally decided to adopt in *Lowe* (2006), but it is often prudent as a way of highlighting which elements of a piece are comment;
- pay extra attention to one's choice of language—conjunctions like "so" or "therefore" are likely to assist in claiming comment defences by avoiding the mixing up of factual bases and factual conclusions, but the preface, "in my opinion" or "we think", will be ineffective if what follows is an allegation of fact;
- if a journalist wishes to deploy a fair comment defence, it is important to analyse in advance what the comment is. In *Irene Adams* (2003) [see **para.26.40**], Lord Reed observed: "When requested by the court to indicate any specific words in the article which were capable of being construed as comment, Counsel [for Guardian Newspapers Ltd] was unable to provide a clear response ... The averment that 'it was fair comment that suspicion attached to the pursuer' is immaterial, since no such comment can be found in the article." Therefore, the judge did not allow the fair comment defence to go forward.

RECENT SCOTTISH CASES ON FAIR COMMENT

27.38   In *Brooks* (2004) [see **para.26.40**], the Inner House of the Court of Session, although awarding damages to the councillor in that case over the suggestion that he had made "a secret agreement", upheld the *Airdrie & Coatbridge Advertiser*'s defence that the reference to "a malicious use of public money" over an earlier defamation action was fair comment:

> "The litigation ... on the face of it was for the private benefit of those pursuing it. The first defender therefore cannot be criticised for forming the view that there had been a deliberate

misuse of public funds. As a matter of fact his concerns were misconceived and without foundation but he had some justification for pursuing the course he did. We would therefore agree with the Lord Ordinary that Mr Lind's letter was not defamatory because it represented fair comment on a matter of public interest. It was not suggested that the Advertiser had not fairly and accurately reported the contents of Mr Lind's letter with reference to the matter of malicious misuse of money. The pursuer did not challenge the Lord Ordinary's apparent view that the report of what was fair comment would itself attract the protection given to fair comment …".

This is appellate-level authority in Scotland that the media will be 27.39
covered by the fair comment defence if they accurately report a criticism which is honestly made, even when the speaker has made the comment in ignorance of an important fact. Presumably the logic here would be that the fact that the council had financially backed actions in the name of a private individual would justify the comment that this was "a malicious misuse of public money" even though, in the light of the unknown fact that the action was intended for the council's benefit, the court considered these "concerns … misconceived and without foundation."

The judge in the *Dickson Minto* **(2002)** case [see **para.26.39**], who 27.40
refused to grant interim interdict against publication of an article suggesting that a solicitor had acted in a conflict of interest, obviously considered that it was at least possible that fair comment would afford a defence there (although he was having to decide in a vacuum, since no article at that stage had been written). In the *Woodland Trust* case [see **para.26.25**], Lord Eassie said, "[w]hile the defender is of course entitled to make criticism of the pursuers … he is not entitled to do so on the basis of statements which convey to the public a factually misleading and untrue account of the pursuers' policies", when he granted interdict against future defamatory publications.

There was a fair comment defence in the *McCormick* **(2006)** case 27.41
[see **para.26.39**] which the jury did not accept. There Lord Menzies, charging the jury, emphasised that comment must be recognisable as comment, based on facts which are true or substantially true and the comment must explicitly or implicitly indicate the facts on which the comment was based:

> "Is the headline 'School Chief's Son Smears Witnesses' comment, or a statement of fact? Was the pursuer the son of a school chief? Did he smear witnesses? Are facts indicated on which the comment is based?"

FAIR RETORT

27.42   A certain latitude is allowed to people who deny charges made publicly against them. Even if the denial is in strong terms, it will not be actionable unless the person making the denial was malicious. It is a kind of privilege—in some respects not dissimilar to the developing privilege of "reportage" [see below]—but can be dealt with conveniently as a "defence". The speaker must not pass from repudiation to the making of separate defamatory allegations against the accuser.

27.43   English defamation law [see **Chapter 31**] has a similar form of qualified privilege called "reply to attack". Although the media have the same privilege that the person making the reply to attack has, that privilege is itself limited by the fact that the reply has to be proportionate. In other words, if a person is attacked by another in a newspaper article, it is reasonable for that target to respond through the media. If, however, the attack is only heard by those who happen to be within earshot, it is unlikely that the target could say that a letter to the newspaper counter-attacking was privileged. It is likely that fair retort in Scotland would take a similar approach; although in one Scottish case, *Gray v The Scottish Society for Cruelty to Animals* **(1890)**, the publications were a letter and advertisement in a newspaper, it was the society and not the newspaper which was sued.

27.44   Certainly, the ambit of fair retort is restricted. In *Blair v Eastwood* **(1935)**, for example, where Eastwood was accused of being the father of the pursuer's child, the reply that she had had intercourse with at least two other men was held not to be a fair retort, as he could have rebutted the charge without accusing her of promiscuity. It would have been relevant, as fair retort, to say that she had slept with one other man, but not with two.

27.45   Nonetheless, fair retort can be useful. In *Carroll v BBC* **(1997)** [see **para.26.56**], an investigative journalist who had been accused of disreputable conduct was held entitled to reply that this was "an outrageous suggestion by a man who is a complete stranger to the truth." Privilege can be defeated by malice, but malice would have to be proved against the newspaper or broadcaster, not just the original speaker, to defeat a fair retort.

27.46   In the *Frances Curran* **(2010)** case [see **para.26.79**], the judge dismissed the action brought by the Scottish Socialist Party MSP against an article in the *Daily Record* in which Tommy Sheridan called her a "political scab". The judge held that this was not defamatory. In any case, "scab" would have been protected, in context, as fair comment. Beyond that, the article was said to fall easily within the privilege of fair retort to a press statement with which Frances Curran had aligned herself, calling Tommy Sheridan a perjurer and a paranoid fantasist. His statements did not go beyond rebutting that attack. The judge held, "nothing ... suggests that the retort must be restricted to a bare denial without emphasis or clarification."

PRIVILEGE

There are two types of privilege—absolute and qualified. If a 27.47 statement has absolute privilege, no action can be based on it, however false, defamatory or malicious it may be. If a statement has qualified privilege, an action can be based on it but the pursuer must prove that it was made with malice. The theory behind both types of privilege is that in some circumstances, the public interest demands freedom to speak without fear of an action for defamation.

MALICE

It is generally very difficult for a pursuer to defeat a plea of qualified 27.48 privilege on the basis of malice. Malice, in the ordinary sense of ill will or spite, is neither necessary nor sufficient. A person who honestly reports a neighbour to the police for wilful fire-raising may very well harbour ill feeling towards the neighbour, but that does not amount to malice so long as the person making a report genuinely thinks that the neighbour starts fires. Conversely, a high degree of recklessness could amount to malice in law even if the publisher (as is typically the case in a journalistic context) has no personal *animus* against the subject of the defamatory statement. Negligence, however, is not malice.

Malice is a state of mind and has to be inferred from the facts and 27.49 circumstances, including, though only in very extreme instances, the intemperance of the language used. Generally, if the facts and circumstances are equally consistent with the publisher not being malicious, the pursuer will lose. In *Thomson* **(2000)** [see **para.28.09**], Lord Eassie said of statements made by the President of the Law Society about two solicitors who had been struck off the roll:

"In my opinion on no reasonable view could the words attributed to the President ever begin to approach the characterisation of violent or extreme language ... I consider that it may thus be said that a pursuer in a defamation action may aver or prove malice either (i) by averring and proving that at the time at which the statement was made its maker knew that what he or she was saying were untrue (or have that wholly reckless indifference to truth which the law in the case of such as fraud equiparates with positive knowledge of untruth) or (ii) by averring and proving that the statement was made predominantly for some private spite or ulterior motive ... The fact that the maker of the statement is by the reason of the matter with which he is concerned ill-disposed or unfriendly towards, or prejudiced against the person who is the subject of the statement ... does not amount to 'malice' in the legal sense ... One who believes another to have been guilty of misconduct will sometimes have no love of that other or be in a popular sense ill-disposed, prejudiced or hostile to that person. However, these sentiments do not constitute malice in the technical sense ...".

27.50 Mere failure to check that what had been said by another was accurate did not deprive the speaker of qualified privilege.

27.51 Despite this high bar, averments that a publisher was malicious are sometimes allowed to go to trial. In ***Hay* (2003)** [see **para.26.39**], the case concerned an Institute of Chartered Accountants of Scotland (ICAS) press release and website about the expulsion of a chartered accountant who had been acquitted of charges involving breach of trust at a criminal trial, but been expelled by the Discipline Committee of ICAS. Lady Paton held that it was not possible, without some enquiry into the facts, to decide whether or not that committee's proceedings attracted absolute privilege, but thought that an inaccurate reference to a not proven verdict was consistent with an inference of malice, as was the content and tone of the ICAS press release. A stronger line was taken in ***Barratt International Resorts Ltd* (2002)** [see **para.30.06**]. In ***Fitchie v Worsnop* (2004)** [see **para.26.40**], the court again thought there was a question as to whether the defender in fact enjoyed absolute privilege, but held that, in any case, there were no sufficient averments of malice.

27.52 In ***McKellar*** [see **para.28.12**], the difference between qualified and absolute privilege was very important. The sheriff held that, even though a schoolboy was entitled to qualified privilege in claiming that a teacher had assaulted him, since the claim was found to be fabricated and he must have known that he was making it up, malice defeated qualified privilege.

27.53 Malice was also significant in ***Westcrowns Contracting Services v Daylight Insulation* (2005)**, because the claim was in verbal injury, not defamation [see **para.30.07**]. Lord MacPhail said there: "The court must be slow to infer malice unless it is satisfied [the defender] did not believe that what he said or wrote was true or that he was indifferent to its truth or falsity." The judge held that, in this case, there was malice, based on a desire to injure Westcrowns' business for commercial advantage and lack of honest belief in what was said about Westcrowns.

In *Fraser* (2010), Sheriff Neilson held that statements made to their 27.54 mutual line manager and other colleagues by the disappointed applicant for a job of the successful applicant did not attract privilege, but even if they had, the privilege would be defeated by the express malice of the speaker, who was accusing the pursuer of assaulting the defender's mother.

ABSOLUTE PRIVILEGE

Absolute privilege applies to statements made in the Westminster 27.55 Parliament, the Scottish Parliament, reports authorised by Parliament and statements made in court with reference to the case in progress by judge, advocate, solicitor or witness. The litigant, however, has only qualified privilege and cannot indulge with impunity in malicious defamation simply by raising an action (*Bernard Hill v Law Society of Scotland* (2005)). In contrast, in England a litigant enjoys absolute privilege [see **Chapter 31**].

By a number of statutes, absolute privilege attaches to certain 27.56 communications by, or to, or arising out of investigations by various commissioners, regulators and ombudsmen. Scottish examples since the millennium include the Commissioner for Children and Young People (Scotland) Act 2003 (s.15 creates both absolute and qualified privilege), the Scottish Public Services Ombudsman Act 2002 (s.18 creates absolute privilege), the Scottish Parliamentary Standards Commissioner Act 2002 (s.17 creates an absolute privilege and a qualified privilege), the Scottish Commission for Human Rights Act 2006 (s.17 creates both absolute and qualified privilege), the Ethical Standards in Public Life etc. (Scotland) Act 2000 (s.27 creates absolute privilege), and the Water Services etc. (Scotland) Act 2005 (Consequential Provisions and Modifications) Order 2005 (SI 2005/ 3172) (art.10 creates absolute privilege).

COURT REPORTING—PRIVILEGE

In terms of s.14 of the Defamation Act 1996, fair and accurate 27.57 contemporaneous reporting of proceedings in public of any UK court, the European Court of Justice, the European Court of Human Rights or an international criminal tribunal established by the United Nations or equivalent (i.e. by a treaty to which the UK is party) is accorded absolute privilege.

27.58   A fair and accurate report of proceedings in public before a court anywhere in the world—contemporaneous or not—gets qualified privilege under s.515 of the 1996 Act.

Contemporaneity

27.59   To get the benefit of absolute privilege, the report needs to be "published contemporaneously with the proceedings", as well as fair and accurate.

27.60   In the case of a weekly newspaper, this will optimally be the next available edition. The concept of contemporaneity has been considered in very few cases in the UK. Clearly, it does not mean literally "contemporaneously", or a verdict could only ever be reported by live broadcast or online. Equally clearly, though, the sooner a fair and accurate court report goes to press, the safer the journalist will be.

27.61   Where a reporting restriction has prevented contemporaneous reporting, e.g. under s.4(2) of the Contempt of Court Act 1981, publication is treated as contemporaneous "if it is published as soon as practicable after publication is permitted." Thus, information about an accused's previous convictions which came out in an unsuccessful plea in bar of trial, or evidence held to be inadmissible, could be included many weeks down the line in a TV backgrounder once the case had ended.

27.62   In the English defamation case of *Bennett* **(2006)** [see **para.20.02**], Eady J. said that he had no doubt that a report published five days after the sentencing would be contemporaneous. The same judge said in *Crossley v Newsquest* **(2008)** that, not only would a report published three days after the hearing still be contemporaneous, but so far as that report went into earlier hearings so as to explain the context for the most recent hearing, that, too, would be absolutely privileged.

What is a court?

27.63   Of course, by no means all legal business is carried out in the civil and criminal courts of the land. There are many other bodies which enjoy the name "court". For example, there is the Valuation Appeal Court, the Restrictive Practices Court, the Scottish Land Court, and the Court of the Lord Lyon, the Court for Trial of Election Petitions. Similarly, there are bodies which exercise functions rather like a court but which do not bear the name "court". In this category we find the Asylum and Immigration Tribunal, the Lands Tribunal for Scotland, the Pensions Appeal Tribunals of Scotland and the Upper Tribunal. Employment tribunals are not called courts, but as of 2007, their chairpeople are called judges [see **Chapter 6**]. The definition of "court" in the 1996 Act includes "any tribunal or body exercising the judicial power of the State", the same definition as in the Contempt of Court Act 1981 [see **paras 15.46 to 15.53**]. In *Trapp v Mackie* **(1979)**, the House of Lords held that witnesses were privileged against a defamation action in a local inquiry into the sacking of a Scottish headmaster where the inquiry had a number of powers similar to those of a normal court.

Reports of inquiries under the Inquiries Act 2005 have the same 27.64 privilege as reports of court proceedings.

OTHER PRIVILEGED REPORTS UNDER THE DEFAMATION ACT 1996

Journalists would do well to study the list of bodies contained in Sch.1 27.65 to the 1996 Act [see **Appendix 4**]. Schedule 1 gives qualified privilege to a range of statements. Other statements can be added to Sch.1 by delegated legislation. Fair and accurate reports of public legislative or judicial proceedings, public inquiries, international organisations and conferences anywhere in the world are covered. So are fair and accurate copies of or extracts from public registers, notices or advertisements published on the authority of a court, copies of or extracts from information published on the authority of a government or legislature, or fair and accurate copies of extracts from information published by an international organisation or conference. Fair and accurate reports of the public proceedings of these bodies are accorded qualified privilege.

Part 1 of Sch.1 has a noticeably global flavour. Part 2 is more 27.66 European. It provides extensive protection to fair and accurate reporting of proceedings and publications under the aegis of the legislatures, governments, authorities performing governmental functions—including police functions—and courts of the Member States and their institutions. The bulk of local authority public activities are covered by Pt 2.

Public companies and press conferences
Protection is also given under Pt 2 to various proceedings of and 27.67 publications by public companies. The definition of "UK public company" for these purposes covers a range of bodies corporate, including those incorporated by Royal Charter, like the BBC. The broadest provision is at para.12, which includes "a fair and accurate report of proceedings at any public meeting held in a member State." A "public meeting" is defined as "a meeting bona fide and lawfully held for a lawful purpose and for the furtherance or discussion of a matter of public concern, whether admission to the meeting is general or restricted." This is potentially quite important for those cases where

the general public are excluded, but the press allowed to remain. It would also appear to cover some meetings which the organisations holding them might regard as quasi-private. In the *McCartan Turkington Breen* (2000) case, the House of Lords held that a press conference counted as a "public meeting" and the contents of the relevant press release would also be protected by privilege, whether or not they had been read aloud during the press conference. Further, protection is provided for a fair and accurate report of findings or decisions of various associations for promoting art, science, religion, education, business or professions, sports or charities, so far as such associations have a regulatory function.

Requirement to publish explanations or contradictions in some cases

27.68   In the case of reports falling under Pt 2, there is an obligation, on request, to publish a reasonable letter or statement by way of explanation or contradiction. It is thought that the letter or statement would have to be of a reasonable length and not contain an attack on third parties. By the same token, it has to be published "in a suitable manner", which is likely to mean "with the same prominence as the original piece to which it is responding."

OTHER STATUTORY PRIVILEGES EXIST

27.69   Statutes other that the Defamation Act 1996 also sometimes create statutory qualified privilege, e.g. the Freedom of Information (Scotland) Act 2002 s.67 (privilege for supplying the information to the person asking for it—*not* to the media; this is also true of s.79 of the Freedom of Information Act 2000, the UK Act); the Broadcasting Act 1996 s.121. Some other examples are given above [see **paras 27.55 to 27.56**]. Reports of inquiries under the Inquiries Act 2005 are protected [see **para.27.64**].

27.70   It is clear from the foregoing that journalists enjoy a substantial degree of protection in their reporting of the proceedings of courts, tribunals and other quasi-judicial bodies. The journalist should have to hand the Schedule to the Defamation Act 1996, reproduced at Appendix 4, to ascertain the type of privilege applying. A fair and accurate report of a legitimate public meeting or body will almost certainly enjoy a degree of privilege, either absolute or qualified.

OTHER FORMS OF QUALIFIED PRIVILEGE— THE COMMON LAW

27.71   The Scottish courts have also long recognised that the protection of privilege arises when someone communicates information being under a social or moral duty to do so. Qualified privilege applies generally to statements made by a person in the discharge of some public or private duty or in matters where his or her own interests are involved. It applies, for example, to statements made by an employer in giving an employee a reference. No action can be founded on such statements unless there is proof of malice (or possibly negligence, according to the House of Lords decision in *Spring v Guardian Assurance Plc* (1994)).

This type of privilege may be relevant for journalists. If a person has 27.72 a duty to make a statement and can only make it adequately in a newspaper, then it seems that qualified privilege may protect not only the person but also the journalist publishing the information: *Brims v Reid* (1885), though the letter to the editor in that case was not held to be privileged, because it was anonymous, leaving the writer's duty or interest in the matter unclear. In *Fraser v Mirza* (1993), a Glasgow justice of the peace had written to the Chief Constable of Strathclyde, complaining of his treatment by Constable Fraser, whom he accused of being motivated by racial prejudice when he arrested the justice of the peace for reset. The House of Lords decided in February 1993 that, although normally a citizen writing to complain about a police officer would be protected by qualified privilege, Mr Mirza had misused the occasion and so no privilege applied. The court awarded the constable £5,000 damages.

UNINTENTIONAL DEFAMATION

As we have seen, people can recover damages for defamation even if 27.73 the statement complained of was not intended to refer to them or was not intended to be defamatory. This has given rise to some hard cases.

In *Morrison v Ritchie* (1902), the *Scotsman* printed "birth notices" 27.74 in August saying that Mrs Morrison had given birth to twins. This statement was false but was printed by the newspaper in good faith. It had no way of knowing that Mrs Morrison had been married for only a month. (An interesting example both of innuendo which would only have been understood by those who knew when the Morrisons married and of an innuendo, i.e. of premarital sex, which would almost certainly not be defamatory nowadays.) The person who inserted the notice could not be traced and an action was raised against the proprietors of the *Scotsman*. They maintained that they were not liable because the notices sent to them for publication were not defamatory on their face and they had no reason to suppose that they were underneath. The court rejected this defence. The defenders could not escape liability by saying that the slander was unintentional.

27.75   Similarly, if a writer does not mean to refer to a particular person or even any real person, but nonetheless writes something which reasonable people reading the article or book will take as a reference to a particular person, that could be defamatory, whether it results from sheer coincidence or not. In *Were v Hodder & Stoughton* **(2006)**, the publishers ended up pulping a novel which contained a character with the same stage name as the claimant's, and paying him substantial damages in England, even though the character was never intended to be based on him. (The novel featured real life events in a way which arguably confused matters.) For this reason, when dealing with a report concerning a real person, it is prudent to give not only a name, but other identifying details such as age, occupation or address.

27.76   This is not foolproof. At the end of the day, this is a factual question: would a reasonable reader/viewer/listener think that the publication referred to the claimant? There are a number of Jim McKenzies in Scotland, so a reasonable person is unlikely to take it that their particular acquaintance of that name is the man being accused of, e.g. fraud in the newspaper. If, however, the piece refers to, "32-year-old Jim McKenzie, a glassblower from Oban", and there are two people fitting that description, the journalist may get a writ from the "wrong" one.

27.77   In *O'Shea v MGN Ltd* (2001), the English courts declined to accept that a "lookalike" could be defamed by an advertisement featuring a photograph of a woman promoting a pornographic internet service. Nonetheless, since journalists, newspapers or broadcasters can in principle be found liable of defaming people of whose existence they are unaware, or whom they believe to be fictional, or by publishing material which on the face of it is totally harmless, it will be obvious that there remains quite some scope for innocent yet expensive error. Here, the offer of amends procedure can help, if not cure.

DEFAMATION ACT 1996—OFFER OF AMENDS

27.78   If the defenders take the view that they were wrong in the original publication, they can make a statutory offer of amends. Such an offer must be in writing, must refer to s.2 of the 1996 Act and must state whether it is a qualified offer or not. If it is a qualified offer, that means that the defender accepts that the words used in the original article were defamatory, but does not accept the meaning attached to them by the potential pursuer. An offer to make amends must offer to publish a suitable correction and a sufficient apology in a manner that is reasonable and practicable. Further, the defender must offer to pay "such compensation (if any) … as may be agreed or determined to be payable", plus legal expenses. The court will decide the amount of compensation if the parties cannot agree. A practice of applying a discount of between one-half and one-third of what the court would otherwise have awarded the aggrieved person, to reflect the speed, willingness, etc. of the offerer, is established in England and, from anecdotal evidence, in Scotland too.

Although this defence can be very useful where a mistake has been made, legal advice should be taken before making such an offer, as the process has its pitfalls. The offer can be made after an action has been brought, but speed is important. It is possible to make a qualified offer of amends, i.e. one which relates only to a particular meaning. | 27.79

In the surprising case of ***Moore v Scottish Daily Record and Sunday Mail Ltd* (2007)**, Lady Paton held that failure to accept an offer of amends and deciding instead to bring an action did not amount to rejecting it, so it was still open for acceptance the day before the hearing was due. In the English case of ***Tesco Stores v Guardian* (2009)**, Eady J. said he did not find ***Moore***'s reasoning persuasive: the person alleging defamation had to choose within a reasonable period whether to accept or to reject it and could not sit indefinitely on the fence. | 27.80

An offer can be withdrawn before acceptance and it can be renewed. If the offer is accepted, that ends the action (unless the offer was a qualified offer). If the offer is not accepted, the pursuer has to show that the defender did not just make an innocent mistake. The offer of amends procedure is not available if the offerer knew or had reason to believe that the statement referred to the aggrieved party or would be taken to refer to him, and was false and defamatory of him. It is presumed that the offerer knew no such thing, but if the aggrieved party can prove the contrary, the offerer is lost. | 27.81

Where the offer of amends has not been accepted, the offerer does not have to rely upon it as a defence—it can be relied upon, instead, to argue that damages should be reduced. However, if the offerer does use it as a defence, no other defence is possible. A journalist cannot rely on an offer of amends and simultaneously argue that the story is true, or is covered by ***Albert Reynolds*** privilege. | 27.82

MINIMISATION OF DAMAGES

Apart from the offer of amends defence, it is right and sensible when a clear mistake has been made to publish an apology/clarification as soon as possible. In particular, this is a sound step where the original publication is still available online [see **para.26.81** and **Chapter 43**]. | 27.83

LAPSE OF TIME

27.84   Under the Prescription and Limitation (Scotland) Act 1973, as
amended in 1985, no action for defamation may be brought unless it
is begun within three years from the date when the publication or
communication first came to the notice of the pursuer. The court has,
however, power to extend this period if it seems to it equitable to do so.
The one year time limit for the rest of the United Kingdom has already
been noted. The continued availability online of many media
publications reduces the helpfulness of statutory time bars for the
media, however [see **Chapter 43** and **para.26.81**].

THE *REYNOLDS* DEFENCE AND REPORTAGE

27.85   The statement by Temporary Judge Gordon Coutts in *Baigent
v McCulloch* **(1998)** that, "[i]t is, in my view, arrogant of the BBC to
consider itself in some way a super-investigative body or a 'watchdog
of society'" was always, from the perspective of the European Court of
Human Rights, remarkably uninstructed. To Strasbourg, a watchdog
of society is exactly what the media should be. The House of Lords
resoundingly endorsed this approach in defamation law in
establishing the *Reynolds* defence.

27.86   In the English case of *Reynolds v Sunday Times*, the House of Lords
accepted that journalists were under a social duty to publish material
about prominent public figures carrying out public functions in
circumstances where the readership/viewership had a legitimate
interest in the subject matter. They stopped short of accepting a
public figure defence of the kind accepted in American courts in
Sullivan v New York Times **(1964)**. In Scots defamation law, public
figures have long been treated differently from ordinary citizens [see
paras 26.77 onwards and para.27.18] but they can and do sue.

27.87   Nevertheless, from a journalist's perspective, *Reynolds* is a welcome
development of the right to comment on public affairs and continues
the trend begun in the *Derbyshire County Council* **(1993)** case which
recognised that if journalists were not given some leeway there would
be a "chilling effect" on public debate. Indeed, whilst *Reynolds*
stopped short of accepting a public figure defence, it created a
privilege which potentially protects the media in a much broader
way, if taken seriously by the lower courts.

27.88   In *Reynolds*, Lord Nicholls in the House of Lords set out a non-
exhaustive, but nonetheless fully comprehensive set of factors
relevant to whether the media would be privileged to report a
defamatory allegation to the world. These are:

"1. The seriousness of the allegation. The more serious the charge, the more the public is misinformed and the individual harmed, if the allegation is not true.
2. The nature of the information, and the extent to which the subject-matter is a matter of public concern.
3. The source of the information. Some informants have no direct knowledge of the events. Some have their own axes to grind, or are being paid for their stories.
4. The steps taken to verify the information.
5. The status of the information. The allegation may have already been the subject of an investigation which commands respect.
6. The urgency of the matter. News is often a perishable commodity.
7. Whether comment was sought from the plaintiff. He may have information others do not possess or have not disclosed. An approach to the plaintiff will not always be necessary.
8. Whether the article contained the gist of the plaintiff's side of the story.
9. The tone of the article. A newspaper can raise queries or call for an investigation. It need not adopt allegations as statements of fact.
10. The circumstances of the publication, including the timing."

In principle, a journalist need not, in all cases, tick every box. In practice, though, the cases where a journalist has been able to use the *Reynolds* defence successfully are few and far between. More successes may be anticipated, perhaps, in the near future, since the House of Lords made in clear in *Mohammed Jameel* **(2006)** that the lower courts in England were wrong in inflexibly interpreting the *Reynolds* factors as a series of hurdles and paying inadequate attention to editorial discretion. Whatever happens, on that front, *Reynolds* is undoubtedly an important tool for the media in a defamation action. If nothing else, it elucidates what the judiciary considers to be the elements of responsible journalism. Strategically, it can take a complex case out of the hands of a jury. It also takes away the onus of proof in an area where the evidence, not atypically, is mostly in the hands of the media's opponent at the time when the story is actually being written. 27.89

However, *Reynolds* is a tool with a sharp edge for the media as well. It puts a focus on journalistic practices which may be uncomfortable, either because the individual journalist's practice in the case will not bear much scrutiny or because the scrutiny itself may create ethical difficulties for the media, for example around source protection or access to un-transmitted material, journalists' notebooks or the like. 27.90

27.91   It is quite possible for the media to fail to establish an *Albert Reynolds* defence, but go on to prove the story true. In *Henry v BBC* **(2005)** for instance, in England, the court took the view that there was no need for the BBC to name the claimant whose hospital had been implicated in wrongdoing by an official enquiry in relation to waiting lists. The BBC went on to prove that the allegations made against the claimant were true and so won the action (*Henry v BBC* **(2006)**). Associated Newspapers had the same experience in the *Miller v Associated Newspapers Ltd* case **(2003; 2005)**.

27.92   What is necessary to prove a defence of *veritas* is very different from what is needed, or even available, to establish *Reynolds* privilege, in everything from philosophy to chronology. If, say, a newspaper finds damning evidence about a pursuer's activities during the preparation for a defamation case, that can be used to bolster a *veritas* defence, but it is likely to be irrelevant to *Reynolds* privilege. One cannot establish that journalism was responsible in a *Reynolds* sense by retrospectively bolstering its accuracy. *Veritas* and *Reynolds* can certainly be argued together, but they need to be argued in quite different ways. That said, the more attention is paid to certain of the *Reynolds* factors, for instance about corroborative investigation and source credibility, the more likely it is that a *veritas* defence will be successful, too.

27.93   There is very little Scottish *Reynolds* jurisprudence, but it is clear from the *Irene Adams* **(2003)** case that the principles of *Reynolds* are uncontroversial in Scotland. In fact, *Reynolds* sits very comfortably with some of the older Scottish case law on public figures.

REPORTAGE

27.94   The English courts are developing a new defence, an offshoot of sorts of the *Reynolds* defence, called reportage. So far, it has covered cases where a newspaper has neutrally reported both sides of a political spat, where allegations and counter-allegations are flying. Although this is sometimes also called "neutral reportage", the newspaper need not be neutral in the sense of being politically impartial: in *Roberts v Gable* **(2008)**, the defender was strongly opposed to the British National Party's politics, but accurately recounted the cross-fire accusations of criminality between one extreme right-wing faction and another. The underlying philosophy, as with court or parliamentary reporting, is that the accurate recounting of an exchange of this sort is sufficiently important, socially, to justify reputational damage.

27.95   There is no indication that it is confined to political speech and it will be interesting to see if it develops to cover other types of controversy. Nor is it confined to covering clashing claims and counter-claims, in theory: "The reportage doctrine ... cannot logically be confined to the reporting of reciprocal allegations. A unilateral libel, reported disinterestedly, will be fully protected" (*Charman* (2008)). In practice, though, it has so far succeeded in cases where claims and counter-allegations have been reported. A reportage defence can be lost when the reporter adopts or embellishes the allegations (*Galloway* (2006)). Some of this speech is already protected by other defences, such as fair comment in the *Simon Singh* (2010) case about the ambit of chiropractics [see **para.27.18**] or fair retort in the *Frances Curran* (2010) case [see **para.26.79**].

Although to some extent the reportage defence has grown out of the   27.96
Albert Reynolds case, it is a very different animal. It has been said that a journalist properly using the *Reynolds* defence is a bloodhound sniffing out the story, whereas a journalist using reportage as a defence is a watchdog barking to wake the public up to a story which is already out there. In *Charman* (2008), above, the Court of Appeal held that the book, *Bent Coppers*, was responsible journalism under *Albert Reynolds*, but was "miles away" from reportage. Lord Justice Sedley observed:

> "... It is the very dependence of a reportage defence on the bald retelling of libels which makes it forensically problematical to fall back upon an alternative defence of responsible journalism. Pleaders may need to decide which it is to be."

KEY POINTS

1. Most unusually, in a defamation action, it is normally not the   27.97
   person bringing the case who has the burden of proof, but rather the defender. Proof is on the balance of probabilities, rather than "beyond reasonable doubt", but that can still be a high standard in cases where seriously defamatory allegations are made.
2. The most common defences on which the journalist may rely are (a) *veritas*; (b) fair comment; (c) absolute privilege; or (d) qualified privilege.
3. Fair comment does not have to be fair in the normal sense. However, it has to be honestly held. If the comment is based on fact, the facts must be accurate.
4. The special "*Reynolds* defence" for responsible journalism is starting to develop, but thus far has rarely succeeded. The availability of the *Reynolds* defence will depend on a number of factors, including the seriousness of the allegation, its

urgency, the credibility of its sources, the steps taken to verify, any existing credible investigations, right of reply, coverage of both sides of the story and tone.

5. The "neutral reportage" defence is still developing, but may well be of great use in governing political controversies in particular.

6. The defence of "fair retort" allows people to counter-attack in relation to charges made against them. However, it does not allow them to make an unrelated defamatory attack on their critics.

7. The defence of qualified privilege can be argued to apply in a good number of situations, especially in regard to public meetings of courts, councils, parliaments, public companies and press conferences. In addition to the common law occasions of qualified privilege, there are the occasions of qualified privilege set out in the Schedule to the Defamation Act 1996. Care should be taken to ascertain into which part of the Schedule the occasion falls. Qualified privilege will be defeated by malice, but proving malice, in the legal sense, is a high hurdle.

8. Fair and accurate court reporting is extensively protected by privilege.

9. Defamation can arise entirely by innocent mistake—for example, when a correct statement about one person is reasonably understood to refer to somebody else of the same name. In news reporting, it is sensible to include not only a name, but other identifying details, to minimise the risk of this happening.

10. The offer of amends procedure under the Defamation Act 1996 can be useful when mistakes happen.

CHAPTER 28

DAMAGES AND OTHER REMEDIES

By ROSALIND MCINNES

Where there is no defence or the defence fails, there will be either a   28.01
settlement or an award of damages. Even when there is no offer of
amends as such [see **paras 27.78 onwards**], prompt action by the
journalist or editor in publishing an apology for a clear error will be
helpful in achieving settlement at a lower figure.

Scots law allows damages for injury to feelings alone. Substantial   28.02
awards may thus be made even although the pursuer has suffered no
financial loss.

JUDGES' AWARDS OF DAMAGES

High damages were awarded in February 1999 by Temporary Judge   28.03
Gordon Coutts QC in the *Baigent v BBC* **(1999)** case [see
para.26.66]. These included £20,000 per head to a daughter and two
sons who were not individually mentioned in the television
programme. Awards of £60,000 and £50,000 were made to their
parents, who also received a further £8,000 each from other
defenders. A single judge decision by Lord Johnston in March 2000
assessed damages due to Jimmy Wray [see **para.26.78**], the
Westminster MP, at £60,000. Both these cases were unsuccessfully
appealed, *Wray* **(2000)** on the outcome, *Baigent* on the amount.
Lord Johnston honestly described his level of award as "almost
instinctive". Compare this to the £2,500 obtained by Mr Brooks [see
para.26.40] or the statement by Lord Milligan that he would have
awarded £30,000 for an allegation that someone was a war criminal
had STV not proved that the allegation was true (*Gecas v Scottish
Television plc* **(1992)**).

JURIES' AWARDS OF DAMAGES

The awards of £45,000 to Father Noel Barry and £120,000 to his co-   28.04
pursuer, Mrs Annie Clinton, have already been noted (*Clinton v News
Group Newspapers Ltd* **(1998)**), ditto £50,000 to prison employee Mrs
Winter. Those cases were decided by a jury. Glasgow solicitor John
McCormick received £45,000 from a jury (*McCormick v Scottish
Daily Record & Sunday Mail Ltd* **(2006)**).

28.05   A jury will always take a somewhat subjective view of the amount of damages to be awarded. Charging the jury in the *Tommy Sheridan* **(2006)** defamation case, Lord Turnbull said:

> "You will have seen in the document called The Issue that there is a figure of £200,000. The first thing that you need to appreciate is that that figure is only there because some figure has to be stated. Its only purpose is to act as an upper limit ... Secondly, you should remember, of course, that damages are not awarded as a punishment ... If you are considering an assessment of damages, you are entitled to take into account factors such as: the circumstances of the publication; the number of times defamatory material is published—because every repetition of a defamation is a new wrong and may increase the level of damages; thirdly, the number of people who are likely to have read the papers concerned; fourthly, the position in life of the Pursuer; fifthly, the gravity of the defamation, and sixthly, the consequent effect, if any, on the Pursuer's reputation and health. You will remember that in this exercise, the principle is compensation and the burden of proof lies on the Pursuer.

> So in deciding on any award that you would make, you should keep, of course, a sense of proportion. You should bear in mind the value of money, and what it costs to pay for things like a holiday or a car or a house, for example."

28.06   The jury awarded the £200,000 stated in the claim and, because under s.8 of the Contempt of Court Act 1981 it is not easy to analyse a jury verdict, it cannot be said how they reached that figure.

DIFFICULTY OF APPEALING AGAINST AMOUNT OF DAMAGES

28.07   So Scottish defamation awards seem to be creeping up and, further, are resistant to appeal. When the BBC appealed the *Baigent* damages, the court said: "The only doubt we have in our minds is whether they are high enough." The Scottish courts will, it seems, decline to interfere unless the figure is at least double what the higher court would have awarded. There is one case, *Wright and Greig v Outram* **(1890)**, where the Inner House slashed a damages award against the *Glasgow Herald* in half as a condition of not ordering a new trial, but in the modern era, Scottish defamation damages are difficult to appeal against with any success.

28.08   Towards the end of the 20th century, the damages awarded by English juries became the subject of much public interest and are naturally of concern to journalists. Examples include the award of half a million pounds, obtained by Jeffrey Archer against the *Star* newspaper over allegations that he had consorted with a prostitute. Archer was later jailed for four years for perjury and perverting the course of justice at the defamation trial. (At the time of writing, Tommy Sheridan, too, is involved in a perjury trial over his defamation case.) The English Court of Appeal had repeatedly had to deal with extremely high defamation damages awarded to, e.g. Elton John and Esther Rantzen (*John v MGN Ltd* (**1996**) and *Rantzen v Mirror Group Newspapers Ltd* (**1993**)), to the point where that court will now substitute its own figure, where necessary. Lord Aldington's £1.5 million damages award over war crime allegations was so high that Strasbourg had to intervene, saying that awards of this level inherently had a "chilling effect" on free expression (*Tolstoy Miloslavsky v United Kingdom* (**1995**)).

WHEN IS JURY TRIAL ALLOWED IN SCOTTISH DEFAMATION CASES?

In the 20th century, Scottish jury trials in defamation cases were rare. 28.09 Increasingly, however, pursuers have seen the advantage of obtaining trial by jury and so have raised proceedings in the Court of Session where jury trial is available. The onus is on the defender to demonstrate to the court why a jury trial should not be allowed. The defender may demonstrate that there is some technical matter with which the jury might struggle—in *Shanks v BBC* (**1993**), the issues involved 27 different companies, nine innuendos, and a £900,000 loss of business claim, and the case was deemed unsuitable for jury trial. Lord Eassie remarked in *Thomson v Ross* (**2000**), dismissing a case brought by solicitors who had been struck off involving allegations of fraud, multiple defenders and arguments about privilege, that he would have considered it wholly unsuitable for a jury. The English courts have taken the view that cases with a *Reynolds* defence [see **paras 27.85 onwards**] are too legally complex for the average juror.

AGGRAVATION

The general rule is that anything which increases the loss or injury to 28.10 the pursuer will aggravate damages. Scots law, unlike English law, does not allow exemplary damages. A successful pursuer is to be compensated—the unsuccessful defender is not to be punished. However, juries may not fully take this on board.

Persistence in, or repetition of, a defamatory allegation, will, as 28.11 Lord Turnbull said, aggravate damages. If a defamation in one edition comes to light, immediate steps should be taken to ensure that it is expunged from later editions. Similarly, as already pointed out, persistence in defence of a defamatory allegation right up to the end of the court hearing will entitle the judge to award a higher sum by way of aggravated damages to the successful pursuer than would have been the case if the defender had admitted the defamation at an earlier point in the proceedings.

28.12   The extent of publication is a relevant factor in assessing damages and a pursuer can bring evidence of a newspaper's circulation in order to aggravate damages. Boasts about circulation may backfire. Remember that mass circulation may not be necessary for the law to regard the publication as particularly damaging. A leaflet distributed to a few well-chosen individuals could ruin, for example, the reputation of a village minister. *Kennedy v Aldington* [see **para.43.15**] involved a specialist magazine, *Automobile*, and allegations about an individual who would only be recognisable to the cognoscenti. The teacher in *McKellar* [see **para.27.52**] was awarded £5,000 for allegations of assault which were never published in the media by the *soi-disant* victim.

MITIGATION

28.13   A prompt apology or explanation will tend to mitigate damages (*Morrison v Ritchie* **(1902)** [see **para.26.59**]). It was formerly thought that evidence of the defender's innocence or good faith in publishing the statement would also be admissible to mitigate damages (*Cunningham v Duncan & Jamieson* **(1889)**), but the case of *Stein v Beaverbrook Newspapers Ltd* **(1968)** throws doubt on this view and suggests that the defender's lack of fault will be relevant to damages only if it affects the extent of the pursuer's injury.

EVIDENCE OF PREVIOUS REPUTATIONAL DAMAGE

28.14   It will, however, be competent to lead evidence of the pursuer's bad reputation in mitigation of damages on the theory that if the pursuer has a bad reputation already, the defamation makes little difference. Evidence of this sort must probably be limited to the particular aspect of character involved in the defamation. Where a woman was said to have had an illegitimate child it was held to be relevant to prove in mitigation of damages that she was well known in the neighbourhood as a person of loose and immoral character. Proof of specific acts of adultery was, however, not allowed. As Lord President Clyde said: "The point of such a defence is not that she is a bad character, but that she has a bad character" (*C v M* **(1923)**). This neatly summarises the maxim that the law of defamation protects the pursuer's reputation (whether deserved or not) and not his or her character. The English courts are more wary of this approach but do now allow evidence of facts about the claimant's past behaviour which are directly relevant to the context in which the defamatory publication was made (*Turner v News Group Newspapers Ltd* (2006); *Warren v Random House Group* (2009)), in mitigation of damages.

SECTION 12 OF THE DEFAMATION ACT 1952: PREVIOUS RECOVERY OF DAMAGES

The Defamation Act 1952 s.12 provides that a defender may prove in mitigation of damages that the pursuer has already recovered damages or raised an action or settled or agreed to settle in respect of publication of words similar to those on which the action is founded. This is of great importance for newspapers. It discourages actions against a series of papers in respect of one defamatory allegation. If defamed in a number of newspapers, the wise pursuer will sue in respect of the most virulent article, and if successful will then usually be able to settle out of court with the publishers of the lesser material. 28.15

INTERDICT

Instead of seeking damages the person complaining of defamation may seek an interdict or interim interdict to prevent publication of the defamatory matter. Scottish journalists do not enjoy the same degree of support from the courts as their colleagues south of the border. The English case *Bonnard v Perryman* (1891) [see **para.31.12**] meant English journalists have been able virtually to ensure publication by telling the court at the injunction hearing that their facts are correct and that they will prove their facts correct if called upon to do so (though that approach may soon face a Human Rights Act 1998-based attack that it fails adequately to balance the art.8 rights of the person bringing the case: *RST v UVW* (2009)). In contrast there is no absolute "right of unrestrained publication" in Scots law (see *Boyd v BBC* (1969); *Waddell v BBC* (1973)). 28.16

However, in practice, the Scottish courts have tended to refuse interim interdicts where the defenders have stated that they are willing to prove that the defamatory allegations are true and to take the risk of being sued for damages after publication. (Both George Galloway MP and the accountants Touche Ross failed to obtain interim interdicts against BBC Scotland programmes in the past and the late Sheriff Ewan Stewart obtained one, but had it recalled within 28.17

days.) The absence of **Bonnard v Perryman** in Scotland nowadays matters still less, because of s.12 of the Human Rights Act 1998.

SECTION 12 OF THE HUMAN RIGHTS ACT 1998—
MEDIA PROTECTION AGAINST INTERIM INTERDICT

28.18 Section 12 applies if a court is considering whether to grant an order which might affect the exercise of the Convention right to freedom of expression.

It provides for notice to be given to the person against whom the order is sought, wherever practicable, unless there are compelling reasons why the respondent should not be notified.

Section 12(3) states "No such relief is to be granted so as to restrain publication before trial unless the court is satisfied that the applicant is likely to establish that publication should not be allowed." "Likely" normally means "more likely than not" (*Cream Holdings* (2004) [see **paras 36.29 onwards**]).

Under s.12(4), "The court must have particular regard to the importance of the Convention right to freedom of expression and, where the proceedings relate to material which the respondent claims, or which appears to the court, to be journalistic, literary or artistic material (or to conduct connected with such material), to—

(a) the extent to which—

(i) the material has, or is about to, become available to the public; or

(ii) it is, or would be, in the public interest for the material to be published;

(b) any relevant privacy code."

28.19 As with the Data Protection Act 1998, then [see **Chapter 10**], the media's nominally self-regulatory codes now have a form of indirect legal enforceability.

28.20 The section does not include any remedy or order sought in criminal proceedings (s.12(5)).

28.21 This section is heavily influenced by the Strasbourg jurisprudence which regards "prior restraint" of publication as a particularly drastic interference with the right to freedom of expression. In the **Dickson Minto** (2002) case [see **para.27.40**], one of the first Scottish cases to deal with s.12, the court refused to grant interim interdict against the publication of any article suggesting that a solicitor had acted in a conflict of interest. The defenders in that case said that they would only publish truthful facts and that they were not making a direct accusation of conflict of interest. Lord Carloway, refusing the interim interdict, said:

"It is difficult to assert that the petitioners will succeed in circumstances in which it is not known what exactly is to be published ... It is very difficult ... to conclude that even a hypothetical article involving an allegation or innuendo of conflict of interest would ultimately, after appropriate enquiry, be prohibited as defamatory in the face of defences of, for example, veritas and/or fair comment ... It is perhaps not without significance that the petitioners are solicitors and their performance in accordance with ethical standards is a matter of public interest."

It is highly unlikely that a Scottish court would nowadays stop a broadcast on the basis that someone claimed it was defamatory. Breach of confidence or contempt would raise different issues, though see *X v BBC* **(2005)** [see **para.34.18**]; *Paterson, Petitioner* [see **para.15.45**]). An interdict against a repetition after a newspaper loses a defamation trial may also be easier to obtain: *Woodland Trust v McMillan* **(2002)**.   28.22

CAVEATS

It is clear from the above that the media, particularly television broadcasters, are in danger of being the recipients of interim interdict applications. The lodging of caveats each year in the Court of Session and the local sheriff court for the main areas of publication or broadcast may be a wise precaution. The lodging of a caveat means that the court will give the caveator the chance to be heard before an interim interdict is pronounced. Section 12 of the Human Rights Act 1998 ought to remove the need for the media to lodge caveats in defamation or breach of confidence cases. The section appears to require the court to give the media the opportunity to be heard in opposition to an application for interim interdict. However, such caveats are still useful to have, in case s.12 is overlooked or where the threat to freedom of expression is subtler.   28.23

KEY POINTS

1. Damages can be awarded for hurt to feelings alone. Such general damages are not likely to be as high as the special damages awarded when actual loss, such as business loss, can be proved. Exemplary damages are not competent in Scotland as they are in England. Aggravated damages are competent in Scotland where the nature or conduct of the defence persists in or exacerbates the defamation.   28.24

2. A journalist can reduce the liability for damages by publishing an immediate apology.

3. Juries can hear suitable defamation cases and are often thought to make higher awards than judges. Defamation damages, whether awarded by a judge or a jury, are difficult to appeal.

4. As an alternative to claiming damages a pursuer can try to prevent publication by seeking an interim interdict. In Scotland in the past it has been much easier for a pursuer to obtain an interim interdict against defamation than it is for a claimant to obtain a similar order in England. It is now likely to be very difficult.

5. Newspapers and broadcasters should lodge caveats annually in the Court of Session and in the case of local newspapers at the local sheriff court—at least until the interpretation of s.12 of the Human Rights Act 1998 is clear.

6. Section 12 of the Human Rights Act 1998 means media outlets should be notified before an order is made in a civil case which could impinge on their freedom of expression. No such order should be granted unless the court thinks that the person seeking it is "likely" to win at the end of the day. Special regard is to be had to the importance of journalistic freedom. However, the court will also pay close attention to the media's own privacy code. Key to such decisions will be what is (a) in the public domain, and (b) in the public interest.

CHAPTER 29

LETTERS, ARTICLES AND ADVERTISEMENTS

BY ROSALIND McINNES

A defamation can be contained in any part of a newspaper. It can lurk   29.01
in a news item or editorial or it can be blazoned forth in a headline or
even on a billboard. In these last two cases, however, the words in the
headline or on the poster are regarded as simply drawing attention to a
specific article and they will not usually be held to be defamatory if not
so when read fairly along with the article (*Leon v Edinburgh Evening
News* (1909) [see **para.26.21**]; *Archer v Ritchie & Co* (1891)). It is
clear and just that a newspaper should be responsible for material
produced in its own offices. It may seem less clear and less just that it
should be responsible for material such as letters, articles or
advertisements contributed by outsiders.

SPOOF ADVERTISEMENTS

An example of a dangerous advertisement was a "spoof" inserted in   29.02
the *Herald* purporting to announce the liquidation of double glazing
company C.R. Smith. It was particularly difficult to spot this hoax as
the letter containing the notice was typed on what appeared to be
lawyers' notepaper. Had this adversely affected that company's
trading it might well have been possible for them to claim damages
for loss of profit against the newspaper. In the event, a clarification
was enough to resolve the matter. However, the case shows the need
for newspapers to have some sort of checking system in place to
avoid the possibility of publication of spoof advertisements. If
spoofed, the offer of amends procedure in the Defamation Act 1996
[see **Chapter 26**] may be of assistance.

LETTERS TO THE EDITOR

A newspaper is liable for a defamation contained in letters to the editor   29.03
and the person defamed can sue both it and the writer. Of the available
defences, the newspaper may be in a much weaker position as regards
assessing or proving the truth of a letter. Fair comment may apply in
some cases, or, in relation to long-running controversies, reply to
attack or reportage [see **paras 27.42 onwards**]. Interestingly, though,

323

in some older cases, the pursuers seem to have gone after the writers of the letters only, not the newspapers (e.g. *Wardlaw*; *Gray*).

PUBLISHERS OF ANONYMOUS CONTRIBUTORS

29.04   Anonymous letters give rise to further difficulties. Recovery, i.e. handing over of documents which might lead to disclosure of the names of anonymous correspondents, has been ordered when the pursuer alleged that a series of letters to the editor were in fact written by the newspaper itself as part of a systematic plan to ruin his reputation (***Cunningham v Duncan & Jamieson* (1989)** [see **para.07.42**]), and a similar order was made when a newspaper put forward a fair comment defence based on the inclusion of letters said to have come from readers in an article critical of a soap manufacturer (***Ogston & Tennant v Daily Record* (1909)**). Nowadays, the editor may be able to argue that this would amount to disclosure of "the source of information contained in a publication for which he is responsible", bringing in s.10 of the Contempt of Court Act 1981, if desired.

29.05   Issues will arise in this context about anonymous internet postings of the sort which provoked George Robertson's action [see **para.43.24**]. Whether or not the court is willing to compel disclosure, there are strong reasons why a newspaper should reveal the names of contributors of defamatory articles. If it does not, it may find itself cut off from a number of important defences.

29.06   It may, for example, lose the defence of qualified privilege. If the name of the writer is not disclosed it cannot be known whether that person had a duty to make the statement complained of or instead was actuated by malice (***Brims v Reid* (1885)**; ***McKerchar v Cameron* (1892)**). It is certainly hard to imagine a *Reynolds* defence being deployed in such circumstances, unless there are other sources or unusual features in the case. It is also possible that a refusal to reveal the author of an anonymous letter will run a newspaper into difficulty should it wish to make an offer of amends, because the identity of the source may be relevant to the newspaper's own good faith in publishing [see **paras 27.78 onwards**].

29.07   The same considerations apply to anonymously published articles contributed by a correspondent.

REPORTAGE

29.08   The defence of reportage [see **paras 27.94 onwards**] may be of help in letters page controversies. In ***Malik v Newspost Ltd* (2007)**, an English case, an MP sued over a letter published in the *Dewsbury Press* and a follow-up article about local election results. Mr Justice Eady held that the letter-writer had no **Reynolds** defence for publishing unsubstantiated defamatory allegations to the world. However, he suggested that the result might have been different for the newspaper's editor and publisher if a response had been obtained or corroborative checks had been carried out. "Moreover, if both sides of the controversy were fairly and disinterestedly reported, there might be a reportage defence ...".

ADVERTISEMENTS

In the case of advertisements and notices of births, marriages and deaths, the newspaper will again be in a weak position if it cannot disclose the name of the contributor and the rules discussed above apply. As advertisements are not usually associated with defamation, it may be of value to mention two Scottish cases where they did lead to litigation.   29.09

In the first case a newspaper published an advertisement which read: 29.10

"A criminal information for conspiracy to defraud is being prepared re the estate of B. Malyon (deceased) 74 Argyle Street. All persons having made payments at the above address since September ... should send immediate information to T Bernstein, private detective, 84 St. John Street."

The pursuer was B. Malyon's trustee and executor and had succeeded to his business which he carried on at 74 Argyle Street. He was allowed to bring an action against the newspaper as well as the private detective on the ground that the advertisement represented that he had been engaged in a fraudulent conspiracy in regard to B. Malyon's estate (*McLean v Bernstein* (1900)).   29.11

The judge did say, however, that the case against the newspaper might be very different from that against the individual, "it being necessary as against the paper to show that they ought to have seen that there lurked in the advertisement a slander".   29.12

In the second case a herbalist inserted an advertisement in a newspaper disclaiming any connection with another herbalist's business and stating that he would not be responsible for any medicines sold at its address "or by any so-called herbalist". The pursuer was a herbalist at the address mentioned, and raised an action against the newspaper, claiming that the advertisement represented that her medicines were dangerous, that she was not a competent herbalist and that she falsely represented herself to be a herbalist. Her action was dismissed on the ground that the advertisement would not reasonably bear this meaning in the circumstances of the case (*Thomson v Fifeshire Advertiser* (1936))   29.13

and would in any case be a verbal injury rather than a defamation [see **Chapter 30**].

29.14   Advertisements are sometimes seen which state that somebody will no longer be responsible for another's debts or which warn the public against imitation goods. Such advertisements can give rise to defamation actions (see, e.g. ***Grainger v Stirling* (1898)**; ***Webster v Paterson & Sons* (1910)**, though in neither case does the newspaper seem to have been sued, only the person who put in the adverts) and should be accepted with caution.

29.15   When Ryanair paid out £50,000 to EasyJet founder Stelios Haji-Ioannou in July 2010, over adverts in the *Guardian* and *Daily Telegraph* suggesting that Sir Stelios was dishonest about EasyJet's punctuality, *Press Gazette* observed "lucky for Guardian and Telegraph Stelios did not sue them". Care should be taken to ensure that adverts are genuine and phrased so as to avoid unnecessary aspersions. In the second type of case, for example, statements which would identify particular traders should be excluded.

KEY POINTS

29.16   1. The media will often publish, and have responsibility as publisher for, material contributed by third parties, such as letters, adverts and blog postings. All of these can pose risks.
2. Newspapers and other media outlets which accept advertising should have a checking system in place to avoid spoof advertisements which may cause people or companies reputational damage.
3. The publication of different sides of a controversy on a letters page may help with a "reportage" defence to defamation actions.
4. Anonymous letters pose particular risks. The newspaper may be ordered to disclose the identities of letter writers in court. Even if they are not, an anonymous contributor is unlikely to be helpful when a newspaper is sued over what Mr X has said.

CHAPTER 30

ACTIONABLE NON-DEFAMATORY STATEMENTS

By Rosalind McInnes

VERBAL INJURY

Statements which are not themselves defamatory may allow a right of   30.01
action on the ground of either (a) verbal injury, or (b) negligence, as
well as by various types of privacy action [see **Chapter 37**]. "Verbal
injury" is here used as a global term for a range of non-defamatory
statements which are nonetheless reckoned to cause such damage.
There has been a fair amount of academic legal debate and judicial
confusion as to how the terms verbal injury, malicious falsehood,
injurious falsehood, slander of title, slander of goods, slander of
business, public hatred, *convicium*, etc. all fit together or otherwise.
The point which matters is that defamation cases are much easier for
the pursuer to win than any action going under any of the former
names. It is hoped that the possibility of journalists and their
employers being sued for negligence are remote. There is, however,
the decision of the House of Lords, *Spring v Guardian Assurance Plc*
(1994), which appears to recognise, at least in English law, the
possibility of actions being based on negligence as an alternative to
defamation. This case is more fully discussed at **para.30.11**.

Sometimes a statement which is not defamatory, because it would   30.02
not lower anyone's reputation in the eyes of right-thinking members
of society generally, is nonetheless highly damaging. Thus, in the
English case of *Grappelli v Derek Block (Holdings) Ltd* **(1981)**, it
was held not to be defamatory to say that a jazz violinist was
seriously ill and might never tour again, but it was, potentially,
malicious falsehood. In 1991, *'Allo 'Allo* actor Gordon Kaye
obtained an injunction in England against the publication of an
article suggesting that he had consented to being interviewed and
photographed while in hospital suffering serious head injuries (*Kaye
v Robertson* **(1991)**). Cases of the *Grappelli* and *Kaye* sort would
nowadays probably be dealt with under privacy law, but malicious
falsehood could be important in other circumstances. For instance, to
say a painting was not a genuine Scottish Colourist work, or cloth not
genuine Harris tweed (*Argyllshire Weavers Ltd v Macaulay (Tweeds)
Ltd (No.3)* **(1965)**), can be actionable. One English claim for "slander
of title" was based on an article saying that the plaintiff's house was
haunted (*Barrett v Associated Newspapers* **(1907)**—the defendant
escaped liability because the house already had a reputation for being
haunted).

30.03   This form of action should give particular concern to journalists working in the area of consumer affairs. Brand names pose particular risk.

ONUS OF PROOF

30.04   The comfort for the journalist is that these actions for verbal injury are the reverse of defamation actions in that the onus of proving falsity lies firmly on the pursuer's shoulders. It is not, as in defamation, necessary for the defender to prove the statements to be true. It is also necessary for the pursuer to show that the statements were maliciously, recklessly or dishonestly made. The pursuer must then go on to show some loss or injury. It might, however, be easy in the case of an individual pursuer to prove some form of injury in the form of hurt feelings.

30.05   It should also be remembered that, in terms of s.3 of the Defamation Act 1952, if an action is raised for verbal injury it is not necessary for the pursuer to prove special damage (i.e. actual pecuniary loss), where the words on which the action is founded are calculated to cause pecuniary damage to the pursuer. The English courts at least have taken the view that it is also necessary for there to be some sort of reference, directly or indirectly, to the claimant's business, where the publication complained of is about that business (*Marathon Mutual v Waters* **(2009)**).

30.06   Recent Scottish examples include *Barratt International* **(2002)** [see **paras 26.60 and 30.06**], and *Westcrowns* **(2005)** [see **para.27.53**]. *Barratt* relates to a timeshare owners' association's dispute with their management company and involved extensive website and paper publications attacking the competency and business behaviour of the company. Lord Wheatley dismissed the claim on a variety of bases, mainly the lack of averments of malice.

30.07   *Westcrowns* was in some ways a more typical verbal injury action. The petitioners sought interdict to stop the respondents, who were competitors, claiming that the former were making false claims about the safety glass they sold. It is an interesting case because the petitioners succeeded in showing malice. Lord Macphail held that the respondents' agent did not believe that what he wrote about the petitioners' product was true, and the publication was actuated by the motive of injuring the competition.

CONVICIUM

30.08   The essence of *convicium*, an old Roman law remedy, was that the pursuer had maliciously been held up to ridicule by the defender and that the latter had intended to bring the pursuer into public hatred, contempt or ridicule. It has been suggested that truth is no defence to *convicium*, but this seems to be a heresy.

In modern times there have been no Scottish proceedings based on 30.09 the remedy of *convicium*, though it still gets the occasional reference (*Barratt International Resorts (2002)*). However, recent developments in privacy law—for instance, Eady J. in the English case of *P, Q and R v Quigley (2008)*, banning an internet novella containing sexual fantasy about pseudonymised but recognisable people—may pose more of a threat to freedom of expression in the name of individual dignity than *convicium* ever did.

BREACH OF PRIVACY

In actions based on privacy—breach of confidence or claims under the 30.10 Data Protection Act 1998 [see **Chapter 10**]—truth is no defence. Once a pursuer has established a legitimate expectation of privacy, unless the public interest justifies the invasion of that privacy, it will be actionable. Breach of confidence claims can be brought by companies or individuals. See, e.g. *Response Handling Ltd v BBC (2008)*, where a call centre company unsuccessfully attempted to stop a BBC Scotland documentary featuring undercover footage.

NEGLIGENT STATEMENTS

Since the case of *Hedley Byrne and Co Ltd v Heller and Partners Ltd* 30.11 *(1963)*, it has been accepted that a statement made negligently which causes the pursuer loss is actionable. From the journalist's viewpoint the problems are obvious. The journalist does not enjoy the possibility of the defences of fair comment or privilege which can be used in cases based on defamation. On the other hand, it is necessary for the pursuer to show that the statement was both false and negligently communicated. The legal principles involved in the *Hedley Byrne* case are complex. In brief:

- A person making a statement on which others may reasonably be expected to rely has a duty to take care that the statement is accurate.
- If an inaccurate statement is made negligently or recklessly, that person can be liable in damages.
- The pursuer must show that the statement was relied upon and that he or she suffered loss as a direct consequence.

The defender can, however, become exempt from liability by issuing a 30.12 reasonable disclaimer—which is precisely what had happened in the *Hedley Byrne* case itself. This is why it is good practice for editors in the likes of financial advice columns in newspapers to include a footnote stating that the editor, staff and the publishing company are not liable for the advice given.

30.13   As stated at the beginning of this chapter, in *Spring v Guardian Assurance Plc* (1994) the House of Lords decided that the terms of an employment reference were actionable under the law of negligence. Normally an employment reference is protected by the law of qualified privilege, so, unless malicious, it would not give ground to an action in defamation. The Lords in the *Spring* case, however, were willing to accept Mr Spring's contention that he had a good ground of action in negligence. If pursuers in Scotland could proceed regularly by way of the law of negligence, journalists might find themselves unable to plead the usual defamation defences of privilege and fair comment. Mr Spring only succeeded by a majority vote in the House of Lords.

30.14   *Spring* has not so far posed a threat to the media, probably because there needs to be a "proximity" between the pursuer and the defender to found a negligence claim (like the employer/employee relationship, giving rise to a duty of care). A later attempt in Scotland to claim in negligence (*Fitchie v Worsnop* [see **para.27.51**]) over an objectionable communication was rejected by the courts. However, the fact that negligence has reared its ugly head in the defamation landscape is yet one more reason for journalists to take the *Albert Reynolds* case seriously [see **paras 27.85 onwards**]: a journalist who meets Lord Nicholls's 10 criteria is most unlikely to be deemed negligent.

KEY POINTS

30.15   1. Some statements which are not defamatory are nevertheless actionable.

2. In such an action of "verbal injury" it is necessary for the pursuer to prove that the statement made by the defender has been made with malice. In addition to proving malice, the pursuer must also prove that the statements were false. Finally, in most cases, the pursuer must also prove that actual pecuniary damage was caused. Remember, however, the terms of s.3 of the Defamation Act 1952 by which the pursuer may be relieved of the obligation of proving pecuniary loss.

3. Negligent statements made by a journalist which are relied upon by others causing them financial loss might be actionable.

CHAPTER 31

DIFFERENCES IN ENGLISH LAW OF DEFAMATION

BY ROSALIND MCINNES

The broad principles of the law of defamation are the same in England   31.01
as in Scotland, but there are several differences on particular points.
The more important of these will now be briefly considered.

NO PUBLICATION NECESSARY TO THIRD PARTIES

Scots law does not require that there be any publication to a third   31.02
party. It is enough that the words are said to the same person who is
defamed by them. The Scots law of defamation compensates for the
insult to the pursuer, not just for damage to reputation.

PUBLIC HATRED AND CONTEMPT

The phrase "ridicule and contempt" and similar phrases are also   31.03
sometimes used differently in the case law of the two countries. North
of the border, these words can suggest a verbal injury case [see
Chapter 30] (though the old Scottish cases do not always use it in this
way). In the south, they are an old-fashioned test concerning whether a
publication is defamatory at all.

DISTINCTION BETWEEN LIBEL AND SLANDER

Roughly speaking, a defamation which is written, or expressed in   31.04
permanent form is a libel in English law, while a defamation which is
spoken or communicated in some other transitory form is slander.
    The showing of a defamatory film (*Youssoupoff v MGN* **(1934)** [see   31.05
para.26.18]) could be libel even at common law and the speaking of
words in a play was similarly treated under the Theatres Act 1968.
Section 166 of the Broadcasting Act 1990 provides that any words
included "in the course of any programme included in a programme
service" count as libel, rather than slander. This appears to include
TV, radio, public teletext services, digital services and internet sites
(although it has been suggested [see **Chapter 43**] that defamatory
remarks on bulletin boards, etc. are in some other respects more akin
to slander than to libel).

31.06   The old Scottish case law often uses the terms "libel" and "slander" interchangeably, to mean simply defamation. There has never been a distinction in principle between the two in Scots law, nor was there in Roman law, from which Scots law in part derives.

31.07   The importance of the distinction is that, with some exceptions, in England, no action will lie for slander unless the claimant proves that the words complained of have caused "special damage", i.e. actual pecuniary damage. The exceptional cases where an action for slander will be allowed without such proof are those involving imputations (a) of a crime punishable by death or imprisonment; (b) of having a contagious or infectious disease; (c) of unchastity in a woman; or (d) calculated to disparage the claimant in any office, profession, calling, trade or business held or carried on at the time of publication. The Slander of Women Act 1891 provides that "words spoken and published which impute unchastity or adultery to any woman or girl shall not require special damage to render them actionable ... This Act ... shall not apply to Scotland." Scottish females are clearly reckoned to be able to defend their own reputations.

CRIMINAL LIBEL

31.08   In English law, libel was, for many years until January 2010, a crime punishable by fine or imprisonment as well as a civil wrong giving rise to a claim for damages. However, criminal libel in England has now been abolished by the Coroners and Justice Act 2009 s.73 along with seditions and obscene libel.

BLASPHEMOUS LIBEL

31.09   In 2007 in England, Mr Green was refused permission to bring a private prosecution against the Director General of the BBC after the broadcast of *Jerry Springer The Opera (R. v City of Westminster Magistrates' Court (2007))* for blasphemous libel. Blasphemy is no longer thought to be a crime in Scotland. It has now been abolished in England by the Criminal Justice and Immigration Act 2008 s.79.

DEFENCES

31.10   Justification is the English term for *veritas*. The same principles apply as in Scotland.

31.11   In England a litigant has absolute privilege with regard to statements made in written pleadings or, by the litigant's instruction, through counsel in court. The Scottish litigant has only qualified privilege (*Bernard Hill v The Law Society of Scotland and Leslie Cumming* (2005)).

REMEDIES

English law, because of *Bonnard v Perryman* [see **paras 28.16 to 31.12 28.17**], refused to stop publication in advance by way of injunction of threatened defamation, where the would-be publisher was stating that the story was true. In Scotland, interim interdict to stop such a story was always competent, if rarely granted. Now Scottish publishers have more protection under s.12 of the Human Rights Act 1998, and English publishers may in future be getting less because of the art.8 reputation right "brought home" by the 1998 Act, challenging *Bonnard v Perryman* (1891). So this distinction is likely to be eroded in the near future [see **para.28.16**].

TIME BAR

Formerly, the period within which an action for defamation had to be 31.13 brought was six years in England. It is now one year in terms of the Defamation Act 1996. In Scotland, it is three years after publication. This has already led to extra litigation for the Scottish courts (*Kennedy v Aldington* (2005) [see **para.43.15**]).

FAIR COMMENT

Motive is irrelevant to fair comment in Scotland. Even malicious 31.14 comment is protected. It has also been suggested that to be "fair" in Scots law the opinion need not even be honestly held by the speaker—it just has to be relevant. In England, there is no defence of fair comment if the opinion is not genuinely held. The Scottish law seems, further, to take a more generous view, from the media's perspective, of how far the facts need to be spelled out for the fair comment defence to succeed (*Wheatley v Anderson & Miller* (1927)) than the traditional English position, though, as with criminal libel, English law now seems to be moving towards the Scottish approach (*Lowe v Associated Newspapers* (2006)).

VERBAL INJURY/INJURIOUS OR MALICIOUS FALSEHOOD

The statements referred to in **Chapter 30**, above as actionable non- 31.15 defamatory statements are sometimes known in English law as injurious falsehoods, though more often, as in Scotland, the phrase "malicious falsehood" is used.

DECLARATOR OF FALSITY

31.16 There can be a declarator of falsity under s.9 of the 1996 Act, but only in England and under the summary procedure. The latter does not apply in Scotland.

FREQUENCY OF ACTIONS/EXEMPLARY OR PUNITIVE DAMAGES

31.17 In England, a libel court may award the claimant exemplary damages as well as compensatory damages. This has almost certainly encouraged libel actions in the High Court in London. Punitive or exemplary damages are rarely awarded in practice.

31.18 The English courts are ready to strike out or to refuse to allow claims for exemplary damages where the court feels they have no prospect of success according to the stringent tests applied to exemplary damages (*John Monks v Warwick District Council* (2009); *Benjamin Pell v Express Newspapers* (2005)). It seems unlikely that exemplary damages will be allowed in England in breach of confidence actions (*Mosley* (2008)).

31.19 The claimant must prove malice or recklessness on the defendant's part to obtain such damages. When exemplary damages are awarded, the figures can be dramatic.

KEY POINTS

31.20
1. To found a defamation action, Scots law does not require that there be any publication to a third party. You can defame someone face-to-face, in the absence of any audience.
2. Many Scots law and English law terms differ.
3. There is no formal distinction in Scots law between libel and slander.
4. In Scotland, a pursuer has three years after publication to raise an action for defamation. In England, there is a one year time limit.

PART 8: INTELLECTUAL PROPERTY

CHAPTER 32

INTELLECTUAL PROPERTY

BY COLIN MILLER

Intellectual property or "IP" is a broad term for a bundle of intangible 32.01
rights which have commercial value. The most important forms of
intellectual property are patents for inventions, trade marks, design
rights, know-how, copyright and database rights. Although these
rights are all different in nature, they do have two things in common.
First they are moveable and can therefore be bought, sold, licensed
and transferred in much the same way as any other moveable
property. Secondly, they are essentially about stopping others from
doing certain things, whether it be pirating, copying, counterfeiting
and in some cases using materials or ideas which have been
independently created.

The most relevant form of intellectual property for journalists is 32.02
copyright. Contrary to popular belief there is no system for
registration of copyright in the United Kingdom. Copyright
protection arises automatically on the act of creation of a copyright
work. The idea behind copyright is that people should be able to
enjoy the benefits of their own original work, in the knowledge that it
will not be pirated or exploited by others. Copyright is in essence a
right to prevent copying (although this definition may come under
strain in the context of the internet). It does not give a monopoly. If
two people by some remarkable coincidence were to write two
identical books and it could be proved that they were in fact
completely independent, the one who got into print first could not
prevent the other from publishing his book. There would be no
copying.

The law of copyright is the same throughout the United Kingdom 32.03
and is contained in the Copyright, Designs and Patents Act 1988. It is a
lengthy and complex Act and there are several sections which are
important to staff journalists, freelancers and photographers in
guiding them as to the use they may make of someone else's work.

32.04   The 1988 Act describes copyright as a property right which covers original literary, dramatic, musical or artistic works, sound recordings, films, broadcasts and typographical arrangements of published editions of literary works.

32.05   In the case of newspapers, does a typographical arrangement of a published edition exist only in the newspaper as a whole or does it also extend to the layout or arrangement of each article? In *The Newspaper Licensing Agency v Marks & Spencer* **(2001)**, the Court of Appeal ruled that typographical arrangement copyright exists only in the newspaper as a whole and not in the arrangement of each article published in a newspaper. In that case Marks & Spencer was licensed to take copies from certain newspapers in exchange for payment of a fee. However Marks & Spencer then made further copies of some of the cuttings which had been sent by fax for daily internal circulation. On appeal to the House of Lords the judges decided that the agency had no copyright in the typographical arrangement of individual articles as such but only in the newspaper as a whole and therefore there was no basis on which to take an action for copyright infringement.

32.06   It is a person's work that is protected, not his ideas. This is an important distinction. Whatever the ethical questions, it is no infringement of copyright to lift the idea of another person's story and use it in a story of your own, expressed in your own words, although it may amount to a breach of confidence [see **Chapter 23**]. This is illustrated in the case of *Baigent v Random House Group* **(2007)**. An action was taken by the authors of the book *The Holy Blood and the Holy Grail* in which it was suggested that Jesus had been married to Mary Magdalene and had children. It contained the story that following the crucifixion, Mary Magdalene and her children escaped to France where Jesus' bloodline survived. The authors took action against the publishers of *The Da Vinci Code* in which it was also suggested that Jesus and Mary Magdalene had been married. The authors argued that the authors of *The Da Vinci Code* had copied this story which was the "central theme" of *The Holy Blood and The Holy Grail*. The action was dismissed by the courts both in the High Court and on appeal on the basis that the story was no more than a collection of ideas at a very general level. The judge said that these were "ideas but not the expression of ideas" and therefore not protectable as copyright.

32.07   Copyright protects only original works but here again it is the form rather than the content which is important. The ideas need not be original provided the form in which they appear is. And this form will be original if it involves the use of some independent knowledge, skill, judgment or labour. There can be copyright in a list of football fixtures or stock exchange prices if skill was required in the selection or arrangement.

On the same principle there can be copyright in verbatim newspaper   32.08
reports of public speeches. Neither the ideas nor the way of expressing them would be commonly regarded as the original work of the reporter, but the conversion of the spoken word into a written report involves the use of independent skill and labour on his part and the report is regarded as an original work for copyright purposes. If, however, the speaker hands the reporter a written copy of his speech and this is published verbatim by the newspaper then there would be no separate copyright in the report. There would be no conversion of the spoken to the written word and no exercise of independent skill or labour.

Another example will help to bring out the meaning of "originality"   32.09
in copyright law. A translation is an "original" work for copyright purposes. The ideas and their arrangement are not original in the ordinary sense but the translation does involve independent knowledge and hard work on the part of the translator. It is therefore protected.

The type of copyright which is of most importance for journalists is   32.10
that existing in "literary works". This term is much wider than might be thought. It certainly does not mean that a work must have literary merit before it is protected. An examination paper has been held to be a literary work for copyright purposes, the judge remarking that if something was worth copying, it was worth protecting.

In the case of "artistic works" too, paintings, drawings, engravings   32.11
and photographs are protected irrespective of artistic quality. A tie-on business label has been held to be an artistic work for copyright purposes (*Walker v British Picker Co* (1961)).

It is clear that a "work" need not be very substantial, but a line must   32.12
be drawn somewhere and in some instances protection has been refused on the ground that there was no "work". Advertising slogans consisting of a few words have been refused protection on this ground. However, attitudes may be changing in this area to allow protection for slender pieces of writing. In a Scottish court action concerning the internet (*Shetland Times v Wills* (1996)), for example, the defenders conceded that there was copyright in the newspaper headlines. A New Zealand court has held that there was copyright in the advertising slogan: "Field friendly—the best choice for field work" (*Sunlec International v Electropar* (1999)).

Titles of newspapers, books and periodicals are not generally   32.13
regarded as copyright. An established newspaper can, however, prevent another paper being sold under the same or a similar title by means of an action for "passing off" and if it has obtained registered trade marks for its titles, an action for trade mark infringement. To

establish passing off it must be proved that the other paper is so similar that it would be likely to deceive the public into thinking that there is an association with the newspaper owner which is seeking to take action. The owners of the magazine *Punch* once failed for this reason to prevent the publication of a much cheaper magazine called *Punch and Judy*.

32.14   This is clearly illustrated in an action taken by Associated Newspapers who are the owners of the *Daily Mail*, the *Mail on Sunday* and the *Evening Standard* (distributed in London) against Express Newspapers (*Associated Newspapers Ltd v Express Newspapers* (2003)). Express are the owners of the *Daily Express*, *Sunday Express*, *Daily Star* and *Daily Star Sunday*. The *Evening Standard* has a virtual monopoly of the evening commuter newspaper market in London and the south east and in 2002 Express decided to attack this market by launching a free newspaper. The proposed names for this newspaper were "*The Evening Mail*" or "*The London Evening Mail*". In its publicity material the title was sometimes referred to as "*The Mail*". Associated Newspapers took action against Express arguing that use of any of the names would amount to both passing off and infringement of its registered trade marks "THE MAIL" "THE DAILY MAIL" and "THE MAIL ON SUNDAY". Associated Newspapers succeeded on both counts. The court decided there was trade mark infringement because the new edition contained the word "Mail" in its title and was also being referred to as "the *Mail*" in marketing materials. Express was therefore using a mark which was identical or at least similar to the registered trade marks owned by Associated Newspapers. The court also accepted there was passing off on the basis that members of the public would be confused into believing that the new publication was in some way associated with the *Daily Mail* and/or the *Mail on Sunday* and that Express was therefore trying to take advantage of the goodwill and reputation of the newspapers published by Associated Newspapers.

32.15   The same considerations apply to a *nom de plume*. There is no copyright, but if the name has become well known the author can bring a passing off action to prevent its use in ways likely to deceive the public.

32.16   To sum up what has been said so far, copyright is a right to prevent copying, not a monopoly. It protects works, not ideas; form, not content. The works must be original, but need not be very original. In most cases, originality means the use of some independent skill, knowledge or labour. Merit is usually unimportant. Works can be small, but not too small. If, like newspaper titles, they are too small, they may nevertheless be protected by the law of passing off.

OWNERSHIP AND INFRINGEMENT

The owner of copyright in a work has the exclusive right to copy it, 32.17
issue copies to the public, rent or lend it to the public, perform, show
or play the work in public, communicate the work to the public and
make an adaptation of it. Copyright is infringed by anyone who
reproduces the whole or a substantial part of the work without the
permission of the copyright owner. To infringe there must be copying
of the whole or a substantial part of the copyright work. Substantiality
is a question of degree. This can be subjective and is often judged more
by quality than quantity. For example the use of 20 seconds worth of
the "Colonel Bogey March" played by a school band and
incorporated into a film of the opening of a Suffolk school was held to
be sufficient to constitute infringement of musical copyright. This issue
was considered recently in the case of the *Newspaper Licensing Agency
v Marks & Spencer* **(2001)**. See **para.32.05** above for details of the
facts. The agency argued that the copyright work was a
"typographical arrangement" of a published edition of a newspaper
and that Marks & Spencer, by making and distributing additional
unauthorised copies, had copied a "substantial part" of the published
editions of the newspaper.

Marks & Spencer argued that there was no infringement because the 32.18
copying of an individual newspaper article on its own was not enough
to satisfy the test of copying a "substantial part" of the typographical
arrangement of a published edition. The court said that the test was
whether sufficient relevant skill or labour had gone into producing
the edition and that in the case of a modern newspaper the skill and
labour invested in a typographical arrangement was expressed in the
overall design of the newspaper as a whole and was unlikely to be
expressed in anything less than a full page. A copy of an article on a
page which gave no indication on how the rest of the page was laid
out was not a copy of a, "substantial part of the published edition
constituted by the newspaper as a whole". None of the individual
cuttings copied by Marks & Spencer sufficiently reproduced the
layout of any page of the newspaper in question and therefore there
was no breach of copyright.

There are various exceptions which allow journalists to make use of 32.19
copyright material for review, criticism and the reporting of current
events. Conversely, a newspaper or broadcasting organisation which
owns copyright of material can prevent anyone else from reproducing
it in public, recover damages and charge a fee for allowing the work to
be published.

Under the 1988 Act s.11(1), the person who first brings a work into 32.20
existence is the owner of any copyright in it. However, where a literary

(or dramatic or musical or artistic) work or a film is made by an employee in the course of his work, the employer is the first owner of copyright unless there is some agreement to the contrary. Therefore a newspaper will retain the entire copyright unless a special agreement has been reached with the staff journalist. A staff journalist is therefore not entitled to use his materials outwith the scope of his employment unless some special agreement has been reached with his newspaper employer. The newspaper also owns copyright in pictures taken by staff photographers.

32.21   The freelance journalist, not working under a contract of service or apprenticeship, is in a different position and owns the copyright in his or her work. This will apply even if a newspaper has ordered the freelance to write an article or series of articles. The position can be altered by a written agreement under which the freelance assigns his copyright. An assignation is different from a licence. An assignation actually transfers ownership of copyright: a licence merely gives permission to do something in spite of the copyright, which remains in the hands of the person granting the licence. Thus, the late Robin Ray, the musicologist and broadcaster, was able to object to Classic FM's selling their database abroad. He had copyright in the documents and catalogue which made up the database and had given Classic FM only an implied licence to use the materials (*Ray v Classic FM Plc* (1998)).

32.22   Before the 1988 Act, where a newspaper commissioned a picture from a freelance or commercial photographer the newspaper owned copyright in the picture. Now, unless there is an agreement to the contrary, copyright belongs to the photographer or his employer. If a member of the public submits a photograph for publication, he will retain the copyright, again subject to any agreement to the contrary.

32.23   However, under s.85 of the Act, a person who, for private and domestic purposes, commissions the taking of a photograph or the making of a film, has the right not to have copies issued to the public, exhibited or shown in public or communicated to the public. This applies only to pictures taken after August 1, 1989, when the 1988 Act came into force. It may well create problems for the newspaper which borrows a wedding picture from a relative after the bride, groom or best man becomes headline news, perhaps years after the wedding. By publishing, the newspaper could be infringing the copyright of the photographer and of the groom who may have commissioned it and would have the right under s.85 not to have it issued to the public. Unauthorised use of photographs or photography can also amount to breach of confidence. [Please see **para.32.06**].

32.24   In *Williams v Settle* (1960), the bridegroom's father-in-law was found murdered. Two national newspapers obtained from a freelance photographer, and published, a photograph of a group at the wedding which included the murdered man. The groom owned the copyright in the photograph in this case and recovered damages and costs from one newspaper and an apology and undertakings from the other. He also recovered substantial damages from the photographer.

The owner of copyright can sue for damages if his right is infringed, 32.25 but the person alleged to have breached copyright has a defence if he can show that at the time of the infringement he did not know and had no reason to believe that there was copyright in the work. In that situation the copyright owner will not be entitled to damages but might still have some other form of remedy such as interdict or accounting of profits.

In an action for infringement, the court has power to award "such 32.26 additional damages as the justice of the case may require"—looking at all the circumstances of the case, particularly the flagrancy of the infringement and any benefit gained by the guilty party.

It is not, of course, an infringement of copyright for a newspaper to 32.27 print and publish letters or manuscripts sent to the editor. The fact that the author sends them implies a licence to publish. An interesting legal situation arises when a letter or article is sent to a newspaper for publication. In the absence of agreement, the position is that the author retains the copyright and the newspaper gets the property in the actual paper on which the words are written and, in addition, implied permission to publish. It is doubtful how far, if at all, the newspaper has implied permission to alter the letter or article. The view of the English courts is that in the absence of express or implied prohibition it has the right, as licensee, to make alterations. Also, a prohibition on reasonable alteration would probably not be implied in the case of ordinary letters and unsigned articles.

FAIR DEALING

As we have seen, the owner of copyright in a work has the exclusive 32.28 right to copy it, issue copies to the public, rent or lend it to the public, perform, show or play the work in public, communicate the work to the public and make an adaptation of it. However, the 1988 Act s.30, contains a provision on "fair dealing" which allows the journalist to reproduce extracts from the work for reporting current events and for criticism and review (but this does not cover a photograph used for reporting current events). The criticism and review can be of the work itself, or of another work altogether, or of a performance of the work. In the case of newspapers the use of the material must also be accompanied by a sufficient acknowledgment provided that the work has been made available to the public. No acknowledgment is needed in reporting current events by means of a sound recording, film or broadcast where this would be impossible for reasons of practicality or otherwise.

32.29   If too much of a work was reproduced (for example lifting another newspaper's story or quotes word for word) that might not be held to be fair dealing. It is not possible to lay down a hard and fast rule on this. To quote a small but crucial part of a book might be regarded as an infringement of copyright, while the use of a longer but less important passage might not. In one case, the use of four lines from a Kipling poem was held to be an infringement of copyright when they were used in an advertisement.

32.30   In January 1991, in the High Court, Scott J. dismissed a breach of copyright action brought by the BBC against British Satellite Broadcasting over the use of BBC football highlights from the World Cup. The judge ruled that BSB's use of clips recorded from the BBC's live coverage was protected by the fair dealing defence allowing limited use of copyright material in reporting current events. The BBC had contended that BSB's use of the "best bits" of its coverage was a breach of copyright (***BBC v British Satellite Broadcasting Ltd* (1991)**. Carlton TV also successfully used the "fair dealing" defence to justify its incorporation of parts of a German TV programme in a documentary about chequebook journalism (***Pro Sieben Media A.G. v Carlton UK Television Ltd* (1999)**. However, the *Sun* was unable to rely on this defence in the case of ***Hyde Park Residence v David Yelland* (2000)**. In that case Mohammed Al Fayed's security services company tried to prevent the *Sun* printing video security stills of the Princess of Wales and Dodi Al Fayed in connection with speculation as to the car crash which killed them. At first the company was unsuccessful but ultimately succeeded on appeal in 2000. The *Sun* had relied on the "fair dealing" defence, arguing that publication of the stills was necessary in order to refute alleged lies told by Al Fayed as to the length and purpose of the Princess of Wales and Dodi Al Fayed's visit to Mohammed Al Fayed's villa in Paris on the day before their death. The courts decided on appeal that in order to rely on the "fair dealing" exemption it was necessary to take into account the motives of the publishers, the extent and purpose of the use of the stills and whether that was necessary for the purposes of reporting current events. The court rejected the *Sun's* argument and ruled that the only relevance of the video stills was to show that the Princess and Dodi Al Fayed had remained at the villa for only 28 minutes. This was a fact already known to the public without the need for publication of the stills. Moreover publication did not prove that the statements made by Mr Al Fayed were untrue. The court's view was that use of the stills was "excessive" and was made for the purposes of increasing newspaper sales. One judge commented that, "to describe what 'the

Sun' did as 'fair dealing' was to 'give honour to dishonour'". Therefore newspapers are unlikely to be able to rely on this defence unless they can show that publication is necessary for reporting a current event. If it is possible to report events based on other available sources of information then the defence is unlikely to be successful, particularly if the work (such as a photograph or in this case a video still) has not been previously published or otherwise circulated to the public.

The "Fair Dealing" exception also allows journalists to reproduce   32.31
extracts for criticism and review. Celebrity photographer Jason Fraser took action against the BBC for copyright infringement over use of 14 of his pictures of the Beckhams in an episode of Piers Morgan's celebrity show, "Tabloid Tales" *Fraser-woodwood v BBC* (2005). In that case the BBC successfully argued that use of the photographs was exempt under the "criticism and review" provisions which allow media organisations to reproduce pictures for the purposes of reviewing them. The BBC argued that the programme was a legitimate review of tabloid journalism and this was accepted by the High Court. In an earlier judgement News Group Newspapers (which owns *The Sun*) was found to have infringed copyright by reproducing the cover of IPC's listings magazine "What's on TV?" *IPC Media Ltd v News Group Newspapers Ltd* (2005). News Group used the "criticism and review" defence, arguing that it was reviewing the magazine. However, the court in that case decided that **The Sun could have levelled criticism without copying the cover of a magazine.**

Where copyright is used in an attempt to gag speech, s.12 of the   32.32
Human Rights Act 1998 will come into play. Section 12 protects freedom of expression. This is illustrated in the case of *Ashdown v Telegraph Group Ltd* (2001). Mr Paddy Ashdown had kept diaries while he was the leader of the Liberal Democrats Party, with a view to later publication. After he relinquished leadership, he prepared materials for publication and showed the material in confidence to representatives of the press. Included in the material was a minute of a particularly important meeting. A copy of the minute was then published by the defendant's newspaper, quoting verbatim from a substantial part of the minute. Mr Ashdown brought an action against the Telegraph Group claiming breach of confidence and copyright infringement. The Telegraph Group sought to rely on s.12 but this was rejected on the basis that although weight had to be given to freedom of expression, on balance the rights of the copyright owner took precedence over freedom of expression.

There is a question as to how far back current events could be said to   32.33
extend. What if evidence of some scandal emerged years after the event, as frequently happens, and, in the course of an investigation, a newspaper gained access to some documents protected by copyright?

Would it be able to quote from the documents by saying it was reporting current events? The position is not clear but recent court decisions indicate that a wide interpretation should be given to "current events". It was argued in the Al Fayed case that the death of Diana and Dodi in August 1997 was no longer "current" when the *Sun* published the video stills two days after the first anniversary of the date of the tragedy. This was rejected by the court as being too narrow a view of the meaning of "current events". The court endorsed the views of the judge in the *Carlton TV* action [see **para.32.30**] who said:

> "[R]eporting current events are expressions of wide and indefinite scope. Any attempt to plot their precise boundaries is doomed to failure. They are expressions which should be construed liberally".

THE SPOKEN WORD

32.34 One of the most important provisions for journalists was the introduction by the 1988 Act for the first time of copyright in the spoken word. Until then, if no notes had been made and the speech was completely off-the-cuff, the speaker had no copyright in his words. There was no "work" to which copyright could attach. Copyright came into existence only when the words were taken down by a reporter and it belonged either to the reporter or his employer. This meant, for example, that although the *Daily Mirror* could sue *Today* newspaper for allegedly "lifting" quotes from an interview with the late show business personality Marti Caine, Miss Caine could not take action because she had no copyright in her words.

32.35 The 1988 Act gives the speaker a copyright which comes into existence as soon as the words are recorded by the journalist. Section 58 provides, however, that where a record of spoken words is made in writing or otherwise for reporting current events or of communicating all or part of the work to the public, it is not an infringement of copyright in the words, provided:

(1) the record is a direct record of the spoken words;
(2) the making of the record was not prohibited by the speaker;
(3) the use made of the material is not of a kind prohibited by the speaker before the record was made; and
(4) the use is by or with the authority of the person lawfully in possession of the record.

32.36 It seems that if a speaker stands up before he makes his speech and makes it known that he does not wish it to be reported in any shape or form, the publisher who chooses to ignore this could be sued for breach of copyright. If the speaker decides after he has made the speech that he does not wish it reported, that will be too late. He must make it clear beforehand. The journalist may also be able to rely on the legal principle that there is no copyright in facts and ideas, and probably on a defence of fair dealing.

The terms of s.58 also suggest that a speaker might be able to dictate 32.37 in what form he wishes his words to appear. The section talks about the use of the material not being of a kind prohibited by the speaker. Suppose an MP was delivering a speech and made it clear that he wanted it reported by certain newspapers and not others? Or that he wished only part of the speech to be reported? The 1988 Act appears to give him the means to sue for breach of copyright if his wishes are ignored.

MORAL RIGHTS

The 1988 Act also gives the author of a copyright literary work the 32.38 moral right to be identified, not to have his work subjected to derogatory treatment, and not to have work falsely attributed to him. The treatment of a work is derogatory if it amounts to a distortion or mutilation of the work or is otherwise prejudicial to the honour or reputation of the author. Treatment is defined as any addition to, deletion from, alteration to or adaptation of the work. The late Alan Clark succeeded against the London *Evening Standard's* spoof diary, using moral rights and "passing off" arguments, although it was the latter which appeared to convince the court—apparently, readers had found the spoof entirely convincing (*Clark v Associated Newspapers Ltd* (1998)).

The right to be identified and not subjected to derogatory treatment 32.39 does not apply to work by employees or reports of current events or to material made available to a newspaper or periodical by the author for publication.

You have to assert your moral rights of paternity. You do not, 32.40 however, have to assert your right not to have your work treated in a derogatory fashion—this is automatic. The exceptions to an action for copyright infringement also apply to infringement of a moral right. Another moral right is "the right of privacy" [dealt with in **Chapter 23** above], i.e. not to have privately commissioned photographs, videos, etc. published or communicated to the public.

RIGHTS IN PERFORMANCES

There are also "rights in performances". A performer in a dramatic 32.41 performance, including dance and miming, musical performance, reading or recitation of a literary work, performance of a variety act and the like (but not live sporting events or public ceremonies) can object to recording or broadcasting of the performance without consent, except for private and domestic use. Amateur performers have these rights. The surviving Beatles and Yoko Ono used this to prevent the marketing of an unauthorised recording of a Beatles performance made in 1962.

32.42   There are various exceptions, e.g. recordings made for the purposes of instruction or examination/recordings made by educational establishments for educational purposes, but only for private use. Persons having "recording rights", i.e. the benefit of an exclusive recording contract in relation to the performance, have similar rights. Trading without consent in such recordings may be a criminal offence.

DURATION

32.43   Copyright lasts for a very long time. In the case of literary, dramatic, musical and artistic works, including photographs, copyright normally lasts for 70 years after the end of the year in which the author dies. This is a change made in 1995 from the previous position, which was only 50 years. Some works which were out of copyright have now come back into copyright as a result. In the case of films, copyright lasts for 70 years from the end of the year of the death of the principal director, screenplay author, dialogue author or the composer of music specially created for and used in the film, whichever dies last. If none of these people is identified, copyright lasts for 70 years from the end of the year the film was made or released. There is a separate right to a 50 year copyright in sound recordings, performances, and communications to the public. Moral rights last as long as copyright does.

32.44   Copyright in a computer program lasts for 70 years from the death of its author. Copyright in a typographical arrangement, for example a cut-out from a newspaper, lasts for 25 years from the end of the year of publication. After the expiry of copyright the work becomes public property and can be freely copied. Protection of sound recordings, computer-generated works and broadcasts is for 50 years. It will be noted that the 50 year period applies only to the recording, program or broadcast itself, not the underlying rights. Recently pressure groups, including a number of high profile rock and pop artists, have campaigned to extend the period to 95 years. This would mean that the owners of the rights (including their representatives) would receive ongoing royalties for 95 years after the work was made. This is the position in the United States but recent attempts by the European Commission to extend the period to 95 years have been unsuccessful.

There is now a proposal for the period to be extended to 70 years but it remains to be seen whether this will be implemented.

The copyrights involved in individual aspects of the work, e.g. the author's in his screenplay or the musician's in his score, exist separately. In other words, a film is a copyright work; the screenplay it uses is also a copyright work, the score written for it is, as is the novel on which it was based. **32.45**

OTHER INTELLECTUAL PROPERTY RIGHTS

As outlined in **para.32.01**, above, there are other intellectual property rights, including patents, trade marks, design rights and know-how. Most of these are more relevant to commerce than journalism, but there are some exceptions. A name, title or device that may be too slight in itself to attract copyright may nonetheless be a registered trade mark. See **para.32.14**, above, on the action taken by Associated Newspapers against Express Newspapers for trade mark infringement and passing off. Trade marks confer a monopoly right, i.e. there are no "fair dealing" or similar defences. Trade mark protection has been extended so as to cover sounds, colours, shapes and packaging, such as the distinctive shape of Toblerone or the Coca-Cola bottle and the Direct Line jingle. There has also been controversy over whether an image is capable of trade mark protection. Most strikingly, there was the failed attempt to register the "image" of the Princess of Wales. Some "images" have been successfully registered as trade marks, however, notably of racing drivers and sporting personalities who clearly "trade off" their names in the matter of sponsorship. Trade marking does not prevent use of the name altogether in Scotland. The band "Wet Wet Wet", having trade marked their name, tried to use the trade mark to prevent use of it as the title of an unauthorised book by Mainstream publishers (*Bravado Merchandising Servicing Ltd v Mainstream Publishing (Edinburgh) Ltd* (1995). This failed as this was use of the name not as a trade mark, but as a title. **32.46**

Unlike copyright, unregistered design rights and know-how, all of which arise naturally, registered trade marks, patents and registered designs all require the owner to undergo a registration process and pay costs. Trade mark registration requires to be renewed once every 10 years from the date of filing. **32.47**

KEY POINTS

32.48

1. Copyright law exists to prevent original work such as literature, drama and music from being exploited without the owner's permission. It protects the expression of an idea, not the idea itself. The law is contained in the Copyright, Designs and Patents Act 1988.

2. Copyright in work produced by an employee such as a journalist belongs to his or her employer, unless there is an agreement to the contrary. A newspaper would also have copyright in pictures taken by a staff photographer. Freelance journalists own the copyright in their own work. Where a newspaper commissions a picture from a freelance photographer, the copyright belongs to the photographer or his employer.

3. The owner of a work has the exclusive right to copy it, issue copies to the public, rent or lend it, show or play the work in public or communicate it to the public. However, the 1988 Act contains a provision on "fair dealing" which allows the journalist to reproduce extracts for reporting current events and for criticism and review.

4. Section 58 of the 1988 Act introduces copyright in the spoken word, and the journalist will infringe this copyright if a speaker makes it clear beforehand that he does not wish his words to be recorded. The Act also gives the copyright owner the moral right to be identified and not have his work subjected to derogatory treatment.

5. Copyright in the written word and photographs normally lasts for 70 years after the end of the year in which the author dies.

PART 9: THE PRINT MEDIA AND THE BROADCASTERS

CHAPTER 33

PRINTER AND PUBLISHER

BY ROSALIND MCINNES

There are various Acts of Parliament which apply primarily to the editorial or managerial side of the newspaper business, but which journalists should know. These provisions apply to both Scotland and England unless otherwise stated.   33.01

NAME OF PRINTER

The name and address of the printer must be printed on the first or last page of every newspaper, periodical and most other printed matter in Scotland or England (Newspapers, Printers and Reading Rooms Repeal Act 1869; Printer's Imprint Act 1961). If this is not done, printers, publishers and distributors can be fined up to £500 for each offending copy. Prosecutions must be brought in the name of the Lord Advocate in Scotland.   33.02

KEEPING COPIES

The printer of a paper (if it is printed for hire, reward, gain or profit— which covers most cases) must keep at least one copy, showing on it the name and address of the person for whom it was printed. The printer must preserve it for six months and show it to any justice of the peace requiring to see it in that time. Failure to comply may result in a fine (Newspapers, Printers and Reading Rooms Repeal Act 1869).   33.03

DELIVERING COPIES TO MUSEUMS AND LIBRARIES

Under the Legal Deposit Libraries Act 2003, the publisher of every newspaper, periodical or book published in the United Kingdom   33.04

must within a month of publication deliver a copy to the British Library Board, at his own expense.

33.05	On written demand within 12 months of publication, he must also deliver a copy to the National Library of Scotland; the Bodleian Library, Oxford; the University Library, Cambridge; the Library of Trinity College, Dublin; and the National Library of Wales. For limited purposes, the Faculty of Advocates counts as a deposit library. A separate demand need not be made for each copy of a newspaper or magazine. One demand can cover all numbers subsequently published.

33.06	In the event of failure to comply, the library may apply to the sheriff for an order requesting the publisher to deposit the material, or, where that is impossible or inappropriate, to pay compensation to the library. It should be noted that the 2003 Act also applies to some electronic and non-electronic deposits, such as CD-Roms and online publications [see **Chapter 43**].

OBSCENE MATERIAL

33.07	Section 51 of the Civic Government (Scotland) Act 1982 makes it an offence to display any obscene material (any book, magazine, bill, paper, print, film, tape, disc or other kind of recording, photograph, drawing or painting) in a public place, which means a place to which the public are allowed access, whether on payment or otherwise. It bans the publication, reproduction, sale, distribution, printing and keeping of obscene material.

33.08	The penalty for contravention is, on summary conviction, a fine not exceeding £10,000 or imprisonment for up to six months, or, on indictment, a fine of no stated limit or imprisonment for up to two years, or both in each case. There is a defence where it can be proved all due diligence was used to avoid an offence.

33.09	The section was extended to television and sound broadcasts by the Broadcasting Act 1990.

KEY POINTS

33.10	1. It is a criminal offence for a newspaper or the like not to have its printer's name on its first or last page.
2. Publishers have an obligation to give copies of their output to certain libraries.
3. Public display of obscene material is a criminal offence.

CHAPTER 34

BROADCASTING

BY ROSALIND MCINNES

The legal principles governing the activities of journalists outlined in 34.01
this book apply also to television and radio broadcasters, particularly
in relation to contempt of court and defamation. Indeed,
broadcasters, particularly television broadcasters, might expect more
severe treatment from the courts than newspaper journalists in view of
the higher public penetration of broadcasting and the higher authority
which radio and TV appear to enjoy, being more strenuously
regulated, in the public mind.

The rules restricting publicity contained in the Contempt of Court 34.02
Act 1981 apply to broadcasts as well as printed publications, but their
effect may be different in practice. Live broadcasts can and
occasionally do catch the commission of crime during transmission
of a news programme. Although strictly speaking the act of arrest
makes proceedings "live" under the 1981 Act, there has not yet been
a case where a broadcaster has been accused of contempt in these
circumstances. Logically, the law cannot strike out what has been
shown on TV up to the point of arrest, but contempt issues may well
arise on repetition of the material after a case becomes active.

As there have been so few cases concerning broadcasters in a 34.03
Scottish court, it is difficult to analyse the approach of the Scottish
judiciary to broadcasting. Possibly, this is in part because
broadcasters—and again, their heavy regulation may be a dominant
factor—take fewer risks. In 2008, ITV Central Ltd (*Att Gen v ITV
Central Ltd* (2008)) was fined £25,000—and offered to pay the third
party costs of postponement of the trial—after it broadcast, on the
morning of the trial, the fact that one of the accused had a murder
conviction. The court said: "We accept that this was a mistake made
by a normally responsible company in an industry which in this respect
is normally responsible."

The transitory nature of a broadcast (unlike the written newspaper 34.04
report which can be read and re-read) can be cited by the broadcasters'
lawyers in court both as a defence and also as a mitigating factor (*Att
Gen v ITN* (1995)). On the other hand, in 1997, where the BBC was
found in contempt over a quip about the Maxwell brothers in *Have I
Got News For You*, Auld L.J.'s reference to "the impermanent
medium of television" was undercut by his later saying "the

offending publicity is great ... because of its medium and repetition ..." (**Att Gen v BBC (1997)**).

34.05 The competing qualities of high penetration and the authority enjoyed by broadcasting on the one hand and the counterbalancing factor of its transitory nature have not been fully discussed in a Scottish case. However, the courts will undoubtedly attach weight to the argument that TV and radio broadcasts reach large audiences and enjoy high authority. It follows that defamation or a contempt by a broadcaster could be regarded as more serious than that by a print journalist.

34.06 In the ***Stuurman*** case (***HM Advocate v Stuurman*** **(1980)**), the *Herald* was fined £20,000 for carrying material which was considered prejudicial about the gangland connections of people arrested on drugs charges, whereas Radio Forth was fined £10,000 for carrying basically the same material. It may be difficult to extract principles from one elderly case, but it is reasonable to suppose that the High Court took the view that the printed words in the *Herald* were more likely to reach and be remembered by the public. The newspaper article, therefore, might have a greater effect on potential jurors than the brief broadcast on Radio Forth. In the ***Derek Riordan*** case (***Scottish Daily Record and Sunday Mail Ltd v Thomson*** **(2009)**) [see **paras 17.29 onwards**], on the other hand, STV was fined £1,750 for showing the footballer's photograph, exactly the same fine as given to the *Sun* and the *Daily Record*. It must also be borne in mind that, with broadcasters' websites being extensive and frequently accessed— allowing material to be read again—the BBC iPlayer, television and radio are less transitory than they used to be.

34.07 As in any contempt case, the locality and penetration of the publication would also tend to be significant—and broadcast penetration can be very high. Here, too, the internet [see **Chapter 43**] may make a difference to how defence arguments are made. It is possible online to make a better-educated guess as to how many times a particular article has been downloaded.

SPECIAL PROBLEMS OF TELEVISION

34.08 Television simultaneously conveys words and visual images. The juxtaposition of the pictures and commentary/script can give rise to accidental and completely unintentional defamation. Tone of voice and expression are also factors which may make broadcasting more vulnerable to arguments about innuendo.

34.09 Court proceedings were raised at Glasgow Sheriff Court by a Glasgow solicitor, John Carroll, who argued that an item on *Reporting Scotland* had been "cut" in such a way as to make it appear that some remarks by Duncan Campbell about Mr Carroll's client applied to Mr Carroll instead. The sheriff principal dismissed Mr Carroll's action (*Carroll v BBC* (1997)) and Mr Carroll later abandoned an appeal to the Court of Session.

The lesson to be learned for journalists working in television is that extreme care must be taken to prevent critical words in news reports which are aimed at one particular target from being accidentally received by another. Television journalists should remember to look at the background of a shot, as well as the foreground. 34.10

It is important to listen for background comments also, as people tend to be self-referential. BBC Scotland received an Ofcom complaint in 2003 from a viewer featured in a programme who said that a policeman had said of him, before going to his house, "This guy's heavy". In fact, the shot had been of the policeman looking up and saying, "The sky's awful heavy." It was successfully defended, but it is as well to be on one's guard against aural ambiguity, because meaning in defamation is what the audience may understand a broadcast to mean. It is good practice for a television journalist to have a colleague who has not been working on the story in question to view the television tape before transmission if there is doubt as to how the viewer would construe critical references in the report. 34.11

LIVE PROGRAMMES

DEFAMATION

Up until 1996 there was no protection given to live programmes: in 1986 BBC Scotland were sued for £500,000 by Robert Maxwell over a remark made by the late Arnold Kemp, much respected editor of the *Herald*, in the live discussion programme on Radio Scotland, *Taking Issue with Colin Bell*. 34.12

Section 1 of the Defamation Act 1996 allows the broadcaster of live programmes protection if one of the participants in the live programme utters defamatory remarks in circumstances where the broadcaster has no control over this, so long as the broadcaster "took reasonable care" and did not have any reason to believe that what it did caused or contributed to the publication of a defamatory statement. 34.13

Section 1 does not protect a broadcaster against what its own employees say on air or post on its websites—only third party content, and only if it can show that the conditions as to reasonable care have been met. Careful preparation and speed of reaction by the broadcaster are likely to be important. Cases on s.1 are few and inconclusive. In the case brought by MORI against the BBC in 1999, 34.14

the "live broadcast defence" was allowed to go to the jury, but the case settled before the verdict. The BBC had broadcast remarks of Sir James Goldsmith on the accuracy of MORI's opinion polls on his Referendum Party's popularity during the 1997 General Election [see **paras 26.08 onwards**].

CONTEMPT

34.15 Live programmes enjoy no special protection regarding contempt of court. If an "active" court case is to be debated in the course of a live programme, it is necessary to take the utmost care that participants say nothing which would cause substantial risk of serious prejudice to the forthcoming trial. Producers and presenters should normally brief participants prior to the programme on the restrictions which apply to any discussion of an outstanding criminal trial, though this may not be necessary with lawyers or other legally experienced interviewees.

WHO MAY BE SUED/ACCUSED IN RESPECT OF A BROADCAST?

34.16 On the analogy of newspaper cases, it appears that the reporter, the editor, the producer and the broadcasting organisation itself could all find themselves involved in court proceedings. In one contempt case in 1987 involving Radio Clyde, however, the fine of £20,000 imposed on the radio station's news editor, Colin Adams, by Lord Allanbridge at Paisley was reduced to nil on appeal by the High Court (*Adams, Petitioner* (1987)).

34.17   This case should not be viewed by news editors as particularly comforting. Mr Adams' pleas that he relied on the expertise of the reporter had more force than normal in that the court reporter in question was a highly experienced freelance. If he had been a staff reporter under the control of Mr Adams, the High Court's attitude would probably have been different. Lord Allanbridge refrained from fining the broadcasting limited company, Radio Clyde. It is interesting to note that the freelance reporter did not appeal the fine of £5,000 imposed on him by Lord Allanbridge, although the reporter's earnings at the relevant time were stated to be £7,000 per annum.

INDEPENDENT PRODUCERS AND CONTEMPT/DEFAMATION/PRIVACY

34.18 Much material broadcast comes from independent producers. It seems clear that Scots law allows the pursuer in a defamation action to sue the independent production company as well as the organisation which broadcast the material. As regards privacy actions, although the law is less developed, it is certainly not unknown for this to happen, too. In *X v BBC* (2005), both the BBC and Lion Television Ltd were sued.

It would be possible therefore to have several defenders when, for 34.19 example, the programme broadcast was produced by an independent production company who employed a freelance reporter. It is suggested that the pursuer could sue all or any of the following:

- the broadcaster;
- the independent production company as producers;
- the reporter(s);
- possibly the editor of the programme;
- a contributor.

There would be no need for the pursuer to sue the broadcasting 34.20 organisation itself. The pursuer could choose to sue the independent producer alone or the reporter alone. In fact, normally a pursuer sues all concerned jointly and severally for the same amount of money. Technically this is incorrect as Lord Fraser's judgment in *Turnbull v Frame* (1966) makes clear. Liability in defamation cases is individual, not joint and several. It may be wise for independent producers and reporters in such programmes to agree in advance what will happen if there is a defamation or privacy/breach of confidence action.

It must be emphasised, however, on the question of contempt, this is 34.21 a quasi-criminal matter over which the court alone has jurisdiction. Nobody can serve a jail sentence for another or accept someone else's criminal conviction. Independent producers and their reporters should be mindful of this fact.

CONTEMPT OF COURT: PARTICULAR PROBLEMS FOR BROADCASTERS

The ability of broadcasters to transmit up-to-the-minute reports of 34.22 developing news stories is one of the principal strengths of TV and radio. But this very strength creates considerable dangers for broadcasters in the area of contempt of court. Television and radio— and, still more, online news, whether from a broadcaster's or a newspaper's website—could broadcast stories of a dramatic bank raid within minutes of the event. The danger, however, of committing the serious offence of contempt of court in this situation is high [see **Chapter 16**]. A broadcaster reporting a bank raid would have to check constantly with the police to see if the case had become active—typically, by an arrest or a warrant for arrest.

34.23   It is therefore suggested that broadcasters should operate a working rule of keeping a record of all enquiries to the police and the times they are made regarding the question of arrest and the granting of arrest warrants in this sort of situation. An unhelpful or sluggish reaction would imperil the Crown's position in any petition for contempt against the broadcasting organisation. The broadcaster could transmit in these circumstances with a reasonable prospect of adopting the innocent publication defence under s.3 of the 1981 Act. It was suggested by Lord Weir in *HM Advocate v Belmonte* (1997) that the Crown Office was the right port of call for such inquiries, but this may be questionable in a 24-hour news environment, given that the police are likely to have information faster and more reliably than the Crown Office about arrests. In other situations—for instance, if the journalist is working on a documentary about released prisoners and needs to know if any of them are accused of re-offending—an approach to the Crown Office *and* the police may be advisable. In news programming, it will be necessary to let the police or Crown know the timescale to publication [see **paras 18.02 to 18.03**].

34.24   Identity is usually an issue in a Scottish criminal case. Once the restrictions of the 1981 Act operate (from arrest, the granting of a warrant, etc.), pictures of the accused cannot normally be used.

34.25   There are some exceptions to this general rule. For example, television pictures of the Govan MP Mohammed Sarwar were used when he gave a press conference after being released on bail, having appeared on petition at Glasgow Sheriff Court in 1998 on electoral offences charges of which he was ultimately acquitted. Generally speaking, the view of media lawyers appeared to be that Mr Sarwar had indicated by his actions, i.e. happily giving full-face interviews to television and newspaper journalists, that he felt his identity was not an issue in the trial and was content for his picture to be used.

34.26   Pictures of the two Libyans accused and, in one case, convicted of the Lockerbie bombing were used by the media without any complaint being made. The highly unusual circumstances of that case included the fact that their photographs had been widely publicised for years, internationally, and the trials occurred over a decade after the bombing.

34.27   Sometimes, very well-known faces accused of a crime are shown, as was that of the boxer Scott Harrison in 2008. Celebrity is not enough: STV and others were found in contempt for showing footballer Derek Riordan's photograph during his assault trial. (He, too, was acquitted.) The contempt findings were upheld on appeal (*Scottish Daily Record and Sunday Mail Ltd v Thomson* (2009) [see **para.17.29**]). Scottish media outlets should be slow to assume that sports personalities are instantly recognisable figures whose photographs can be shown while cases against them are active. These cases are the exception. Television journalists, like newspaper journalists, must exercise extreme caution before using the picture of an accused person who has not yet been tried.

In attempting to conceal someone's identity generally—whether because of concerns about contempt, defamation, privacy or statutory breach—there is a particular risk in using moving footage. It tends to show details like a person's height, voice or gait in a way which photographs do not. It is not impossible to anonymise a person on television or film, but it takes more thought and effort than in a newspaper still. 34.28

POLICE POWERS

In terms of the Broadcasting Act 1990 s.167 a justice of the peace or sheriff may authorise a police constable to require a broadcaster to produce a visual or sound recording of any matter contained in a programme where there is reasonable ground for suspecting that an offence under s.51 of the Civic Government (Scotland) Act 1982 or under s.22 of the Public Order Act 1986 has been committed. These offences relate to obscene or racially inflammatory material. 34.29

Section 167 appears only to cover the situation where the material has already been broadcast. 34.30

RACIAL HATRED: PUBLIC ORDER ACT 1986

Section 164 of the 1990 Act extends the law in the Public Order Act 1986 relating to incitement to racial hatred to apply to broadcasting. So, if a programme involves threatening or abusive or insulting visual images or sounds, each of a group of persons will be guilty of an offence if (a) he intends to stir up racial hatred, or (b) having regard to all the circumstances racial hatred is likely to be stirred up. Those who may be guilty of an offence are: 34.31

- the person providing the broadcast;
- any person by whom the programme was produced or directed; and
- any person by whom offending words or behaviour are used.

It is a defence for the person providing the service, or a person by whom the programme was produced or directed, to prove that (a) he did not know and had no reason to suspect that the programme would involve the offending material, and (b) having regard to the circumstances in which the programme was broadcast it was not 34.32

reasonably practicable for him to secure the removal of the material. While this defence might well apply to the broadcasting organisation providing the service, it is difficult to see that either a producer or director is likely to be able to use it; by the nature of their job, it would be difficult to claim ignorance.

OBSCENITY

34.33 Section 163 of the 1990 Act modifies the terms of the Civic Government (Scotland) Act 1982 so as to allow prosecution of anyone responsible for the inclusion of any obscene material in a programme. The section appears wide enough to include the reporter, an independent production company (if there is one) and the broadcasting organisation itself, and possibly also the editor and producer of such a programme.

34.34 The Obscene Publications Act 1959 (covering the broadcasting of obscene material in England) does not apply in Scotland. There are of course a variety of other criminal provisions prohibiting child pornography, in the Protection of Children and Prevention of Sexual Offences (Scotland) Act 2005 and earlier. Criminal provisions of this sort could in certain cases pose a threat to freedom of political and artistic expression, but in practice, at least since the passage of the Human Rights Act 1998, there has been little sign of use of the criminal law to censor programme content.

OFCOM

34.35 Ofcom—the Office of Communications—regulates commercial TV and radio in the UK. It also regulates the BBC in several respects. Ofcom can impose fines—it fined the BBC £150,000 in 2009 over Jonathan Ross and Russell Brand's abusive telephone messages on air to the actor Andrew Sachs—it can also grant or withhold licences to broadcasters. Its decisions are subject to judicial review. Ofcom is covered by the Freedom of Information Act 2000.

THE BBC

34.36 The BBC is a body incorporated under Royal Charter. It, too, is covered by the Freedom of Information Act 2000, in relation to information held for purposes other than those of journalism, art or literature. It is a legal entity and can sue and be sued in the courts. It does not enjoy any special rights or privileges, under the laws of defamation or contempt of court. It has constitutional obligations of due accuracy and due impartiality. As well as Ofcom's regulation, the BBC is also self-regulated, presently by the BBC Trust. One of the BBC's public purposes, under its agreement of July 2006 with the Secretary of State for Culture, Media and Sport, is to represent the nations, regions and communities of the UK, and to make appropriate provision for minority languages, such as Gaelic. There is an Audience Council Scotland, with a remit to advise on how well the BBC meets the needs of licence fee-payers in Scotland, headed by a National Trustee for Scotland with a seat on the BBC Trust. The running of BBC Scotland is in the hands of the Director Scotland, Ken MacQuarrie.

KEY POINTS

1. The broadcast industry is more heavily regulated than the print media. In many cases, broadcasters also reach a bigger audience. For these reasons, the legal consequences when they fail to meet their obligations may be more severe. In the past, this has been offset to some extent by the evanescence of broadcasting. In the world of the internet and the iPlayer, that is changing.   34.37
2. In television, the combination of pictures, words and sounds may give rise to particular risks of accidental defamation.
3. Section 1 of the Defamation Act 1996 creates protections for the broadcasters of live programmes if a contributor blurts out something defamatory on air, but only if the broadcaster has taken reasonable care. Section 1 can also be helpful with defamatory postings on websites. A fast response to close down the defamatory attack is important, if s.1 is to work.
4. There is no particular protection for live broadcasting as regards contempt of court, so live broadcasting in relation to criminal proceedings needs to be considered with particular care.
5. Television broadcasters, and anyone using photographs online, must keep in mind that use of a visual image of the accused may very well be contempt of court.
6. A broadcaster may be ordered to produce a recording where there is reasonable ground for suspecting that a public order offence has been committed.
7. Broadcasts which are likely to stir up racial hatred can be a criminal offence for which a producer or director can incur responsibility.
8. The principal regulator of UK broadcasting is Ofcom, which has the power to impose heavy fines.

CHAPTER 35

ADVERTISEMENTS

BY DAVID MCKIE

35.01   The publication of certain advertisements is illegal and can result in a fairly heavy fine or imprisonment or both.

MEDICAL ADVERTISEMENTS

35.02   It is an offence to take part in the publication of an advertisement containing an offer to treat any person for cancer, or to prescribe a remedy or give advice on the treatment of that disease (Cancer Act 1939 s.4).

35.03   The Medicines Act 1968 introduced a set of offences concerning medical advertisements generally. Under the Act it is an offence to issue, at the request or with the consent of "a commercially interested party" (a term which includes most manufacturers and suppliers of medicines), a false or misleading advertisement relating to medicinal products.

35.04   An advertisement is false or misleading for this purpose if it falsely describes the medicinal products or if it is likely to mislead as to their nature, quality, uses or effects.

35.05   In the case of certain medicinal products which are subject to a licence it is also an offence to issue an advertisement containing recommendations other than those authorised by the licence. In both cases, however, it is a defence for an accused person to prove that he did not know, and could not with reasonable diligence have discovered, that the advertisement was false or misleading or contained unauthorised recommendations.

35.06   Where a product licence is in force for medicinal products of a particular description only the holder of the licence can authorise advertisements relating to such products. Accordingly, it is an offence under s.94 of the Medicines Act 1968 to issue any such advertisement at the request or with the consent of any other commercially interested party. It is, however, a defence for an accused person to prove (a) that he exercised all due diligence to secure that the section would not be contravened, and (b) that the contravention was due to the act or default of another person.

35.07   The Medicines Act 1968 also empowers the appropriate Ministers to make regulations prohibiting, or regulating, particular types of advertisements for medicinal products. The regulations may, for example, prohibit the advertising of treatments for particular diseases, or prohibit advertisements containing particular misleading words or phrases, or require medical advertisements to take a certain form and contain specified particulars. The defence mentioned above is available where a contravention of these regulations is alleged.

FOOD ADVERTISEMENTS

Section 8 of the Food Safety Act 1990 states: 35.08

(1) Any person who—

(a) sells for human consumption, or offers, exposes or advertises for sale for such consumption, or has in his possession for the purpose of such sale or of preparation for such sale; or

(b) deposits with, or consigns to, any other person for the purpose of such sale or of preparation for such sale,

any food which fails to comply with food safety requirements shall be guilty of an offence.

EXPERIMENTS ON ANIMALS

It is an offence to publish an advertisement of a public exhibition of an   35.09
experimental or scientific procedure on an animal which may have the effect of causing the animal pain, suffering, distress or lasting harm (Animals (Scientific Procedures) Act 1986).

FRAUDULENT ADVERTISEMENTS

It is a serious offence to distribute circulars which to one's knowledge   35.10
fraudulently induce or attempt to induce people to invest money. This will not involve a newspaper proprietor, publisher or distributor in liability unless he knows of or is a party to the fraud (Prevention of Fraud (Investments) Act 1958).

CONSUMER CREDIT ADVERTISEMENTS

The Consumer Credit Act 1974 contains provisions on consumer   35.11
credit advertisements, such as most advertisements of hire-purchase facilities and most moneylenders' advertisements. Regulations will provide for the form and content of such advertisements to ensure,

among other things, that they give a fair indication of the credit or hire facilities offered and of their true cost. The 1974 Act itself makes it an offence to publish a consumer credit advertisement which conveys information which is misleading in a material respect. It also prohibits certain advertisements of credit facilities for goods or services which are not available for cash. There are similar restrictions on advertisements by credit brokers, debt adjusters and debt counsellors.

35.12   All these provisions apply expressly to the publisher of an advertisement as well as to the advertiser, but newspapers and others are protected by a provision that it is a defence for a person charged to prove (a) that the advertisement was published in the course of a business carried on by him, and (b) that he received the advertisement in the course of that business, and did not know and had no reason to suspect that its publication would be an offence.

ADOPTION AND CARE OF CHILDREN

35.13   It is an offence to publish knowingly an advertisement indicating that a parent or guardian wants a child adopted, or that a person wants to adopt a child or that any person other than a registered adoption society or local authority is willing to make arrangements for the adoption of a child.

35.14   The Children Act 1958 makes it an offence to publish knowingly an advertisement that a person will undertake or will arrange for the care and maintenance of a child, unless the advertisement truly states the person's name and address.

LICENSED BETTING OFFICE ADVERTISEMENTS

35.15   It was formerly an offence to publish or permit to be published an advertisement of a particular licensed betting office or of licensed betting offices in general. However, first of all, the Deregulation (Betting and Gaming) Order, which came into effect in April 1997 allowed the advertisement of betting shops in the print media, although not the broadcast media. It also removed all restrictions on bingo advertising including advertising on radio and television. Then in 2005, with the passing of the Gambling Act 2005, bookmakers became permitted to advertise on radio and television, but subject to the strong caveat that their advertising was responsible, with a strong emphasis on protecting the young and socially vulnerable, and subject to strict regulation by the Advertising Standards Authority.

LOTTERIES AND GAMING

The laws relating to lotteries and gaming were all brought together 35.16
under the Gambling Act 2005. A lottery is a scheme for distributing
prizes by lot or chance. The 2005 Act explains the differences between
lotteries, betting and gaming—playing a game of chance for a prize.

A "skill test" is not a lottery under the 2005 Act as it does not 35.17
involve the same level of chance. If a competition involves a
particular level of skill, such as a prize awarding crossword or sudoku
in the newspaper, this falls outwith the ambit of the 2005 Act. Quizzes
with answers which are too easy, such as "who is the Prime Minister",
will not meet the "skill" threshold and therefore fall under the 2005
Act, although a multiple choice example which covers reasonably
viable alternative answers may fall outwith the scope of the
legislation and therefore be able to be published without fear of any
possible action.

If there is no skill element, the competition is regarded as a lottery 35.18
unless it is free to enter. Normal posting or standard rate telephone
calls are still regarded as free, but calls to premium rate numbers are
not. Payment can include paying a premium on a product, such as a
box of cereal. If there is no premium on the price for the
"competition" product, that is not regarded as payment. The internet
has created logistical problems for free entry, as many people in the
UK still do not have free entry to the internet. A recent survey
indicated that as many as nine million adults in the UK had never
used the internet. The Gambling Commission therefore look to
alternative options such as postal options and making the
competition last longer than three days to allow for postal entries to
be permitted.

Lotteries can be criminal to run unless you have an operating 35.19
licence, or it is exempt under the 2005 Act. An exempt lottery can
include a privately run lottery which is normally for non-commercial
or charitable purposes and are generally small in nature (e.g. raffles at
charity events, tombolas at coffee mornings, etc.). Any individual or
organisation found guilty of running or promoting an illegal lottery
can be a fined up to £5,000 and/or imprisoned for up to six months.

The general exempt categories of lottery include the following 35.20
conditions: the lottery is not for private benefit or gain and is part of,
but incidental to a non-profit making event, at which tickets are to be
supplied for the lottery to take place there; there is to be no rollover;
those in charge are not allowed to deduct from the lottery proceeds
more than the total sum designated for prizes or other expenses; and
the outcome is determined and announced at the event.

BETTING

35.21 Competitions which involve guessing the result, such as a race night or a "what happened next" type of question are betting, provided that payment is an essential term of entry. If so, an operating licence is needed. This does not apply if you have paid the normal price for something. If for example you entered a "spot the ball" competition on a pack of football stickers, provided the price of the stickers remains the same as if the competition were not being run, it does not fall foul of the 2005 Act.

GAMING

35.22 Gaming is a skill competition which involves playing a game of chance. This might include such games as blackjack or roulette, and therefore usually require a casino operating licence. Games of chance involve, either or both, chance and skill.

GAMBLING COMMISSION

35.23 The Gambling Act 2005 set up the commission as the regulatory body for all matters relating to betting, gaming, casinos and lotteries. They are an independent non-departmental body sponsored by the Department of Culture, Media and Sport with UK wide authority. They do not have any responsibility for the National Lottery, but do regulate bookmakers, arcades, bingo halls, casinos and other organisations in which gambling or betting is at the forefront of activities. Their stated aims include keeping crime out of gambling and to protect the young and vulnerable from harm or exploitation in gambling

35.24 Their website provides regular written guidance notes and updates on the legislation. It also provides detailed guidance on the law, on licensing, regulation and enforcement. The commission has prepared its own licence conditions and has codes of practice, all prepared under the authority of s.24 of the 2005 Act. The latest *Licence Conditions and Codes of Practice* (Gambling Commission, 2008) is available on the commission's website. This covers the general licensing operating conditions required and codes of practice, covering among other matters financial requirements, protection of the young and vulnerable, marketing and complaints and disputes.

FALSE TRADE DESCRIPTIONS

The Trade Descriptions Act 1968 prohibits false trade descriptions (as 35.25
defined in the Act) and various other mis-statements, such as false
indications that goods are being offered at a cut price. The 1968 Act
also gives the Department of Trade power to require certain
advertisements to include certain particulars if they think this is
necessary or expedient in the interests of consumers. Although the
Act is aimed primarily at misstatements by those supplying goods
and services, certain of its provisions apply to publishers of
advertisements. If a newspaper knew that an advertisement
contained a false trade description, e.g. that goods advertised as new
were in fact second-hand or reconditioned, it would be guilty of an
offence under the 1968 Act if it published it. Obviously, however,
newspapers cannot be expected to investigate the accuracy of every
statement made in their advertising columns. The 1968 Act therefore
provides that it shall be a defence for the publisher of an advertisement
to prove that he is a person whose business it is to publish or arrange
for the publication of advertisements and that he received the
advertisement for publication in the ordinary course of business and
did not know and had no reason to suspect that its publication would
amount to an offence under the 1968 Act.

PIRATE RADIO STATIONS

Under the Marine, &c., Broadcasting (Offences) Act 1967 it is an 35.26
offence to publish the times or other details of broadcasts to be made
from pirate radio stations or to publish advertisements calculated to
promote their interests.

CARS

An advertisement for new cars which contains any statement about 35.27
fuel consumption must include information about results of relevant
official tests.

SURROGACY ARRANGEMENTS

The Surrogacy Arrangements Act 1985 makes it an offence to publish 35.28
any advertisement containing an indication (a) that any person is or
may be willing to enter into a surrogacy arrangement or to negotiate
or facilitate the making of a surrogacy arrangement, or (b) that any
person is looking for a woman willing to become a surrogate mother

or is looking for persons wanting to carry a child as a surrogate mother.

OBSCENE PUBLICATIONS

35.29 Obscenity is an offence at common law in Scotland. The broad test is whether the publication complained of is calculated to deprave and corrupt those who are likely to read it. The Indecent Advertisements Act 1889 deals mainly with placing indecent advertisements on walls and similar places and the distribution or exhibition of indecent matter in the streets. The Civic Government (Scotland) Act 1982 makes it an offence to publish any advertisement to the effect that the advertiser distributes or intends to distribute an indecent photograph of a child under 16.

HARMFUL PUBLICATIONS

35.30 It is an offence to print, publish, sell or hire "horror comics" (Children and Young Persons (Harmful Publications) Act 1955). This will not affect the average newspaper as the statute applies only to works which consist wholly or mainly of picture stories portraying the commission of crimes or acts of violence or cruelty or incidents of a repulsive or horrible nature in such a way that the work as a whole would tend to corrupt a child or young person into whose hands it might fall. It would apply, e.g. to "video nasties". A child is defined as someone under 14 and a young person as someone under the age of 17.

ELECTION MATTER

35.31 It is an offence to incur expense without the written authority of the election agent in issuing advertisements, circulars or publications with a view to promoting or procuring the election of a candidate at an election (Representation of the People Act 1983). This does not prevent newspapers commenting on an election with complete freedom and presenting a candidate or his views or disparaging another candidate. It has been held that there was an offence when a publication advised electors to vote against a candidate but did not advise them to vote for his opponent. It nevertheless tended to promote the opponent's election.

35.32   But to offend, the publication must tend to promote or procure the election of a particular candidate and not merely a political party as a whole. This was decided in a case (***R. v Tronoh Mines Ltd* (1952)**) in which the proprietors of *The Times* and others were prosecuted over an advertisement condemning the financial policy of the Labour Party and saying that an election would give an opportunity of saving the country from being reduced to bankruptcy through the policies of a socialist government. The judge observed that no reasonable jury could find that this advertisement presented to the electors of any particular constituency any particular candidate.

It is also an offence to print, publish, post or distribute any bill, 35.33 placard or poster referring to an election unless the name and address of the printer and publisher appear on its face (Representation of the People Act 1983). This provision might apply, for example, to newspaper posters proclaiming, "Vote for Blogg".

ACCOMMODATION AGENCIES

It is an offence under the Accommodation Agencies Act 1953, to issue 35.34 any advertisement describing any house as being to let without the authority of the owner of the house or his agent. It is also an offence under the 1953 Act to demand or accept certain illegal commissions for registering people seeking tenancies or for supplying particulars of houses to let. However, the 1953 Act expressly provides that:

> "[A] person shall not be guilty of an offence under this section by reason of his demanding or accepting any payment in consideration of ... the publication in a newspaper, of any advertisement or notice, or by reason of the ... publication ... of an advertisement or notice received for the purpose in the ordinary course of business".

ADVERTISING STANDARDS

Publishers should be familiar with the British Code of Advertising, 35.35 Sales Promotion and Direct Marketing (CAP Code) and broadcasters with the TV and Radio Advertising Standard Codes, both administered by the Advertising Standards Authority (ASA).

Although the code is not statutory, the authority has power, where 35.36 an advertisement is found to have contravened the code, to order the advertiser to amend or withdraw it from publication. The aim of the code is to protect consumers from unacceptable or misleading advertising, its philosophy, in brief, being that, "if an advertiser can't prove it, he can't say it"; and the authority summarises its message thus: "All advertisements should be legal, decent, honest and truthful".

35.37   The code, which is under constant review, makes special provision for political and religious advertising, to avoid undue suppression of freedom of speech. Publishers of newspapers and periodicals are entitled to withdraw any advertisement they think is contrary to the code. There are separate codes dealing with television, radio, cable and satellite broadcasting.

35.38   The Advertising Standards Authority deals with complaints. In 2008, it dealt with a total of 26,000 complaints, which in turn led to 2,500 advertisements either being amended or withdrawn. The types of complaints they are most likely to encounter will involve those which offend, harm or mislead. Complaints can come from competitors, consumers or anyone who has a direct or indirect interest in the matter. Complaints can be made via the ASA website, post or fax.

35.39   The outcome of complaints are set out in the adjudications section of the ASA website. The range of different complaints referred to are wide ranging, from advertisements about the wording of particular advertisements, to the tone and content of leading television and radio advertisements. The sanctions for upheld complaints can include the advertiser being referred to in news alerts to other CAP members, a simple agreement that the advertisement must not recur in the same format as the "offending one", withdrawal of trade privileges and in the worst case scenarios, for misleading or unfair advertising, referral to the Office of Fair Trading. In broadcast advertising breaches, sanctions can include publication or broadcast of a retraction and correction, or referral of the matter to Ofcom, the broadcast industry regulator.

35.40   The British Code of Advertising Practice says advertisements should contain nothing which might cause children physical, mental or moral harm, or which exploits their credulity, lack of experience or sense of loyalty and should not encourage them to be a nuisance to their parents or anyone else with the aim of persuading them to buy an advertised product.

KEY POINTS

35.41   1. A fine and/or imprisonment can be imposed for the publication of certain types of illegal advertisement. For example, it is an offence to publish false or misleading advertisements about medicines or medical treatment, food and drugs.

2. There are also strict rules governing advertisements on consumer credit, betting and lotteries.

3. Advertisements are supposed to be "legal, decent, honest and truthful" and the Advertising Standards Authority has power to order an advertiser to amend or withdraw an advertisement which fails to meet these criteria.

PART 10: THE HUMAN RIGHTS ACT 1998, PRIVACY AND BREACH OF CONFIDENCE

CHAPTER 36

THE HUMAN RIGHTS ACT 1998

BY ROSALIND MCINNES

36.01   From a journalistic point of view, the European Convention on Human Rights contains two rights of overarching importance: art.8, the right to privacy; and art.10, the right to freedom of expression.

36.02   Despite being an early signatory to it, the United Kingdom did not incorporate the Convention into domestic law. Therefore, when a United Kingdom citizen felt that these rights had been breached, his or her only redress was to go to the European Court of Human Rights in Strasbourg. Neither the court nor the Convention has any connection with the European Union.

36.03   With the coming into force of the Human Rights Act 1998, however, United Kingdom citizens can rely upon their Convention rights in "domestic courts, tribunals and 'disputes with public authorities'." Scottish courts and tribunals are public authorities (see s.6), as is "any person certain of whose functions are functions of a public nature."

36.04   The most important decision makers, i.e. the courts, have to take account of European Convention rights in deciding disputes, even between individuals. The courts and tribunals also require to take account of existing Strasbourg case decisions, though they are not "bound" by them. First, individual States have what Strasbourg calls a "margin of appreciation"—a degree of cultural discretion as to how they implement law within their own courts. Secondly, the Convention is to be a "living instrument", growing and changing to meet particular social circumstances. It would doubtless have startled the drafters of the Convention, acutely conscious of totalitarian horrors and zealous to protect human dignity and family life, to see privacy used to censor information about the eroticisation of violence against "prisoners of war" by a married man concealing this from his wife; or to see freedom of expression used to justify the mass publication of a video showing the latter. But this is where we are in the UK, as the *Mosley* **(2008)** case [see **paras 23.56**] vividly shows. Thirdly, membership of the court has changed often and newer democracies are joining, so the approach of Strasbourg will not be static or even predictable.

ACTS OF PARLIAMENT

The Human Rights Act 1998 does not permit the courts to strike down 36.05 Westminster legislation because it does not comply with the Convention. Instead, if they cannot, by any stretch of interpretation, reconcile the domestic legislation with the Convention right, they are to issue a "declaration of incompatibility". Remedial legislation can then be put in place.

In relation to the Scottish Parliament, the position is somewhat 36.06 different. Since the Scotland Act 1998 does not permit the Scottish Parliament to legislate in contravention of international treaty obligations (including the European Convention on Human Rights), Scottish Acts which the Scottish judiciary considers do not comply with the Convention may be struck down. The legislation is also supposed to be looked at carefully before it is passed, to check for compatibility.

PRIVACY

Article 8 of the Convention states: 36.07

1. Everyone has the right to respect for his private and family life, his home and his correspondence.

2. There shall be no interference by a public authority with the exercise of this right except such as is in accordance with the law and is necessary in a democratic society in the interests of national security, public safety or the economic well-being of the country, for the prevention of disorder or crime, for the protection of health or morals, or for the protection of the rights and freedoms of others.

FREEDOM OF EXPRESSION

36.08   Article 10 states:

> 1. Everyone has the right to freedom of expression. This right shall include freedom to hold opinions and to receive and impart information and ideas without interference by public authority and regardless of frontiers. This Article shall not prevent States from requiring the licensing of broadcasting, television or cinema enterprises.
>
> 2. The exercise of these freedoms, since it carries with it duties and responsibilities, may be subject to such formalities, conditions, restrictions or penalties as are prescribed by law and are necessary in a democratic society, in the interests of national security, territorial integrity or public safety, for the prevention of disorder or crime, for the protection of health or morals, for the protection of the reputation or rights of others, for preventing the disclosure of information received in confidence, or for maintaining the authority and impartiality of the judiciary.

FREEDOM OF EXPRESSION AND OTHER HUMAN RIGHTS

36.09   Other Articles of the Convention may also be of significance to the journalist. The art.6 right to a fair trial may be expected to have a place in arguments about contempt of court, open justice and disclosure of sources. The art.11 right of freedom of assembly and association may be of assistance in relation to the investigative and reporting process. The art.2 right to life and art.3 right not to be subjected to torture or to inhuman or degrading punishment or treatment can also arise from time to time. The lifelong anonymity given by the English court to the 10-year-old killers of James Bulger after they had grown up and been released (though, at the time of writing, Jonathan Venables is once more detained) was awarded on the basis that they would be at risk of vigilante attacks.

36.10   Even art.1 of the First Protocol, which protects the right to peaceful enjoyment of one's possessions, can crop up in media law. In *Response Handling Ltd v BBC* (2007), for instance [see **paras 37.15 and 37.86**], when a call centre company tried unsuccessfully to stop a *Frontline Scotland* documentary including undercover filming at its premises, Lord Bracadale accepted in principle that this "would include intellectual property, such as their work systems, procedures and employment protocols." The mere fact that information is confidential does not render it property as such (*Douglas v Hello!*

(2007)), but a case can raise both breach of confidence and intellectual property issues, as did the ones raised by Prince Charles (*HRH Prince of Wales v Associated Newspapers Ltd* **(2007)**) and Paddy Ashdown (*Ashdown v Telegraph Group Ltd* **(2001)**) over their diaries.

However, it is the interplay between the art.8 right of privacy and   36.11
the art.10 right of freedom of expression which is likely to be of most interest to the journalist.

WHAT IS PRIVACY?

There has never been a coherent attempt of the Strasbourg Court to   36.12
draw the line between public and private life. Many of the cases relate either to children or to sexuality, although some deal with physical invasion of the home or sometimes professional space, access to leisure facilities, noise and other environmental pollution. Significance has been attached to whether the person concerned had "a legitimate expectation of privacy" in the circumstances, e.g. in using the telephone in her own office (*Halford v UK* **(1997)**), see below). The right to private life includes the right to protection of one's reputation (*Pfeifer v Austria* **(2009)**), so art.8 comes into defamation claims as well as more obviously privacy-based actions.

HOME AND FAMILY

There have been cases where search of a home for civil or criminal   36.13
proceedings in the United Kingdom has been held to amount to violation of art.8, even if the premises are partly used for business purposes. In particular circumstances, however, this may be justified as being for protection of the rights of others.

Family life includes the extended family, grandparents and   36.14
grandchildren. What is necessary is evidence of a genuine and close family tie—fostering, step-parenting, cohabitation and adoption have all been included. Something may fall within the "private life" category even if it does not fall within the "family" as such.

PRISONERS

The position of prisoners has generated a lot of art.8 case law. In   36.15
particular, the European Court has allowed substantial freedom to a prisoner to correspond with lawyers and to seek media intervention to investigate an alleged miscarriage of justice.

TELEPHONE TAPPING

36.16 Telephone tapping is accepted in principle by the United Kingdom, but has to be "prescribed by law" and kept within bounds. The United Kingdom lost a case brought by senior policewoman Alison Halford because the safeguards then in place were inadequate [see **para.36.12** above].

FREEDOM OF EXPRESSION: THE PAPARAZZI

36.17 The European Court has consistently held that freedom of expression, including unpopular expression, is an essential foundation of democracy and an important line of defence for human rights. Therefore, any limit on freedom of expression must be "proportionate" to the aim pursued. There are certain limits on freedom of expression. On the whole, Strasbourg has limited interest in what it considers to be "junk" journalism or intrusive journalism.

36.18 In its most significant decision on photographs, *Von Hannover v Germany* **(2004)**, it was willing to outlaw a series of photographs of Princess Caroline of Monaco, even in an innocuous setting and a public place. In light of the Court of Appeal's decision in the case brought by J.K. Rowling on behalf of her small son, this may be the shape of things to come in our domestic courts [see **Chapter 23**].

36.19 The fact that someone who was physically in the place where the photograph was taken at the time could have seen what the photograph records, is not the end of any privacy argument. In *Peck v United Kingdom* **(2003)**, the European Court of Human Rights held that the broadcast of CCTV footage of a man carrying a knife violated his art.8 rights. The man was, he said, suicidal at the time and carrying the knife for that reason. The court said:

> "Private life is a broad term not susceptible to exhaustive definition ... [Art.8] protects a right to identity and personal development, and the right to establish and develop relationships with other human beings and the outside world and it may include activities of a professional or business nature. There is, therefore, a zone of interaction of a person with others, even in a public context, which may fall within the scope of 'private life' ... [His carrying the knife] was viewed to an extent which far exceeded any exposure to a passer-by or to security observation and to a degree surpassing that which the applicant could possibly have foreseen ...".

THE PUBLIC'S RIGHT TO BE INFORMED

The European Court found against the United Kingdom and for the 36.20
Sunday Times on the Thalidomide issue in a decision which was partly
responsible for the passage of the Contempt of Court Act 1981. There
was an injunction against the appearance of an article on the
Thalidomide tragedy whilst there was an ongoing litigation on the
amount of compensation due. The court said:

> "The Thalidomide disaster was a matter of undisputed public
> concern ... Article 10 guarantees not only the freedom of the
> press to inform the public but also the right of the public to be
> properly informed" (*Sunday Times v United Kingdom* (1979)).

DEFAMATION DAMAGES AND "THE CHILLING EFFECT"

The court has also looked increasingly closely at large defamation 36.21
awards. Regardless of the facts of the case, the mere size of the
damages, in an extreme case, may breach art.10 (*Tolstoy Miloslavsky
v United Kingdom* (1995)—an award of £1.5 million).

NATIONAL SECURITY AND PRIOR RESTRAINTS

The Strasbourg jurisprudence is especially wary of "prior restraint", 36.22
i.e. gagging orders. In relation to the famous *Spycatcher* excerpts to
be published by the *Observer*, *Sunday Times* and *Guardian*, the court
held that the original injunctions were valid because the State was
given great leeway in the name of national security. However, after
the book had been published in the United States, national security
no longer amounted to an adequate reason for restriction. Sensitive
information was already "out there"—a factor of ever-greater
potential significance in the internet age [see **Chapters 38** and **43**].

LICENSING

Article 10 allows States to licence broadcasting. Article 10 does not 36.23
constitute a right of access to broadcasting facilities, but it does
include the right not to have properly-licensed broadcasts jammed or
disrupted and not to suffer politically motivated refusals of a licence.

COMMERCIAL SPEECH

36.24 Advertising and commercial activities are protected as exercises of free speech, although the level of protection is less than that accorded to the expression of political ideas.

POLITICAL SPEECH AND POLITICIANS

36.25 A high level of protection is given to political speech, a widely defined notion covering many types of public interest debate. The limits of criticism are wider in relation to a politician, or public figure of a similar role, than in relation to a private citizen. They are still wider in relation to government figures and to elections (*Filatenko v Russia* **(2010)**). However, even politicians like Jean Marie Le Pen (*Lindon v France* **(2008)**) have a right to reputation which can result in defamation findings being upheld in Strasbourg, as not violating art.10.

FACTS, VALUE JUDGMENTS, PROVOCATION AND EXAGGERATION

36.26 Strasbourg distinguishes between factual allegations and "value judgments" which cannot be proved. There must be a sufficient factual basis to support a value judgment (*Pedersen v Denmark* **(2006)**).

THE JOURNALISTIC PACKAGE

36.27 The European Court emphasises the right of journalists to tell their stories in the style and tone of their choosing:

> "The Court reiterates ... that Article 10 protects not only the substance of the ideas and information expressed, but also the form in which they are conveyed. Consequently, it is not for this Court, nor for the national courts for that matter, to substitute their own views for those of the press as to what technique of reporting should be adopted by journalists" (*Stoll v Switzerland* **(2007)**).

SECTION 12: A LIMIT ON PRIOR RESTRAINT, INTERIM INTERDICT, ETC.

Section 12 of the Human Rights Act 1998 was introduced as a result of strong representations from the media. However, s.12 can be employed by anyone, not just "the media". It applies if a court is considering whether to grant any relief which, if granted, might affect the exercise of the Convention right to freedom of expression. This section reflects the weight given to the art.10 right to freedom of expression by the European Court jurisprudence and its distaste for prior restraints. Section 12 is intended to stop gagging orders from being obtained behind the journalist's (or other defender's) back. The defender has to be notified of the hearing unless "there are compelling reasons" why not. There is to be no restraint on publication unless the court is satisfied that the applicant is "likely to establish that publication should not be allowed" in a full hearing at the end of the day.

36.28

WHAT DOES "LIKELY" MEAN IN SECTION 12?

The House of Lords said in *Cream Holdings v Banerjee* (2004):

36.29

"There can be no single, rigid standard covering all applications for interim restraint orders. Rather ... the effect of Section 12(3) is that the court is not to make an interim restraint order unless satisfied the applicant's prospects of success at the trial are sufficiently favourable ... The general approach should be that courts will be exceedingly slow to make interim restraint orders where the applicant has not satisfied the court he will probably ('more likely than not') succeed at the trial."

In that case, where a dismissed in-house accountant had given, unpaid, information to the *Liverpool Daily Post & Echo* which she saw as showing illegal and improper activity by her former employers, the court took the view that the Cream Group's prospects of success at trial were not sufficiently likely to justify such an order. They were more likely to fail than to succeed at the trial and there were no grounds to apply a lower meaning of "likely" than "more likely than not" in that case.

36.30

However, the floating standard of "likely" does mean that s.12(3) can lack rigour at the very stage where it is intended to operate, i.e. at the interim stage. In *X v BBC* (2005), the pursuer, who had signed a consent form and participated in filming over a period of weeks for a documentary about Glasgow Sheriff Court, sought to stop the broadcast of the footage featuring her. She claimed that her

36.31

psychological fragility was such that she would harm herself if the programme were broadcast. The programme, which was filmed in 2003, was delayed for a period of 18 months, until a full hearing on the case. The action was settled on the morning of the proof, i.e. full hearing on the evidence, and the programme broadcast in 2006.

36.32   Section 12 does not cover merely obvious areas such as defamation cases, but any order which, in effect, would operate as a gag. Thus, breach of confidence and breach of copyright actions may also come under this heading. So might orders preventing the identification of people involved in civil actions.

36.33   The court must have particular regard to the importance of the Convention right to freedom of expression. Where the proceedings relate to material which the respondent claims, or which appears to the court, to be journalistic, literary or artistic material (or to conduct connected to such material), the court must give weight to: (a) the extent to which: (i) material has, or is about to become, available to the public; or (ii) it is, or would be, in the public interest for the material to be published; (b) any relevant privacy code. This would include the Press Complaints Commission Code (*LNS (John Terry) v Persons Unknown* (2010)) and the Ofcom Code (*Response Handling Ltd* (2007)) [see **paras 37.15 and 37.86**].

36.34   "Courts" includes a tribunal and "relief" includes, "any remedy or order (other than in criminal proceedings)".

CONTEMPT OF COURT AND ARTICLE 6

36.35   Contempt of court rulings which affect freedom of expression may bear—at any rate as regards pre-trial publicity—on the right to a fair trial. This right is guaranteed by art.6 of the Convention and is also regarded as extremely important by the European Court of Human Rights. This art.6 right does not relate simply to criminal trials, but applies to the determination of "civil rights and obligations". This could be pled against the media when they are refusing to reveal sources who may be in breach of, for example, their contracts of employment or duties of confidentiality. On the other hand, art.6 also reinforces the existing common law position that court proceedings ought normally to take place in public.

KEY POINTS

36.36   1. The Human Rights Act 1998 requires public authorities— including courts—to respect the fundamental rights set out in the European Convention on Human Rights, and to have regard to the decisions of the Strasbourg Court. Two of these fundamental rights are the art.10 right to freedom of expression and the art.8 right to privacy. Freedom of expression covers political, commercial and other speech and writing in all media. Privacy covers the home, family life, correspondence and associated areas. Balancing these rights when they conflict may not be easy or obvious, but a high value is given to freedom of expression.

2. Section 12 of the 1998 Act is intended to operate to prevent prior restraints on freedom of expression in most cases. Although reporting restrictions on trials, contempt findings, etc. will require to be justified as necessary, the right to a fair trial is also enshrined in the Convention and 1998 Act, so there needs to be a balance there also.

3. The Act gives added emphasis to voluntary codes like the Press Complaints Commission Code.

4. The European Court of Human Rights jurisprudence has favoured the media in a range of cases dealing with high defamation damages, access to prisoners, source protection and reporting of matters of public interest. It regards the media as an important watchdog of society. However, the European Court has been protective of the right to privacy as extending to unwanted paparazzi photographs and individual reputation.

CHAPTER 37

PRIVACY AND BREACH OF CONFIDENCE

BY ROSALIND MCINNES

37.01   Privacy is the area of media law which has changed most dramatically since the last edition of this book, and on which it is hardest to give legal advice. Geoffrey Robertson and Andrew Nicol say in *Media Law*, 5th edn (London: Sweet and Maxwell, 2007) of art.8:

> "Each state party [to the European Convention] has a duty to ensure that there is a legal power to deny the media entry to privacy zones that can be geographically defined: the cradle, the school and the hospital, the toilet, the bedroom and the grave."

37.02   Though this is deliberately simplified (it omits the church, for instance, and a Narcotics Anonymous meeting need not take place in a hospital), it aptly captures areas of especial sensitivity. Moreover—and controversially—the art.8 privacy right is increasingly being treated as containing a right to reputation.

37.03   Some academic ink has been spilt over whether, despite the incorporation of the European Convention on Human Rights and the Human Rights Act 1998 with its art.8 guarantee of a right of privacy, it can be said that there is an action of privacy, properly called, in the UK at all.

37.04   Clearly, however, there are actions of breach of confidence—sometimes now called in the English media cases, "misuse of private information"—and rights under the Data Protection Act 1998 and the Protection from Harassment Act 1997, to name but three of the ways in which the law within the UK protects what may conveniently be called the right of privacy.

RELATIONSHIP BETWEEN CONFIDER AND CONFIDANT

37.05   The main way in which privacy law has developed is by the action of breach of confidence. This action has existed for centuries, growing arms and legs to fill the perceived gap caused by the former lack of a legal right to privacy.

37.06   Originally it required there to be some sort of relationship between the confider and the person who was said to have breached the confidence. This might be commercial, e.g. an employee who illicitly left the job and took with him a customer list might be sued for breach of confidence. It might be professional: the relationship of

380

doctor and patient, solicitor and client, priest and confessor could all give rise to an actionable breach of confidence. Or, increasingly, it could be personal: the secrecy of matrimonial confidences could be enforced even between divorced spouses, as was held in the notorious *Argyll v Argyll* (1967) case. This expanded later in the 20th century to cover lovers. One of the earliest cases, of the commercial type, with a media law slant was **Prince Albert v Strange (1849)**. In that case, Queen Victoria and Prince Albert had produced and kept etchings of the Royal Family, friends, dogs and the like. A publisher had, by undisclosed means, got hold of these and wished to produce a catalogue listing and describing them. It was held that this was a breach of confidence.

MISUSE OF PRIVATE INFORMATION

The breach of confidence action has continued to be the principal 37.07 vehicle for developing the right of privacy in the UK since the Human Rights Act 1998 came into force. The search for a confidential relationship began to look increasingly strained and unnecessary. In the *Naomi Campbell* (2004) case in the House of Lords, Lord Nicholls said,

> "This cause of action has now firmly shaken off the limiting constraint of the need for an initial confidential relationship. In doing so it has changed its nature ... Information about an individual's private life would not, in ordinary usage, be called 'confidential' ... The essence of [new-style breach of confidence] is better encapsulated now as misuse of private information."

Nonetheless, where there is an old-style confidential relationship, that 37.08 fact remains of great assistance to a pursuer or claimant making a privacy case.

Niema Ash, whose biography of Canadian singer Loreena 37.09 McKennitt ended up being pulped as a consequence of McKennitt's breach of confidence action against her, was not helped by the fact that the book was subtitled, *My Life As A Friend*. The Court of Appeal upheld the injunction against the biography (*McKennitt v Ash* (2007)). Similarly, in the *Mosley* (2008) case, that the prostitute must have, as Eady J. saw it, betrayed Max Mosley by secretly filming the orgy, was a significant factor.

CONTRACT

The existence of a contract between the two is another potent pointer 37.10 to the likelihood that a breach of confidence action will succeed.

Continuing the tradition set by Prince Albert, Prince Charles sued Associated Newspapers over publication of his diaries concerning overseas State visits (*HRH Prince of Wales v Associated Newspapers* **(2006)**). As with the *McKennitt* case, there was also a pre-existing relationship: "The information was disclosed in breach of a well-recognised relationship of confidence, that which exists between master and servant"; though the court held that in any case "[t]he journals were paradigm examples of confidential documents" which would have been protected even if found in the street rather than, as here, handed to a newspaper by a member of the Prince's staff.

37.11   Diaries—at least of the personal journal type—are indeed typically regarded as private. Nonetheless, upholding that decision, over arguments that some of the information, e.g. the Prince's attitude towards China's politics, was in the public interest, the Court of Appeal emphasised the importance of contract. The test, they said, was not simply whether the information was a matter of public interest, but whether in all the circumstances it was in the public interest that the duty of confidence should be breached.

37.12   Mr Justice Tugendhat took the same view in *Northern Rock Plc v FT Ltd* **(2007)**, when he granted an injunction against a repetition of financial details from a "briefing memorandum" concerning Northern Rock's difficulties and how they might be fixed. There, the memorandum details had probably been leaked by an employee who would, it was claimed, be subjected to a contractual obligation of confidentiality.

37.13   It is not, however, impossible to defend oneself in an action of breach of confidence even where a contractual obligation of confidence is in place. This was done in *LRT & London Underground v The Mayor of London* **(2001)** about a public works contract. There, the Court of Appeal said: "No authority has been cited to the Court establishing that an apparent breach of a contractual duty of confidence is more serious ... than other apparent breaches."

37.14   In Scotland, in *Dr Avril Osborne v BBC* **(2000)**, the Inner House of the Court of Session lifted an interim interdict based on a minute of agreement between Orkney Islands Council and its outgoing Director of Community Social Services which contained a clause saying that neither party would make a public statement about her retirement except for an agreed press release. The court said:

> "No argument was put before us to support reliance on the Agreement in itself as extending confidentiality to any information which was not already confidential for other reasons ... In our view, the argument advanced on behalf of the

respondents that an agreement between the Council and the petitioner could not bind third parties such as the respondents is clearly correct."

Most recently, in Scotland, in *Response Handling Ltd v BBC* (2008), 37.15
an interim interdict application in relation to undercover filming at a call centre showing gaps in security was defeated, despite a confidentiality clause in the undercover journalist's contract.

PUBLIC INTEREST

The traditional defence to a breach of confidence action would be that 37.16
"there is no defence in iniquity"—in other words, the wrongdoer is not entitled to keep wrongdoing quiet. Nowadays, that is both too narrow and too wide a proposition. Too narrow, because the essential issue is not whether the party who wishes the matter kept quiet is guilty of iniquity, but whether it is in the public interest to reveal it. Too wide, in that the mere fact that behaviour might reasonably be censured, or might even be illegal, does not mean that a journalist is entitled to reveal it.

Journalists should be mindful of the fact that although public 37.17
interest may well provide a defence to an action of breach of confidence, the courts define "public interest" in a way quite different from that of journalists. Judges have repeatedly told the press that "public interest" in law does not mean that in which the public has an interest, such as celebrity gossip. In law, the public interest in this context is confined to the likes of exposure of fraudulent activity, discovery of a crime or revelation of hypocrisy.

PUBLIC FIGURE

In the early days of the Human Rights Act 1998, the status of someone 37.18
as a public figure or even "role model" was thought to be important—
see the *Flitcroft* (2002) and *Theakston* (2002) cases. Undoubtedly, a campaigner, church leader or other spokesperson will have a different set of legitimate expectations of privacy in relation to their public role. In the case of someone whose public role embraces a wide range of responsibilities and discretionary decision-making on behalf of the public—quintessentially, a politician—their legitimate expectations will be very different from that of an ordinary citizen. However, a number of privacy cases have been launched by royals, captains of industry (e.g. *Lord Browne* (2007)) and statespeople, as well as celebrities exerting a greater or lesser practical influence on the public. In art.8 terms, everyone has a right to privacy, even though

their public role and pronouncements will affect the ambit and nature of that right.

37.19   After the death of the Princess of Wales, the Parliamentary Assembly of the Council of Europe passed Resolution 1165 (1998) on the right to privacy. It defined public figures as, "persons holding public office and/or using public resources and ... all those who play a role in public life, whether in politics, the economy, the arts, the social sphere, sport or in any other domain." Whilst the Resolution stated that "public figures must recognise that the special position they occupy ... automatically entails increased pressure on their privacy", it made it clear that the public is not entitled to know everything about public figures.

37.20   In the *Von Hannover* case [see **para.23.48**], which concerned a series of paparazzi shots of Princes Caroline of Monaco shopping, horse-riding, etc. the European Court of Human Rights held that her privacy rights had been violated. They laid emphasis on the facts that she did not exercise official functions, that the pictures related to her personal life only and that they were not capable of "contributing to a debate in a democratic society."

37.21   Scottish defamation law has always recognised the decreased right to reputational protection of the public figure [see **paras 26.77 onwards**], but their broader privacy rights may now receive greater protection. Of course, more will typically be in the public domain about public figures, their pronouncements are more likely to be public and they are more likely to wield the sort of power which relevantly affects the degree of reasonable public interest in how they behave. Depending on their public actions and official functions, their right to privacy will be curtailed to a greater or lesser extent.

37.22   Politicians, by dint of their representative functions, can expect a very high degree of legitimate scrutiny in their lives as a whole. Heads of state and religious leaders will be in a similar category. Spokespeople for particular charities, campaigns or policies can scarcely object to exposure if their words and actions do not march together. But actors, singers, reality TV figures, sportsmen, etc. are not automatically to be investigated or publicly criticised if they fall short of their own declared ideals (*McKennitt v Ash* (2007)) or for subsequent failure in their relationships (*LNS* (2010)). Imperfection is not always hypocrisy, and when it is, the media will not be able to declare open season on every weathergirl with a substance addiction or a married lover, in the matter of photos, details, or the like. Even in public figures of greater constitutional significance, there will be limits on extreme intrusion. In fact, in the Prince Charles Hong Kong journals case (*HRH Prince of Wales v Associated Newspapers* (2006)), the court suggested that the private space for reflection afforded by a diary might be *more* protected because of the constant public scrutiny experienced by the heir to the throne. In short, there is no straightforward expectation that a public figure must be "robust" in relation to invasive coverage of personal life.

HYPOCRISY

Naomi Campbell's lying about her drug use was accepted as providing justification for the *Mirror's* exposing her as an addict. She won her case against them on other grounds, prominently the sensitivity of medical information and the use of photographs, but her hypocrisy was accepted as grounds for exposure of her drugs habit. However, "hypocrisy" is not a catch-all justification.   37.23

In ***McKennitt v Ash*** **(2007)**, where it was argued that Loreena McKennitt was not living up to the values which she had espoused on her website, the Court of Appeal was dismissive of these claims of falling from grace. Whilst it "may well go too far" to say that a very high degree of misbehaviour was required to trigger a public interest defence, Loreena McKennitt had not behaved disreputably or insincerely, according to the judge's findings.   37.24

FACT SENSITIVITY OF PRIVACY CASES

Alter a few facts in almost any of the breach of confidence cases considered below and it is possible to imagine a quite different outcome. For example, if Naomi Campbell had been photographed shooting up, rather than after a Narcotics Anonymous meeting? Or suppose, instead of publishing online a sexually explicit video shot undercover, the *News of the World* had simply reported that the president of the *Federation Internationale de l'Automobile* regularly engaged in activities involving violence against prostitutes, which he concealed from his wife and which possibly rendered him vulnerable to blackmail? If Lord Browne [see **para.37.34**] had not involved BP in any way? If Loreena McKennitt had lost her property dispute with Niema Ash, her unauthorised biographer?   37.25

In the teeth of all this, it is tempting for a legal commentator just to say of the developing privacy law, in the manner of the medieval cartographers: here be dragons. However, this is the environment in which we work, so it is perhaps useful to look at clusters of cases where particular privacy-related legal concerns arise.   37.26

PERSONAL ASSISTANTS

37.27   Niema Ash acted as a personal assistant to Loreena McKennitt and that combination of a commercial relationship which entails a large degree of personal involvement and the holding of a great deal of personal information, has proved a particularly potent source of breach of confidence actions: Naomi Campbell sued her personal assistant, Vanessa Frisbee, on breach of confidence grounds (*Campbell v Frisbee* (2003)), and Mary Archer got an injunction and damages against her personal assistant (*Lady Archer v Williams* (2003)).

SEXUALITY

37.28   Particular leeway is increasingly given on matters of sexual morality, mainly arising out of the English decisions of Eady J. The marriage contract, despite its social and often financial significance, is not treated in the same way as other contracts (see above). Mr Justice Eady has successively regarded adultery as a private matter in *CC v AB* (2006) (where he granted an injunction sought by an adulterer against his lover's spouse), and similarly Max Mosley's paying a number of women to strike him and vice versa (above). In *P v Quigley* [see **para.30.09**], Eady J. went so far as to injunct a threatened internet novella on privacy grounds because it contained sexual fantasy content about "thinly disguised" identifiable people.

37.29   Mr Justice Eady said in *Mosley* (2008):

> "It is not for journalists to undermine human rights, or for judges to refuse to enforce them, merely on grounds of taste or moral disapproval ... The fact that a particular relationship happens to be adulterous, or that someone's tastes are unconventional or 'perverted', does not give the media carte blanche ... I am conscious that the decision in CC v AB was subjected to a number of criticisms, the more restrained of these being directed to its 'moral relativism'. This is, I believe, ... a failure to appreciate the task which judges are now required to carry out in the context of the rights-based environment introduced by the Human Rights Act ... It is not simply a matter of personal privacy versus the public interest. The modern perception is that there is a public interest in respecting personal privacy."

37.30   If that is correct—and the Court of Appeal upheld Eady J.'s decision here—then decisions which raised the hopes of tabloid journalists in the early years of the Human Rights Act 1998—the Court of Appeal's refusal, for instance, to uphold an injunction against the revelation that footballer Garry Flitcroft (*A v B Plc* (2002)), had been having affairs with two women, one a lap-dancer, or to prohibit the publication of the fact that children's presenter Jamie Theakston had been to a brothel [see **para.23.52**]—are now unreliable guides to judicial reactions in this extremely fact-sensitive area.

The upshot is the opposite of "moral relativism", on one view. 37.31 Assuming a competition of rights, a judge like Eady J. cannot simply be declining to enforce an outdated moral consensus, but he is choosing, positively, to value the secrecy of sexual autonomy above, say, the claims of the marriage bond, or above the freedom of a person whose wife has had an affair to disclose true facts about his own life.

It may be intellectually dishonest of a judge to disclaim the role of 37.32 moral arbiter in a breach of confidence action, but it is also unreasonable, in the light of s.6 of the Human Rights Act 1998, to expect him or her to do anything else. Section 6 says that it is unlawful for a court, or any other public authority, to act in a way which is incompatible with a Convention right.

The big challenge to the media is to wait in hope until sufficient 37.33 moral inter-subjectivity evolves around privacy issues to enable them to conform to the judicially accepted values. Such a shakedown is, however, some way off at present.

Clearly the kiss-and-tell culture is under serious threat, but even the 37.34 parameters of that are not sharp. In *Lord Browne of Madingley v Associated Newspapers* (2007), a good deal of information was released about a businessman's relationship after the escort boy whom he had been "keeping" told his story to the newspaper. A lie which Lord Browne told to Eady J.'s court was probably a major factor in that decision. The public interest elements relied upon, about alleged misuses of BP resources—modest use of BP computers and personnel to set up a company trading in mobile ring tones— might not be thought to amount to a "high degree of misdemeanour".

In the *John Terry* (2010) case, Tugendhat J. refused to grant an 37.35 injunction over the reporting of allegations that the England football captain had had an adulterous affair. He said:

"The fact that conduct is private and lawful is not, of itself, conclusive of the question whether or not it is in the public interest that it be discouraged. There is no suggestion that the conduct in question in the present case ought to be unlawful ... But in a plural society there will be some who would suggest that it should be discouraged. That is why sponsors may be sensitive to the public image of those sports persons whom they pay to promote their products ... Exploitation of weaker persons ... commonly occurs in private places, including within families. Those who are exploited do not always protest ..."

MEDICAL INFORMATION

37.36   Information about, including simply photographs of, the human body does seem to attract a higher order level of privacy protection. Even higher risk than publishing about another's sexuality, it is suggested, is publishing another's medical information. As well as the intimacy and physicality of medical information, there can be a wider public interest in encouraging people to be frank with their medical advisers so that people can get healthy or at least avoid passing on diseases.

37.37   Strasbourg has rated medical confidentiality as engaging the art.8 privacy right to an exceptionally high degree. In ***Plon v France (2006)***, for instance, where President Mitterand's widow and children brought an action to stop a book written by his doctor after his death called *Le Grand Secret* and describing the late President's cancer, the court held that stopping distribution of the book was initially justified, although its continued prohibition many months after the President's death, and where 40,000 copies had already been sold, was a violation of art.10.

37.38   The fact that Naomi Campbell's attendance at Narcotics Anonymous was viewed through the lens of medical treatment, rather than as an oblique admission of criminal drug-taking, was an important part of her victory over the *Mirror*.

37.39   Baroness Hale observed in the ***Naomi Campbell (2004)*** case:

> "Not every statement about a person's health will carry the badge of confidentiality ... The privacy interest in the fact that a public figure has a cold or a broken leg is unlikely to be strong enough to justify restricting the press's freedom to report it ... Sometimes there will be other justifications for publishing, especially where the information is relevant to the capacity of a public figure to do the job. But that is not this case ... People trying to recover from drug addiction need considerable dedication and commitment ... Blundering in where matters are acknowledged to be at a 'fragile' stage may do great harm."

37.40   Similarly, Lord Buxton in the Court of Appeal in the ***Loreena McKennitt (2007)*** biography case referred to:

> "[R]evelations about the state of Ms McKennitt's health, their intrusive nature being made the worse by her fragility having been associated with [her fiancé's death by drowning]. A

person's health is in any event a private matter ... It is doubly private when information about it is imparted in the context of a relationship of confidence."

The stigma attaching to AIDS was the determinant factor in Sir Mark   37.41
Potter's decision in 2005 *A Local Authority v W* **(2005)** to grant anonymity to a convicted woman and the partner she had knowingly infected with the virus, to protect her two small children. This is an extremely unusual decision, in that the open justice principle almost invariably succeeds over the privacy claims of the children of criminals [see **paras 25.23 to 25.28**]. It was based significantly on the factor that neighbours might, wrongly but damagingly, assume that the children were infected, too.

MEDICAL CONFIDENTIALITY AFTER DEATH

The Information Tribunal, south of the border, have said that medical   37.42
confidentiality survives death for the purposes of freedom of information (*Bluck v Information Commissioner* **(2007)**). The view that medical confidentiality might well survive a patient's death was taken in *Dr Nicholas Lewis v Secretary of State for Health in England* **(2008)**, though there the doctor was ordered, in the public interest, to hand over health records of deceased patients who had worked in the nuclear industry and whose tissue was now the subject of the Redfern Inquiry. The European Court of Human Rights in *Plon v France* **(2006)** [see **para.37.37**] clearly recognised that surviving relatives had a legitimate interest in trying to keep medical secrets after death. Under the Data Protection Act 1998, relatives have no right to access the medical records of the deceased, though they may sometimes be available under the Access to Health Records Act 1990. The Data Protection Act 1998 makes it void to contract to require an individual to hand over his or her health records.

The Freedom of Information (Scotland) Act 2002 specifically   37.43
exempts a deceased person's health record from the definition of information.

LIMITS TO MEDICAL CONFIDENTIALITY

Again, even medical confidentiality has its limits. In *Three Rivers &*   37.44
BCCI v Bank of England **(2005)**, Mr Quinn sought a private hearing because the information revealed would concern his medical condition. The Court of Appeal held that this was a public litigation of great importance between the Bank of England, a form of public body, and arising out of the collapse of BCCI, a matter of deep public

concern. Mr Quinn was a witness because he was a former senior officer who had been accused of dishonesty and the medical details in question were in no way embarrassing. Once again, the claims of open justice in the court setting triumphed.

37.45　　In 2006, Davis J. in England allowed the full publication of a report into Michael Stone's treatment, notwithstanding a high degree of medically confidential material. Michael Stone's conviction for murdering two members of the Russell family meant that he was responsible for making his medical background the legitimate concern of the public (***Stone v South East Coast SHA* (2007)**).

PHOTOGRAPHY AND AUDIO TAPES

37.46　　The use of photographs, visual images or audio tapes also raise special sensitivities, dealt with at **Chapter 23**. Among the four most significant breach of confidence cases so far, the Naomi Campbell ("Narcotics Anonymous") story (***Campbell v MGN Ltd* (2004)**), the Catherine Zeta-Jones and Michael Douglas wedding case (***OBG Ltd v Allan* (2007)**), J.K. Rowling's action on behalf of her son (which addresses both photography in public places and the protection to be accorded to children (***Murray v Express Newspapers* (2008)**), and the European Court of Human Rights' decision in *Von Hannover v Germany* **(2005)** concern photographs. Photographs are different in quality from the written word, as no television journalist could deny, and audio tapes may have something of the same quality.

CHILDREN

37.47　　Children receive particular protection where their private and family lives are concerned, especially, but not exclusively, in court proceedings [see **Chapter 25**]. Outside of the statutory exceptions, though, open justice is a very powerful countervailing factor against claims based on children's privacy.

37.48　　In Scotland, the parents of the children removed by the social work department from Orkney were successful in November 1992 in obtaining an interim interdict in the Court of Session against the BBC *Panorama* programme from using tapes of the disclosure sessions between the children and officials of the Royal Scottish Society for the Prevention of Cruelty to Children. The interim interdict was granted by Lord Cameron, despite the fact that the BBC had given an undertaking that the children could not be seen in the interview and their voices would be disguised.

37.49　　In *Green Corns v Claverley* **(2005)** [see **para.25.83**], Tugendhat J. granted an injunction against publication of addresses of children's home containing troubled children, some of whom were sex offenders. He said that: "The public policy in disclosing the addresses of children's homes has received statutory recognition."

The *Murray* (2008) case, involving J.K. Rowling's son, suggests   37.50
that the children of celebrities may be protected against unwelcome and identificatory photographs even of innocuous content and in a public place.

THE HOME

There is a line of cases concerning what one might call hearth and   37.51
home. In the *McKennitt* (2007) case, descriptions of the interior of Loreena McKennitt's Irish holiday cottage were considered to be particularly offensive, even though they do not appear to have been especially critical. The Court of Appeal there endorsed the trial judge's protection of:

> "[T]he traditional sanctity accorded to hearth and home ... To convey such details [as décor, layout, cleanliness et al], without permission, to the general public is almost as objectionable as spying into the home with a long distance lens and publishing the resulting photographs."

Similarly, an injunction is granted against photographs of the interior   37.52
of Victoria and David Beckham's house (*Beckham v MGN Ltd* (2001)). The same trial judge, Eady J., had said in the *Lord Browne of Madingley* (2007) case that:

> "One would expect most people from time to time to come home from work and to feel free to unburden themselves about the horrors of the day ... People feel free in the privacy of their own homes to have a moan about colleagues or employees."

Thus even business matters, where discussed in a domestic context,   37.53
may receive a greater degree of protection as being private.

In *D v L* (2003) [see **para.23.52**], where the Court of Appeal refused   37.54
an injunction to stop publication of secretly recorded tapes containing sexual information made by an estranged spouse, Waller L.J. said: "It may be less wrong for this to have been done by L in her own shared space than if she had put a listening device into what was D's space."

There does seem, therefore, to be a territorial aspect to privacy, even   37.55
though privacy claims can still be made in relation to public places.

FINANCE

In the *Naomi Campbell* (2004) case, Lady Hale referred to   37.56
"information which is obviously private, including information

about health, personal relationships or finance." The Data Protection Act 1998 does not include personal finance as "sensitive personal information." That said, though, it is likely that a court would treat personal finance as attracting some privacy protection.

37.57 As with all breach of confidence considerations, everything turns on the facts. An MP's allowances are likely to be open to scrutiny. The items on his own credit card bill are likely to be protected unless they suggest wrongdoing, or are met out of the public purse.

37.58 In *Long Beach v Global Witness Ltd* (2007), for instance, the English court refused to stop Global Witness from publishing on its website the credit card statements of the free-spending son of the President of the impoverished Republic of Congo, when they had been used in a Hong Kong court, even though the Hong Kong court had ruled that they remained confidential.

37.59 The breach of confidence cases which have involved financial details most sharply (*Northern Rock* (2007) [see **para.37.12**]; *Barclays v Guardian News and Media* (2009)) related to the activities of corporate bodies of clear public interest and had mixed results.

37.60 Thus far there have been few privacy cases turning on an individual's financial affairs. In the English case of *Crossley* (2008) [see **para.27.62**], Eady J. stated that: "[w]hile I would accept that ordinary people may expect their financial affairs to be accorded privacy", once such information had come out in court, that expectation was lost.

"SPYCATCHERS"

37.61 The *Spycatcher* (1991) litigation [see **paras 22.07 onwards**] in England and the *Cavendish* litigation in Scotland both involved the law of confidence. It is sometimes supposed by journalists that these cases are of limited relevance because they involved the use by journalists of material obtained by Peter Wright and Anthony Cavendish when both were working for the security services as spies. However, the law of confidence is not restricted to matters involving State secrets. Nor is it restricted to cases, such as *Spycatcher* and *Cavendish*, in which the duty of confidence is owed to the government.

37.62 The obligation of confidentiality may not be confined to the two parties to the confidential communication. It can extend to third parties who come into possession of inherently and clearly confidential information. As the *Cavendish* litigation made clear, the obligation will extend even to situations where the third party comes into possession of the confidential information without any positive steps on his or her part. The law of confidence will apply just as much to the journalist who receives the confidential information anonymously in a brown paper parcel as to the journalist who, in the course of an investigative piece of work, uncovers the confidential information by his or her own efforts. The law, of course, requires that there is knowledge that the material is of a confidential nature. However, it seems clear that the courts will take the view that certain material, by its very nature, must put the recipient on guard that it is confidential. If it is obvious that the material is of a confidential nature, then the journalist takes a risk in publishing without making further inquiries [see **Chapter 38**].

VULNERABLE ADULTS

Some English cases concern the rights of vulnerable adults. As with   37.63
children, they too have positive rights under art.8. In 2003, in *A Local Authority and a Health Authority v A* **(2004)**, Dame Butler-Sloss refused to allow publication of part of a local authority inquiry report into a home looking after vulnerable adults, on the grounds that the media interest would be detrimental to them. In *E v Channel Four* **(2005)**, Munby J. refused the Official Solicitor's attempt to ban a documentary concerning a vulnerable adult diagnosed with a dissociative identity disorder, Pamela Edwards, when the adult herself wished the programme to be broadcast. A different view was taken by Eady J. in *T v BBC* **(2008)**, where he granted an injunction against the identification of a vulnerable adult, forced to give up her child for adoption. She had an IQ of 63 and was regarded by the judge as incapable of giving consent.

All investigative journalists will be familiar with the person who   37.64
threatens self-harm or suicide if the article is published or the programme broadcast. There have been two cases in Scotland so far where the BBC has had written consents, in one case from a 17-year-old self-harmer (*X v BBC* **(2005)**) and in the other from a 14-year-old criminal detained in an educational establishment (his mother's consent in writing had also been obtained), who had changed their minds about being included in documentaries in which the teenagers had extensively participated. In both cases, the pursuers obtained legal aid. As a result, some thoughtful broadcasters are veering away from consent-led documentaries, particularly in enclosed institutions, where participant stories will tend to become intertwined.

INTERACTION OF DEFAMATION AND PRIVACY CLAIMS

It should be noted that one can sue both in defamation and for   37.65
invasion of privacy. It is also not unknown, at least in England, for claimants to make "false privacy" claims, refusing to state whether

or not a defamatory allegation is true, on the basis that, even if it is, it is no business of the press. Most such claims relate to adulterous affairs or the like.

ULTIMATE BALANCING TEST?

37.66 What happens, essentially, in the standard breach of confidence (misuse of private information) action is a four stage process. In the unanimous House of Lords decision in *Re S* **(2004)** [see **para.25.23**], Lord Steyn said:

> "First, neither [the art.8 privacy right nor the art.10 freedom of expression right] has *as such* precedence over the other. Secondly, where the values under the two Articles are in conflict, an intense focus on the comparative importance of the specific rights being claimed in the individual case is necessary. Thirdly, the justifications for interfering with or restricting each right must be taken into account. Finally, the proportionality test must be applied to each. For convenience, I will call this the ultimate balancing test."

37.67 The privacy claimant has to establish first that he or she has a reasonable expectation of privacy. That, it is becoming clear, is quite a low threshold. Sometimes the information will be held to be obviously private, like a personal diary. Where there is no pre-existing confidential relationship between the people involved, the primary focus is on the nature of the information. Where the parties have been friends, spouses, employee and employer or the like, trivial information may still be held to be private.

ARTICLE 8 CLAIMS IN FAVOUR OF
FREEDOM OF EXPRESSION

37.68 Most privacy-based actions against the media boil down to a clash between the art.8 privacy rights of one side and the art.10 freedom of expression rights of the other, resolved by the degree of perceived intrusion, the legitimacy of the public interest and all the circumstances of the individual case. However, it is perfectly coherent to argue that one has rights under art.8 and art.10. In the *E v Channel Four* (2005) case about the woman with dissociative identity disorder, for instance, the judge said that both her art.8 right to tell her story and the art.10 right to freedom of expression supported the broadcast of the documentary. Some cases involve the balancing of the art.8 rights of different parties, e.g. *Southend on Sea Borough Council v RS-H* **(2008)**, where the court decided to name names about inadequate service from a DNA testing company, on the basis that the art.8 rights of anyone who had used the company trumped the art.8 rights of its director.

FREED CRIMINALS

Mary Bell, who killed two children in Newcastle in 1968 when she was 11, and her daughter were given lifetime injunctions protecting their anonymity in 2003, the mother having been given a new identity (*X v SO* (2003). Mary Bell's new grandchild's identity has also been protected since the baby's birth in 2009. In 2001, Robert Thompson and Jonathan Venables, the two boys who, at 10, killed toddler James Bulger, were given new identities on their release from prison (*Venables v News Group Newspapers Ltd* (2001)). Maxine Carr, the then girlfriend of child murderer Ian Huntley and who assisted in covering up his crimes and was sentenced to three and a half years, obtained another such injunction *Carr v News Group Newspapers Ltd* (2005). In June 2004, Lord Menzies granted an interim interdict banning Scottish media outlets from revealing her new identity or location. An injunction was granted in *Re KT* (2004) in England to protect a young adult who, in his teens, had been accused, but not convicted, of sexual offences. Lisa Healey, who at 15 murdered pensioner Lily Lilley, has also received a new identity, initially in December 2009 to protect the child whom she conceived on day release from prison, but now it is proposed to extend it directly to her. 37.69

The recall of Jonathan Venables to prison for child pornography offences reignited the commentary on whether the young man should still have his new identity protected. In July 2010, an application for interdict to extend the effect of the injunction protecting his anonymity was dropped in Scotland following the giving of undertakings not to publish by many of the Scottish media. A reluctance to name new child offenders is evident [see **para.25.12**]; the complications naming creates for rehabilitation attempts may be driving this. 37.70

In 2001, granting the Thompson and Venables injunctions, Dame Elizabeth Butler-Sloss emphasised that "the claimants are uniquely notorious ... Their case is exceptional." The word "exceptional" recurs in her judgment. The trajectory, in less than a decade, however, has seen similar protection extended from two child murderers who killed at 10, to one woman who at 11 was convicted of manslaughter, to a woman who, as an adult, was convicted of deception, to a young man who had not been convicted of any offence. In sufficiently emotive cases, the exception may be becoming the rule. 37.71

37.72   Incarcerated criminals are obviously in a very different position. The Yorkshire Ripper was refused anonymity in 2010 on his application to court for a ruling on how much longer he must serve before being eligible for parole.

ARTICLE 2 AND ARTICLE 3 RIGHT TO LIFE AND PROTECTION FROM TORTURE, ETC.

37.73   The Thompson and Venables anonymity cases touch on the art.2 right to life and the art.3 right of criminals to be protected from inhuman or degrading punishment or torture. Right to life arguments for anonymity can come from the other side of the law as well. In ***R. v Her Majesty's Coroner for Inner South London* (2004)**, two police officers successfully sought anonymity (under s.11 of the Contempt of Court Act 1981), claiming to fear for their own safety as regards giving evidence in the inquest into Derek Bennett's death. Both of the officers had been present at the shooting and one of them had fired the fatal bullet.

37.74   The House of Lords looked at the art.2 right of police witnesses to the Hamill Inquiry (***Re Officer L* (2007)**), accepting in principle that preventing loss of life could justify granting anonymity to witnesses. In ***Times Newspapers v R* (2008)**, the Courts Martial Appeal Court upheld anonymity orders under s.11 of the Contempt of Court Act 1981 protecting soldiers charged with conspiracy to defraud, on the basis of risk to their lives. (Anonymity had been given on similar art.2 grounds to former soldiers suspected of having fired the Bloody Sunday shots, in their evidence to the Saville Inquiry in 1999.) The successor to the House of Lords, the Supreme Court, said in ***Guardian News and Media* (2010)**, although refusing anonymity to suspected potential terrorists and strongly censuring attacks on open justice: "In an appropriate case, where threats to life or safety are involved, the right of the press to freedom of expression obviously has to yield".

37.75   Section 90 of the Criminal Justice and Licensing (Scotland) Act 2010 provides for the granting of witness anonymity orders in specified cases.

37.76   Between the courts claiming inherent jurisdiction to protect the administration of justice and the Human Rights Act 1998's focus on privacy as well as the right to life, the power to anonymise witnesses can look shapelessly discretionary, even where no specific statutory power exists—and, as the House of Lords pointed out in ***Re S* (2004)** [see **para.37.66**], many such statutory powers do exist. However, appellate courts have clear concerns about the risks of anonymisation to open justice in all but the most compelling cases. In criminal trials, in particular, anonymisation of the accused looks extremely unlikely in most cases.

Occasionally, too, this emphasis on the right to life can be of 37.77 advantage to the journalist. The Recorder of Belfast refused to order investigative journalist Suzanne Breen to hand over her notes about the Real IRA to the police in 2009, mainly on the grounds that it endangered her and her family's lives. In 2006, however, investigative journalist Mazher Mahmood [see **para.23.58**] unsuccessfully argued for an injunction against publication of his photograph on the website of the political party, Respect, arguing that this would put his life in danger. The judge was sceptical, saying, "[f]or photographs of Mr Mahmood to be of any use [to potential assailants] they would have to have a whole package of further information ... as to his whereabouts and habits", and anyone who had that, would be able to find out what he looked like.

Considerations about the art.2 right to life and the art.3 right to be 37.78 protected from inhuman or degrading punishment or torture may also be relevant when it comes to s.12(3) of the Human Rights Act 1998, because such considerations may be particularly apt to persuade a court to accept a weaker threshold for "likely" under s.12.

PUBLIC DOMAIN

Traditionally, breach of confidence cases fail where the information 37.79 sought to be protected is in the public domain. Section 12(4) of the Human Rights Act 1998 requires a court considering whether, e.g. to grant an interdict against publication, to consider "the extent to which the material is or is about to become more available to the public ...". A year after the *Naomi Campbell* case, Eady J. refused to grant an injunction against possible disclosures of drug taking and treatment to the media by an estranged wife, where the husband had already discussed his drug problems in the media in the past (*A v B* (2005)).

It matters how much is in the public domain. That defence is less 37.80 clear-cut now than it was when the European Court of Human Rights was deciding that it had been a violation of freedom of expression to ban the publication of *Spycatcher* in the UK once it was readily available in the rest of the world. In the matter of *X & Y (Children), F v Newsquest Ltd* (2004) [see **para.25.31**], where an injunction was sought to protect two handicapped and motherless children from the consequences of a sex offences trial against their father's identical twin brother, the English judge, Munby J. said: "With the advent of the internet, and in a world where there is an almost infinite quantity of accessible information, it is impossible to see the public domain as something which has clear boundaries." He also took the view that, even where some information was in the public domain, re-publication of it could cause an unacceptable intrusion into the private lives of the children.

37.81   In *Northern Rock Plc v FT Ltd* **(2007)** [see **para.37.12**], an injunction against repetition of information from a briefing memorandum concerning Northern Rock's difficulties was refused so far as it had appeared in the *Daily Telegraph*, the BBC, the *Evening Standard* and in the website of Reuters and the *Guardian*, but granted in relation to detailed financial calculations which had appeared only on the *FT.com* website. Favouring "a qualitative and not just a quantitative assessment" of the public domain, Tugendhat J. said that:

> "The FT.com website, while available to anyone, is unlikely to have a readership of anything like the same magnitude ... And none of the other media have published the full and detailed figures contained on the pages published on FT.com."

37.82   In *Barclays Bank v Guardian News and Media* **(2009)** [see **para.37.12**], where documents about tax avoidance had been on the "very widely used" *Guardian* website, but only for a brief period, Blake J. thought the bank could realistically argue that the material was still confidential. Both of these cases relate to the sort of commercial confidentiality which pre-dated the Human Rights Act 1998 by centuries and has comparatively little to do with privacy.

37.83   The re-publication of material like intimate photographs [see **paras 23.52 to 23.53**] is not so readily defended by using public domain arguments. Ultimately, though, there does come a degree of exposure at which the courts will refuse to ban re-publication. The law does not like to make itself an ass. In the Alfie Patten case (*Re Stedman* **(2009)**) [see **para.23.67**], where a 12-year-old said to have fathered a child was ultimately found out not to have done so, King J., whilst clearly appalled at the media circus instigated by the putative grandparents, declined to ban re-publication of the known facts and photographs on the basis that, "the dam ... has indeed burst". This does not, of course, mean that re-publication would not result in a fresh action for damages.

COMPANIES

37.84   Improbable as it may seem, companies have been held to have a right to privacy. In *R. v BSC Ex p. BBC* **(2000)**, the Court of Appeal upheld a decision by the Broadcasting Standards Commission (a predecessor of Ofcom) that secret filming by the BBC had infringed the privacy of electrical store Dixons. Partly this decision turned on the deference the courts pay to regulatory bodies. Lord Mustill observed:

"Can a company say that it is aggrieved by an invasion of its own privacy? As a matter of ordinary language, I would not have thought so. The context ... is, however, special ... [In] general I find the concept of a company's privacy hard to grasp".

Lady Justice Hale expressed similar reservations, but the BBC was 37.85 refused leave to appeal by the House of Lords.

Whether "privacy" is a word aptly used or not, a company can 37.86 certainly claim that some of its information is confidential and it frequently does. In *Response Handling Ltd v BBC* **(2008)** [see **para.37.15**], a call centre company attempted to stop broadcast of a BBC Scotland documentary about credit card fraud, containing footage, filmed undercover in the call centre, alleging flaws in the security system. The undercover journalist had a confidentiality clause in her employment contract with the call centre company. The call centre company did not argue about art.8 privacy rights. Instead, it argued that confidential information was its intellectual property under art.1 of the First Protocol to the European Convention on Human Rights. The BBC won the case. Lord Bracadale considered that the public interest in the security of call centres was very high and the material sought to be protected as confidential "not highly sensitive".

Sometimes, a company is better advised to keep privacy (as opposed 37.87 to commercial confidentiality) arguments out of it. *BKM Ltd v BBC* **(2009)** concerned another BBC documentary with undercover filming, this time in a care home in Wales. Mr Justice Mann said that it was "not wholly satisfactory" for BKM to argue that it was entitled to argue for the protection of the privacy rights of the care home residents whose identities were being concealed by the BBC:

"BKM is (understandably) sensitive to its own reputational position ... Its commercial interests lie in playing down the allegations, not having them broadcast ... I think that this might explain why a lot of the emphasis ... was to prevent the broadcast of the programme at all, as opposed to a broadcast which did not render residents identifiable ..."

Again, the BBC was allowed to broadcast the documentary.

BREACH OF CONFIDENCE AND COPYRIGHT CLAIMS

An action for breach of confidence is sometimes made as an 37.88 alternative to breach of copyright. For example, if an unsolicited script treatment or manuscript is sent to a publisher or broadcaster which rejects it, and a book or programme of considerable similarity later appears from that stable, the writer may argue that it was a breach of confidence to "steal" the idea. The writer would require to prove that the script was confidential; that the idea was developed to an extent that showed it was not common knowledge or unoriginal; and that unauthorised use was made of it. Because copyright does not protect ideas—only their expression—a breach of confidence action might succeed where a copyright action would fail.

37.89   Sometimes the reverse is true: the Court of Appeal decided the Paddy Ashdown (2001) case in his favour, which concerned the *Telegraph's* publication of his leaked minute about Labour/Liberal Democrat coalition plans, on copyright grounds, whilst suggesting that the newspaper might have had a defence to a breach of confidence argument [see **para.36.10**].

37.90   The Prince of Wales successfully sued for both breach of confidence and infringement of copyright in relation to his leaked, handwritten travel journals [see **para.36.10**].

REMEDIES

DAMAGES

37.91   There is limited Scottish authority on damages for non-commercial breach of confidence. The major recent cases (e.g. *X v BBC* **(2005)** [see **para.36.31**]) have been about interim interdict—stopping the publication in the first place. In England, though, such damages seem to be creeping upward, with Max Mosley receiving £60,000 and then raising a defamation action, seeking further damages.

ACCOUNT OF PROFITS

37.92   The English courts have allowed an "account of profits" in breach of confidence cases on a discretionary basis, i.e. required the breaker of the confidence to pay the profit made by leaking the information instead of damages. This may also be possible in Scotland where the claim involves a breach of copyright or of a fiduciary duty, but it is not clear how a Scottish court would react to such a claim in an action, e.g. involving a paparazzi photograph, which was held to invade the subject's privacy right.

INTERDICT

37.93   In defamation, courts were always likely to permit publication on the premise that success and damages restore reputation. In cases involving confidential information, however, the mere fact of publication can mean that the information loses its confidential quality. It might be felt that it is more invidious to ban publication of something that is admittedly true than something which is said to be false, but the courts have typically been quicker to grant interim interdict on confidentiality grounds than in defamation.

Actions seeking interdict for anticipated breach of confidence 37.94 against the media will now normally fall under s.12 of the Human Rights Act 1998 (see above).

Journalists are only too aware of the fact that, although an interim 37.95 interdict can be overturned once the court has heard all the evidence, the newsworthiness of the material is unlikely to endure until the court hears the evidence, often a year or two later. So victory at the interim stage is vital for the media.

CODES

The Human Rights Act 1998 attaches significance to codes such as the 37.96 Press Complaints Commission and Ofcom produce. In some cases, these guidelines (e.g. the BBC's Editorial Guidelines) may be a good deal more restrictive than the law would require, and failure to follow them will be a factor weighing against the journalist before the court in resisting an interdict against a broadcast or article. It should also be remembered that the Human Rights Act 1998 does not exist in isolation from other important contemporary legislation on access to personal information—notably the Data Protection Act 1998 [see **Chapter 10**] and the Protection from Harassment Act 1997 [see **paras 41.06 and 41.07**].

A real concern about the developing privacy law is that it will choke 37.97 off investigation and evidence-gathering for journalistic purposes, e.g. undercover filming. The right to publish or broadcast is, however, strengthened because of the emphasis in the Strasbourg jurisprudence on freedom of expression.

KEY POINTS

1. Within the UK, most privacy claims are made by an action for 37.98 breach of confidence, though claims may also be made under, for instance, the Data Protection Act 1998 and the Protection from Harassment Act 1997. Actions for breach of confidence against the media are now quite often described as actions for "misuse of private information."

2. Medical and sexual information, private diaries, detailed information about family or home life, photographs of weddings and funerals and coverage of children attract

particular scrutiny from the courts. Some additional protection is also given to vulnerable adults. The existence of a contractual obligation can bolster a privacy claim.

3. The public interest is always a defence to an action for breach of confidence. However, the courts make a rigid distinction between what is in the public interest and that which is merely of interest to the public. The courts are involved in weighing up competing values of privacy and freedom of expression, and sometimes also other human rights. The existence of a legitimate public interest in some information will not necessarily be strong enough to trump public interest in, for instance, contract keeping, the protection of children or the social benefits of keeping medical records secret.

4. Neither the fact that someone is a public figure, nor that certain behaviour took place in public, automatically means that there is no privacy right in play.

5. Privacy cases depend very much on their individual facts and the subjective response of the judge, making it difficult to predict the outcome.

6. The law of breach of confidence has been used to protect the identities of released criminals and their children.

7. Where information—even photographs or footage—is very much in the public domain, courts may be reluctant to grant orders preventing its re-publication on privacy grounds, even if the matters are highly private.

8. Some information can be in the public domain, but there may still be private information which the courts will deem worthy of protection. Where detailed financial information has appeared on one website, for instance, the court may still make an order against its wider repetition. Where general information has appeared in a national newspaper, the court may still make an order against the release of detailed information.

9. As well as interim interdict to stop the publication before it happens, people raising a privacy action may seek damages or an account of profits.

PART 11: THE JOURNALIST AND THE STATE: POLITICS, TERRORISM AND OFFICIAL SECRETS

CHAPTER 38

OFFICIAL SECRETS

By LAURA C R MACPHEE

Inherent in the very nature of secrets is the desire of outsiders to 38.01 discover and relay the sacred information. Indeed, the investigative journalist is often, appropriately, congratulated for the successful achievement of this aim. However, she must beware the specific category covered by the Official Secrets Acts.

OFFICIAL SECRETS ACT 1911

Section 1 of the 1911 Act disallows presence in or around a prohibited 38.02 place for any purpose prejudicial to the interests of the State (Official Secrets Act 1911 s.1). What, one might ask, constitutes a prohibited place in this context? The list includes aircraft and ships; naval and air force establishments; factories; dockyards; camps; arsenals; British Nuclear Fuels Plc and Atomic Energy Authority sites; signals stations occupied by on or behalf of Her Majesty. Also covered by this section are places where munitions or documents relating thereto are kept by the Crown. Other specific places may be declared to be "prohibited places" if information relating to them is judged potentially helpful to an enemy. If it can be shown that a journalist's purpose was prejudicial to the interests of the State, in the light of his conduct or the circumstances, he may be convicted. The prosecution does not require to prove this purpose.

Furthermore, the 1911 Act prohibits the making of models, 38.03 sketches, notes or photographs which could be of use to an enemy. All the stages of obtaining, communicating or publishing such information also amount to offences in themselves. Generally, in such a situation, it will be presumed that the journalist was acting for

403

a purpose prejudicial to the safety of the State, unless the alternative is specifically evidenced (Official Secrets Act 1911 s.1).

OFFICIAL SECRETS ACT 1989

38.04 The Official Secrets Act 1989 protects against disclosure of material in several classes:

- security and intelligence;
- international relations;
- crime (this covers disclosures which does, or is likely to, lead to the commission of a crime, facilitate an escape from custody or thwart the process of discovering or intercepting offences);
- defence (details such as policy and strategy, as well as the organisation, size, deployment and training of the armed forces);
- material which has been imparted in confidence to international organisations or other States; and
- special powers of investigation (relating to the interception of communications such as letters including State telephone-tapping). Anyone who contravenes this measure and deliberately discloses the protected information risks the maximum penalty—two years' imprisonment.

38.05 Journalists are included within the scope of this Act, although admittedly it was predominantly directed towards representatives of the intelligence and security services, government contractors and civil servants. If a journalist were to divulge information pertaining to the sensitive areas of defence, security, intelligence and international relations, then it would be for the prosecution to demonstrate that the journalist was aware, or had "reasonable cause to believe" that this disclosure would be "damaging" (if, for example, it jeopardised the United Kingdom's interests overseas), and that it in fact was.

38.06 The case is slightly different where the information related to the categories of crime or special investigation powers. In this situation damage is assumed, so there is no onus on the prosecution to evidence this, or the level of knowledge possessed by the journalist.

38.07 Public interest does *not* serve as a defence under the 1989 Act, as confirmed by the House of Lords in *R. v Shayler* (2002), which also held that the absence of a public interest defence in those circumstances did not violate art.10 freedom of expression. In practice, the existence of a public interest, or even the legitimate perception of a public interest, will be of considerable importance.

The prosecution of civil servant Derek Pasquill who leaked documents about dealings with Islamic extremists to the *Observer* was dropped, apparently on the evidence that other officials did not believe that the leaks had threatened national security and were against the prosecution. Nor is prior publication a defence per se. However, the latter would have a high chance of success if presented in the European Court of Human Rights, as demonstrated by the *Spycatcher* case. Prior publication may also be beneficial to the journalist, since this is an indicator that further publication could not result in any more damage. In 2007, the Parliamentary Assembly of the Council of Europe passed Resolution 1551 stating:

> "Information that is already in the public domain cannot be considered as a state secret and divulging such information cannot be punished as espionage, even if the person concerned collects, sums up, analyses or comments on such information."

OFFICIAL SECRETS ACTS 1920 AND 1939

There are circumstances in which a police inspector has the capacity to require a person to provide information concerning an offence or suspected offence under the Official Secrets Acts. Failure to provide such information would in itself constitute an offence, as would consciously providing false information. However, this will be academic unless the officer has the authority of the chief officer of police. Unless it is an emergency, the Secretary of State must also have given express permission for this. 38.08

INCURSIONS INTO OPEN JUSTICE

Article 6 of the European Convention specifically provides an exemption from the right to public trial in the interests of national security. 38.09

Section 8 of the Official Secrets Act 1920 gives the power to exclude the public from proceedings under the Official Secrets Acts on the basis that, if the evidence were to be published, it would pose a risk to national safety. The Investigatory Powers Tribunal (IPT), which hears a number of sensitive cases involving the intelligence service, sits in private: see *R. v B* (2009), where the Supreme Court held that the IPT had exclusive and final jurisdiction over whether a former member of the security service should be allowed to publish a book about his work there, largely on the basis that the hearings would be secret. 38.10

Before we embark upon a tour through the specifics of the relevant case law, and what this means for journalists, it would be helpful to 38.11

consider the social and political context in which these rules operate. Since 9/11 there has been an increase in government control and very liberal measures have been adopted. This has inevitably led to a relaxation in the law of contempt of court. However, it is important to remember that this represents a significant *cultural* change as opposed to a legal one.

THE ZIRCON CASE

38.12   The Zircon (***BBC v Jessop* (1987)**) affair which sparked such political controversy during 1987 demonstrated the bite retained by s.9 of the 1911 Act in the field of investigative journalism. This provision allows the wide use of searches in circumstances where there is, "reasonable ground that an offence ... has been or is about to be committed". The scope of this section is rendered so extensive by its stipulation that, "*any* constable may enter at *any* time *any* premises or place named in the warrant" (emphasis added), as the BBC were to discover.

38.13   The incident consisted of a weekend raid which was mounted on the corporation's Glasgow offices. The detectives were in possession of a warrant. This allowed them to search the offices and confiscate material pertaining to a planned programme concerning the Zircon satellite (which was used to garner intelligence). The intention was that this should form part of BBC Scotland's six-part documentary series, *Secret Society*, presented by the journalist Duncan Campbell, which suggested that the £300 million cost of the satellite had been contested by the Public Accounts Committee.

38.14   A particularly contentious point of note was that the critical warrant was granted by a sheriff as opposed to a magistrate. Provision for this is explicitly made in the Broadcasting Act 1990, which clarifies that this is not the exclusive domain of the magistrates. It is within the sheriff's ambit to issue warrants which authorise the removal of film and other relevant articles from a body responsible for broadcasting such material.

THE DA-NOTICE SYSTEM

38.15   One cannot consider fully the issues posed by the protection of official secrets without addressing the DA-Notices System (comprising Defence Advisory Notices), which has been in existence since 1912. The Defence, Press and Broadcasting Advisory Committee (composed of representatives from the fields of media and civil service) governs the administration of this system.

38.16   This is a protocol and as such is not *legally* binding, but it still retains its significance as an important form of self-regulation by the press. The system is effectively a code which is entered voluntarily by members of the British media which advises on the broadcasting or publication of information relating to national security. These were known as D-Notices until 1993. As of May 2000 there are five standing DA-Notices, covering: "military operations, plans and capabilities"; "nuclear and non-nuclear weapons and equipment"; "ciphers and secure communications"; "sensitive installations and home addresses"; and "United Kingdom Security and Intelligence Services and Special Services".

These five have been reached as a result of diligent examination and revision throughout the years since 1982. That year saw the removal of four subjects from the system's scope: prisoners of war and evaders; aircraft and aero-engines; Royal Navy warship construction and equipment; and the whereabouts of Vladimir Petrov (the former KGB chief in Canberra) and his wife, who had defected to Australia in 1954.   38.17

The 1982 version expressly incorporated terrorism into its list, and contained within the introduction is the caution that, "dissemination of sensitive information ... can also be of value to terrorist groups who lack the resources to obtain it through their own efforts".   38.18

Concerns were raised in 1988 by members of the media who held positions on the Defence, Press and Broadcasting Committee. The government had, on a number of occasions, pursued legal action against the press despite the fact that the offending information had been presented to the D-Notice Committee's secretary, who had opted to take no further action. In response to this apprehension, the government reasserted its commitment to the system. Furthermore, the chairman stated that the D-Notice Committee did not have jurisdiction on these issues, which related to breaches of the duty of confidentiality which members (and former members) of the intelligence and security services owe to the Crown.   38.19

In this historical progression, we are now entering the realm of the First Gulf War. During the December of 1990, a D-Notice was issued entreating the media not to publish information relating to the theft of a laptop and classified documents from an RAF officer's car. Following a widespread search, the computer was returned to the Ministry of Defence in January 1991.   38.20

In the October of the subsequent year, the Defence, Press and Broadcasting Committee called for an extensive review of the system, allegedly driven by a combination of the end of the Cold War and John Major's aspiration for increased government openness. In July 1993, the contemporaneous update of the system was completed and the six standing DA-Notices were published, which number was reduced to five in May 2000.   38.21

38.22   Now that we have covered the background to this area, how does the system actually work? The committee deliberates over cases presented to it by service departments, who divulge their opinions on whether or not the material ought to be published. The DA-Notices convey which information is not suitable for publication, and are distributed to the implicated sections of the media. The committee's secretary is responsible for the resolution of any queries as to how the notices are to be applied or interpreted.

38.23   Until recently there had been little complaint about the functioning of the system, which is deemed to have been generally successful. However, mention must be made of the "D-Notice Affair" which took place during 1967. This controversy stemmed from the *Daily Express'* revelation that the security authorities had regular access to and opportunity to scrutinize cables sent out from Britain. The government's argument was that this breached D-Notices, but the *Express* unsurprisingly contested this. The *Express'* view was upheld by a committee of inquiry, but this was "rejected" by the government.

38.24   Forty years later, representatives of Eton College were censured for publishing a photograph of the head of the SAS in his uniform on their website. The committee's secretary informed the school that the photograph was to be removed at once. Its publication was in breach of two DA-Notices prohibiting the identification of anyone working for the SAS. This notice also applies to those who are no longer serving, and the school's action constituted a very serious breach.

38.25   The next year, 2008, saw further controversy surrounding the DA-Notice System, as Rear-Admiral Nick Wilkinson tried to publish the entirety of his work, *Secrecy and the Media*. Wilkinson had been Secretary of the DA-Notice Committee between 1999 and 2004, and the book was intended to be a history of the committee. Ironically, a DA-Notice was placed on this by current secretary Air Vice-Marshall Andrew Vallance. The Ministry of Defence requested that the book should end at 1991, however a compromise was reached and it now extends to 1997, thanks to the intervention of Cambridge historian Christopher Andrew. The committee's secretary said that he wanted the book withdrawn for "reasons of style and structure". However the Ministry of Defence seem generally to wish to prevent insiders from discussing its relations with the media during recent years.

38.26   Importantly, also in 2008, the system came under criticism from the Intelligence and Security Committee, which asserted in its last general report that the DA-Notice System was not working "as effectively as it might" and this was "putting lives at risk." This condemnation was expressed in response to the leak of information concerning the imminent arrests of terrorist suspects in Birmingham, in the "Gamble" operation. The aim of this was to counter a plot to kidnap and murder a British serviceman during 2007. It has been suggested that an extension of the DA-Notice System may be required, although at present no such action has been taken. The DA-Notice website is at *http://www.dnotice.org.uk* [Accessed September 24, 2010].

SPYCATCHER

The biggest cases in this field involving the media have not involved 38.27 prosecutions under the Official Secrets Acts, but rather civil actions for breach of confidence [see **Chapter 37**] concerning memoirs of former intelligence officers. Undoubtedly, the most famous case concerned the British Government's 1987 bid to stop the publication of excerpts from Peter Wright's book *Spycatcher*. This was an extremely large scale endeavour—spanning jurisdictions including Hong Kong and New South Wales. Wright had formerly been an MI5 officer, so when he produced this work during his retirement (in Australia) he breached his lifelong obligation of confidentiality to the government.

Throughout the judicial proceedings in England, the book, which 38.28 was being published in the United States, was entering Britain unimpeded. Injunctions made in the English courts did not hold in Scotland, as editors north of the border were well aware. Accordingly, some published reports of the Sydney proceedings and passages lifted from the infamous book.

The ban on the book, upheld by the decision in the House of Lords, 38.29 was considered to be in the interests of national security, in the light of Mr Wright's forthcoming trial. It was also necessary to dissuade other secret service officers from breaching *their* duty of confidentiality. No action was taken in the Scottish courts against any publication which breached the House of Lords' prohibition, despite the Lord Advocate's threat.

That demonstrates most profitably the independence of the Scottish 38.30 legal system and what that means for Scottish editors, but what, one might reasonably ask, was the eventual outcome of the *Spycatcher* case itself? On the basis that there had been very extensive prior publication in other jurisdictions, notably the United States, the United Kingdom's national security would *not* be threatened by further publication, and as such the injunctions governing such publication were lifted.

This issue was raised once more in the European Court of Human 38.31 Rights, which came to the conclusion that the Crown had infringed art.10 (freedom of expression) of the European Convention on Human Rights when it had prohibited the publication of information from *Spycatcher* during the period between July 1987 and October 1988. The question which the European Court was asking themselves was: "Is a ban necessary in a democratic society?" The answer to this was essentially "no". The relevant confidentiality had already been lost when the book was published in its entirety in other countries. Nonetheless, the government were *not* deemed to have breached art.10 in 1986, when it gained the original injunctions, since the information had not yet been disclosed in America

JAMES STEEN AND DAVID SHAYLER

38.32   We now have a more modern example of a similarly styled dilemma posed for journalists by the protection of official secrets. A highly significant judgment was handed down by the House of Lords in the case of *Att Gen v Punch & James Steen* (2002). In this decision, James Steen, the editor of *Punch* magazine, was found to be in contempt of court. He was found to have breached a non-disclosure order against ex-security services officer David Shayler in publishing an article he had written on the Bishopgate bombing. This was published during the course of a trial against Mr Shayler, the intention of which was to determine which material ought to remain confidential.

38.33   Several points were raised here, awareness of which is essential for the prudent journalist. Chief amongst these is that whilst Steen had no *intention* of damaging national security, in cases such as this the court will treat the journalist as having known that he was undermining the court's order. Accordingly, it would be advisable to become aware of the terms of any orders preventing potential authors from publishing certain information. Mr Steen himself had done this, and had acquired copies of the relevant injunctions from the Treasury Solicitor. His publication in spite of this was contempt.

38.34   It is important to understand the court's rationale. The injunction was intended "to serve the interests of the administration of justice by preserving the confidentiality of the information until trial". Naturally, through this publication, the confidentiality was irredeemably lost. A short-term injunction prior to a trial might be required in order to protect national security. If this is to be effective, then it is essential that this should be respected not only by parties to the proceedings, but also by third parties. Journalists will be in contempt of court if they prevent the court from achieving its purpose.

38.35   It was held in the case of *Times Newspapers Ltd v R* (2007) that restriction on publication is justified where the restriction is necessary to protect the *overall* object of proceedings, and official secrets was cited as an apt example of such an object. The overall object dealt with in the case of *Steen* was the protection of official secrets through the preservation of confidentiality.

However, there is still hope for a third party whose work has been 38.36
impacted upon as a result of such an order. She may apply to the court
for the order to be varied. Moreover, there will be no contempt unless
the act had some "significant and adverse affect on the administration
of justice" throughout the legal proceedings.

There were other consequences for journalists of the David Shayler 38.37
affair, even though no journalist was prosecuted under the Official
Secrets Acts. In *R. v Central Criminal Court Ex p. Bright, Alton and
Rusbridger* **(2001)**, the *Guardian* and *Observer* successfully appealed
blanket orders for the production of documents relating to the
publication of a letter by him in the *Guardian* and an article in the
Observer. The Court of Appeal observed that inconvenient or
embarrassing revelations about the security services should not be
suppressed.

INSIDE INTELLIGENCE

Continuing our theme of *Spycatcher* style litigation, let us examine the 38.38
closest example offered by Scots law—*Lord Advocate v The Scotsman
Publications Ltd* **(1989)**, which is often referred to as the *Inside
Intelligence* case. This was the title written by Anthony Cavendish,
formerly of MI6. The Lord Advocate sought, by means of an
interdict, to ban its publication. An injunction was granted in the
English courts after the *Sunday Times* published passages taken from
the book. This was prior to the Scottish litigation.

Once again, the House of Lords did eventually decide that 38.39
publication was to be permitted on the basis that it was conceded that
the contents of the book were not themselves damaging to national
security; that there had been limited publication already (a few
hundred copies); and that the newspapers involved had not in any
way encouraged Mr Cavendish to breach his obligations.

In situations where the contents of the book threatened national 38.40
security, or there had been *no* prior publication, it logically follows
that the Crown's chances of success would be very much improved.
The Official Secrets Act 1989 further outlines the types of case where
publication is impermissible.

Another issue which has been raised by the *Inside Intelligence* case 38.41
was the potential ambit of the interdict. The Scottish courts are
unwilling to grant an interdict effective against the "world in
general". On the other hand, it is unclear whether a third party who
disclosed information affected by a court order which prohibited
publication would be in contempt of court. The English *Spycatcher*
decision in the House of Lords suggests that they might well be.

ENGLISH INJUNCTIONS AND SCOTTISH INTERDICTS

38.42 That English injunctions are impotent in the Scottish courts has continued to be reaffirmed, such as in the case of the *Herald's* publication in 1986 of the pertinent information contained within a confidential dispatch to Saudi Arabia from Her Majesty's Ambassador. The English courts issued an injunction to prevent the *New Statesman* from publishing the report. Although the *Herald's* editor was aware that this injunction had been granted, it was assumed that this would be ineffective in Scotland. The Crown sought an interim interdict against the *Herald,* however this proved to be too little too late. By the time Lord Davidson had granted such an interdict the newspaper containing the entirety of the report had been published and distributed.

38.43 Moreover, details of Mr Paddy Ashdown's extra-marital affair in 1992 were published by the *Scotsman* despite an injunction banning such publication having been granted by the English courts. The English injunction even went so far as to prohibit any acknowledgment that it had ever been granted. It seems irrefutable that injunctions granted in England will not be applicable within the Scottish legal system, and as such will not serve their purpose of preventing the information from being published. Of course, though, some Scottish media outlets are vulnerable to the English courts' jurisdiction, since many media outlets operate across the border.

ATTORNEY GENERAL v BLAKE (2001)

38.44 The House of Lords allowed an order stripping George Blake—a convicted spy who was sentenced to 42 years in prison, before escaping to Moscow—of the anticipated profits of his autobiography, *No Other Choice.* They did so on the basis of his breach of his contractual obligation of lifelong silence, even though the book's content contained nothing which was still confidential. They stressed this was exceptional and driven by public policy. Blake's application to Strasbourg on freedom of expression grounds was declared inadmissible in 2005, though he did ultimately receive 5,000 compensation under art.6 (fair trial), owing to the "unreasonable" time the proceedings took. Authorisation disputes regarding books by former members of the security services now fall to the Investigatory Powers Tribunal: *R. v B* (2009).

OFFICIAL SECRETS AND ACCESS TO INFORMATION

No contemporary discussion of the Official Secrets Acts could be   38.45
complete without some consideration of their interaction with
information law. One of the most significant pieces of legislation
passed at the dawn of this century was the Freedom of Information
Act 2000. This Act confers a "general right of access to information
held by public authorities". However, official secrets are exempted
from being the subject matter of this right by virtue of s.24 of the
2000 Act. This section provides that such information may be exempt
if such exemption would serve to safeguard national security. Official
secrets are obvious candidates for such protection. It is also worth
noting that the definition of a "public authority" under the 2000 Act
does not extend to include MI5, MI6 or GCHQ.

We are arguably entering a period of reform in relation to the   38.46
treatment of official secrets in the light of information law. Under the
Constitutional Reform and Governance Act 2010, there is to be a
change from the current position whereby government documents of
historical relevance are automatically transferred to the National
Archive after *30* years with the result that this transfer will take place
after just 20 years.

KEY POINTS

1. Section 1 of the Official Secrets Act 1911 makes it an offence to   38.47
   be in or around a prohibited place for a purpose prejudicial to
   the interests of the State. The list includes a variety of vehicles
   and installations used by the armed forces, nuclear
   installations and the like. The 1911 Act also prohibits the
   making of notes, photographs, etc. which could be of use to
   an enemy.
2. The Official Secrets Act 1989 protects against the disclosure of
   a variety of material about security, intelligence, international
   relations, crime, defence and special investigation. In some
   cases, to divulge information is assumed to be damaging. In
   other areas, the prosecution would have to demonstrate that,
   for instance, a journalist had reasonable cause to believe that
   the disclosure was damaging and that it did in fact do harm.
   Public interest is no defence under the 1989 Act, though in
   practice public interest factors will almost certainly play a
   role in whether a journalist is prosecuted or convicted. Prior
   publication is also not a defence, although, again, in practice,
   it will be significant.

3. The Official Secrets Acts 1920 and 1939 allow a police inspector, under certain circumstances, to require a person to provide information concerning a suspected offence under the Official Secrets Acts.

4. Section 8 of the Official Secrets Act 1920 gives the power to exclude the public from proceedings under the Act in order to protect national security. Article 6 of the European Convention also provides for the possibility of trials being held in private, for national security reasons. The Investigatory Powers Tribunal, which hears a number of sensitive cases involving the intelligence service, sits in private.

5. In addition to the law, the DA-Notice System, which involves self-regulatory restraint by the media in relation to the publication of information feared to affect national security, is an important check upon the media's actions.

6. Aside from criminal prosecution, a number of former intelligence officers have become embroiled in civil litigation over their memoirs. Ultimately, in *Spycatcher*, the injunction was lifted, but there is no doubt that a Scottish court could grant an interim interdict to stop publication of information said to threaten national security.

7. Newspapers, books and broadcasters must be wary of undermining court orders to protect the confidentiality of material, including material which is said to be damaging to national security, even if the court's order is against another newspaper, etc. If the *Herald* was banned from publishing excerpts from a book, and the *Scotsman* then published an excerpt from the same book, that could be contempt of court, because it would undermine the administration of justice in the court case against the *Herald*.

8. Any such orders should be granted in order to protect the administration of justice or national security—not to suppress inconvenient or embarrassing revelations about the security services.

9. Escaped spy George Blake was stripped of the anticipated profits of his autobiography in 2001, even though the book's content contained nothing which was still confidential.

10. The Scottish courts will not grant an interdict against the world in general—only against named individuals or corporations. Nor will an English injunction have direct effect in Scotland. The Scottish media must, however, remain alert to the risk of being in contempt of court by deliberately undermining the administration of justice in interdict proceedings against other people. Pragmatically, too, a Scottish media outlet may be vulnerable to the decisions of

an English court because the newspaper operates throughout the UK and has assets or employees on both sides of the border.

11. MI5, MI6 and GCHQ are not covered by the Freedom of Information Act 2000 and there is an exemption under the Act for official secrets.

CHAPTER 39

ELECTIONS

By ROSALIND MCINNES

PRINT MEDIA

39.01   There is no general obligation of political neutrality on a newspaper. At election time print journalists are entitled to be (and frequently are) extremely selective and biased in their reporting of events. The newspapers do, however, have some obligations.

39.02   During an election period, it is a criminal offence under s.106 of the Representation of the People Act 1983 to publish a false statement of fact about the personal character or conduct of an election candidate for the purpose of influencing the vote. There is a defence if the publisher can show reasonable grounds for believing that the statement was true. False statements about paedophilia led to a conviction in 2006 of a Labour candidate in London, and in 1997 a journalist was fined under the Act for falsely stating that a candidate was homosexual. It is also an offence under s.106 knowingly to publish falsely that a rival candidate has withdrawn. Advertising is regulated too [see **Chapter 35**].

39.03   It is an offence under s.66A of the 1983 Act to publish an exit poll before voting has ended. The Ofcom Broadcasting Code also prohibits publication of opinion polls during this period.

39.04   Section 10 of the Defamation Act 1952 specifically provides that there is no special privilege for an election address as regards defamation actions.

BROADCASTERS

39.05   Broadcasters have to be particularly aware of the obligations imposed upon them to be impartial.

39.06   Section 4 of the BBC's Editorial Guidelines states:

> "The Agreement accompanying the BBC's Charter requires us to do all we can to ensure controversial subjects are treated with due impartiality in our news and other output dealing with matters of public policy or political or industrial controversy".

The BBC is required by law to adopt a code of practice at each election 39.07
to govern the participation of candidates in each constituency or
electoral area, having regard to the views of the Electoral
Commission. Impartiality need not be achieved within a particular
programme, but can be across the coverage of the campaign period as
a whole.

In the case of the independent broadcasting companies, the 39.08
obligation arises in terms of the Ofcom Code, section 6 of which sets
out the broadcasters' impartiality obligations in relation to elections
and referendums. In addition, s.127 of the Political Parties, Elections
and Referendums Act bans broadcasters from influencing a
referendum.

Ofcom has a duty under s.319 of the Communities Act 2003 to do all 39.09
it can to ensure due impartiality by the broadcasters it regulates on
matters of political or industrial controversy, or relating to current
public policy, even outside elections.

The old law, under which all constituency candidates had a veto on 39.10
programmes about their constituency featuring any candidate, was
abolished by the Political Parties, Elections and Referendums Act
2000.

PARTY POLITICAL BROADCASTS

Section 333 of the Communications Act 2003 permits Ofcom to 39.11
require a licensed public service television channel and a national
radio service to carry party political broadcasts and referendum
campaign broadcasts. The BBC has a parallel obligation under cl.48
of its current Agreement, with the BBC Trust determining which
registered parties are entitled to a party political broadcast or party
referendum broadcast, how often and for how long. Broadcasters
should stick to the times arranged once a firm arrangement is in
place: *Evans v BBC and IBA* **(1974)**.

Unsuccessful challenges by political parties and candidates
The broadcasters still have legal responsibilities as publishers, even 39.12
though the parties make the broadcasts. A judicial review against the
BBC's refusal to screen the ProLife Alliance's party election broadcast
because its footage of mutilated foetuses breached its taste and
decency obligations, failed (**R. (*on the application of ProLife Alliance
v BBC* (2003))**. (The ProLife Alliance's earlier challenge on similar
grounds had been declared inadmissible by Strasbourg in 2000.)
Another judicial review against the BBC because it insisted on the
change of two words in the Christian Choice party election broadcast
on defamation grounds, also failed in 2008 (***Craig v BBC and ITV***
(2008)).

39.13   Courts have allowed the broadcasters very extensive discretion in the allocation of party political broadcasts and the like. The Referendum Party's challenge to the BBC, ITV and Independent Television Commission in London before the May 1997 election claiming that the party had been given insufficient broadcasts failed (*R. v BBC Ex p. Referendum Party* (1997)), as did earlier challenges in *Wilson v IBA (No.2)* (1988) by the SNP to the Independent Broadcasting Authority allocation in Scotland. The SNP complained that it received only two broadcasts, as compared to five for the other main Scottish parties, but the Scottish court held that, since of the five broadcasts, two would go out in Scotland, the SNP had equality "as regards Scottish issues". Similar deference to discretion was shown in *Marshall v BBC* (1979), *R. v BBC Ex p. Owen* (1985) and in *SNP v STV* (1998), where the SNP failed to stop a party leaders' debate on STV and Grampian from being broadcast without the inclusion of Alex Salmond (now First Minister).

39.14   In April 2010, Lady Smith refused the SNP's application to stop the Prime Ministerial debates among Gordon Brown, David Cameron and Nick Clegg from gong out without SNP representation "on equal terms". She said:

> "[Impartiality] cannot be a simple matter of giving each and every political party equal coverage. Nor can it be a simple matter of taking one point in time during the election period and examining the coverage on a single channel at that stage ..." (*SNP v BBC* (2010)).

Broadcasters' defeats

39.15   However, this tolerance is not limitless. In *Wilson v IBA (No.1)* (1979), the Scottish court intervened when three of the main political parties had broadcasts favouring the same side in the 1979 referendum on Scottish devolution. Lord Ross, granting an interdict, said, "It will be necessary ... to ensure that the same time is given to the proponents of the 'yes' as is given to the proponents of the 'no'." In *Houston v BBC* (1995), a local election candidate in a Scottish election persuaded the Scottish court to grant interim interdict against a *Panorama* consisting of an interview with the Prime Minister, postponing its broadcast until after the Scottish local elections.

BROADCASTING AND THE SCOTTISH PARLIAMENT

39.16   Broadcasting is not a devolved function. It follows that the Scottish Parliament has no legal role to play in this area. However Scottish broadcasters have agreed to appear before the committees of the Parliament.

KEY POINTS

1. During an election period, it is a criminal offence to publish a 39.17 false statement of fact about the personal character or conduct of an election candidate for the purpose of influencing the vote; knowingly to publish falsely that a rival candidate has withdrawn; or to publish an exit poll before voting has ended.
2. Broadcasters have an obligation of political impartiality.
3. Public service broadcasters also have an obligation to carry party political broadcasts. The courts have allowed the broadcasters extensive discretion in the allocation and treatment of politically sensitive broadcasts.
4. Broadcasting is reserved under the Scotland Act 1998 to Westminster.

CHAPTER 40

TERRORISM

By Rosalind McInnes

40.01 Since the last edition of this book, 9/11, 7/7, the attempted attack on Glasgow Airport and similar events have transformed everything from air travel to terrorism law as it affects journalists. In particular, three major statutes have been passed: the Terrorism Act 2000; the Terrorism Act 2006; and the Counter-Terrorism Act 2008. All three affect or will affect Scotland.

ANONYMITY AND CONTROL ORDERS

40.02 In addition, the Prevention of Terrorism Act 2005 created yet another statutory reporting restriction. People subject to control orders, i.e. suspected of involvement in terrorism, but not being prosecuted, can apply to the court for anonymity in media reports of the orders. The Supreme Court endorsed such an order in *Secretary of State for the Home Department v AP (No.2)* **(2010)**, where the person subject to the control order had been forced to live in a town where some racist and anti-Islamic feeling was evident.

DEFINITION OF "TERRORISM"

40.03 Section 1 of the Terrorism Act 2000 defines terrorism as meaning the use or threat of action designed to influence the government or an international governmental organisation or to intimidate the public, for the purpose of advancing a political, religious, racial or ideological cause. The actions have to involve serious violence against a person, serious damage to property, danger to human life or serious risk to public health and safety. But it also includes action designed to disrupt an electronic system.

FAILURE TO DISCLOSE INFORMATION TO THE POLICE

40.04 It is now a crime to fail to disclose to police, as soon as reasonably practicable, information that you know or believe might be of material assistance in preventing an act of terrorism or catching a terrorist. There is a defence of "reasonable excuse" which may well protect, but does not exclude, an investigative journalist.

COLLECTING INFORMATION LIKELY
TO BE USEFUL TO A TERRORIST

It is also an offence to collect or make a record of information of a kind 40.05
likely to be useful to a terrorist or merely having a record of that kind.
Again, there is a defence of reasonable excuse, but no blanket
exemption for journalists. Similarly, it is an offence to "elicit or
attempt to elicit" information about a member of the armed forces,
the intelligence services or the police if the information is of a kind
likely to be useful to a terrorist. There is a separate offence of
publishing the information—with a maximum 10 year jail term.
Again, there is a defence of reasonable excuse, but its limits have yet
to be tested.

"GLORIFICATION"

The Terrorism Act of 2006 prohibits "glorification" of terrorism, 40.06
including the publication of a statement which glorifies terrorism. If
the accused did not intend to encourage terrorism, there is a defence
that what was published or broadcast was clearly not endorsed by
(for instance) the journalist. This would protect the reporting of
threats or propaganda uttered by terrorists in, for example, "videos"
of kidnap victims. The police can give websites notice that a particular
statement is said to encourage terrorism on their websites. The
publishers then have two working days to take down the publication.

SEIZURE OF JOURNALISTIC MATERIAL

The Terrorism Act 2000 also gives extensive power to the police to 40.07
seize material for the purposes of investigations into terrorism. The
2000 Act provides some protection for journalistic material, but it is
far from absolute and the protection does not apply in Scotland at all.
In *Shiv Malik v Chief Constable of Greater Manchester Police* (2008),
the co-author of *Leaving Al-Qaeda: Inside the Mind of a British
Jihadist* appealed against an order to disclose such material,
including sources. The court narrowed the order granted, but stated
that:

> "[J]ournalists who investigate the world of terrorism must be
> taken to be aware of the fact that it is a criminal offence not to
> disclose to the police information relating to terrorism that is
> caught by ... the 2000 Act." [see **para.23.71**]

CONTEMPT OF COURT

40.08   The growing fear of terrorism has had a complex impact on contempt of court. On the one hand, it is felt in some quarters that the desire to promote public vigilance has led to the police and other state authorities giving out prejudicial information about suspects and accused persons which in earlier days they would have kept to themselves. On the other, in *Att Gen v Random House Group* **(2009)**, Tugendhat J.—a judge with a sophisticated regard for freedom of expression and open justice—granted an injunction to stop the publication of a book titled, *The Terrorist Hunters*, written by a former Assistant Commissioner of the Metropolitan Police, Andy Hayman [see **Chapter 15**].

40.09   The judge emphasised that the case was unique—a retrial of those accused of the "airline plot" to use explosives in soft drinks bottles on board transatlantic flights. Nine pages of the book contained a detailed, albeit purportedly anonymised, narrative of the police operation into the airline plot. Andy Hayman's word would be highly credible to any juror who read the book. Crucially, the book would have been published at the very end of the trial, in the middle of closing speeches. Mr Justice Tugendhat said that he was not sure that its publication would represent a substantial risk of serious *prejudice* to the trial, but was sure that there would be a substantial risk that the course of justice would be seriously *impeded*, because of the likely defence applications, e.g. to find out if the jury had read the book and consequent delay. Although the book was of a high order of public interest, being political speech, the public interest in the fair and smooth running of this particular trial could not be higher.

KEY POINTS

40.10
1. Terrorist suspects subject to control orders may be anonymised under the Prevention of Terrorism Act 2005.
2. It is a crime to fail to disclose to police, as soon as reasonably practicable, information which may be of material assistance in preventing terrorism or apprehending a terrorist.
3. It is an offence to collect, record or publish information likely to be useful to a terrorist, or to "attempt to elicit" information from forces, intelligence services or the police of a kind likely to be useful to a terrorist.
4. All these offences are subject to a defence of "reasonable excuse", which remains to be interpreted.
5. "Glorification" of terrorism, including the publication of a statement which glorifies terrorism, is also an offence.

6. The police have extensive power to seize material for the purposes of terrorism investigations.

CHAPTER 41

SUNDRY CRIMINAL OFFENCES

By Rosalind McInnes

41.01 With Holyrood, Westminster and Europe all making law, there is a new offence born every minute. It is not possible to list all the ways in which a journalist may commit a crime. Some particular criminal offences, such as those under the data protection and regulation of investigatory powers legislation, are discussed elsewhere [see **Chapters 10, 12, 34 and 40**]. Journalists should, however, remember that they are subject to the ordinary law of the land and can be prosecuted for offences such as breach of the peace, assault, fraud and harassment.

BREACH OF THE PEACE

41.02 In 1998 a reporter and photographer from the *Daily Record* stood trial at Edinburgh Sheriff Court for breach of the peace. The reporter was fined £1,500 and the charge against the photographer was found not proven.

41.03   Both men had denied committing a breach of the peace by pursuing and photographing two women, uttering threats and placing them in a state of fear and alarm. The reporter was also alleged to have placed his foot in the door of a house and prevented it from closing. One of the women was due to be married to a man called Archie McCafferty, who had been deported from Australia to Scotland after serving 25 years for multiple murder. The case aroused tremendous interest in the media who referred to McCafferty as "Mad Dog". Sheriff Peter McNeill QC at Edinburgh was told that the *Record* reporter thought he had arranged an exclusive interview with McCafferty and his pregnant fiancée. The reporter and photographer turned up for the interview, but McCafferty and his girlfriend did not.

41.04   According to the *Record* reporter, when he tracked down the fiancée to her friend's house he called through the letterbox, asking why the interview had not taken place. He denied putting his foot through the door, shouting or swearing or threatening the women. The women claimed that the reporter and photographer had come "storming up" and chased them to the door. They alleged that the reporter had been "very aggressive and intimidating" and had put his foot in the door to prevent it closing. The procurator fiscal submitted that the behaviour of the journalists had gone beyond their legitimate duties as reporter and photographer and that it had been made clear to them that their presence was unwanted. Defence solicitors argued that both journalists had been carrying out their lawful business and that the Crown had failed to prove that the taking of pictures had caused fear and alarm.

A postman who took an amateur, mobile phone snap of a woman 41.05 being sick in Edinburgh in 2008 was convicted of breach of the peace [see **para.23.38**]. Accredited journalists would have been better placed to deploy a Human Rights Act 1998-based defence as to their freedom of expression. The unwilling subjects of photographs have art.8 privacy rights which have to be balanced with journalists' rights to freedom of expression, but Strasbourg has looked askance at criminal penalties for legitimate journalistic activity. If the postman had been a journalist making a programme about Saturday night in a capital city, for instance, different arguments could have arisen.

PROTECTION FROM HARASSMENT ACT 1997

There is also the Protection from Harassment Act 1997 to be 41.06 considered. Despite free expression considerations, *Esther Thomas v News Group Newspapers Ltd* **(2001)** saw the *Sun* newspaper fighting a damages claim under the 1997 Act over a series of articles concerning police demotions over allegedly racist remarks. The Court of Appeal took the view that she had an arguable claim that she had been harassed by racist criticism.

A similar view was taken in *Howlett v Holding* **(2006)**, to grant an 41.07 injunction against flying banners with abusive messages. A claim has also been made in relation to anonymous postings on the internet: *Gentoo Group v Hanratty* **(2008)** [see **Chapter 43**]. "Conduct" in the 1997 Act is specifically defined as including speech. There is a defence under the Act where the harassing course of conduct is for the purpose of preventing or detecting crime; lawful; or "in the particular circumstances … reasonable". Sienna Miller, Lily Allen and Amy Winehouse have all used harassment-based claims against paparazzi photographers.

USING FALSE NAMES

In 2009, BBC Scotland journalist Arifa Farooq was arrested and 41.08 charged under the Police Act 1997 for using a false first name whilst working under cover as a carer to expose malpractice, in an award-winning *Panorama* documentary. There was an outcry and the fiscal ultimately declined to prosecute the case.

FILMING OR PHOTOGRAPHING CRIMINAL ACTS

41.09 It is not a criminal offence, usually, merely to film a criminal act, so long as one does not facilitate or encourage that act. Journalists will often find themselves filming such acts unintentionally, when covering riots, protests or even football matches. Sometimes, too, they will film violence or fraud.

INVOLVEMENT IN CRIMINAL OFFENCES

41.10 When a journalist goes further—buys guns, for instance, or counterfeit goods, to prove how easily this can be done—the risk of prosecution arises. That such prosecutions are, in practice, extremely rare, is down to the discretion and good sense of the fiscal service, rather than to any journalistic privilege.

41.11 Prosecutions in Scotland are not allowed unless the fiscal considers that they are in the public interest. Nonetheless, journalists as a category are normally bound, like other citizens, by the ever-expanding criminal law. As with contempt of court, journalists should remember that to breach the criminal law may get them into the form of legal jeopardy from which their employers, however well-intentioned, cannot protect them. Arrest is rarely pleasant and conviction can be career-limiting.

KEY POINTS

41.12 1. The journalist, like any other citizen, is subject to the criminal law.
2. Particular issues arise in relation to the Data Protection Act 1998, the regulation of investigatory powers legislation, the Protection from Harassment Act 1997, the terrorism legislation and the laws in relation to public order, incitement to racial hatred and obscenity. However, "ordinary" offences, like breach of the peace, can also create problems for a journalist.
3. It is not usually an offence to record a criminal act, without facilitating or encouraging it.
4. Prosecutions in Scotland should not be commenced unless they are in the public interest. Therefore, a journalist who is contemplating committing a crime in good faith and for professional reasons, should analyse, in advance, what the

public interest would be in committing that crime, as well, of course, as what harm might result to individuals or to the general public as a result of its commission.

CHAPTER 42

RACE RELATIONS

By David McKie

42.01   It is an offence under s.19 of the Public Order Act 1986 to display, publish or distribute written material which is threatening, abusive or insulting if the intention is to stir up racial hatred or, taking all the circumstances into account, racial hatred is likely to be stirred up. The penalties for a breach of the 1986 Act are up to six months' imprisonment or a fine or both for summary conviction and up to two years' imprisonment or a fine or both on indictment. The Broadcasting Act 1990 extended these provisions to radio and television broadcasts [see **Chapter 34**].

42.02   The important point to note is that an offence can be committed under the 1986 Act without any intention of stirring up racial hatred. An editor could be prosecuted for publishing a racist speech, just as an extremist politician could be for making it. The editor would have to decide whether in all the circumstances racial hatred was likely to be stirred up. He might have to consider toning down the language of the original by taking the controversial parts out of direct speech so that they were no longer threatening, abusive or insulting in terms of the 1986 Act.

42.03   Under s.22 of the 1986 Act journalists involved in television or radio broadcasts may be guilty of an offence if the programme involves the use of threatening, abusive or insulting visual images or sounds in circumstances in which racial hatred is likely to be stirred up. The offence covers each of the people providing the programme service; any person by whom the programme is produced or directed and any person by whom the offending words or behaviour are used [see **para.34.29**].

42.04   The 1986 Act defines racial hatred as hatred against a group of people in Great Britain by reference to colour, race, nationality (including citizenship) or ethnic or national origins. This can include a particular racial group such as Jews, Sikhs or Romanies. In October 1991 the Dowager Lady Birdwood was conditionally discharged and ordered to pay £500 towards prosecution costs after being convicted of distributing anti-Jewish leaflets intended to stir up racial hatred.

42.05   In a test case in 1983, the House of Lords, overruling the English Court of Appeal, decided that Sikhs qualify for protection under the Race Relations Act 1976 as a racial group. The Court of Appeal had held that they were a religious community and did not enjoy such protection. The Lords ruled that a Birmingham headmaster unlawfully discriminated against a Sikh pupil in refusing to allow him to wear a turban in the school. Lord Fraser of Tullybelton (a Scottish Lord of Appeal), said the Sikhs were a group defined by reference to ethnic origins for the purposes of the 1976 Act. The court laid down a test of whether a group regarded itself and was seen by others as a distinct community because of certain characteristics such as a long shared history, a cultural tradition of its own, a common ancestry, common language and literature, a common religion and being a minority.

In a case in April 1991 an employment appeal tribunal decided that 42.06 Rastafarians were a religious sect but not a racial group defined by ethnic origin within the meaning of the Race Relations Act 1976. In allowing an appeal from an employer from a finding of racial discrimination by an industrial tribunal, the employment appeal tribunal stated that Rastafarians were not sufficiently distinguishable from the rest of the African-Caribbean community. It also took the view that as a movement which went back only 60 years, the Rastafarians did not possess a long shared history, one of the tests for establishing a racial group.

It is a defence for someone who is not shown to have intended to stir 42.07 up racial hatred to prove that he was not aware of the content of the material or did not suspect, and had no reason to suspect that it was threatening, abusive or insulting. The defence must be proved on a balance of probabilities.

The 1986 Act does not apply to fair, accurate and contemporaneous 42.08 reports of public hearings before any court or tribunal exercising judicial authority, or to reports of proceedings in Parliament.

During 1986 the Press Council dealt with a series of complaints 42.09 about the practice of some newspapers of specifying the skin colour or race of the offender or defendant in reports of cases of violence or serious crime dubbed by some writers "adjectival racism". Its decisions had no legal force, but they at least gave editors a basis for considering how to proceed in this sensitive area. One of the grounds of complaint was that while reports sometimes described offenders as black, no mention was made of the fact, in other similar kinds of case, that the offenders were white.

In 2002, the first conviction of a man, David Wilson, a member of 42.10 the British National Party, led to his imprisonment for a breach of the Public Order Act 1986. Mr Wilson was convicted of inciting racial hatred by delivering leaflets in Pollokshields, Glasgow, home of the largest Muslim community in Scotland. His campaign group, Families Against Immigrant Racism, alleged white people were being subjected to a series of violent attacks that would get worse if the "militants" were not stopped.

42.11 The subject of discrimination is dealt with in the Editors' Code of Practice drawn up by the Press Complaints Commission (PCC). The code states:

> "i) The press must avoid prejudicial or pejorative reference to an individual's race, colour, religion, gender, sexual orientation or to any physical or mental illness or disability.

> ii) Details of an individual's race, colour, religion, sexual orientation, physical or mental illness or disability must be avoided unless genuinely relevant to the story."

42.12 A number of complaints have been upheld by the PCC on articles deemed to have transgressed cl.12 (Discrimination) of the code. One recent example involved a complaint by an Albanian national (and the chief editor of the *Albanian Times* in London) over a very critical travel piece written by A.A. Gill in the *Sunday Times*. The commission decided that the code of practice allows journalists the freedom to write robust and provocative pieces with which many people may disagree. However, it also requires comment to be distinguished from fact. In this case, the complainant objected to a number of statements about Albania, many of which constituted the journalist's own view of the country which were formed during a visit there. He was entitled to take a negative view of the place and to share it with the newspaper's readers, who would have been aware from the manner in which it was presented that the article represented his own subjective position rather than an indisputable statement of fact. The journalist had clearly upset the complainant with the strident and challenging nature of the article, but given that it was clearly presented as a partisan view of Albania—and given that the newspaper had been able to point to the evidence on which the analysis was based—the tone of the article was not a matter for the commission. That said, the commission noted that the newspaper had subsequently published a variety of contrary views from readers, which, considering the strength of feeling that the article had aroused, seemed to be a sensible approach. With regard to cl.12, the commission emphasised that this clause relates to individuals, and is not applicable to groups of people. The journalist's references to Albanians in general—for instance, to their "surprisingly fair skin"—were not matters that raised a breach of this clause.

42.13 A person is guilty of an offence in Scotland under s.50A of the Criminal Law (Consolidation) (Scotland) Act 1995 if he:

"(a) pursues a racially-aggravated course of conduct which amounts to harassment of a person and—

(i) is intended to amount to harassment of that person; or

(ii) occurs in circumstances where it would appear to a reasonable person that it would amount to harassment of that person; or

(b) acts in a manner which is racially aggravated and which causes, or is intended to cause, a person alarm or distress."

It carries a six month maximum term of imprisonment for summary crimes and seven years for solemn. 42.14

"Conduct" includes speech; "harassment" of a person includes causing the person alarm or distress; "racial group" means a group of persons defined by reference to race, colour, nationality (including citizenship) or ethnic or national origins, and a course of conduct must involve conduct on at least two occasions. 42.15

KEY POINTS

1. It is an offence to publish threatening, abusive or insulting material with the intention of stirring up racial hatred, or if racial hatred is likely to be stirred up (Public Order Act 1986). Racial hatred is defined as hatred against a group of people by reference to colour, race, nationality or ethnic or national origins. 42.16

2. Guidelines for dealing with issues of race and colour are contained in the Editors' Code of Practice drawn up by the Press Complaints Commission.

3. Statute has created a specific form of breach of the peace offence which is designed to create an aggravated element involving racial harassment or distress. The general approach of the courts is to increase the sentence if an individual is convicted.

PART 12: THE INTERNET

Chapter 43

THE INTERNET: JURISDICTION, DEFAMATION, CONTEMPT AND PRIVACY

By Rosalind McInnes

43.01 The growth of the internet has had an impact upon every area of the law. Already there have been international cases involving harassment by email, obscenity, defamation, commercial disputes, data protection and privacy. The culture of the country (privacy-centred, freedom of speech-centred, public order-centred, etc.) will strongly colour its attitude towards regulation of the internet.

43.02 The difficulty with this, obviously, is that the internet is global. For those who wish to control content on the internet, the fact that the "wrong-doers" may be in another jurisdiction thousands of miles away makes the task acutely complicated. For the internet user to know, and abide by, the laws of all the countries to which one transmits materials, is equally impossible on the face of it.

JURISDICTION IN INTERNET CASES: THE SCOTTISH VIEW

43.03 In a Scottish case, ***Bonnier Media v Smith and Kestrel* (2003),** the now defunct *Business am* newspaper obtained interim interdict against defenders who, they said, threatened to breach their trademark by registering confusingly similar domain names to the newspaper's online service's domain name. Lord Drummond Young said:

> "The critical question for present purposes is the location of a wrong that is said to have been committed by way of the Internet … In my opinion it is not appropriate to regard the Internet for legal purposes as a mere static physical entity: nothing more than a group of computers containing information which are linked physically to one another. The Internet should rather be viewed as a process of communication … It follows, in my opinion, that

the person who sets up the website can be regarded as potentially committing a delict in any country where the website can be seen, in other words in any country in the world. It does not follow that he actually commits a delict in every country in the world, however. It is obvious that the overwhelming majority of websites will be of no interest whatsoever in more than a single country ... In my opinion a website should not be regarded as having delictual consequences in any country where it is unlikely to be of significant interest ..."

That case involved England, Greece and Mauritius, but it was followed in the less exotic setting of Largs, Troon and Wemyss Bay in another Scottish case, *Mackie (t/a 197 Aerial Photography) v Askew* **(2009)**, where a photographer in Troon claimed a landlady had uploaded his aerial photographs from his website to hers without permission or acknowledgment. The issues are obvious. 43.04

THE INTERNET: SPONTANEOUS, INFECTIOUS, UNSTOPPABLE

Apart from its global reach, the internet has various features as a means of communication which make it particularly risky in legal terms. It is rapid, so there can be no adequate time for second thoughts. It is easy to publish, for example, a defamatory statement by mistake, sending it to the wrong person, or even to the wrong list of people, at the press of a button. Because it is easy to forward emails, objectionable material can very quickly be further distributed. It is easier to tell, face-to-face, if someone will find material objectionable. As well, the culture of the internet is informal and uninhibited. Large and searchable archives can grow, not to mention blogs, *Facebook* and other social networking sites—a potent if unreliable source for journalists. It appears informal and anonymous, but actually e-communication leaves a long "paper trail". Furthermore, footage can readily be embedded in other sites once put on one. An English judge, sentencing in September 2009 a former member of the British National Party, Matthew Single, for breach of the Data Protection Act 1998 by publishing names and contact details of party members online, likened internet posting to "opening a Pandora's Box". 43.05

Part of the explanation of the distinctive and informal culture lies in its origins. The internet is about 30 years old. It developed from the United States military-sponsored ArpaNet. This was deliberately designed to create a means of communication which operated so randomly that it would not be possible to prevent messages getting through altogether, even if individual elements of the system were 43.06

attacked or sabotaged. Later, university researchers and government agencies began to use it. So its whole background is one of unstoppable, international, interactive communication, making it highly difficult to control.

43.07   Although all areas of law will have an impact on the internet (and vice versa), four areas in particular are of concern to the journalist: intellectual property rights [see **Chapter 44**]; defamation; contempt of court; and privacy.

DEFAMATION

43.08   When a statement has gone over the world, whose laws should govern content? And where, in which "jurisdiction", can one sue? In many cases, there will be an embarrassment of choices of courts in different countries, leading Lars Davies, Research Fellow in Internet Law at University College London to remark: "The Internet is the most regulated entity in existence … it is impossible to avoid infringing regulations."

FORUM SHOPPING

43.09   In practice, this means that those making claims in defamation go "forum shopping" and choose the courts that award higher damages. London is already a popular choice in "forum shopping" for defamation actions against the international press. Whether the court of a particular country will regard itself as having jurisdiction is a matter for that country. Dow Jones was highly, but pointlessly, affronted at being sued in Australia in 2002 (*Dow Jones v Gutnick* **(2002)** by Joseph Gutnick over a publication of *WSJ.com*, a subscription news website, in a case so alarming to some United States websites, including Amazon.com Inc, that they arranged to be represented in court too. The United States has now passed the Securing the Protection of our Enduring and Established Cultural Heritage ("SPEECH") Act, to curb "libel tourism". The Act prohibits federal courts from recognising foreign defamation judgments which do not meet the high standard for freedom of expression set by the First Amendment in the United States Constitution. On the other hand, the Court of Appeal in Ontario declined to entertain a claim of defamation by its resident, Cheickh Bangoura, over two *Washington Post* articles, in 2005. It should also be borne in mind that defamation can be a criminal offence in some countries, though it no longer is in England and never was in Scotland.

43.10   In reality, there is no way to comply in each and every jurisdiction. The journalist has to make a risk assessment. Where do those likely to take umbrage at a publication live? Where are their families? Do they have an international reputation? Where are the media outlet's assets? Where are its people? Perhaps the majority of media publications today are international in one sense, but equally, most of the world is unlikely to care about them, still less be in a position to make any objection felt.

Nonetheless, the risks are there. Hence the flow of American stars and Russian businessmen to the libel judges in London and the ongoing pressure to reform defamation law in the UK. As Lord Hoffmann said in his dissenting judgment in **Berezowsky v Forbes (2000)**: 43.11

> "The commonsense of the matter is that [Berezowsky] wants the verdict of an English court that he has been acquitted of the allegations in the article, for use wherever in the world his business may take him. He does not want to sue in the United States because he considers that New York Times v Sullivan [a seminal case, making defamation action against public figures contingent on proof of malice] ... makes it too likely that he will lose. He does not want to sue in Russia for the unusual reason that other people might think it was too likely that he would win."

This does not mean that the English courts will automatically decide claims brought before them. Often, the right jurisdiction will depend on international treaty. Sometimes, the publisher will be able to convince the court that the case would be more suitably heard in another jurisdiction. 43.12

In **Dow Jones v Jameel (2005)**, for instance, the claim was dismissed in the Court of Appeal because only five Dow Jones subscribers in England appeared to have read the internet article in question. The case was accordingly dismissed, there, as an abuse of process: "The game will not merely not have been worth the candle, it will not have been worth the wick." It is not impossible that a Scottish judge would have taken a different view in this case. Traditionally, in Scots law, it is not necessary to prove damage to your reputation to bring a defamation claim: hurt feelings are sufficient, so publication to the defamation pursuer alone is, in theory, sufficient in Scotland. However, a Scottish court might well reject a case like Jameel's on the basis that it would more suitably take place in the court of a country with a stronger connection with the parties. 43.13

Much will depend on the facts of the case. A year earlier, in **Lennox Lewis v Don King (2004)**, the Court of Appeal allowed Don King, a boxing promoter and a United States citizen, to sue Lennox Lewis, a British citizen who lived in New York and two other United States-based defendants to sue over allegations on two websites. The Court of Appeal said: 43.14

"A global publisher should not be too fastidious as to the part of the globe where he is made a libel defendant. We by no means propose a free-for-all for claimants libelled on the internet. The court must still ascertain the most appropriate forum; the parties' connections with this or that jurisdiction will still have to be considered; there will be cases ... where only two jurisdictions are really in contention. We apprehend ... no more than this, that in an internet case the court's discretion will tend to be more open-textured than otherwise ..."

43.15   Jurisdictional issues can also be significant within the UK. In ***Kennedy v Aldington* (2005)** [see **para.26.60**], an English pursuer raised a defamation action in Scotland, because Scotland has a three-year time bar for such claims and he had missed his chance in England, which has a one-year time limit [see **Chapter 31**]. He was suing over a magazine which had only 60 Scottish subscribers, but the case (not an internet one) was nonetheless allowed to go to proof in Scotland, with damages confined to the harm done to Kennedy's reputation in Scotland.

ELECTRONIC COMMERCE DIRECTIVE

43.16   Some effort is being made at least in the European countries to set common standards. There is already a European Commission Electronic Commerce Directive (Directive 2000/31 [2000] OJ L178/ 1). This aims, amongst other things, to protect internet service providers when they host material which they did not, and could not, know was unlawful.

43.17   In *Bunt v Tilley* (2006), an English court held that an internet service provider (ISP) which performed no more than a passive role in facilitating postings on the internet could not be a publisher at common law. (The ISPs sued there did not even host the websites.) In any case, they were protected by the Electronic Commerce (EC Directive) Regulations 2002 (SI 2002/2013) and by s.1 of the Defamation Act 1996. In ***Metropolitan International Schools Ltd v Designtechnica* (2010)**, the same English judge held that the Google Inc search engine was not a publisher when a search automatically threw up defamatory "snippets" from someone else's website. Those regulations may also prove useful to those who host websites (***Kaschke v Gray* (2010)**).

SECTION 1 OF THE DEFAMATION ACT 1996

Other forms of protection exist for ISPs. In an early English case, 43.18
Godfrey v Demon Internet (1999), the defamatory material was
posted to a Demon Internet news-group, purporting to come from
one of its subscribers, an academic named Laurence Godfrey. He
asked for it to be removed as it was a forgery, but Demon failed to do
so. They were held liable for defamation, not so much for hosting the
material as for failing to remove it when asked.

Section 1 of the Defamation Act 1996 says that, where a person is 43.19
not the author, editor or publisher of the statement complained of in
a defamation action, took reasonable care in relation to its
publication, and did not know, and had no reason to believe, that
what he did caused or contributed to the publication of a defamatory
statement, that person has a defence.

The section specifies that a person will not be considered the author, 43.20
editor or publisher if only involved as the broadcaster of a live
programme containing the statement in circumstances in which he
has no effective control over the maker of the statement [see
Chapters 27 and 34] and is only involved "as the operator of or
provider of access to a communication system by means of which the
statement is transmitted, or made available, by a person over whom he
has no effective control." Section 1 also says that the court may have
regard to these provisions "by way of analogy in deciding whether a
person is to be considered the author, editor or publisher of a
statement".

In determining whether a person took reasonable care, or had no 43.21
reason to believe that what he did caused or contributed to the
publication of a defamatory statement, regard is to be had to: the
extent of his responsibility for the content of the statement or the
decision to publish it; the nature or circumstances of the publication;
and the previous conduct or character of the author, editor or
publisher.

There is presently little case law on how this applies on the internet, 43.22
or, specifically, how it applies to newspapers and broadcasters who
invite user-generated content of various kinds, readers' letters,
viewers' photographs, comments, criticisms, debates. In *Godfrey
v Demon Internet* (1999), s.1 was held to apply, in principle, where an
ISP carried a usenet "news group" which could be accessed by its
users, even though the defence was defeated by Demon Internet's
delay in removing the posting once the complaint had been made.

The general feeling—perhaps better expressed as a rational hope— 43.23
is that the media will be able to use s.1 in relation to third party
contributions to their website, so long as contributions are not vetted

in advance (which would mean that the media outlet was an "editor" of the online debate), and provided that defamatory postings are removed as soon as possible once a complaint has been made. Much of this, however, remains to be tested. For instance, if a newspaper's website invites comments on, say, the behaviour of Fred Goodwin, former Chief Executive of the Royal Bank of Scotland, at a time when his pension arrangements are controversial, and defamatory comments are made, does that meet the "reasonable care" criterion? There is a tension between ensuring that one is not acting as editor, on the one hand, and the requirement to take reasonable care, on the other, for the majority of media outlets with online presences who allow third party content.

43.24   In 2006, former NATO chief George Robertson raised a defamation action against the *Sunday Herald* over a post by an anonymous contributor to its online reader forum about the Dunblane massacre. The *Sunday Herald* deleted the contribution within 15 minutes of Lord Robertson's drawing it to their attention, the newspaper said. They intended to run a defence under s.1, but a settlement offer, of one-eighth of the amount originally claimed, was accepted by Lord Robertson. So that case came to nothing—except that the *Sunday Herald* was again sued, unsuccessfully, by Lord Robertson over the newspaper's reporting of the reasons for the settlement [see **para.26.13**].

RE-PUBLICATION ON EACH DOWNLOADING

43.25   One of the difficulties for the media in the UK is the lack of a so-called single publication rule. If there were a "single publication rule" within the UK, the time limits for raising a defamation action would start to run from the date at which the offending publication was first put online. Effectively, this means that a claimant in England would have one year from that date to bring a defamation action, and in Scotland, a pursuer would have three years from that date to bring a defamation action, but once those periods had expired, the defamation claim would be time-barred. The Court of Appeal rejected this, on the basis of an 1849 English case where the Duke of Brunswick, 17 years after the publication of an article in the *Weekly Dispatch* about him, when his defamation claim was time-barred, sent his manservant to the *Weekly Dispatch* office to purchase a back number containing the relevant article. The Victorian court had held that this constituted a new publication and that he could bring a claim (***Duke of Brunswick v Harmer* (1849)**). Although the Court of Appeal later said in the ***Yousef Jameel v Dow Jones* (2005)** case [see **para.43.13**] that the ***Duke of Brunswick*** case would have been dismissed nowadays as an abuse of process, it said in **Loutchansky v Times Newspapers Ltd (No.2) (2002)** that the rule that each communication was grounds for its own defamation action ought to stand:

> "We accept that the maintenance of archives, whether in a hard copy or on the internet, has a social utility, but consider that the maintenance of archives is the comparatively insignificant aspect of freedom of expression. Archive material is stale news ...".

This case was brought to defend the reputation of Grigor 43.26 Loutchansky, an international businessman of Russian and Israeli dual nationality who at the time had been excluded from the UK by the Home Secretary on the grounds—challenged by him—that his presence would not be conducive to the public good. The Court of Appeal did, however, throw the media a sop:

> "Nor do we believe that the law of defamation need inhibit the responsible maintenance of archives. Where it is known that archive material is or may be defamatory, the attachment of an appropriate notice warning against treating it as the truth will normally remove any sting from the material."

Refused leave to appeal to the House of Lords, *The Times* took their 43.27 case to the European Court of Human Rights, which also held against them on this point. Strasbourg took a somewhat stronger view of the importance of internet archives than had the Court of Appeal:

> "In light of its accessibility and its capacity to store and communicate vast amounts of information, the internet plays an important role in enhancing the public's access to news and facilitating the dissemination of information generally. The maintenance of internet archives is an important aspect of this role ... Such archives constitute an important source for education and historical research ... However, the margin of appreciation afforded to states in striking the balance between the competing rights [of freedom of expression and right to reputation] is likely to be greater where news archives of past events, rather than news reporting of current affairs, are concerned ... The court recalls the conclusion of the Court of Appeal that the attachment of a notice to archived copies of material which it is known may be defamatory would 'normally remove any sting from material'. ... It is also noteworthy that the Court of Appeal did not suggest that potentially defamatory articles should be removed from archives altogether."

The Strasbourg court warned that, if a newspaper were called into 43.28 court suddenly years after the original publication to defend themselves, that might well amount to a violation to their right to freedom of expression (*Times Newspapers Ltd v United Kingdom* **(2009)**).

NO PRESUMPTION THAT WEBSITE HAS BEEN READ

43.29 According to the English courts, there is no presumption that, just because a story was put online, anyone in a court's jurisdiction had read it. In *Al-Amoudi v Brisard* **(2006)**, an Ethopian-born Saudi resident, who said he spent about two months a year in England, was suing Brisard, a French national resident in Switzerland, over claims about terrorism funding, in the London libel courts. Mr Justice Gray held that it was for the claimant to prove that a substantial number of people saw the publications.

43.30 Substantial publication in an online defamation can be established as a matter of inference, as in *Gregg v O'Gara* **(2008)**. In *Christopher Carrie v Royd Tolkien* **(2009)**, Eady J. said that there must be some solid basis for the inference. Another reason why the claimant failed in this case was that the posting was made on his own website and he could have removed it at any time.

ONLINE STATEMENTS CAN BE TAKEN LESS SERIOUSLY—SOMETIMES

43.31 It should also be noted that the meaning to be drawn from certain types of online statement might be different from the meaning which would be drawn in more formal publications. In *Smith v ADVFN* **(2008)** [see **para.27.16**], in the English courts, Eady J. said of bulletin board communications:

> "Particular characteristics ... are that they are read by relatively few people, most of whom will share an interest in the subject-matter; they are rather like contributions to a casual conversation (the analogy sometimes being drawn with people chatting in a bar) which people simply note before moving on; they are often uninhibited, casual and ill thought out; those who participate ... expect a certain amount of repartee or 'give and take' ... People do not often take a 'thread' and go through it as a whole like a newspaper article ... In the case of a bulletin board thread it is often obvious to casual observers that people are just saying the first thing that comes into their heads and reacting in the heat of the moment. The remarks are often not intended, or to be taken, as serious."

He emphasised: "I would not suggest for a moment that blogging 43.32 cannot ever form the basis of a legitimate libel claim. I am focusing only on these particular circumstances."

There are also early indications that the qualified privilege attaching 43.33 to certain types of publication would receive a generous interpretation, even when they form part of an online or other archive: *Stuart Bray v Deutsche Bank AG* (2008).

CONTEMPT OF COURT

Although there are signs of a growing synthesis, the Scots and English 43.34 courts have traditionally interpreted the same Contempt of Court Act 1981 in different ways—sometimes to the disadvantage of Scots journalists. In part, this arises from fundamental differences in the legal systems of the two countries. In a Scottish criminal trial, identification of the accused is typically in issue, so the use of photographs poses risks. Moreover, cultural differences between countries can make it very difficult for them to agree upon issues such as the pre-trial publicity and the identification of underage offenders.

DIFFICULTIES IN CONTROLLING PRE-TRIAL PUBLICITY IN CASES OF INTERNATIONAL INTEREST

The trial of Al Megrahi and Khalifa Fhima in 2000 for the Lockerbie 43.35 bombing took place without a jury, in the Netherlands, in front of a panel of senior judges. The Scottish court—wherever it was sitting— would have been in no position to prevent an influx of American comment through the internet.

Canada found this out, to its cost (*R v Bernardo* (1995); *R v* 43.36 *Williams and Tumata* (2008)), when it imposed a highly controversial publication ban on the 1993/1994 trials of Karla Homolka and Paul Bernardo in connection with grotesque double murders. Internet users criticised, ignored and ultimately substantially undermined the ban. The trial took place in Ontario, just on the border with the United States, so the free speech of the American conventional media was also a major factor. In New Zealand, in August 2008, Judge David Harvey took the unusual step of banning news websites from naming two men charged with murder, whilst allowing newspapers, radio stations and TV networks to name them. He took the view that the "tomorrow's fish and chip wrapping" philosophy no longer applied in the context of internet reporting. However, his order was recalled within a month.

Whatever the proper position in law, the effect of a ban on the 43.37 conventional media can be to create a *cordon-sanitaire* in relation to the immediate geographical surroundings of the trial. Analogue signals and newspaper distribution can overlap jurisdictions; media outlets can have assets or personnel in more than one jurisdiction of the UK. On the internet, however, the sender of the information can be a very long way from the scene of any enforcement action.

43.38	This is not a matter which is likely to be resolved by international agreement. Canada, New Zealand and Scotland traditionally have legal systems which believe strongly that the accused has a right to be protected from the potentially damaging effects of adverse pre-trial publicity; the United States believes strongly that freedom of expression is a primary social good. In relation to trials of international interest, a state can only attempt physically to exclude foreign journalists. This is plainly easy to circumvent in a variety of ways. Few democracies, whatever their attitude to the purity of the trial process, are willing to ban journalists altogether. Nor, obviously, would that operate to prevent the leakage, through the internet, of information from other sources.

JURIES, CONTEMPT AND THE INTERNET

43.39	Most trials are not of international interest. In relation to those that are, however, countries with a Scottish approach are going to be unable to enforce their usual standards in relation to control of pre-trial publicity. Solutions may have to be practical. The Lockerbie trial arrangements were plainly elaborate, but they set a precedent for trial by a high-calibre judicial panel, rather than by a jury. Alternatively, one could favour tactics such as examination of the jury before its selection, sequestration of it, or, simply, careful instructions to jurors to disregard extraneous information. The last route is obviously the simplest. This has been regarded as adequate when the likes of William Beggs, Raymond Coia, Nat Fraser, Mags Haney and Angus Sinclair have unsuccessfully argued that hostile publicity meant that they could not get a fair trial. In *Beggs* **(2010)**, the Appeal Court rejected the suggestion that the original trial judge should have specifically instructed the jury not to surf the web for information about William Beggs—"Whether such an injunction is a good idea is a matter of debate"—and openly scorned the idea of jury sequestration:

> "The notion that the members of the jury should be sequestered in hotel accommodation every night and every weekend in conditions, even within the hotel, precluding access to the internet, is so disproportionate that it can readily be rejected. In

reality, of which we think trial counsel would be very conscious, such sequestration of the jury might be likely to 'backfire' seriously against the accused."

In July 2010, however, Lord Judge, the Lord Chief Justice of England, commented that it was apparent that the use of the web "is so common that some specific guidance must now be given to jurors".   43.40

Research into ways in which juries actually reach their decisions is itself limited at present by the Contempt of Court Act 1981.   43.41

HYPERLINKS

Hypertext linking is an internet phenomenon on which there are few cases [see **para.44.02**]. In *Islam Expo v The Spectator* **(2010)**, an English judge held that it was at least arguable that, in deciding what a publication meant, he had to have regard to hyperlinked documents.   43.42

ARCHIVES

Before the original trial, Lord Osborne had decided that, in relation to internet archives about William Beggs, every fresh downloading constituted a new publication for contempt purposes: *HM Advocate v Beggs (No.2)* **(2002)**. A similar view, in the defamation context, was taken by the English court in *Loutchansky* **(2002)** [see **para.43.25**], though in *Bedeau v Newham LBC* **(2009)**, Holroyde J. held that the rule that fresh publication occurred every time a website was accessed could not apply where a broadcaster had been unable to comply with an injunction requiring it to remove material from a website.   43.43

In *Budu v BBC* **(2010)**, an English judge dismissed as an abuse of process a case brought over archived articles on the BBC website. The judge said that anyone who looked under Mr Budu's name would find articles updating the story and read all three together. The BBC was not liable for a *Google* snippet drawn from part of a BBC article: 43.44

> "Search engines after all are not used by accident. In the 21st century, they are accessed and used by computer literate individuals ... It might also be thought that those who use Google search engines are well aware that such a snippet is merely a fragment ...".

She implied, too, that actions brought late in the day over archived articles would be looked on with disfavour by the courts.   43.45

UPDATING ARTICLES

43.46 Purging articles would be a source of profound ethical concern to journalists internationally, involving, as it does, a rewriting of history. However, it ought to be possible to add material, updating a story where addition or clarification is in order. If a story moves on, it is sensible to add a modification or correction online, even if the subject of the article will not agree a form of words (*Flood v Times Newspapers Ltd* (2010)).

PRIVACY

43.47 Keeping secrets online can be very difficult, for all the reasons already looked at in this chapter: ease of access to the internet, ease of transmission of information; lack of international control; perceived anonymity.

43.48 "Perceived" is used for a reason. In England, Eady J. refused an interim injunction sought by a police officer who wrote a blog known as "Night Jack" against his identity being revealed, despite arguments about potential prejudice to the policeman's undercover work. The journalist said he had worked out the policeman's identity by a process of deduction, mainly using information available on the internet, and not through breach of confidence. There was no pre-existing relationship of confidence, no discussion of sexual relationships, mental or physical health, financial affairs or the claimant's family or domestic arrangements. The mere fact that bloggers might not want their identity known did not mean that they had a reasonable expectation of privacy. It was possible that the police officer was in breach of internal regulations in writing the blog the way he did. The judge held that blogging was essentially a public, rather than a private activity (*Author of a Blog v Times Newspapers Ltd* (2009)).

43.49 In the *Mahmood v Galloway* (2006) case, a judge refused to grant an injunction against publishing photographs of a *News of the World* investigative journalist on a website controlled by George Galloway [see **para.23.58**].

43.50 The courts will, however, provide remedies if convinced that someone's privacy has been invaded online. In *Applause Store Productions Ltd v Raphael* (2008), Matthew Firsht was awarded £2,000 for misuse of private information by the creation of a fake *Facebook* profile giving information as to sexual orientation, relationship status, birthday, political and religious views (some accurate, some not), all conceded to be private, by an estranged former friend. There was also a libel claim, resulting in a further award of £20,000 in total.

Conversely, although internet sites are accessible throughout the world, it does not follow that substantial numbers of people actually will access them, or even be able to find them, still less that they will implicitly believe in their contents if they do. The fact that the internet is a free-for-all might be felt to diminish its credibility as a purveyor of information as to someone's past behaviour, present whereabouts or reputation, or in relation to the details of a trial, where the jurors are being provided with high-quality evidence designed to convince.   43.51

Ready correction is also possible. The Court of Session once agreed to issue an opinion reflecting that the Law Society had withdrawn allegations of dishonesty against two disbarred solicitors, because the earlier opinion suggesting the contrary had been published online (***Thomson, Petitioners* (1999)**). This is one of the ways in which analogies with conventional print media may be false.   43.52

The Federal District Court in Philadelphia said in the *ACLU v Reno* **(1997)** case that four characteristics of the internet were "of transcendent importance":   43.53

> "First, the Internet presents very low barriers to entry. Second, these barriers to entry are identical for users and listeners. Third, as a result of these low barriers, astoundingly diverse content is available on the Internet. Fourth, the Internet provides significant access to all who wish to speak ... and even creates a relative parity ... The Internet is a far more speech-enhancing medium than print, the village green, or the mails ...''

Later, the United States District Court agreed that: "Just as the strength of the Internet is chaos, so the strength of our liberty depends upon the chaos and cacophony of the unfettered speech the First Amendment protects." The United States First Amendment is, of course, very different from the balancing approach between freedom of expression and other values which dominates the UK.   43.54

Emphasis on "soft law", such as ethical codes, is suggested as a solution in some American quarters. This amounts to a recognition of the fact that "hard law" may make itself look ridiculous. Moreover, codes have recently been given emphasis in the United Kingdom by s.12 of the Human Rights Act 1998.   43.55

ORDERING REVELATION OF THE IDENTITIES
OF WEBSITE USERS

43.56 As with all privacy cases, *"Night Jack"* [see **para.43.48**] and *Mahmood* [see **para.43.49**] turn on their own facts, but they do show that the seductive facelessness of internet communication can be illusory. The English courts on more than one occasion have ordered those who own and operate websites to identify posters of defamatory messages, although the courts there are discriminating with care. As Richard Parkes QC said in *Sheffield Wednesday Football Club v Hargreaves* **(2007)**:

> "Where the proposed order will result in the identification of website users who expected their identities to be kept hidden, the court must be careful not to make an order which unjustifiably invades the right of an individual to respect for his private life, especially when that individual is in the nature of things not before the court."

43.57 Relevant factors in making or refusing an order are the gravity of the defamatory allegations, the strength of the claimant's apparent case, whether there was a concerted campaign online against the claimant, the size and extent of the potential readership, whether the claimant could identify the person who had made the posting in any other way, and whether there was a policy of confidentiality for users of the website. In the *Sheffield Wednesday* case, the judge granted some of the disclosure orders sought, but refused others:

> "I do not think that it would be right to make an order for the disclosure of the identities of the users who have posted messages which are barely defamatory or are little more than abusive or likely to be understood as jokes."

43.58 So out of 14 total postings, he only ordered disclosures of the identity of the poster in relation to five of them, which he thought alleged greed, selfishness, untrustworthiness and dishonest behaviour, such that the claimants' entitlement to reputation outweighed the right of the authors to maintain their anonymity and to express themselves.

43.59 In *Smith v ADVFN* **(2008)** [see **para.27.16**], the Court of Appeal took a similar, restricted approach. It is interesting to see reluctance, in these cases, on the part of the courts to interfere too aggressively in the rough and tumble culture of, in this case, bulletin boards.

43.60 In *G and G v Wikimedia Foundation* **(2009)**, Tugendhat J. ordered disclosure of the IP address of a *Wikipedia* user who had made an amendment to an article which, according to G, revealed sensitive information about her and her child, possibly linked to a blackmail attempt. The Wikimedia Foundation removed the amendment and said that it would "comply with a properly issued court order normally limited", even though it did not accept the jurisdiction of the UK courts.

PUBLIC DOMAIN AND THE INTERNET

The new identities of the James Bulger killers were protected in 2001 **43.61** by an injunction, based on breach of confidence (*Venables and Thompson v News Group Newspapers Ltd* **(2001)**). The injunction was served on internet service providers. In a judgment granting it, Dame Elizabeth Butler-Sloss said:

> "I am, of course, aware that injunctions may not be fully effective to protect the claimants from acts committed outside England and Wales resulting [in] information about them being placed on the internet. Injunctions can, however, prevent wider circulation of that information through the newspapers or television and radio. To that end, therefore, I would be disposed to add, in relation to information in the public domain, a further proviso, suitably limited, which would protect the special quality of the new identity, appearance and addresses of the claimants or information leading to that identification, even after that information has entered the public domain to the extent that it had been published on the internet or elsewhere such as outside the UK."

There was a contempt prosecution over an online breach of the Bulger **43.62** injunction, against Greater Manchester Newspapers Ltd, *Att Gen v Greater Manchester Newspapers* **(2001)**, but the article objected to had also been published in the paper edition of the *Manchester Evening News*.

The internet changes not only the probability of keeping a secret, **43.63** but muddies the waters of when a secret may be said to have been kept. In *F v Newsquest Ltd, X and Y* **(2004)** [see **para.25.31**], an English judge said:

> "There is, I think, considerable force in the point … that, with the advent of the internet … it is impossible to see the public domain as something which has clear boundaries."

All that said, there does come a tipping point beyond which **43.64** information is irretrievably, practically, in the public domain. This is no new phenomenon—it happened, for instance, when Peter Wright's memoir *Spycatcher* could be easily purchased outside the UK. However, such a situation could occur more suddenly and dramatically nowadays through the internet. Injunctions anonymising the killers of baby Peter Connolly in 2007 and the non-golfing activities of Tiger Woods in 2009 were fatally undermined by the availability of the information online. Milton's statement that, "[p]romiscuous reading is necessary to the constituting of human nature. The attempt to keep out evil doctrine by licensing is like the exploit of that gallant man who thought to keep out the crows by shutting his park gate ...", seems remarkably prescient in the internet age.

43.65   Little as judges like to acknowledge impotence, they prefer that to demonstrating it. The classic recent example is *Mosley v News Group Newspapers Ltd* (2008). Mr Justice Eady accepted that the footage in question was a serious violation of Max Mosley's privacy which would be repeated every time the *News of the World* S&M orgy footage was downloaded [see **para.23.56**] but he nonetheless declined to grant to grant an injunction. The footage had been viewed over one million times in two days, either on the *News of the World* website or by visitors to other websites on which the footage had been embedded. The judge said:

> "If someone wishes to search the internet for the content of the edited footage, there are various ways to access it notwithstanding any order the court may choose to make imposing limits on the content of the News of the World website. The court should guard against slipping into playing the role of King Canute. Even though an order may be desirable for the protection of privacy ... there may come a point where it would simply serve no useful purpose ... It is inappropriate for the court to make vain gestures."

43.66   The same approach was taken by King J. in deciding to allow re-publication of material in the Alfie Patten/Chantelle Stedman case, where, amidst a blaze of adult-orchestrated publicity, a 12-year-old boy was wrongly said to have fathered a baby. The judge said:

> "I have to deal with the reality ... There are not just hundreds of public domain photographs of Chantelle, Maisie [the baby] and Alfie in existence, there are tens of thousands all over the world and largely on the internet ... [It] is a matter of public record that newspaper circulation is suffering as a consequence of the large number of (particularly younger) people reading the news online ..." [see **para.37.83**].

43.67   More commonly, though, public domain is a continuum. In *Northern Rock* (2007), for instance [see **Chapter 37**], Tugendhat J. refused an injunction about extracts of information from a briefing memorandum about Northern Rock's financial difficulties, to the extent that the extract had been published in the *Daily Telegraph*, the *Evening Standard*, the BBC and other outlets. However, he granted an injunction in relation to detailed financial information posted on the *FT.com* website on the basis that it was commercially detailed to a greater extent than the rest of the publications and that it was unlikely to have readership of the same magnitude of the BBC, the hard copy newspapers or the *Guardian* website.

Timing matters, too. In ***Barclays Bank v Guardian News and Media***   43.68 **(2009)** [see **para.37.82**], in England, Blake J held that publication for some hours on the *Guardian* website had not destroyed the confidentiality of documents, including legally privileged documents, about tax avoidance schemes.

TERRORISM

The Electronic Commerce Directive (Terrorism Act 2006)   43.69 Regulations 2007 (SI 2007/1550) provide a defence under the 2006 Act for ISPs who act only as conduits, cache or host terrorist material, so long as they were unaware of it or quickly took steps to remove it [see **Chapter 40**].

KEY POINTS

1. The internet is a fast-growing and hard to control medium of   43.70 mass communication. There is at present no international consensus as to whether and how content should be regulated.
2. Particular challenges lie ahead in terms of dealing with defamation risk, the keeping of secrets and in reassessing contempt law in internationally-reported trials or trials of previous high-profile offenders.
3. Although states vary enormously in their views on appropriate controls, they nonetheless can and do attempt to enforce their existing laws on defamation, privacy and contempt in the context of the internet; individuals and companies have fallen foul of such attempts already. Pragmatically, avoiding this is an issue of risk assessment and likely to remain so for some time.
4. The Scottish courts have said that a person who sets up a website can be regarded as potentially committing a delict in any country where the website can be seen. In the ***William Beggs* (2002)** case, the Scottish courts also held that, in terms of contempt of court, every time someone downloaded an archived piece, this was a fresh publication.

5. Some protection for internet service providers, and possibly also to those who host websites, is provided by the Electronic Commerce Directive and by s.1 of the Defamation Act 1996. Special protection is given to ISPs who unknowingly harbour terrorist material, so long as they quickly remove it.

6. The view in the UK courts as a whole has been that, for defamation purposes, there is a fresh publication of a defamatory article or programme every time it is downloaded. The European Court of Human Rights has declined to interfere. The English Court of Appeal has suggested that the attachment of a notice to archived copies of material which it is known may be defamatory would protect the media.

7. Libel tourism is perceived to be a problem in the London courts, certainly by the American media. The United States has legislated to curb this and the matter is under consideration in the Westminster Parliament.

8. The courts, certainly in England and probably in Scotland, will order the identification of website users who make defamatory postings or reveal sensitive personal information on line.

9. When publication occurs on the internet, it can be particularly difficult to say whether the information has gone into the public domain, or merely possibly been seen by a small number of readers.

CHAPTER 44

THE INTERNET: COPYRIGHT AND OTHER INTELLECTUAL PROPERTY

BY COLIN MILLER

Intellectual property rights—copyright, moral rights, trade marks, and so on—are increasingly valuable. Furthermore (unlike contempt of court or defamation), considerable international efforts have already been made to secure a baseline for them to be protected, by treaty.   44.01

Nonetheless, novel questions have been raised by the internet. In an early Scottish case, the electronic publisher "Shetland News" created unauthorised hypertext linking from its own website to the *Shetland Times* site [see **para.32.12**]. *Shetland Times* sued for copyright infringement. (The problem from the *Shetland Times*' perspective is that the hypertext links enabled the reader to go straight to the *Shetland Times* piece, bypassing the advertising on the front pages.) Lord Hamilton granted interim interdict to stop Shetland News from doing this. He took the view that the *Shetland Times* website was a cable programme and rights in it were infringed by the links to it, which were themselves items in a cable programme. This case is quite unusual on its facts—for example, it was conceded by both sides that the headlines which formed part of the links were protected by copyright. Some commentators think that the case might have gone against the *Shetland Times* at the end of the day. In any event, it settled out of court.   44.02

Analogies with existing means of communication, like print, are not very exact. In the *Shetland Times* case, for example, it was not the Shetland News as such which was making use of the *Shetland Times*' copyright material, rather, it was showing other users where they could read it. Also, the new technology is much more concerned with using the material, rather than the old-fashioned act of "copying". Some people argue that every act of access entails breach of copyright.   44.03

However, straightforward commercial piracy of intellectual property rights over the internet is unlikely to appeal to judges in the United Kingdom. "Cyber-squatting", i.e. unrelated parties registering famous names like "Scottish Widows" and then trying to sell the domain names to those companies, has been attacked successfully, as "passing off", on both sides of the Border.   44.04

The internet has changed beyond recognition since the last edition of this book in 2000. A new generation of sophisticated internet users   44.05

has emerged, whose talents and aptitude go far beyond the skills of their predecessors. We have been bombarded with a wide range of challenging new phenomena such as the search engine, peer-to-peer file sharing, e-commerce, internet shopping, online gambling and the boom in social networking to name but a few.

44.06 Similarly, internet law has mushroomed and there have been significant developments in a wide range of areas such as data protection, privacy, electronic surveillance, cyber crime, cyber security, cryptography and electronic signatures, intellectual property, e-commerce, contracting online and distance selling.

44.07 Although the internet now impacts on almost all areas of law there are some issues which are of particular interest to the journalist, such as intellectual property and the role of copyright in the digital age. Copyright raises a number of questions for consideration such as how to regulate infringement on a global scale and in particular peer-to-peer file sharing. Another issue is the digitisation of books and the treatment of "orphan works" whose author cannot be identified or located. The role of the search engine has also stimulated extensive legal debate. To what extent does use of a search engine for aggregating news information infringe copyright? Should the benefits of such a service outweigh the right of the owner to protect its copyright? To what extent does operation by *Google* of its AdWords service infringe the trade marks of those whose brands appear under "sponsored links"? These issues are considered below.

INTELLECTUAL PROPERTY RIGHTS—COPYRIGHT

44.08 Intellectual property rights are discussed in **Chapter 32**, above. Considerable international efforts have been made over the years to secure a base line for intellectual property rights to be protected by treaty and this has considerably helped regulation of infringement on the internet. Global regulation of the internet remains a perennial problem, particularly with the existence of so many contrasting legal systems with their own separate rules and regulations. However for those of us who live in the EU, there have been a number of legal developments over recent years which have helped to regulate the use of the internet in so far as it is used within the EU. The Directive on Copyright In The Information Society (Directive 2001/29 [2001] OJ L167/10) created a new "public communication right" which was implemented in the UK in 2003 by the Copyright and Related Rights Regulations 2003 (SI 2003/2498). This heralded the introduction of a new right to allow for distribution on the internet. The 2003 Regulations now make it clear that only a copyright owner or an authorised licensee is entitled to transmit its work on the internet.

Any other person who downloads or makes copies of such material will be an infringer.

There is no doubt that private copying and in particular the downloading of music and films from the internet, has cost the music industry millions if not billions of pounds of lost revenue. Attempts have been made by the UK Government to address this. For example and as mentioned above, the 2003 Regulations provide a new form of "copyright" in the form of an exclusive public communication right. The 2003 Regulations also provide for an extension of criminal liability to individuals who not only copy (by transmission, downloading or copying on the internet) in the course of a business but also in any private capacity if this in any way prejudices the owner of the copyright. However the 2003 Regulations did little to stem the tide of widespread piracy as acknowledged in the Gowers Report (the Gowers Report was published in December 2006 after a committee was commissioned by the Treasury to review and make recommendations on reform of intellectual property in the United Kingdom): "The fact that the letter of the law is rarely enforced only adds to the public sense of illegitimacy surrounding copyright law" (*Gowers Review of Intellectual Property Law* (The Stationery Office, 2006), para.3.29).   44.09

This remained a serious concern and the government has taken further steps to address abuse by adopting new measures in the Digital Economy Act 2010 (see below).   44.10

A constant concern has been the difficulty and indeed the desirability of taking action against millions of individual infringers. As a result regulatory authorities have focused on controlling the activities of those involved in making the equipment available to facilitate online infringement on a wide scale. There has been some regulation within the EU on this subject. The Electronic Commerce Directive (which was implemented in the UK under the Electronic Commerce (EC Directive) Regulations 2002 (SI 2002/2013) states that an internet service provider (ISP) is exempt from criminal liability if the ISP transmits offending material provided by a subscriber or if such material is cached or hosted by the ISP provided the ISP has no knowledge of the illegal content. Similarly an ISP will be immune from any civil liability, including copyright infringement or defamation, insofar as the ISP has no actual knowledge of illegal content. Moreover, there is no obligation on an ISP to monitor the contents of its sites with a view to deciding whether or not material might be considered to be unlawful.   44.11

However immunity will only be available if the ISP acts "expeditiously" to remove or disable access to the offending material. The question of how "expeditiously" an ISP must take down material in order to benefit from immunity remains untested. To date there   44.12

have been no cases on immunities from a copyright perspective but the cases on defamation imply that if the ISP complies with take down notices, it is likely to escape liability for any users' infringement. This may not be a major issue for large sophisticated ISPs who operate speedy take down systems, but it may be of concern to smaller organisations who cannot act so quickly.

44.13   However, the nature and scale of online copyright infringement remained a major concern for the UK Government and in June 2009 the Department for Business Innovation and Skills (BIS) and the Department for Culture, Media and Sport (DCMS) published the *Digital Britain Final Report* (The Stationery Office, 2009). The government noted that the UK was a world leader in culture and media and highlighted the threats which widespread copyright infringement was having on the financial future of the creative industries within the UK. The report recommended various ways of reducing widespread online copyright infringement. Those measures were introduced quickly into the Digital Economy Bill in Autumn 2009 and rushed on to the statute book before the general election in May 2010.

44.14   The Digital Economy Act 2010 has been welcomed by many. Several of the key creative trade unions, (such as the Writers' Guild and Equity), supported the Bill's passage:

> "For too long, this illegal activity [web piracy] has been threatening the livelihoods of thousands of workers throughout our sector. Looking to the future, we now face the challenge of ensuring that the system outlined in the Bill functions properly in order to allow industry to focus on developing new business models that can flourish without having to compete with illegal file-sharing, downloading and streaming. Only with this protection will the UK's creative industries be able to continue to invest in the TV programmes, films, books, sporting events and music which are loved by millions across the UK and throughout the world."

44.15   The Digital Economy Act 2010 contains important new provisions to tackle online copyright infringement. There are two key reforms. First a copyright owner may now make a copyright infringement report to an ISP if it appears to him that:

(1) a subscriber to an internet access service has infringed the owner's copyright by means of the service; or
(2) a subscriber to an internet access service has allowed another person to use the service, and that other person has infringed the owner's copyright by means of the service.

The ISP is now required to notify its subscribers of complaints of   44.16
copyright infringement received from a copyright owner. A
notification must include specified information including evidence of
the infringement, the subscriber's IP address and the time at which
the evidence was gathered, information for the subscriber about
appeals and the grounds on which they may be made and
information to enable the subscriber to obtain lawful access to
copyright works, such as securing a proper licence. The ISP is
required to provide the copyright owner with a list of the subscribers
to whom the report of infringement has been sent and in a form in
which the subscriber remains anonymous. Ofcom will be responsible
for the procedural and enforcement aspects of these new obligations
through the adoption of a legally enforceable code of practice.

The second key reform is that the Secretary of State has the power to   44.17
make regulations to provide for the courts to grant orders blocking
access. The Secretary of State may not make regulations under these
provisions unless he is satisfied that the use of the internet for activities
that infringe copyright is having a serious adverse effect on businesses
or consumers and that the making of the regulations is a proportionate
response and will not prejudice national security or the detection of
crime. More draconian remedies were put forward by the
government during the Bill's passage throughout Parliament. One
proposal was the grant of an order on ISPs to take action against
subscribers, including limiting internet connection speed or
suspending access. Concerns were raised that this would infringe
provisions of the European Convention on Human Rights which
entitle everyone to a fair and public hearing within a reasonable time
by an independent court. These provisions were retained in the Act but
subject to significant safeguards, including the right to appeal against
a decision made to block access.

Following a report from Ofcom, it will be for the Secretary of State   44.18
to decide whether any "technical obligations" should be imposed on
the ISP to take technical measures such as suspending internet access
to a subscriber. Any such order by the Secretary of State must be laid
in draft before Parliament along with an explanation of the proposal,
and there will be a 60 day period for making representations or
recommendations in relation to the proposed order. However it
remains to be seen how these new measures will be applied in practice
and how this will address the ongoing threat of web piracy.

THE SEARCH ENGINE

Almost everyone who wants to find information on the internet will   44.19
probably start by using a search engine. The search engine is

fundamental to the success of the work of the journalist. The engine
has the potential to create or block a new story at the press of a
button. Intellectual property law is now being used to regulate the use
of the search engine, particularly in trade marks and copyright.

44.20   In 2010 the European Court of Justice held that the operation by
Google of its AdWord service did not amount to trade mark
infringement by *Google* (***Google* (2010)**). This service allows
individuals to purchase key words, such that when the key word is
entered into *Google's* search engine by an internet user, advertising
links to others' sites will be displayed on screen under the heading
"sponsored links". The European Court has held that the storing of
key words and organising the display of advertisements on the basis
of those key words does not constitute trade mark infringement. The
function of a trade mark is to operate as a "badge" of origin. *Google*
did not itself infringe because it was not holding itself out as being
connected with the goods or services which originated from the
owner of the trade mark. *Google* was not itself using the brands in
this way but merely allowing others (namely their subscribers to the
sponsored link) to use those brands. What is clear from this decision
is that although *Google* or any other similar reference service will not
infringe by providing an AdWords service, a trade mark owner will
still have the right to take action against a display of adverts which
internet users think are coming from or associated with that trade
mark owner. So for example, Calvin Klein can oppose the use of
"Calvin Klein" as a key word by a retailer if the advert suggests that
the retailer does sell such products or if it suggests the retailer is in
some way linked to or authorised by Calvin Klein to do so, when in
fact this is not the case.

44.21   *Google* and other referencing service providers now have clarity
that the storage and use of key words to display other persons'
adverts will not render them liable for trade mark infringement.
Similarly, those individuals who try to take advantage of an
AdWords service by suggesting that they are in some way linked to
the trade mark owner, may now find themselves liable for trade mark
infringement.

44.22   In a more recent decision in 2010, the European Court of Justice
held that use of a competitor's trade mark as a key word is only
infringed if the advert creates confusion about the identity of the
company which is creating the advert. This arose from a dispute
between Portakabin and "Primakabin". The European Court of
Justice ruled that a competitor's trade mark will infringe a trade
mark owner's right if it "does not enable average internet users, or
enables them only with difficulty, to ascertain whether the goods or
services referred to by the ad originate from the proprietor of the
trade mark or from an undertaking economically linked to it". As a

result of this case Google has now announced that it will allow companies to use their competitors' trade marks as key words to trigger search adverts not just in the UK but in all European countries.

There have also been some developments in the law of copyright 44.23 particularly in the context of news aggregation. A "news aggregator" will collate online news from different sources and make them available online or sometimes will email subscribers directly if they have chosen a particular area of interest such as sport or politics. A journalist who uses such a service will save an enormous amount of time and effort in getting to grips with a particular news event.

An extract will typically contain a headline and a short summary 44.24 together with a link to the website of the author of the original news excerpt. Does the provision of such a service infringe copyright and if so what should be done if anything to curb such activity? To succeed in any action for copyright infringement it is necessary to show that copying is of a "substantial part" of the original work. It is questionable whether a short list of excerpts of news is sufficient to constitute a "substantial part". In *Infopaq International A/S v Danske Dagblades Forening* (2009), the European Court of Justice held that the sorting and printing out of 11-word extracts from newspaper articles amounted to copyright infringement provided the elements reproduced were the "expression of the intellectual creation of their author". However, the European Court left this issue for the national courts to determine. Arguably this should also be excluded under the defence of reporting of current events [see comments in **Chapter 32** above]. This issue has been considered by the courts in Germany and Belgium but remains to be decided in the UK. If this is considered by the courts in this country, it is hoped that some of the wider public interest issues should come to the fore as it is clear that there are many benefits in having such a service available at the press of a button. It will be disappointing if the journalist is prevented from using this service but it remains to be seen whether the courts will give priority to the wider public interest issues at the expense of copyright.

In September 2010 the Australian courts held that there was no 44.25 copyright in newspaper headlines—*Fairfax Media Publications PTV Limited v Reed International Books Australia PTY Limited*. In that case Reed offered a service called ABIX. Subscribers received abstracts of articles published in various newspapers and magazines. The subscriber usually received the original headline together with the journalist's by-line and a summary of the article written by Reed. Fairfax claimed that, inter alia, each individual headline was an original literary work and that Reed had infringed copyright. However, the courts did not agree and said *"headlines generally are, like titles, simply too insubstantial and too short to qualify for copyright protection as literary works"*. This decision brings some clarity to news aggregators and gives them some scope to focus on their activities, albeit in Australia.

ONLINE DIGITISING OF BOOKS—ORPHAN WORKS

44.26   To what extent is digitising of books permitted if the author cannot be identified or located? This has created difficulties for book publishers and libraries engaged in projects for digitisation of books. As we have outlined in **Chapter 32** above, in the case of books, the copyright term expires 70 years after the end of the year in which the author dies. If the author is unknown or cannot be located compliance will prove extremely difficult. The Copyright, Designs and Patents Act 1988 currently states that no use can be made of anonymous works without following some process of "reasonable enquiry" about the author's identity.

44.27   This problem is recognised by the government and proposals for reform were outlined in the government's report on *Digital Britain* in June 2009 [see **para.44.13** above]. Those measures included a requirement that any operator who wished to use orphan works had to obtain approval from the government which would only be granted if the proposed operator could establish that its business methods and procedures met certain minimum standards, including making relevant searches for the actual author. Provisions were included in the Digital Economy Bill but were shelved in the race to get to the statute book before the general election in May 2010.

44.28   The proposals met with opposition, particularly from photographers who argued that it would create a situation in which anyone would be able to use works simply by claiming that they could not trace the author/owner. Others complained about the fact that any proposed licence fees would have gone to a government regulatory body rather than the owner. The removal of the treatment of orphan works from the 2010 Act was no doubt welcomed by copyright owners but less so for those who need access to copyright works whose owner cannot be identified or located. It is hoped that the new government will take steps to improve access to orphan works particularly those which have been digitised but are otherwise out of print. This will allow journalists to have certainty that access and use of such books will not infringe copyright.

ONLINE DIGITISING OF BOOKS—*GOOGLE*

Google has taken its own approach to digitising books. All books have   44.29
been made available online on the basis that it is up to the copyright
owner to identify himself/herself and object to infringement. *Google*
scans books and provides very short summaries of the book without
the consent of the author. *Google* gives the author the opportunity to
opt out either before the scanning takes place or after the book is
published. If an objection is made *Google* will remove the text. This
has resulted in a longstanding legal battle in the United States. The
Authors' Guild raised an action against *Google* claiming copyright
infringement of their members' copyright as a result of complete
scanning of books without the consent of the author. *Google* on the
other hand argued that there was no infringement because the author
was given the right to object to online publication. *Google* has also
raised some public interest arguments including the need to access
works of authors, particularly orphan works. A settlement was
reached in 2008 pursuant to which it was proposed that a registry
would be set up to maintain a database of authors, their details and
information about requests to use of their books. The proposal was
that *Google* would pay a proportion of the set-up costs of the registry
and share any resulting revenue with the registry and the authors.

The settlement was subject to a Fairness Hearing which took place   44.30
in February 2010 and a ruling from the New York District Council is
awaited.

It remains to be seen how this battle will be won and indeed the   44.31
outcome of any similar issues in the UK. At the end of the day some
kind of balance will need to be struck between protecting the interests
of the author/publisher on the one hand and to enable access to texts,
the authors of which are often unidentified or cannot be found. Should
the role of copyright therefore be changed to support digitising
initiatives, even if at the expense of the author?

KEY POINTS

1. The internet has changed beyond recognition in the past 10   44.32
   years. There have also been significant developments in
   internet law including electronic surveillance, cyber crime,
   cyber security, e-commerce, contracting online and distance
   selling.
2. The role of copyright in the digital age raises a number of
   issues for journalists. There are difficulties in regulating
   copyright infringement on a global scale and in particular
   peer-to-peer file sharing.

3. There has been a limited amount of regulatory intervention on controlling global infringement. There has been some regulation within the EU with controls on the activities of those involved in making equipment available to facilitate online infringement. The activities of ISPs are regulated under the Electronic Commerce (EC Directive) Regulations 2002.

4. The Digital Economy Act 2010 contains new provisions to tackle online copyright infringement.

5. The search engine is fundamental to the success of the work of the journalist. It is now clear that operation by Google of its AdWord service does not amount to trade mark infringement by Google. However it is still not clear to what extent the provision of a news aggregation service will constitute copyright infringement. This will depend on whether the courts take the view that there has been copying of a "substantial part" of the original work.

6. Clarification is required on the extent to which digitisation of books infringes copyright in circumstances where the owner cannot be identified or located. Proposals by the government to reform copyright law on the treatment of orphan works was abandoned before the general election in 2010. It remains to be seen what steps will now be taken to improve access to orphan works, particularly those which have been digitised but are otherwise out of print.

CONTEMPT OF COURT ACT 1981 (C.49)

Strict liability

The strict liability rule

1.—In this Act "the strict liability rule" means the rule of law whereby conduct may be treated as a contempt of court as tending to interfere with the course of justice in particular legal proceedings regardless of intent to do so.

Limitation of scope of strict liability

2.—[1](1) The strict liability rule applies only in relation to publications, and for this purpose "publication" includes any speech, writing, programme included in a cable programme service or other communication in whatever form, which is addressed to the public at large or any section of the public.

(2) The strict liability rule applies only to a publication which creates a substantial risk that the course of justice in the proceedings in question will be seriously impeded or prejudiced.

(3) The strict liability rule applies to a publication only if the proceedings in question are active within the meaning of this section at the time of the publication.

(4) Schedule 1 applies for determining the times at which proceedings are to be treated as active within the meaning of this section.

[2](5) In this section "programme service" has the same meaning as in the Broadcasting Act 1990.

NOTES
1. As amended by the Broadcasting Act 1990 (c.42), s. 203(1), Sch.20 para.31(1)(a).
2. Inserted by Broadcasting Act 1990 (c.42), s. 203(1), Sch. 20, para.31(1)(b).

Defence of innocent publication or distribution

[1]**3.**—(1) A person is not guilty of contempt of court under the strict liability rule as the publisher of any matter to which that rule applies if at the time of publication (having taken all reasonable care) he does not know and has no reason to suspect that relevant proceedings are active.

(2) A person is not guilty of contempt of court under the strict liability rule as the distributor of a publication containing any such matter if at the time of distribution (having taken all reasonable care)

he does not know that it contains such matter and has no reason to suspect that it is likely to do so.

(3) The burden of proof of any fact tending to establish a defence afforded by this section to any person lies upon that person.

NOTE
1. Amended by Administration of Justice Act 1960 (c. 65), s. 11.

Contemporary reports of proceedings

4.—(1) Subject to this section a person is not guilty of contempt of court under the strict liability rule in respect of a fair and accurate report of legal proceedings held in public, published contemporaneously and in good faith.

(2) In any such proceedings the court may, where it appears to be necessary for avoiding a substantial risk of prejudice to the administration of justice in those proceedings, or in any other proceedings pending or imminent, order that the publication of any report of the proceedings, or any part of the proceedings, be postponed for such period as the court thinks necessary for that purpose.

[1](2A) Where in proceedings for any offence which is an administration of justice offence for the purposes of section 54 of the Criminal Procedure and Investigations Act 1996 (acquittal tainted by an administration of justice offence) it appears to the court that there is a possibility that (by virtue of that section) proceedings may be taken against a person for an offence of which he has been acquitted, subsection (2) of this section shall apply as if those proceedings were pending or imminent.

[2](3) For the purposes of subsection (1) of this section a report of proceedings shall be treated as published contemporaneously—

(a) in the case of a report of which publication is postponed pursuant to an order under subsection (2) of this section, if published as soon as practicable after that order expires;

(b) in the case of a report of committal proceedings of which publication is permitted by virtue only of subsection (3) of section 8 of the Magistrates' Courts Act 1980, if published as soon as practicable after publication is so permitted.

NOTES
1. Inserted by the Criminal Procedure and Investigations Act 1996 (c.25), s.57.
2. Amended by Defamation Act 1996 (c.31), Sch.2.

Discussion of public affairs
5.—A publication made as or as part of a discussion in good faith of public affairs or other matters of general public interest is not to be treated as a contempt of court under the strict liability rule if the risk of impediment or prejudice to particular legal proceedings is merely incidental to the discussion.

Savings
6. —Nothing in the foregoing provisions of this Act—

(a) prejudices any defence available at common law to a charge of contempt of court under the strict liability rule;
(b) implies that any publication is punishable as contempt of court under that rule which would not be so punishable apart from those provisions;
(c) restricts liability for contempt of court in respect of conduct intended to impede or prejudice the administration of justice.

...

Other aspects of law and procedure

Confidentiality of jury's deliberations
8.—(1) Subject to subsection (2) below, it is a contempt of court to obtain, disclose or solicit any particulars of statements made, opinions expressed, arguments advanced or votes cast by members of a jury in the course of their deliberations in any legal proceedings.

(2) This section does not apply to any disclosure of any particulars—

(a) in the proceedings in question for the purpose of enabling the jury to arrive at their verdict, or in connection with the delivery of that verdict, or
(b) in evidence in any subsequent proceedings for an offence alleged to have been committed in relation to the jury in the first mentioned proceedings,
or to the publication of any particulars so disclosed.

(3) Proceedings for a contempt of court under this section (other than Scottish proceedings) shall not be instituted except by or with the consent of the Attorney General or on the motion of a court having jurisdiction to deal with it.

Use of tape recorders
9.—(1) Subject to subsection (4) below, it is a contempt of court—

(a) to use in court, or bring into court for use, any tape recorder or other instrument for recording sound, except with the leave of the court;

(b) to publish a recording of legal proceedings made by means of any such instrument, or any recording derived directly or indirectly from it, by playing it in the hearing of the public or any section of the public, or to dispose of it or any recording so derived, with a view to such publication;

(c) to use any such recording in contravention of any conditions of leave granted under paragraph (a).

(2) Leave under paragraph (a) of subsection (1) may be granted or refused at the discretion of the court, and if granted may be granted subject to such conditions as the court thinks proper with respect to the use of any recording made pursuant to the leave; and where leave has been granted the court may at the like discretion withdraw or amend it either generally or in relation to any particular part of the proceedings.

(3) Without prejudice to any other power to deal with an act of contempt under paragraph (a) of subsection (1), the court may order the instrument, or any recording made with it, or both, to be forfeited; and any object so forfeited shall (unless the court otherwise determines on application by a person appearing to be the owner) be sold or otherwise disposed of in such manner as the court may direct.

(4) This section does not apply to the making or use of sound recordings for purposes of official transcripts of proceedings.

Sources of information

10. —No court may require a person to disclose, nor is any person guilty of contempt of court for refusing to disclose, the source of information contained in a publication for which he is responsible, unless it be established to the satisfaction of the court that disclosure is necessary in the interests of justice or national security or for the prevention of disorder or crime.

Publication of matters exempted from disclosure in court

11.—In any case where a court (having power to do so) allows a name or other matter to be withheld from the public in proceedings before the court, the court may give such directions prohibiting the publication of that name or matter in connection with the proceedings as appear to the court to be necessary for the purpose for which it was so withheld.

...

Penalties for contempt and kindred offences

...

Penalties for contempt of court in Scottish proceedings

[1]**15.**— (1) In Scottish proceedings, when a person is committed to prison for contempt of court the committal shall (without prejudice to the power of the court to order his earlier discharge) be for a fixed term.

(2) The maximum penalty which may be imposed by way of imprisonment or fine for contempt of court in Scottish proceedings shall be two years' imprisonment or a fine or both, except that—

(a) where the contempt is dealt with by the sheriff in the course of or in connection with proceedings other than criminal proceedings on indictment, such penalty shall not exceed three months' imprisonment or a fine of level 4 on the standard scale or both; and

(b) where the contempt is dealt with by the district court, such penalty shall not exceed sixty days' imprisonment or a fine of level 4 on the standard scale or both.

[2] (3) The following provisions of the Criminal Procedure (Scotland) Act 1995 shall apply in relation to persons found guilty of contempt of court in Scottish proceedings as they apply in relation to persons convicted of offences—

(a) in every case, section 207 (restrictions on detention of young offenders);

(b) in any case to which paragraph (b) of subsection (2) above does not apply, sections 58, 59 and 61 (persons suffering from mental disorder);

and in any case to which the said paragraph (b) does apply, subsection (5) below shall have effect.

[3](5) Where a person is found guilty by a district court of contempt of court and it appears to the court that he may be suffering from mental disorder, it shall remit him to the sheriff in the manner provided by section 7(9) and (10) of the Criminal Procedure (Scotland) Act 1995][1] and the sheriff shall, on such remit being made, have the like power to make an order under section 58(1) of the said Act in respect of him as if he had been convicted by the sheriff of an offence, or in dealing with him may exercise the like powers as the court making the remit.

NOTES
1. Amended by Prisoners and Criminal Proceedings (Scotland) Act 1993 (c.9), Sch.7.

2. Substituted by Criminal Procedure (Consequential Provisions) (Scotland) Act 1995 (c.40), Sch.4.
3. Amended by Substituted by Criminal Procedure (Consequential Provisions) (Scotland) Act 1995 (c.40), Sch.4.

...

Supplemental

[1]19. Interpretation

In this Act—

"court" includes any tribunal or body exercising the judicial power of the State, and "legal proceedings" shall be construed accordingly;

"publication" has the meaning assigned by subsection (1) of section 2, and "publish" (except in section 9) shall be construed accordingly;

"Scottish proceedings" means proceedings before any court, including the [Court Martial Appeal Court][1], the Restrictive Practices Court and the Employment Appeal Tribunal, sitting in Scotland, and includes proceedings before the Supreme Court in the exercise of any appellate jurisdiction over proceedings in such a court;

"the strict liability rule" has the meaning assigned by section 1;

"superior court" means the Supreme Court, the Court of Appeal, the High Court, the Crown Court, the Court Martial Appeal Court, the Restrictive Practices Court, the Employment Appeal Tribunal and any other court exercising in relation to its proceedings powers equivalent to those of the High Court.

NOTE
Amended by Constitutional Reform Act (2005 c.4), sched.9; sched.9, para35(3); sched.18, prt 5 and the Armed Forces Act (2006 c.52), sched.16, para.91.

20.— Tribunals of Inquiry

(1) In relation to any tribunal to which the Tribunals of Inquiry (Evidence) Act 1921 applies, and the proceedings of such a tribunal, the provisions of this Act (except subsection (3) of section 9) apply as they apply in relation to courts and legal proceedings; and references to the course of justice or the administration of justice in legal proceedings shall be construed accordingly.

(2) The proceedings of a tribunal established under the said Act shall be treated as active within the meaning of section 2 from the time when the tribunal is appointed until its report is presented to Parliament.

21.— Short title, commencement and extent

(1) This Act may be cited as the Contempt of Court Act 1981.

(2) The provisions of this Act relating to legal aid in England and Wales shall come into force on such day as the Lord Chancellor may appoint by order made by statutory instrument; and the provisions of this Act relating to legal aid in Scotland and Northern Ireland shall come into force on such day or days as the Secretary of State may so appoint.

Different days may be appointed under this subsection in relation to different courts.

(3) Subject to subsection (2), this Act shall come into force at the expiration of the period of one month beginning with the day on which it is passed.

(4) Sections 7, 8(3), 12, 13(1) to (3), 14, 16, 17 and 18, Parts I and III of Schedule 2 and Schedules 3 and 4 of this Act do not extend to Scotland.

(5) This Act, except sections 15 and 17 and Schedules 2 and 3, extends to Northern Ireland.

SCHEDULE 1

TIMES WHEN PROCEEDINGS ARE ACTIVE FOR PURPOSES OF SECTION 2

Preliminary

1. In this Schedule "criminal proceedings" means proceedings against a person in respect of an offence, not being appellate proceedings or proceedings commenced by motion for committal or attachment in England and Wales or Northern Ireland; and "appellate proceedings" means proceedings on appeal from or for the review of the decision of a court in any proceedings.

[1]**1A.** In paragraph 1 the reference to an offence includes a service offence within the meaning of the Armed Forces Act 2006.

2. Criminal, appellate and other proceedings are active within the meaning of section 2 at the times respectively prescribed by the following paragraphs of this Schedule; and in relation to proceedings in which more than one of the steps described in any of those paragraphs is taken, the reference in that paragraph is a reference to the first of those steps.

Criminal Proceedings

[2]**3.** Subject to the following provisions of this Schedule, criminal proceedings are active from the relevant initial step specified in paragraph 4 until concluded as described in paragraph 5.

4. The initial steps of criminal proceedings are:—

    (a) arrest without warrant;

    (b) the issue, or in Scotland the grant, of a warrant for arrest;

    (c) the issue of a summons to appear, or in Scotland the grant of a warrant to cite;

(d) the service of an indictment or other document specifying the charge;

(e) except in Scotland, oral charge.

[2]**4A.** Where as a result of an order under section 54 of the Criminal Procedure and Investigations Act 1996 (acquittal tainted by an administration of justice offence) proceedings are brought against a person for an offence of which he has previously been acquitted, the initial step of the proceedings is a certification under subsection (2) of that section; and paragraph 4 has effect subject to this.[1]

5. Criminal proceedings are concluded—

(a) by acquittal or, as the case may be, by sentence;

(b) by any other verdict, finding, order or decision which puts an end to the proceedings;

(c) by discontinuance or by operation of law.

[3]**6.** The reference in paragraph 5(a) to sentence includes any order or decision consequent on conviction or finding of guilt which disposes of the case, either absolutely or subject to future events, and a deferment of sentence under section 1 of the Powers of Criminal Courts (Sentencing) Act 2000][1], section 219 or 432 of the Criminal Procedure (Scotland) Act 1975 or Article 14 of the Treatment of Offenders (Northern Ireland) Order 1976.

7. Proceedings are discontinued within the meaning of paragraph 5(c)—

(a) in England and Wales or Northern Ireland, if the charge or summons is withdrawn or a nolle prosequi entered;

(b) in Scotland, if the proceedings are expressly abandoned by the prosecutor or are deserted *simpliciter*;

(c) in the case of proceedings in England and Wales or Northern Ireland commenced by arrest without warrant, if the person arrested is released, otherwise than on bail, without having been charged.

8. [*Repealed by Armed Forces Act 2006 (c.52), sched.17.*]

9. Criminal proceedings in England and Wales or Northern Ireland cease to be active if an order is made for the charge to lie on the file, but become active again if leave is later given for the proceedings to continue.

10. Without prejudice to paragraph 5(b) above, criminal proceedings against a person cease to be active—

(a) if the accused is found to be under a disability such as to render him unfit to be tried or unfit to plead or, in Scotland, is found to be insane in bar of trial; or

[4](b) if a hospital order is made in his case under section 51(5) of the Mental Health Act 1983 or paragraph (b) of subsection (2) of section 62 of the Mental Health Act (Northern Ireland) 1961 or, in Scotland, where an assessment order or a treatment order ceases to have effect by virtue of sections 52H or 52R respectively of the Criminal Procedure (Scotland) Act 1995,

but become active again if they are later resumed.

11. Criminal proceedings against a person which become active on the issue or the grant of a warrant for his arrest cease to be active at the end of the period of twelve months beginning with the date of the warrant unless he has been arrested within that period, but become active again if he is subsequently arrested.

NOTES

1. Amended by Armed Forces Act 2006 (c.52), Sch.16, para.92.

2. Amended by Criminal Procedure and Investigations Act 1996 (c.25), s.57(4).

3. Amended Powers of Criminal Courts (Sentencing) Act 2000 (c.6), Sch.9, para.86.

4. Amended by Mental Health (Care and Treatment) (Scotland) Act 2003 (Modification of Enactments) Order 2005 (SSI 2005/465), Sch.1, para.11(2).

Other proceedings at first instance

12. Proceedings other than criminal proceedings and appellate proceedings are active from the time when arrangements for the hearing are made or, if no such arrangements are previously made, from the time the hearing begins, until the proceedings are disposed of or discontinued or withdrawn; and for the purposes of this paragraph any motion or application made in or for the purposes of any proceedings, and any pre-trial review in the county court, is to be treated as a distinct proceeding.

....

14. In Scotland arrangements for the hearing of proceedings to which paragraph 12 applies are made within the meaning of that paragraph—

    (a) in the case of an ordinary action in the Court of Session or in the sheriff court, when the Record is closed;

    (b) in the case of a motion or application, when it is enrolled or made;

    (c) in any other case, when the date for a hearing is fixed or a hearing is allowed.

Appellate proceedings

15. Appellate proceedings are active from the time when they are commenced—

    (a) by application for leave to appeal or apply for review, or by notice of such an application;

    (b) by notice of appeal or of application for review;

    (c) by other originating process,
    until disposed of or abandoned, discontinued or withdrawn.

16. Where, in appellate proceedings relating to criminal proceedings, the court—

    (a) remits the case to the court below; or

    (b) orders a new trial or a venire de novo, or in Scotland grants authority to bring a new prosecution,
    any further or new proceedings which result shall be treated as active from the conclusion of the appellate proceedings.

OFCOM CODE

Section 1: Protecting the Under-Eighteens

Relevant legislation includes, in particular, sections 3(4)(h) and 319(2)(a) and (f) of the Communications Act 2003, Article 22 of the Audiovisual Media Services and Article 10 of the European Convention on Human Rights.)

This section must be read in conjunction with Section Two: Harm and Offence.

Principle

To ensure that people under eighteen are protected.

Rules

Scheduling and content information

1.1 Material that might seriously impair the physical, mental or moral development of people under eighteen must not be broadcast.

1.2 In the provision of services, broadcasters must take all reasonable steps to protect people under eighteen. For television services, this is in addition to their obligations resulting from the Audiovisual Media Services Directive (in particular, Article 22, see Appendix 2).

1.3 Children must also be protected by appropriate scheduling from material that is unsuitable for them.

Meaning of "children":

Children are people under the age of fifteen years.

Meaning of "appropriate scheduling":

Appropriate scheduling should be judged according to:

- the nature of the content;
- the likely number and age range of children in the audience, taking into account school time, weekends and holidays;
- the start time and finish time of the programme;
- the nature of the channel or station and the particular programme; and
- the likely expectations of the audience for a particular channel or station at a particular time and on a particular day.

1.4 Television broadcasters must observe the watershed.

Meaning of "the watershed":
The watershed only applies to television. The watershed is at 2100.
Material unsuitable for children should not, in general, be shown
before 2100 or after 0530.

On premium subscription film services which are not protected as
set out in Rule 1.24, the watershed is at 2000. There is no watershed
on premium subscription film services or pay per view services which
are protected as set out in Rules 1.24 and 1.25 respectively.

1.5   Radio broadcasters must have particular regard to times when
       children are particularly likely to be listening.

Meaning of "when children are particularly likely to be listening":
This phrase particularly refers to the school run and breakfast time,
but might include other times.

1.6   The transition to more adult material must not be unduly abrupt
       at the watershed (in the case of television) or after the time when
       children are particularly likely to be listening (in the case of
       radio). For television, the strongest material should appear
       later in the schedule.

1.7   For television programmes broadcast before the watershed, or
       for radio programmes broadcast when children are particularly
       likely to be listening, clear information about content that may
       distress some children should be given, if appropriate, to the
       audience (taking into account the context).
       (For the meaning of "context" see Section Two: Harm and
       Offence.)

**The coverage of sexual and other offences in the UK involving under-
eighteens**
1.8   Where statutory or other legal restrictions apply preventing
       personal   identification,   broadcasters   should   also   be
       particularly careful not to provide clues which may lead to the
       identification of those who are not yet adult (the defining age
       may differ in different parts of the UK) and who are, or might
       be, involved as a victim, witness, defendant or other
       perpetrator in the case of sexual offences featured in criminal,
       civil or family court proceedings:

•   by reporting limited information which may be pieced
     together with other information available elsewhere, for
     example in newspaper reports (the 'jigsaw effect');
•   inadvertently, for example by describing an offence as
     "incest"; or
•   in any other indirect way.

(Note: Broadcasters should be aware that there may be statutory reporting restrictions that apply even if a court has not specifically made an order to that effect.)

1.9 When covering any pre-trial investigation into an alleged criminal offence in the UK, broadcasters should pay particular regard to the potentially vulnerable position of any person who is not yet adult who is involved as a witness or victim, before broadcasting their name, address, identity of school or other educational establishment, place of work, or any still or moving picture of them. Particular justification is also required for the broadcast of such material relating to the identity of any person who is not yet adult who is involved in the defence as a defendant or potential defendant.

Drugs, smoking, solvents and alcohol

1.10 The use of illegal drugs, the abuse of drugs, smoking, solvent abuse and the misuse of alcohol:

- must not be featured in programmes made primarily for children unless there is strong editorial justification;
- must generally be avoided and in any case must not be condoned, encouraged or glamorised in other programmes broadcast before the watershed (in the case of television), or when children are particularly likely to be listening (in the case of radio), unless there is editorial justification;
- must not be condoned, encouraged or glamorised in other programmes likely to be widely seen or heard by under-eighteens unless there is editorial justification.

Violence and dangerous behaviour

1.11 Violence, its after-effects and descriptions of violence, whether verbal or physical, must be appropriately limited in programmes broadcast before the watershed (in the case of television) or when children are particularly likely to be listening (in the case of radio) and must also be justified by the context.

1.12 Violence, whether verbal or physical, that is easily imitable by children in a manner that is harmful or dangerous:

- must not be featured in programmes made primarily for children unless there is strong editorial justification;
- must not be broadcast before the watershed (in the case of television) or when children are particularly likely to be

listening (in the case of radio), unless there is editorial justification.

1.13 Dangerous behaviour, or the portrayal of dangerous behaviour, that is likely to be easily imitable by children in a manner that is harmful:

- must not be featured in programmes made primarily for children unless there is strong editorial justification;
- must not be broadcast before the watershed (in the case of television) or when children are particularly likely to be listening (in the case of radio), unless there is editorial justification.

(Regarding Rules 1.11 to 1.13 see Rules 2.4 and 2.5 in Section Two: Harm and Offence.)

Offensive language

1.14 The most offensive language must not be broadcast before the watershed (in the case of television) or when children are particularly likely to be listening (in the case of radio).

1.15 Offensive language must not be used in programmes made for younger children except in the most exceptional circumstances.

1.16 Offensive language must not be broadcast before the watershed (in the case of television), or when children are particularly likely to be listening (in the case of radio), unless it is justified by the context. In any event, frequent use of such language must be avoided before the watershed.(Regarding Rules 1.14 to 1.16 see Rule 2.3 in Section Two: Harm and Offence.)

Sexual material

1.17 Material equivalent to the British Board of Film Classification ("BBFC") R18-rating must not be broadcast at any time.

1.18 'Adult sex material' - material that contains images and/or language of a strong sexual nature which is broadcast for the primary purpose of sexual arousal or stimulation - must not be broadcast at any time other than between 2200 and 0530 on premium subscription services and pay per view/night services which operate with mandatory restricted access.

In addition, measures must be in place to ensure that the subscriber is an adult.

Meaning of "mandatory restricted access":
Mandatory restricted access means there is a PIN protected system (or other equivalent protection) which cannot be removed by the user, that restricts access solely to those authorised to view.

1.19   Broadcasters must ensure that material broadcast after the watershed which contains images and/or language of a strong or explicit sexual nature, but is not 'adult sex material' as defined in Rule 1.18 above, is justified by the context.
       (See Rules 1.6 and 1.18 and Rule 2.3 in Section Two: Harm and Offence which includes meaning of "context".)

1.20   Representations of sexual intercourse must not occur before the watershed (in the case of television) or when children are particularly likely to be listening (in the case of radio), unless there is a serious educational purpose. Any discussion on, or portrayal of, sexual behaviour must be editorially justified if included before the watershed, or when children are particularly likely to be listening, and must be appropriately limited.

Nudity
1.21   Nudity before the watershed must be justified by the context.

Films, premium subscription film services, pay per view services
1.22   No film refused classification by the British Board of Film Classification (BBFC) may be broadcast unless it has subsequently been classified or the BBFC has confirmed that it would not be rejected according to the standards currently operating. Also, no film cut as a condition of classification by the BBFC may be transmitted in a version which includes the cut material unless:

       ●   the BBFC has confirmed that the material was cut to allow the film to pass at a lower category; or
       ●   the BBFC has confirmed that the film would not be subject to compulsory cuts according to the standards currently operating.

1.23   BBFC 18-rated films or their equivalent must not be broadcast before 2100 on any service (except for pay per view services), and even then they may be unsuitable for broadcast at that time.

1.24   Premium subscription film services may broadcast up to BBFC 15-rated films or their equivalent, at any time of day provided that mandatory restricted access is in place pre-2000 and post-0530.

In addition, those security systems which are in place to protect children must be clearly explained to all subscribers.

(See meaning of "mandatory restricted access" under Rule 1.18 above.)

1.25 Pay per view services may broadcast up to BBFC 18-rated films or their equivalent, at any time of day provided that mandatory restricted access is in place pre-2100 and post-0530.

In addition:

- information must be provided about programme content that will assist adults to assess its suitability for children;
- there must be a detailed billing system for subscribers which clearly itemises all viewing including viewing times and dates; and
- those security systems which are in place to protect children must be clearly explained to all subscribers.

(See meaning of "mandatory restricted access" under Rule 1.18 above.)

1.26 BBFC R18-rated films must not be broadcast.

Exorcism, the occult and the paranormal

1.27 Demonstrations of exorcisms, occult practices and the paranormal (which purport to be real), must not be shown before the watershed (in the case of television) or when children are particularly likely to be listening (in the case of radio). Paranormal practices which are for entertainment purposes must not be broadcast when significant numbers of children may be expected to be watching, or are particularly likely to be listening. (This rule does not apply to drama, film or comedy.) (See Rules 2.6 to 2.8 in Section Two: Harm and Offence and Rule 4.7 in Section Four: Religion.)

The involvement of people under eighteen in programmes

1.28 Due care must be taken over the physical and emotional welfare and the dignity of people under eighteen who take part or are otherwise involved in programmes. This is irrespective of any consent given by the participant or by a parent, guardian or other person over the age of eighteen in loco parentis.

1.29 People under eighteen must not be caused unnecessary distress or anxiety by their involvement in programmes or by the broadcast of those programmes.

1.30 Prizes aimed at children must be appropriate to the age range of both the target audience and the participants.(See Rule 2.16 in Section Two: Harm and Offence.)

Section 2: Harm and Offence

(Relevant legislation includes, in particular, sections 3(4)(g) and (l) and 319(2)(a), (f) and (l) of the Communications Act 2003, and Articles 10 and 14 of the European Convention on Human Rights.)

This section must be read in conjunction with Section One: Protecting the Under-Eighteens. The rules in this section are designed not only to provide adequate protection for adults but also to protect people under-eighteen.

Principle

To ensure that generally accepted standards are applied to the content of television and radio services so as to provide adequate protection for members of the public from the inclusion in such services of harmful and/or offensive material.

Rules

Generally Accepted Standards

2.1 Generally accepted standards must be applied to the contents of television and radio services so as to provide adequate protection for members of the public from the inclusion in such services of harmful and/or offensive material.

2.2 Factual programmes or items or portrayals of factual matters must not materially mislead the audience. (Note to Rule 2.2: News is regulated under Section Five of the Code.)

2.3 In applying generally accepted standards broadcasters must ensure that material which may cause offence is justified by the context (see meaning of "context" below). Such material may include, but is not limited to, offensive language, violence, sex, sexual violence, humiliation, distress, violation of human dignity, discriminatory treatment or language (for example on the grounds of age, disability, gender, race, religion, beliefs and sexual orientation). Appropriate information should also be broadcast where it would assist in avoiding or minimising offence.

Meaning of "context":
Context includes (but is not limited to):

- the editorial content of the programme, programmes or series;

- the service on which the material is broadcast;
- the time of broadcast;
- what other programmes are scheduled before and after the programme or programmes concerned;
- the degree of harm or offence likely to be caused by the inclusion of any particular sort of material in programmes generally or programmes of a particular description;
- the likely size and composition of the potential audience and likely expectation of the audience;
- the extent to which the nature of the content can be brought to the attention of the potential audience for example by giving information; and
- the effect of the material on viewers or listeners who may come across it unawares.

Violence, dangerous behaviour, and suicide

2.4   Programmes must not include material (whether in individual programmes or in programmes taken together) which, taking into account the context, condones or glamorises violent, dangerous or seriously antisocial behaviour and is likely to encourage others to copy such behaviour. (See Rules 1.11 to 1.13 in Section One: Protecting the Under-Eighteens.)

2.5   Methods of suicide and self-harm must not be included in programmes except where they are editorially justified and are also justified by the context. (See Rule 1.13 in Section One: Protecting the Under-Eighteens.)

Exorcism, the occult and the paranormal

2.6   Demonstrations of exorcism, the occult, the paranormal, divination, or practices related to any of these that purport to be real (as opposed to entertainment) must be treated with due objectivity. (See Rule 1.27 in Section One: Protecting the Under-Eighteens, concerning scheduling restrictions.)

2.7   If a demonstration of exorcism, the occult, the paranormal, divination, or practices related to any of these is for entertainment purposes, this must be made clear to viewers and listeners.

2.8   Demonstrations of exorcism, the occult, the paranormal, divination, or practices related to any of these (whether such demonstrations purport to be real or are for entertainment purposes) must not contain life-changing advice directed at individuals. (Religious programmes are exempt from this rule but must, in any event, comply with the provisions in Section Four: Religion. Films, dramas and fiction generally are not bound by this rule.)

Meaning of "life-changing":

Life-changing advice includes direct advice for individuals upon which they could reasonably act or rely about health, finance, employment or relationships.

Hypnotic and other techniques, simulated news and photosensitive epilepsy

2.9   When broadcasting material featuring demonstrations of hypnotic techniques, broadcasters must exercise a proper degree of responsibility in order to prevent hypnosis and/or adverse reactions in viewers and listeners. The hypnotist must not broadcast his/her full verbal routine or be shown performing straight to camera.

2.10   Simulated news (for example in drama or in documentaries) must be broadcast in such a way that there is no reasonable possibility of the audience being misled into believing that they are listening to, or watching, actual news.

2.11   Broadcasters must not use techniques which exploit the possibility of conveying a message to viewers or listeners, or of otherwise influencing their minds without their being aware, or fully aware, of what has occurred.

2.12   Television broadcasters must take precautions to maintain a low level of risk to viewers who have photosensitive epilepsy. Where it is not reasonably practicable to follow the Ofcom guidance (see the Ofcom website), and where broadcasters can demonstrate that the broadcasting of flashing lights and/or patterns is editorially justified, viewers should be given an adequate verbal and also, if appropriate, text warning at the start of the programme or programme item.

Broadcast competitions and voting

2.13   Broadcast competitions and voting must be conducted fairly.

2.14   Broadcasters must ensure that viewers and listeners are not materially misled about any broadcast competition or voting.

2.15   Broadcasters must draw up rules for a broadcast competition or vote. These rules must be clear and appropriately made known. In particular, significant conditions that may affect a viewer's or listener's decision to participate must be stated at the time an invitation to participate is broadcast.

2.16 Broadcast competition prizes must be described accurately.
(See also Rule 1.30 in Section One: Protecting the Under-Eighteens, which concerns the provision of appropriate prizes for children.)

Note
For broadcast competitions and voting that involve the use of premium rate services (PRS), broadcasters should also refer to Rules 10.9 to 10.12.

Meaning of "broadcast competition":
A competition or free prize draw featured in a programme in which viewers or listeners are invited to enter by any means for the opportunity to win a prize.

Meaning of "voting":
Features in a programme in which viewers or listeners are invited to register a vote by any means to decide or influence, at any stage, the outcome of a contest.

Section 3: Crime
(Relevant legislation includes, in particular, sections 3(4)(j) and 319(2)(b) of the Communications Act 2003, Article 3(b) of the Audiovisual Media Services Directive, and Article 10 of the European Convention on Human Rights.)

Principle
To ensure that material likely to encourage or incite the commission of crime or to lead to disorder is not included in television or radio services.

Rules
3.1 Material likely to encourage or incite the commission of crime or to lead to disorder must not be included in television or radio services.

3.2 Descriptions or demonstrations of criminal techniques which contain essential details which could enable the commission of crime must not be broadcast unless editorially justified.

3.3 No payment, promise of payment, or payment in kind, may be made to convicted or confessed criminals whether directly or indirectly for a programme contribution by the criminal (or any other person) relating to his/her crime/s. The only exception is where it is in the public interest.

3.4 While criminal proceedings are active, no payment or promise of payment may be made, directly or indirectly, to any witness or any person who may reasonably be expected to be called as a witness. Nor should any payment be suggested or made dependent on the outcome of the trial. Only actual expenditure or loss of earnings necessarily incurred during the making of a programme contribution may be reimbursed.

3.5 Where criminal proceedings are likely and foreseeable, payments should not be made to people who might reasonably be expected to be witnesses unless there is a clear public interest, such as investigating crime or serious wrongdoing, and the payment is necessary to elicit the information. Where such a payment is made it will be appropriate to disclose the payment to both defence and prosecution if the person becomes a witness in any subsequent trial.

3.6 Broadcasters must use their best endeavours so as not to broadcast material that could endanger lives or prejudice the success of attempts to deal with a hijack or kidnapping.

Section 4: Religion
(Relevant legislation includes, in particular, sections 319(2)(e) and 319(6) of the Communications Act 2003, and Articles 9, 10 and 14 of the European Convention on Human Rights.)
The rules in this section apply to religious programmes.

Principles
To ensure that broadcasters exercise the proper degree of responsibility with respect to the content of programmes which are religious programmes.

To ensure that religious programmes do not involve any improper exploitation of any susceptibilities of the audience for such a programme.

To ensure that religious programmes do not involve any abusive treatment of the religious views and beliefs of those belonging to a particular religion or religious denomination.

Rules
4.1 Broadcasters must exercise the proper degree of responsibility with respect to the content of programmes which are religious programmes.

Meaning of a "religious programme":
A religious programme is a programme which deals with matters of religion as the central subject, or as a significant part, of the programme.

4.2   The religious views and beliefs of those belonging to a particular religion or religious denomination must not be subject to abusive treatment.

4.3   Where a religion or religious denomination is the subject, or one of the subjects, of a religious programme, then the identity of the religion and/or denomination must be clear to the audience.

4.4   Religious programmes must not seek to promote religious views or beliefs by stealth.

4.5   Religious programmes on television services must not seek recruits. This does not apply to specialist religious television services. Religious programmes on radio services may seek recruits.

Meaning of "seek recruits":
Seek recruits means directly appealing to audience members to join a religion or religious denomination.

4.6   Religious programmes must not improperly exploit any susceptibilities of the audience.(See Rules 10.15 to 10.18 in Section 10: Commercial References and Other Matters, regarding appeals.)

4.7   Religious programmes that contain claims that a living person (or group) has special powers or abilities must treat such claims with due objectivity and must not broadcast such claims when significant numbers of children may be expected to be watching (in the case of television), or when children are particularly likely to be listening (in the case of radio).

Section 5: Due Impartiality and Due Accuracy and Undue Prominence of Views and Opinions
(Relevant legislation includes, in particular, sections 319(2)(c) and (d), 319(8) and section 320 of the Communications Act 2003, and Article 10 of the European Convention on Human Rights.)
     This section of the Code does not apply to BBC services funded by the licence fee, which are regulated on these matters by the BBC Trust.

Principles
To ensure that news, in whatever form, is reported with due accuracy and presented with due impartiality.
     To ensure that the special impartiality requirements of the Act are complied with.

Rules

Meaning of "due impartiality":
"Due" is an important qualification to the concept of impartiality. Impartiality itself means not favouring one side over another. "Due" means adequate or appropriate to the subject and nature of the programme. So "due impartiality" does not mean an equal division of time has to be given to every view, or that every argument and every facet of every argument has to be represented. The approach to due impartiality may vary according to the nature of the subject, the type of programme and channel, the likely expectation of the audience as to content, and the extent to which the content and approach is signalled to the audience. Context, as defined in Section Two: Harm and Offence of the Code, is important.

Due impartiality and due accuracy in news

5.1   News, in whatever form, must be reported with due accuracy and presented with due impartiality.

5.2   Significant mistakes in news should normally be acknowledged and corrected on air quickly. Corrections should be appropriately scheduled.

5.3   No politician may be used as a newsreader, interviewer or reporter in any news programmes unless, exceptionally, it is editorially justified. In that case, the political allegiance of that person must be made clear to the audience.

Special impartiality requirements: news and other programmes
Matters of political or industrial controversy and matters relating to current public policy

Meaning of "matters of political or industrial controversy and matters relating to current public policy":
Matters of political or industrial controversy are political or industrial issues on which politicians, industry and/or the media are in debate. Matters relating to current public policy need not be the subject of debate but relate to a policy under discussion or already decided by a local, regional or national government or by bodies mandated by those public bodies to make policy on their behalf, for example non-governmental organisations, relevant European institutions, etc.

The exclusion of views or opinions
(Rule 5.4 applies to television and radio services except restricted services.)

5.4   Programmes in the services (listed above) must exclude all expressions of the views and opinions of the person providing the service on matters of political and industrial controversy and matters relating to current public policy (unless that person is speaking in a legislative forum or in a court of law). Views and opinions relating to the provision of programme services are also excluded from this requirement.

The preservation of due impartiality
(Rules 5.5 to 5.12 apply to television programme services, teletext services, national radio and national digital sound programme services.)

5.5   Due impartiality on matters of political or industrial controversy and matters relating to current public policy must be preserved on the part of any person providing a service (listed above). This may be achieved within a programme or over a series of programmes taken as a whole.

Meaning of "series of programmes taken as a whole":
This means more than one programme in the same service, editorially linked, dealing with the same or related issues within an appropriate period and aimed at a like audience. A series can include, for example, a strand, or two programmes (such as a drama and a debate about the drama) or a 'cluster' or 'season' of programmes on the same subject.

5.6   The broadcast of editorially linked programmes dealing with the same subject matter (as part of a series in which the broadcaster aims to achieve due impartiality) should normally be made clear to the audience on air.

5.7   Views and facts must not be misrepresented. Views must also be presented with due weight over appropriate timeframes.

5.8   Any personal interest of a reporter or presenter, which would call into question the due impartiality of the programme, must be made clear to the audience.

5.9   Presenters and reporters (with the exception of news presenters and reporters in news programmes), presenters of "personal view" or "authored" programmes or items, and chairs of discussion programmes may express their own views on matters of political or industrial controversy or matters relating to current public policy. However, alternative viewpoints must be adequately represented either in the programme, or in a series of programmes taken as a whole. Additionally, presenters must not use the advantage of regular appearances to promote their views in a way that compromises the requirement for due impartiality. Presenter phone-ins must encourage and must not exclude alternative views.

5.10 A personal view or authored programme or item must be clearly signalled to the audience at the outset. This is a minimum requirement and may not be sufficient in all circumstances. (Personality phone-in hosts on radio are exempted from this provision unless their personal view status is unclear.)

Meaning of "personal view" and "authored":
"Personal view" programmes are programmes presenting a particular view or perspective. Personal view programmes can range from the outright expression of highly partial views, for example by a person who is a member of a lobby group and is campaigning on the subject, to the considered "authored" opinion of a journalist, commentator or academic, with professional expertise or a specialism in an area which enables her or him to express opinions which are not necessarily mainstream.

Matters of major political or industrial controversy and major matters relating to current public policy

5.11 In addition to the rules above, due impartiality must be preserved on matters of major political and industrial controversy and major matters relating to current public policy by the person providing a service (listed above) in each programme or in clearly linked and timely programmes.

Meaning of "matters of major political or industrial controversy and major matters relating to current public policy":
These will vary according to events but are generally matters of political or industrial controversy or matters of current public policy which are of national, and often international, importance, or are of similar significance within a smaller broadcast area.

5.12 In dealing with matters of major political and industrial controversy and major matters relating to current public policy an appropriately wide range of significant views must be included and given due weight in each programme or in clearly linked and timely programmes. Views and facts must not be misrepresented.

The prevention of undue prominence of views and opinions on matters of political or industrial controversy and matters relating to current public policy
(Rule 5.13 applies to local radio services (including community radio services), local digital sound programme services (including

community digital sound programme services) and radio licensable content services.)

5.13 Broadcasters should not give undue prominence to the views and opinions of particular persons or bodies on matters of political or industrial controversy and matters relating to current public policy in all the programmes included in any service (listed above) taken as a whole.

Meaning of "undue prominence of views and opinions":
Undue prominence is a significant imbalance of views aired within coverage of matters of political or industrial controversy or matters relating to current public policy.

Meaning of "programmes included in any service Taken as a whole":
Programmes included in any service taken as a whole means all programming on a service dealing with the same or related issues within an appropriate period.

Section 6: Elections and Referendums

(Relevant legislation includes, in particular, sections 319(2)(c) and 320 of the Communications Act 2003, and Article 10 of the European Convention on Human Rights. Broadcasters should also have regard to relevant sections of the Representation of the People Act 1983 (as amended) ("RPA") see in particular sections 66A, 92 and 93 (which is amended by section 144 of the Political Parties, Elections and Referendums Act 2000).)

This section of the Code does not apply to BBC services funded by the licence fee, which are regulated on these matters by the BBC Trust.

Rules made under section 333 of the Communications Act 2003 (regarding party election broadcasts, party political broadcasts and referendum campaign broadcasts) and paragraph 18 of Schedule 12 are contained in Ofcom Rules on Party Political and Referendum Broadcasts on the Ofcom website. However, such broadcasts are also required to comply with the relevant provisions of this Code, for example the provisions regarding harm and offence notwithstanding that the content is normally the responsibility of the relevant political parties.

Principle

To ensure that the special impartiality requirements in the Communications Act 2003 and other legislation relating to broadcasting on elections and referendums, are applied at the time of elections and referendums.

Rules

Programmes at the time of elections and referendums

6.1   The rules in Section Five, in particular the rules relating to matters of major political or industrial controversy and major matters relating to current public policy, apply to the coverage of elections and referendums.

Programmes at the time of elections and referendums in the UK

The remainder of this section only applies during the actual election or referendum period which is defined below.

Meaning of "election":
For the purpose of this section elections include a parliamentary general election, parliamentary by-election, local government election, mayoral election, Scottish Parliament election, Welsh, Northern Ireland and London Assembly elections, and European parliamentary election.

Meaning of "referendum":
For the purpose of this section a referendum (to which the Political Parties,Elections and Referendums Act 2000 applies) includes a UK-wide, national or regional referendum but does not extend to a local referendum.

6.2   Due weight must be given to the coverage of major parties during the election period. Broadcasters must also consider giving appropriate coverage to other parties and independent candidates with significant views and perspectives.

Meaning of "major party":
At present in the UK major parties are the Conservative Party, the Labour Party and the Liberal Democrats. In addition, major parties in Scotland and Wales respectively are the Scottish National Party and Plaid Cymru. The major parties in Northern Ireland are the Democratic Unionist Party, Sinn Fein, Social Democratic and Labour Party, and the Ulster Unionist Party.

Meaning of "election period":
For a parliamentary general election, this period begins with the announcement of the dissolution of Parliament. For a parliamentary by-election, this period begins with the issuing of a writ or on such earlier date as is notified in the London Gazette. For the Scottish Parliament elections, the period begins with the dissolution of the Scottish Parliament or, in the case of a by-election, with the date of the occurrence of a vacancy. For the National Assembly for Wales, the Northern Ireland Assembly, the London Assembly and for local

government elections, it is the last date for publication of notices of the election. For European parliamentary elections, it is the last date for publication of the notice of election, which is 25 days before the election. In all cases the period ends with the close of the poll.

Meaning of "candidate":
Candidate has the meaning given to it in section 93 of the Representation of the People Act 1983 (as amended) and means a candidate standing nominated at the election or included in a list of candidates submitted in connection with it.

6.3   Due weight must be given to designated organisations in coverage during the referendum period. Broadcasters must also consider giving appropriate coverage to other permitted participants with significant views and perspectives.

Meaning of "designated organisation" and "permitted participants":
Designated organisations and permitted participants are those that are designated by the Electoral Commission.

Meaning of "referendum period":
For referendums different periods may apply. A referendum held under the Northern Ireland Act 1998 (as amended) begins when the draft of an Order is laid before Parliament for approval by each House. In the case of a referendum held under other Acts, the time at which a referendum period commences is given in the individual Acts. In the case of an Order before Parliament, the time will be given in that Order. In all cases the period ends with the close of the poll.

6.4   Discussion and analysis of election and referendum issues must finish when the poll opens. (This refers to the opening of actual polling stations. This rule does not apply to any poll conducted entirely by post.)

6.5   Broadcasters may not publish the results of any opinion poll on polling day itself until the election or referendum poll closes. (For European Parliamentary elections, this applies until all polls throughout the European Union have closed.)

6.6   Candidates in UK elections, and representatives of permitted participants in UK referendums, must not act as news presenters, interviewers or presenters of any type of programme during the election period.

6.7   Appearances by candidates (in UK elections) or representatives (of permitted participants in UK referendums) in non-political programmes that were planned or scheduled before the election or referendum period may continue, but no new appearances should be arranged and broadcast during the period.

Constituency coverage and electoral area coverage in elections
(Rules 6.8 to 6.13 will only apply to S4C if S4C has adopted them under the RPA as its Code of Practice.)

6.8   Due impartiality must be strictly maintained in a constituency report or discussion and in an electoral area report or discussion.

Meaning of "electoral area":
Electoral area (for example electoral division, borough ward or other area) is the local government equivalent to the parliamentary term "constituency".

6.9   If a candidate takes part in an item about his/her particular constituency, or electoral area, then candidates of each of the major parties must be offered the opportunity to take part. (However, if they refuse or are unable to participate, the item may nevertheless go ahead.)

6.10   In addition to Rule 6.9, broadcasters must offer the opportunity to take part in constituency or electoral area reports and discussions, to all candidates within the constituency or electoral area representing parties with previous significant electoral support or where there is evidence of significant current support. This also applies to independent candidates. (However, if a candidate refuses or is unable to participate, the item may nevertheless go ahead.)

6.11   Any constituency or electoral area report or discussion after the close of nominations must include a list of all candidates standing, giving first names, surnames and the name of the party they represent or, if they are standing independently, the fact that they are an independent candidate. This must be conveyed in sound and/or vision. Where a constituency report on a radio service is repeated on several occasions in the same day, the full list need only be broadcast on one occasion. If, in subsequent repeats on that day, the constituency report does not give the full list of candidates, the audience should be directed to an appropriate website or other information source listing all candidates and giving the information set out above.

6.12   Where a candidate is taking part in a programme on any matter, after the election has been called, s/he must not be given the opportunity to make constituency points, or electoral area points about the constituency or electoral area in which s/he is standing, when no other candidates will be given a similar opportunity.

6.13 If coverage is given to wider election regions, for example in elections to the Scottish Parliament, Welsh Assembly, Northern Ireland Assembly, London Assembly or European Parliament, then Rules 6.8 to 6.12 apply in offering participation to candidates. In these instances, all parties who have a candidate in the appropriate region should be listed in sound and/or vision, but it is not necessary to list candidates individually. However, any independent candidate who is not standing on a party list must be named. Where a report on a radio service is repeated on several occasions in the same day, the full list need only be broadcast on one occasion. If, in subsequent repeats on that day, the constituency report does not give the full list of candidates, the audience should be directed to an appropriate website or other information source listing all candidates and giving the information set out above.

Section 7: Fairness

(Relevant legislation includes, in particular, sections 3(2)(f) and 326 of the Communications Act 2003 and sections 107(1) and 130 of the Broadcasting Act 1996 (as amended), Article 23 of the Audiovisual Media Services Directive and Article 10 of the European Convention on Human Rights.)

Foreword

This section and the following section on privacy are different from other sections of the Code. They apply to how broadcasters treat the individuals or organisations directly affected by programmes, rather than to what the general public sees and/or hears as viewers and listeners.

As well as containing a principle and a rule this section contains "practices to be followed" by broadcasters when dealing with individuals or organisations participating in or otherwise directly affected by programmes as broadcast. Following these practices will not necessarily avoid a breach of this section of the code (Rule 7.1). However, failure to follow these practises will only constitute a breach where it results in unfairness to an individual or organisation in the programme. Importantly, the Code does not and cannot seek to set out all the "practices to be followed" in order to avoid unfair treatment.

The following provisions in the next section on privacy are also relevant to this section:

- the explanation of public interest that appears in the meaning of "warranted" under Rule 8.1 in Section Eight: Privacy;
- the meaning of surreptitious filming or recording that appears under "practices to be followed" 8.13 in Section Eight: Privacy.

Principle

To ensure that broadcasters avoid unjust or unfair treatment of individuals or organisations in programmes.

Rule

7.1   Broadcasters must avoid unjust or unfair treatment of individuals or organisations in programmes.

Practices to be followed (7.2 to 7.14 below)

Dealing fairly with contributors and obtaining informed consent

7.2   Broadcasters and programme makers should normally be fair in their dealings with potential contributors to programmes unless, exceptionally, it is justified to do otherwise.

7.3   Where a person is invited to make a contribution to a programme (except when the subject matter is trivial or their participation minor) they should normally, at an appropriate stage:

- be told the nature and purpose of the programme, what the programme is about and be given a clear explanation of why they were asked to contribute and when (if known) and where it is likely to be first broadcast;

- be told what kind of contribution they are expected to make, for example live, pre-recorded, interview, discussion, edited, unedited, etc.;

- be informed about the areas of questioning and, wherever possible, the nature of other likely contributions;

- be made aware of any significant changes to the programme as it develops which might reasonably affect their original consent to participate, and which might cause material unfairness;

- be told the nature of their contractual rights and obligations and those of the programme maker and broadcaster in relation to their contribution; and

- be given clear information, if offered an opportunity to preview the programme, about whether they will be able to effect any changes to it.

Taking these measures is likely to result in the consent that is given being 'informed consent' (referred to in this section and the rest of the Code as "consent").

It may be fair to withhold all or some of this information where it is justified in the public interest or under other provisions of this section of the Code.

7.4   If a contributor is under sixteen, consent should normally be obtained from a parent or guardian, or other person of eighteen or over in loco parentis. In particular, persons under sixteen should not be asked for views on matters likely to be beyond their capacity to answer properly without such consent.

7.5   In the case of persons over sixteen who are not in a position to give consent, a person of eighteen or over with primary responsibility for their care should normally give it on their behalf. In particular, persons not in a position to give consent should not be asked for views on matters likely to be beyond their capacity to answer properly without such consent.

7.6   When a programme is edited, contributions should be represented fairly.

7.7   Guarantees given to contributors, for example relating to the content of a programme, confidentiality or anonymity, should normally be honoured.

7.8   Broadcasters should ensure that the re-use of material, i.e. use of material originally filmed or recorded for one purpose and then used in a programme for another purpose or used in a later or different programme, does not create unfairness. This applies both to material obtained from others and the broadcaster's own material.

Opportunity to contribute and proper consideration of facts

7.9   Before broadcasting a factual programme, including programmes examining past events, broadcasters should take reasonable care to satisfy themselves that:

- material facts have not been presented, disregarded or omitted in a way that is unfair to an individual or organisation; and
- anyone whose omission could be unfair to an individual or organisation has been offered an opportunity to contribute.

7.10   Programmes such as dramas and factually-based dramas should not portray facts, events, individuals or organisations in a way which is unfair to an individual or organisation.

7.11   If a programme alleges wrongdoing or incompetence or makes other significant allegations, those concerned should normally be given an appropriate and timely opportunity to respond.

7.12   Where a person approached to contribute to a programme chooses to make no comment or refuses to appear in a broadcast, the broadcast should make clear that the individual concerned has chosen not to appear and should give their explanation if it would be unfair not to do so.

7.13   Where it is appropriate to represent the views of a person or organisation that is not participating in the programme, this must be done in a fair manner.

Deception, set-ups and 'wind-up' calls

7.14   Broadcasters or programme makers should not normally obtain or seek information, audio, pictures or an agreement to contribute through misrepresentation or deception. (Deception includes surreptitious filming or recording.) However:

- it may be warranted to use material obtained through misrepresentation or deception without consent if it is in the public interest and cannot reasonably be obtained by other means;
- where there is no adequate public interest justification, for example some unsolicited wind-up calls or entertainment set-ups, consent should be obtained from the individual and/or organisation concerned before the material is broadcast;
- if the individual and/or organisation is/are not identifiable in the programme then consent for broadcast will not be required;
- material involving celebrities and those in the public eye can be used without consent for broadcast, but it should not be used without a public interest justification if it is likely to result in unjustified public ridicule or personal distress. (Normally, therefore such contributions should be pre-recorded.)

(See "practices to be followed" 8.11 to 8.15 in Section Eight: Privacy.)

Section 8: Privacy
(Relevant legislation includes, in particular, sections 3(2)(f) and 326 of the Communications Act 2003, sections 107(1) and 130 of the Broadcasting Act 1996 (as amended), and Articles 8 and 10 of the European Convention on Human Rights.)

Foreword
This section and the preceding section on fairness are different from other sections of the Code. They apply to how broadcasters treat the individuals or organisations directly affected by programmes, rather than to what the general public sees and/or hears as viewers and listeners.

As well as containing a principle and a rule this section contains "practices to be followed" by broadcasters when dealing with individuals or organisations participating or otherwise directly affected by programmes, or in the making of programmes. Following these practices will not necessarily avoid a breach of this section of the Code (Rule 8.1). However, failure to follow these practises will only constitute a breach where results in an unwarranted infringement of privacy. Importantly, the Code does not and cannot seek to set out all the "practices to be followed" in order to avoid an unwarranted infringement of privacy.

The Broadcasting Act 1996 (as amended) requires Ofcom to consider complaints about unwarranted infringement of privacy in a programme or in connection with the obtaining of material included in a programme. This may call for some difficult on-the-spot judgments about whether privacy is unwarrantably infringed by filming or recording, especially when reporting on emergency situations ("practices to be followed" 8.5 to 8.8 and 8.16 to 8.19). We recognise there may be a strong public interest in reporting on an emergency situation as it occurs and we understand there may be pressures on broadcasters at the scene of a disaster or emergency that may make it difficult to judge at the time whether filming or recording is an unwarrantable infringement of privacy. These are factors Ofcom will take into account when adjudicating on complaints.

Where consent is referred to in Section Eight it refers to informed consent.

Please see "practice to be followed" 7.3 in Section Seven: Fairness.

Principle
To ensure that broadcasters avoid any unwarranted infringement of privacy in programmes and in connection with obtaining material included in programmes.

Rule
8.1   Any infringement of privacy in programmes, or in connection
       with obtaining material included in programmes, must be
       warranted.

Meaning of "warranted":
In this section "warranted" has a particular meaning. It means that
where broadcasters wish to justify an infringement of privacy as
warranted, they should be able to demonstrate why in the particular
circumstances of the case, it is warranted. If the reason is that it is in
the public interest, then the broadcaster should be able to demonstrate
that the public interest outweighs the right to privacy. Examples of
public interest would include revealing or detecting crime, protecting
public health or safety, exposing misleading claims made by
individuals or organisations or disclosing incompetence that affects
the public.

Practices to be followed (8.2 to 8.22)

Private lives, public places and legitimate expectation of privacy

Meaning of "legitimate expectation of privacy":
Legitimate expectations of privacy will vary according to the place and
nature of the information, activity or condition in question, the extent
to which it is in the public domain (if at all) and whether the individual
concerned is already in the public eye. There may be circumstances
where people can reasonably expect privacy even in a public place.
Some activities and conditions may be of such a private nature that
filming or recording, even in a public place, could involve an
infringement of privacy. People under investigation or in the public
eye, and their immediate family and friends, retain the right to a
private life, although private behaviour can raise issues of legitimate
public interest.

8.2   Information which discloses the location of a person's home or
       family should not be revealed without permission, unless it is
       warranted.

8.3   When people are caught up in events which are covered by the
       news they still have a right to privacy in both the making and the
       broadcast of a programme, unless it is warranted to infringe it
       This applies both to the time when these events are taking place
       and to any later programmes that revisit those events.

8.4   Broadcasters should ensure that words, images or actions filmed
       or recorded in, or broadcast from, a public place, are not so
       private that prior consent is required before broadcast from the

individual or organisation concerned, unless broadcasting without their consent is warranted.

Consent

8.5 Any infringement of privacy in the making of a programme should be with the person's and/or organisation's consent or be otherwise warranted.

8.6 If the broadcast of a programme would infringe the privacy of a person or organisation, consent should be obtained before the relevant material is broadcast, unless the infringement of privacy is warranted. (Callers to phone-in shows are deemed to have given consent to the broadcast of their contribution.)

8.7 If an individual or organisation's privacy is being infringed, and they ask that the filming, recording or live broadcast be stopped, the broadcaster should do so, unless it is warranted to continue.

8.8 When filming or recording in institutions, organisations or other agencies, permission should be obtained from the relevant authority or management, unless it is warranted to film or record without permission. Individual consent of employees or others whose appearance is incidental or where they are essentially anonymous members of the general public will not normally be required.

- However, in potentially sensitive places such as ambulances, hospitals, schools, prisons or police stations, separate consent should normally be obtained before filming or recording and for broadcast from those in sensitive situations (unless not obtaining consent is warranted). If the individual will not be identifiable in the programme then separate consent for broadcast will not be required.

Gathering information, sound or images and the re-use of material

8.9 The means of obtaining material must be proportionate in all the circumstances and in particular to the subject matter of the programme.

8.10 Broadcasters should ensure that the re-use of material, i.e. use of material originally filmed or recorded for one purpose and then used in a programme for another purpose or used in a later or different programme, does not create an unwarranted infringement of privacy. This applies both to material obtained from others and the broadcaster's own material.

8.11 Doorstepping for factual programmes should not take place unless a request for an interview has been refused or it has not been possible to request an interview, or there is good reason to believe that an investigation will be frustrated if the subject is approached openly, and it is warranted to doorstep. However, normally broadcasters may, without prior warning interview, film or record people in the news when in public places. (See "practice to be followed" 8.15).

Meaning of "doorstepping":
Doorstepping is the filming or recording of an interview or attempted interview with someone, or announcing that a call is being filmed or recorded for broadcast purposes, without any prior warning. It does not, however, include vox-pops (sampling the views of random members of the public).

8.12 Broadcasters can record telephone calls between the broadcaster and the other party if they have, from the outset of the call, identified themselves, explained the purpose of the call and that the call is being recorded for possible broadcast (if that is the case) unless it is warranted not to do one or more of these practices. If at a later stage it becomes clear that a call that has been recorded will be broadcast (but this was not explained to the other party at the time of the call) then the broadcaster must obtain consent before broadcast from the other party, unless it is warranted not to do so.
(See "practices to be followed" 7.14 and 8.13 to 8.15.)

8.13 Surreptitious filming or recording should only be used where it is warranted. Normally, it will only be warranted if:

- there is prima facie evidence of a story in the public interest; and
- there are reasonable grounds to suspect that further material evidence could be obtained; and
- it is necessary to the credibility and authenticity of the programme.

(See "practices to be followed" 7.14, 8.12, 8.14 and 8.15.)

Meaning of "surreptitious filming or recording":
Surreptitious filming or recording includes the use of long lenses or recording devices, as well as leaving an unattended camera or recording device on private property without the full and informed consent of the occupiers or their agent. It may also include recording telephone conversations without the knowledge of the other party, or

deliberately continuing a recording when the other party thinks that it has come to an end.

8.14 Material gained by surreptitious filming and recording should only be broadcast when it is warranted. (See also "practices to be followed" 7.14 and 8.12 to 8.13 and 8.15.)

8.15 Surreptitious filming or recording, doorstepping or recorded wind-up' calls to obtain material for entertainment purposes may be warranted if it is intrinsic to the entertainment and does not amount to a significant infringement of privacy such as to cause significant annoyance, distress or embarrassment. The resulting material should not be broadcast without the consent of those involved. However if the individual and/or organisation is not identifiable in the programme then consent for broadcast will not be required. (See "practices to be followed" 7.14 and 8.11 to 8.14.)

Suffering and distress
8.16 Broadcasters should not take or broadcast footage or audio of people caught up in emergencies, victims of accidents or those suffering a personal tragedy, even in a public place, where that results in an infringement of privacy, unless it is warranted or the people concerned have given consent.

8.17 People in a state of distress should not be put under pressure to take part in a programme or provide interviews, unless it is warranted.

8.18 Broadcasters should take care not to reveal the identity of a person who has died or of victims of accidents or violent crimes, unless and until it is clear that the next of kin have been informed of the event or unless it is warranted.

8.19 Broadcasters should try to reduce the potential distress to victims and/or relatives when making or broadcasting programmes intended to examine past events that involve trauma to individuals (including crime) unless it is warranted to do otherwise. This applies to dramatic reconstructions and factual dramas, as well as factual programmes.

 • In particular, so far as is reasonably practicable, surviving victims and/or the immediate families of those whose experience is to feature in a programme, should be informed of the plans for the programme and its intended broadcast, even if the events or material to be broadcast have been in the public domain in the past.

People under sixteen and vulnerable people

8.20   Broadcasters should pay particular attention to the privacy of people under sixteen. They do not lose their rights to privacy because, for example, of the fame or notoriety of their parents or because of events in their schools.

8.21   Where a programme features an individual under sixteen or a vulnerable person in a way that infringes privacy, consent must be obtained from:

- a parent, guardian or other person of eighteen or over in loco parentis; and
- wherever possible, the individual concerned;
- unless the subject matter is trivial or uncontroversial and the participation minor, or it is warranted to proceed without consent.

8.22   Persons under sixteen and vulnerable people should not be questioned about private matters without the consent of a parent, guardian or other person of eighteen or over in loco parentis (in the case of persons under sixteen), or a person with primary responsibility for their care (in the case of a vulnerable person), unless it is warranted to proceed without consent.

Meaning of "vulnerable people":
This varies, but may include those with learning difficulties, those with mental health problems, the bereaved, people with brain damage or forms of dementia, people who have been traumatised or who are sick or terminally ill.

Section 9: Sponsorship

(Relevant legislation includes, in particular, sections 319(2)(i) and (j) and 319(4)(e) and (f) of the Communications Act 2003, Articles 1, 3(e), 3(f) and 10(1), of the Audiovisual Media Services Directive, and Article 10 of the European Convention on Human Rights.)

This section of the Code does not apply to BBC services funded by the licence fee.

Principle

To ensure that the unsuitable sponsorship of programmes on radio and television is prevented, with particular reference to:

- transparency to ensure sponsorship arrangements are transparent;
- separation to ensure that sponsorship messages are separate from programmes and to maintain a distinction between advertising and sponsorship; and

- editorial independence to ensure that the broadcaster maintains editorial control over sponsored content and that programmes are not distorted for commercial purposes.

In this Principle, programmes include "channels" as defined below.

Rules

Meaning of "sponsored programme", "sponsored channel" and "sponsor":
A sponsored programme, which includes an advertiser-funded programme, is a programme that has had some or all of its costs met by a sponsor with a view to promoting its own or another's name, trademark, image, activities, services, products or any other direct or indirect interest.

A channel is a television or radio service. A sponsored channel is a channel that has had some or all of its costs met by a sponsor with a view to promoting its own or another's name, trademark, image, activities, services, products or any other direct or indirect interest.

Costs include any part of the costs connected to the production or broadcast of the programme or channel.

A sponsor is any public or private undertaking (other than the broadcaster or programme producer), who is sponsoring the programme, programming or channel in question with a view to promoting their or another's name, trademark, image, activities, services, products or any other direct or indirect interest. This meaning extends to those who are otherwise supplying or funding the programme or channel.

Content that may not be sponsored
9.1   The following may not be sponsored:

- news bulletins and news desk presentations on radio; and
- news and current affairs programmes on television.

Meaning of "current affairs programme(s)":
A current affairs programme is one that contains explanation and analysis of current events and issues, including material dealing with political or industrial controversy or with current public policy.

Prohibited and restricted sponsors
9.2   No channel or programme may be sponsored by a sponsor that is not allowed to advertise on the relevant medium.

9.3   Sponsorship on radio and television must comply with both the advertising content and scheduling rules that apply to that medium.

The content of sponsored output
9.4   A sponsor must not influence the content and/or scheduling of a channel or programme in such a way as to impair the responsibility and editorial independence of the broadcaster.

9.5   There must be no promotional reference to the sponsor, its name, trademark, image, activities, services or products or to any of its other direct or indirect interests. There must be no promotional generic references. Non-promotional references are permitted only where they are editorially justified and incidental.

Meaning of "promotional reference":
This includes, but is not limited to, references that encourage, or are intended to encourage, the purchase or rental of a product or service.

Sponsorship credits

Television and radio
9.6   Sponsorship must be clearly identified as such by reference to the name and/or logo of the sponsor. For programmes, credits must be broadcast at the beginning and/or end of the programme.

9.7   The relationship between the sponsor and the sponsored channel or programme must be transparent.

Radio
9.8   During longer sponsored output, credits must be broadcast as appropriate to create the degree of transparency required.

9.9   Credits must be short branding statements. However, credits may contain legitimate advertising messages.

9.10 Credits must be cleared for broadcast in the same way as advertisements.

9.11 Programme trails are treated as programmes and the same sponsorship rules apply.

Television
9.12 Sponsorship credits must be clearly separated from programmes by temporal or spatial means.

9.13 Sponsorship must be clearly separated from advertising. Sponsor credits must not contain advertising messages or calls to action. In particular, credits must not encourage the purchase or rental of the products or services of the sponsor or a third party.

9.14 Where a programme trail contains a reference to the sponsor of the programme, the sponsor reference must remain brief and secondary.

Section 10: Commercial References and Other Matters

Relevant legislation includes, in particular, sections 319(2)(f) and (i) and 319(4)(e) and (f) of the Communications Act 2003, Articles 1, 3(e), 10(1), and 18 of the Audiovisual Media Services Directive, section 21(1) of the Financial Services and Markets Act 2000, paragraph 3 of the Investment Recommendation (Media) Regulations Act 2005, and Article 10 of the European Convention on Human Rights.)

This section of the Code does not apply to BBC services funded by the licence fee, which are regulated on these matters by the BBC Trust.

The rules in this section are subject to, and supplemented by, Ofcoms Cross-promotion Code.

Principles

To ensure that the independence of editorial control over programme content is maintained and that programmes are not distorted for commercial purposes.

To ensure that the advertising and programme elements of a service are clearly separated.

Rules

10.1 Broadcasters must maintain the independence of editorial control over programme content.

10.2 Broadcasters must ensure that the advertising and programme elements of a service are kept separate.

Products or services in programmes

10.3 Products and services must not be promoted in programmes.

This rule does not apply to programme-related material.
(See Rule 10.6.)

10.4 No undue prominence may be given in any programme to a product or service.

Note

Undue prominence may result from:

- the presence of, or reference to, a product or service (including company names, brand names, logos) in a programme where there is no editorial justification; or
- the manner in which a product or service (including company names, brand names, logos) appears or is referred to in a programme.

10.5   Product placement is prohibited.

Meaning of product placement:

Product placement is the inclusion of, or a reference to, a product or service within a programme in return for payment or other valuable consideration to the programme maker or broadcaster (or any representative or associate of either).

- Prop placement: For the purpose of this rule, references to products or services acquired at no, or less than full, cost, where their inclusion within the programme is justified editorially, will not be considered to be product placement. On television, a brief, basic text acknowledgement of the provider of these products or services may be included within the end credits of the programme. This is permitted only where the identity of the product is not otherwise apparent from the programme itself.
- Acquired programmes: With the exception of childrens programmes produced after 19 December 2009, Rule 10.5 does not apply to arrangements covering the inclusion of products or services in a programme acquired from outside the UK and films made for cinema provided that no broadcaster regulated by Ofcom and involved in the broadcast of that programme or film directly benefits from the arrangement.

Childrens programmes in this context are programmes commissioned for, or specifically directed at, audiences below the age of 16.

Broadcasters should note that all acquired programmes or films must nevertheless comply with all other relevant rules in this Code. In relation to references to products and services in acquired programmes that may have resulted from commercial arrangements, broadcasters should pay particular attention to the requirements of Sections One, Two and Ten of the Code.

Programme-related material
10.6 Programme-related material may be promoted in programmes only where it is editorially justified.

10.7 The broadcaster must retain responsibility for all programme-related material.

10.8 Programme-related material may be sponsored, and the sponsor may be credited when details of how to obtain the material is given.

Any credit must be brief and secondary, and must be separate from any credit for the programme sponsor.

Meaning of programme-related material:
These are products or services that are both directly derived from a specific programme and intended to allow listeners or viewers to benefit fully from, or to interact with, that programme.

Premium rate numbers
10.9 Where a broadcaster invites viewers or listeners to take part in or otherwise interact with its programmes, it may only charge for such participation or interaction by means of premium rate telephone services or other telephony services based on similar revenue-sharing arrangements.

10.10 Premium rate services will normally be regarded as products or services, and must therefore not appear in programmes, except where:

- they enable viewers/listeners to participate directly in or otherwise contribute directly to the editorial content of the programme; or
- they fall within the meaning of programme-related material.

Each of the above exceptions is subject to the undue prominence rule.
10.11 Where a premium rate service is featured in a programme, the primary purpose of the programme must continue to be clearly editorial. Promotion of the featured premium rate service must be clearly subsidiary to that primary purpose.

10.12 Any use of premium rate numbers must comply with the Code of Practice issued by PhonepayPlus.

Competitions
10.13 References to brands within competitions must be brief and secondary.

(See Rule 1.30 in Section One: Protecting the Under-Eighteens and Rules 2.13 to 2.16 in Section Two: Harm and Offence.)

Use of advertisements in programmes
10.14 Advertising must be clearly separated from programmes. Advertisements must not appear in programme time, unless editorially justified.

Charity appeals
10.15 Charity appeals that are broadcast free of charge are allowed in programmes provided that the broadcaster has taken reasonable steps to satisfy itself that:

- the organisation concerned can produce satisfactory evidence of charitable status, or, in the case of an emergency appeal, that a responsible public fund has been set up to deal with it; and
- the organisation concerned is not prohibited from advertising on the relevant medium.

10.16 Where possible, the broadcast of charity appeals, either individually or taken together over time, should benefit a wide range of charities.

Appeals for funds for programmes or services
10.17 Broadcasters may broadcast appeals for donations to make programmes or fund their service. The audience must be told of the purpose of the donation and how much has been raised as a result of the appeal. All donations must be separately accounted for and used for the purpose for which they were donated.

Financial promotions and investment recommendations
10.18 When broadcasting financial promotions and investment recommendations broadcasters must comply with the relevant provisions in Appendix 4 to this Code.

Meaning of financial promotion(s):
A financial promotion is an invitation or inducement to engage in investment activity (in accordance with section 21(1) of the Financial Services and Markets Act 2000 (Restrictions on financial promotion).)

Meaning of investment recommendation(s):
An investment recommendation occurs when someone directly recommends a particular investment decision, for example, buying or selling a particular share or underwriting a particular share offer.

Virtual advertising
Television
10.19 The use of electronic imaging systems during broadcast coverage of an event must comply with the following requirements:

- broadcasters and viewers must be informed in advance of the presence of virtual images;
- virtual advertising may only replace existing on-site advertising virtual advertising messages must not be more visible or conspicuous than the actual advertising at the venue;
- rules relating to prohibited advertisers also apply to virtual advertising; and the broadcaster may not trade in virtual advertising.

Meaning of virtual advertising:
Virtual advertising normally (but not exclusively) takes place at events, for example, sporting events, and involves altering the broadcast signal to replace existing venue advertising with other advertising in the television picture (potentially targeted at a particular geographical audience).

APPENDIX 3

PRESS COMPLAINTS COMMISSION
CODE OF PRACTICE

All members of the press have a duty to maintain the highest professional standards. The Code, which includes this preamble and the public interest exceptions below, sets the benchmark for those ethical standards, protecting both the rights of the individual and the public's right to know. It is the cornerstone of the system of self-regulation to which the industry has made a binding commitment.

It is essential that an agreed code be honoured not only to the letter but in the full spirit. It should not be interpreted so narrowly as to compromise its commitment to respect the rights of the individual, nor so broadly that it constitutes an unnecessary interference with freedom of expression or prevents publication in the public interest.

It is the responsibility of editors and publishers to apply the Code to editorial material in both printed and online versions of publications. They should take care to ensure it is observed rigorously by all editorial staff and external contributors, including non-journalists, in printed and online versions of publications.

Editors should co-operate swiftly with the PCC in the resolution of complaints. Any publication judged to have breached the Code must print the adjudication in full and with due prominence, including headline reference to the PCC.

DEFAMATION ACT 1996 (C.31)

Schedule 1

QUALIFIED PRIVILEGE

STATEMENTS HAVING QUALIFIED PRIVILEGE WITHOUT EXPLANATION OR CONTRADICTION

1. A fair and accurate report of proceedings in public of a legislature anywhere in the world.

2. A fair and accurate report of proceedings in public before a court anywhere in the world.

3. A fair and accurate report of proceedings in public of a person appointed to hold a public inquiry by a government or legislature anywhere in the world.

4. A fair and accurate report of proceedings in public anywhere in the world of an international organisation or an international conference.

5. A fair and accurate copy of or extract from any register or other document required by law to be open to public inspection.

6. A notice or advertisement published by or on the authority of a court, or of a judge or officer of a court, anywhere in the world.

7. A fair and accurate copy of or extract from matter published by or on the authority of a government or legislature anywhere in the world.

8. A fair and accurate copy of or extract from matter published anywhere in the world by an international organisation or an international conference.

STATEMENTS PRIVILEGED SUBJECT TO EXPLANATION OR CONTRADICTION

9.—(1) A fair and accurate copy of or extract from a notice or other matter issued for the information of the public by or on behalf of—

    (a) a legislature in any member State or the European Parliament;

    (b) the government of any member State, or any authority performing governmental functions in any member State or part of a member State, or the European Commission;

    (c) an international organisation or international conference.

(2) In this paragraph "governmental functions" includes police functions,

10. A fair and accurate copy of or extract from a document made available by a court in any member State or the European Court of

507

Justice (or any court attached to that court), or by a judge or officer of any such court.

¹**11.**— (1) A fair and accurate report of proceedings at any public meeting or sitting in the United Kingdom of—

    (a)   a local authority, local authority committee or in the case of a local authority which are operating executive arrangements the executive of that authority or a committee of that executive;

    (b)   a justice or justices of the peace acting otherwise than as a court exercising judicial authority;

    (c)   a commission, tribunal, committee or person appointed for the purposes of any inquiry by any statutory provision, by Her Majesty or by a Minister of the Crown, a member of the Scottish Executive, the Welsh Ministers or the Counsel General to the Welsh Assembly Government or a Northern Ireland Department;

    (d)   a person appointed by a local authority to hold a local inquiry in pursuance of any statutory provision;

    (e)   any other tribunal, board, committee or body constituted by or under, and exercising functions under, any statutory provision.

(1A) In the case of a local authority which are operating executive arrangements, a fair and accurate record of any decision made by any member of the executive where that record is required to be made and available for public inspection by virtue of section 22 of the Local Government Act 2000 or of any provision in regulations made under that section.

(2) In sub-paragraphs (1)(a) and (1A)—

"executive" and "executive arrangements" have the same meaning as in Part II of the Local Government Act 2000;

"local authority" means—

    (a)   in relation to England and Wales, a principal council within the meaning of the Local Government Act 1972, any body falling within any paragraph of section 100J(1) of that Act or an authority or body to which the Public Bodies (Admission to Meetings) Act 1960 applies,

    (b)   in relation to Scotland, a council constituted under section 2 of the Local Government etc. (Scotland) Act 1994 or an authority or body to which the Public Bodies (Admission to Meetings) Act 1960 applies,

    (c)   in relation to Northern Ireland, any authority or body to which sections 23 to 27 of the Local Government Act (Northern Ireland) 1972 apply; and

"local authority committee" means any committee of a local authority or of local authorities, and includes—

(a) any committee or sub-committee in relation to which sections 100A to 100D of the Local Government Act 1972 apply by virtue of section 100E of that Act (whether or not also by virtue of section 100J of that Act), and

(b) any committee or sub-committee in relation to which sections 50A to 50D of the Local Government (Scotland) Act 1973 apply by virtue of section 50E of that Act.

(3) A fair and accurate report of any corresponding proceedings in any of the Channel Islands or the Isle of Man or in another member State.

12.—(1) A fair and accurate report of proceedings at any public meeting held in a member State.

(2) In this paragraph a "public meeting" means a meeting bona fide and lawfully held for a lawful purpose and for the furtherance or discussion of a matter of public concern, whether admission to the meeting is general or restricted.

13.—(1) A fair and accurate report of proceedings at a general meeting of a UK public company.

(2) A fair and accurate copy of or extract from any document circulated to members of a UK public company—

(a) by or with the authority of the board of directors of the company,

(b) by the auditors of the company, or

(c) by any member of the company in pursuance of a right conferred by any statutory provision.

(3) A fair and accurate copy of or extract from any document circulated to members of a UK public company which relates to the appointment, resignation, retirement or dismissal of directors of the company.

(4) In this paragraph "UK public company" means—

²(a) a public company within the meaning of section 4(2) of the Companies Act 2006 or

(b) a body corporate incorporated by or registered under any other statutory provision, or by Royal Charter, or formed in pursuance of letters patent.

(5) A fair and accurate report of proceedings at any corresponding meeting of, or copy of or extract from any corresponding document circulated to members of, a public company formed under the law of any of the Channel Islands or the Isle of Man or of another member State.

14. A fair and accurate report of any finding or decision of any of the following descriptions of association, formed in the United Kingdom or another member State, or of any committee or governing body of such an association—

(a) an association formed for the purpose of promoting or encouraging the exercise of or interest in any art, science, religion or learning, and empowered by its constitution to exercise control over or adjudicate on matters of interest or concern to the association, or the actions or conduct of any person subject to such control or adjudication;

(b) an association formed for the purpose of promoting or safeguarding the interests of any trade, business, industry or profession, or of the persons carrying on or engaged in any trade, business, industry or profession, and empowered by its constitution to exercise control over or adjudicate upon matters connected with that trade, business, industry or profession, or the actions or conduct of those persons;

(c) an association formed for the purpose of promoting or safeguarding the interests of a game, sport or pastime to the playing or exercise of which members of the public are invited or admitted, and empowered by its constitution to exercise control over or adjudicate upon persons connected with or taking part in the game, sport or pastime;

(d) an association formed for the purpose of promoting charitable objects or other objects beneficial to the community and empowered by its constitution to exercise control over or to adjudicate on matters of interest or concern to the association, or the actions or conduct of any person subject to such control or adjudication.

15.— (1) A fair and accurate report of, or copy of or extract from, any adjudication, report, statement or notice issued by a body, officer or other person designated for the purposes of this paragraph—

(a) for England and Wales or Northern Ireland, by order of the Lord Chancellor, and

(b) for Scotland, by order of the Secretary of State.

(2) An order under this paragraph shall be made by statutory instrument which shall be subject to annulment in pursuance of a resolution of either House of Parliament.

SUPPLEMENTARY PROVISIONS

16.— (1) In this Schedule—

"court" includes any tribunal or body exercising the judicial power of the State;

"international conference" means a conference attended by representatives of two or more governments;

"international organisation" means an organisation of which two or more governments are members, and includes any committee or other

subordinate body of such an organisation; and
"legislature" includes a local legislature.

(2) References in this Schedule to a member State include any
European dependent territory of a member State.

(3) In paragraphs 2 and 6 "court" includes—

(a) the European Court of Justice (or any court attached to
that court) and the Court of Auditors of the European
Communities,

(b) the European Court of Human Rights,

(c) any international criminal tribunal established by the
Security Council of the United Nations or by an
international agreement to which the United Kingdom is a
party, and

(d) the International Court of Justice and any other judicial or
arbitral tribunal deciding matters in dispute between
States.

(4) In paragraphs 1, 3 and 7 "legislature" includes the European
Parliament.

17.— (1) Provision may be made by order identifying—

(a) for the purposes of paragraph 11, the corresponding
proceedings referred to in sub-paragraph (3);

(b) for the purposes of paragraph 13, the corresponding
meetings and documents referred to in sub-paragraph (5).

(2) An order under this paragraph may be made—

(a) for England and Wales or Northern Ireland, by the Lord
Chancellor, and

(b) for Scotland, by the Secretary of State.

(3) An order under this paragraph shall be made by statutory
instrument which shall be subject to annulment in pursuance of a
resolution of either House of Parliament.

NOTES

1. Amended by Scotland Act 1998 (c.46), Sch.8, para.33(3); Local
Authorities (Executive and Alternative Arrangements) (Modification of
Enactments and Other Provisions) (Wales) Order 2002 (SI 2002/808),
art.30; Government of Wales Act 2006 (c.32), Sch.10, para.40.

2. Amended by Companies Act 2006 (Consequential Amendments,
Transitional Provisions and Savings) Order (SI 2009/1941), Sch.1,
para.159.

DATA PROTECTION PRINCIPLES:

DATA PROTECTION ACT 1998 (c.29)

Schedule 1

THE DATA PROTECTION PRINCIPLES

The principles

1. Personal data shall be processed fairly and lawfully and, in particular, shall not be processed unless—

(a) at least one of the conditions in Schedule 2 is met, and

(b) in the case of sensitive personal data, at least one of the conditions in Schedule 3 is also met.

2. Personal data shall be obtained only for one or more specified and lawful purposes, and shall not be further processed in any manner incompatible with that purpose or those purposes.

3. Personal data shall be adequate, relevant and not excessive in relation to the purpose or purposes for which they are processed.

4. Personal data shall be accurate and, where necessary, kept up to date.

5. Personal data processed for any purpose or purposes shall not be kept for longer than is necessary for that purpose or those purposes.

6. Personal data shall be processed in accordance with the rights of data subjects under this Act.

7. Appropriate technical and organisational measures shall be taken against unauthorised or unlawful processing of personal data and against accidental loss or destruction of, or damage to, personal data.

8. Personal data shall not be transferred to a country or territory outside the European Economic Area unless that country or territory ensures an adequate level of protection for the rights and freedoms of data subjects in relation to the processing of personal data.

Interpretation of the principles in Part I

The first principle

1.—(1) In determining for the purposes of the first principle whether personal data are processed fairly, regard is to be had to the method by which they are obtained, including in particular whether any person from whom they are obtained is deceived or misled as to the purpose or purposes for which they are to be processed.

(2) Subject to paragraph 2, for the purposes of the first principle data are to be treated as obtained fairly if they consist of information obtained from a person who—

(a) is authorised by or under any enactment to supply it, or

(b) is required to supply it by or under any enactment or by any convention or other instrument imposing an international obligation on the United Kingdom.

2.—(1) Subject to paragraph 3, for the purposes of the first principle personal data are not to be treated as processed fairly unless—

(a) in the case of data obtained from the data subject, the data controller ensures so far as practicable that the data subject has, is provided with, or has made readily available to him, the information specified in sub-paragraph (3), and

(b) in any other case, the data controller ensures so far as practicable that, before the relevant time or as soon as practicable after that time, the data subject has, is provided with, or has made readily available to him, the information specified in sub-paragraph (3).

(2) In sub-paragraph (1)(b) "the relevant time" means—

(a) the time when the data controller first processes the data, or

(b) in a case where at that time disclosure to a third party within a reasonable period is envisaged—

  (i)   if the data are in fact disclosed to such a person within that period, the time when the data are first disclosed,

  (ii) if within that period the data controller becomes, or ought to become, aware that the data are unlikely to be disclosed to such a person within that period, the time when the data controller does become, or ought to become, so aware, or

  (iii) in any other case, the end of that period.

(3) The information referred to in sub-paragraph (1) is as follows, namely—

(a) the identity of the data controller,

(b) if he has nominated a representative for the purposes of this Act, the identity of that representative,

(c) the purpose or purposes for which the data are intended to be processed, and

(d) any further information which is necessary, having regard to the specific circumstances in which the data are or are to be processed, to enable processing in respect of the data subject to be fair.

[1]**3.**—(1) Paragraph 2(1)(b) does not apply where either of the primary conditions in sub-paragraph (2), together with such further conditions as may be prescribed by the Secretary of State by order, are met.

(2) The primary conditions referred to in sub-paragraph (1) are—

(a) that the provision of that information would involve a disproportionate effort, or

(b) that the recording of the information to be contained in the data by, or the disclosure of the data by, the data controller is necessary for compliance with any legal obligation to which the data controller is subject, other than an obligation imposed by contract.

[1]4.—(1) Personal data which contain a general identifier falling within a description prescribed by the Secretary of State by order are not to be treated as processed fairly and lawfully unless they are processed in compliance with any conditions so prescribed in relation to general identifiers of that description.

(2) In sub-paragraph (1) "a general identifier" means any identifier (such as, for example, a number or code used for identification purposes) which—

(a) relates to an individual, and

(b) forms part of a set of similar identifiers which is of general application.

The second principle

5. The purpose or purposes for which personal data are obtained may in particular be specified—

(a) in a notice given for the purposes of paragraph 2 by the data controller to the data subject, or

(b) in a notification given to the Commissioner under Part III of this Act.

6. In determining whether any disclosure of personal data is compatible with the purpose or purposes for which the data were obtained, regard is to be had to the purpose or purposes for which the personal data are intended to be processed by any person to whom they are disclosed.

The fourth principle

7. The fourth principle is not to be regarded as being contravened by reason of any inaccuracy in personal data which accurately record information obtained by the data controller from the data subject or a third party in a case where—

(a) having regard to the purpose or purposes for which the data were obtained and further processed, the data controller has taken reasonable steps to ensure the accuracy of the data, and

(b) if the data subject has notified the data controller of the data subject's view that the data are inaccurate, the data indicate that fact.

The sixth principle

[2]**8.** A person is to be regarded as contravening the sixth principle if, but only if—

(a) he contravenes section 7 by failing to supply information in accordance with that section,

(b) he contravenes section 10 by failing to comply with a notice given under subsection (1) of that section to the extent that the notice is justified or by failing to give a notice under subsection (3) of that section,

(c) he contravenes section 11 by failing to comply with a notice given under subsection (1) of that section, or

(d) he contravenes section 12 by failing to comply with a notice given under subsection (1) or (2)(b) of that section or by failing to give a notification under subsection (2)(a) of that section or a notice under subsection (3) of that section.

The seventh principle
9. Having regard to the state of technological development and the cost of implementing any measures, the measures must ensure a level of security appropriate to—

(a) the harm that might result from such unauthorised or unlawful processing or accidental loss, destruction or damage as are mentioned in the seventh principle, and

(b) the nature of the data to be protected.

10. The data controller must take reasonable steps to ensure the reliability of any employees of his who have access to the personal data.

11. Where processing of personal data is carried out by a data processor on behalf of a data controller, the data controller must in order to comply with the seventh principle—

(a) choose a data processor providing sufficient guarantees in respect of the technical and organisational security measures governing the processing to be carried out, and

(b) take reasonable steps to ensure compliance with those measures.

12. Where processing of personal data is carried out by a data processor on behalf of a data controller; the data controller is not to be regarded as complying with the seventh principle unless—

(a) the processing is carried out under a contract—

   (i)   which is made or evidenced in writing, and

   (ii) under which the data processor is to act only on instructions from the data controller, and

(b) the contract requires the data processor to comply with obligations equivalent to those imposed on a data controller by the seventh principle.

The eighth principle
13. An adequate level of protection is one which is adequate in all the circumstances of the case, having regard in particular to—

(a) the nature of the personal data,

(b) the country or territory of origin of the information contained in the data,

(c) the country or territory of final destination of that information,

(d) the purposes for which and period during which the data are intended to be processed,

(e) the law in force in the country or territory in question,

(f) the international obligations of that country or territory,

(g) any relevant codes of conduct or other rules which are enforceable in that country or territory (whether generally or by arrangement in particular cases), and

(h) any security measures taken in respect of the data in that country or territory.

[2]**14.** The eighth principle does not apply to a transfer falling within any paragraph of Schedule 4, except in such circumstances and to such extent as the Secretary of State may by order provide.

15.—(1) Where—

(a) in any proceedings under this Act any question arises as to whether the requirement of the eighth principle as to an adequate level of protection is met in relation to the transfer of any personal data to a country or territory outside the European Economic Area, and

(b) a Community finding has been made in relation to transfers of the kind in question,

that question is to be determined in accordance with that finding.

(2) In sub-paragraph (1) "Community finding" means a finding of the European Commission, under the procedure provided for in Article 31(2) of the Data Protection Directive, that a country or territory outside the European Economic Area does, or does not, ensure an adequate level of protection within the meaning of Article 25(2) of the Directive.

NOTES
1. Amended by Secretary of State for Constitutional Affairs Order 2003 (SI 2003/1887), Sch2, para9(1)(b).
2. Amended by Data Protection Act 1998 (c.29), Sch.13, para.5.

Schedule 2

CONDITIONS RELEVANT FOR PURPOSES OF THE FIRST PRINCIPLE: PROCESSING OF ANY PERSONAL DATA

1. The data subject has given his consent to the processing.

2. The processing is necessary—

(a) for the performance of a contract to which the data subject is a party, or

(b) for the taking of steps at the request of the data subject with a view to entering into a contract.

3. The processing is necessary for compliance with any legal obligation to which the data controller is subject, other than an obligation imposed by contract.

4. The processing is necessary in order to protect the vital interests of the data subject.

[1]**5.** The processing is necessary—

(a) for the administration of justice,

(aa) for the exercise of any functions of either House of Parliament,

(b) for the exercise of any functions conferred on any person by or under any enactment,

(c) for the exercise of any functions of the Crown, a Minister of the Crown or a government department, or

(d) for the exercise of any other functions of a public nature exercised in the public interest by any person.

6.—(1) The processing is necessary for the purposes of legitimate interests pursued by the data controller or by the third party or parties to whom the data are disclosed, except where the processing is unwarranted in any particular case by reason of prejudice to the rights and freedoms or legitimate interests of the data subject.

[2](2) The Secretary of State may by order specify particular circumstances in which this condition is, or is not, to be taken to be satisfied.

NOTES
1. Amended by Freedom of Information Act 2000 (c.36), Sch.6, para.4.
2. Amended by Secretary of State for Constitutional Affairs Order 1887 (SI 2003/1887), Sch.2, para.9(1)(b).

Schedule 3

CONDITIONS RELEVANT FOR PURPOSES OF THE FIRST PRINCIPLE: PROCESSING OF SENSITIVE PERSONAL DATA

1. The data subject has given his explicit consent to the processing of the personal data.

2.—(1) The processing is necessary for the purposes of exercising or performing any right or obligation which is conferred or imposed by law on the data controller in connection with employment.

[1](2) The Secretary of State may by order—

(a) exclude the application of sub-paragraph (1) in such cases as may be specified, or

(b) provide that, in such cases as may be specified, the condition in sub-paragraph (1) is not to be regarded as satisfied unless such further conditions as may be specified in the order are also satisfied.

3. The processing is necessary—

(a) in order to protect the vital interests of the data subject or another person, in a case where—

    (i)   consent cannot be given by or on behalf of the data subject, or

    (ii) the data controller cannot reasonably be expected to obtain the consent of the data subject, or

(b) in order to protect the vital interests of another person, in a case where consent by or on behalf of the data subject has been unreasonably withheld.

4. The processing—

(a) is carried out in the course of its legitimate activities by any body or association which—

    (i)   is not established or conducted for profit, and

    (ii) exists for political, philosophical, religious or trade-union purposes,

(b) is carried out with appropriate safeguards for the rights and freedoms of data subjects,

(c) relates only to individuals who either are members of the body or association or have regular contact with it in connection with its purposes, and

(d) does not involve disclosure of the personal data to a third party without the consent of the data subject.

5. The information contained in the personal data has been made public as a result of steps deliberately taken by the data subject.

6. The processing—

(a) is necessary for the purpose of, or in connection with, any legal proceedings (including prospective legal proceedings),

(b) is necessary for the purpose of obtaining legal advice, or

(c) is otherwise necessary for the purposes of establishing, exercising or defending legal rights.

7.—(1) The processing is necessary—

(a) for the administration of justice,

[2](aa) for the exercise of any functions of either House of Parliament,

(b) for the exercise of any functions conferred on any person by or under an enactment, or

(c) for the exercise of any functions of the Crown, a Minister of the Crown or a government department.

(2) The Secretary of State may by order—

(a) exclude the application of sub-paragraph (1) in such cases as may be specified, or

(b) provide that, in such cases as may be specified, the condition in sub-paragraph (1) is not to be regarded as satisfied unless such further conditions as may be specified in the order are also satisfied.

[3]**7A.**—(1) The processing–

(a) is either–
   (i)   the disclosure of sensitive personal data by a person as a member of an anti-fraud organisation or otherwise in accordance with any arrangements made by such an organisation; or
  (ii) any other processing by that person or another person of sensitive personal data so disclosed; and
(b) is necessary for the purposes of preventing fraud or a particular kind of fraud.

(2) In this paragraph "an anti-fraud organisation" means any unincorporated association, body corporate or other person which enables or facilitates any sharing of information to prevent fraud or a particular kind of fraud or which has any of these functions as its purpose or one of its purposes.

8.— (1) The processing is necessary for medical purposes and is undertaken by—
  (a) a health professional, or
  (b) a person who in the circumstances owes a duty of confidentiality which is equivalent to that which would arise if that person were a health professional.

(2) In this paragraph "medical purposes" includes the purposes of preventative medicine, medical diagnosis, medical research, the provision of care and treatment and the management of health care services.

9.— (1) The processing—
  (a) is of sensitive personal data consisting of information as to racial or ethnic origin,
  (b) is necessary for the purpose of identifying or keeping under review the existence or absence of equality of opportunity or treatment between persons of different racial or ethnic origins, with a view to enabling such equality to be promoted or maintained, and
  (c) is carried out with appropriate safeguards for the rights and freedoms of data subjects.

[1](2) The Secretary of State may by order specify circumstances in which processing falling within sub-paragraph (1)(a) and (b) is, or is not, to be taken for the purposes of sub-paragraph (1)(c) to be carried out with appropriate safeguards for the rights and freedoms of data subjects.

[1]**10.** The personal data are processed in circumstances specified in an order made by the Secretary of State for the purposes of this paragraph.

NOTES
1. Amended by Amended by Secretary of State for Constitutional Affairs Order 1887 (SI 2003/1887), Sch.2, para.9(1)(b).

2. Inserted by Amended by Freedom of Information Act 2000 (c.36), Sch.6, para.5.
3. Inserted by Serious Crime Act 2007 (c.27), Pt3, s.72.

APPENDIX 6

DATA PROTECTION (PROCESSING OF SENSITIVE PERSONAL DATA) ORDER 2000 (SI 2000/417)

1.— (1) This Order may be cited as the Data Protection (Processing of Sensitive Personal Data) Order 2000 and shall come into force on 1st March 2000.

(2) In this Order, "the Act" means the Data Protection Act 1998.

2. For the purposes of paragraph 10 of Schedule 3 to the Act, the circumstances specified in any of the paragraphs in the Schedule to this Order are circumstances in which sensitive personal data may be processed.

Schedule 1

CIRCUMSTANCES IN WHICH SENSITIVE PERSONAL DATA MAY BE PROCESSED

1.—(1) The processing—

(a) is in the substantial public interest;

(b) is necessary for the purposes of the prevention or detection of any unlawful act; and

(c) must necessarily be carried out without the explicit consent of the data subject being sought so as not to prejudice those purposes.

(2) In this paragraph, "act" includes a failure to act.

2. The processing–

(a) is in the substantial public interest;

(b) is necessary for the discharge of any function which is designed for protecting members of the public against–

   (i) dishonesty, malpractice, or other seriously improper conduct by, or the unfitness or incompetence of, any person, or

   (ii) mismanagement in the administration of, or failures in services provided by, any body or association; and

(c) must necessarily be carried out without the explicit consent of the data subject being sought so as not to prejudice the discharge of that function.

3.— (1) The disclosure of personal data—

(a) is in the substantial public interest;

(b) is in connection with–

   (i) the commission by any person of any unlawful act (whether alleged or established),

521

(ii) dishonesty, malpractice, or other seriously improper conduct by, or the unfitness or incompetence of, any person (whether alleged or established), or

(iii) mismanagement in the administration of, or failures in services provided by, any body or association (whether alleged or established);

(c) is for the special purposes as defined in section 3 of the Act; and

(d) is made with a view to the publication of those data by any person and the data controller reasonably believes that such publication would be in the public interest.

(2) In this paragraph, "act" includes a failure to act.

4. The processing—

(a) is in the substantial public interest;

(b) is necessary for the discharge of any function which is designed for the provision of confidential counselling, advice, support or any other service; and

(c) is carried out without the explicit consent of the data subject because the processing–

(i) is necessary in a case where consent cannot be given by the data subject,

(ii) is necessary in a case where the data controller cannot reasonably be expected to obtain the explicit consent of the data subject, or

(iii) must necessarily be carried out without the explicit consent of the data subject being sought so as not to prejudice the provision of that counselling, advice, support or other service.

5.— (1) The processing—

(a) is necessary for the purpose of—

(i) carrying on insurance business, or

(ii) making determinations in connection with eligibility for, and benefits payable under, an occupational pension scheme as defined in section 1 of the Pension Schemes Act 1993;

(b) is of sensitive personal data consisting of information falling within section 2(e) of the Act relating to a data subject who is the parent, grandparent, great grandparent or sibling of–

(i) in the case of paragraph (a)(i), the insured person, or

(ii) in the case of paragraph (a)(ii), the member of the scheme;

(c) is necessary in a case where the data controller cannot reasonably be expected to obtain the explicit consent of that data subject and the data controller is not aware of the data subject withholding his consent; and

(d) does not support measures or decisions with respect to that data subject.

[1](2) In this paragraph–
(a) "insurance business" means business which consists of effecting or carrying out contracts of insurance of the following kind—
    (i) life and annuity,
    (ii) linked long term,
    (iii) permanent health,
    (iv) accident, or
    (v) sickness; and
(b) "insured" and "member" includes an individual who is seeking to become an insured person or member of the scheme respectively.
[2](2A) The definition of "insurance business" in sub-paragraph (2) above must be read with—
(a) section 22 of the Financial Services and Markets Act 2000;
(b) any relevant order under that section; and
(c) Schedule 2 to that Act.

NOTES
1. Amended by Financial Services and Markets Act 2000 (Consequential Amendments and Repeals) Order 2001 (SI 2001/3649), Pt9, art.587(2).
2. Inserted by Financial Services and Markets Act 2000 (Consequential Amendments and Repeals) Order (SI 2001/3649), Pt9, art.587(3).

6. The processing—
(a) is of sensitive personal data in relation to any particular data subject that are subject to processing which was already under way immediately before the coming into force of this Order;
(b) is necessary for the purpose of–
    [1](i) effecting or carrying out contracts of long-term insurance of the kind mentioned in sub-paragraph (2)(a)(i), (ii) or (iii) of paragraph 5 above.
    (ii) establishing or administering an occupational pension scheme as defined in section 1 of the Pension Schemes Act 1993; and
(c) either—
    (i) is necessary in a case where the data controller cannot reasonably be expected to obtain the explicit consent of the data subject and that data subject has not informed the data controller that he does not so consent, or
    (ii) must necessarily be carried out even without the explicit consent of the data subject so as not to prejudice those purposes.

NOTE
1. Amended by Financial Services and Markets Act 2000 (Consequential Amendments and Repeals) Order (SI 2001/3649), Pt9, art.587(4).

7.— (1) Subject to the provisions of sub-paragraph (2), the processing–

(a) is of sensitive personal data consisting of information falling within section 2(c) or (e) of the Act;

(b) is necessary for the purpose of identifying or keeping under review the existence or absence of equality of opportunity or treatment between persons–

    (i) holding different beliefs as described in section 2(c) of the Act, or

    (ii) of different states of physical or mental health or different physical or mental conditions as described in section 2(e) of the Act,

with a view to enabling such equality to be promoted or maintained;

(c) does not support measures or decisions with respect to any particular data subject otherwise than with the explicit consent of that data subject; and

(d) does not cause, nor is likely to cause, substantial damage or substantial distress to the data subject or any other person.

(2) Where any individual has given notice in writing to any data controller who is processing personal data under the provisions of sub-paragraph (1) requiring that data controller to cease processing personal data in respect of which that individual is the data subject at the end of such period as is reasonable in the circumstances, that data controller must have ceased processing those personal data at the end of that period.

8.—(1) Subject to the provisions of sub-paragraph (2), the processing—

(a) is of sensitive personal data consisting of information falling within section 2(b) of the Act;

(b) is carried out by any person or organisation included in the register maintained pursuant to section 1 of the Registration of Political Parties Act 1998 in the course of his or its legitimate political activities; and

(c) does not cause, nor is likely to cause, substantial damage or substantial distress to the data subject or any other person.

(2) Where any individual has given notice in writing to any data controller who is processing personal data under the provisions of sub-paragraph (1) requiring that data controller to cease processing personal data in respect of which that individual is the data subject at the end of such period as is reasonable in the circumstances, that data

controller must have ceased processing those personal data at the end of that period.

9. The processing—

(a) is in the substantial public interest;

(b) is necessary for research purposes (which expression shall have the same meaning as in section 33 of the Act);

(c) does not support measures or decisions with respect to any particular data subject otherwise than with the explicit consent of that data subject; and

(d) does not cause, nor is likely to cause, substantial damage or substantial distress to the data subject or any other person.

10. The processing is necessary for the exercise of any functions conferred on a constable by any rule of law.

FREEDOM OF INFORMATION (SCOTLAND) ACT 2002 (c.13)

Schedule 1

PART 1: Ministers, the Parliament
1 The Scottish Ministers.
2 The Scottish Parliament.
3 The Scottish Parliamentary Corporate Body.

PART 2: Non Ministerial Office Holders in the Scottish Administration
4 The Chief Dental Officer of the Scottish Administration.
5 The Chief Medical Officer of the Scottish Administration.
6 Her Majesty's Chief Inspector of Constabulary.
7 Her Majesty's Chief Inspector of Prisons for Scotland.
[1]**7A** The Drinking Water Quality Regulator for Scotland.
8 Her Majesty's Inspector of Anatomy for Scotland.
[2]**9** [Her Majesty's Chief Inspector of Fire and Rescue Authorities]
10 Her Majesty's inspectors of schools (that is to say, the inspectors of schools appointed by Her Majesty on the recommendation of the Scottish Ministers under the Education (Scotland) Act 1980 (c.44)).
11 The Keeper of the Records of Scotland.
12 The Keeper of the Registers of Scotland.
[3]**12A** The Office of the Scottish Charity Regulator.
13 A procurator fiscal.
14 The Queen's and Lord Treasurer's Remembrancer.
15 The Queen's Printer for Scotland.
16 The Registrar General of Births, Deaths and Marriages for Scotland.
17 The Registrar of Independent Schools in Scotland.
18 A rent officer appointed under section 43(3) of the Rent (Scotland) Act 1984 (c.58).
[4]**18A** The Scottish Court Service.
[5]**19** A social work inspector appointed under section 4 of the Joint Inspection of Children's Services and Inspection of Social Work Services (Scotland) Act 2006 (asp 3).

PART 3: Local Government
20 An assessor appointed under section 27(2) of the Local Government etc. (Scotland) Act 1994 (c.39).
21 A council constituted by section 2 of that Act.

22 A joint board, within the meaning of section 235(1) of the Local Government (Scotland) Act 1973 (c.65).

[6]**23** A licensing board [continued in existence by or established under section 5 of the Licensing (Scotland) Act 2005 (asp 16).

24 The Strathclyde Passenger Transport Authority.

[7]**24A** A Transport Partnership created under the Transport (Scotland) Act 2005 (asp 12).

PART 4: The National Health Service

25 [*Repealed.*]

26 The Common Services Agency for the Scottish Health Service.

27 A Health Board, constituted under section 2 of the National Health Service (Scotland) Act 1978.

28 [*Repealed.*]

29 [*Repealed.*]

30 A local health council, established under section 7 of the National Health Service (Scotland) Act 1978.

31 A National Health Service trust.

32 NHS 24.

[8]**32A** NHS Education for Scotland.

[8]**32B** NHS Health Scotland.

[8]**32C** NHS Quality Improvement Scotland.

[9]**33** A person providing primary medical services under a general medical services contract (within the meaning of the National Health Service (Scotland) Act 1978) or general dental services, general ophthalmic services or pharmaceutical services under Part II of that Act, but only in respect of information relating to the provision of those services.

[9]**34** A person providing primary medical services or personal dental services under arrangements made under section 17C of that Act, but only in respect of information relating to the provision of those services.

35 A person providing, in Scotland, piloted services within the meaning of the National Health Service (Primary Care) Act 1997 (c.46), but only in respect of information relating to the provision of those services.

36 [*Repealed.*]

37 The Scottish Advisory Committee on Distinction Awards.

38 [*Repealed.*]

39 The Scottish Ambulance Service Board.

40 [*Repealed.*]

41 The Scottish Dental Practice Board.

42–44 [*Repealed.*]

45 The State Hospitals Board for Scotland.

46 [*Repealed.*]

PART 5: Educational Institutions

47 The board of management of a college of further education (expressions used in this paragraph having the same meaning as in section 36(1) of the Further and Higher Education (Scotland) Act 1992 (c.37)).

48 A central institution within the meaning of the Education (Scotland) Act 1980.

[10]**49** An institution in receipt of funding from the Scottish Further and Higher Education Funding Council other than any institution whose activities are principally carried on outwith Scotland.

PART 6: Police

50 A chief constable of a police force in Scotland.

51 A joint police board constituted by an amalgamation scheme made or approved under the Police (Scotland) Act 1967 (c.77).

52 The Police Advisory Board for Scotland.

[11]**52A** The Scottish Police Services Authority, but only in respect of information relating to the provision of the police support services within the meaning of section 3(2) of the Police, Public Order and Criminal Justice (Scotland) Act 2006.

PART 7: Others

53 The Accounts Commission for Scotland.

54–56 [*Repealed.*]

57 Audit Scotland.

58 The Auditor General for Scotland.

59 The Board of Trustees for the National Galleries of Scotland.

60 The Board of Trustees of the National Museums of Scotland.

61 The Board of Trustees of the Royal Botanic Garden, Edinburgh.

[12]**61A** Bòrd na Gàidhlig.

62 The Central Advisory Committee on Justices of the Peace.

[13]**62ZA** The Commissioner for Children and Young People in Scotland.

[14]**62A** A community justice authority.

[15]**62B** The Convener of the Water Customer Consultation Panels (appointed under paragraph 5(1) of schedule 1 to the Water Industry (Scotland) Act 2002 (asp 3)) and those Panels.

[16]**62C** Creative Scotland.

63 The Crofters Commission.

64–65 [*Repealed.*]

66 The General Teaching Council for Scotland.

[17]**66A** Her Majesty's Chief Inspector of Prosecution in Scotland.

67 Highlands and Islands Enterprise.

67A–68 [*Repealed.*]

[18]**68A** The Judicial Appointments Board for Scotland.

69 A justice of the peace advisory committee.

71 The Local Government Boundary Commission for Scotland.
72 The Mental Welfare Commission for Scotland.
73 A National Park authority, established by virtue of schedule 1 to the National Parks (Scotland) Act 2000 (asp 10).
74 The Parole Board for Scotland.
75 A person appointed for Scotland under section 3(1) of the Local Government and Housing Act 1989 (c.42).
[19]**75A** The Public Transport Users' Committee for Scotland.
[20]**75AA** The Police Complaints Commissioner for Scotland.
[21]**75B** Quality Meat Scotland.
[21]**75C** The Risk Management Authority.
76 The Royal Commission on the Ancient and Historical Monuments of Scotland.
77 The Scottish Agricultural Wages Board.
78–79 [*Repealed.*]
80 The Scottish Children's Reporter Administration.
[22]**80B** The Scottish Commission for Human Rights.
81 The Scottish Commission for the Regulation of Care.
82 [*Repealed.*]
83 The Scottish Criminal Cases Review Commission.
84 Scottish Enterprise.
85 The Scottish Environment Protection Agency.
[23]**85A** The Scottish Further and Higher Education Funding Council.
86–89 [*Repealed.*]
90 The Scottish Information Commissioner.
91 The Scottish Law Commission.
92 The Scottish Legal Aid Board.
[24]**92A** The Scottish Legal Complaints Commission.
[25]**92B** The Scottish Local Authorities Remuneration Committee.
93 Scottish Natural Heritage.
94 The Scottish Prison Complaints Commission.
95 The Scottish Public Services Ombudsman.
96 The Scottish Qualifications Authority.
97 [*Repealed.*]
[26]**97A** The Scottish Road Works Commissioner.
98 [*Repealed.*]
99 The Scottish Social Services Council.
100 The Scottish Sports Council.
101 [*Repealed*]
102 Scottish Water.
103 [*Repealed.*]
104 The Standards Commission for Scotland.
105 The Trustees of the National Library of Scotland.
[27]**105A** VisitScotland.
106 The Water Industry Commissioner for Scotland.

NOTES
1. Inserted by Freedom of Information (Scotland) Act 2002 (Scottish Public Authorities) Amendment Order 2008 (SSI 2008/297), Sch.1
2. Amended by Fire (Scotland) Act 2005 (asp 5), Sch.3, para.22.
3. Inserted by Freedom of Information (Scotland) Act 2002 (Scottish Public Authorities) Amendment Order 2008 (SSI 2008/297), Sch.1.
4. Inserted by Judiciary and Courts (Scotland) Act 2008 (asp 6), Sch.3, para.18.
5. Amended by Joint Inspection of Children's Services and Inspection of Social Work Services (Scotland) Act 2006 (asp 3), Pt3, s.8(2).
6. Amended by Licensing (Scotland) Act 2005 (asp 16), Sch.6, para.10.
7. Inserted by Transport (Scotland) Act 2005 (asp 12), Sch.1, para.20.
8. Inserted by Freedom of Information (Scotland) Act 2002 (Scottish Public Authorities) Amendment Order 2008 (SSI 2008/297), Sch.1.
9. Amended by Primary Medical Services (Scotland) Act 2004 (asp 1), Sch.1, para.5(a)(ii).
10. Amended by Further and Higher Education (Scotland) Act 2005 (asp 6), Sch.3, para.12(a).
11. Amended by Police, Public Order and Criminal Justice (Scotland) Act 2006 (asp 10), Sch.6, para.11(a).
12. Amended by Gaelic Language (Scotland) Act 2005 (asp 7), Sch.2, para.3.
13. Inserted by Freedom of Information (Scotland) Act 2002 (Scottish Public Authorities) Amendment Order 2008 (SSI 2008/297), Sch.1.
14. Inserted by Management of Offenders etc. (Scotland) Act 2005 (asp 14), s.21(12).
15. Inserted by Water Services etc. (Scotland) Act 2005 (asp 3), Sch5, para.9(a).
16. Inserted by Public Services Reform (Scotland) Act 2010 (asp 8), Sch.10, para.3(a).
17. Inserted by Freedom of Information (Scotland) Act 2002 (Scottish Public Authorities) Amendment Order (SSI 2008/297), Sch.1.
18. Inserted by Judiciary and Courts (Scotland) Act 2008 (asp 6), Sch.1, para.21.
19. Inserted by Transport (Scotland) Act 2005 (asp 12), Pt3, s.41(4).
20. Possible drafting issue, para.75A previously inserted, new para.75A inserted immediately after by Police, Public Order and Criminal Justice (Scotland) Act 2006 (asp 10), Sch.6, para11(b).
21. Inserted by Freedom of Information (Scotland) Act 2002 (Scottish Public Authorities) Amendment Order 2008 (SSI 2008/297), Sch.1.
22. Inserted by Scottish Commission for Human Rights Act 2006 (asp 16), Sch.1, para17.
23. Inserted by Further and Higher Education (Scotland) Act 2005 (asp 6), Sch.3, para.12(b).
24. Inserted by Legal Profession and Legal Aid (Scotland) Act 2007 (asp 5), Sch.5, para.5.
25. Inserted by Freedom of Information (Scotland) Act 2002 (Scottish Public Authorities) Amendment Order 2008 (SSI 2008/297), Sch.1.
26. Inserted by Transport (Scotland) Act 2005 (asp 12), Sch.2, para.4.
27. Inserted by Tourist Boards (Scotland) Act 2006 (asp 15), Sch.2, para.8(b).

GLOSSARY

absolvitor	decree absolving defender
ad factum praestandum	obligation to perform an act other than payment of money
adhere	(court) affirm; (spouse) live with
ad interim	in the interval; meantime
Adjournal, Acts of	procedural rules made by High Court
adminicle	piece of supporting evidence
ad valorem	according to value
advise	give judgment
advocation	form of criminal appeal usually by prosecution at preliminary stage
agnate	related through father
alibi	elsewhere (special defence plea)
aliment	maintenance enforceable by law
a mensa et thoro	from bed and table (separation)
apparent insolvency	insolvency which has become public
appoint	to order, direct
arbiter	one chosen by parties to settle difference (in England - arbitrator)
as accords (of law)	in conformity with the law
assize	jury
assoilzie (z silent)	absolve
aver	to state in written pleadings
avizandum	to be considered (reserved judgment)
back letter	document qualifying another which purports to give an absolute right
bill of suspension	form of appeal to Justiciary Appeal Court
brevi manu	short cut; summarily
calling	first step in civil action
casual homicide	blameless killing
caution (pronounced "cay-shun")	security
caveat	"let him take care"; legal document lodged by part to ensure no order passes against him in his absence
certiorate	give formal notice of a fact
circumvention	dishonest taking advantage of a vulnerable ("facile") person for gain
cite	to summon to court
cognate	related through mother
commit	consign to prison to await further procedure
compear	to appear and participate in an action
conclusion	relief sought in an action
condescendence	statement of averred facts or contentions
conditio si testator	principle by which a will not dealing with children is

sine liberis decesserit	revoked by birth of a child
consanguinean	relationship between brothers or sisters who have the same father but different mothers
consistorial	relating to questions of status, such as matrimonial proceedings
contra bonos mores	in breach of moral law
contumacy	failure to obey court order
crave	formally ask court (as in petition)
curator ad litem	officer appointed by court to assume responsibility for interests of litigant
curator bonis	officer appointed by court to manage a person's estate
cy-pres	as near as possible (applied to necessary variation of terms of trust, will, etc.)
damnum	harm, loss
damnum fatale	loss due to act of God
decern	give formal, final decree
declarator	binding statement of rights of a party issued by court
declinature	refusal of judge to take jurisdiction because of his interest or relationship
de die in diem	from day to day
deforcement	offence of resisting officer of law to prevent him carrying out his duties
de jure	in point of law; legal (as opposed to actual)
delectus personae	choice of person
de minimis (non curat lex)	the law ignores trifles
de novo	of new; afresh
de plano	summarily; simply; without further procedure
de presenti	now
desert	to abandon (diet)
design	to set forth person's occupation and address
dies non	a non-legal day
diet	date fixed for a hearing of a case
diligence	execution against a debtor; procedure for recovery of document
dispone	to convey (land)
DA-notice	Defence Advisory (see Chapter 38)
dominus litis	person controlling lawsuit who is not actually a party to it
edictal citation	method of citing persons who are outside of Scotland or sheriffdom
effeir	to correspond, appertain
esto	assuming; let it be assumed
ex adverso	opposite to; adjacent
excambion	contract for exchange of one piece of land for another
ex concesso	from what has been admitted
executor-dative	executor appointed by court
executor-nominate	executor appointed by testator
ex facie	on the face of it
ex hypothesi	by the hypothesis
ex justa causa	for just cause or sufficient reason
ex officio	by virtue of office
ex parte	in absence of a party; one-sided; partisan

expenses	payment for legal services (in England—costs)
ex proprio motu	on (the court's) own initiative
ex re	arising in the circumstances
extract	authenticated copy of decree, etc.
fee	full right of property (as opposed to liferent, q.v.)
fiar	owner of a fee
force and fear	duress vitiating a contract
force majeure	something beyond control; that cannot be prevented
forisfamiliation	departure of child from family on becoming independent
forum	platform; court; tribunal
fund in medio	amount under dispute in action of multiplepoinding (q.v.)
furth	outside (e.g. the country)
grassum	single payment made in addition to periodic one, such as rent
habile	apt
habit and repute	reputation of being married without formal ceremony, entitling parties to declarator of marriage
haver (pronounced as in "to have")	person holding documents he is required to produce in court
heritage	land and buildings passing to an heir on owner's death
holograph	wholly handwritten and signed by the author
homologate	approve and thereby validate
hypothec	security for debt, such as right of landlord over tenant's goods in premises let to him
in camera	behind closed doors
in causa	in the case (of)
incompetent	in conflict with the law applicable
incrimination	special defence accusing another of the crime charged
indictment	accusation of a crime made in name of Lord Advocate
induciae	time limit
in extenso	in full
in faciendo	in doing
infeft	having a feudal title to heritage
in foro	in court
in gremio	in the body (of a deed, etc.)
in hoc statu	at this stage; in the present state of affairs
in initio litis	at the outset of the action
in jure	in right
in limine	at the outset (threshold)
in loco parentis	in the place of a parent (e.g. guardian)
Inner House	appellate department of Court of Session comprising First and Second Divisions
in re	in the case of
in rem suam	in one's own affairs
in retentis	kept for the record
in solidum	for the whole sum
interdict	judicial prohibition (in England-injunction)
interlocutor	formal minute of court decision
interpone	authority to give court's approval to

interrogatories	written questions put to witness excused from attending court
inter vivos	between living persons (with reference to deeds)
intromit	to handle, deal with, funds, property, etc.
ipse dixit	bare assertion
ipso jure	by the force of law alone
irritancy	forfeiture of a right due to neglect or contravention (e.g. lease)
irrelevant	even if proved, would not justify remedy sought
ish	termination, usually of lease
joint minute	agreement between parties
judicial factor	person appointed by court to manage affairs of another
jus quaesitum tertio	contractual right of a person arising out of a contract between two others to which he is not a party
justifiable homicide	killing in exercise of public duty
lawburrows	ancient process for security against apprehended molestation
lenocinium	procuring by husband of his wife's adultery
lesion	detriment, loss, injury
lex loci contractus	law of the place where contract was made
lien	right to retain property of a debtor until payment
liferent	right entitling a person for life to use of another's property
liquid (sum)	of ascertained amount
locus	place
locus standi	right to be heard in court
medium concludendi	ground of action
minute	document by which party defines his position to the court
missives	writings exchanged by parties negotiating for a contract
modus	mode, manner
Moorov doctrine	the principle that, where an accused is charged with a series of similar offences closely linked in time and circumstances, the evidence of one witness as to each offence will be taken as mutually corroborative
mora	delay in making claim
mortis causa	to take effect after death
multiplepoinding (pronounced "multiple pinding")	action raised nominally by one party but in which a number of conflicting claims are made to a fund *in medio*
murmur	to slander a judge
nobile officium	equitable jurisdiction of High Court of Justiciary or Inner House of Court of Session by which strictness of common law may be mitigated, or a remedy given where not otherwise available
nomine damni	in name of damages
nominal raiser	holder of fund in a multiplepoinding when another initiates proceedings
non constat	it is not evident, not agreed
nonfeasance	omission to do a legal duty

notour	bankruptcy insolvency which has become public, a prerequisite in most cases of sequestration now, apparent insolvency
obiter dictum	judge's expression of an opinion not forming part of court's decision
obtemper	obey (court order)
onerous	granted for value
onus	burden (e.g. of proving case)
oppression	use of office or process of law to commit injustice
Outer House	department of Court of Session exercising jurisdiction of first instance
pactum illicitum	unlawful contract
panel, pannel	prisoner at bar
pari passu	share and share alike; side by side
parole (evidence)	oral (term borrowed from England)
particeps criminis	accomplice
patrimonial	pertaining to property; pecuniary
party-minuter	party entering proceedings by lodging a minute
per capita	divided equally among persons
per incuriam	by mistake
per stirpes	division among children of the shares that would have been their parents' (as opposed to per capita)
plagium	child-stealing
poind (pronounced "pind")	to take debtor's moveable property by way of execution
precognition	statement from witness of evidence he is prepared to give
prescription	restriction of a right owing to passage of a specific period of time
probative document	one which by its nature appears to afford proof of its contents
process	documentary course of an action from first step to final judgment
pro hac vice	for this occasion
pro indiviso	undivided
pro loco et tempore	for the place and time
proof before answer	hearing of evidence before the legal arguments are determined
proof	hearing of evidence by a judge
prorogate	extend time allowed; or submit to court's jurisdiction
protestation	procedure whereby defender compels pursuer to proceed with his case or end it
prout de jure	by all the means known to the law
pro veritate	as if true
quantum lucratus	as much as he has profited
quantum meruit	as much as he has earned; what is due
quantum valeat	for what it is worth
quoad ultra	otherwise; with regard to other matters
rank	to admit a claimant to his rightful place (e.g. in multiplepoinding)
ratio decidendi	line of reasoning; basis of judgment

real raiser	party who, holding fund in medio, initiates action of multiplepoinding
reclaim	to appeal to Inner House of Court of Session against Outer House judgment
record (pronounced with accent on second syllable)	statement by parties to an action of their claims and answers; document containing these
reduce	annul; rescind; set aside (by action of reduction)
rei interventus	rule barring a party, who knowingly permits another to depart from form, to challenge the resulting contract
relevant	applied to case where, if facts stated are proved, pursuer would be entitled to remedy he seeks
relocation	re-letting
repel	reject (a plea or objection)
repone	to restore a party as a litigant
res gestae	things done
res judicata	matter already judicially decided
res noviter	information newly discovered
res publicae	things owned by the state
rolls	list of cases to be heard in court
roup	auction
rubric	head-note; summary given at head of law report
sasine	a putting into possession of land
Sederunt, Acts of	procedural rules made by Court of Session
separatim	separately
sequestrate	render bankrupt (strictly it is the estate which is sequestrated)
seriatim	singly, in regular order
serve	to deliver (a court document)
servitude	burden or obligation on a piece of land
simpliciter	simply, absolutely, without qualification
sine die	without a date being fixed
Single Bill	motion in the Inner House of the Court of Session
singular successor	person obtaining property otherwise than as heir
sist	to stay or stop a process; to summon or call a party
socius criminis	accomplice in a crime
solatium	damages for injured feelings, grief, pain
spes successionis	hope of succession (as heir apparent)
sui generis	of its own kind
summons	court writ bearing royal mandate; document served on defender by which pursuer initiates civil action
superior	grantor of a feu
supersede	postpone
suspension	stay of diligence
tacit relocation	implied re-letting
taciturnity	keeping silent about a debt leading to inference of payment
tender	offer in settlement made by defender to pursuer
tenor, proving the	establishing the effect of a document (e.g. will) the principal copy of which has been lost
thole an assize	undergo trial, after which no further trial on same charge may take place
title to sue	legal right to bring an action

ultra vires	beyond (one's legal) powers
unum quid	one thing; single unit
upset price	price at which property is exposed for sale by auction
uterine	born of same mother but different father
utter	to put false writing or currency into circulation
veritas	truth (defence to action of slander)
vis et metus	force and fear (q.v.)
volenti non fit injuria	no injustice is done to a party by an act to which he consents (defence to action for damages)
warrandice	guarantee of a right contained in a deed, usually disponing heritage
writ	a writing possessing legal significance
writer	old name for solicitor

INDEX

breach of confidence actions,
36.32
copyright actions, 36.32, 36.33
gagging orders, 36.22, 36.28
interim interdicts, 36.28
interim restraints, 36.29
likely prospect of success, 36.28–
36.32
national security, 36.22
prior restraints, 36.28, 36.36
value judgments, 36.26
Freedom of information
access to information, 38.45, 38.46
see also **Access to information**
appeals, 11.09
applications
advice/assistance, 11.08, 11.15,
11.16
procedure, 11.08
cost considerations, 11.06, 11.19
derogation (journalism/art/
literature), 11.10
environmental information, 11.18,
11.19
exemptions, 11.02, 11.04, 11.05,
11.19
legislation, 11.01, 11.02, 11.19
ministerial veto, 11.07
National Archive, 38.46
news, 11.12–11.14
publication schemes, 11.11
Scottish Information Commissioner,
11.03, 11.16, 11.19
substantial prejudice, 11.02
timescales, 11.06
UK Information Commissioner,
11.03, 11.19
wholly-owned companies, 11.17

Gaming
see also **Lotteries and gaming**
advertisements, 35.22
Gaming Commission, 35.23, 35.24
Gill Review
case management, 05.02, 05.03, 05.33
changes affecting journalists, 05.03
district judges, 05.03
docket system, 05.03
financial constraints, 05.01
implementation, 05.01, 05.04, 05.05
information technology, 05.02
judicial review, 05.02, 05.46
mediation, 05.02
multiple claims procedure, 05.03
personal injury court, 05.03

pre-action protocols, 05.02
procedural changes, 05.02, 05.03
publication, 05.01
scope, 05.02
Sheriff Appeal Court, 05.03
Sheriff Court jurisdiction, 05.03
simplified procedure, 05.03
specialist sheriffs, 05.03
Government Legal Service for Scotland
constituent offices, 03.16
legal staff, 03.16
workload, 03.16

High Court of Justiciary
appeals, 04.31
Court of Criminal Appeal, 04.42–
04.45
judges, 03.03, 03.04, 04.28
jurisdiction, 04.01, 04.30, 04.42,
04.101, 06.03
Justiciary Appeal Court, 04.31
Parliament House, 04.29
prosecutions, 04.30
retrials, 04.101
sittings, 04.29
Horror comics
prohibition on publication, 35.30
Human rights
see also **European Convention on
Human Rights; Freedom of
expression**
breach of confidence cases, 14.29
journalist's sources, 19.07–19.09,
19.25
rape cases, 07.37
rehabilitation of offenders, 13.29
right to life
see **Right to life**
Scottish case law, 01.31
sexual offences, 07.37
Human Rights Act 1998
Convention rights
declarations of incompatibility,
05.81, 36.05
legislative compatibility, 05.79,
36.05
legislative incorporation/
interpretation, 05.79, 05.80,
36.03, 37.03
margin of appreciation, 36.04
privacy rights, 28.18, 28.19,
28.24
public authorities, 05.79, 36.03,
36.04
remedial legislation, 36.05